Psychology

SECOND EDITION

Morris K. Holland

University of California, Los Angeles

D. C. HEATH AND COMPANY

Lexington, Massachusetts Toronto

Psychology

An Introduction
to Human Behavior

Consulting Editors

Paul Mussen
Mark R. Rosenzweig
University of California, Berkeley

Acknowledgments

The author wishes to thank Becky Schworer for her valuable support and assistance, Milton Zolotow for his creative artwork and Mike Berlin for his research.

Appreciation is also expressed to the following— users of the first edition who have suggested changes and reviewers of the manuscript for the second edition:

Bart B. Bare, Caldwell Community College
Ellen Beck, Sinclair Community College
Ervin Betts, Norwalk Community College
Larry Bloom, Colorado State University
James F. Bray, Bristol Community College
Jack Brigham, Florida State University
Lucy Champion, Southern Union State Junior College
R. D. Chapman, State University of New York, Morrisville
Paul DellaRocca, New Hampshire Technical Institute
Joyce Dennis, Southern Union State Junior College
Ed Edmonds, Augusta College
Juanita Field, New Hampshire Technical Institute
Joseph Gutenson, Thornton Community College
Brian Hayden, Brown University
Janet Hyde, Bowling Green State University
Barbara Kabat, Sinclair Community College
Daniel Kimble, University of Oregon
Nancy King, Iowa Central Community College
Mark Muradian, Bristol Community College
Leonard B. Neil, Worthington Community College
Daniel O'Neill, Bristol Community College
Carl Peters, Normandale Community College
Patsy S. Pierce, Wake Technical Institute
R. W. Pratt, Kettering College of Medical Arts
Tom Staton, Huntington College
Tom Steiner, San Diego City College
William Struhar, Sinclair Community College

Grateful acknowledgment is made to the following publishers and authors for permission to quote from their works.

H. P. Laughlin, *The neuroses.* Washington, D. C.: Butterworth, 1967.
D. Freedman, An etiological approach to the genetical study of human behavior. In S. G. Vandenberg (Ed.), *Methods and goals in human behavior genetics.* New York: Academic Press, 1965.
A. A. Milne, *Now we are six.* Copyright 1927 by E. P. Dutton & Co.; renewal © 1955 by A. A. Milne. Reprinted by permission of the publishers, E. P. Dutton.

continued on p. xvi

A Personal Note to the Student

This book is about human psychology, the fascinating study of how we behave and why we behave the way we do. For the most part, it is about normal individuals, like yourself, and their reactions to each other and to life. You will read about many questions you have wondered about: Was your personality shaped by your parents? How can you improve your memory? How can you gain some control over your bad habits? How often do you dream and what do your dreams mean? How can you improve your relationships? What are the origins of prejudice? Can other people control your mind? Are you normal? This book will help you answer these questions, and will raise other questions about human behavior that you may not have thought about.

Psychology is constantly in the news. Books and magazine articles spread the story of psychology and its discoveries; television programs are more and more often based on psychological principles; and psychological explanations are increasingly offered for many of the ills of society. Why the great interest in psychology? One reason is that we have begun to realize that all of our sophisticated machines and expensive technology will not, in themselves, solve all of our problems: most problems that we face are fundamentally problems that we ourselves create, are human problems, and must have human solutions. We all face complex, often frustrating, personal and social problems in this crowded world, and we need to understand one another better in order to survive. Psychology can aid that understanding.

Psychology: An Introduction to Human Behavior is the result of ten years of teaching beginning classes in psychology to students at UCLA. During this time I've learned a lot about the problems students have, the concepts they find particularly difficult, the topics they are most interested in, and the aspects of psychology that are most relevant to their lives. I've also learned a lot about psychology. This book reflects what I've learned as a student of psychology and later as a teacher of the introductory course.

Learning psychology requires more than reading the material over once or twice before the exam. Some ways of studying work better than others. Effective study methods are discussed in detail in Chapter 3 of this book, and this discussion provides you with the tools you will need to get off to a good start in your efforts to learn psychology. In addition, each chapter is designed to support your learning efforts. The material is presented in relatively small, easily read sections, followed by brief summaries. At the beginning of each chapter you will find a list of three or four basic questions that the chapter answers. Then at the end of each chapter you will find the answers to these questions along with a glossary of terms and their definitions. Learning psychology is in some ways like learning a foreign language: you must master a new vocabulary of terms, special words that are used in psychology and which must be understood in order to follow a lecture, newspaper article, or textbook discussion of psychology. It is important that you learn these glossary terms in each chapter as you read the book.

With this book you are undertaking an adventure into the human mind. You will learn the basic principles of human behavior and will increase your understanding of yourself and of other people. This will be no small achievement, because we are wonderfully complicated creatures.

A Note to the Instructor

Although the second edition of this book represents a substantial revision, its primary aim has not changed: to be an effective teaching text, one that will be easy to read, easy to master, flexible, and comprehensive.

Psychology: An Introduction to Human Behavior treats all of the basic material typically covered in introductory or general psychology courses; however, the presentation of the material is unique. The fundamental facts and principles of psychology are presented within the broader context of contemporary personal and social concerns rather than within the historic divisions of the discipline. Students in increasing numbers are turning to psychology to seek answers to personal and social problems. They are concerned with understanding themselves, their friends, and the social forces at work around them. But our students are often disappointed when they find that their psychology texts contain little about meaningful human behavior; they read the quantitative predictions of sensory capacities and the laws that apply to memory of nonsense syllables; they read endless variations of laboratory simulations and complicated descriptions of how simple animals learn. But psychology is more than that. Psychology has something meaningful to say about important social problems such as prejudice, drugs, sex, and ecology; and it is time that this research was communicated. This text discusses directly the psychological research

on these important problems. The traditional areas of psychology are well covered but they are presented within chapters dealing with meaningful human issues. Specific chapters covering the traditional divisions of the discipline are listed below:

Area of Psychology	Text Coverage (Chapters)
Background, History	1, 3
Scientific Method	2 and all Research Methods units
Child Development	4, 5, 6
Motivation	14, 15, 18, 24
Consciousness	10, 11
Perception	12, 27
Learning	3, 7, 9
Memory	8
Biological	10, 14
Personality	13, 16, 17, 19, 28, 29
Abnormal	20, 21
Social	22, 23, 24, 25, 26, 30
Measurement, Statistics	Research Methods III, VI

As the preceding table indicates, physiological processes are discussed within the context of states of consciousness (Chapter 10) and within the context of the biological foundations of sexual arousal (Chapter 14). Students find the principles of the nervous system more intriguing when they are discussed as part of a problem that they can relate to. The psychological development of the child is discussed in Chapters 5 and 6 within a context of the growth of personal identity, another problem of great significance to young adults. The traditional area of motivation is presented in chapters on aggression, sexual arousal, and actualization. Instead of an isolated chapter on social psychology, the text presents chapters that confront real problems: aggression and war, prejudice, conformity, and ecology. Within the three chapters on ecology, the text introduces concepts such as adaptation and stress, social isolation, crowding and social space, sensory overload and sensory deprivation, and environmental complexity. Recent research on these topics is presented, and the question is raised of what the human cost might be of adapting to a rapidly changing environment.

Understanding sexual identity, sexual feelings, and sexual behavior is an area of human concern that is discussed in three chapters in the text. The text introduces the concept of sexual identity and presents research findings on sex-role acquisition; homosexuality is discussed from the point of view of sexual preference, not pathology. The discussion of the biological foundations of sexual arousal includes basic information about the principles of the nervous system. The question is raised of whether we are in the process of a sexual revolution, and it is concluded that there is a revolution in attitudes about sex but not in sexual behavior.

The research methods units are a unique addition to the text. Distributed throughout the book, these brief units provide a broad understanding of how psychologists think, how they ask questions, how they collect data, and how they come to conclusions about human behavior. Students are stimulated to question their own beliefs about themselves and the behavior of other people and to examine the variety of ways in which scientific

knowledge about behavior is accumulated. The scientific method is presented as one of several ways of knowing; it is not value-free, but rests on specified assumptions and values concerning the natural world. The research methods units present the experimental method of controlled experiments as well as a variety of other methods for answering questions about people. These research units are separate sections and are designed to be easily skipped by students in courses with a more humanistic emphasis. Some instructors will want to use the research methods units as advanced, extra reading for interested students or for students who are considering psychology as a major or as a profession.

Psychology: An Introduction to Human Behavior is a book with a personal/social orientation; but it is also designed to be a flexible text, one that can fit a variety of courses. For example, you may choose to include or to exclude the research methods sections. The continuum of possible courses is represented by the four sample course assignments shown in the table.

The second edition of this book is an improvement in many ways over the first edition. Content, organization, and format have been significantly changed. New chapters include Chapter 3 (Learning Psychology), Chapter 5 (Childhood), Chapter 10 (Consciousness and the Brain), and Chapter 29 (Self Control). All chapters have been made more readable and have been updated. The Research Methods units have been revised and two new ones have been written. The organization of the book has also been revised. Chapters on Learning, Memory, and Teaching are now introduced early in the sequence because of the importance of learning principles to psychological theory. Chapters on social psychology have been grouped more logically. The format of the book has also been revised by adding certain didactic features to support student learning. Chapter glossaries, interim

Section	Strong Research Focus	General Course with Research	General Course	Strong Personal/ Social Focus
I	1	1	1	1
	2	2	2	
	3	3	3	3
	RM I	RM I		
II	4	4	4	
	5	5	5	5
	6	6	6	6
	RM II	RM II		
III	7	7	7	7
	8	8	8	8
	9	9	9	9
	RM III	RM III		
IV	10	10	10	
	11	11	11	
	12	12	12	
	RM IV	RM IV		
V	13	13	13	13
	14	14	14	14
		15	15	15
	RM V	RM V		
VI		16	16	16
		17	17	17
		18	18	18
	RM VI	RM VI		
VII	19	19	19	19
	20	20	20	20
	21	21	21	21
	RM VII	RM VII		
VIII	22	22	22	22
	23	23	23	23
	24	24	24	24
	RM VIII	RM VIII		
IX	25	25	25	25
	26	26	26	26
	27	27	27	
	RM IX	RM IX		
X	28	28	28	28
	29	29	29	29
		30	30	30
	RM X	RM X		

summaries, and study questions have been designed and included to promote efficient mastery of the material. The changes in the second edition of *Psychology: An Introduction to Human Behavior* make it a more effective teaching text.

The Learning Support System for the Student

- **Easy to read.**   (1) Complex jargon has been reduced drastically; whenever possible, plain English words replace the unnecessary technical vocabulary.   (2) When words are used that may be unfamiliar, they are explicitly defined in the text and also included in the glossary even if they are not highly technical—e.g., "response," "facilitate," "stage," and "symptom."   (3) Sentences are direct and relatively brief.   (4) Concepts are explained verbally, without resorting to graphs or statistical tables, which so many students find confusing.   (5) Sexist language has been eliminated.

- **Easy to master.**   (1) Short chapters enable full concentration while reading.   (2) Study questions precede each chapter to help students focus their reading.   (3) Interim summaries reinforce each small unit of reading.   (4) Chapter summaries help students review major points.   (5) Glossaries at the ends of chapters provide an easy way for students to study important terms.

- **Fun to read.**   (1) The writing style is personal and informal.   (2) Many concrete details and interesting case histories are used.   (3) Numerous photographs and original works of art illustrate the text, making reading more enjoyable.   (4) Active learning and involvement are encouraged through self-tests, inventories, and questionnaires.

- **Supplemental materials.**   (1) The *Study Guide* is designed to help students master the course content. Many activities and sample tests are provided to aid learning.   (2) The *Individualized Study Program* is designed to support PSI courses or other individualized programs.

The Teaching Support System for the Instructor

- **Comprehensive and accurate coverage.**   (1) The full range of important introductory topics is presented. Each major academic area in psychology is represented in this survey.   (2) Instructors with students who plan to continue to more advanced courses in the field can be confident that they will have an appropriate foundation in the principles of psychology.   (3) The text is based on a strong research foundation; over 800 references are cited from the scientific literature.

- **Social/personal focus.**   (1) The book focuses on social issues and personal concerns, in contrast to a biological or quantitative emphasis.   (2) The text reflects the author's humanistic value system and his respect for the scientific method.   (3) The principles of psychology are related to the lives of students through chapters on the psychology of consciousness, sex, prejudice, war, environment, and revolution.

- **Flexible organization.**   (1) Chapters can be assigned in an order that fits your personal course outline. Each chapter is relatively independent and can stand on its own.   (2) Separate research methods units are distributed throughout the text. The text can be further tailored to your course by either requiring or excluding these units.

- **Supplemental materials.**   (1) The *Instructor's Manual* is designed to assist instructors in teaching the beginning course by identifying difficult concepts, suggesting ideas for lectures or demonstrations, and recommending films.   (2) The *Test Item File* provides hundreds of true-false and multiple-choice questions for testing the students' understanding of the text.

Contents

S. Fleck. Family dynamics and origin of schizophrenia. *Psychosomatic Medicine*, 1960, *22*, 333–343.

David Elkind, "Giant in the Nursery," May 26, 1968 © 1968 by The New York Times Company. Margaret Mead, "One Vote for This Age of Anxiety," May 20, 1956 © 1956 by The New York Times Company. Reprinted by permission.

W. Penfield, The interpretive cortex. *Science*, 1959, *129*, 1719–1725. S. Milgram, The experience of living in cities. *Science*, 1970, *167*, 1461–1468. Copyright 1970 by the American Association for the Advancement of Science. C. R. Rogers & B. F. Skinner, Some issues concerning the control of human behavior: A symposium. *Science*, 1956, *124*, 1057–1066.

W. Dement & E. Wolpert. Relationships in the manifest content of dreams occurring on the same night. *Journal of Nervous and Mental Disease*, 1958, *126*, 568–578. © 1958 The Williams & Wilkins Co., Baltimore.

C. R. Leon. *Case histories of deviant behavior: A social learning analysis*. Boston: Holbrook Press, 1974.

S. Milgram. Some conditions of obedience and disobedience to authority. *Human Relations*, 1965, *18*, 57–75.

D. J. Bem. *Beliefs, attitudes, and human affairs*. Copyright © 1970 by Wadsworth Publishing Company, Inc. Reprinted by permission of the publisher, Brooks/Cole Publishing Company, Monterey, California.

R. Dubos. *Man adapting*. New Haven: Yale University Press, 1965.

Publications of the American Psychological Association and of the American Psychiatric Association and articles in *Psychology Today* magazine.

Photo Credits

ACTION 356

Jeff Albertson/Stock, Boston 102, 229, 241

Barbara L. Baumann 3, 4, 10, 12, 35, 37, 46, 47, 121, 126, 216, 227, 327, 329, 330, 342, 361, 429, 504, 576, 586

Marion Bernstein 21, 70, 86, 93, 101, 259, 390, 391, 396, 402, 430, 438, 526

John H. Breck, Inc. 432

Daniel S. Brody/Stock, Boston 315, 575, 576

Ingbert Brüttner for Rockefeller University Press 22, 31

Ken Buck 253, 254, 258, 262, 264, 280, 287, 307, 559, 562, 574, 587

Ed Buryn 191, 199, 343, 359, 474, 491, 509, 511, 560, 561, 563, 568

Canadian Government Travel Bureau 493, 499

H. Cartier-Bresson/Magnum 512

Children of Crisis by Robert Coles, Figures 1 and 2. Copyright © 1964, 1965, 1966, 1967 by Robert Coles. Reprinted by permission of Little, Brown and Co. in association with The Atlantic Monthly Press. 455

Terry Corey Collection. From the motion picture *Dirty Harry* courtesy of Warner Bros. Inc. copyright © 1971. 467

Culver Pictures 222

Bruce Davidson/Magnum 583

Irven De Vore/Anthro-Photos 407, 412, 470

Donald Dietz/Dietz-Hamlin 7, 106, 159, 293, 496, 522, 532

Rohn Engh/Photo Researchers 283

Elliott Erwitt/Magnum 507

Martin Etter/Anthro-Photos 320

Bob Fletcher/Barboza 95

Owen Franken/Stock, Boston 17, 257, 515

Arthur Furst 79, 81, 120, 124, 161, 162, 163, 166, 445

Len Gittleman 189

Dorothy Gloster/Luba-Lunda Agency 59, 64, 141

Arthur Grace/Stock, Boston 465

Nikki Grimes 308, 317

Elizabeth Hamlin/Dietz-Hamlin 8, 17, 30, 36, 44, 119, 164, 173, 175, 255, 261, 284, 295, 326, 333, 374, 382, 444, 450, 492, 494, 503

Harry F. Harlow, University of Wisconsin Primate Laboratory 96, 527

Jim Harrison 577

Steven Hersch 549

Ellis Herwig/Stock, Boston 312

Jerome Kagan/Harvard Infant Study 27

B. A. King title page, 38, 75, 310

Eric Kroll 66, 92, 104, 270, 271, 275, 278, 309, 322, 325, 378, 436, 521, 573, 580

Peter Laytin 18, 211, 212, 213, 218, 220, 373, 389, 405, 409

Jean Claude Lejeune/Stock, Boston 341

The Levinson Institute 14

The Lipton Kitchens 231

Chris Maynard/Magnum 406, 413

Sheila Metzner 197

The Museum of Modern Art/Film Stills Archive. Copyright © 1970, United Artists Corporation, all rights reserved. 94

Museum of Natural History 62, 510

National Institute of Mental Health, photo by Nilo Olin 508, 517

Jack Prelutsky/Stock, Boston 466, 468

Rudolph R. Robinson 289

John Running/Stock, Boston 228, 230

Schick Laboratories 130

Judy Sedwick 5, 11, 13, 18, 23, 25, 43, 61, 67, 543, 545, 556

Peter Simon 201, 208

Frank Siteman/Stock, Boston 269

United Press International 400

University of Denver 80

Peter Vandermark 87

Alex Webb/Magnum 443

Wide World 554

John Young 29, 76, 78, 82, 91, 125, 142, 145, 160, 169, 476

Milton Zolotow 501

Cover: Design by Len Gittleman. Photos by Barbara L. Baumann, Marion Bernstein, and Louis Draper/Luba-Lunda Agency

Illustrations: Milton Zolotow and B. J. & F. W. Taylor.

Psychology

Introduction

1 The Nature of Psychology

CHAPTER OUTLINE

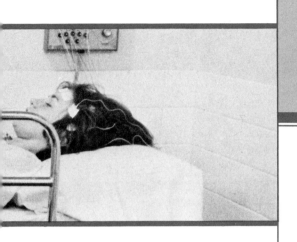

KEY QUESTIONS

1. What is psychology?
2. What are the goals of psychology?
3. What do psychologists do?

Wondering about people can be a full-time occupation.

You watch people constantly—in classrooms, restaurants, and on the street—and you listen to what they say. What could possibly be more interesting than people? You find them amusing, delightful, fascinating, and sometimes appalling or terribly annoying. And you wonder. Why do they do what they do? What are they thinking? Why do they act that way?

Each day the newspaper reports unusual accounts of human behavior. A recent article reported that fourteen high school students from Arlington Heights, Illinois, leap-frogged for twelve hours, traveling 56 miles, and beating the 1973 record by 6 miles.[1] The same day another story reported that a California artist bought ten tons of clay and molded 5,000 giant shark teeth; he then arranged them on a dry lake bed in the desert.[2] A third newspaper story reported that a seventeen-year-old boy hanged himself from a persimmon tree.[3] At the foot of the tree a jar was found with a note inside addressed to

5

"Mom and Dad." The note said, "When you stop growing you are dead. I stopped growing long ago."

When you read stories like the last one, you wonder: Why did he do it? In his circumstances, would I have done it? You wonder about yourself, your life, your growth. You wonder how you came to think, feel, and act the way you do. You review your memories and study your behavior to seek an understanding of yourself.

You are a student of human behavior and you already know a lot about psychology. The purpose of this book is to deepen that understanding.

What Is Psychology?

You are at a noisy party; a friend walks up to talk, but you can hear only part of what she says: "Hello! How are . . . ? Where have you been? I haven't seen you in a long . . .'' Can you supply the missing words? You understand what is being said even when you can't hear all the words. That is because you can predict what the missing words should be, and can fill them in yourself. You know the missing words are "you" and "time." You have learned to predict what other people will do.

You are out shopping; when the light turns red, you cross a busy downtown street, hardly glancing at the cars speeding toward you. You are predicting that they will stop, and you are betting your life on that prediction. A lot of the time you know what people are going to do before they do it. You understand other people fairly well.

Understanding other people is possible because, to a certain extent, they act consistently. There are two kinds of consistency that are important in the understanding of other people. First, a person is relatively consistent from day to day; if you know what the person did in the past, you can predict (with some accuracy) what the person is going to do in the future. Your shy, soft-spoken little sister is not likely to suddenly start shouting and fighting; although everybody changes, large and sudden changes are rare. Second, there is consistency among different people; your behavior is similar to the behavior of other people in similar circumstances. Because you are similar to other people, I can, for example, predict that you are reading this book right-side-up, not upside-down. Everybody is unique, but we are also all alike in some ways.

Because of these two kinds of consistencies in people, a science of behavior is possible. Psychology is that science.

Definition of Psychology

Psychology is the science of behavior. It is the study of individual people and what they do. It is a *science* because it is a systematic study, involving observation, description, and explanation. Psychology is a science of *behavior;* the term **behavior** refers to activities, things that you do. Psychology studies the activities of the mind (mental activities such as thinking and experiencing) as well as the activities of the body (motor activities such as moving and talking). All of the things that you do are types of behavior studied by psychology.

For example, one type of behavior that psychology studies is aggression. Why do you think people fight, kill, and make war? Some have argued that people have "killer instincts," but there is little evidence to support this claim. Do children grow up to be aggressive adults because of their continual exposure to TV violence? These questions have been examined in hundreds of psychological studies.

An example of a different type of behavior is dreaming. In a recent study of dreaming, sixteen college students slept in a laboratory for three nights.[4] On one of these nights a stressful film, showing a terrible accident, was shown just before the students went to sleep. Later, the students reported dreaming about parts of the film. This study and other similar studies show that dreams often incorporate aspects of waking experience.

Another example of behavior is language. Psychologists are very interested in studying how children's use of language begins and how it grows. Typically this research involves observing infants, but a recent case was dramatically different. Genie, a girl of 13 years 9 months, was taken into protective custody by the police; her parents had kept her isolated in a small closed room, tied to a chair, for her entire life.[5] Genie was extremely thin and unable to stand erect. She did not speak and did not seem to understand language. Within a few weeks, however, she began to imitate words, and was using sentences within a year after her discovery. Studies of Genie's language development showed that she progressed through the same stages of growth that an infant displays in learning language.

Psychologists have developed a special vocabulary for discussing behavior. The term **response** refers to behavior and is used in a fairly general sense. For example, a psychologist might write, "Aggressive responses were found to increase following exposure to TV violence." This sentence means that after people watched violent TV programs they became more aggressive. Another general word referring to behavior is **tendency.** For example, a psychologist might write, "The new drug reduces aggressive tendencies." This sentence means that people who take this drug act, on the average, less aggressively. A more complex behavioral word is the term **trait,** which refers to a

Watching people can be fun.

relatively enduring personal characteristic or way of behaving. For example, a psychologist might write, "The trait of aggressiveness is not universally evident among human beings." This sentence means that not all peoples in the world have an aggressive way of behaving. The term **state** refers to a temporary condition, a way of reacting or behaving that does not endure. For example, a psychologist might write, "Pain sometimes produces an immediate state of aggressiveness." This sentence means that a temporary condition of aggressiveness is sometimes caused by pain. The terms "response," "tendency," "trait," and "state" are used to refer to a wide variety of behavior.

Goals of Psychology: The Example of Anxiety

Psychology is the science that seeks to understand behavior of all kinds. As a science, it has the goals of *description, prediction, explanation,* and *control.* We seek to describe a particular behavior so that we can understand what it is. We seek to predict it so that we can understand who will behave in that manner, and when and where they will do so. We seek to explain a behavior so that we can understand why it occurs. We seek to control a behavior so that we can manage our lives better and help others manage theirs. These goals of psychology can be demonstrated by considering the problem of anxiety.

■ *Describing Anxiety* Anxiety is a feeling of worry, tension, dread, or foreboding. It is a feeling that something terrible is about to happen, a feeling of despair and of hopelessness. Everyone has felt anxiety at one time or another; in fact, we live with mild anxiety every day. Extreme anxiety can be an unpleasant problem for some people.

Anxiety and fear are so closely related that there is no clear dividing line between the two concepts. The term **fear** is used to describe a person's reaction to a specific threatening object (you may fear a snarling

Wondering about people can be a full-time occupation.

dog or a loaded gun pointed at you). The term **anxiety** is used to describe a vague worry or apprehension that has no specific cause (you may feel anxiety when in crowds or when talking to strangers). Anxiety may be acute or chronic. **Acute anxiety** is a reaction of anxiety that happens suddenly and does not last for long. **Chronic anxiety** is anxiety that is continual; it does not come and go. In the description below, a young woman explains her acute anxiety to her roommate:

I'm on edge tonight. I feel worried, but I don't know what it's about. My heart is pounding, and I'm perspiring more than usual. It's almost like I was waiting for something to happen. . . . I feel frightened and fearful, but I don't really know why I feel this way. . . . Things seem to be going well, and I shouldn't have any reason to be so uneasy![6]

■ *Predicting Anxiety* Who, where, and when will anxiety strike? Psychologists have been able to make certain predictions. By studying what happens just before people feel anxious, we have found certain regularities. Anxiety often follows some kind of *threat*, either real or imagined, and either physical or psychological. Anxiety is aroused by the stress of failure, by the anticipation of being evaluated, by the loss of a loved one, by punishment, and by uncertainty. We can predict that almost everyone in these **aversive** (unpleasant) circumstances will feel anxious, and our predictions will be confirmed. There are also individual reactions of anxiety, ones not shared by the majority. For example, some people are made anxious by open spaces, cats, clocks, or closets.

One of the ways psychologists can predict anxiety is to study individual differences in anxiety. Some people are frequently anxious and some are not; in a particular situation, some people will be extremely anxious while other people will not be anxious at all. Psychologists can predict who will and who will not be anxious by asking people to report their reactions. This is typically done with a questionnaire. For example, the following items come from a questionnaire concerned with **test anxiety,** the anxiety aroused by tests and exams. How anxious are you during tests?

Generally	Rarely or Never	
☐	☐	While taking a test, I feel nervous, tense, or upset.
☐	☐	While taking a test, I perspire a lot.
☐	☐	While taking a test, my hands shake or tremble.
☐	☐	While taking a test, my heart "pounds."
☐	☐	While taking a test, I experience an upset stomach.
☐	☐	While taking a test, I experience a shortness of breath.
☐	☐	While taking a test, I experience an ache in the back of my neck.

Each of the above is a **symptom** of anxiety; that is, each of the above is characteristic of, or indicates the presence of, anxiety. Answers to questionnaires like this one can be used to predict how people will react to taking tests.

■ *Explaining Anxiety* Psychology has studied the **physiology** of anxiety (the bodily processes involved in the experience of anxiety). It is now known that certain brain structures are activated in the anxious person

Anxiety aroused by tests can interfere with your performance.

and that this leads to the secretion of chemicals called **hormones** into the bloodstream. The body reacts with trembling, sweaty palms, muscular tension, an increased heart rate, and a dry mouth.

Sigmund Freud, the founder of psychoanalysis, believed that anxiety was due to **unconscious conflicts,** internal "tugs-of-war" between biological impulses for sex or violence on the one hand and moral standards of conduct on the other. More recently psychologists have stressed other sources of internal conflicts, such as dependence versus independence or trust versus mistrust.

Is anxiety a result of the activity of the brain or is it a result of conflicts in the unconscious mind? The answer is both, and more besides. The effect of significant conflicts in your life may be to arouse certain brain structures, causing the bodily signs of anxiety. However, the causes of anxiety are not as well understood as this explanation

implies. Many psychologists reject Freud's theory of the unconscious, proposing instead a variety of other ideas. The facts are not certain and the issue is not yet settled.

Many questions about anxiety have not been answered. For the time being, psychology is proceeding in several directions at once in its effort to understand this problem. Single explanations are often inadequate. Most behavior can be understood in more than one way.

Psychologists study and attempt to explain many human problems and experiences. For some of these problems, they have developed multiple explanations, each contributing to our understanding on a different level.

■ *Controlling Anxiety* Anxiety can be controlled in a variety of ways. One way is through the use of tranquilizing drugs. Another way is through training in muscle relaxation. The experience of anxiety is associated with muscle tension; by learning to control muscle tension, people can control anxiety. The following case shows how a student with test anxiety learned to control it.

Susan, an 18-year-old freshman, came for help with extreme nervousness over taking tests . . . . Susan stated that, while she studied 25–30 hours each week on her coursework, she had received only D's and F's on her exams and quizzes. She felt that in each case she knew the material prior to the exam, but was "unable to put it down on paper." Discussion revealed that Susan came from a small rural high school where exams were rarely given.[7]

Susan came to the counseling center at her college and was taught a special type of deep muscle relaxation; she was taught how to relax when she needed to do so. Her performance on examinations improved dramatically, and she finished the term with a B average. Many studies have shown that anxiety **impairs** (interferes with) academic achievement, while relaxtion **facilitates** it (makes it easier).

Relation to Other Sciences

Psychology is not a narrowly defined field of study; instead—like the object of its study, human beings—it is broad in scope, deep, and very complex. It involves *biology*, because behavior and experience depend upon the structure and function of the body, particularly the nervous system. Psychologists with a special interest in biology, for example, may study the electrical activity of individual cells in the brain. Psychology involves *chemistry*, because the chemistry of the body—particularly of the brain—is important in understanding behavior. Psychologists with special training in chemistry, for example, may focus their study on the effects of various drugs on chemical changes in the brain.

Psychology involves *sociology* (the study of social groups), because individual behavior always occurs within the context of a social system. Psychologists with special interests in social processes, for example, may study how an individual's attitudes and values are affected by other people. Psychology involves *anthropology* (the comparative study of culture), because most behavior is relative to its culture. A psychologist with an anthropological orientation, for example, may study the cross-cultural differences in child-rearing practices in Asia and Africa. Psychology involves *mathematics*, because the tools of mathematics are needed to draw conclusions from complex data concerning human behavior. These and other sciences are used by psychologists and, in turn, many of these sciences draw upon the knowledge of psychology.

What then is the difference between psychology and biology? Where is the line between psychology and sociology? There is no clear line, but there is a general rule: common

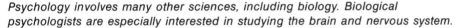

Psychology involves many other sciences, including biology. Biological psychologists are especially interested in studying the brain and nervous system.

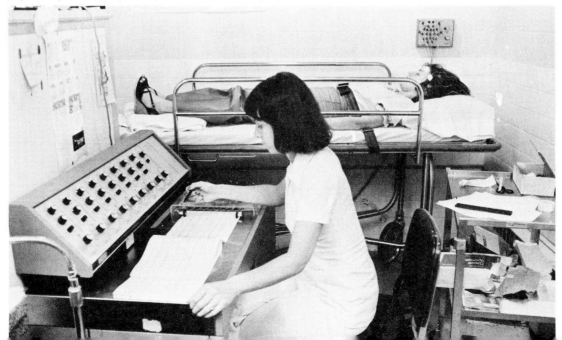

to the variety of ways of studying psychology is the goal of understanding *individual behavior*. When psychology uses other sciences, it is always in pursuit of this goal.

ⓢ Psychology is the science of behavior. The term "behavior" refers to such varied activities as talking, moving, thinking, perceiving, and feeling. The goals of psychology are the description, prediction, explanation, and control of behavior. Psychology uses and is related to many other sciences but is unique in its emphasis on understanding individual behavior.

Careers in Psychology

Many different kinds of people become psychologists. Psychologists are teachers, scientists, counselors, and therapists. Psychologists teach psychology in high school and college classes as an academic discipline; they do research in psychology to advance scientific knowledge of human behavior; and, as professionals, they apply psychological principles to help individuals, schools, businesses, and communities. Many psychologists work in more than one area; they combine the roles of teacher and researcher, or the roles of researcher and professional, or the roles of teacher and professional.

Teaching Psychology

Teaching psychology occupies an increasing number of psychologists every year. Throughout the country interest in psychology is growing as people begin to see the task of understanding each other as a greater challenge than the task of conquering nature. Psychology is chosen by more and more students as a college major, and so more and more teachers of psychology are needed.

A psychologist teaching college students.

Why do people become teachers of psychology? One prominent teacher of psychology is Bill McKeachie, a professor at the University of Michigan who has taught psychology and studied the psychology of teaching for many years. McKeachie described his initial exposure to the field of psychology as follows:

In 1935 I was fourteen years old, an ardent baseball player, a dedicated Presbyterian, and secretary-treasurer of the Sunday school of the small rural church near my home in White Lake Township, Oakland County, Michigan. Each Sunday afternoon I counted the collection (average per Sunday, 77 cents), checked the date on each penny for my penny collection, and read the Sunday school paper, Young People. *It was on a Sunday afternoon that I read the half-page article on psychology as a vocation, and from that day to this, psychology has seemed to me the most fascinating field in which one could work.*[8]

A psychologist studying human learning.

Research in Psychology

The scientific investigation of human behavior is the full- or part-time work of thousands of psychologists. Many researchers conduct their studies at colleges and universities. In addition to their research in psychology they may also teach.

Researchers in psychology are motivated by a driving curiosity to understand behavior. They have many questions about people that they want to answer, and they find their answers by systematically observing behavior. Recently researchers have asked, "What is the effect on the minds of children of observing violence on TV?" Their conclusions are reported later in this book. Researchers have asked, "How can memory be improved?", "How often do people dream?", and "What causes schizophrenia?" The re-

sults of their studies are discussed in later chapters.

Scientific psychology is both a method of investigation and a body of accumulated knowledge. Researchers in psychology use this method to discover facts and principles that can be added to this body of knowledge about human behavior. This method will be discussed in greater detail in the next chapter.

Professional Psychological Services

Psychology is a helping profession; psychologists provide their professional services to individuals and groups who seek help. Over the hundred years or so during which psychology has flourished as a science, many

A clinical psychologist, Dr. Harry Levinson, conducting a seminar for business executives on how to deal with stress.

theories and principles have been developed that can be applied to specific psychological problems. These principles are applied by professional psychologists who are actively engaged in practical problem solving.

■ *Clinical and Counseling Psychology* Clinical and counseling psychologists advise and help people who have personal problems. A **counselor** may offer advice and guidance on educational and vocational decisions and may provide assistance in solving personal and marital problems. A **clinical psychologist** does similar work but typically concentrates on such tasks as diagnosing and treating personality disorders and providing therapy for individuals facing crises in their lives or for those who wish to promote their personal growth and development. A clinical psychologist typically has a Ph.D. in psychology with training in testing and research. **Psychiatrists** differ from clinical psychologists in that (1) psychiatrists are medical doctors and are licensed to prescribe drugs and (2) clinical psychologists receive extensive training in research while psychiatrists do not.

The work of a counseling psychologist in a university counseling center has been described as follows:

Robert Franklin, Ph.D., counseling psychologist . . . interviews and tests students to assess ability, motivation, and interests, . . . works intensively with students who are having serious difficulty adjusting to college or are experiencing emotional problems which hamper their college work, . . . conducts group meetings in reading and study skills, . . . supervises three interns enrolled in the university's doctoral program in counseling psychology, . . . teaches undergraduate courses in child psychology, psychology of personality, and tests and measurements, . . . is faculty adviser to a group of student volunteers in mental hospitals.[9]

■ *School and Industry* Counselors and clinical psychologists sometimes work in the public school system where they provide help to students and teachers with personal or educational difficulties and collect psychological information on students for purposes of guidance. **School psychologists** give psychological tests to students in order to learn how best to advise them. One such test is the standard IQ test of intelligence; another is a vocational aptitude test, which attempts to identify suitable career choices. Psychologists in industry also use tests; with the data gathered they help to select qualified personnel for various tasks. In addition, they study ways of improving working conditions and employee motivation.

■ *Criminology* Psychologists working in prisons provide diagnosis and treatment for psychological problems of prisoners, and they participate in the selection of prisoners to be paroled. Psychologists also work in special treatment programs for drug addicts, sexual offenders, and juvenile delinquents. Increasing attention is being given to crime prevention, through the early identification and treatment of potential criminals and through efforts to modify harmful environments; psychologists study ways of changing neighborhoods and schools to make them less likely to produce juvenile delinquents.

⑤ Psychologists work in many different capacities. Teaching psychology is a popular and demanding career. Conducting research in psychology to answer questions about human behavior is another full- or part-time career. Finally, psychologists provide services to people asking for help. For example, a clinical psychologist provides therapy for people facing crises in their lives.

How Much Do You Know About Psychology?

You have been struggling to understand yourself and others for many years, and you have learned a lot in the process. You already know many things about psychology which you have learned by observing yourself and other people. For example, you probably know that these are true statements:

Rewards and punishments change behavior.

People learn to behave differently in different cultures.

Sometimes people may be doing or feeling something that they are not aware of at the time.

Some people learn quickly, others slowly.

When some people are frustrated, they become aggressive.

Your brain is the "master control organ" for your behavior.

This book is about these important things that you already know, plus many others that you may not yet know. Below is a list of thirty-four statements, some of which are true and some false. How much do you know about psychology? Test yourself by marking each one true or false, then continue reading to check your answers.

True or false?

___ 1. Babies need loving in order to grow up to be healthy adults.

___ 2. Eye color may be inherited, but not intelligence.

___ 3. Parental attention and love can increase a child's IQ.

___ 4. Your personality is completely determined by the age of three.

___ 5. For the first week after birth, most babies are unable to see or hear.

___ 6. Pigeons can be taught to play Ping-Pong.

___ 7. It doesn't matter whether you learn something a little at a time or all at once.

___ 8. Most of your fears consist of inborn reactions.

___ 9. Everybody dreams several times each night.

___ 10. You can tell when people are dreaming by watching their eyelids.

___ 11. What you see is influenced by what you expect to see.

___ 12. Of all the different drugs in the news recently, only alcohol seems relatively harmless.

___ 13. In all cultures men are more aggressive than women.

___ 14. A person who has homosexual experiences as a child will likely turn out to be a homosexual adult.

___ 15. Masturbation can cause mental illness.

___ 16. Highly creative people are frequently mentally disturbed.

___ 17. In the formation of relationships, the rule is that opposites attract.

___ 18. Psychoanalysis is the most common form of psychotherapy.

___ 19. People who go to psychologists or psychiatrists for help are generally crazy.

___ 20. Mentally healthy individuals have no psychological problems.

___ 21. People who are mentally disturbed are clearly different from people who are not.

___ 22. What it means to be psychologically normal depends upon who you are and where you live.

___ 23. Most people who are confined to mental hospitals are dangerous.

___ 24. It is possible to become blind or deaf with no physical injury.

___ 25. If electricity is applied to a certain part of your brain, you may become violent.

___ 26. Prejudiced persons tend to have different personalities than nonprejudiced persons.

___ 27. Most people would not obey an order to injure someone else.

___ 28. When you are extremely bored, you may begin to see things that aren't there.

___ 29. Rock music can make you partially deaf.

___ 30. Animals and people behave in more socially acceptable ways when they are crowded.

___ 31. Muscle relaxation reduces nervousness.

___ 32. By deliberately practicing a bad habit, you may be able to break it.

___ 33. You can learn to control your own blood pressure and heart rate.

___ 34. In recent years there has been a sexual revolution, in that young men and women are acting much more permissively than ever before.

These statements concern some of the many issues discussed in the chapters to come. They follow the outline of the book; the first few come from the section entitled "Identity" and the last few come from the last section of the book, entitled "Freedom." These nine sections of the book are previewed in the discussion which follows, and the answers to the thirty-four true and false items are listed at the end of this chapter.

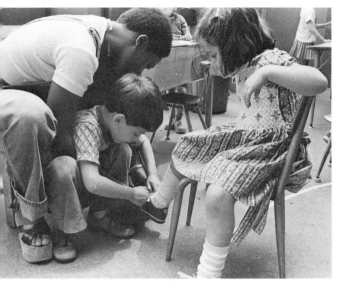

Preview of the Book

This book is an introduction to the science of psychology, the problems psychologists study, and the methods used in psychological inquiry. Chapters are organized by groups of three into clusters or sections, according to the major problems with which they are concerned. A discussion of research methods appears at the end of each section. The nine sections which follow are summarized below.

Identity, the second section, will give you a clearer view of how you came to be who you are. Who you are—your identity—was partially inherited from your parents and partially results from your experiences growing up in your family and community.

Education, the third section, deals with the effect of your experience on feelings, actions, and understanding. Most of your behavior, attitudes, and feelings were learned. You learn from experience and are able to profit from the past because of your memory. Teaching involves applying principles of psychology to promote learning.

Experience, the fourth section, shows how your consciousness is related to the brain and nervous system, and how consciousness can be altered through hypnosis or drugs. It discusses how people experience the sensory world and the inner world of dreams. Both the perception and the dream are to some degree a personal construction, affected by memories, personality, and physical energies in the world.

Sex, the fifth section, provides an overview of many aspects of the psychology of sex. Psychologists have studied the origins of sexual identity, the dependence of sexual arousal on physiology and learning, and the forms of sexual expression. Studies of sexual arousal and response show that men and women are remarkably similar.

Growth, the sixth section, is about the normal personality and your potential for personal growth. An important aspect of psychological growth is increasing interpersonal effectiveness. Growing toward health is possible for those who wish to do so; the human personality is not fixed—it holds the potential for change.

Conflict, the seventh section, deals with the feelings of anxiety, the disabling consequences of neurosis, and the severe psy-

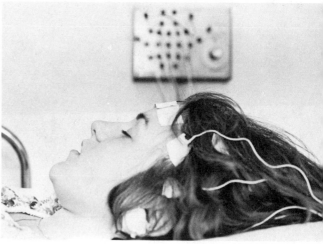

chological disturbance called insanity or psychosis. These psychological problems are discussed in terms of their symptoms and possible causes.

Groups, the eighth section, is about how individual behavior is influenced by others. Most of your behavior is social; you are strongly influenced by your interactions with other people. Conformity and aggression are two ways of responding to others, by either going along with the crowd or by fighting it.

Ecology, the ninth section, concerns the psychological effects of the social and physical environments. You are part of a network of relationships, a system in which you change your world and in turn are changed by it. In the urban environment, sensory stimulation is sometimes excessive. Crowding and noise pollution are harmful to human health; because of the urban stresses, more and more people are leaving the cities.

Freedom, the tenth section, is about freedom and the dangers of losing it. This last section deals with the new tools for controlling the mind, the psychology of self-control, and the coming social and psychological revolutions that may lead to a new society. Psychology is a revolutionary activity; it teaches us that old habits can be broken, that we are not doomed to relive our history.

Summary

KEY QUESTIONS

1. What is psychology?

   Psychology is the science of behavior. As a science, it involves systematic study and careful observation and description. Its subject matter is behavior—activities, things that you do. The concept of behavior includes physical actions, such as fighting, as well as mental processes, such as thinking or remembering.

2. What are the goals of psychology?

The goals of psychology are the description, prediction, explanation, and control of individual behavior. Psychologists seek to describe behavior so they can understand what it is. They seek to predict it so they can understand what it is related to. They seek to explain it so they can understand why it occurs. And they seek to control it so they can change it for the better.

3. What do psychologists do?

Psychologists are teachers, scientists, counselors, and therapists. Teaching psychology has occupied more and more people as the interest in psychology has expanded. Scientific research in psychology is aimed at discovering facts and principles to increase our understanding of human behavior. Clinical psychologists and counselors provide a variety of psychological services to individuals and groups seeking help.

KEY CONCEPTS

psychology	The science of behavior.
behavior	Activities; things that are done; includes actions, thoughts, attitudes, memories, perceptions, language, feelings, etc.
response	Any kind of behavior or reaction.
tendency	How people are inclined or prone to behave; an "aggressive tendency" refers to behavior that is, on the average, somewhat aggressive.
trait	A relatively enduring characteristic; a way of reacting or feeling that is lasting; for example, "She displays the trait of dominance."
state	A relatively temporary characteristic or way of behaving; for example, "Following her accident, she was in a highly anxious state."
fear	The reaction of dread or apprehension to a specific threatening object; a person may feel fear when confronted with a loaded gun.
anxiety	The vague worry or apprehension that has no specific known cause; a person may feel anxiety in crowds, but not know the reason for this feeling.
acute anxiety	A reaction of anxiety that happens suddenly and does not last for long; it has an abrupt onset.
chronic anxiety	Anxiety that is continual.

aversive	Unpleasant or punishing; for example, pain and nausea are aversive.
test anxiety	Anxiety concerning examinations.
symptom	Something that is a characteristic of, or an indication of, a problem.
physiology	The functions and processes of the body.
hormone	A chemical produced by a gland and deposited into the bloodstream.
unconscious conflict	An internal conflict of which a person is unaware; an example might be the conflict between moral standards and sexual desire.
impair	To interfere with or reduce in effectiveness; for example, "The damage to his eye impaired his vision."
facilitate	To make easier.
counselor	A psychologist who specializes in offering advice and guidance.
clinical psychologist	A psychologist who specializes in treating personality disorders and providing therapy; typically has a Ph.D. degree with training in testing and research.
psychiatrist	A medical doctor trained in the treatment of personality disorders and licensed to prescribe drugs; has MD degree.
school psychologist	A psychologist who works in the schools, counseling and testing students.

Answers to the true-false questions on page 16.
1-T, 2-F, 3-T, 4-F, 5-F, 6-T, 7-F, 8-F, 9-T, 10-T, 11-T, 12-F, 13-F, 14-F, 15-F, 16-F, 17-F, 18-F, 19-F, 20-F, 21-F, 22-T, 23-F, 24-T, 25-T, 26-T, 27-F, 28-T, 29-T, 30-F, 31-T, 32-T, 33-T, 34-F

2 The Science of Psychology

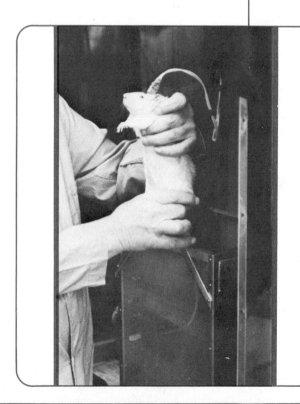

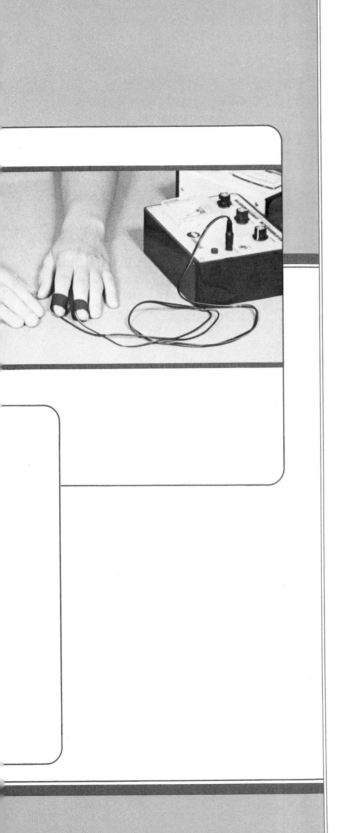

KEY QUESTIONS

1. What is science?
2. What is the scientific method?
3. How is the scientific method applied in psychology?

Why do you dream?

This is a question that people have tried to answer for thousands of years. How might the answer be found? How can you determine what is true and what is false?

There are many possible ways for deciding what to call true and what to call false. You can decide on the basis of your intuitions or hunches ("My guess is that dreams are our contact with the spirit world"); you can decide on the basis of a popularity poll ("Everybody who believes that dreams are the work of the devil, raise your hand"); or you can decide on the basis of the opinion of some authority ("Just ask Holland"). Finally, you can decide on the basis of systematic study of dreams and people who dream; this is the way of science.

Science

Science is a method of acquiring knowledge and also the body of knowledge acquired by that method. Chemistry is a science because it uses this method and has accumulated such a body of knowledge. Psychology is a science, too, though it rarely uses test tubes.

The method used in science—the **scientific method**—is a method for deciding what is probably true and what is probably false. The method consists of a set of rules for testing and observing the world. People who "play the game" of science agree to follow these rules. This minimizes disagreements. There are of course still quarrels among scientists about what is true and what is false. It is just that there are fewer disagreements among scientists than among, say, politicians.

The Rules of Science

What are the rules of science? One rule is the **principle of empirical verification.** According to this principle, a scientific claim should be regarded as true only if it agrees with experience. To discover whether a statement is true, you must test it against your observation of the world. According to this principle, the opinion of an expert does not count; you must rely on experience, not opinion.

A second rule of science is the **principle of reliable and public evidence.** According to this principle, no claim should be accepted without sound evidence, evidence that is both reliable and public. *Reliable evidence* is evidence that can be repeatedly observed. Under given circumstances, consistent observations should be made. If something happens only once, it cannot be checked, and—according to this principle—should not be given much weight. A second aspect of this principle is the notion of public evidence. *Public evidence* is accessible to many people; your observations can be checked against theirs. Private evidence is accessible only to one person and therefore cannot be checked. Evidence that is both reliable and public is regarded as sound evidence and is scientifically acceptable.

The Scientific Method

The scientific method is a method of acquiring knowledge based on the rules of science. The method consists of classifying the events of the world ("This is a dream, this is a cow, this is a book"); of observing the various relations between events ("After reading this book I dreamed of a cow"); and of developing theories that attempt to make sense of those relations ("Dreams are fragments of memories and the book in question was about cows").

When you classify things and observe relations among them, you are collecting facts or data. There are many different ways psychologists collect facts: surveys, tests, interviews, experiments. Suppose, for example, you wanted to know the relation between dreaming and taking drugs. Do drugs increase or decrease dreaming? After taking drugs, a person might be more likely or less likely to dream. How could you collect the facts that would help you to answer the question?

One possibility would be to **interview** one group of people who take drugs and a second group of people who do not, getting them to report how often they remember dreaming. You might find that the group which takes drugs reports fewer dreams than the group which does not take drugs. It is, however, not possible to conclude from this observation that taking drugs *causes* people to dream less. There are other possible explanations of the observed relationship: it is possible (though unlikely) that the experience of not dreaming compels people to take drugs. It is also possible that people who tend to take drugs are the sort of people who tend not to

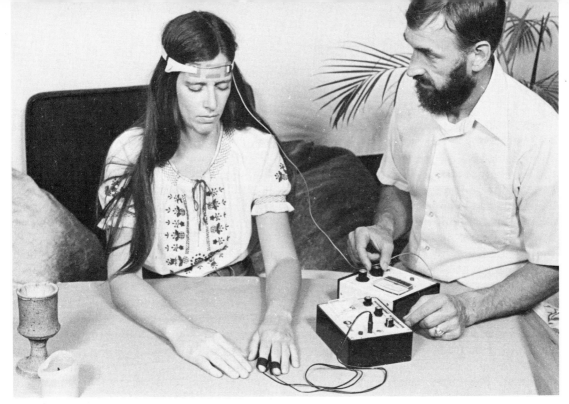

Scientific research involves systematic observation and measurement.

dream, and that drugs and dreaming are not related in terms of **causation;** that is, neither one causes or produces the other.

A second possible way to collect facts relevant to the relation between drugs and dreaming would be to conduct an experiment. In an **experiment,** the scientists not only observe what happens; they partially control what happens. A psychologist might conduct an experiment on drugs and dreaming by getting a number of volunteers who had not recently used drugs, and dividing them into two groups that were as equal as possible in terms of their frequency of dreaming. Members of one group (the **experimental group**) would then be given pills containing a drug, while members of the other group (the **control group**) would be given pills containing only sugar or some other inactive substance. The data for the experiment would be the later reports from the participants concerning the frequency of their dreams. If the frequency of dreaming

was different between the two groups, you would have confidence that the drug was somehow responsible for causing the difference. As a matter of fact, experiments of this sort have shown that many drugs do have the effect of reducing dreaming.

⑤ Science is both a particular method for acquiring knowledge and the body of knowledge acquired by that method. The method is the scientific method, a set of rules for observing and testing the world in order to decide what is probably true. One such rule is the principle of empirical verification, the idea that you must rely on experience, not opinion, to decide what is true. A second rule of science is the principle of reliable and public evidence, the idea that truth is decided on the basis of sound evidence. One way to obtain sound evidence is to conduct an experiment, a type of controlled observation in which the researcher manipulates one thing and then observes the consequences.

Research Methods: The Example of Marijuana Effects

In their study of behavior, psychologists use a variety of methods. Some of these involve a laboratory and complicated electronic equipment; other methods are used in the observation of behavior in natural settings in the world. Common to all the methods is a procedure for objective and systematic observation.

The dramatic increase in the use of marijuana in the past ten years has stimulated much research on the effects of marijuana smoking. Hundreds of studies of both the long-term and short-term effects of smoking marijuana have been conducted. Conclusions from these studies are reported in Chapter 10. Three studies of marijuana smoking are discussed below because they demonstrate three important but different methods of research in psychology.

Observation

One important research method in psychology is the systematic observation of behavior. Science is a way of knowing that is based on experience. Since science resolves issues and answers questions by referring to experience, the gathering of that experience is especially important. Although we all are constantly experiencing the world, these experiences are casual and informal. By contrast, **systematic observation** involves careful and specific attention given to different aspects of experience; it involves noting relationships among behaviors; and it involves detailed description.

An example of systematic observation is the study of the influence of context on marijuana effects. Researchers have found that one problem in discovering the effect of smoking marijuana is that the effects are different in different settings. The circumstances in which the marijuana is smoked seem to influence the psychological effect. The effect of marijuana also depends upon the set of expectations of the person smoking it. Under these circumstances, how can you observe the effect of smoking marijuana? Observations done in a laboratory will be different from those done in a home. Legal and moral attitudes toward marijuana smoking should influence the effect, since they affect expectations. Different countries have different attitudes toward marijuana smoking. This means that observations done in this country may be different from observations done elsewhere.

One researcher carefully observed marijuana smoking in Africa, among a group of people called the Plateau Tonga of Zambia.[1] He found their attitudes to be permissive and their expectations about the subjective effects to be different from the expectations of American smokers. Smoking "lubanje" (marijuana) is regarded as quite acceptable in Zambia; most Tonga respond to it as we respond to alcoholic beverages. When they smoke marijuana, they expect to feel confident and to become talkative and boastful. They do not focus on how they are feeling, on their change in consciousness or experience; instead they engage in lively conversation. This contrasts with observations of American smokers of marijuana; they expect to become more aware, detached, and relaxed. Because of these expectations they pay close attention to their internal, subjective changes. Descriptions of their subjective feelings usually conform to these expectations. Thus, this study showed that the effects of marijuana depend upon the cultural context.

Correlation

The term **correlation** refers to the correspondence or relationship between two things. Sometimes things vary together—like height and weight, the more of one the more of the other; or like exercise and weight, the more of one the less of the other. Two things are correlated when they vary together in some way. For example, the amount of your fuel bill and the frequency of lawn mowing are correlated. They vary together; when the weather is cold, you spend more for fuel and also mow the lawn less often. Cigarette smoking and cancer are correlated; in addition, there is evidence that cigarette smoking causes cancer. When two things are correlated, one may or may not cause the other. For example, the amount of your fuel bill and the frequency of your lawn mowing are correlated, but neither causes the other.

What is the correlation between marijuana smoking and academic performance in college? It's possible that students who smoke marijuana do more poorly than those who abstain; that is, it may be that the higher the marijuana smoking, the lower the grade point average in college. It is also possible that the reverse is true. A study was con-ducted to resolve this issue.[2] The researchers sent to 335 randomly selected students questionnaires about their use of marijuana and alcohol. The results showed no correlation between marijuana use and grade point average; marijuana users had about the same GPA as abstainers. There was a correlation, however, between marijuana use and scholastic *aptitude*, as measured by the college's admissions examination. Marijuana users scored more highly on this exam than abstainers. The marijuana users were apparently more capable, but were performing no better than the abstainers.

Experimentation

In an **experiment,** the researcher controls what happens. The experimenter manipulates a condition or situation and then measures the consequence. An experimenter interested in how a setting can influence a marijuana smoker's behavior would change the setting and determine the consequence.

In an experiment, the researcher controls what happens, then observes the response.

An experimenter interested in the effect of marijuana smoking on academic performance would control the amount of marijuana smoking, then measure the effect on GPA. All experiments involve some aspect of control or manipulation; the experimenter changes one thing and then observes the effect.

How would you determine the effect of marijuana on human memory? In one experiment, paid volunteers were tested for memory after smoking marijuana.[3] Eighteen young adults who were experienced with marijuana participated in the study. Each was given material to study and was later asked to recall it. The study session, the memory test, or both could be given under the influence of marijuana; the condition encountered by each participant was determined and controlled by the experimenter. The results of the experiment showed that more errors were made when the study session and the memory test were given under the influence of marijuana; marijuana interfered with memory. Even more errors were made when the study session was given under the influence of marijuana and the memory test was given without this influence. This result suggests that students who smoke marijuana while studying should have difficulty later on an examination remembering what was studied.

⑤ Observation, correlation, and experimentation are all used in the scientific study of behavior. Systematic observation involves careful and specific attention given to various aspects of experience. Correlation refers to the correspondence or relationship between two things; things that are correlated co-vary, or vary together. In an experiment, the researcher partially determines what happens, then observes the consequences.

Research in Psychology

The scientific method has been applied to the study of human behavior for about a hundred years. Many facts, principles, and theories about behavior have developed from research in psychology. The kind of research that is done is classified into one of several different areas, depending upon both the method used in the research and the subject being studied.

Developmental Psychology

The study of the changes in behavior and ability that occur as a child grows is called **developmental psychology.** Theorists have attempted to identify the important stages of development of the child, from birth to adulthood. A **stage** is a period of growth, a step toward greater maturity. The development of language, thinking abilities, motor coordination, moral beliefs, and sexual identity has been an important research area in developmental psychology. In this book, some general principles of developmental psychology are presented in Section II.

Jerome Kagan, a researcher in developmental psychology at Harvard University, has studied the perception and attention of infants; he has shown that important changes occur in the mind of a child between the ages of nine and twelve months. Kagan's dedication to scientific research was highly influenced by his mother:

My mother viewed knowledge as a sacrament and must have reminded me hundreds of times that her father, whom I had never known and to whom she felt strong affection, died quietly in a stuffed living-room chair with an open book on his chest. This image, which never

Developmental psychologists study the behavior of children.

had the opportunity to become tarnished, exerted its strong influence years later when I began to brood about a vocation.[4]

Kagan eventually decided to study psychology and to specialize in the study of children.

Personality and Clinical Psychology

Your **personality** is your typical way of behaving and relating to others. Research on personality attempts to identify the important ways in which people are psychologically different and to relate these differences to significant aspects of behavior and experience. For example, how can personality best be described—in terms of different types of people, different ways in which people differ, or different interactions between people and situations in the world? Research in **clinical psychology** examines the causes of personality disorders and the relative effectiveness of various types of treatment or **therapy** for these disorders. Clinical research also attempts to discover ways to promote self-development and personal growth.

A prominent modern researcher in clinical psychology is Carl Rogers. Rogers is a practicing therapist, a theorist, and an investigator in the techniques of psychotherapy. He originated a method of psychotherapy called nondirective or **client-centered therapy.** This is a form of therapy in which the therapist establishes a close and open relationship in which the clients can explore their own feelings safely. Rogers explains some of the things he has learned in the course of his study:

I would like to take you inside, to tell you some of the things I have learned from the thousands of hours spent working intimately with individuals in personal distress.

In my relationship with persons I have found that it does not help, in the long run, to act as though I were something that I am not.

I have found it highly rewarding when I can accept another person.

The more I am open to the realities in me and in the other person, the less do I find myself wishing to rush in to "fix" things.[5]

Roger's approach to personality and psychotherapy will also be discussed in Chapter 18 of this book.

Social Psychology

Research in **social psychology** investigates how individual behavior is influenced by the groups to which individuals belong. The effects of group pressure on an individual's beliefs and actions, the way social attitudes are formed and changed, the basis for interpersonal liking or attraction, the effects of different types of leadership on small groups, and the causes and cures of intergroup prejudice—these are some of the important research problems investigated by social psychologists. Many of these topics are discussed in Section VIII of this book.

Stanley Milgram is a social psychologist who has studied the psychological basis for obedience to authority. At first Milgram believed that the people who blindly obeyed the Nazi authorities during Hitler's control of Germany were different from other people. To find out for sure, he devised a study in which participants were instructed to press a lever which, they believed, would cause a dangerous electric shock to be delivered to another person. Most participants obeyed. The details of this experiment are discussed in Chapter 22.

Educational Psychology

Research on the psychology of classroom teaching and learning is called **educational psychology.** Types of teaching, methods of organizing and presenting material, ways of improving special skills such as reading, and methods for evaluating the results of instruction have been important research areas. Educational psychologists ask questions: Is TV instruction as effective as traditional "live" teaching? Are discussion groups superior to large lecture classes? Should rewards and punishments be used in the classroom? What is the most effective way to teach a retarded child to read?

A psychologist who is a theorist and researcher in educational psychology (in addition to other areas) is Jerome Bruner. Bruner's studies of the development of chil-

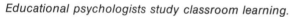

Educational psychologists study classroom learning.

dren's minds led him to propose an approach to teaching that is called the **discovery method.** Children who are taught by the discovery method of teaching are led to discover important principles themselves rather than to receive them passively from the teacher. The psychology of teaching and the discovery method are discussed in Chapter 9 of this book.

Experimental Psychology

Experimental psychology is a broad area of research defined by its unique method of investigation, the experiment. In an experiment researchers manipulate what they are studying and then observe the effects of their manipulation. Experimental psychologists studying perception may place participants in a specially constructed sound-proof room and then, in different trials, present very quiet tones to them in order to determine the lower limits of human hearing. The experimenter is controlling the physical environment of the participant and is observing the effects. Experimental psychologists studying learning may vary the time allowed for rehearsal of a passage to be learned; they then measure the amount of learning that takes place. Perception and learning are discussed in Chapters 12 and 7. The psychology experiment is discussed in detail in the research methods unit at the end of Section VIII of this book.

Neal Miller is an experimental psychologist who has studied learning for many years. While most of Miller's work involves studies of the rat, he believes that the same learning principles that apply to rats also apply to human beings. In his recent experiments he has studied how rats can be taught to control their heart rate, blood pressure, and other supposedly involuntary bodily reactions. Some progress has been made in applying his discoveries to human

Physiological psychologists, like Professor Neal E. Miller of Rockefeller University, study how the brain and nervous system control behavior. In such studies, rats are often used as experimental subjects.

problems of high blood pressure and heart irregularities.

Physiological Psychology

Physiological psychology is the study of how bodily processes relate to behavior. Some of the most important advances in scientific knowledge made by psychologists in recent years have been made by researchers studying the brain and its direction and control of behavior. It is known that body chemistry affects behavior (consider what happens when drugs change body chemistry) and that brain structures affect behavior (consider what happens to behavior when the brain is damaged). Studies of these effects now form an important body of knowledge in psychology. Physiological psychology is discussed in several of the chapters of this book, particularly Chapters 10 and 14.

⑤ Research in psychology is conducted in many areas of study. Developmental psychology involves the study of changes in behavior and ability that occur with increasing age. Research in personality and clinical psychology involves studying individual differences in behavior and experience and ways to promote personal growth. Social psychology is concerned with how individual behavior is influenced by groups. Educational psychology involves studying classroom learning and teaching. Experimental psychology involves studying behavior by means of the psychology experiment. Physiological psychology involves studying how bodily processes relate to behavior.

Summary

KEY QUESTIONS

1. What is science?

   Science is both a particular method of acquiring knowledge and the body of knowledge acquired by that method. Scientific psychology offers a unique way of understanding yourself and other people; rather than deciding what to believe on the basis of intuition or the opinion of some "authority," scientific psychology arrives at truth on the basis of systematic study and the scientific method.

2. What is the scientific method?

   The scientific method is a set of rules for deciding what is probably true. According to this method, you must rely on experience, not opinion, in the search for truth; and you must insist on sound evidence, evidence that is both reliable and public. Through observation, correlation, and experimentation, researchers in psychology seek facts and principles to better understand human behavior.

3. How is the scientific method applied in psychology?

   The scientific method is applied in many different areas of study in psychology. For example, researchers are interested in how behavior changes with age and how it is influenced by other people; researchers are interested in understanding the origins of personality problems and in developing effective means to treat problems.

KEY CONCEPTS

science	A method of acquiring knowledge and also the body of knowledge acquired by that method.
scientific method	A method for acquiring knowledge based on the rules of science.
principle of empirical verification	The rule of science that a scientific claim should be regarded as true only if it agrees with experience or observation.
principle of reliable and public evidence	The rule of science that no claim should be accepted as true without sound evidence, evidence that is accessible to many people and is repeatable.
interview	A conversation with the purpose of obtaining information.
causation	A cause-and-effect relationship; a relationship in which one thing influences another.
experiment	A form of controlled observation in which the researcher manipulates one thing and then observes the consequence.
experimental group	In an experiment, the group receiving a special treatment.
control group	In an experiment, the group receiving no special treatment.
systematic observation	A way of acquiring knowledge that involves careful and specific attention to different aspects of experience; it involves noting relationships, classifying, and detailed description.
correlation	The correspondence or relationship between two things; the degree to which things vary together.
developmental psychology	The study of the changes in behavior and ability that occur with age.
state	A period of growth in which behavior can be distinguished from that of other periods.
personality	A person's typical way of behaving and relating to others.
clinical psychology	The study of the causes of personality disorders and the effectiveness of different types of treatment.
therapy	Treatment.
client-centered therapy	A form of therapy based on a close and open relationship between therapist and client.
social psychology	The study of how individual behavior is affected by groups.

educational psychology   The study of teaching and school learning.

discovery method   A method of teaching that encourages students to discover important principles on their own.

experimental psychology   The study of behavior through the use of experiments.

physiological psychology   The study of how bodily processes, such as the activity of the brain, relate to behavior.

3 Learning Psychology

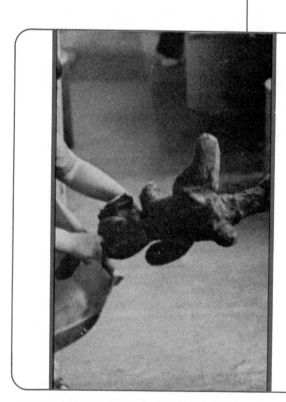

CHAPTER OUTLINE

KEY QUESTIONS

1. What is the history of psychology?

2. How do psychologists think about behavior?

3. What are the principles of effective study?

You know a great deal about psychology and have been using psychology all your life. You spend a lot of time thinking about the behavior of certain other people; you think about how to describe, predict, explain, and, possibly, control their behavior. For the most part, what you have learned about human behavior you have learned by direct experience.

This book is about the science of psychology and will require different learning skills. You will be reading and studying what psychology has to say about many different aspects of human behavior. Psychologists have a special point of view about behavior, a perspective that can be understood by learning the history of the discipline. Learning psychology will require not only that you study the facts and principles of the science but also that you understand the history and way of thinking of psychology.

History of Psychology

How are we to understand ourselves? People have wondered about their own behavior and have invented theories to explain it for thousands of years. Two early influential psychologists were the Greek philosophers Plato and Aristotle. Plato (about 400 B.C.) believed that the world known by the senses, the perceptual world, is but a faint copy of the perfect world of ideas. This world of ideas, Plato believed, exists quite separately from human beings, and is permanent and unchangeable. We are born, according to Plato, with knowledge of this world of ideas; that is, we have **innate ideas** (inborn ideas). Although knowledge of this perfect world of ideas is inborn, awareness of the ideas re-

What is the source of her knowledge—experience or innate ideas?

quires meditation and rational thought. Plato's student Aristotle held a different view; he believed that all knowledge comes from experience. According to Aristotle, no ideas are innate. The mind at birth is quite empty, like a "blank tablet," or **tabula rasa**. Aristotle was a careful student of human behavior and wrote about the human personality, the senses, memory, and thinking. Plato's conception of innate ideas and Aristotle's emphasis on the role of experience both have strongly influenced the past two thousand years of psychological thought.

Origins of Scientific Psychology

Modern scientific psychology is believed to have started in about 1879 with a German named Wilhelm Wundt. Wundt defined psychology as the science of **consciousness** (awareness); he believed that the task of psychology was to analyze and classify experience into elementary sensations and feelings. Wundt's method of investigation was **trained introspection,** or self-observation. We are all occasionally introspective; we pay attention to our inner feelings and experiences. But Wundt's approach was more systematic. In his laboratory people were trained to be careful and reliable observers of their experiences. Furthermore, Wundt was not interested in experiences that were random or accidental; he controlled the experiences by controlling the **stimuli**—tones, lights, odors, or other events that stimulated reactions. Wundt believed that people could be understood by studying a person's conscious experience produced by simple stimuli.

As a child in Germany, Wundt did so poorly in school that he was held back a year; but he was a determined student and eventually earned a degree in medicine. After years of teaching physiology in the university, he

Wilhelm Wundt

established in 1879 the world's first laboratory for the scientific study of psychology. Wundt was a methodical and humorless man who had little tolerance for any views except his own. He was a popular lecturer in the university but had a rather stiff classroom manner. Try to imagine yourself sitting in his class in 1880:

Wundt would appear at exactly the right minute—punctuality was essential—dressed all in black and carrying a small sheaf of lecture notes. He clattered up the side aisle to the platform with an awkward shuffle and a sound as if his soles were made of wood. . . . His voice was weak at first, then gained in strength and emphasis. . . . He seldom referred to the few jotted notes. As the clock struck the end of the hour he stopped and, stooping a little, clattered out as he had clattered in.[1]

Wundt's approach to studying psychology by analyzing conscious experience was later attacked as unscientific. The mind, it was argued, cannot be reliably observed, and therefore cannot be objectively studied. After a lapse of about 60 or 70 years, psychology is once again studying consciousness with great interest, this time with modern objective methods.

People Who Made the Science

The history of psychology is a history of our conception of our own nature. Over the years psychologists have offered a variety of views to explain human nature. What are your views on human nature?

Freud, Watson, and Maslow represent three views that still influence modern psychology. The ideas of each of these men all stem from their different opinions on one central issue: What is human nature? How can we understand ourselves?

■ *Freud* Sigmund Freud believed that people can be understood only by understanding the contents of their unconscious minds. Like other animals, Freud believed, we have biological impulses and drives that compel us to irrational violence or sexual gratification. These impulses are unconscious, below the surface of awareness, in the dark unconscious mind.

Freud grew up and spent his life in Vienna, Austria. A small lively man with a moustache and pointed beard, Freud developed a theory of personality that has influenced Western thought more than that of any other psychologist.

Freud's theory of personality development was very controversial because he stated that infants have sexual impulses and seek sexual gratification. Adult personality, according to Freud, is highly influenced by experiences that occur before the age of three, particularly by experiences arising from the infant's sexual desires. Freud's ideas about sex are discussed in Chapter 13.

Freud emphasized the importance of **unconscious motivation:** people are often unconscious (unaware) of their motives (why they do what they do). Personality, Freud wrote, consists of three basic processes: the **id** (storehouse of unconscious impulses, often sexual or aggressive in nature); the **superego**

Sigmund Freud

John Watson

(conscience, the guardian of right and wrong); and the **ego** (the rational self which attempts to satisfy the demands both of the id and of the superego). Freud's method of treating personality disorders is called **psychoanalysis.** The goal of psychoanalysis is to make conscious what is presently unconscious, to bring unconscious memories and impulses to the light of day. Psychoanalysis is discussed in more detail in Chapter 18.

What was Freud like? Freud had an unorthodox and brilliant mind, capable of intense concentration in the search for truth. Even the smallest detail would capture his attention, for he was convinced that everything a person did was meaningful, even small "slips of the tongue" (now called Freudian slips). As one person described him:

The half-peering and half-piercing gaze beneath the heavy brows showed a power to see beneath the surface and beyond the boundaries of ordinary perceptions. But it also expressed a capacity for patient, careful scrutiny and for suspended judgment so rare as to

be unrecognizable by many; his cool skepticism has even been misread as cynicism or pessimism. There was in him a conjunction of the hunter on an endless trail and the persistent immovable watcher who checks and revises; it was from this conjunction that his power of discovering and understanding the sources of the feelings and behavior of men and women sprang[2]

Freud lived a long and full life. For most of his adult years he was a heavy cigar smoker, often smoking as many as twenty cigars a day.[2] This habit may have contributed to the fact that he died of cancer of the mouth.

■ *Watson* John Watson, an American psychologist, disagreed with both Wundt and Freud. People are to be understood, Watson believed, only by understanding their observable behavior. Psychology should be the science of publicly observable behavior, not the science of the conscious or unconscious mind. Behavior, Watson argued, is controlled by the **environment,** the physical and psychological context of behavior; people are

Abraham Maslow

into body movements or glandular secretions. Watson later claimed that thinking consisted of "subvocal speech," and could be studied by measuring small movements of the vocal cords and tongue.

Watson believed that adult intelligence and personality could be attributed to **conditioned reflexes,** involuntary reactions acquired through an elementary form of learning. According to Watson, these reactions developed through the years by the interaction of a child with the environment. He made the startling claim that he could take any baby at random and make it into a lawyer, thief, or Indian chief by properly conditioning its feelings and actions.

■ *Maslow* Abraham Maslow believed that Wundt, Freud, and Watson were wrong. According to Maslow, people cannot be understood by analyzing their elementary sensations; they cannot be understood as controlled by animalistic impulses or by external forces. Instead, human beings are conscious, creative, and unique among other creatures, Maslow wrote. They transcend their environment and are free agents, not robots.

Maslow objected to psychology's focus on rats, schizophrenics, involuntary reactions, and the negative side of people's nature. He advocated the study of the normal, healthy, and creative person. According to Maslow, people are born inherently good, with an inner motivation toward fulfilling their potential. They become bad, abnormal, or destructive only when the environment blocks or frustrates this inner nature.

Fulfilling your potential is termed **self-actualization.** Maslow wrote:

All the evidence that we have . . . indicates that it is reasonable to assume in practically every human being, and certainly in almost every newborn baby, that there is an active will

like machines run by external forces and can be understood by studying the ways the environment controls their observable behavior.

John Watson was born near Greenville, South Carolina, in 1878, and as a child attended a one-room rural schoolhouse. His teachers reported that he was a poor student, and was lazy and argumentative. He went to the University of Chicago for graduate study in psychology, working his way through school as a waiter and janitor. His Ph.D. thesis involved a study of how rats learn to run through a maze after they have been made blind or deaf.

Watson became a professor at Johns Hopkins University in Baltimore and published a paper in 1913 that launched a radical new movement in psychology, **behaviorism.** Watson called for a purely objective approach to psychology, defining the task of the science as the prediction and control of observable behavior. Thinking, feeling, and dreaming could not be publicly observed and so, according to Watson, could not be studied scientifically unless they could be translated *towards health, an impulse towards growth, or towards the actualization of human potentialities.*[3]

Maslow studied the lives of a few unusual individuals who, he believed, had fulfilled their potential; he called these rare persons self-actualized. He found that these self-actualized people experienced more moments of intense happiness, awe, or wonder than most other people. During these "peak" experiences, the individuals tended to become less conscious of themselves and to feel more spontaneous and in touch with the world. While these moments occur only rarely for most people, self-actualized persons experienced them more often. Maslow's theories are discussed in more detail in Chapter 18.

Maslow's research and theories have stimulated the development of an important new direction in psychology—**humanistic psychology.** Maslow called humanistic psychology the "third force" in psychology, the first two forces being psychoanalysis and behaviorism. Humanistic psychology is more concerned with human potential than with personality disorders; it seeks ways to promote self-development and growth.

Psychology Today

Modern psychology is enormous in its scope. It includes Freud's psychoanalysis, Watson's behaviorism, and Maslow's humanism in various modified and modernized versions. Modern views of the human personality and neurotic and psychotic disorders have been strongly influenced by Freud. Although there are many different types of psychotherapy that have been developed since Freud, most are still variations of the "talking cure" that he used, psychoanalysis. The influence of Watson's behaviorism can be seen in most areas of modern psychology

today. The study of conditioning and conditioned reflexes, which Watson popularized, has been a consistent interest in psychology ever since. The view that human beings are controlled by their environments is a belief still held by many psychologists. Maslow's humanism—the "third force" in psychology—has formed the basis for the development of the recent emphasis on human potential. The concepts of self-actualization and personality growth have inspired many best-selling self-improvement books.

The study of the conscious mind—systematically begun by Wundt, but long out of favor—has recently been a major focus in modern psychology. The study of the conscious mind involves studying perception, imagery, thinking, and memory and is now referred to as **cognitive psychology.** Cognitive psychologists today are interested in how people perceive their worlds, how they acquire and retain knowledge, and how they solve problems.

Ⓢ Modern scientific psychology began with Wilhelm Wundt, a German who established the world's first laboratory for the scientific study of psychology. Wundt was interested in studying conscious experience, an area of study now currently popular that is called cognitive psychology. Sigmund Freud, the founder of psychoanalysis, emphasized the importance of the unconscious mind in influencing behavior; he developed a theory of personality based on three processes: the id, ego, and superego. John Watson denied that psychology should study either the conscious or the unconscious mind; instead, he stated, psychology should be the science of publicly observable behavior. Abraham Maslow emphasized the uniqueness of human beings and their natural drive for growth; people are not like machines or lower animals, he argued, but are conscious and creative free agents.

Thinking Psychologically

How do psychologists think about behavior? They begin with a curiosity, a questioning, an urge to know, that is probably not much different from yours. Their desire to understand people is similar to your desire. However, what they do with this desire, this urge, is different.

Analysis, Precision, and Measurement

When psychologists think about behavior, study individuals, or try to solve people's problems, their approach is highly analytic. **Analysis** consists of separating something into its component parts; it involves categorizing and clarifying these parts, and studying their relations to each other. A related characteristic of how psychologists think is precision. **Precision** involves being exact and specific; psychologists dislike being vague and general and want instead to be precise and detailed. This need for precision is often served by measuring behavior. **Measurement** involves assigning a number to behavior; for example, rather than saying a child is very intelligent, a psychologist might say that the child has an IQ of 130. The concepts of analysis, precision, and measurement describe how psychologists approach the study of behavior.

How would you study personality? Your curiosity about people has led you to notice the many differences among individuals in their personalities. Some people tend to behave fairly consistently in one way, while other people behave in other ways. Psychologists in their study of personality take a somewhat different approach. Their interest in analysis leads psychologists to divide up the concept of personality into many different aspects or traits. Their interest in

The time required to solve a puzzle is one measure of intelligence.

precision leads psychologists to define these traits as exactly as possible. Their interest in measurement leads psychologists to develop personality tests, ways of measuring personality traits so that individual differences can be precisely described.

Types of Psychological Questions

In studying behavior, psychologists tend to ask certain kinds of questions. A common question is, "What is the origin of this behavior?" By this question the psychologist is asking how the behavior began. Was it innate or was it learned? If it was learned, how and when was it learned? A second common

Psychologists are interested in the origins of aggression and in individual differences in aggressiveness.

question is, "What is the course of development of this behavior?" How did it change as the individual grew older? A third common question is, "What are the individual differences in this behavior?" In regard to this behavior, are certain types of people different from others? A fourth common question is, "What is the present context of this behavior?" What typically precedes this behavior (What are its **antecedents**)? What typically follows this behavior (What are its **consequences**)? In what kinds of situations does it occur? A fifth common question is, "What are the biological foundations of this behavior?" Is it influenced by hormones or drugs? What brain structures control this behavior? Finally, a sixth common question is, "What can be done to manipulate this behavior?" How can it be increased, decreased, or otherwise changed?

How do psychologists think about behavior? Consider their approach to the problem of aggression. They have wondered about its *origin*—is it innate or is it learned? They have found that we are born with the

potential for aggression, but learn how and when to be aggressive. Psychologists have wondered about how aggression develops in children; what is its *course of development?* They have learned, for example, that aggressive parents tend to increase the aggressiveness in their children. Psychologists have wondered about *individual differences* in aggressiveness. They have learned that these differences exist and can be measured. In this society, but not in certain others, men tend to be more aggressive than women. Psychologists have wondered about the context and *antecedents* for aggression. They have found that aggression frequently follows frustration, but not always. They have wondered about the *biological foundations* of aggression. They have found that certain brain structures control aggression; aggression can be reduced if these brain structures are cut. Finally, psychologists have wondered how aggression can be *manipulated;* in particular, they want to discover how to reduce it. They have learned that certain drugs reduce aggression.

⌷ When psychologists think about a problem or investigate behavior, their approach involves analysis, precision, and measurement. They tend to categorize behavior and to separate it into component parts; they tend to be exact and detailed, not vague or general, in their study; and they tend to measure the behavior they are studying. By using this approach, they try to answer such questions as "What is the origin of this behavior?", "What are the antecedents of this behavior?", or "How can this behavior be changed?"

Studying Psychology

In the hundred years of its existence, scientific psychology has accumulated a vast body of knowledge about human behavior; psychological facts, principles, theories, and methods now fill whole libraries of books and journals. Learning psychology requires a considerable amount of reading and studying. To master psychology, you must become an efficient learner.

An important principle psychologists have repeatedly confirmed is that people can learn how to be more effective learners. You can learn to read faster and better, to study more effectively, to retain what you learn for a longer time, and to improve examination performance. But first you must determine what your present habits are.

Inventory of Study Habits

How well do you typically study? The test below will help you assess your present habits. Read each of the items below; check those that are generally true for you.

☐ 1. Before reading an assignment in the textbook, I first attempt to get an overview of the material.

☐ 2. After reading passages in the text, I restate to myself the key ideas.

☐ 3. When I am reading I write down on paper the most important ideas in my own words.

☐ 4. As I read the text I think of questions that the text has answered.

☐ 5. While studying for a test I go over important concepts and definitions by repeating them out loud.

☐ 6. While studying for a test I make up and give myself practice tests, and I write out the answers.

☐ 7. While studying for a test I classify, organize, and summarize the important concepts to be covered on the exam.

☐ 8. I study small units of material frequently, rather than large units less often.

☐ 9. I study every week and do not depend just on cramming before the exam.

☐ 10. After I have learned a concept I continue to study it some more.

☐ 11. I hardly ever study in front of the TV or in bed.

☐ 12. I have a special place set aside for studying that is fairly free from distractions, and I almost always study there.

☐ 13. I quit studying for a while when I find I have trouble concentrating.

☐ 14. In studying, after I have completed a unit of work, I "reward" myself by doing something else I like.

☐ 15. I manage my time so that going to shows, talking to friends, and other activities do not prevent me from studying.

☐ 16. I have a schedule for studying and I follow it fairly well.

Each of the items on the study inventory describes a principle for effective study. The higher the number of items that you were able to check, the more effective your study habits are. The specific principles on which the inventory is based are discussed in the following section.

Principles of Effective Study

There are a number of principles that can be applied to improve your study skills. The first is the principle of *active reading*. When most people read, they do little more than move their eyes. Active reading requires more work, but it has a payoff: when you are through, you know what you've read. When you read actively, you begin by skimming your assignment to get an overview. You can do this by reading the paragraph headings, the summaries, and an occasional topic sentence. Then when you begin to read, you stop after key passages and restate the main points to yourself. You write down the key concepts as you go through. You try making up questions that are answered in the material you are reading. In these ways your reading will be active; you will continually interact with the material you are reading. Students who read in this way comprehend what they read better and remember it longer.

A second principle of effective study is *active practice*. In your earlier schooling you may have been able to do well by reading your assignments only once. Mastering more difficult material requires not only effective reading but also effective practice. Active practice involves reviewing the assignment after you have read it once; it involves rehearsing the main points by repeating them out loud or writing them down; it involves putting main points into your own words by paraphrasing; it may involve using "flash

Studying effectively.

cards" to practice the vocabulary of terms you must master. By practicing in an active way you will learn the material better.

A third principle of effective study is *spaced practice*. Many students depend upon cramming the night before the exam, studying in one long period what had been weekly assignments. Cramming in this way is called "massed practice." The alternative is "spaced practice." Spaced practice involves distributing or spacing your study periods so that you do not wind up studying everything all at once. If you study psychol-

Studying ineffectively.

A fifth principle is *controlled concentration.* Many students complain that they are often distracted from studying, or have difficulty with daydreaming or feeling sleepy. These are failures of concentration, but concentration can be controlled. One way to do this is to find a quiet study place, always study there, and do nothing else there but study. If you feel like daydreaming, sleeping, eating, or talking to friends, you should go somewhere else to do these things. If you follow this rule, you will find it easier and easier to concentrate on studying in your special study place. A second way to strengthen your concentration is to stop studying. Take a break when you feel your mind wandering. Stop for a while when you have completed a unit of studying. These breaks will strengthen your ability to study with full concentration.

A sixth principle of effective study is *time management.* Many students feel that they just do not have the time to keep up with their studies. Many demands are being made on your time by school, friends, family, and perhaps work. You can, however, make more efficient use of the limited time you have. The first step is to record how you have been spending your time. Next, make a schedule that includes enough time for studying and try to stick to it. Make sure that you leave yourself time for fun too; otherwise, following the schedule will become too unpleasant and you will abandon it.

Now, when you are preparing to read this book, is a good time to evaluate your study habits and consider trying some new techniques. Use the principles of psychology to help you learn psychology.

⬚ Six principles of effective studying are (1) active reading, (2) active practice, (3) spaced practice, (4) overlearning, (5) controlled concentration, and (6) time management. These principles make learning both more efficient and more lasting.

ogy a little bit each day, you will learn it much better than if you study it all just before the exam. The rule here is plan, don't cram.

A fourth principle is *overlearning.* When you study something just until you feel you know it, you will often forget it later. Overlearning involves continuing to study for a while after you feel you have mastered it. You must assume that you will forget some between the time you last study something and the time you are tested on it. By overlearning the material, you give yourself a margin for forgetting.

Summary

KEY QUESTIONS

1. What is the history of psychology?

The history of psychology is the history of our attempts to understand ourselves. It is the history of our conceptions of our own nature. Plato and Aristotle disagreed on the role of experience in shaping human nature. Wundt and Freud disagreed on the significance of conscious experience in shaping human nature. Maslow and Watson disagreed on whether people were controlled by their environments or were free agents. The present attitudes of psychology can best be understood within the context of this history.

2. How do psychologists think about behavior?

Psychologists think about behavior and approach problems differently from many other people. They emphasize analysis, precision, and measurement in their attempts to understand behavior. They insist on being exact and detailed, on analyzing behavior into its component parts, and on measuring behavior.

3. What are the principles of effective study?

The material in this book and in other books can be studied effectively or ineffectively. To learn psychology effectively requires the use of study skills. These techniques make learning both more efficient and more lasting. Active, rather than passive, reading and rehearsal lead to better comprehension and better retention. Studying small units and studying not just to mastery, but beyond mastery, will provide insurance against forgetting. Other principles involve ways of controlling concentration during studying and establishing a study schedule.

KEY CONCEPTS

innate ideas	Ideas present at birth; inborn ideas.
tabula rasa	View of the mind as a "blank tablet," empty at birth.
consciousness	Awareness.

trained introspection	A method of studying experience through self-observation under controlled conditions.
stimulus (one) stimuli (plural)	Anything that is sensed or that produces a reaction; at the simple level, these can be lights, tones, or odors; more complexly, they can be events, people, situations, words, or even books.
unconscious motivation	Desires or needs of which a person is unaware.
id	According to Freud, that aspect of personality that is a storehouse of sexual and aggressive impulses.
superego	According to Freud, that aspect of personality that is the guardian of right and wrong; conscience.
ego	According to Freud, that aspect of personality that attempts to deal with reality in a rational manner.
psychoanalysis	A form of therapy developed by Freud.
environment	The physical and psychological context of behavior; trees, storms, your mother, school, and this book all form a part of your context.
behaviorism	A system of psychology started by John Watson; according to this system, psychology is limited to the study of publicly observable behavior.
conditioned reflexes	Involuntary reactions acquired through an elementary form of learning; for example, when your mouth waters in reaction to a picture of food.
self-actualization	An individual fulfilling his or her potential.
humanistic psychology	The "third force" in psychology; emphasizes personal growth and creativity.
cognitive psychology	The study of mental activities such as thinking, knowing, perceiving, and remembering.
analysis	The act of separating something into its component parts.
precision	Accuracy; being exact and specific.
measurement	Assigning a number to behavior on the basis of a rule (for example, by using an IQ test).
antecedents	The prior context; the events that precede behavior.
consequences	The events that follow a behavior.

Suggested Readings

Psychology: The Science of Mental Life by George A. Miller & Robert Buckout. New York: Harper & Row, 1962. A group of essays surveying the historical development of the science of psychology. Highly readable.

A Brief History of Psychology by Michael Wertheimer. New York: Holt, Rinehart and Winston, 1970. An overview of the people and ideas of psychology, from the Greeks to the twentieth century.

The Mind of Man: A History of Psychotherapy and Psychoanalysis by Walter Bromberg. New York: Harper & Row, 1954. The evolution of psychotherapy as an art and science, from magic and faith-healing to behavior therapy and group therapy.

The Life and Work of Sigmund Freud by Ernest Jones. New York: Basic Books, 1961. A lengthy but interesting biography of the life of Freud. Full of fascinating personal details.

Erik H. Erikson: The Growth of His Work by Robert Coles. Boston: Little, Brown, 1970. A biography of Erikson, the man and his work.

The Psychologists: What They Do and How They Came to Do It ed. by T. S. Kraiwiec. New York: Oxford University Press, 1972. Twelve psychologists from various research fields describe their work and lives.

Psychology as Science and Art by James Deese. New York: Harcourt Brace Jovanovich, 1972. Introduction to the philosophy, theories, and methods of psychology in a readable paperback.

The Psychology Experiment by Barry F. Anderson. (Second edition.) Belmont, Calif.: Brooks/Cole, 1971. A simple well-organized book explaining the applications of the scientific method in psychology. Describes how to design and conduct a psychology experiment. Includes a section on elementary statistics.

The Nature and Study of Psychology by John Wallace & Lee Sechrest. Itasca, Ill.: F. E. Peacock Publishers, 1973. Nontechnical orientation to psychology. Examines psychology's scientific basis, its relationship to other disciplines and society, and its possible future applications.

Psychology's Scientific Endeavor by Christopher F. Monte. New York: Praeger Publishers, 1975. A lively supplementary text for beginning psychology students. Explains why and how psychologists use the scientific method to explore human behavior.

Research Methods

1 Questioning

Are you the sort of person who often wonders, "What would happen if . . .," "Why do people do . . .," or "What causes . . ."?

The first step in research occurs when one person wonders about something. Research psychologists wonder about a lot of things, and then they take the next step and try to find the answers to their questions. Scientific research is a way of asking and answering questions; so research begins with questioning.

Asking questions is not as easy as you might think. Some scientists say that asking exactly the right question is nine-tenths of the work in research. For scientific purposes, some questions are much better than others; some lead directly to important research while others are useless for research. How can you tell the difference?

Asking Scientific Questions

To be valuable for scientific research, questions should satisfy two rules: (1) they must be significant (meaningful), and (2) they must be answerable.

There is no simple way to tell when your question is significant and when it is not; many scientists ask questions that later prove to be insignificant; and a question that is insignificant today may be significant tomorrow. Some questions are significant because they concern practical problems and their solutions: Is psychoanalysis an effective treatment for drug addiction? Some questions are significant because they concern basic psychological processes: What is the effect of anxiety on learning? Some questions are significant because they are related to an important theory in psychology: Are dreams of sex, as Freud would have predicted, more common during sexual abstinence?

The second criterion that scientific questions should satisfy is that they should be answerable by the **scientific method.** This method answers questions by seeking the facts, by observing what is, by referring to experience; popular opinion, fond wishes, expert judgment, and the dreams of gurus do not count. The term **fact** refers to information based on observation. Science accepts as fact only the results of careful observation. Some questions are not answerable by the scientific method. The question "Is murder evil?" is not answerable by carefully observing the world. The answer to this question rests on human values and moral beliefs.

Facts and Value Judgments

An **empirical question** is a question that can be answered by observation or by referring to experience. An example of an empirical question is the following: What is the effect of alcohol on behavior? This is an empirical question because it can be answered by carefully observing the behavior of people who are intoxicated. The results of your observations are *facts*—not just opinions—and these facts can then be used to answer the original question. The scientific method answers empirical questions by seeking facts through careful observation.

A **value question** is different from an empirical question. Value questions cannot be answered by observation but instead must be answered by preference, opinion, or belief. An example of a value question is the following: Should people drink alcohol? This is a value question because it asks for a judgment of good and bad, a moral conclusion. To answer a value question, you must

refer to your beliefs or values; the result will be a **value judgment,** not a fact. A value judgment is a conclusion based on values or beliefs. The scientific method cannot answer value questions.

A Test to Take

Here are twenty questions; some can be answered by the scientific method and some cannot. Can you tell the difference? Check the questions you think are answerable scientifically.

- [ ] 1. Should mothers work or stay home with their children?
- [ ] 2. What are the psychological differences between the children of working and nonworking mothers?
- [ ] 3. Is premarital sexual intercourse wrong?
- [ ] 4. What is the relation between premarital intercourse and later marital sexual adjustment?
- [ ] 5. Is it bad for teachers to spank their students?
- [ ] 6. What proportion of teachers use physical punishment in classes?
- [ ] 7. Should people who are mentally disturbed be confined in mental hospitals even if they do not agree to it?
- [ ] 8. What is the effect of hospitalization on the severity of psychotic symptoms?
- [ ] 9. Should drug addicts be forced to accept psychotherapy?
- [ ] 10. What proportion of drug addicts remain drug-free five years after psychotherapy?
- [ ] 11. Is it better to be a conformist or a nonconformist?
- [ ] 12. What are the family backgrounds of conformists and nonconformists?
- [ ] 13. Is smoking marijuana wrong?
- [ ] 14. What is the effect of marijuana on thinking and memory?

□ 15. Should homosexuality be a crime?

□ 16. What are the causes of homosexuality?

□ 17. Which is a better place to live—the country or the city?

□ 18. What are the psychological effects of rural and urban environments?

□ 19. Should all mothers love their babies?

□ 20. What is the effect of inadequate love during infancy?

In the list above only the even-numbered questions can be answered by the scientific method. The odd-numbered questions are *value questions*, employing such terms as "should," "right," "wrong," "good," and "bad." The even-numbered questions are *empirical questions*, asking about the facts as they are in the world. Psychology uses the scientific method to find answers to empirical questions; however, there are many questions about human behavior that cannot be answered by psychology because they involve values, moral and religious beliefs, or the laws of society.

The Philosophy of Science

The requirement to find answers empirically, in experience, is a philosophical position called **logical positivism.** According to this school of philosophy, in order to know what is true you must refer to the facts of experience; observation of fact is the only solid basis for human knowledge. Some logical positivists express the more radical view that it is meaningless to talk about the "soul" or about what is "good," since these terms do not refer to things that can be observed in the world. Most psychologists would probably accept the more modest position that the limitations of the scientific method prevent questions about the "soul" or about what is "good" from being investigated

scientifically; such questions fall within the legitimate province of other disciplines.

Sources of Questions

Where do psychologists get the questions that they ask? Although the method psychologists use in answering questions is systematic and objective, the method they use in generating significant and interesting questions is highly subjective and is more of an art than a science. Many questions stem from the psychologist's intuition, hunches, or informed guesses. Questions have been known to be stimulated by dreams, fantasies, novels, and myths. More often, scientific questions are the result of being observant, of noticing the details of what happens in the world, of attending to your own experience and the behavior of others without preconceptions.

Questions are also stimulated by theories that psychologists have devised to account for their findings. For example, Freud's theory of personality development assumed that the repression of sexual feelings was a universal problem. This theory stimulated other psychologists to ask whether repressed sexuality was evident even in primitive cultures or was a feature only of so-called civilized societies. Some theories provide more interesting questions than others; theories such as Freud's which provoke many questions are regarded by psychologists as superior to those which do not.

A Question Cookbook

Psychological questions that are significant and answerable come in many varieties. They can be classified in different ways: one way to classify them is to relate them to the main goals of the science of psychology. Psychology has four important goals: description, prediction, control, and explanation. Each of these goals is advanced by a different type of psychological question.

Consider hallucinations (perceiving things that are not there). You can ask (1) What is a *hallucination?* (description); (2) What is the relation of *hallucinations* and *mental disturbance?* (prediction); (3) What is the effect of *LSD* on *hallucinations?* (control); and (4) What causes *hallucinations?* (explanation). The italicized terms in the four questions can be replaced with almost any other psychological term in order to generate other interesting questions. The four forms are like recipes for cooking up interesting questions.

1. What is _____?
2. What is the relation of _____ and _____?
3. What is the effect of _____ on _____?
4. What causes _____?

Try substituting each of the following ingredients in the standard question-recipes listed above: anxiety, conformity, prejudice, learning, memory, and aggression. The substitution is demonstrated below for dreaming and for psychosis (mental disturbance).

The Example of Dreaming

Description
What is a dream? What is the most common content of dreams? What is the subjective experience of dreaming? What is the frequency of dreaming?

Prediction
What is the relation between wishes or needs and dream content? What is the relation between dreaming and bodily movements in sleep? What is the relation between dreaming and the electrical activity of the brain?

Control
What is the effect of drugs on dreaming? What is the effect of sounds in the night on the content of dreams? What is the effect of the previous day's experience on the content of dreams?

Explanation
What causes dreams? Why do people dream?

The Example of Psychosis

Description
What is psychosis? What are the symptoms of psychosis? What is the most common psychosis?

Prediction
What is the relation between psychosis and the type of family background? What is the relation between psychosis in one twin and psychosis in the other twin? What is the relation of psychosis and the chemical composition of the blood?

Control
What is the effect of tranquilizing drugs on psychosis? What is the effect of shock treatment on psychosis? What is the effect of rewards and punishments on psychotic behavior?

Explanation
Why do people become psychotic?

Now think about your own behavior and experiences and your observations of others. Do you have some particular areas of interest? Pick an area and try listing some questions that can be answered empirically. The question cookbook method may help you do this.

KEY CONCEPTS

scientific method	A method for acquiring knowledge based on the rules of science; questions are answered by seeking facts from observations.
fact	Information based on observation; a statement based on careful observation or experience.
empirical question	A question that can be answered by observation.
value question	A question that must be answered by preference, opinion, or belief; it cannot be answered by observation.
value judgment	A conclusion based on values or beliefs.
logical positivism	A school of philosophy that emphasizes the basis of knowledge in observation and experience; according to this school, observation of fact is the only valid basis for human knowledge.

Identity

4 Heredity

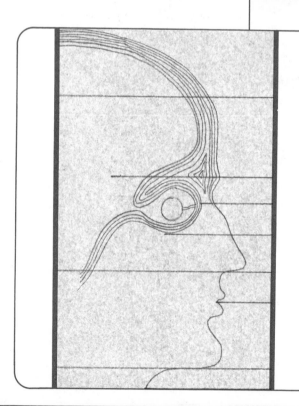

KEY QUESTIONS

1. Can behavior be inherited?
2. How is behavior inherited?
3. What is the relation of heredity to intelligence, schizophrenia, and personality?

Could you have been someone else?

Suppose some family in another part of the world had adopted you at birth. Your home and experiences would have been entirely different. Would you be similar to the person you are now? You would look about the same. Your eye, hair, and skin color are physical characteristics you were born with; they were determined genetically. But are there aspects of your behavior, your personality, your *identity*, that were not formed uniquely by your life experiences but were inherited from your parents?

Behavioral Genetics

To some degree your behavior and personality are inborn; some aspects of your behavior you inherited from your parents. **Genetics** is the study of inherited characteristics, and **behavioral genetics** is the study of the inheritance of behavior. Scientists typically

61

separate two general influences on behavior, heredity and the environment. Some characteristics are influenced strongly by heredity; like hair color they are primarily inborn. Others are strongly influenced by the environment, that is, by what happens in the womb and after birth. However, all behavior involves both hereditary and environmental influences; both must be considered to understand behavior.

Human beings are, of all animals, the least determined by hereditary influences. The most important forces affecting your behavior come from your experiences in the world and with the people around you. Simple animals like insects and fish, however, are under much stronger hereditary control.

Instincts

Behavior can be inherited: the migration of birds at the change of seasons; salmon returning from the sea to spawn; the spider building its complex web; the bee storing its honey; the moth flying to its death in the flame. Complex unlearned behaviors such as these are called **instincts.** These behavior sequences are as characteristic of a particular animal species as is its physical appearance. Because of this, they are called **species-specific behaviors.** Typically, an instinctual behavior pattern appears to be adaptive and purposeful, in that it contributes to the capacity of the species to survive. Human beings, however, do not appear to be born with instincts.

■ *Rat Mothers* A pregnant rat that is kept in a cage will begin to build a nest just before her litter is born. After she gives birth, she cleans her tiny babies carefully and allows them to nurse. When the young begin to scatter about the cage, she carries them back to the protection of the nest. This

sequence of behavior is inborn, not learned. The instinctive behavior is the same for a rat's first litter as it is for its fifth; it is not dependent upon previous experiences and is displayed in exactly the same fashion by rats reared completely apart from other rats.[1] Mothering is not unique to people.

■ *Birds Who Paint and Use Tools* Certain birds from the Galapagos Islands, a species of finch, eat insects from the bark of trees as do the various woodpeckers of the Americas. Unlike the woodpeckers, however, the Galapagos finch lacks a long and pointed bill for probing into the bark; instead the finch collects and uses the sharp spine of a cactus as a crowbar held in its mouth, digging out the grubs with the sharp point. Only one species of finch uses tools in this fashion, and the young apparently do not learn the habit from their parents.[2] People are not the only users of tools.

The male satin bower bird of Australia builds a small structure of twigs and branches in which to court the female bower bird. To attract a mate, the bower bird places small colored shells and stones on the ground around this structure, giving the appearance

Australian bower birds.

of a garden. To complete his work, he paints the inside of his love house with charcoal from a burnt twig or purple juice from a berry held in his mouth. This elaborate courtship display is apparently an inborn behavior.[3] People are not the only architects.

■ *Triggers* These instinctive sequences of behavior do not occur at random; they are typically triggered by some specific stimulus, sometimes called a **releasing stimulus.** The releasing stimulus for the fighting behavior of the male stickleback fish is a small red spot on another fish. In nature, the red spot normally occurs on a rival male stickleback. For this fish, the red spot on another male triggers instinctive fighting behavior. Not all releasing stimuli are external to the organism. The instinctive maternal behavior of the rat, for example, is released by a hormone called "prolactin," normally associated with the production of milk. If the male rat is injected with this hormone, he too will begin building a nest.

Releasing stimuli are sometimes very specific. Certain newly hatched birds automatically crouch down when a hawk flies overhead. The releasing stimulus for this instinctive crouching behavior is a hawklike shadow—the shadow of some other bird will not initiate the response.

Chromosomes and Genes

The instinctive behavior just described follows a genetic blueprint or program; the program is set to go into operation when the conditions, either body chemistry or external stimulation, are exactly right. How does a species-specific sequence of behavior continue, generation after generation?

Genetic programming of behavior is transmitted from parent to young in **chromosomes,** small rodlike structures within the

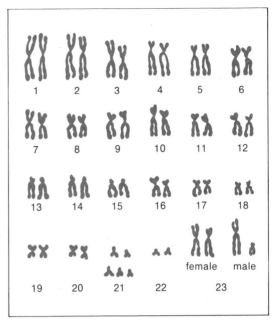

The 46 human chromosomes.

nucleus of each cell of the body. Each chromosome has many **genes**—the basic units of genetic information. Genes are composed of **DNA,** a complex molecule that has the capacity to duplicate itself. Half of your chromosomes came from your mother, and half from your father.

You began when a sperm cell from your father united with an egg cell from your mother—a chance meeting of two cells from each parent's population of reproductive cells. The sperm and egg each brought 23 chromosomes to the union. The resulting fertilized cell (you), containing 46 chromosomes, began its growth through a long process of multiplying by dividing. During cell division each chromosome duplicates itself, so that the resulting two cells each contain exactly the same genetic information. On rare occasions two individuals, each having the same 46 chromosomes, result from a single fertilized egg. These babies will be **identical twins.** Identical twins look almost exactly alike because they have the same genetic structure. **Fraternal twins** result from two eggs being fertilized by two sperm cells at about the same time; the genetic structure of fraternal twins may be similar but it is not identical. Fraternal twins are no more similar than other brothers and sisters.

Because of the enormous number of possible combinations of genetic structures, human beings are very different from each other. The single exception is the case of identical twins, the individuals who share the same genetic structures as a consequence of originating from a single egg. Identical twins are always of the same sex and look very much alike. They also show similarity in measures of respiration rate, motor performance,[4] and patterns of brain-wave activity.[5] Findings such as these indicate the genetic basis for these characteristics.

Your sex was determined by one pair of your chromosomes known as **X and Y chromosomes.** If you are a female, this pair consists of two X chromosomes; if you are a male, this pair has an X and a Y member. About half of the male sperm cells contain an X chromosome and the other half contain a Y chromosome. All female egg cells contain X chromosomes. If a sperm containing an X chromosome unites with the egg, the resulting cell will have two X chromosomes, one from the sperm and one from the egg, and a female baby will result. If a sperm containing a Y chromosome unites with the egg, a male will result.

Genotype and Phenotype

The sum of your biological inheritance is contained in your genes, and this inheritance is called your **genotype.** Your genotype is your genetic makeup, and it remains constant from conception, to birth, to death. By contrast, your appearance and behavior change

Mothers and daughters resemble each other (have similar phenotypes) because they have similar, but not identical, genotyptes.

with time and are affected by the environment in which you live. The sum of your observable characteristics such as your appearance and behavior is called your **phenotype.** The phenotype is not inherited directly, but results from the interaction of the genotype and the environment. For example, the phenotype of shortness may result from an inherited tendency to be short, from a living environment with poor nutrition, or from an interaction between heredity and environment.

The phenotype and genotype are often different. As an extreme example, it is possible for an individual to have a male genotype (an XY chromosome pair) but a female phenotype (as a result of a special hormone treatment and a sex-change operation). An important way in which genotypes and phenotypes differ results from the effect of combining genes from your father and mother. Inherited characteristics result from the influence of pairs of genes, one from your father and one from your mother. Sometimes these pairs combine genes for the same trait, for example, two genes for blue eyes or two genes for curly hair. In these cases, the resulting phenotype (your appearance) will simply reflect this genotype by showing blue eyes or curly hair. Sometimes, however, these pairs combine genes for opposing traits, for example, the combination of genes for blue and brown eye color or straight and curly hair. Under these circumstances, one trait—the **dominant trait**—determines your actual appearance (your phenotype), while the other trait—the **recessive trait**—has no effect. Genes for brown eyes, curly hair, black hair, and the lack of musical ability are all dominant; genes for blue eyes, straight hair, blond hair, and musical ability are all recessive. If you have musical ability, this means you must have inherited this tendency from both parents; however, you could have curly hair as a result of your inheritance from only one parent.

☒ Behavioral genetics is the study of the inheritance of behavior. Behavior can be inherited, but the behavior of human beings is not as influenced by genes as is the behavior of insects, fish, and birds. These animals display many instincts, complex species-specific behaviors that are triggered by releasing stimuli. The inheritance of behavior occurs through chromosomes that are passed on from parents to their children. Each chromosome has many genes, the basic unit of heredity that is composed of molecules called DNA. You are the product of both heredity and experience. Your genotype is your genetic makeup, the sum of your inheritance from your parents; your phenotype is your actual behavior and appearance, the sum of your observable characteristics. Under certain conditions, a trait can be inherited from your parents—and therefore found in your genotype—but not be expressed in your phenotype; such a trait is called recessive.

Intelligence and Heredity

As a general rule, the children of bright parents are bright and the children of dull parents are dull. The extent of this relationship was examined in a study comparing the IQ's of parents and children in 428 father-child pairs and 538 mother-child pairs. In general, the children's IQ's resembled the IQ's of their parents.[6]

What accounts for the intellectual resemblance of children and their parents? One possibility is that intelligence, like physical appearance, is inherited. If this were true, bright parents would tend to have bright children for the same reason that tall parents tend to have tall children—they pass this trait on through their genes. However, a second possibility is that intelligence is a consequence—not of heredity—but of the child's home and school environment. If this were true, bright parents would tend to have bright children because they rear their children in homes that are intellectually more stimulating. Which of these two possibilities is correct? To put the question more generally, what are the relative effects of heredity and environment on intelligence?

Adopted Children

In an attempt to separate the effects of heredity from the effects of environment, psychologists have compared the intelligence levels of adopted children with that of both their biological and foster parents. Although adopted children share their genetic makeup with their biological parents, their home environments are entirely the products of their foster parents. Therefore, evidence for genetic or hereditary effects on intelligence would be found if the adopted children's intelligence levels were more similar to that of

Identical twins have identical genotypes.

their biological parents. For example, finding a bright child whose biological parents were bright—but whose foster parents were dull—would support the argument that intelligence has a genetic basis. By contrast, finding a bright child whose biological parents were dull—but whose foster parents were bright—would support the argument that intelligence is primarily determined by the home environment. Thus, the relative effects of heredity and environment on intelligence can be examined in a study of adopted children.

A study of this kind was made using 194 children who were placed in foster homes before the age of six months and another 194 children living with their biological parents.[7] The IQ's of the parents and children were tested and compared. It was found that the IQ of a child resembles more closely the IQ of biological parents than the IQ of foster parents. A child born of bright parents but living with dull foster parents is more likely to be bright than dull. This shows the important effect of heredity on intelligence.

Identical Twins

If intelligence is hereditary, you would expect that persons of identical genetic structure would have very similar IQ's, and this was proved to be the case. The IQ scores of two identical twins are typically about equal, while the IQ's of fraternal twins are much less similar.[8] Identical twins are very similar in intelligence, even when they have been separated at birth and reared apart. Numerous pairs of *separated* identical twins have been tested and found to have IQ's that differed by only a few points.[9] If the IQ of one twin is known, the IQ of the identical twin can be predicted quite accurately.

Super-rats

Additional evidence on the genetic basis of intelligence comes from attempts to selectively breed more intelligent animals. Using a population of rats, it is possible to mate the brights to the brights and the dulls to the dulls. The brightest offspring of the brights are mated with each other and the dullest offspring of the dulls are mated. This procedure of **selective breeding** will, over a period of a few generations of rats, produce two strains—one strain of bright rats and one strain of dull rats.

Using a maze as an intelligence test, one psychologist was able to develop a maze-bright strain and a maze-dull strain of rats in only six generations. The brights had only half as many errors as the dulls in solving the maze.[10] These rats were found to be bright only at solving mazes, not bright in general. Such experiments, of course, are not possible for human beings. But since mate selection is not random, often involving consideration of traits such as intelligence, selective breeding in effect does take place among humans as well.

Mental Retardation

Mental retardation in some cases has a genetic basis. In the middle 1930's a Norwegian biochemist discovered that certain children inherit a deficiency that prevents an essential amino acid, phenylalanine, from being processed in the liver. The result is a progressive and severe form of mental retardation known as **PKU.** Phenylalanine, a common substance in food, builds up in the blood and tissues because it cannot be excreted adequately by the kidneys. Affected infants appear normal at first but show gradual mental deterioration as the accumulated phenylalanine blocks the action of the nervous system. Fortunately, if PKU is discovered early in an infant, retardation can be prevented with the use of a diet lacking phenylalanine. Newborn infants are now routinely checked for this genetic problem. PKU is a *recessive* trait. It appears only when both parents contribute genes for PKU.

The normal human cell has 46 chromosomes; the cells of persons with **Down's syndrome,** or **mongolism,** have 47. How the extra chromosome has its effect is not known, but mongoloids have smaller brains and are usually retarded. In addition, they may have a round face with almond-shaped eyes, a skull flattened in back, short stature, and a thick fissured tongue.

Schizophrenia and Heredity

A genetic tendency for certain forms of mental disorders may be inherited.[11] The closer the family relationship of two persons, the greater the likelihood that if one is mentally disturbed, the other will be also. **Schizophrenia** is a type of severe mental disturbance characterized by withdrawal from reality. Less than 1 percent of the overall

Down's syndrome baby and mother.

population of the United States becomes schizophrenic, but 14 percent of the siblings (brothers and sisters) of schizophrenics develop the disorder, including the siblings who are fraternal twins. If one parent is a schizophrenic, about 16 percent of the children become schizophrenic.[12] The chances of a child developing schizophrenia more than double if both parents are schizophrenic.

Identical Twins

If a psychological characteristic is genetically based, identical twins with identical genetic structures should resemble each other closely on this trait. This is true for schizophrenia. In a study of 268 schizophrenics with identical twins, it was found that 86 percent of the co-twins suffered from the disorder.[12] A more recent study of 57 pairs of identical twins found that the co-twin of a schizophrenic eventually became schizophrenic in 76 percent of the cases. Furthermore, the chance of a twin developing this disorder was highest during the two-year period following the onset of schizophrenia in the co-twin.[13] Based on data such as these, it has been argued that the similarity in the mental condition of identical twins is a direct result of their identical genetic structures and that schizophrenia is an inherited disorder.

This conclusion can be criticized on the grounds that identical twins also usually have very similar home environments. Thus, a similarity in psychological condition between two identical twins may be due to the similarity in the environments in which they grew up. For example, they were reared by the same mother. Furthermore, the home experience of identical twins is probably more similar than the home experience of fraternal twins or other siblings.[14] Identical twins are treated more alike by their parents,[15] tend to study more together, and share more close friends and interests than fraternal twins.[16]

If identical twins were reared apart, however, their environments would be different but their genetic structures would be identical, so similarities between them in psychological condition could be attributed only to heredity. Reports of separated identical twins are uncommon. The following case is one of the few on record.

The Case of Lisa and Kaete

The identical twin girls Lisa and Kaete were reared apart from early infancy by uncles living in different cities who had little contact with each other.[17] They were difficult children but bright. Even though they were reared separately, they showed several similarities. They looked alike; they were the same size and both had blue eyes and blond hair. They began to menstruate in the same month of their twelfth year. And they both developed schizophrenia at about the same time in their late teens. It is not clear in this case how similar the homes of the two uncles were. Since the two uncles were related, the two home environments may have been similar. While the story of Lisa and Kaete suggests that schizophrenia is inherited, the conclusion is not yet proved.

It is difficult to interpret cases like that of Lisa and Kaete. Why should they show so much similarity when they were separated at birth and were not brought up in the same home? Perhaps the similarity can be accounted for by the similarity of their genes. However, they also had a similar prenatal environment; like all identical twins, they shared a common womb and circulatory system. Because of the common blood system, a biochemical abnormality in one would be shared by the other. Fraternal twins and other siblings do not share a common circulatory system.

Personality and Heredity

Individuals seem to have consistent differences in temperament observable from birth. For example, some babies from the beginning are more active and energetic than other babies;[18] some babies are cuddlers while others consistently avoid human physical contact whenever possible.[19] These differences may be inborn and may underlie personality differences that can be seen in adults. How can the influences of genetic structure on personality be investigated?

Alcoholic Rats

If a procedure of selective breeding can develop strains that are clearly separated on some psychological trait such as intelligence, the trait can be considered as inherited to some extent. This method has been used to study the problem of alcoholism. A tendency toward alcoholism has been selectively bred in mice.[20] After many generations of breeding the extremes, one strain was developed that consistently preferred to drink a 10 percent solution of alcohol rather than water; another strain was developed that consistently refused to drink alcohol.

A psychological dependence on morphine has also been selectively bred in rats.[21] The procedure was first to create a morphine addiction in a population of rats. Following a two-week waiting period without morphine, the rats were given the opportunity to drink morphine again. The extent of psychological dependency, indicated by the rats returning to morphine this time, showed great individual variability. By selectively breeding the extremes, two different strains of rats were produced within three generations. One strain had an inborn tendency for morphine addiction, while the other strain did not.

In order to determine whether the tendency for addiction was general or was specific to morphine, each of the two strains was later made dependent on alcohol. After a dry period, the rats were again given the opportunity to drink alcohol. The strain with an inborn tendency for morphine addiction drank significantly more alcohol. This result showed that the dispositions toward a psychological dependence on morphine and a psychological dependence on alcohol have similar genetic roots, at least in rats. Perhaps there is a genetically based "addictive personality."

Aggressive Dogs

Different breeds of dogs show the effects of centuries of selective breeding. Some have been bred for showing the behavior of aggressive protection, and others have been bred for retrieving fowl or herding sheep. A study of 5,000 puppies showed clear breed differences in emotionality and capacity for problem solving and learning.[22] For example, fox terriers are more aggressive and dominant than beagles, even when the terriers are raised by beagle mothers and the beagles are raised by terrier mothers.[23] In the case of these puppies, behavior was more predictable from knowing genetic structure than from knowing the mother or the environment.

Twin Similarities

There are personality similarities among family members. Identical twins are more similar than fraternal twins or other siblings, although their similarity in personality is not so great as their similarity in physical characteristics or in intelligence.[24] This similarity in temperament of identical twins can be seen even during the first year of life.

The similarity of twins is due not only to their genes but also to the experiences they share.

One psychologist studied twenty pairs of twins over this one-year period.[25] Each baby was observed at home by independent judges and was rated on the extent of social smiling and on the extent of fear of strange persons and objects. The nine pairs of identical twins were more alike, or concordant, than the eleven pairs of fraternal twins.

In the second month, it usually took some external stimulation to elicit smiling. . . . This was the case with Arturo, a fraternal twin, who was a sleepy-head and rarely wide awake. His fraternal brother, Felix, was a remarkable contrast. He was wide eyed and very watchful—but he was unremittingly sober and rarely smiled. This difference in amount of smiling persisted throughout the first year.

While infants under 5 months of age will usually smile at any person, after this age they become increasingly discriminating, and smiles are increasingly reserved for familiar persons. Discrimination turns to wariness some time in the third or fourth trimester of the first year, and most infants begin to react with fear when with a stranger. . . . Lori and

Lisa, an identical pair, were both very wary of strangers from 5 months of age through 8 months, when fear gave way to rather easy acceptance. As in the majority of identical pairs, the timing and intensity of their reactions were very similar over the entire period.[25]

Even infants who are deaf or blind from birth exhibit patterns similar to those of their normal twin in the development of social smiling. Yvonne, congenitally blind from cataracts, smiled and consistently turned her blind eyes toward the person holding her. Smiling seems to be a response under strong biological control. The study of infant twins concludes:

Heredity plays a role in the development of positive social orientation (including smiling) and in the fear of strangers. Our evidence for this is that identical twins show greater concordance than fraternal twins in these two areas of behavior over the first year of life. There seems to be no reasonable alternate explanation of these results.[25]

Personality tests have also been used in the study of the genetic basis of personality. One study of identical and fraternal twins found that identical twins were more similar than fraternal twins on several personality traits, as measured by a personality test.[26] Another study of twins that used personality tests found that identical twins were very similar and fraternal twins were only slightly similar on the psychological dimension defined as "neuroticism." If one identical twin tended to be neurotic, the co-twin did also. The similarity was much less between fraternal twins.[27]

The evidence presented here does not mean that your personality is entirely inherited. There are many factors that have a strong influence on the development of your

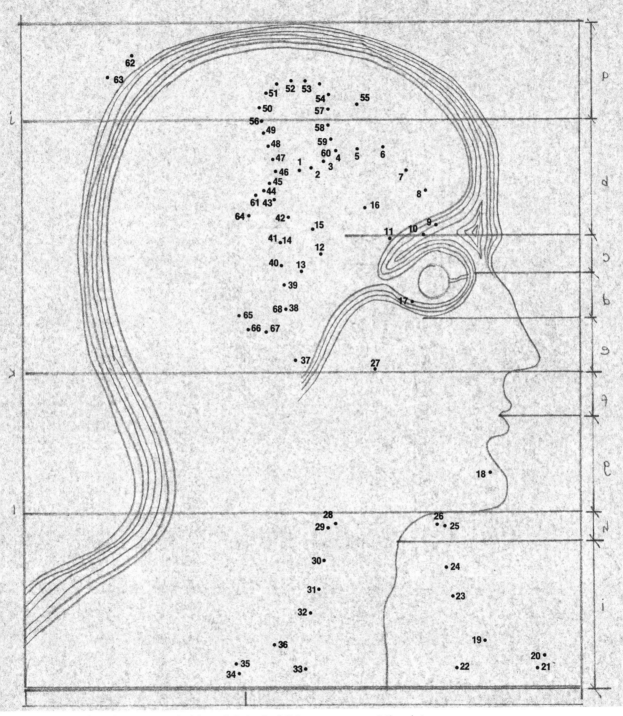

Each of us has a genetic blueprint; to find this one, connect the dots.

personality. Your home and parents and your early experiences were especially important in shaping your personality. But it is also clear, from the studies presented here, that personality is not independent of genetic influences. Your personality was to some extent inherited from your parents.

How could your personality be inherited? We are not simply born "pre-wired" with built-in reactions. What we do inherit is the genetic blueprint for physical structures that control important bodily functions. The systems of our bodies and their functioning affect our behavior. Does this mean that we are fated from birth to live a future laid down in our chromosomes or can we overcome our heredity? Neither. Our identity is formed by the interaction between our genetic structures and the experiences we encounter during our lives.

⑤ The influence of heredity on intelligence can be seen from studies of the similarity in IQ among family members, from the selective breeding of bright and dull strains of animals, and from the study of mental retardation. Evidence for a genetic tendency for schizophrenia comes primarily from studies of families; studies show that the identical twin of a schizophrenic is likely also to be schizophrenic. There are personality similarities among family members: the closer the family relationship, the more similar the personalities; however, the evidence from family similarities is difficult to interpret. Family members usually experience similar environments and may be treated and even dressed alike. Furthermore, identical twins share a common womb and circulatory system. Thus, similarities among family members may not all be due to heredity.

Summary

KEY QUESTIONS

1. Can behavior be inherited?

Behavior can be inherited. Birds, fish, and insects display instincts, complex species-specific behavior that is inherited. For example, the behavior of ants and bees is largely inborn, genetically determined; nest-building among birds is largely an inborn instinct. Human beings are less determined by their genes, but do, nevertheless, inherit behavior tendencies.

2. How is behavior inherited?

The inheritance of behavior is based on chromosomes found within each cell in the body. Chromosomes contain genes, the basic unit of heredity. Half of your chromosomes came from your mother and half from your father. Of your 46 chromosomes, your sex was determined by one pair, known as the X and Y chromosomes. Your physical and psychological characteristics have been influenced by the information carried on your chromosomes.

3. What is the relation of heredity to intelligence, schizophrenia, and personality?

Studies of families show that the closer the family relationship, the more similar people are in intelligence, mental disorder, and personality. Identical twins—individuals with exactly the same genetic structures—are typically very similar both physically and psychologically. It is likely that many psychological characteristics, such as intelligence and personality, are influenced by heredity, but the evidence for this is difficult to interpret.

KEY CONCEPTS

genetics	The study of inherited characteristics.
behavioral genetics	The study of the inheritance of behavior.
instinct	A complex unlearned behavior sequence, such as nest-building in some birds.
species-specific behavior	A behavior pattern that is characteristic of a species, and distinguishes it from other species; for example, in a bird species, the inborn tendency to build a particular type of nest; an instinct.
releasing stimulus	A stimulus that triggers an instinctive sequence of behavior; for example, a hawklike shadow causes certain newly hatched birds to crouch down.
chromosome	A rodlike structure within the nucleus of each cell in the body that carries hereditary information.
genes	The basic units of genetic information found on chromosomes.
DNA	The complex molecule that makes up the genes.
identical twins	Twins resulting from a single fertilized egg, each having exactly the same genes; they are therefore always of the same sex and of very similar physical appearance.
fraternal twins	Twins resulting from two eggs being fertilized by two sperm cells at about the same time; their genetic structure is no more similar than that of other siblings.
X and Y chromosomes	Chromosomes determining sex; an XX pair is female and an XY pair is male.
genotype	The sum of your biological inheritance; your genetic makeup.
phenotype	The sum of your observable characteristics.

dominant trait   The trait that will appear in the phenotype when a pair of genes reflects opposing traits.

recessive trait   The trait that will not appear in the phenotype when a pair of genes reflects opposing traits.

selective breeding   A procedure for strengthening a trait in a population by mating only those animals from each generation which show the trait in the extreme.

PKU   A form of progressive mental retardation resulting from the accumulation of phenylalanine; an inherited recessive disorder.

Down's syndrome   A condition associated with mental retardation and physical abnormality; results from an additional chromosome (47 instead of 46).

mongolism   A common name for Down's syndrome.

schizophrenia   A type of severe mental disturbance characterized by withdrawal from reality; often involves disorders in thought, perception, and language.

5 Childhood

CHAPTER OUTLINE

KEY QUESTIONS

1. What is the relation of maturation and learning?
2. What is unique about the mind of a child?
3. How can the growth of personality be described?

What is your earliest memory? Can you remember what you were like as a young child? How did you see the world? What did you think about? In the past few years, psychologists studying children have made remarkable discoveries about the world of the very young. Understanding the world of childhood is an important step in understanding yourself. By tracing your journey from infancy, you can better understand where you are, and perhaps where you are going.

How did you become what you are today? Some would stress the importance of heredity, while others would stress the effects of experience or learning. The debate about the relative effects of learning and heredity in shaping human behavior is called the **nature-nurture issue.** Your personality may result from "nature" (you were born that way) or from "nurture" (you were brought up that way). The seventeenth-century philosopher John Locke believed that all aspects of human character resulted from learning; he argued that babies are born with a **tabula rasa,** a "blank slate" or empty mind. The eighteenth-century philosopher Immanuel Kant disagreed. He wrote that people are born with certain inborn ways of perceiving the world, that babies' minds are not blank but instead hold **innate ideas.** For example, Kant believed that we are born with the ideas of time, space, cause, and effect. During the first half of this century psychologists strongly emphasized the effects of learning in human development—that is, the "nurture" side of the issue. Today psychologists tend to take a more balanced approach in which the effects of heredity are given equal weight.

The age of walking is determined by maturation, not training.

Physical Development

Human infants are truly remarkable. Although newborns typically sleep about 20 hours a day, they can be quite active. They cry, suck, cough, spit, sneeze, burp, turn away, and move their arms, legs, and fingers; they react to light, sound, touch, smell, and taste. Some of the actions of infants are automatic and are responses to specific stimuli. For example, the **rooting reflex** occurs in response to the infants' cheek being touched; if a finger or nipple touches their cheek, they will turn and try to contact the object with their mouth. This simple inborn reaction is soon modified by learning; the infant rapidly becomes better and better at locating the nipple.

As children grow older they become capable of more and more complex behavior. These changes result both from learning and from maturation. The term **learning** refers to changes in behavior or potential that result from experience; the term **maturation** refers to developmental changes that are relatively independent of experience. Maturation is a

genetically programmed growth process in which muscles, bones, and nerves become increasingly mature. Walking seems to depend very little on learning or practice. Children walk, on the average, by about 12–14 months whether or not they have been trained in the art of walking; walking follows a schedule based on maturation rather than learning. Individual differences in the age of walking depend primarily on individual differences in maturation.

Although children from different cultures have widely different early experiences, most begin to walk at about the same age. The Hopi Indians restricted their infants' movements by tying them to cradleboards until about nine months of age. A study compared two groups of Hopi Indian infants—one group was confined to cradleboards and the other was not.[1] Cradleboards prevent babies from moving their bodies. Although the infants of one group spent much more time moving about, both groups walked at the same age. Apparently the age of walking

The ability to climb requires a certain level of physical maturation.

depended more on the level of maturation than on practice.

Learning many motor skills is possible only after an appropriate level of maturation is reached. The ability to type or ride a bicycle depends upon delicate muscular coordination not available to infants. Control of bladder or bowels requires the maturation of muscles and nerves to a level typically reached only in the second year of life; before this level of maturation is reached, toilet training will be unsuccessful.

To study the effect of learning and maturation on the development of a simple skill, a psychologist observed two groups of young children, two to three years of age.[2] One group was allowed to practice climbing a small ladder each day for twelve weeks. These toddlers slowly got better and better at the task until at the end they were able to climb it quite well. The second group of children had no opportunity to climb the ladder until the first group had finished their twelve-week practice period; then the second group was allowed to practice. Rather than taking them twelve weeks to master the task, it took them only one week. Less practice was required because they had reached a more advanced stage of maturation.

⑤ At birth infants are already capable of a wide range of behavior. Some skills, however, require a later stage of maturation before they can be mastered. For example, the age of walking is primarily dependent upon physical maturation and is little influenced by practice.

Cognitive Development

While your body matured and your skills increased with age, your intelligence and knowledge also increased. The word **cognition** refers to such activities as thinking, perceiving, knowing, and understanding. The study of **cognitive development** is the study of how these activities change with age; it is the study of the growth of the mind.

Perceptual Development

What did the world look, sound, and feel like when you were young? What kind of world does an infant perceive? The senses of the infant are working from birth, or in some cases, even before birth. For example, there is evidence that the fetus in the womb can hear and can respond to touch, temperature, and pain.

The visual world of the infant is different from the visual world of the adult. At birth, the infants' ability to discriminate fine lines or points is rather poor; even if they knew how to read, their vision is not well enough developed at birth to see the difference between the letters. They also have difficulty adjust-

Infant on visual cliff apparatus, unwilling to crawl from shallow to deep side toward mother.

ing the focus of their eyes to see things at different distances; the eyes of infants are like fixed-focus cameras set at about eight inches, so that things closer or farther are out of focus.

Depth perception is the awareness of the distance between yourself and objects in the world; it is the ability to see things in three dimensions. There has been a long debate in the history of philosophy and science on the question of whether depth perception is innate or learned. If depth perception is innate, then infants at birth can see things in three dimensions. But infants can't talk, so how could you ever find out how they see the world?

One way of studying depth perception in infants is by using an apparatus called the **visual cliff.** This consists of a large sheet of very heavy glass suspended a foot or two above the floor, to form a kind of table. A checkered cloth is attached to the undersurface of half of the glass; under the other half of the glass the material is placed on the floor below. An infant is placed in the middle of the glass. To one side the glass appears solid;

to the other side it appears to drop off, like a cliff. Infants old enough to crawl (6 months) tend to be willing to crawl across the "shallow" side but not the "deep" side of the glass; apparently, by this age, infants are able to see in depth.[3] A follow-up study showed that infants respond to depth even before they are able to crawl. Infants that were 55 days old were placed on either the shallow or the deep side of the visual cliff.[4] Their heart rates were monitored and it was found that there was a significant difference in the heart rate on the two sides. This evidence shows that human infants can see things in three dimensions at a very early age. Depth perception is either innate or it is learned within the first few months of life.

Language Development

Have you tried to learn a foreign language? For most of us this is a painfully difficult task. How easy it would be if you were born with the ability to speak and comprehend the language, rather than hav-

Baby saying "bye-bye."

ing to spend time in painstaking study. Yet, remarkably enough, there is evidence that you were born with such an ability.

The general sequence of language development appears to be universal, as if reflecting a genetic program that is unfolding. Although different children proceed through these stages at different rates, all seem to follow the same order in moving from stage to stage.[5] The first stage begins with the birth cry of the newborn; for the next three weeks or so the infant is limited to variations on this basic cry. From about three weeks to about five months of age, in the second stage, the infant begins making vowel-like sounds, often through a partly open mouth. These sounds appear to indicate comfort or pleasure. In the third stage, during the last half of the first year, the infant begins "babbling," a continual stream of articulated vowel-like sounds. These sounds appear to be independent of what the infant hears, since they are very similar across cultures with different languages. By the end of the first year, in stage four, the beginnings of patterned speech are heard as the infant begins to use single words meaningfully. Initially, these words may simply accompany actions ("bye-bye"); later, they may involve commands ("Cookie!"). Finally, at around two years of age, in stage five, the infant begins to use two-word phrases and sentences. These two-word sentences are not simply random pairings of words; they are put together according to certain rules; that is, they follow a grammar. **Grammar** is a term referring to the rules that people follow when they construct sentences.

As the child grows older, longer and more complex sentences are constructed. An interesting paradox is that children are able to construct grammatical sentences that they have never heard before; they are able to create correct new sentences that they could not possibly have learned by imitation. This fact suggests that a basic competence in language is inborn.[6]

Intellectual Development

How does intelligence grow? The author A. A. Milne, who wrote the delightful children's book *Winnie the Pooh*, gave a child's perspective on this question in *Now We Are Six*.[7]

> When I was One,
> I had just begun.
>
> When I was Two,
> I was nearly new.
>
> When I was Three,
> I was hardly Me.
>
> When I was Four,
> I was not much more.
>
> When I was Five,
> I was just alive.
>
> But now I am six, I'm as
>   clever as clever.
> So I think I'll be six now
>   for ever and ever.

■ *The Growth of Intelligence* According to some psychologists, you were very clever indeed by the age of six; they find that six-year-olds have attained about two-thirds of the adult level of intelligence.[8] Other psychologists would argue that it is not so much a matter of *how much* intelligence is acquired, but rather of *what kind.*

The Swiss psychologist Jean Piaget is the best-known child psychologist in the world today. He has devoted his life to the careful study of the minds of children. According to Piaget, in each stage of development the quality of intelligence is somewhat different. Piaget's **theory of cognitive stages** states that intellectual development occurs through a sequence of stages, the order of which remains constant, although, for different individuals, the rate of development may vary.

Jean Piaget

■ *Piaget's Theory of Cognitive Stages* According to Piaget, children in the first stage of cognitive development, the **sensorimotor stage,** live in a world of sensation and motor movement. From birth until about age two, the life of the infant is dominated by sucking, sniffing, tasting, and moving arms and legs. During the early part of this stage, infants lack the concept of **object permanency;** as far as they are concerned, objects that are not perceived simply do not exist. If a ball rolls out of sight behind a chair, the ball, for the infant, ceases to exist. Later in this stage, the infant learns object permanency, so that objects are considered to continue to exist even though they may not currently be seen.

In the sensorimotor stage, it's "out of sight, out of mind."

PIAGET'S STAGES OF COGNITIVE DEVELOPMENT

Stage	Approximate Age	Description
1. Sensorimotor	0–2	World of sensation and motor movement; learns object permanency
2. Preoperational	2–7	Learns language, can represent things symbolically; is egocentric
3. Concrete operations	7–11	Achieves conservation; becomes capable of logical thought
4. Formal operations	11–up	Capable of abstract and hypothetical thinking

The **preoperational stage,** from about age two to seven, begins with the emergence of language; now children can represent objects by words. Children in this stage can think, but cannot think very abstractly. An important feature of this stage is the child's **egocentrism,** the tendency to see things only from his or her own point of view. Egocentrism does not mean "selfish," but refers instead to a limitation on perspective so that a child cannot see the world from someone else's point of view. For example, children in the preoperational stage may think that the sun follows them as they travel; from their point of view, the world revolves around them.

In the **concrete operations stage,** from about seven to eleven, children are able to think logically for the first time, but only about fairly concrete things. During this stage children develop the concept of **conservation**—the idea that things retain their general character even though their appearance may change. Before the concept of conservation is acquired, children believe that the number of things in a collection changes just because they are spread out; for example, before conservation, children believe there are more marbles if they are scattered than if they are in a pile. Before the concept of conservation is acquired, children believe that a ball of clay, when rolled out in a snake, becomes more clay. After conservation, children believe that number, weight, mass, volume, and other properties of objects remain unchanged when the shape is changed.

In the **formal operations stage,** from about eleven on up, children acquire their adult level of intelligence. During this stage children become capable of abstract and hypothetical thinking. The child can design and conduct scientific experiments; hypothetical possibilities can be imagined, then systematically tested. In this stage the child develops the capacity to think about thinking, to examine and evaluate personal thoughts as well as thoughts of others.

S Babies have all their senses at birth, but their perceptual worlds are different from the perceptual world of an adult. They have less ability to focus their eyes at different distances and to see fine lines and points. We do not know whether they have depth perception at birth, but we do know, from studies using the visual cliff, that they have depth perception at two months of age.

It appears that language competence is inborn. The development of language follows a sequence of stages that are similar for people in different cultures. According to Piaget, intellectual development also follows a set sequence of stages for children everywhere. Children's view of reality and way of thinking is qualitatively different in each stage.

Personality Development

Your **personality** is your unique way of re-acting to the world and relating to the people around you; it is your psychological self. Although there is some evidence that personality characteristics can be influenced by heredity, for the most part you are who you learned to be. Your personality developed through a history of experiences with the world and with people. There are different views of how personality development can best be understood.

Freud's Psychoanalytic Theory

According to Freud's **psychoanalytic theory,** personality is fixed or determined at an early age, as a consequence of certain crucial experiences. Social practices centering around food habits and cleanliness training are important learning experiences early in life. Freud considered these experiences as significant in determining the adult personality.

■ *Weaning* Weaning is the procedure for changing the infant from nursing to drinking and eating. The transition from dependence on sucking to the ability to drink or eat from a spoon can be a difficult period of adjustment both for the infant and the mother. There are wide cultural differences in how and when weaning occurs, but in this society it usually begins between six and ten months of age. In some societies weaning does not occur until the child is several years old.

■ *Toilet Training* Another critical period in an infant's early life, according to Freud, is toilet training. This period involves one of the first major learning tasks for the child that requires performance (doing something).

Many parents attempt toilet training before the infant is capable of acquiring the necessary control. Such attempts lead to failure and frustration for both the infant and the parent. The average age at which a baby has the physical maturity to achieve good control over the bladder and bowels is about eighteen months. Toilet training is easiest and least frustrating when the child is about twenty months of age.[9] Yet American parents, with their drive for performance, typically attempt toilet training when the child is about eleven months of age, long before the average infant has the capacity for success.[9]

■ *Oral and Anal Characters* Weaning plays an important role in Freud's psychoanalytic theory. Freud believed that sucking was more than a way to get food; it was a basic need and a source of sexual pleasure for the infant. The frustration of this need, according to Freud, led to an adult personality disturbance, a pattern of traits called the **oral character.** This pattern includes traits of excessive dependency, passivity, sarcasm, and pessimism. Furthermore, because the need to suck was frustrated and ungratified, adults having "oral characters" would be expected to chew, smoke, and talk excessively in order to achieve oral compensation. While Freud's hypothesis is an intriguing one, the idea that early and severe weaning causes adult personality maladjustment has not been substantiated.

Freud believed that elimination, like sucking behavior, produced sexual gratification for the infant. He argued that the blocking or frustration of this need led to later personality disturbance, a pattern called **anal character.** Freud described the anal character as consisting of traits of stinginess, stubbornness, compulsive cleanliness and punctuality, and extreme orderliness. If Freud were right about the origins of the anal character, we might expect these traits to characterize the "American personality," since we in this culture employ relatively harsh toilet training practices.

Harsh toilet training has a variety of unpleasant consequences in the development of the personality.[10,11,12,13] Freud's hypothesis, that frustrations associated with toilet training will lead to the development of such "anal" traits as stinginess and excessive orderliness, has not, however, been substantiated. A review of research on this problem shows that the evidence does not generally support the Freudian position.[14]

It is clear, however, that the interactions of parents and infants are especially significant for the development of the personality, especially during certain periods in the early life of the infant. Infants with harsh weaning and with severe and early toilet training experiences are more likely to become poorly adjusted adults. Infants with close and warm contact with their parents, with gradual and permissive weaning, and with bladder and bowel training attempted only when such control is easy and natural, tend to develop more healthy adult personalities.

Erik Erikson

Erikson's Psychosocial Theory

Unlike Freud, who believed that the personality was fixed early in childhood, Erik Erikson believes that the personality continues to develop throughout life. Erikson identified eight stages of development, from birth to death.[15] These **psychosocial stages** describe the progressive development of a person's orientation to society. During each of the eight stages, individuals face a crisis in their relationship to the social world—a crisis that can be resolved either positively or negatively. If it is resolved positively, a

THE EIGHT STAGES OF PSYCHOSOCIAL DEVELOPMENT

Crisis	Age	Outcome
1. Trust vs. Mistrust	0–1	Hope
2. Autonomy vs. Doubt	2–3	Self-control
3. Initiative vs. Guilt	4–5	Direction and Purpose
4. Industry vs. Inferiority	6–11	Competence
5. Identity vs. Role Confusion	12–18	Devotion
6. Intimacy vs. Isolation	Young Adulthood	Love
7. Generativity vs. Stagnation	Middle Age	Production and Care
8. Integrity vs. Despair	Old Age	Wisdom

Interactions between parent and child influence personality development.

new dimension of social interaction becomes possible.

In the first stage—*Trust vs. Mistrust* (age 0–1)—infants learn to trust other people if adequate care and loving are provided. If their needs are not met, they develop attitudes of suspicion and mistrust toward the world.

In the second stage—*Autonomy vs. Doubt* (age 2–3)—infants begin to explore and manipulate their world and gain an increasing sense of independence (autonomy) and self-control. With overly critical or impatient parents, children develop an excessive doubt about their abilities to control the world and themselves.

In the third stage—*Initiative vs. Guilt* (age 4–5)—parents either support the self-initiated activities of their children by allowing them relative freedom to act and to think, or they inhibit their initiative by telling them that their activities are stupid, silly, or bad. With the former, the children gain a stronger sense of freedom and initiative; with the latter, they develop a sense of guilt over their activities.

In the fourth stage—*Industry vs. Inferiority* (age 6–11)—children learn how to do things in the world and become concerned with how things are made and how they work. When children are encouraged in productive activities, their sense of competence is strengthened; when their efforts are discouraged, they develop a sense of inferiority. During these elementary school years the school contributes to the children's sense of competence or inferiority.

In the fifth stage—*Identity vs. Role Confusion* (age 12–18)—adolescents attempt to put together a firm identity, a sense of who they are and where they are going. Throughout childhood they have played different parts or roles—at home, among peers, and at school—and they must now unify these various images into one whole distinct identity. If they fail to do so, they experience role confusion, a sense of not knowing who they are or where they belong.

In the sixth stage—*Intimacy vs. Isolation* (young adulthood)—individuals seek to establish deep relationships with friends or with a mate; failure to do so means being isolated and alone.

In the seventh stage—*Generativity vs. Stagnation* (middle age)—individuals begin to be concerned with others besides their immediate family, for example, with society and future generations. "Generativity" is the concern with guiding the next generation. If a sense of generativity is not achieved, the individuals will be concerned only with their own personal needs and comforts.

In the eighth and final stage—*Integrity vs. Despair* (old age)—individuals reflect on their lives and the coming of death. Acceptance of life and a feeling of satisfaction with it lead to a sense of integrity or completeness. Despair is experienced by individuals who see their lives as missed opportunities and who know it is too late to start over.

Social-Learning Theory

According to **social-learning theory,** your personality results from your experiences interacting with your environment and with other people. In other words, your personality consists of learned behavior patterns. Unlike psychoanalytic theory, social-learning theory does not focus on a few "crucial" early experiences but regards all experiences as significant. Furthermore, social-learning theory assumes that people continue to grow and to change throughout life. Unlike Erikson's psychosocial theory, social-learning theory rejects the notion of universal stages of personality development and stresses the wide range of individual differences.

Like father, like son.

■ *The Inconsistent Woman* Social-learning theory rejects the idea that individuals have a set personality trait or character that is displayed in all situations. Instead, the pattern of your reaction will be different in different situations; that is, your behavior is situation-specific. How you act depends on the situation. As one author wrote, a woman can be inconsistent; she can be

a hostile, fiercely independent, passive, dependent, feminine, aggressive, warm, castrating person all in one. Which of these she is at any particular moment would not be random and capricious; it would depend on . . . whom she is with, when, how, and much more. But each of these aspects of her self may be a quite genuine and real aspect of her total being.[16]

■ *Imitating Models* The different ways that people have of reacting to the world are learned. Much of this learning results from watching other people and imitating them. Do you remember being told that you acted just like your father or that you were the image of your mother? Because you were

closest to them as you grew up, you observed them and in many instances imitated what you saw. This is the process of **identification.** Boys are taught to identify with their fathers and girls with their mothers. Children learn from their parents of the same sex what is expected of them and how they are to act as males or females. What is learned—that is, what is not biologically determined—is influenced by a particular culture. Sex-role learning appears early in childhood. Indications of masculine identification are present in boys as young as three.[17] The process of identification serves the function of transferring the values and behaviors of a culture from one generation to the next.

How does this process of identification work? As you grew up, you copied a parent, who served as your **model.** You learned by observation; you acquired new behaviors simply by watching your parents behave. Sometimes the act of imitating or copying the parent is itself rewarded by the parent, and the act of imitating may thereafter increase.

Sometimes, however, a kind of second-hand reward system seems to be working; the child receives a kind of indirect reward by observing the parent receive a direct reward.

The more a child envies the status of another with respect to the control of a given resource, the more he will covertly practice that role. By covert practice we mean that he will indulge in phantasy in which he sees himself as the envied person, controlling and consuming the valued resources of which he has been deprived. It is the phantasy of being someone other than himself that we would like to define as identification.[18]

A boy observes a parent act and obtain rewards and the child indirectly enjoys the reward himself. A boy, in his fantasy, becomes his father, has competence, and is rewarded.

■ *The Girl Who Limped* Children imitate the parent with whom they identify. The process can be seen in the following example. A psychologist visited a poor Puerto Rican family near San Juan to interview the mother about one of her several children.[19] One child, a small three-year-old girl, re-

mained quite close to the mother throughout the visit. The mother, a woman in her early thirties, walked with a slouch and a slight limp. She made a noise—a loud whispered "ooph"—whenever she had to bend over to pick up something from the floor. The little girl was perfectly healthy but also walked with a slouch and a limp, and each time she bent down she uttered a loud "ooph." The mother said to the psychologist, "I don't know what drives her to make that awful sound every time she bends down."

⑤ According to Freud's psychoanalytic theory of personality, an individual's personality is fixed at an early age; weaning and toilet training experiences are of particular significance in personality development. According to Erikson, personality continues to develop throughout life and follows a sequence of stages; each stage describes the development of a person's orientation to society. According to social-learning theory, personality is learned, and results from interactions with other people and the environment. Observational learning and imitation of adults are the ways that children develop traits and habits similar to their parents.

Summary

KEY QUESTIONS

1. What is the relation of maturation and learning?
   The mastery of many skills depends upon a certain degree of maturation; nerves and muscles are apparently incapable of supporting certain kinds of skilled movements before a necessary level of maturity is reached. For example, the ability to walk is little influenced by practice but is greatly influenced by maturation. Toilet training is of little use before nerves and muscles are mature enough for voluntary control.

2. What is unique about the mind of a child?

Children's views of reality and ways of seeing and thinking are qualitatively different at different ages. The perceptual worlds of infants are different from those of adults. According to Piaget, children progress through a fixed sequence of stages of intellectual development, and are not able to think like adults until they reach adolescence.

3. How can the growth of personality be described?

Three different views are presented—those of Freud, Erikson, and social-learning theory. According to Freud, personality is fixed at an early age, and is profoundly affected by certain experiences early in life. Erikson argues that personality continues to develop throughout life, following a set sequence of stages of social orientation. Social-learning theory proposes that personality is learned through interactions with other people. According to this theory, observational learning and imitation are particularly important in personality development.

KEY CONCEPTS

nature-nurture issue	The debate about the relative effects of heredity and learning in determining human behavior.
tabula rasa	A "blank slate," or empty mind; according to Locke, the state of the mind before any outside impressions.
innate ideas	Ideas, concepts, or ways of perceiving the world that are inborn or present at birth.
rooting reflex	An automatic response of infants to being touched on the cheek; they turn toward the source of stimulation and try to take it into their mouths.
learning	Changes in behavior or potential that result from experience.
maturation	Developmental changes that are relatively independent of experience, but result instead from genetically programmed growth processes.
cognition	Mental activities such as thinking, perceiving, knowing, or understanding.
cognitive development	The changes that occur with age in cognitive activities.
depth perception	The ability to see in three dimensions; the awareness of the distance between yourself and objects.

visual cliff	An apparatus used for studying depth perception in infants; consists of a piece of heavy glass covering shallow and deep surfaces.
grammar	The rules that people follow when they construct sentences.
theory of cognitive stages	Piaget's theory that intellectual development proceeds through a succession of qualitatively different stages.
sensorimotor stage	The first of Piaget's cognitive stages, from birth until about age two.
preoperational stage	The second of Piaget's cognitive stages, lasting from two to seven.
concrete operations stage	The third of Piaget's cognitive stages, lasting from about seven to eleven.
formal operations stage	The fourth and last of Piaget's cognitive stages, beginning about eleven and continuing throughout adulthood.
object permanency	The concept that objects continue to exist even when they cannot be perceived.
egocentrism	The tendency to see things only from one's own point of view.
conservation	The idea that things retain their properties of weight, number, and volume, even though their surface appearance may change.
personality	A person's unique way of reacting to the world and relating to people.
psychoanalytic theory	Freud's theory of personality; according to this theory, personality is determined at an early age.
oral character	A personality pattern of excessive dependency, passivity, sarcasm, and pessimism.
anal character	A personality pattern of stinginess, stubbornness, compulsive cleanliness and punctuality, and extreme orderliness.
psychosocial stages	Erikson's description of the eight stages of personality development, beginning with birth and ending with death.
social-learning theory	The theory that a person's pattern of behavior is learned and results from experiences with other people and the environment.
identification	The process by which children observe and imitate adults.
model	A person who is observed and imitated.

6 The Family

CHAPTER OUTLINE

KEY QUESTIONS

1. Do babies need families?
2. How do children and parents influence each other?
3. What are the types of families?

Anna was found in an attic room when she was six. She had skeletonlike legs and a bloated abdomen. She could not talk or walk and appeared as a wild animal, without human intelligence. Anna had lived her life without care and attention and with only enough food to be kept barely alive. She was removed from her mother's house by the authorities and placed in a county institution; no special treatment was provided her. Two years later she could walk and she had achieved the mental age of an infant of about one year old.[1]

Isabelle was discovered when she was six and a half years of age. Her mother was a deaf mute, and they had lived together since her birth in a dark room completely isolated from the rest of the mother's family. Isabelle acted like an infant; she was unable to relate to people or care for her own needs. She made only a strange croaking sound. She was given an IQ test and scored close to the zero point of the scale. The authorities removed her from her room and put her under the care of a psychologist and a speech specialist. Within two months she was using

93

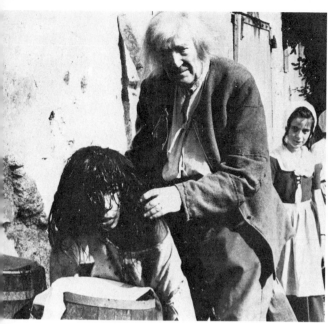

An abandoned child, as portrayed in the movie "Wild Child of Aveyron."

sentences; nine months later she began to read and write. By the time she was eight and a half she was intellectually and psychologically normal.[1]

These and similar cases show the terrible consequences when children are raised in extreme isolation, away from a normal human family.[2,3] Because they are deprived of human contact, these children do not learn to be human. Interaction with loving adults, usually in the context of a family, is necessary for healthy development. Sometimes, as in the case of Isabelle, the damage of early neglect can be undone; sometimes the damage is more permanent.

Babies Without Families

Babies are helpless and must have their physical needs satisfied in order to live. They need caretaking, or **parenting,** by mothers, fathers, or both. But parenting is more than meeting basic physical needs—parenting is also holding, hugging, caressing, loving the infant. Remarkably enough, these other aspects of caring for children are also matters of life or death.

Infants who lack adequate loving, who suffer from **love deprivation,** may develop a condition called **marasmus.** Marasmus is a condition of increasing physical weakness, loss of appetite, and apathy.

Love Deprivation

Orphans in institutions have no real families, and so some orphanages have tried to provide loving care. Because of overcrowding and lack of money, some institutions are unable to provide more than the basic physical requirements for their children. Cases of gross neglect are fairly rare now, but conditions used to be much worse.

■ *The Nursery and the Foundlinghome* Some years ago, a scientist named Spitz studied infants in two institutions. The two places equally met the physical needs of their babies for food and warmth, but differed in the amount of emotional interchange offered.[4]

In one institution, the "Foundlinghome," the infants were attended by overworked nursing personnel who had minimal contact with each child. In the other institution, the "Nursery," the children were cared for by their own mothers with much emotional interchange. Spitz was particularly interested in determining the effect of warm interactions between mother and infant, under conditions where other differences between infants might be small. He described the results:

While the children in "Nursery" developed into normal healthy toddlers, a two-year observation of "Foundlinghome" showed that the

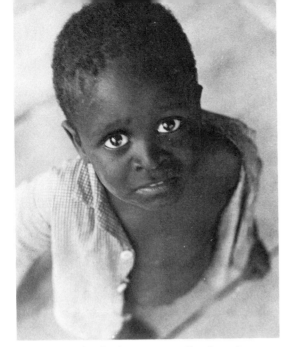

Orphans in institutions may suffer from love deprivation.

emotionally starved children never learned to speak, to walk, to feed themselves. With one or two exceptions in a total of 91 children, those who survived were human wrecks.[4]

The infants cared for by their own mothers developed normally. On the other hand, the unloved infants failed to develop normally (inferior intelligence and motor ability). Among the unloved infants, about one child in three died during its first two years of life. Furthermore, the early experience of love deprivation for the infants in the "Foundlinghome" affected their adult personalities. Those who survived grew up to be maladjusted and neurotic adults.[5]

■ *The Case of Paul and His Mother*
Fortunately most orphans in this country are now placed in foster homes as early as possible, where they receive the love and care they need to develop normally. It is important that such placement occur as soon as possible, because in the early years of childhood parenting is especially important. The case

of Paul shows some of the effects of the lack of love.

Paul's parents were separated before his birth. As a small child, he scarcely had any contact with his father. . . . As for Paul's mother, she had always been a profoundly unhappy woman. Paul never knew a family life. He scarcely knew what being loved meant. . . . From the maternity ward of the hospital in which he was born, Paul went directly to a nursery, where he lived out his first four years of life. . . . The occasional night spent with his mother meant very little to Paul. She worked so late that when she did bring him home he was half asleep, and in the morning she deposited him again at the nursery before he was really awake. . . . When he was not yet six, his mother . . . placed him in an orphanage.[6]

Paul's mother, an extremely disturbed woman, was ridden by guilt for having neglected him, yet could not cope with the responsibility of functioning as his mother. Her confused feelings toward her son can be seen in the fact that she would plan grand birthday parties for him and then forget his birthday. Paul did not do well at the orphanage, becoming more and more violent. During his last several months there, Paul—screaming that he wanted to die—made several suicide attempts. He was referred to the Orthogenic School for emotionally disturbed children.

When we met him, Paul was ten years old. The psychiatric examination that was given him when he entered the School did not so much reveal murderous and depressive phantasies—as might have been expected from his suicidal and homicidal attempts—as emptiness, great flatness and instability of emotion, inability to relate, extreme detachment, and markedly infantile behavior.[6]

After years of care in the controlled environment of the school for emotionally disturbed children, Paul was able to achieve a relatively good adjustment and was placed in a foster home.

Monkeys Without Mothers

The need for love is not unique to human children; infant monkeys need love too. Infant monkeys are helpless and dependent at birth, as are human infants, and monkey mothers show much affection and care for their babies. The infants of monkeys and humans show about the same pattern of development—infant monkeys just mature more rapidly. The similarities of humans and monkeys make the study of monkeys relevant to the understanding of human behavior.

■ *Mothers Made of Wire and Wood* Psychologist Harry Harlow raised monkeys both with and without mothers.[7] Harlow wanted to investigate the love bond between mother and infant in order to see the effects of love deprivation on adult behavior. Many scientists believed that a baby loves its mother because the mother feeds the infant; according to this view, the rewarding effects of being fed result in the infant's positive reactions to the mother. Harlow, however, suspected that the stimulation of warmth and holding was responsible for the development of the love bond. He tested this idea by building a **surrogate mother,** an artificial "mother" made of wire and cloth.

We had . . . discovered . . . that a baby monkey raised on a bare wire-mesh cage floor survives with difficulty, if at all, during the first five days of life. If a wire-mesh cone is introduced, the baby does better; and, if the

Baby monkey and its surrogate mother.

cone is covered with terry cloth, husky, healthy, happy babies evolve. It takes more than a baby and a box to make a normal monkey. . . .

We built a surrogate mother . . . from a block of wood, covered with sponge rubber, and sheathed in tan cotton terry cloth. A light bulb behind her radiated heat. The result was a mother, soft, warm, and tender, a mother with infinite patience, a mother available twenty-four hours a day, a mother that never scolded her infant and never struck or bit her baby in anger. . . . It is our opinion that we engineered a very superior monkey mother, although this position is not held universally by the monkey fathers.[8]

Harlow gave the infant monkeys a choice of two surrogate mothers: one was made of bare wire mesh but contained a bottle from which the infant received all its meals; the other, containing no bottle, was constructed of wire mesh covered with soft terry cloth. Harlow observed the infant monkeys to find which type of mother they preferred. He found that, except at meal times, the baby monkeys spent all their time clinging to the terry-cloth mother. The infant monkeys reacted to their terry-cloth surrogates very much like they would have reacted to their real mothers.

When the cloth mother was present . . . the babies rushed to her, climbed up, clung tightly to her, and rubbed their heads and faces against her body. . . .

During the last two years we have observed the behavior of two infants raised by their own mothers. Love for the real mother and love for the surrogate mother appear to be very similar. The baby macaque spends many hours a day clinging to its real mother. If away from the mother when frightened, it rushes to her and in her presence shows comfort and composure. As far as we can observe, the infant monkey's affection for the real mother is strong, but no stronger than that of the experimental monkey for the surrogate cloth mother, and the security that the infant gains from the presence of the real mother is no greater than the security it gains from a cloth surrogate.[8]

■ *The Infant Monkeys Grow Up* The comfort offered by the soft surrogate mothers is sought by the infant monkeys, but the artificial cloth mothers are not an adequate replacement for real mothers. Motherless monkey infants tend to grow up to be aggressive and isolated; they often do not mate, or if females do mate, they are poor mothers. Sometimes they are brutal and rejecting to their own infants.[9] They behave as if they do not know how to be a loving parent. On the other hand, infant female monkeys raised by their own mothers develop normally and usually grow up to be mothers who love, protect, and care for their babies.

Substitute Families

The warmth and affection of parenting are essential for the development of the healthy personality. Love deprivation in the early years of infancy often has persisting effects on adult personality. Can these effects be undone? Can the emotional damage be repaired? Yes—to some extent, but it is not yet clear exactly what rehabilitation program works best.

■ *Foster Homes* Institutionalized children who have suffered love deprivation make considerable gains when placed in foster homes.[10] Thirty children who had experienced extreme love deprivation up to age two and one-half were placed in foster homes with special programs designed to make up for the lack of loving relationships that they had experienced. Most of these children showed rapid growth and a healthy potential.[11]

■ *Enrichment Programs* If foster parents are not available, special enrichment programs may be helpful.[12] In one early study a psychologist transferred a group of orphan babies diagnosed as mentally retarded from their own overcrowded institution to a nearby institution for feeble-minded older girls. The brighter girls were selected to care for the infants. During a two-year period the orphans cared for by the feeble-minded girls experienced an average gain in IQ of over 25 points, while a similar group of infants left in the orphanage experienced a drop of over 25 points in IQ.[13] What became of the orphan babies? Thirty years later they were located as adults. All the infants cared for by the feeble-minded girls were found to be normal adults, while most of those left in the orphanage were still institutionalized as mentally retarded.

How do you measure up to your parents' expectations?

Even small amounts of loving in infancy may have long-lasting positive effects on the development of personality. One psychologist selected twelve six-month-old babies from an institution and provided extra loving to half of them each day for a period of eight weeks.[14] The six babies she did not visit were cared for normally by the institutional staff. At the end of the experimental eight-week period, the psychologist measured how all twelve babies responded to people, using a series of specially designed behavioral tests. For example, in one test a baby received a high score for "social responsiveness" if it smiled when the experimenter stood by its crib. The social responsiveness score was high when a baby reacted positively to people. The responsiveness of the twelve babies to strangers was also tested. The psychologist found that the experimental babies who were given extra loving were more responsive, both to the experimenter and to strangers.

You might wonder about the six "control" babies who did not receive the extra attention. Were they treated fairly? In order to find out whether this kind of "short-term loving" was beneficial, a comparison had to be made between some infants who got it and some who did not. Because it was discovered that short-term loving was effective, programs are now being designed to provide this kind of care to all institutionalized children. Effective enrichment programs, however, are only short-term solutions, designed to fix the problems that result from troubled families.

S Babies are helpless. To survive they must have someone provide for their physical needs, but they also must receive love. Infants suffering from love deprivation may develop marasmus, a condition of extreme weakness. The need for parental love was studied in monkeys by Harry Harlow. He provided motherless infant monkeys with a wire and cloth surrogate, then observed the effect on them as adults. He found that the motherless monkeys grew up to be aggressive and poor parents. Studies show that foster homes and certain enrichment programs can reverse the bad effects of love deprivation.

Children and Parents

Because of your genes and your unique experiences, you are a unique person; there is no one else just like you. You may have inherited your mother's hair color or your father's build. But you receive much more than physical characteristics from your parents. You learned to speak their language, you learned to use their manners, you learned to adopt their values and prejudices. Your parents actively prepared you to become a member of their culture, and you may or may not accept the invitation to join.

This process of learning how to be a member of the human community is called **socialization.** From earliest infancy children begin to learn how they are to act as they relate to others. These parent-child interactions can have great significance. Because of the dependence of children on their parents, emotional bonds develop that invest the parents with enormous powers of reward and punishment. Parents use these powers in enforcing their expectations through the use

of discipline. For example, parents may reward children for their achievement with praise, love, or even money; withholding such rewards can be punishing.

Parental Expectations

You have felt the weight of parental expectations, both spoken and unspoken. What did your parents expect of you? What kind of person did they expect you to be? You may or may not have been able to live up to their expectations, and their expectations may or may not have been realistic. Realistic or not, parental demands for conformity begin in infancy. Even before the child is born, parents may have hopes and expectations about what the child will be.

Often before the infant is born adults may have decided what sex the infant should be, and also have a number of other expectations that may or may not be congruous with or appropriate for the actual child who arrives.[15]

Parental expectations have persisting effects on the personality. Children internalize the expectations of their parents and make them their own. These expectations then live on, long after the parents are gone. You may be reading this page—a small part of your effort to be educated—in order to satisfy an expectation your parents have of your future. These expectations are communicated in a variety of different ways.

■ *A Hopi Indian Child*   Hopi parents expect their children to be peaceful and nonaggressive. An autobiography of a Hopi Indian gives an idea of how this cultural value is communicated to the young.

As soon as I was old enough to take advice, he (my grandfather) taught me that it was a disgrace to be called kahopi *(not Hopi, not peaceful). He said, "My grandson, old people are important. They know a lot and don't lie. Listen to them, obey your parents, work hard, treat everyone right. Then people will say, 'That boy Chucka is a good child. Let's be kind to him.' If you do these things you will live to be an old man yourself and pass away in sleep without pain. That is the trail that every good Hopi follows."*[16]

The Hopi Indians place great significance on peace. The grandfather ensures the continuity of his culture by transferring his values and expectations to the coming generation.

■ *The Case of the Teen-aged Thief*   The following paragraph shows how a boy became what his mother expected of him.

A middle-class family's 15-year-old son stole a car. His mother told the psychiatrist that she had anticipated something of the kind ever since the boy had stolen, six years earlier, a pack of cigarettes. She had disciplined him at the time, but . . . she had never really ex-pected her son to stop stealing. Instead, the mother classified him in her mind as a potential thief. . . . From then on, whenever anything was missing from the house she immediately questioned him about it. The boy soon realized that his mother expected him to steal.[17]

Parental expectations are experienced as pressure to conform to whatever standard of behavior is expected. When expectations are high, there is pressure to do better; when expectations are low, there is pressure to do worse.

Obedience and Achievement

A recent study of adolescents shows the influence of parental expectations.[18] Three groups of teen-agers were compared: those who were classified as independent, those who were dependent, and those who were rebellious. The study revealed that children in these different groups came from different types of families. The independent adolescents tended to grow up in homes where parents expected independent thinking, where rules were consistent and explanations for rules were freely given. The adolescents who were dependent tended to have another type of parents. Their mothers and fathers tended to expect respect for authority and absolute obedience above all. Rules in these homes were not made and enforced consistently. The rebellious adolescent group had parents remarkably like those of the dependent adolescents. That is, the parents of the rebellious adolescents expected absolute obedience—but their children, rather than submitting, rebelled and failed to conform to this expectation. Think about your parents. Did they expect you to be independent or did they expect you to submit to their absolute authority? Did you turn out to be independent, dependent, or rebellious?

The need for achievement motivates people to succeed.

Most parents, particularly those in a competitive society, expect their children to achieve success. The children eventually accept this expectation and make it their own. Psychologists have called this motive the **need for achievement.** You probably know people who have an unusually high need for achievement—they seem driven to succeed. This need for achievement is highly influenced by parental expectations. Mothers of boys with a high need for achievement tend to expect and encourage independence and accomplishment. Such mothers also expect achievement of their sons at an earlier age than mothers whose sons have a low need for achievement.[19] Your need for achievement and success probably reflects the expectations of your parents.

Discipline

Many parental expectations are imposed on children through the use of discipline. When children violate their parents' expectations, they are scolded; when they conform, they are praised. This is how parents teach their children to become acceptable members of their culture. Try to recall the last time you were punished as a child. What parental expectation did you violate? Is this an expectation that you now have of yourself?

■ *The Law of Effect* Discipline is a powerful tool of socialization. Parents, in effect, shape the behavior of the child through interactions involving rewards and punishments. Sometimes the rewards and punishments are obvious, such as giving candy or a spanking; more often less direct techniques are employed. The smiles or frowns of your parents, their praise or criticism, the raising of an eyebrow or a quick penetrating glance, the subtle sound of the voice—these have acquired powers of reward and punishment for you. The meaning of these subtle signs, and thereby their rewarding or punishing power, is learned in the family situation. The frown, infants learn, precedes the spanking; the smile, they eventually discover, precedes the caress or the candy. After a period of learning, the smile and frown themselves can reward or punish behavior.

Children's behavior occurs, not in isolation, but in a responsive system: the family unit. Occurring in this responsive system, children's behavior is typically followed by some kind of a reaction. The reaction or **feedback** has the effect of modifying the children's later behavior. Children adjust their behavior to make it adaptive to their family system. When a particular behavior is followed by rewarding feedback, children tend to repeat it; when a behavior is followed

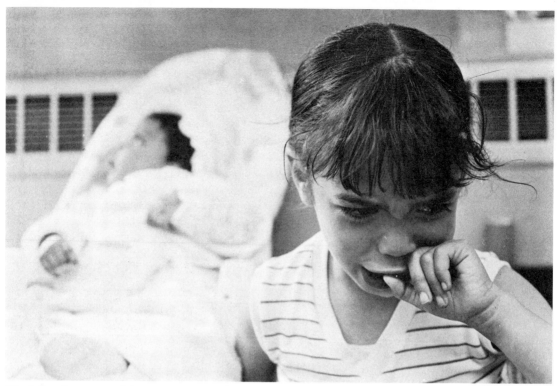

Discipline is a powerful tool of socialization.

by punishing feedback, children under certain circumstances tend to abandon that behavior. The principle shown here is called the **Law of Effect:** acts followed by rewards tend to be repeated and acts followed by punishment tend to be abandoned.

■ *Punishment* Patterns of discipline characterized by domination, rigidity, and excessive control through physical punishment typically produce children who are submissive, inhibited, and respectful to authority.[20] Punishment, however, often does not eliminate the behavior that is being punished. A study by Sears compared the child-rearing practices of 379 suburban New England mothers in two different towns and assessed the consequences of parental punishments and rewards.

In our discussion of the training process we have contrasted punishment with reward.

Both are techniques for changing the child's habitual ways of acting. Do they work equally well? The answer is unequivocally "no." . . . Punitiveness, in contrast with rewardingness, was a quite ineffectual quality for a mother to inject into her child's training.

The evidence for this conclusion is overwhelming. . . . Mothers who punished toilet accidents severely ended up with bed-wetting children. Mothers who punished dependency to get rid of it had more dependent children than mothers who did not punish. Mothers who punished aggressive behavior severely had more aggressive children than mothers who punished lightly.[21]

But the Law of Effect states that behavior that is rewarded should increase in frequency and behavior that is punished should be abandoned. In this case, however, the punishment of aggression caused aggressive acts to increase. Why would a child tend to repeat what he or she has been severely punished for? Sears explains:

Punishment [of aggression] seems to have complex effects. While undoubtedly it often stops a particular form of aggression, at least momentarily, it appears to generate more hostility in the child and lead to further aggressive outbursts at some other time or place. Furthermore, when the parents punish—particularly when they employ physical punishment— they are providing a living example of the use of aggression at the very moment they are trying to teach the child not to be aggressive. The child, who copies his parents in many ways, is likely to learn as much from this example of successful aggression on his parent's part as he is from the pain of punishment. Thus, the most peaceful home is one in which the mother believes aggression is not desirable . . . but who relies mainly on nonpunitive forms of control.[21]

The use of physical punishment can also have effects unrelated to the behavior punished. Harsh and arbitrary punishment has been shown to precede later prejudice[20] and also delinquency.[22] An important part of this problem is whether the strict discipline occurs within a context of rejection and hostility or whether it occurs within the context of acceptance and love.

Children Influence Parents

Parents shape the personality of their children and teach them to become members of their culture, but they are part of a relationship. Obviously, children are more than lumps of clay molded by their parents. Children can also influence their parents.[23] The family is an interacting system of relationships in which each member affects, and is affected by, other members.

The fact that troubled children tend to have troubled parents does not necessarily mean that the parents are at fault. It could be that troubled children are so hard to live with that their parents develop mixed attitudes of love and anger. Perhaps troubled children produce troubled parents, or, what is more likely, each influences the other.

The impact of children on parents begins before birth. Mothers may experience nausea, anxiety, or depression with pregnancy; and complications of pregnancy sometimes result from an abnormal fetus.[24] These experiences may shape the attitudes of mothers toward their infants. Infants behave differently from birth; some are easier to care for than others because of their activity levels and their reactions to being held. Mothers of infants that are easy to care for develop strong positive feelings toward their infants more often than mothers of infants that are difficult.[25] Thus, while parental behavior and attitudes may influence the personality and development of children, the personality of children also influences parental behavior and attitudes.

S   Parents actively prepare their children to be members of their culture; this process of learning is called socialization. Children internalize parental expectations and make them their own. Expectations for obedience and achievement are particularly strong in this culture. Most parents expect their children to be successful; the acceptance of this expectation results in children with a strong need for achievement. Parents differ in their expectations for obedience and in their patterns of discipline. Harsh and arbitrary punishment in childhood has been shown to precede a variety of adult personality problems. While parents influence their children in a variety of ways, it is also true that children influence their parents. The impact of children on parents begins before birth and continues throughout childhood.

Family Types

Each family is different, because the family is a system composed of unique individuals. But similar families can be grouped together for the purpose of description. In this way we can talk about family types.

Typical Families

Different family organizations can be viewed as different solutions to the various needs and problems that arise in life. On the basis of the way they cope with these needs and problems, most families can be classified as being one of three types: child-centered, home-centered, or parent-centered.[26]

The parents in the **child-centered family** willingly sacrifice their needs and desires for the sake of their children. The happiness and health of their children are more important than any other considerations. Typically in the child-centered family, a division of labor occurs in which the father specializes in maintaining economic security and in ensuring a respected place for the family in the community; the mother specializes in taking care of the needs of the children.

A second type of family is **home-centered.** In home-centered families priority is also given to the needs of the children. The difference between home-centered and child-centered families is that home-centered families are not oriented toward socioeconomic achievement. The father of home-centered families does not specialize in maintaining economic security and social status. Instead, both the father and mother give priority to personal relationships among family members; emotional security and companionship are highly valued. The family's energy is spent on family life, rather than on the community.

The self-esteem of a child is influenced by the parents' interest and affection.

The third type of family is **parent-centered.** In parent-centered families priority is given to the needs and problems of the parents, not of the children. Family life is not the focus of interest or attention; the parents are committed to obtaining success and rewards from the community, not the home. Mothers in parent-centered families are more likely to work in the community instead of spending all of their time and energy on the family life. Which of these three types is your family?

Disturbed Families

Some families have an emotional climate of rejection and hostility and are centered around unhappy parents. Such **disturbed families** may be unable to provide the love and stability necessary for the normal development of a child's personality. Disturbed families are more likely to produce disturbed children.

The most common type of severe mental disturbance is **schizophrenia.** Schizophrenics withdraw from reality into a world of their own and often show bizarre thought processes and perceptual disturbances. It has been found that children and adults suffering from schizophrenia often were raised in disturbed families. They tend to come from homes with emotional climates that differ in specific ways from the homes of healthy individuals. In some cases one parent dominated the family and the other parent withdrew completely. One study showed that male schizophrenics, as compared with normal males, more often had a weak father and a strong dominant mother. These women rejected their sons, but encouraged their dependency, a combination of attitudes that put the sons in a **double-bind** with no way to please their mothers.[27] The sons were given a double message: come close but stay away. They could not do both.

■ *The Son of Mr. Lamb—A Case Study*
The parents of some schizophrenics compete for the affection of the child; the mother wants all of the child's love but so does the father. These parents may also use inconsistent discipline, giving the child two conflicting sets of expectancies and standards.[28] Here is an account of the family history of one such schizophrenic patient.

Mr. Lamb (the father of the patient) was a very successful businessman but a most inadequate parent. As a young adult he had been an outstanding athlete but had to leave his school for disciplinary reasons. . . . From the time of the son's conception on, he made every possible effort to retain all of his wife's attention and affection, and to keep her away from his son, who later was our patient. . . . Instead of standing up to the father and objecting
to his behavior, she tended to look at times to the son for emotional support that the husband could not give her. Moreover, she encouraged the talented son to fulfill her own artistic tendencies. These were entirely lost on her husband, who openly criticized the son as effeminate, weak, and unathletic, after having thwarted the son's earlier efforts to be physically active by sneering at the child's performance in games or sports.[29]

In the Lamb family all the relationships among the family members were disturbed. The relationship of the parents was not one of confidence and love. The father was jealous of the child and was hostile and rejecting toward him, while the mother turned away from the father to seek a close relationship with the son. In turning toward the son for the love she could not find with the father, the mother in a sense was relying on the son to be the lover that her husband never was. The son could not adjust to the demands made by his disturbed family; he became schizophrenic.

Only autistic withdrawal seemed open to him. To live up to his father's "expectations," he had to be weak and passive in one sense, and an athlete in another; to please his mother he had to be artistic; but to assume a male role in any area carried the threat of incestuous closeness to his mother and indeed constituted a threat to his father's shaky masculinity.[29]

Loving Families

From birth until death we seek love, for not to be loved is to be separate and alone. For most people love is provided within the living environment of a family. The family serves the important functions of overcoming separateness and fostering strength and growth.

A loving family.

Love begins in the family when we are infants. The experience of unconditional acceptance, warmth, caressing, food, and security provides an environment of trust within which the personality can grow. As one author put it:

When the baby is genuinely loved and given much-needed, warm, reassuring mothering, with consideration for his helpless dependency and also his individuality, he begins to develop an image of the self, with feelings and expectations toward the world, that evokes his many capacities and latent potentialities. This prepares him for the experience of being transformed into a personality, the core of which is the image of the self that becomes symbolically expressed as I, me, my and mine.[30]

In other words, when babies are genuinely loved by their family, their identity begins developing and they are given the freedom to grow.

Just as the families of schizophrenics can be studied in search of the origins of mental disturbance, so the families of outstandingly successful persons can be studied in search of the origins of health. One psychologist studied the childhood histories of twenty eminent geniuses. He hoped to find a consistent pattern of experiences to help explain their intellectual achievements.[31] He concluded that most of the twenty had received in early childhood a large amount of loving and intellectually stimulating attention from their fathers and mothers. Families that are loving and democratic not only have children who are brighter than families that are cold and autocratic, but also tend to have children whose IQ's *increase* while in school rather than decrease.[32]

Attention and interest also affect a child's feelings of worth. Do you feel your parents were indifferent toward you or were they interested in you? A recent study of adolescents showed that parents who are relatively indifferent toward their children tend to have children with low self-esteem, while parents who are relatively interested in their children tend to have children with high self-esteem.[33]

The self-esteem of the child is affected much more by the interest and attitudes of the parents than by the social position or income of the family, the physical attractiveness of the child, or the child's ability in academics or sports.[34]

In other parts of the world parents interact with their children differently from the ways typical to American society. Studying families in other cultures sometimes shows the consequences of different family patterns. In a comparison of forty-eight other societies, it was found that the frequency of theft by adults was low when the cultural pattern for child-rearing included a high level of parental indulgence and affection.[35] Similar effects have been found for individuals within our culture. Those parents who show affectionate warmth toward their children have children with a lower incidence of juvenile delinquency.[22] Interest and affectionate warmth in the home are important for the growing personality.

S   Child-centered families focus on the needs and desires of their children and are dedicated to providing economic security for them. Home-centered families give priority to relationships among family members, and are more concerned with emotional security and family life. Parent-centered families are focused on the needs and desires of the parents. Disturbed families display an emotional climate of hostility and rejection, while loving families show love, caring, and attention among family members.

Can the Family Survive?

The family is the basic social unit of society, but the American family is in trouble. The signs of trouble have been widely publicized. The divorce rate is increasing; now about one out of every three marriages ends in divorce. Increasing numbers of young people express the determination never to get married. Family conflict is increasing: runaway teen-agers, child beating, and even murder are becoming more common occurrences in American families.

The traditional family structure has been changed by the changing roles of men and women in family life. Women used to do a great deal of menial work in the home, serving the men and children; now women want the same choices as men. A large proportion of women work but find that their families still expect them to play the role of "homemaker" full time, an impossible job. Family structure has been changed by families moving from place to place. Families used to settle and remain close to grandparents and other relatives, but the new mobile family leaves relatives behind.

Family structure has been weakened because the traditional functions of the family unit have been taken over by other social agencies. The education of children is increasingly done by schools. Child care is being taken over by child-care centers. Welfare and security needs are increasingly met by government. Families used to serve many important purposes, but these purposes are diminishing. Do you think the family unit can survive these changes?

Anthropologist Margaret Mead is optimistic. She has studied families in different cultures all over the world and is convinced that the family will survive. She writes:

If we go back into history we find over and over again, in moments of revolutionary change, that people start talking about the family, and what they're doing to it, and what's wrong with it. They even predict it's going to disappear altogether. It is in fact the only institution we have that doesn't have a hope of disappearing.[36]

Summary

KEY QUESTIONS

1. Do babies need families?

   Babies need families to provide not only for their physical needs but also for their emotional needs. Babies without loving may die. Even monkeys without mothers develop abnormally and later turn out to be poor parents.

2. How do children and parents influence each other?

   Parents shape their children to be members of their culture. Parental expectations and discipline influence the behavior and personality of children; children later assimilate these expectations and make them their own. The influence that parents have on their children is great, but children also influence their parents. The effect of children on parents begins even before birth.

3. What are the types of families?

   Families differ in terms of their focus; some are focused on the children, others on the home, and still others on the parents. These differing family organizations result in different experiences for growing children. In addition, families differ in terms of their emotional climate; some families are disturbed, with consistent patterns of hostility and rejection, while others are loving and supportive. The type of family can have long-lasting effects upon the personalities of the children.

KEY CONCEPTS

parenting	Taking care of children; serving as a caretaker.
love deprivation	For children, the condition of experiencing inadequate love.
marasmus	A condition of extreme weakness, loss of appetite, and apathy found in infants experiencing prolonged love deprivation.
surrogate mother	A fake or artificial mother; for example, in Harlow's work, a "mother" made of wire and wood.
socialization	The process by which children are shaped to become members of their culture.

need for achievement	The motivation to succeed or win.
feedback	Knowledge of results; knowing whether an action was or was not successful.
Law of Effect	The principle that actions with favorable consequences tend to be repeated, while actions with unfavorable consequences tend to be abandoned; for example, an action followed by reward is more likely to recur than an action followed by punishment.
child-centered family	A type of family that emphasizes the health and happiness of the children above all else.
home-centered family	A type of family that gives priority to personal relationships among family members.
parent-centered family	A type of family that gives priority to the needs of the parents.
disturbed family	A family with a climate of hostility or rejection; a family in which the personal relationships among family members are distorted.
schizophrenia	The most common type of severe mental disturbance; characterized by disturbances in thought processes, perceptions, and communication.
double-bind	A condition in which two opposing attitudes have been communicated; a double message, such as, "I love you" and also "I hate you."

Suggested Readings

Culture and Human Development: Insights into Growing Human edited by Ashley Montagu. Englewood Cliffs, N.J.: Prentice-Hall, 1974. A collection of articles examining the cultural influences on child development. Montagu and other noted authorities argue that an unfavorable cultural environment can cause retardation and other handicaps in children, but a favorable environment can reverse these effects.

The Process of Child Development edited by Peter Neubauer. New York: New American Library, 1976. Brings together the work of seventeen authorities in child development, including John Watson and Jean Piaget. Presents theories of intellectual development, sexual development, and parent-child relationships.

The Widening World of Childhood: Paths Toward Mastery by Lois Barclay Murphy. New York: Basic Books, 1962. A leading child psychologist reports on the study of thirty-two children selected as "normal" in infancy. The book demonstrates the varied and unique ways in which children encounter new situations in growing up. Concludes that mastery and coping ability are closely involved with the sense of identity.

Liberated Parents, Liberated Children by Adele Faber & Elaine Mazlish. New York: Avon Books, 1974. Presents the theories of Dr. Haim Ginott on parent-child interactions. Ginott advised parents to stop evaluating children and start respecting them as people. A down-to-earth child-raising manual for parents looking for a better way of communicating with their children.

Piaget's Theory of Intellectual Development: An Introduction by Herbert Ginsberg & Sylvia Opper. Englewood Cliffs, N.J.: Prentice-Hall, 1969. Clear presentation of Piaget's major theories of the intellectual development of children.

Children's Liberation edited by David Gottlieb. Englewood Cliffs, N.J.: Prentice-Hall, 1973. Collection of articles detailing the legal, moral, and institutional discrimination faced by children in our society.

Becoming: Basic Considerations for a Psychology of Personality by Gordon W. Allport. New Haven: Yale University Press, 1955. Presents the view that personality is not rigidly set but is always in a process of growth. A brief classic.

The Importance of Infancy by Lawrence K. Frank. New York: Random House, 1966. A survey of research on infant development. Discusses the effects of types of infant care on learning, coping, and personality. A technical book but well written.

Childhood and Society by Erik H. Erikson. (Rev. ed.) New York: Norton, 1963. A classic study in the social significance of childhood. Numerous case histories.

A Primer of Freudian Psychology by Calvin S. Hall. New York: New American Library, 1954. The best summary of Freud's psychoanalytic theory; a brief and easy-to-read paperback.

Sanity, Madness, and the Family by R. D. Laing & A. Esterson. Baltimore, Md.: Penguin Books, 1970. A study of the families of schizophrenics that concludes that the symptoms of schizophrenia are adaptive responses to disturbed family relationships.

Research Methods

II Observing Behavior

All science begins with observing nature, and psychology is no exception. The facts of psychology come from observations of behavior; for psychologists, behavior is the special part of nature that is most interesting.

Psychologists are not unique in observing behavior. We all spend time paying attention to our own behavior and the behavior of others. For example, parents typically find their newborn babies fascinating to watch; babies change rapidly during their early months of life and their growth is fun to observe. But what if you are both a parent and a psychologist?

Piaget: A Gifted Observer

Jean Piaget, a Swiss psychologist, has published over thirty books on children; his theories of child development have had widespread influence among psychologists and educators around the world. Yet Piaget's conclusions about children are based primarily on his observations of his own three children.

One psychologist described Piaget as follows:

It is Piaget's genius for empathy with children, together with true intellectual genius, that has made him the outstanding child psychologist in the world today and one destined to stand beside Freud with respect to his contributions to psychology, education and related disciplines. Just as Freud's discoveries of unconscious motivation, infantile sexuality and the stages of psychosexual growth changed our ways of thinking about human personality, so Piaget's discoveries of children's implicit philosophies, the construction of reality by the infant and the stages of mental development have altered our ways of thinking about human intelligence.

The man behind these discoveries is an arresting figure. He is tall and somewhat portly, and his stooped walk, bulky suits and crown of long white hair give him the appearance of an . . . Einstein.[1]

From his careful observations of his own three children, Piaget concluded that children not only reason differently from adults, but they also see the world differently. Piaget noted that when his children were in their first year of life they acted as if hidden objects no longer existed; that is, they did not have the concept of **object permanency.** He wrote:

At six months and nineteen days Laurent immediately began to cry from hunger and impatience on seeing his bottle (he was already whimpering, as he does quite regularly at mealtime). But at the very moment when I make the bottle disappear behind my hand or under the table—he follows me with his eyes— he stops crying. As soon as the object reappears, a new outburst of desire; then flat calm after it disappears. I repeat the experiment four more times; the result is constant until poor Laurent, beginning to think the joke bad, becomes violently angry.[2]

As far as Piaget's son was concerned, when the bottle could no longer be seen, it simply did not exist. It was "out of sight, out of mind."

From his records of his observations of his own children as they developed, Piaget reached certain conclusions about the minds of children that have, in general, been confirmed in many other studies. Piaget's observational techniques, however, differed from your methods of casual observation.

Observational Techniques

Psychologists are especially concerned that their observations are accurate and reliable. **Reliability** refers to dependability or consistency. If several different observers all agree with your observation, your observation is reliable.

One of the techniques psychologists use to increase the accuracy and reliability of their observations is to establish behavioral categories. Behavior is continuous and constantly changing; no two behaviors are identical. To make sense out of their observations, psychologists create **category systems,** procedures for grouping behavior into classes. Just as every tree is unique, but can be grouped into types of trees, so every behavior is unique, but can be grouped into types of behavior, or categories of behavior. For example, a wide variety of different behaviors can be grouped into the category "aggressive behavior." Other behaviors could be grouped into the category "helping behavior."

In order to study how members of a group interact, one psychologist developed a category system for classifying group interactions.[3] Some of these categories were the following:

1. Gives opinion or expresses a feeling
2. Gives information or clarifies
3. Asks for information
4. Asks for opinion or evaluation
5. Agrees
6. Disagrees
7. Shows tension, asks for help
8. Shows tension release, jokes, laughs
9. Shows antagonism
10. Shows solidarity, gives help

Trained observers were able to categorize most of the interactions in groups they observed into one of the above categories.

There are sometimes disagreements about category systems. There are many different ways of classifying behavior. One person may prefer one way, while a second person may prefer another way. The category system for classifying types of psychosis has long been controversial. One of the problems with all category systems for psychosis is that different trained observers classify people differently. These systems then are unreliable.

Observer Bias

Perhaps you have heard someone say, "Seeing is believing."

But can you believe your eyes? Sometimes different people see different things. What you see is sometimes ambiguous or unclear. To most people, the figure shown here looks like a three-dimensional glass box. But which corner of the box is closest to you, corner A or B? Look again, and you may change your mind.

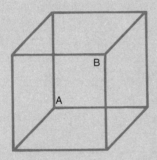

Distortions and Prejudice

Observations are sometimes distorted or biased. We have a tendency to oversimplify people, to see them as stereotypes. It is as if we put an imaginary "halo" over some people's heads—from our perspective, they can do no wrong. This kind of bias is called the **halo effect**—the tendency of people who have been judged positively in one respect to be judged positively in other respects.

Physical appearance biases our judgment and creates a kind of halo effect. In one study students were shown photographs of strangers and asked to rate their personalities.[4] The photographs had been previously separated by judges into categories of high, medium, or low attractiveness. Pictures of highly attractive people were rated as more

confident, happy, active, serious, perceptive, and flexible. Even though the pictures were of complete strangers, the students rated the attractive ones as positive and the unattractive ones as negative on a wide variety of personality traits.

Expectancy

Expectations can bias observations. You may have heard, "What you expect is what you get." There is some truth in that. Expectations have a way of coming true. It is widely believed that a lion tamer who expects to be bitten has a greater chance of being attacked. Many experiments in the psychology of perception have shown that, to some extent, you see what you expect to see. For example, what do you see at the center of the figure below?

12
A 13 C
14

Whether you see it as a "B" or as a "13" depends upon whether you are expecting a letter or a number; exactly the same figure can be seen as two different things. The results of psychology experiments can sometimes be influenced by the expectations of the experimenter, and the IQ of a child can be influenced by the expectations of the teacher.[5] The tendency for your expectations to come true is called a **self-fulfilling prophecy.**

Selectivity and Bias

As far as your senses are concerned, the world has a great excess of information. How can you cope with the all the sounds and sights that demand your attention? You cannot pay attention to everything at once; you notice some things and ignore others. According to the **principle of selective attention,** you are able to attend to and perceive only a small portion of the information available in the world.

Magicians would be out of work were it not for this principle. Most magic tricks are based on your tendency to pay attention only to part of what is going on. Magicians learn how to divert your attention so that their hands are faster than your eyes. Early in this century a psychologist demonstrated this effect in front of his class:

I stood on the platform behind a low desk and begged the [psychology class] to watch and to describe everything which I was going to do from one given signal to another. As soon as the signal was given, I lifted with my right hand a little revolving wheel with a color-disk and made it run and change its color, and all the time, while I kept the little instrument at the height of head, I turned my eyes eagerly toward it. While this was going on, up to the closing signal, I took with my left hand, at first, a pencil from my vest pocket and wrote something at the desk; then I took my watch out and laid it on the table; then I took a silver cigarette box from my pocket, opened it, took a cigarette out of it, closed it with a loud click, and returned it to my pocket; and then came the ending signal.[6]

The observers then wrote down everything they observed. The results showed that 18 out of the 100 students failed to observe *anything* that he did with his left hand.

Recording Observations

Memory can play tricks on you. You not only tend to observe selectively, but you also tend to remember selectively. Your story of an auto accident or some other event you have observed slowly changes over time. You tend to remember certain parts of the story better than others. To avoid the biasing effects of a selective memory, psychologists try to record their observations as accurately as possible and with as little delay as possible. One way to do this is to write down everything that happens, as it happens. Another way is to check off categories of behavior as they occur, counting the frequency of aggressive behavior, for example. An increasingly popular technique is to record the behavior on film or videotape.

Psychologists are aware of the sources of potential bias in their observations and consequently work to prevent their distorting influence. They, like all scientists, have a stake in accuracy.

KEY CONCEPTS

object permanency	The concept that objects continue to exist even when they cannot be perceived.
reliability	Dependability or consistency.

category system	A way of classifying objects or events; a set of groups or types of behavior.
halo effect	The tendency of people who have been judged positively on one trait to be judged positively on other traits.
self-fulfilling prophecy	The tendency for expectations to come true.
principle of selective attention	The idea that a person can attend to and perceive only a small portion of information available.

Education

7 Learning

KEY QUESTIONS

1. What is the difference between learned and unlearned behavior?
2. How do you know what you know?
3. How can learning a skill or learning from a book be made easier?
4. How are habits and emotional reactions learned?

You are learning as you read this book. And reading this book is something you learned how to do. Most of what you do, or could do, are things you learned how to do; but some things are *innate*—you could do them from birth or as soon after as your body was able. You did not know how to read when you were born—you had to learn how to read. But you have always known how to sneeze because your ability to sneeze is innate, not learned.

What Is Learning?

Most of your intellectual abilities, your feelings about things, and your skills have been learned. You learned how to read; you learned to fear spiders; and you learned how to ride a bike. Learning is necessary for all these activities. What is learning? Psychologists define **learning** as a change in behavior or behavior potential as a result of experience.

Unlearned Behavior

The word "change" is important in the definition of learning. Some of human behavior, and much of animal behavior, does not change with time and experience; it is therefore not learned behavior. For example, certain complex behaviors called *instincts* are present at birth in some animals. The songs and nest-building of many birds are the result not of learning but of inborn instinctual behavior patterns

Simpler, more specific inborn reactions are called **reflexes.** Reflexes are involuntary reactions occurring to specific stimulation. If you tickle a dog on the right spot on its side, its back legs will move in a scratching motion. This is a reflex. You can demonstrate one of your own reflexes. Remain seated in your chair and cross your legs so that your right leg rests on top of your left leg and can swing freely. With the edge of your hand tap your right leg directly below your kneecap. If you miss the right spot, nothing will happen; but if you hit your leg just right, the result will be a reflex knee jerk. You have a variety of other highly specific built-in reactions. The hair on your forearm stands up when you are chilled ("goosebumps"); your eye blinks when an object comes too close or a loud noise occurs; your hand pulls back rapidly when it is burned; you sneeze when you have dust or pepper in your nose; you salivate when you put food in your mouth. You do not have to think about these reactions—they are involuntary. The event producing the reflex is called the *stimulus* (e.g., pepper) and the reaction is called the *response* (e.g., a sneeze). Reflexes are inborn;

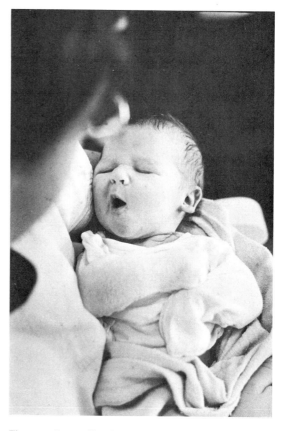

The rooting reflex is an inborn behavior. Babies turn toward and try to suck something that touches their cheek.

they do not develop as a result of experience and are therefore not learned. You do not have to learn how to sneeze.

In order for learning to occur, behavior must change *as a result of experience.* Certain kinds of behaviors change, not as a result of experience in the world, but for other reasons. For example, drugs and disease change behavior; but these changes are not termed "learning," because the changes are not caused by experience. Another important type of behavior change occurs as a result of *maturation,* the physical growth and development of the body. As your body develops and matures, you are able to do more and more things. Changes due to maturation are not called "learning" because these changes are not caused by experience.

Most infants are able to sit without support by eight months, but not by four months; most are able to crawl by ten months, but not by five months; most are able to walk alone by fifteen months, but not by ten months.[1,2] These changes in behavior are made possible by the development and increasing maturation of muscles, bones, and nerves in the infant's body. The rate of this development and maturation seems little affected by experience. In some cultures, infants spend most of their early life completely restricted, yet this does not slow down their motor development. They are able to walk at the same age as other children.[3,4]

Learning and Experience

Learning is a change in behavior or behavior potential that results from *experience*. Simple reflexes and instincts are not learned behavior, and changes due to maturation and development are not considered learning. Learning results from experience. Reading this book is a kind of experience, and from it you are learning about psychology. Your knowledge of the English language was learned from experience. Your habits and skills were learned from experience. From the pattern of experiences in your life, you have learned your beliefs, attitudes, and to some extent your personality. You have learned to be human.

The behavior that is learned from experience can be simple or complex; you can learn to do something or you can learn not to do something; sometimes what is learned is demonstrated right away in behavior and sometimes it is stored away but never used. In any case, if behavior changes are the consequence of experience, then learning has occurred.

When learning occurs, what is it that is learned? Some learning involves learning simple reactions. For example, your mouth learns to anticipate the candy with the flow of saliva juices. This kind of learning by association is seen in primitive animals as well as humans. Some learning consists of learning the consequences of different actions. Both animals and humans learn which actions are followed by favorable consequences and which by unfavorable consequences. Some psychologists believe that these two types of simple learning—by association and by consequences—are the only kinds of learning possible. Most psychologists, however, believe that human learning is generally more complex and consists primarily of knowledge about ourselves, other people, and the world. This kind of learning cannot be reduced to simple behavioral reactions.

⑤ Instincts and reflexes are inborn reactions, do not develop from experience, and are therefore not learned. Changes in behavior due to the physical maturation of the body are also not a result of learning. Learning is a change in behavior as a result of experience. Learning can be simple or complex; your habits, emotional reactions, and knowledge are the result of learning.

Learning as Knowing

You know many things about yourself and the world. Some of this learning came from school and books, some from your parents and friends, and some from your other life experiences. Much of what you initially learned you have since forgotten; and, perhaps, some of what you now know you would like to forget. Sometimes you learned by

Some learning requires rote memorization, but most learning involves meaningful relationships.

rote, memorizing lists of words or numbers that made little sense at the time. For example, your initial learning of the multiplication table was rote learning. Most learning, however, involves meaningful relationships; it is organized or structured.

Structure and Relationships

Why is psychology easier to learn than nuclear physics? An important reason is that nuclear physics, unlike psychology, consists of concepts with which you have little or no familiarity. You have had little experience observing the physical structure of the atom, but have been observing human behavior all of your life. Meaningful human learning requires relating new material to what you already know or discovering new relationships among things you have experienced. The term *relationship* is important here.

Your knowledge of the world consists, not of lists of unrelated information, but of a body of related facts and rules. Your knowledge of psychology consists of facts, concepts, and their relationships.

A pile of unconnected boards and nails is of little use; but if they are connected and related they form a *structure*, a house. Ideas are like that. Unconnected concepts or ideas appear meaningless to us, but a set of related or organized ideas form a kind of **mental structure;** and this is what we call knowledge. Through experience we acquire a structured mental representation of reality. When we add to our knowledge, we add to this mental structure. Child psychologists such as Piaget have shown that as children develop mentally they acquire more complex mental structures for understanding the world.

If knowledge consists of mental structures, learning should be made easier when the material to be learned is itself structured. It turns out that this is so. Learning an organized or structured set of ideas is far easier than learning an unrelated list of ideas. In addition, unrelated details are easily forgotten, while those that are part of a structure of ideas are more likely to be remembered.

Book Learning

Books are not lists of random words; they are organized or structured. Much of human learning involves written or spoken words, but in the animal world few species have any ability to understand symbolic language. Chimpanzees have recently been taught a form of human sign language used by the deaf,[5] but the tremendous efficiency of learning information from books remains beyond the capacity of any organisms but ourselves.

Learning verbal material is affected by

other material learned either before or after the material in question. Your ability to remember a particular passage, for example this one, may be blocked by material read on the preceding page and on the following page. Learning verbal material is also affected by the meaningfulness of the material. In general, the more meaningful the material, the better it is learned. In order for an idea to be meaningful, it must be easily related to what is already known; that is, it must be related to an existing mental structure. How verbal material is organized also affects the learning process. Apparently human memory is best suited to remember material that is organized or structured into meaningful clusters, rather than material that is relatively unrelated. Thus, learning material from books is made easier when the material is meaningful and organized, and is hindered by interference from other learned material.

Social Learning

How did you learn to dance and to sing? Chances are, you learned how to do these things from social learning, by carefully observing and listening to other people. A person who is observed and copied is a **model.**

Much of human behavior is learned socially, through observing and imitating models. There are three types of models: real-life, symbolic, and representational. *Real-life models* are parents and teachers, for example, whose behavior is copied by children. Models presented to us through symbolic language, such as the heros of novels, are classified as *symbolic models*. Models presented through television and films are classified as *representational models*.[6] Observing and imitating models can teach not only what to do but also what not to do. A child seeing an adult receive a painful shock

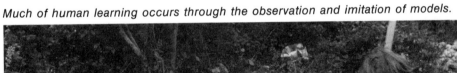

Much of human learning occurs through the observation and imitation of models.

when touching an electric wire will learn not to touch the wire. Observing models can also teach when to do something, that is, the appropriate time for behaving in a particular manner. A boy may learn to yell at football games but not at weddings by observing and imitating his father.

Social learning occurs in all cultures. Among the Canadian Ojibwa Indians, a young boy may follow his father as he traps, hunts, and fishes. Learning initially is solely by observation, not by teaching or explanation. The boy's father is a real-life model that the child watches and imitates.

Skill Learning

An important consideration involved in learning a skill is the method of *practice*. For example, should you practice the whole act every time, or should you practice a part of the act until you achieve competency with it, then practice another part? This has been identified as the **whole-part issue,** and the answer depends upon the structure of the skill to be learned. The method of practice (whole or part) should reflect whether the skill is organized as a whole or as separate parts. Research on this issue shows that when a skilled act is made up of a group of relatively independent parts, then practicing the several parts of the skill separately works better; but when the skilled act involves a highly integrated group of parts, ones that are highly interdependent, then it is better to practice the whole act. For example, the serve in the game of tennis is relatively independent from the other parts of the game and can effectively be practiced separately (part-practice); but the various movements that make up the serve are highly inter-dependent—they form an integrated act—and should be practiced together (whole-practice).

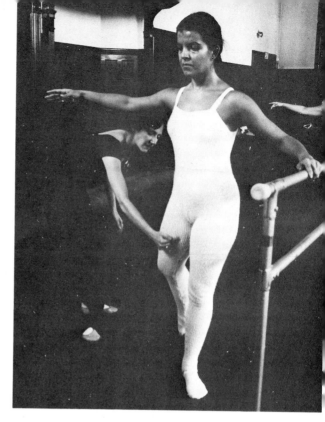

Skill learning requires practice.

Another important question involved in how to practice is the question of *when*. This is the **massed-spaced issue** in learning. Should your practice occur all together in one long session (cramming or *massed practice*) or should your practice periods be interrupted by rest periods (*spaced practice*)? The evidence on this question shows that concentrated or massed practice does not work as well as spaced practice for most skills.

Recent studies show that certain skills can be practiced effectively just by thinking about them; mental or imaginary practice improves performance. Studies show dramatic improvement following the imaginary practice of perceptual-motor skills.[7] Can you imagine yourself shooting baskets in a game of basketball, or serving a ball in tennis, or throwing a dart? Once you know what to do and have tried it a few times you can practice in your imagination and get better and better.

Learning to Learn

Most human learning is not the result of a single learning situation; a typical learning problem has been preceded by many other similar problems. Because problems are similar, there is usually some transfer of learning from one learning problem to another. If you know two foreign languages, you may find that learning your third foreign language is easier than learning your first or second; you may have learned *how to learn* a foreign language. If you learn several new dance steps, you may find that learning the fifth dance is easier than learning the first; you may have learned *how to learn* dancing. Learning how to learn a particular kind of problem provides you with a **learning set.**[8]

If you didn't develop learning sets, you would approach each new problem as if it were entirely new and unrelated to other problems you have successfully solved in the past. Your ability to develop learning sets means that you can adjust to new situations rapidly by taking advantage of similar situations in the past. You gain learning efficiency by taking advantage of the transfer of learning from one situation to the next. You develop general learning strategies.

The development of transfer and learning sets is more likely when the material to be learned is organized and structured. As the psychologist Jerome Bruner wrote,

The teaching and learning of structure, rather than simply the mastery of facts and techniques, is at the center of the classic problem of transfer. . . . If earlier learning is to render later learning easier, it must do so by providing a general picture in terms of which the relations between things encountered earlier and later are made as clear as possible.[9]

Psychologists have shown that learning sets are not unique to human beings. Other animals can also learn how to learn. Learning sets have been demonstrated in persons of all ages,[10] in monkeys,[8] cats,[11] and even in rats.[12]

⑤   Meaningful human learning involves acquiring or modifying mental structures, sets of related or organized ideas. Learning is made easier when the material to be learned is organized or structured. Social learning occurs by observing models (other people) and imitating them. The best method of learning a skill involves a method of practice that reflects whether the skill is organized as a whole or as separate parts. There is usually some transfer of learning from one situation to another; with experience, you develop learning sets which make future learning easier.

Learning as Conditioning

Your habits and emotional reactions were learned as a result of experience. Animals as well as humans learn to adjust their responses to the world. Behavioral psychologists studying this kind of learning focus on how new responses are learned and emphasize the influence of the environment in controlling behavior. They are concerned with reducing complex experience to measurable behavior, then studying the conditions in which that behavior changes. An example is the very simple kind of learning called *conditioning.* A response can be conditioned by *association* or by its *consequences.* Under the proper circumstances, a response that is repeatedly associated with a stimulus will become conditioned to that stimulus. Whenever the stimulus occurs, the response will follow. A response can also be conditioned by its consequences. If your dog gets a bit of food as a consequence of doing its trick, it will continue to perform it. Conditioning was initially studied by psychologists in laboratories using animals, such as dogs, rats, and pigeons. More recently, conditioning principles have been applied to change human behavior.

Conditioning by Association

Virginia was involved in a serious accident—in a compact car—but fortunately escaped with only minor injuries. For several weeks thereafter, however, she found herself unable to ride in any car. Whenever she got into a car, she would feel extremely anxious; her limbs would tremble and her heart would race. The stimulus of cars and the response of fear had become associated through *conditioning*, so that the sight of a car gained the power to produce fear.

Steven, an alcoholic, was treated with a drug called Antabuse, which has a highly specific effect: any alcohol, even a small drink, causes severe nausea and vomiting. After several experiences of drinking and vomiting, Steven found that even thinking about taking a drink would make him slightly ill. When he went off the drug and tried to take a drink of whiskey, he became nauseated and vomited. The stimulus of whiskey and the response of nausea had become associated through *conditioning*, so that whiskey gained the power to cause nausea.

Ivan Pavlov

Conditioning by association, or **classical conditioning,** was first investigated systematically by Ivan Pavlov, a Russian physiologist born in 1849. Pavlov, the son of a Russian priest, spent his entire life studying the physiology and psychology of the digestive sys-

Ivan Pavlov

tem. He was fanatically dedicated to pure science and in 1904 won the Nobel Prize for his physiological discoveries.

What kind of a man was Pavlov? He was so dedicated to his work that there was little room in his life for anything else. Only one thing really mattered—his research.

After one taste of research all the practical issues—his position, salary, living conditions, even the clothes he wore—became little more than unavoidable annoyances intruding upon the only part of life that really mattered. . . . Only unwavering faith enabled his wife and friends to put up with him. His complete inability to manage his financial affairs was not his only peculiarity: he was equally difficult in other matters. For example, he liked to take long walks with his wife, but he set such a strenuous pace that she often had to run to keep up. . . . During the [Russian] revolution he scolded one of his assistants for arriving ten minutes late for an experiment; shooting and fighting in the streets should not interfere when there was work to be done in the laboratory.[13]

Pavlov was concerned only with the physiology of the body and with observable behavior. There was no room in Pavlov's laboratory for such expressions as "consciousness" or "mind." If Pavlov's assistants mistakenly used one of these expressions, they were promptly fined. The "errors" added up to a comfortable petty-cash fund.

Pavlov and His Dogs

Pavlov's interest in digestion led him to study the salivary response in dogs—that is, how a dog's mouth waters when the dog eats food. One day, when studying how a dog salivates, Pavlov made an important psychological discovery, and he spent the next 30 years investigating it. Pavlov noticed that the dog began to salivate *before* it was fed, whenever it heard someone approaching with food.[14]

Just as your mouth begins to water before you bite into an apple, dogs learn to salivate in anticipation of food. This kind of automatic involuntary reaction Pavlov called a *reflex*. Salivating to the sound of footsteps signaling that food is coming is a learned or conditioned reflex. If a bell repeatedly accompanies a dog's feeding, the dog will salivate whenever it hears the bell. Pavlov established a new response in his dogs by pairing a bell with the presentation of meat powder. The bell and the presentation of meat powder in the mouth occurred at the same time. Following repeated pairings of meat powder and bell, the bell eventually acquired the power to produce salivation by itself. Thus, a new response—salivating to a bell—was learned. Whenever Pavlov rang a bell, his dogs began to salivate.

Law of Contiguity

In classical conditioning a connection is established between a stimulus and a response, in which the stimulus acquires the power to produce the response. In order for this stimulus-response connection to be made, they must occur at nearly the same time; that is, they must be *contiguous* (close together) in time. Classical conditioning is based on the **Law of Contiguity:** under certain circumstances, a stimulus that occurs at about the same time as a response will acquire the power to produce that response.

This law can be applied to the following everyday example of classical conditioning. Your saliva juices may flow when you see pictures of certain kinds of food, such as a slice of orange or lemon. In the past on many occasions, the sight of an orange slice has been closely followed by the experience of putting the orange into your mouth and chewing it. The presence of food in your mouth is a stimulus that elicits an automatic-reflex response of salivation. Thus, the sight of an orange slice (stimulus) and salivation (response) have occurred together repeatedly in the past. Because of the Law of Contiguity, the response of salivating has become classically conditioned to the sight of oranges so that now the sight alone is sufficient to produce salivation.

In this example, salivating to food in the mouth is an automatic reflex and is termed the **unconditioned response (UCR).** Salivating at the sight of food is a learned response and is termed the **conditioned response (CR).** The food in the mouth that causes the reflex response of salivation is termed the **unconditioned stimulus (UCS).** The sight of food, which—after learning—acquires the power to produce salivation, is termed the **conditioned stimulus (CS).** The procedure of classical conditioning consists of pairing the CS (the sight of food) with the UCS (food in the mouth) so that they both occur at about the same time and both slightly precede the UCR (the response of salivating to the food in

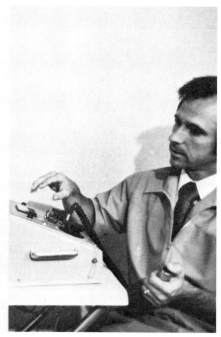

A program based on classical conditioning designed to help people stop smoking.

the mouth). With this procedure a connection is established, and the CS (the sight of food) eventually produces the CR (salivation).

Once a response has been classically conditioned to a particular stimulus, it may also be produced by other similar stimuli. This effect is called **stimulus generalization.** For example, if you were conditioned to salivate at the sight of an orange, you might also salivate at the sight of a tangerine or even at the sight of an orange balloon. Stimulus generalization occurred for Virginia, who was conditioned to fear a car; her fear response generalized to cars unlike those in which she had her accident. If stimulus generalization had not occurred, she might feel afraid only in small compact cars like the one she was in during her accident; the response would be elicited selectively, only by certain kinds of cars. This process of selective responding is termed **discrimination.** Ultimately, Virginia's fear of cars may disappear—it extinguishes. When the conditioned response no longer occurs to the conditioned stimulus, the response is said to be extinguished. Re-

sponse **extinction** occurs when the unconditioned stimulus and the conditioned stimulus are no longer paired—the sight of food is not followed by food in the mouth; riding in a car is not accompanied by a painful accident.

Albert's Problem

Albert was an unusually fearless baby before John Watson decided to use him in his psychology experiment. Watson chose Albert for this experiment on the origins of fear because he appeared to be "stolid and unemotional" and hardly ever cried. When Albert was about one year old, Watson decided to find out whether he could teach Albert to be afraid.

Watson first tested Albert to find out what would make Albert cry. He confronted him suddenly with a white rat, but Albert showed no fear. He presented him with a monkey, a rabbit, a mask, burning newspapers, but Albert showed no fear. But when, unexpectedly, a loud noise was made behind his head,

Albert broke into a sudden crying fit. Watson had found the stimulus he needed for his conditioning experiment.

In order to prove that Albert could learn to fear something, Watson had to find something that Albert at first did not fear and then teach him to fear it. Watson chose a white rat because he knew that Albert was not afraid of rats. Watson walked close to Albert, reached into a basket, and suddenly pulled out a large white rat. As Albert smiled and reached for it with his left hand, Watson's assistant suddenly made a loud noise directly behind Albert's head by striking a hammer against a piece of metal. Albert jumped violently and slumped forward, covering his face. The rat and the loud noise were presented to Albert five more times. On the sixth trial the rat was presented alone, without the noise; the instant the rat was shown, Albert began to cry and to turn away.[15] Albert had learned to fear rats.

The procedure Watson used was classical conditioning. The loud noise was an unconditioned stimulus and the fear reaction to the noise was an unconditioned response. The white rat was the conditioned stimulus and the fear reaction to the rat was a conditioned response. By repeatedly pairing the CS and the UCS, the CS acquired the power to elicit the CR. You may be wondering about the ethics of this kind of research with children. This experiment was done over fifty years ago and would not be consistent with the ethical standards of modern researchers in psychology.

Ⓢ Classical conditioning is based on the Law of Contiguity: under certain circumstances, a stimulus that repeatedly occurs at about the same time as a response will acquire the power to produce that response. In the case of Pavlov's dogs, the stimulus was a bell, the response was salivation, and the dogs were conditioned to salivate to the bell.

The following are major concepts in classical conditioning:

1. Unconditioned stimulus—a stimulus that automatically causes a response, for example food powder in the mouth.
2. Unconditioned response—a response to the unconditioned stimulus, for example salivating to food powder.
3. Conditioned stimulus—the initially neutral stimulus that is paired with the unconditioned stimulus, for example a bell.
4. Conditioned response—the learned reaction to the conditioned stimulus, for example learning to salivate to the bell.
5. Stimulus generalization—a conditioned response to stimuli similar to the conditioned stimulus.
6. Discrimination—responding to certain stimuli but not to others.
7. Extinction—the disappearance of the conditioned response brought about in classical conditioning by presenting the conditioned stimulus without the unconditioned stimulus.

Conditioning by Consequence

A cat is put into a box from which it can escape and be fed only if it presses a lever. The cat tries to get out of the box, but doesn't know how; it turns this way and that, then, by accident, sits down on the escape lever. The door to the box opens and the cat leaves and is fed. The next time that the cat is put into the box, it goes to the lever and sits down on it again, opening the door right away. Because the cat's behavior was rewarded, it was learned and could be repeated. This kind of conditioning by consequences is called **operant conditioning** or **instrumental conditioning.**

An infant is lying in its crib making babbling noises and its mother is working nearby. By chance, the infant babbles "ma-ma, ma-ma"; smiling, the mother picks the baby up and snuggles it. The baby received attention and affection as a consequence of babbling in a particular way; such rewards make it likely that "ma-ma" will be said more often in the future. The response of saying "ma-ma" in the presence of its mother will be learned through *operant conditioning.*

Skinner and His Rats

One of the most influential figures in modern psychology is B. F. Skinner, a man who has devoted his life to the study of operant conditioning. One of Skinner's early contributions was the invention of a special box for studying animal learning (the "Skinner box"). When a rat, pigeon, or other small animal is placed in this box and it pushes a lever, a mechanism delivers a small pellet of food to the animal. The Skinner box automatically rewards the animal for pressing the lever; lever-pressing is learned through operant conditioning. The Skinner box makes it possible for psychologists to study the effects of various kinds of rewards and reward schedules on the behavior of animals. For example, it has been learned that responses rewarded occasionally but not consistently do not extinguish very easily. They become very persistent habits.

Skinner contends that the world is like the Skinner box. People are like rats: their behavior is controlled by the environment, which rewards some activities and not others. As Skinner put it in an interview:

The world at large is a laboratory. Take the people in Las Vegas, pulling levers on slot machines. They are in a laboratory situation, and very willingly. The slot machines simply

B. F. Skinner

use a schedule of conditioning and reinforcement similar to those we use in the laboratory—with money dropping down the chute instead of food.[16]

Skinner argues that freedom is an illusion. People are not free; their behavior is controlled by their environment. The problem for people to solve is how to gain control over the rewards and punishments in their environment by applying the principles learned in the Skinner box to the design of future society.

Law of Effect

In operant conditioning a response is learned because of the favorable consequences that follow it; these consequences, typically rewards, are called **reinforcers** (the reward reinforces or strengthens the response). The procedure of giving rewards following a response is called **reinforcement.** An example of reinforcement is giving your dog some meat after it performs a trick.

Operant conditioning is based on the **Law of Effect:** responses followed by reinforcement will tend to be repeated. If a dog's trick is followed by a reinforcer (food), the trick will probably be repeated. The reinforcer is given only when the appropriate response is made; that is, reinforcement is dependent upon making the appropriate response. The response-reinforcement dependency is the key to the operant-conditioning procedure.

There are many different kinds of rewards. Some events are quite directly gratifying, such as food when you are hungry or water when you are thirsty. These are called **primary reinforcers.** Other events are only indirectly rewarding; money, for example, is an indirect or **secondary reinforcer,** since food can be purchased with it. There are many varieties of secondary reinforcers. A smile is a secondary reinforcer; it has developed the power to reward because it has been associated with direct rewards in the past. Words can be secondary reinforcers; if a mother says "good" when her son behaves correctly, he is more likely to behave correctly in the future.

Initially, infants are rewarded with attention for saying anything even slightly like "ma-ma"; later they are rewarded only for saying it correctly. The improvement is a consequence of **shaping** the response. The parents reward only closer and closer approximations to the final desired response. In language, as with other skills, the rules for what is rewarded become stricter as greater competency is acquired; the skill is *shaped* through gradual approximations.

Initially infants say "ma-ma" to all adults; later they say it only to women; still later they say it only to their mothers. The change is a result of increasing **stimulus control;** the response becomes under the control of a particular stimulus (the mother) because the response is rewarded only in the presence of the mother.

Eventually the reward becomes inconsistent; sometimes they are rewarded for saying "ma-ma" to their mothers and sometimes they are not. When reinforcers are given only part of the time, this is called **partial reinforcement.** If no reinforcers are given, the response eventually stops altogether; this is called response **extinction.**

How to Train Animals

Have you ever taught a dog a trick? If you have, you have used the procedures of operant conditioning. Operant conditioning is an easy and fast method for teaching tricks to all kinds of animals. There are seven easy steps:

1. Get some food that the animal likes and cut it up into a large number of very small pieces.

2. Wait until a time that the animal is hungry—such as right before dinner. To make sure that the animal is really hungry it may be necessary to withhold one meal.

3. Establish a "secondary reinforcer"—a signal that the animal is conditioned to associate with food. A whistle or a clap will work as a secondary reinforcer. To make a whistle become a secondary reinforcer, you whistle, then immediately give the animal a small tidbit of food; whistle, then feed. This pattern is repeated several times until the whistle becomes a signal for the animal that food is available.

4. Decide on a simple trick you want the animal to perform. Then break the behavior up into a series of simple steps. For example, suppose you want to teach your dog to come to you and sit down by your

feet when you say "come." The first step of the trick involves the dog coming toward you. The second step involves the dog going to your right side. The third step requires the dog to orient its body in the same direction as your body, with its head pointing forward. The last step involves the dog sitting down.

5. Shape the desired behavior by gradual approximation or guidance. To do this, you begin by rewarding the animal for completing the first step of the trick. You say "come" and reward the animal if it comes toward you. Sometimes the first step is not something that the animal will naturally do, so you must reward it for doing something approximately like the first step. The way to reward the animal is first to signal it with the secondary reinforcement, then to feed it a tidbit of food. Another way an animal can be helped to perform a physical movement is by guidance; you can help a dog sit, for example, by pressing gently on its rear end. By breaking the trick down into a series of small steps, the animal can gradually learn how to do a complicated trick; but each small step must be fairly easy.

6. Establish stimulus control. Once the animal can perform the trick and is rewarded, you want to train the animal to do it only at certain times; for example, only when it is told to do so. This is getting the behavior under the control of a verbal stimulus. You do this by providing the stimulus *"Come,"* then rewarding the animal if it performs its trick; if the trick is performed at some other time, when you have not provided the appropriate verbal stimulus, you do not reward it. In this way a discrimination is established; the animal learns to perform the trick only following the appropriate stimulus.

7. Introduce partial reinforcement. After the animal is able to perform the trick perfectly every time, you should begin to withhold the food reward occasionally (but not the secondary reinforcement). At first withhold the food every second or third time the trick is performed; later, withhold the food most of the time, providing the food reward only rarely. This way you won't have to carry dog food with you all of the time. Also, behavior that is only partially rewarded is less likely to extinguish.

Different people respond to different types of reinforcements.

■ **Priscilla, the Dainty Pig** Keller and Marian Breland have made a career of training animals with operant-conditioning procedures. In their trained chicken acts, which were exhibited in county fairs in different parts of the country, one chicken was trained to play a five-note tune on a small piano and another performed a tap dance in costume and shoes. They also developed a trained pig show, featuring Priscilla. Priscilla was able to turn on the radio, eat breakfast at a table, pick up the dirty clothes and put them in a hamper, run the vacuum cleaner around the rug, and take part in a quiz program. She would answer "yes" or "no" to questions to her from the audience by lighting up the appropriate signs.[17]

■ **Superstitious Pigeons** Pigeons have been used extensively in operant-conditioning studies. A pigeon can be put into a Skinner box and taught to peck at a small disk or key in order to receive a reward of grain. Stimulus control can be established by rewarding the pigeon only when the key is colored a particular color, but not rewarding it when the color changes; soon the pigeon will peck only at the rewarded color. Some studies have shown that pigeons can distin-

guish colors about as well as people can.[18,19] In the normal procedure, the pigeon works for its reward by pecking at the key in the box; the reinforcer is not given unless the pigeon pecks at the key.

Skinner wondered what pigeons would do if they were reinforced with grain no matter what they did. Several pigeons were put into Skinner boxes and rewarded every fifteen seconds with a tidbit of grain; the delivery of the grain was not dependent upon what any bird was doing. In effect, these birds were put on welfare; they did not have to work in order to be fed. After some time had passed, Skinner looked into the boxes to see what the birds were doing. He found that each bird was performing some highly patterned act. One bird was turning counterclockwise around the cage, making two or three turns between each feeding; another was repeatedly thrusting its head into the far upper corners of the cage; a third was rocking with a pendulum motion; another bird developed a kind of rhythmic dance. Skinner described the behavior as *superstitions.*[20]

The birds seemed to be repeating what they were doing when they received their reward of grain. Their responses were irrelevant, but they had been conditioned by the reward. The rewards actually appeared by chance and had nothing to do with what the pigeons did. The food dance of the pigeon and the rain dance of Indians might have similar origins in the accidental pairing of food or water with the occurrence of some behavior.

Breaking Bad Habits

Unlearning something can be much more difficult than learning. Perhaps you have learned certain habits that you would like to get rid of. How can you break your bad habits? Many techniques have been developed to help you unlearn your bad habits. One of these approaches will be presented here; namely, the approach based upon the principles of operant conditioning.

■ *Tantrums*   A twenty-one-month-old boy had a tantrum every night at bedtime. If one of his parents left the room after putting him to bed, he would scream and fuss until the parent returned to the room; as a result, the parent could not leave the room until the child was asleep. This required from one-half hour to two hours of time each night.

What could be done about the problem? From the point of view of conditioning, the problem was to *extinguish* the tantrum behavior. One of the principles of conditioning states that a response will extinguish if it has no rewarding consequences. In this case the rewarding consequence of the boy's tantrums was that the parents stayed in his room and gave him attention. Each tantrum was followed by a reward: parental attention. Upon the advice of a psychologist the parents began to put the boy to bed and, after kissing him goodnight, leave the room and close the door. On the first night this was tried the boy screamed and raged for forty-five minutes, but the parents did not reward his behavior by giving him attention. By the tenth night of "no reward," the boy's tantrums had extinguished; when he was put to bed he smiled and quietly went to sleep.[21]

■ *Smoking*   What is the reward for smoking? One psychologist reasoned that the reward for the act of reaching for a cigarette and smoking was the experience of smoking; then the reward for smoking could be withdrawn only by preventing the experience of smoking. To withdraw the reward, the cigarettes were put into a special case that had a unique lock allowing the case to be opened only at certain times. A timer could be set that would allow the case to be opened only every hour. The response of reaching for a cigarette would be rewarded only if the case could be opened; thus the response of reaching for a cigarette sooner than once every hour was extinguished.[22] Other psychologists have taken the approach of trying to diminish the rewarding effect of the experience of smoking by getting smokers to overdo it. Just as chocolate might not be rewarding after you had eaten a pound of chocolate, smoking was no reward for persons who were made to smoke almost constantly for a period of several hours. In effect, this procedure attempts to satiate the desire to smoke by overdoing it.[23]

■ *Overeating*   The response of eating is rewarded by food; if the reward could be withdrawn, the response would extinguish. One approach to the problem of overeating is to extinguish attempts to eat between meals. This approach depends upon the removal of the food reward except at mealtimes. When this is accomplished, the attempts to eat between meals will, over a period of time, extinguish.

A conditioning-based approach to the problem of overeating attempts to remove the stimulus for overeating and to strengthen behavior that is incompatible with overeating.[24]   Eating, especially the relatively unconscious automatic eating between meals, is a learned behavior, a response that has been conditioned to a variety of stimuli and situations.   If you eat in bed for a period of time, for example, the response of eating will be conditioned to the stimulus conditions of the bed.   When the stimulus occurs (you are in bed), the response tends to automatically follow (you eat); that is, eating is under the stimulus control of the bed.   By restricting your eating to only one place, and only to mealtimes, you will weaken and eventually extinguish the response of eating in bed, in the living room, or in the movies.

A second part of this program depends upon strengthening behavior that is incompatible with overeating.   The Law of Effect states that responses followed by rewards will be strengthened and will recur.   Staying on a diet is behavior that might be rewarded by attention and approval from your family and friends; if staying on a diet is rewarded, that behavior will be strengthened.

⬓ Operant conditioning is based on the Law of Effect: responses followed by reinforcement will tend to be repeated.   In the case of Skinner's rats, when a response (lever-pressing) was followed by reinforcement (delivering a small pellet of food to the animal), the response tended to be repeated.   When responses are followed only part of the time by reinforcement, using a schedule of partial reinforcement, the response becomes a very persistent habit and does not easily extinguish.

Primary reinforcers, such as food, have a reinforcing effect without the need of prior learning.   Secondary reinforcers, such as money, develop a reinforcing effect as a result of prior learning; the significance of money must be learned.   Shaping is a training procedure that involves reinforcing closer and closer approximations to the final desired response.   "Superstitious" behavior in animals can develop by occasionally giving them reinforcement regardless of their behavior; under these conditions they may develop rigid, stereotyped actions.

A Humanistic Perspective

How can human learning be understood? Psychologists do not agree on a single theory to explain learning but have developed different points of view.   The humanistic theory of learning focuses on the experiencing person and emphasizes human choice, values, and creativity.   Humanistic psychologists such as Abraham Maslow and Carl Rogers argue that the goal of learning is personal growth and self-realization.   They insist that meaningful learning can be understood only in terms of the life experiences of the whole person; they reject attempts to reduce learning to simple reactions to external events. From this point of view, the only learning that is significant is *intrinsic* learning— learning that is internally motivated and self-discovered.   Intrinsic learning follows from a craving to learn, to grow, to become fully human.   By contrast, *extrinsic* learning is meaningless; it is external to the learner, arbitrary, and impersonal.   It lasts only so long as external conditions of reward or punishment support it; it is easily forgotten. The humanistic psychologists consider the simple stimulus-response reactions studied by the behaviorists to be insignificant, extrinsic learning.

Summary

KEY QUESTIONS

1. What is the difference between learned and unlearned behavior?

   For the most part, who you are and what you can do are the result of learning. Instincts and reflexes are not learned because they are not acquired from experience; but knowledge, habits, and emotional reactions are built from a history of interaction with the world and are therefore the product of learning.

2. How do you know what you know?

   Knowledge consists of mental structures, or sets of related ideas; meaningful learning involves acquiring these structures. To be meaningful, new material must be related to what is already known; that is, it must be related to existing mental structures.

3. How can learning a skill or learning from a book be made easier?

   Because knowledge is structured, the structure of the skill or material to be learned influences the ease of learning it. The method of practice chosen should reflect whether the skill is organized as a whole or can be broken down into separate parts. Structured material is easier to learn than unstructured material.

4. How are habits and emotional reactions learned?

   Habits and emotional reactions are learned by conditioning. A response can be conditioned by association (classical conditioning) or by consequences (operant conditioning). For example, an emotional reaction of fear may be classically conditioned to automobiles if you are hurt while driving. As an example of operant conditioning, a child may learn to throw tantrums if tantrums are rewarded with parental attention.

KEY CONCEPTS

learning	A change in behavior or behavior potential as a result of experience.
reflex	A simple, involuntary reaction occurring to a specific stimulus; for example, a sneeze.
mental structure	A set of related or organized ideas that represents reality.

model	A person who is observed and imitated.
whole-part issue	The question of whether it is better to practice the whole act every time or to practice one part at a time until it is mastered.
massed-spaced issue	The question of whether it is better to practice something in one long session or in several shorter sessions.
learning set	A learned ability to learn, making later learning easier. For example, after learning one foreign language, it may be easier to learn others.
classical conditioning	Conditioning by association.
Law of Contiguity	Under certain circumstances, a stimulus that occurs about the same time as a response will acquire the power to elicit that response.
unconditioned stimulus	A stimulus that automatically elicits a response; for example, food powder in the mouth elicits salivation.
unconditioned response	A response to an unconditioned stimulus; for example, the response of salivating to food powder in the mouth.
conditioned stimulus	The initially neutral stimulus that is paired with the unconditioned stimulus; for example, a bell.
conditioned response	The learned reaction to the conditioned stimulus; for example, the reaction of salivating to a bell.
stimulus generalization	A conditioned response to stimuli similar to the conditioned stimulus; for example, the response of salivating to a whistle after being conditioned to salivate to a bell.
discrimination	Responding to certain stimuli but not to others as a result of learning.
extinction	The disappearance or stopping of the conditioned response; in classical conditioning, brought about by presenting the conditioned stimulus without the unconditioned stimulus; in operant conditioning, brought about by withholding reinforcement.
operant conditioning	Conditioning by consequences; instrumental conditioning.
reinforcer	A favorable consequence; for example, a reward.
reinforcement	The procedure of providing a reward or other favorable consequence following a response.
Law of Effect	Responses followed by reinforcement will tend to be repeated.
primary reinforcer	An event having a reinforcing effect without the need of prior learning; for example, food.

secondary reinforcer	An event having a reinforcing effect as a consequence of prior learning; for example, money.
shaping	A training procedure that involves reinforcing closer and closer approximations to the desired response.
stimulus control	In operant conditioning, the power of a prior stimulus to influence the production of a response; brought about by reinforcing the response only in the presence of the stimulus.
partial reinforcement	The procedure of giving reinforcement after some correct responses but not after others; for example, a slot machine provides partial reinforcement, because only occasionally does it reinforce with money.

8 Memory

CHAPTER OUTLINE

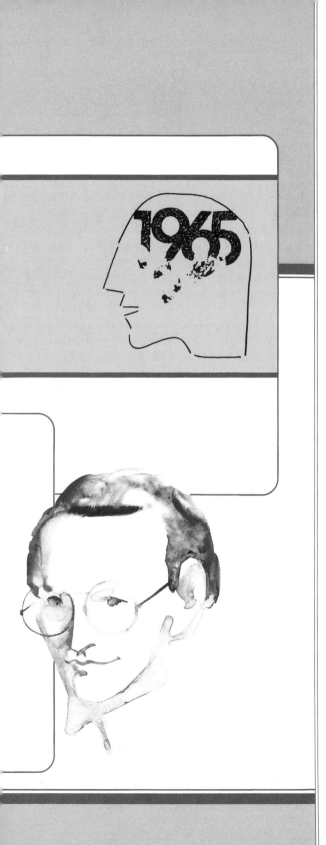

KEY QUESTIONS

1. How do you remember?
2. Where in the brain are memories located?
3. Why do you forget?
4. How can you improve your memory?

And there was the man who couldn't remember three things: names, faces, and—he forgot what the third was. His wife, however, had the worst memory in the world: she remembered everything.[1]

What did you eat for lunch yesterday? If you know, you must have a memory of it. Your memory preserves the past, so the experience of yesterday can, in a sense, be relived today. Many older people can relive and remember experiences in great detail that occurred over fifty years ago. We have a remarkable ability to retain the past.

What would you be like without memory? Even the simplest task would be impossible. For example, you could not repeat your name and could not find your way home. You could not read this sentence. You would have no knowledge of the beginning of the sentence by the time your eyes reached the end of the sentence. Without memory you would not learn from experience. Without the ability to learn from the past you would begin anew at every moment. In effect, you would remain an infant throughout your life.

How You Remember

How are you able to remember past experiences and events? Since you do not have a camera in your mind, how can you remember a picture? Since you do not record music with your brain, how can you remember a song once heard? Human memory is still a mysterious process that we know relatively little about. Logically, however, we know that remembering requires at least three processes: getting information in the mind, retaining it, and then getting it out. These processes are called encoding, storage, and retrieval.

Encoding

Memories are not the same as real events; I do not have actual music in my mind; my house is not actually in my head. Memories can be thought of as consisting of information, rather than of physical objects such as houses. **Encoding** is the process of changing physical scenes and events into the form of information that can be stored in memory. The memory code is the form of information used in recording memories. Thus the process of encoding consists of changing the physical energy in the environment (for example, a sound) into memory codes.

What is this code? Evidence shows that memories of recent letters or words are often encoded into labels or sounds. In a complex experiment designed to test the capacity of memory, Sperling[2] allowed participants one very brief glance at a group of twelve letters printed on a card, then asked them to name as many letters as they could remember. On the average, they were able to name only about four or five letters. But the errors that they made were very interesting. Although the letters were presented visually, the participants tended to confuse letters that *sounded* alike; for example, they would mix up D and E or B and C. This finding indicates something about the nature of the memory code in this task: people must be encoding what the letters sound like, and then storing the sound-codes. If people encoded what the letters looked like, they would have made more confusions among letters that looked alike than among letters than sounded alike. Other experimenters have confirmed that errors made in recalling visually presented items tend to be acoustically related (related by sound) to the missed item.[3,4] That is, people are more likely to confuse E with C (an acoustic confusion) than they are to confuse E with F (a visual confusion). These brief memories of recent events are sometimes encoded into the spoken sounds of letters or words.

More permanent memories are not influenced so much by sound similarity. The memory for material that is highly practiced tends to be influenced more by semantic similarity—similarity in meaning.[5] Apparently, material that is more permanently stored in memory is encoded into meanings rather than into sounds. Since you can remember pictures of all sorts—even abstract designs—it is clear that the sound code and the meaning code are not the only memory codes we have available. An image code is also used.

Storage

After an event is encoded, the information must be retained. How is it stored? We know that memory **storage** is not a random filing away of information; the information is systematically organized or structured. Things that are related to each other tend to be stored together. This can be shown by the fact that you tend to remember things in

Musicians must be able to memorize hundreds of musical scores.

chunks, and the process of grouping items into such units is called **chunking.**[8]

Research has shown that our ability to recall material that is presented only once is quite limited, and that our capacity depends upon the number of chunks involved, not the number of individual items of information. On the average, the limit to the amount that we can recall seems to be about five to seven chunks.[8,9] You can increase the amount of information you can recall by increasing the number of items in each chunk. In the example using digits, if you have one digit per chunk you would be able to recall only five to seven digits; if you increased the number of digits per chunk to three, you would be able to recall fifteen to twenty-one digits.

clusters. If you put a random list of words into memory, an organized list tends to come out.[6] If you were to read the words: green, north, red, blue, south, yellow, east, you would later tend to recall the directional words in one group and all the color words in another group. Apparently memory storage is organized around units of meaning.

Another type of organization depends not upon meaning but upon the order of occurrence. Events that occur at about the same time tend to be clustered or grouped together. Memorize these numbers:

6 4 9 5 1 7 8 2 3

Chances are, you learned the numbers not as nine individual digits, but as two or three groups of digits, like this:

649   517   823

Memorizing numbers like these is easier when you group them in clusters of three or four.[7] These clusters or groups are called

Retrieval

In order to remember an event, you must first get the information about the event into a usable form in memory; this is the encoding process. Then you must retain the information for some period of time until you need it; this is the storage process. The third essential feature of the memory process is **retrieval:** finding and using the stored information. How do you retrieve your memory of the meaning of the word "chunk"? In a sense you have the word and its meaning "on file" and you "look it up"; but your mind is not a dictionary and memory retrieval is not the same as looking something up in a book.

■ *Your Mental Library* If your "filing system" were completely random and mixed up, you would never be able to find what you need. You can retrieve memories because memory storage is organized. It can be compared to a library. Libraries use complex filing systems, typically grouping books together that are meaningfully related. Different books concerning psychology would be filed in the same general area, for example. Sometimes libraries keep "recent arrivals" separate, so that you can quickly find the newest books in print. Your memory storage and retrieval system in certain ways resembles a library. Your memory is a library of information, organized so that those items are grouped together that are meaningfully related. In addition, the "recent arrivals" (the most recent events) are kept separate, so as to be quickly accessible.

■ *On the Tip of Your Tongue* Sometimes when you try to retrieve from your memory the name of a person, you fail. You know that you have it in memory, but you can't quite locate it. You describe what happened to you by saying that the person's name was "on the tip of your tongue." This frustrating experience has been called the **tip of the tongue phenomenon.** The remarkable

Do your memories slip off the tip of your tongue?

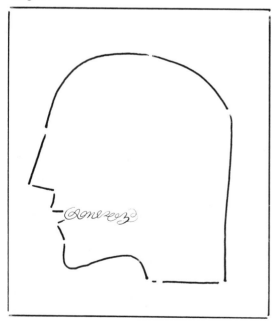

thing about the experience is that you often know about how long the word is, you may know the number of syllables, you may even know the beginning letter of the word, but you cannot recall the word.[10] It is as if you know part of the library "call number" for the book, but not the remainder and can therefore not find the book. If your memory filing system uses the first letter of words in its indexing system, you would expect that it would be easier to recall a word if you were provided with its first letter, and this has been demonstrated to be the case.[11]

Photographic Memory

Photographic memory is the rare ability to remember in great detail whole scenes or pages from books that were once looked at. Incredibly, such persons are able to retain visual information in memory in a form similar to a photograph. A more technical name for photographic memory is **eidetic imagery.** Children seem to have this ability more often than adults. In one study, 151 children were tested for eidetic imagery and 12 children were found who showed this remarkable memory ability.[12] Although 5 to 10 percent of children have some eidetic ability, almost no adults have been found to have this ability. It is not known why the ability disappears with age, but one possibility is that the culture and the educational system destroy it.[13] This is a "brass-tacks" culture; it is factually oriented, verbally oriented, and distrustful of the visual imagination.

■ *Elizabeth* Rarely is an adult found who possesses this remarkable ability. One of the few documented cases is that of a woman named Elizabeth.[14] Elizabeth showed an amazing talent for remembering visual information in great detail. A demonstration of her memory capacity was her

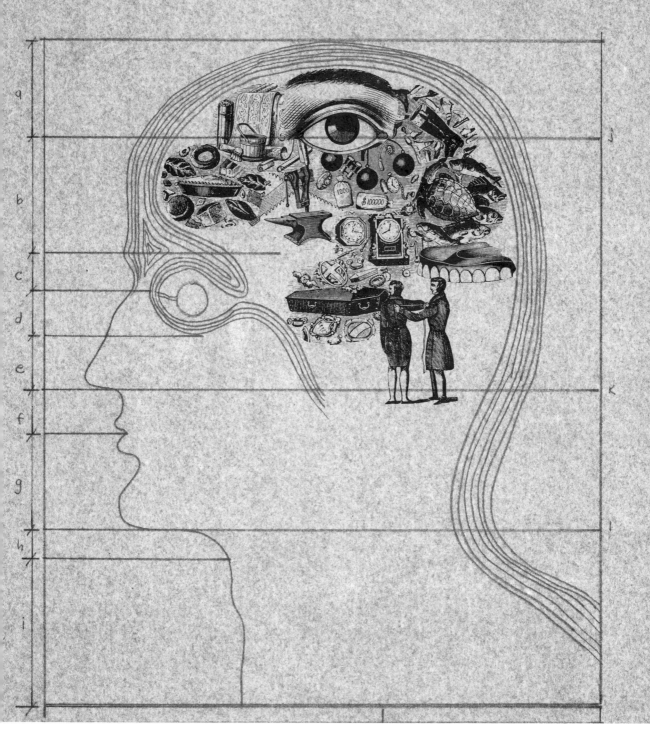

People with photographic memories have a remarkable ability to retain visual information.

ability to look at one picture of thousands of random dots with her right eye, then, *weeks later,* look at another similar but slightly different picture with her left eye and combine them into a single pattern. Apparently she could take the information given separately to each of her eyes and put together the picture she would have seen if the information had been originally presented to both her eyes simultaneously. She "saw," using her memory, although she had never actually seen with her eyes this complete pattern.

■ *The Case of S.*   One of the most carefully documented cases of photographic memory was investigated by A. R. Luria, a famous Russian psychologist. Luria had the opportunity to study the mind of the man he called S. for thirty years. Luria set out to test the limits of S.'s memory.

When I began my study of S. it was with much the same degree of curiosity psychologists generally have at the outset of research, hardly with the hope that the experiments would offer anything of particular note. However, the results of the first tests were enough to change my attitude and to leave me, the experimenter, rather than my subject, both embarrassed and perplexed.

I gave S. a series of words, then numbers, then letters, reading them to him slowly or presenting them in written form. He read or listened attentively and then repeated the material exactly as it had been presented. I increased the number of elements in each series, giving him as many as thirty, fifty, or even seventy words or numbers, but this, too, presented no problem for him. . . .

As the experimenter, I soon found myself in a state verging on utter confusion. An increase in the length of a series led to no noticeable

increase in the difficulty for S., and I simply had to admit that the capacity of his memory had no distinct limits. . . . *Experiments indicated that he had no difficulty reproducing any lengthy series of words whatever, even though these had originally been presented to him a week, a month, or even many years earlier.*[15]

How was S. able to remember so much? When S. was asked how he did it, he described the process as reading off the words or numbers from the paper on which they were originally written; it was as if he continued to see the list. If words were read out loud to him, the sound of each word would produce a visual image; the sounds were changed into colored splotches, lines, or splashes. S.'s visual imagery was very vivid and sometimes bothersome. As S. described it:

To this day, I can't escape from seeing colors when I hear sounds. What first strikes me is the color of someone's voice. Then it fades off . . . for it does interfere. If, say, a person says something, I see the word; but should another person's voice break in, blurs appear. These creep into the syllables of the words and I can't make out what is being said.[15]

For S. all sounds seemed to be encoded into colored visual images, and it was the images that were remembered.

A Memory Test

Test your memory for the sentences below.[16] Follow these instructions carefully: Read each sentence, count to five, answer the question on the right, then go on to the next sentence; continue until you have read all of the sentences and answered all of the questions on the right.

Sentence	Question
The hill was steep.	What was?
The cat, running from the barking dog, jumped on the table.	From what?
The old car climbed the hill.	What did?
The cat running from the dog jumped on the table.	Where?
The car pulled the trailer.	Did what?
The scared cat was running from the barking dog.	What was?
The scared cat jumped on the table.	Did what?
The old car climbed the steep hill.	What did?
The large window was on the porch.	Where?
The car pulling the trailer climbed the steep hill.	Did what?
The cat jumped on the table.	Where?
The car pulling the trailer climbed the hill.	What did?
The dog was barking.	Was what?
The window was large.	What was?

STOP. Cover the sentences above so you cannot see them. Now read the sentences below and mark each as "old" (in the list above) or "new" (not in the list above).

The car climbed the hill.	(old____, new____)
The scared cat, running from the barking dog, jumped on the table.	(old____, new____)
The window was on the porch.	(old____, new____)
The barking dog jumped on the table.	(old____, new____)
The scared cat was running from the dog.	(old____, new____)
The old car pulled the trailer.	(old____, new____)
The cat was running from the barking dog.	(old____, new____)
The old car, pulling the trailer, climbed the hill.	(old____, new____)
The cat was running from the dog.	(old____, new____)
The car was old.	(old____, new____)
The scared cat, running from the dog, jumped on the table.	(old____, new____)
The old car pulling the trailer climbed the steep hill.	(old____, new____)
The car climbed the steep hill.	(old____, new____)
The cat was scared.	(old____, new____)

STOP. Count the number of sentences judged "old," then read the explanation that follows in order to understand what this means about your memory.

Which sentences did you remember from the first list and mark as "old"? Check the ones you marked as "old" to determine whether they were in fact in the first list. You will find that none of the sentences were actually repeated; every one of them was "new." How can you explain the fact that you "remembered" sentences that you had not read before?

Sometimes your memory plays tricks on you. You think you remember seeing something that you have never seen before. The face of a stranger in a crowd somehow seems familiar.

Memory mistakes are sometimes useful. They help to show how memory works. Theories of memory are concerned with how past experiences are used in remembering and how they are retained over time. One theory, the **duplication theory of memory,** proposes a relatively exact storage system, in which the details of past experience are "filed away" and copies later retrieved. From this point of view, memory mistakes might come from mis-filing information or failing to retrieve it properly.

A second theory, the **reconstructive theory of memory,** proposes that memory is creative and that duplications or copies of experience are not retained. According to this theory, remembering involves an imaginative reconstruction made from past experience as a whole. The memory test you have just taken shows that this reconstructive theory has some merit. If you can "remember" things you have never seen before, remembering must involve a creative or reconstructive process. Remembering must be more like creating a painting of a past scene than like pulling a photo out of a file. One study of memory used sentences like the ones in the preceding memory test, and found that people were quite sure that they had seen sentences before that were completely new.[17]

When a new, complex sentence combined several parts of old sentences, people were especially sure that they had seen it before.

ⓢ   Remembering requires three basic processes: encoding, storage, and retrieval. Encoding involves putting information into memory by changing the physical energies in the world into memory codes that can be retained. Verbal items like letters and words are initially encoded acoustically; that is, they are changed into labels or sounds. Storage is the process of retaining information over time. Memory storage is organized, with similar items linked together by associations; sometimes items are clustered, or chunked. Retrieval refers to the process of getting at the stored information so that it can be used. The "tip of the tongue" phenomenon is an example of a failure of retrieval. Photographic memory, or eidetic imagery, is the rare ability to encode, store, and retrieve whole scenes or pages of information. The duplication and reconstruction theories of memory are two different ways of accounting for remembering.

Memories in the Brain

Thinking and remembering are activities of the brain, a complicated structure composed of over 10 billion nerve cells. If you were to look at a human brain, what you would see is the outer surface of the brain, the cerebral cortex, a gray wrinkled covering in which many of the most important brain processes occur. Among other things, the brain is a storehouse of memories.

The Search for the Engram

Where is memory in the brain? Is there a *place* in the brain where the memory of your

Karl Lashley

name might be located? Your body has the ability to retain past experience, but where is it kept? In a series of experiments with rats many years ago, Karl Lashley[18] searched the brain for the physical location of memory. He believed that memories stored in the brain must have a physical form, something he called the **engram.** He reasoned that if he could cut out different parts of the brain he might find where memories are kept. If the memory were cut out with the piece of brain, the animals would not be able to remember. Lashley began by teaching rats to solve a maze, then cutting out particular parts of their brains. He would then test them to see if they remembered how to solve the maze. Surprisingly, Lashley found that in rats memory does not seem to be located in a particular place in the brain; instead, widespread areas of the surface of the brain are involved in each memory. We know today that memory seems to be spread out all through the cortex, but that there are partic-

ular brain structures which are essential in order to memorize anything; these structures lie hidden beneath the cortex on each side of the brain.[19]

The Man with Half a Brain

Along the midline of the brain from the front to the back is a deep fold, dividing the brain into two halves called cerebral hemispheres. The left hemisphere controls most of the right side of the body and the right hemisphere controls most of the left side of the body. What do you suppose would happen to you if you lost half your brain?

Small injuries to the brain sometimes produce rapid death; extensive damage to the brain sometimes has little effect. The important factor, of course, is what part of the brain is damaged. You might expect that if you could survive the loss of half your brain, you would wind up with only half a mind. The following case describes what actually happened to one man.[20]

A forty-seven-year-old right-handed man came to the hospital with complaints of being speechless and having seizures in the right arm and face. Five months later a brain operation was performed and a tumor was removed from his left hemisphere. The tumor recurred, so a year later the entire left hemisphere was removed in one piece. Because the left hemisphere was removed and it controls the right side of the body, the operation resulted in paralysis on the right side. The man could not move his right arm and right leg. Remarkably, however, the man's hearing, personality, intelligence, and memory were essentially unaffected by the operation. In this case, half a brain was almost as good as a whole brain. Apparently removing half the brain had little effect on the mind itself.

Brain Chemistry

Recently scientists have proposed that memory may be based on chemical changes in the brain. The search for the physical basis of memory (the engram) has focused on certain kinds of brain chemicals called "protein molecules."[21] Brain cells continuously manufacture protein molecules, a process guided by a substance called RNA (ribonucleic acid). The physical basis of memory may involve these protein molecules. Interfering with the manufacture of these protein molecules has been shown to produce memory loss in animals.[22] Furthermore, the amount of RNA in the brain seems to increase after learning.[23]

Remembering with the Help of Electricity

A famous brain surgeon, Wilder Penfield, investigated the function of the brain by stimulating the cerebral cortex at different points with a weak electrical current. The current was applied by gently touching the brain surface with a fine wire electrode during a brain operation in which the patient was awake. The operation can be carried out under local anesthesia because the brain itself has no pain receptors and is quite insensitive to pain. Penfield found that electrically stimulating the brain in certain areas occasionally causes past sensory experiences to recur. Old memories are suddenly brought to life again. Penfield described this procedure and the experiences of two of his patients.[24]

Occasionally during the course of a neurosurgical operation under local anesthesia, gentle electrical stimulation in this temporal area, right or left, has caused the conscious patient to be aware of some previous experience. The experience seems to be picked out at random from his own past. It comes back to him in great detail. . . .

A woman heard an orchestra playing an air while the electrode was held in place. The music stopped when the electrode was removed. It came again when the electrode was reapplied. On request, she hummed the tune, while the electrode was held in place, accompanying the orchestra. It was a popular song. Over and over again, restimulation of the same spot produced the same song. The music seemed always to begin at the same place and to progress at the normally expected tempo. All efforts to mislead her failed. She believed that a Gramophone was being turned on in the operating room on each occasion, and she asserted her belief stoutly in a conversation some days after the operation.

A boy heard his mother talking to someone on the telephone when an electrode was applied to his right temporal cortex. When the stimulus was repeated without warning, he heard his mother again in the same conversation. When the stimulus was repeated after a lapse of time, he said, "My mother is telling my brother he has got his coat on backwards. I can just hear them." The surgeon then asked the boy whether he remembered this happening. "O yes," he said, "just before I came here."

S A particular memory is apparently not located in a particular place in the brain. Instead, as Lashley discovered, widespread areas of the brain may be involved in each memory. Some researchers now believe that certain complex chemicals are produced when learning occurs and these are the key to the physical basis of memory. The electrical activity of the brain is important also. It has been found that electrical stimulation of certain parts of the brain can bring old memories back to life.

Why You Forget

Often memory fails and you forget. Why do you forget? Can you remember the exact wording of the first sentence of this chapter? You most likely have forgotten. There are two general possible explanations for the fact that you have forgotten the sentence: first, a certain amount of time has passed, and second, other sentences you have read more recently may have disrupted the memory of the first sentence. These two general explanations are the basis for prominent theories of forgetting, the decay theory and the interference theory.

Decay

The **decay theory** states that memories weaken spontaneously with time; that is, they "decay."[25] According to this theory, you have forgotten the first sentence of this chapter because you read it some time ago; the memory of the sentence decayed or weakened more and more as time passed until the memory was too faint or weak to remember. One way memory decay has been studied is with memories over very short intervals. Evidence shows, for example, that there are brief sensory memories that fade rapidly with time, both for visual events[2] and for auditory events.[26] It is difficult to prove that decay occurs, however, in the forgetting of complex material. The problem is the difficulty of deciding whether forgetting was due simply to the passage of time or to interference coming from the activities that occurred in that time period.

Interference

The **interference theory** states that memories weaken because of the action of other memories interfering with them.[27] Learning the name of one new friend is a lot easier than

Memories may decay with time.

New memories may interfere with old.

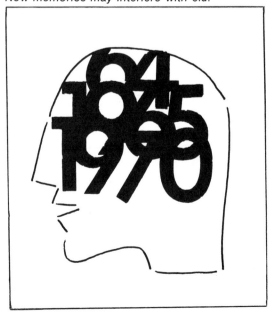

learning the names of ten new friends; the memory of each name may suffer from interference due to the other memories. According to the interference theory, you have forgotten the first sentence of this chapter because you have read many other sentences before it and after it, and the memories of these other sentences create interference.

Two kinds of interference have been identified: **proactive interference,** resulting from older memories, and **retroactive interference,** resulting from newer memories. Proactive interference from the sentences in the previous chapter may have caused you to forget the first sentence of this chapter; or retroactive interference from the other later sentences of this chapter may have caused your memory loss; or both kinds of interference may have been working together. When you read Chapters 7, 8, and 9, your memory of Chapter 8 may be interfered with by the material in Chapter 7 (proactive interference) and by the material in Chapter 9 (retroactive interference).

It has proved very difficult to establish which one of the two theories of forgetting, the decay theory or the interference theory, is the best explanation of why we forget. Probably both theories are right and some forgetting is due to decay and some to interference.

Repression

When you repress a memory, you block it from consciousness. It is possible that certain memories are too painful to relive and so are forgotten. According to Freud, **repression** is a major psychological defense we all use against anxiety; we repress painful experiences in order not to feel the anxiety that would accompany their memories. Our everyday failures of memory are sometimes due to repression. Freud cites the case of a man who repeatedly forgot the name of an ac-

quaintance, and he shows how the forgetting may be explained as repression; it seems that the acquaintance had married a woman whom the man had hoped to marry himself. His forgetting was a way of dealing with the anxiety of this painful experience.

Amnesia

Amnesia is a loss of memory due to shock or injury. Sometimes the loss of memory is for the immediate past and at other times it is for events in the remote past. Persons with amnesia cannot remember certain facts of their histories; sometimes they cannot even remember their own names. What is it like to experience amnesia? One person described it this way:

With an assurance to my wife that I would be back in a minute or two, I went out and failed to return. The next thing that I remember is a sound of rifle shots and some short bursts of machine-gun fire coming from the other side of a hill on the right of a road on which I was walking. I was conscious of being dirty, unshaven and footsore. I did not seem to be particularly hungry or thirsty. I had a feeling of puzzlement upon my mind, not unlike that which one may experience on waking from a deep sleep in a strange place. Where was I? Who was I? Something was wrong, but what was it? I knew my own name and recognized my own writing when I jotted it down on a bit of paper, but everything else seemed uncertain and unstable. . . . It was some few minutes before I realized fully that I had absolutely no recollection of any course of events which could have brought me to the existing position. The immediate past seemed to be "a perfect and absolute blank." [28]

Shortly afterward the man went to the police who located his wife and family. He still could not remember the events of the past twenty years of his life. Gradually his memory returned, and he wrote a book about his experiences, but he never learned what caused the amnesia.

■ *Brain Injury* Sometimes amnesia results from a blow to the head or an injury to the brain. Often when people are knocked unconscious, they fail to remember the blow that did it and also the events occurring just before the blow.[29] Memory for these prior events usually recovers fairly quickly following the return of consciousness, but a memory failure for the events of the few seconds preceding the loss of consciousness may last even after recovery from the head injury.[30] One patient suffered severe memory loss following a brain operation:

He could no longer recognize the hospital staff, apart from Dr. Scoville himself, whom he had known for many years; he did not remember and could not re-learn the way to the bathroom, and he seemed to retain nothing of the day-to-day happenings in the hospital. . . . The same forgetfulness applies to people he has met since the operation, even to those neighbors who have been visiting the house regularly for the past six years. He has not learned their names and he does not recognize any of them if he meets them in the street.[31]

This patient experienced amnesia for events preceding the operation, and in addition was unable to retain new information in memory after the operation.

■ *The Case of the Anxious College Student* Occasionally amnesia has an emotional origin. To experience severe loss of memory can be a defense against unbearable anxiety. If you lose all memory of your identity, you start anew, with no painful conflicts. The case of G. R. is an example of amnesia with a psychological origin:

Mr. G. R. was a twenty-four-year-old college student. He was the only son of an extremely ambitious father who was a very successful engineer. His mother was perfectionistic, obsessional, and domineering. The young man was in his third year of university study, struggling to get through a pre-engineering course, in which he was not in the slightest bit interested. However, he felt he had to continue, largely as a result of irresistible parental pressure. He had already failed one year in this course.

His third year was further complicated by the fact that he had made a marriage which had been kept secret, in as far as his parents were concerned. . . .

The marriage had involved emotional and time demands, which had still further interfered with his college performance. He had become extremely anxious about the probable results of examinations, which were due to begin in a few weeks time. One Friday afternoon, after classes, he took part in a "bull session" in the college dormitory. This left him thoroughly convinced that he would not be able to pass his examinations. This served as the precipitating event.

He started for home, but did not arrive there. Late that evening he was found wandering in the streets of a city some two hundred miles away from the site of his college.[32]

The loss of personal identity is a terrible price to pay for the relief from anxiety. Individuals suffering from anxiety-induced amnesia typically recover from their amnesia and are able to develop less destructive solutions to their conflicts. A trained psychotherapist can sometimes help with this transition.

⑤   Two theories that explain forgetting are the decay theory and the interference theory. According to the decay theory, people forget because memories fade or decay over time. According to the interference theory, people forget because one memory has been interfered with by other memories. This interference can be either proactive (from older memories) or retroactive (from newer memories). Forgetting can also be due to repression, a defensive process in which painful memories are blocked from consciousness. Amnesia is a loss of memory for past events or personal identity resulting from a brain injury or from emotional distress.

Improving Your Memory

The challenge of how to improve memory is an old one. The Greeks invented the "art of memory," creating memory systems by which memory could be improved.[33] Since that time innumerable systems have been invented, most of which depend upon the **principle of orderly association:** items to be remembered are paired with concrete and orderly images. New items to be remembered are matched up with old images already familiar. The set of old images serves, in a sense, as a filing system for the new material.

For one system, you must learn the following rhyme:

One is a bun,
Two is a shoe,
Three is a tree,
Four is a door,
Five is a hive,
Six is sticks,
Seven is heaven,
Eight is a gate,
Nine is wine, and
Ten is a hen.

The rhyme matches a specific image of an object with each number. When you have learned this system, you are able to remember a list of words by combining and associating the words to be remembered with the image from the rhyme. For example, if the first word to be remembered is "wheel," you might imagine a bun with wheels on it speeding around a track. If the second word is "flower," you might imagine a flower growing out of a shoe. The system has been shown to improve memory dramatically.[34] Why don't you try it?

Another popular memory system, using the principle of orderly association, involves imagining items to be remembered in different places. The Russian psychologist Luria studied a man with a photographic memory (mentioned earlier) who went on to become a professional entertainer specializing in feats of memory. One of his techniques for remembering lists of words was to distribute images of them along some roadway or street he visualized in his mind. When it came time to remember the words, he would imagine himself walking along the roadway looking for words. On the rare occasions when S. made an error, it was often attributable to some difficulty in the placement of the word.

I put the image of the pencil *near a fence . . . the one down the street, you know. But what happened was that the image fused with that of the fence and I walked right on past without noticing it. The same thing happened with the word* egg. *I had put it up against a white wall and it blended in with the background. How could I possibly spot a white egg up against a white wall?*[15]

You will not develop the fantastic ability of S. for memorizing material, but your memory can be improved by using the principle of orderly association.

[s] Most systems for improving memory are based on the principle of orderly association. According to this rule, a number of images are arranged in an organized fashion (as in the "one is a bun" rhyme), then the images are used as a filing system to store new material. The procedure involves combining the new material with the old images.

Summary

KEY QUESTIONS

1. How do you remember?

   Remembering past events requires three important processes: encoding, storage, and retrieval. Two theories of remembering are the duplication theory and the reconstructive theory; according to the latter theory, remembering is a creative process.

2. Where in the brain are memories located?

   One attempt to find the physical basis of memory involved cutting out parts of brain tissue in rats and then testing for memory loss. It was found that memories are not located in one spot, but are widespread throughout the cortex. Recent studies on memory have focused on brain chemistry and the effects of electrical stimulation of the brain.

3. Why do you forget?

   Two general explanations have been proposed to account for why you forget: the decay theory and the interference theory. According to the decay theory, forgetting occurs because memories fade with time. According to the interference theory, forgetting results from memories being disrupted by other memories. Repression and amnesia are special cases of forgetting and may serve the function of providing relief from anxiety.

4. How can you improve your memory?

   Improving your memory is possible by using the principle of orderly association. According to this principle, items to be remembered should be paired with concrete and orderly images. When this has been done, items can be retrieved from memory by consulting the associated images.

KEY CONCEPTS

encoding	Putting information into memory by changing the physical energy in the environment into memory codes.
storage	The process of retaining information over time.
retrieval	The process of getting out the stored information so that it can be used.
chunking	Grouping items to be remembered into units or clusters.
tip of the tongue phenomenon	Knowing that a memory is in storage, but being unable to retrieve it.
eidetic imagery	A kind of photographic memory in which whole pictures or scenes can be remembered in detail.
duplication theory of memory	A theory that remembering involves retrieving copies of past experience.
reconstructive theory of memory	A theory that remembering involves an imaginative reconstruction of the past.
engram	The physical basis of memory in the brain.
decay theory	The theory of forgetting that memories fade with time.
interference theory	The theory of forgetting that memories are disrupted by newer and older memories.
proactive interference	Older items in memory interfere with the memory for more recent items.
retroactive interference	More recent items in memory interfere with the memory for older items.
repression	A defensive process in which painful memories are forgotten by being blocked from consciousness.
amnesia	A loss of memory for past events or personal identity as a result of brain injury or psychological stress.
principle of orderly association	A rule for improving memory that suggests associating material to be remembered with an organized set of images.

9 Teaching

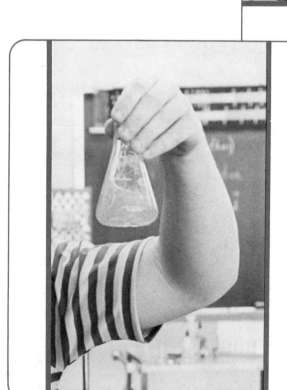

CHAPTER OUTLINE

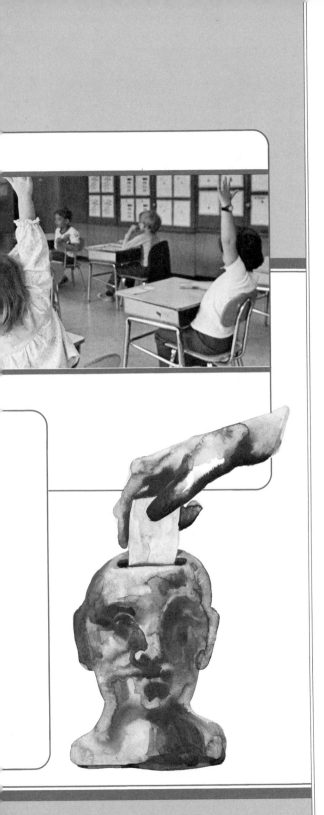

KEY QUESTIONS

1. What differences among students are important for teachers?
2. What differences among teachers are important for students?
3. How can teachers communicate factual information to their students?
4. How can teachers change the behavior of their students?
5. How can teachers promote the personal growth of their students?

"Face the front and pay attention!"

"No talking or gum chewing."

"Raise your hand and ask permission if you have to go to the bathroom."

"Don't move until you hear the bell!"

How much of your life have you spent "facing the front" and listening to teachers talk? Most of your life you have been a student. You have had many different teachers, some good and some bad, and they have influenced your life. How can these influences be understood? Psychology, the science of human behavior, includes the study of teachers and students. Many psychologists are concerned with understanding how students learn in the classroom and how teachers can help students to learn better.

Students

Differences among students present a great challenge to teachers. Although students in a classroom may be of approximately the same age, their personalities and levels of maturation and intelligence are very different. A single, standard teaching method is bound to fail with some students because of these differences; students do not come in a single, standard form. Thus, teachers must recognize the individual differences among their students.

Readiness

When is the best time to teach a child a particular skill? When, for example, are children ready to learn how to read? Most would agree that trying to teach a two-week-old baby to read would be a wasted effort. But should you wait until the child is six? The concept of **readiness** refers to the level of development or preparation required for a child to learn a particular skill. There are two views of readiness. Those on one side argue that readiness can be taught, so that, with proper preparation, any child can be taught any subject. Those on the other side argue that teachers must wait for the "teachable moment"—that special time, in the development of children, when they are ready to learn. One learning expert wrote:

When the body is ripe, and society requires, and the self is ready to achieve a certain task, the teachable moment has come. Efforts at teaching which would have been largely wasted if they had come earlier give gratifying results when they come at the teachable moment.[1]

This author wrote in favor of waiting for the natural development of readiness and argued

A child's readiness to read may depend upon prior mastery of simple skills.

against trying to teach students skills before they were ready.

■ *Piaget*   Jean Piaget, a world authority on child development, has described at length the mental growth of children. According to Piaget's model, each child passes through a series of stages of intellectual development (see Chapter 5). The first of these stages, during the first two years of life, is the sensorimotor period; in this stage the infant is primarily concerned with sensory stimulation—touching and tasting—and with motor movement—such as manipulating and moving its own body. With increasing age the child passes through other developmental stages in which more complex and abstract thinking becomes possible.

Piaget believes that teaching must take into account these stages of development by presenting children with problems appropriate to their level of growth. Piaget states that parents and teachers should not try to speed up these stages of development, but should wait for intellectual growth to occur naturally. There is, he believes, an optimum time, a time of maximum readiness, for learning:

It is probably possible to accelerate the stages of development, but maximum acceleration is not desirable. There seems to be an optimum time; what this optimum time is will surely depend upon each individual and on the subject matter. We still need a great deal of research to know what the optimal time would be.[2]

■ *Bruner* Jerome Bruner, a Harvard psychologist, does not believe in waiting for an optimal time for learning. Although Bruner, like Piaget, argues that intellectual development occurs in stages, he insists that these stages can be accelerated by experience. Rather than waiting for readiness, he believes in teaching readiness. He writes:

The idea of "readiness" is a mischievous half-truth. It is a half-truth largely because it turns out that one teaches *readiness or provides opportunities for its nurture; one does not simply wait for it. Readiness, in these terms, consists of mastery of those simple skills that permit one to reach higher skills.*[3]

Bruner believes that the intellectual development of children can be speeded up by presenting problems that "tempt" them into the next stage of development. Furthermore, according to Bruner, the stages of intellectual development should not restrict learning; children in earlier stages can and should be taught complex subject matter. He writes, "Any subject can be taught effectively in some intellectually honest form to any child at any stage of development."[4]

Achievement Motivation

Why do some students work so hard and others loaf? One way of explaining this is to say that the students have different levels of motivation. The term **motivation** refers to the forces or drives behind a person's actions; motivation is what causes a person to begin an activity and to follow it through. There are many different kinds of motivation. The desire to succeed and do things well has been called **achievement motivation.** Students with low achievement motivation tend to be underachievers—they do not perform up to their level of ability. Students with high achievement motivation try harder and strive for success. How great is your achievement motivation? How important is it for you to achieve success in school?

Children differ in their levels of achievement motivation.

Studies have shown that parents influence their children's achievement motivation. Children with high achievement motivation typically have parents who expected them to be independent at an early age and who rewarded them for their successes. For example, their parents may have expected them, at an early age, to take care of themselves, to choose their own clothes, and to earn their own money.[5] Another study found that children with high achievement motivation tended to have parents who also had high achievement motivation; the study concluded that children learn the value of achievement from their parents.[6]

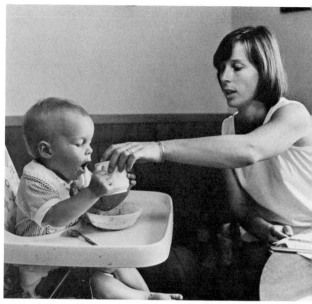

Children strive to master the world around them. They enjoy doing things themselves.

Competence Motivation

Neither animals nor human beings like to be bored; we seem to have a need to be active, to work, and to solve problems. Harry Harlow has found that monkeys will work hard to solve puzzles apparently just to satisfy their curiosity.[7] We, too, are curious about the world and strive to explore and understand it. What drives us to do this? Robert White, a Harvard psychologist, says that we are—from birth—motivated to explore and deal with our environment; we are born with a desire to be effective or competent. This desire is called **competence motivation.** White writes:

The many hours that infants and children spend in play are by no means wasted. . . . Play may be fun, but it is also a serious business in childhood. During these hours the child steadily builds up his competence in dealing with the environment.[8]

Children strive to master the world around them, to be active and competent. Abraham Maslow wrote, "Observation of children shows more and more clearly that healthy children *enjoy* growing and moving forward, gaining new skills, capacities and powers."[9]

Feelings of competency vary greatly among individual students; some, those with high self-esteem, feel confident and capable, while others, with low self-esteem, feel inadequate. Success experiences strengthen feelings of competence and failure experiences weaken these feelings. Have you ever failed an exam? Do you remember how you felt afterward? Parents and teachers can influence the self-esteem and feelings of competence of their children; children with high self-esteem are more likely to have parents who encourage their desire for competence and provide them with opportunities to achieve success.[10]

Learning Styles

The way you learn is different from the way other people learn, both in terms of your learning *style* and your learning *ability*. Although there are general principles of learning that apply across persons, there are important differences too. Not all people learn in the same way.

Your **learning style** is the way you, as an individual, learn. The term "style" is not used here to refer to your overall capacity in learning, but rather to that particular pattern of preferences and abilities that makes you different from others. For example, although men and women are of equal intellectual capacity, they differ in where their talents lie. Women tend to make high scores on *verbal* types of tests, and men make high scores on *mathematical* types of tests. This stylistic difference is apparently not innate but learned.[11]

Some persons learn better in highly structured situations; others prefer independent study. Some students prefer learning by listening; others prefer learning by looking. What is your learning style? Some learning styles that have been studied recently by psychologists are the reflective/impulsive styles and the relational/analytic styles.

Whether people are *reflective* or *impulsive* in their approach to learning is determined by the extent to which they consider and think about the alternative solutions to a problem.[12,13] People with a **reflective style** consider and evaluate the alternatives before they respond; since this takes time, they are consistently slower to respond. People with an **impulsive style** spend less time considering and evaluating the possible alternative answers before responding; they are therefore faster. Contrary to the myth that girls are more impulsive than boys, most investigators have found no difference between boys and girls in measures of reflection/impulsivity.[14,15] It is possible that impulsive persons would excel at tasks requiring spontaneity.

Some persons have a tendency to analyze their experience by breaking it down into separate parts; others respond less to the elements of their experience than to the context, the experience as a whole, and the relationships among the parts. The former person has adopted an **analytic style,** and the latter person has adopted a **relational style.**[16] The school system requires, with each additional grade level, an increasing degree of analytic skills. The school focuses on the development of analytic talent and offers little reward for individuals with a relational style.[17] The interpersonal and environmental problems facing society today are different from the technological problems of the past; today's problems seem to require a more relational and contextual approach. People and environment are increasingly related and interdependent. For these reasons the present focus of the school system on the development of analytic skills should, perhaps, be modified so that the relational styles are also fostered.[18]

⑤ To be most effective, teachers must be sensitive to differences among students. One important difference is that some students may be ready to master a particular skill while others are not. Certain authorities, such as Piaget, argue that teachers should wait for the time of maximum readiness on the part of their students; other authorities, such as Bruner, argue against waiting. Another difference among students is in their level of achievement motivation (the desire for success) and competence motivation (the striving to master problems and gain new skills). Students also differ in their styles of learning. Some have a reflective learning style, while others have an impulsive learning style; some have an analytic style, while others have a relational style. These differences in learning styles reflect differences in how students learn.

Teachers

Think back. Can you remember a great teacher that you have had? What was this teacher like? Did this person influence your life? Chances are, you have had a teacher sometime in school who has changed the direction of your life. We know that teachers exert a powerful influence on students, for good and, sometimes, for bad. One study shows that the IQ of some students increased over the period of the school year simply because their teacher believed (incorrectly) that they were "more promising" than the other students in the class.[19] Teachers have power. How this power is used depends upon the personality of the individual teachers. What makes a great teacher? Although much research has been done, we still know very little.[20]

One study showed that there was a relationship between student learning and type of teacher for elementary school classes.[21] Teachers who were rated as understanding, friendly, organized, stimulating, or original, tended to have students who were more confident, more alert, and more responsible. Another study showed that children who had harsh and punishing teachers, as compared with children who had nonpunishing teachers, tended to show more aggression, to be more unsettled, and to display more misconduct.[22] These relationships are not extremely informative. It is not surprising that there should be a relationship between the behavior of the teacher and the behavior of the class. Each probably contributes to the behavior of the other. It may be that the relationships found in these studies reflect only that teachers are influenced by the character of their classes.

A more informative study was one that asked high school students who had won

Who was your favorite elementary school teacher?

National Merit Scholarships to identify and describe the one teacher who had contributed most to their desire to learn.[23] Common characteristics reported for these teachers were (1) they allowed time in the classroom for discussion, (2) they modified the course in accordance with student interests, (3) they treated students as equals, and (4) they took a personal interest in students.

Carl Rogers, a well-known teacher and therapist, has described the qualities of teachers that promote and facilitate learning among their students.[24] These qualities are similar to the qualities a person must have to be a good therapist; according to Rogers, both teachers and therapists must be primarily concerned with helping other people grow. Rogers identifies good teachers as having three essential characteristics: (1) realness or genuineness—the good teacher is a real person, without pretense and without a false front; (2) acceptance and trust—the good teacher accepts the feelings of students without putting them down; and (3) empathic understanding—the good teacher has the ability to understand students from the inside and has a sensitive awareness of the students' point of view. Have you had teachers with these qualities?

Teachers differ not only in personality but also in the type of teaching method that they use in the classrooms. Different methods of teaching are concerned with different aspects of the lives of students. Some teachers are concerned primarily with communicating ideas; others use an approach designed to change the students' behavior; a third approach focuses on the feelings and experiences of students. Most teachers today combine these three approaches.

[S]   Teachers have a strong influence on their students. Good teachers have been described as friendly, organized, stimulating, understanding, and original. Acording to Carl Rogers, good teachers resemble good therapists—they are genuine, accepting, and have empathic understanding.

Cognitive Teaching Methods

The oldest, most traditional approach to teaching involves the communication of information—the **cognitive teaching method.** This method is called *cognitive* because it is concerned with thoughts, ideas, and factual knowledge. A cognitive teaching method is regarded as successful to the extent that students learn the facts and concepts taught. There are two varieties of this method: the expository approach and the discovery approach.

The Expository Method

An ancient teaching method, and still the most popular, is a cognitive approach that consists of giving information through talking and lecturing—the **expository method.** According to this approach, learning should take place when the teacher presents information and the students receive it. In effect, the teacher is assumed to deposit knowledge in the student's empty mind, like depositing money in a bank. This has been called the "banking" method.[25]

The expository method has been studied extensively, with much of the interest in the particular technique of conveying information. For example, could a teacher be effectively replaced by a television set? If so,

The expository method involves "depositing" knowledge.

there would be a tremendous economic advantage. Research on this question shows that in many comparisons of conventional instruction and television instruction there is no substantial difference in academic performance on the part of students, although conventional instruction typically turns out to be very slightly superior.[26] Students, however, tend not to like television teaching as well as a live performance.

Another method of presenting information is through textbooks. Several studies have compared the academic performance of students who attended lectures and students who only read the textbook.[27,28,29] These studies demonstrated that college students learned as much from reading as from hearing lectures on the same material. I taught one undergraduate psychology course by lecturing to half of the class and providing the other half with detailed instructions for reading outside of class. Both groups did the readings but the one group never attended lectures. At the end of the term, all the students were given the same test over the material, and the two groups performed equally well.[30] When the lecture method has been compared to small discussion sections, there typically is no difference found in exam scores over the material,[31,32] but student attitude toward the material and their ability to use the material in problem solving are superior with the discussion approach.[33]

A defender of the expository method claims that it can be highly effective when it is not misused.[34] Ausubel, an educational psychologist, characterizes the method as involving expository instruction and receptive learning; but receptive learning need not be rote and passive. The communication of organized information, according to Ausubel, is one of the principal functions of pedagogy (the art of teaching). If students are motivated, Ausubel believes, they will actively consider, criticize, rework, and integrate new ideas no matter how the material is taught. Ausubel writes:

It is fashionable in many quarters to characterize reception learning as parrot-like repetition and rote memorization of isolated facts, and to dismiss it disdainfully as an archaic remnant of discredited educational tradition. . . .

Some . . . speak with disdain about the school's role of imparting knowledge, contrasting it with the allegedly more desirable role of helping children learn by themselves. . . . Symbolic exposition is actually the most efficient way of teaching subject matter. . . . Thus the art and science of presenting ideas and information effectively— so that clear, stable and unambiguous meanings emerge and are retained over a long period of time as an organized body of knowledge—is really one of the principal functions of pedagogy. This is a demanding and inventive rather than a routine or mechanical task. . . . If it is done properly it is the work of a master teacher, and is not a task to be disdained.[34]

Thus one advantage of the expository method used by an effective teacher may be its efficiency in communicating an organized body of knowledge.

The Discovery Method

A second major cognitive approach to teaching is the **discovery method,** which was made popular by the psychologist Jerome Bruner.[35,36,37] According to the discovery method, learning consists not in passively accepting the "deposits" of the instructor, but rather in actively discovering ideas on your own. The role of the teacher is to provide situations that will encourage students to gain new insights. Bruner criticizes the expository method on the grounds that it is based on "extrinsic rewards" (that is, students learn in order to gain the approval of other persons, such as parents or teachers). The discovery method, on the other hand, involves "intrinsic rewards," since gaining insights is itself a reward. Bruner writes:

Much of the problem in leading a child to effective cognitive activity is to free him from the immediate control of environmental rewards and punishments. Learning that starts in response to the rewards of parental or teacher approval or to the avoidance of failure can too readily develop a pattern in which the child is seeking cues as to how to conform to what is expected of him. . . . The hypothesis I would propose here is that to the degree that one is able to approach learning as a task of discovering something rather than "learning about" it, to that degree there is a tendency for the child to . . . be rewarded by discovery itself.[35]

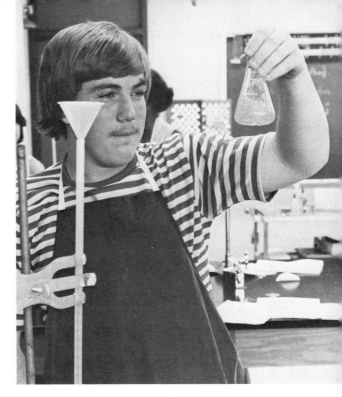

The discovery method of teaching involves intrinsic rewards.

The discovery method has been compared with the more conventional expository method in many studies. The results of one such study showed that the discovery method was superior to the conventional method because it motivated students to practice more and thus remember more of the material.[38] This result is consistent with one of Bruner's claims for the discovery method, namely, that material learned with the discovery method could be better remembered, since it would be organized in terms of the students' own interests.[35]

Another study compared three approaches to teaching high school boys a mathematical principle. One approach gave the rule and taught the students how to apply it (the expository method); a second approach required students to discover the principle for themselves after some hints

were given (the discovery method); and the third approach broke the problem down into forty small steps, requiring discovery for each step (the guided discovery method). When tested on a new problem, the expository method was the worse by far, and the guided discovery method was somewhat superior to the discovery method.[39]

The discovery method has been criticized for a variety of reasons. One claim against it is that it is not efficient. It takes longer for students to discover a rule in mathematics than it takes for the teacher to tell them about it. Another criticism that has been made is that it is naive to believe that students within one term of chemistry or mathematics will be able to discover all the principles that scientists took centuries to discover originally.[40] Because of the information explosion in the world today, it seems unlikely that students would have time to keep up with what is known if they must rediscover everything themselves.

⑤ Cognitive teaching methods are those concerned primarily with communicating ideas and factual knowledge. Two types of cognitive approaches are the expository method and the discovery method. The expository method consists of giving information through lecturing and talking; the discovery method consists of providing situations for students in which they can discover principles on their own.

Behavioral Teaching Methods

A second major approach to teaching is to focus on behavior instead of ideas. This approach—the **behavioral teaching method**—is regarded as successful to the extent that students acquire certain desired responses or behaviors. Behavioral teaching methods are based on the principles of conditioning.

The method of learning known as conditioning has been discussed before. Briefly, **operant conditioning** is based on the **Law of Effect,** which states that behavior which is followed by rewarding consequences will tend to recur, while nonrewarded behavior will tend to disappear or extinguish. Behavior, from this point of view, can be modified or changed, depending upon the rewards in the environment. About a half century ago one enthusiast of conditioning went so far as to say that he could condition anybody to do anything:

Give me a dozen healthy infants, well-formed, and my own special world to bring them up in and I'll guarantee to take anyone at random and train him to become any type of specialist I might select—doctor, lawyer, artist, merchant-chief and, yes, even beggerman and thief, regardless of his talents, penchants, tendencies, abilities, vocations, and race of his ancestors.[41]

Conditioning in the Classroom

Learning, according to the behavioral method, is assumed to follow automatically from rewarded practice; all teachers must do, therefore, is to get the students to act as they want them to and then reward them for it. In an article entitled "Good-bye, teacher . . ."[42] one psychologist reported how he employs conditioning principles in his psychology class. His approach is to break down the material into very small units, get students to study each unit on their own and then go to a student proctor to be tested and rewarded (with approval and encouragement). Lectures are provided only for students who have successfully completed a certain number of these units; thus the lecture is used as the students' "reward." This method has been elaborated and is now being successfully applied in college classrooms all over the country.

■ *Working for a Smile* In the conventional classroom, conditioning techniques are often used freely. For example, a teacher who smiles and responds "Good" to a student's answer is giving the student a kind of reward, and, according to the Law of Effect, the student should thereafter be more likely to respond correctly in the future. A teacher who refuses to call on students who wildly wave their arms in the air is withholding a reward from the students; arm-waving thereafter should tend to decrease and eventually extinguish. Grades, of course, are powerful reinforcers or rewards, and teachers use them to increase the behavior leading to the *A*.

When students find out how their behavior is being manipulated by the teacher's control over rewards, they sometimes react. It is rumored that in one class the students decided that they controlled a form of reward for the teacher—their attention and ap-

With the behavioral teaching method, good students get rewarded.

■ *Rewarding Learning with Candy* One group of psychologists tried the conditioning method in order to teach children in a preschool classroom to say "Good morning" to their teacher. The principle they applied was the familiar Law of Effect. The psychologists began by giving "social approval" as a reward to the children, that is, by smiling or saying "Good." Later, a more powerful reward was tried.

As each child entered the preschool in the morning, removed his coat, and proceeded to his seat, each of the three teachers . . . smiled at him and said, "Good morning." At the beginning of the school year, only about 20 percent of the children answered any teacher appropriately. These the teachers would reinforce with social approval. Over the next three months, the average number of children answering the teachers' greetings rose from 20 percent to between 70 and 80 percent. . . .

However, our aim was to teach the children to say "good morning" whether greeted first by the teacher or not. Therefore we brought a more powerful reinforcer into play. Each teacher gave an M & M to each child who answered her greeting appropriately. The number of children replying rose at once to 100 percent and remained there for the last five days of this condition. Then the teachers . . . discontinued their initial greetings. . . . As long as the M & Ms were used, about 95 percent continued to greet the teachers despite the teachers' silence.[43]

proval. They decided to use that reward to shape the behavior of the teacher, and they applied conditioning principles in the following way. Whenever the teacher moved to the right of the room the class looked at him attentively; whenever he moved to the left of the room, the class looked away with lack of interest. According to the Law of Effect, behavior that is followed by rewarding consequences will tend to recur and become stronger. In this situation, if the attention of the class was in fact a reward for the teacher, the behavior that preceded it—moving to the right—should become stronger; and since moving to the left was followed by no rewards, it should tend to extinguish. This is supposedly what happened. According to the story, the "moving to the right" behavior of the teacher became stronger and stronger, until the teacher was standing in the exit doorway at the right of the room!

Programmed Learning

One example of a behavioral teaching method is a kind of teaching method called **programmed instruction.** Programmed instruction is a teaching method that breaks down the subject matter into very small steps. In order to try it out for yourself, get a piece of paper and cover everything in the list that follows except the first question. Each of the questions that follow is actually a sentence to be completed. Your task is to supply the missing words, and then check your answer. The answers are provided on the right-hand side of the page. Be sure to keep the answer covered until after you have responded.

1. In programmed learning the subject matter to be taught is composed into a *program*. _____ learning makes use of many different forms of these programs.

(Programmed)

2. The subject matter of some programs is programmed learning. In fact, the subject matter of the program you are now reading is pro-grammed _____.

(Learning)

3. In programmed learning, each program consists of a series of *frames*. A f_____ is a unit of the program that requires a response from the reader, such as completing the sentence. This paragraph is a frame in this program.

(Frame)

4. An important principle of programmed learning is that each frame should add only a small amount to what you already know. Rather than proceeding in large steps, programmed learning proceeds in _____ steps.

(Small)

5. The answer to each small step is made easier by providing *hints* or *prompts*. Hints or p_____ for the answer are often contained in each frame.

(Prompts)

6. Since programmed learning is based on operant conditioning, the program must provide rewards or reinforcements for your responses. According to operant conditioning, learning occurs when responses are followed by rewards or rein _____.

(Reinforcements)

7. Immediate reinforcement follows each response in programmed learning. Thus, programmed learning is an example of learning based on op_____ conditioning.

(Operant)

8. In programmed learning the reinforcement is not money or candy, but is the knowledge that your response was correct. A principle of programmed learning is that knowing that your response was _____ is a reinforcement.

(Correct)

9. All programs are extremely easy. Making a mistake or error is not rewarding, and learning is believed to occur only with rewards. An important principle of programmed learning is that students should make almost no errors. If this is a successful program, you will have made almost no e_____ in your response to it.

(Errors)

Programmed learning follows the old rule: The best way to eat an elephant is to cut it up into small pieces. The subject matter of the program is broken up into a number of small pieces, and each small piece is dealt with one at a time. This form of instruction has been the subject of numerous research studies. A basic question is, Do you learn anything with programmed learning? The answer is definitely yes. A second important question is, How does programmed learning compare to the conventional expository method? The answer to this question is less certain. A review of thirty-six different studies comparing the two methods of instruction concludes that about half found no difference between them and the remaining half found that programmed instruction was superior.[44]

Why doesn't everybody switch to programmed instruction? There are many educators and psychologists who are not at all enthusiastic about its promise. The method has been criticized on the grounds that it is of use only for communicating simple facts, material that a student might learn through rote drill and practice. It fails to communicate what is not known or what remains to be discovered; worse, it fails to develop in students a thirst for discovery. It may be superior as a method of teaching a large number of isolated responses, but fails as a method of teaching an understanding of the whole. It fosters a dependency on external rewards rather than promoting the self-satisfaction that results from gaining insights. With programmed instruction, learning occurs wholly outside of the student-teacher relationship; there is the risk that learning made impersonal may be less meaningful to students.

Research on programmed learning has raised questions about the basic assumptions underlying the method. For example, a number of studies have compared programs requiring responses from students to those in which the answers are already filled in. The results of these studies show that there is no difference in performance between these two types of programs; that is, making actual responses and receiving reinforcements seemed not to be as necessary as operant-conditioning principles proclaim.[45,46,47] It may be that subjects in these studies were making unspoken responses to the material, and that was sufficient to produce learning.

Robots as Teachers

Ideally, each student should have his or her own teacher. Since this is too expensive, scientists have begun to develop various kinds of teaching robots. Teaching robots are machines designed to teach. These robots vary all the way from the simple machine that presents the frames of a program one at a time to the multimillion-dollar computer that carries on a dialogue with the student about the subject matter.

Computers can be robot teachers.

In some ways these complex computer robots are better than human teachers. They do not have "bad days"; they have a perfect memory and are able to analyze each student's history to select the most useful present focus; they are easily modified and updated; and they can provide instant feedback to the student.[48] In other ways, however, the computer robot leaves something to be desired. The function of education is broader than the transmission of facts; an important function of school concerns the social interaction among peers and between teacher and student. The whole context of human relationship is absent with the mechanized teacher. Furthermore, the computer robot can only respond in predetermined ways; it cannot respond creatively and spontaneously to new situations as can a good teacher.

[s] Behavioral teaching methods are based on the principles of operant conditioning and are concerned with changing the behavior of students. Teachers following this approach provide either explicit or implicit rewards for learning. One behavioral approach is programmed instruction, which breaks down the material to be learned into small units, each of which requires a response. The knowledge that your response is correct is considered to be a reinforcement. Computers are sometimes used in programmed instruction.

Humanistic Teaching Methods

A third major approach to teaching includes an aspect of human life that the cognitive and behavioral approaches exclude: the rich emotional life of the learner. The **humanistic teaching method** is concerned with the experience, emotional life, and goals of students. From this point of view, direct experience rather than abstract thinking or conditioned behavior is primary.

Because this approach centers on the experience of the student, it is more student-centered than the other two approaches. The teacher-centered class typically has goals determined by the teacher; the teacher lectures, criticizes, and corrects. The student-centered class encourages greater student participation and responsibility; goals for the class are partially or wholly determined by the students. Interactions within class are facilitated. Research studies comparing student-centered and teacher-centered classes typically show either no measurable differences on tests or show superiority for the student-centered approach.[49,50,51]

Whether the humanistic method is better than the other two approaches probably depends upon a variety of factors, including the type of students and the type of subject matter to be taught. According to Carl Rogers, there are two distinct types of learning, nonsense learning and experiential learning.

Learning, I believe, can be divided into two general types, along a continuum of meaning. At one end of the scale is the kind of task psychologists sometimes set for their subjects—the learning of nonsense syllables. To memorize such items as baz, ent, nep, arl, lud, and the like, is a difficult task. Because there is no meaning involved, these syllables are not easy to learn and are likely to be forgotten quickly.

We frequently fail to recognize that much of the material presented to students in the classroom has, for the student, the same perplexing, meaningless quality that the list of nonsense syllables has for us. . . . Such learning involves the mind only. It is learning which takes place "from the neck up." It does not involve feelings or personal meanings; it has no relevance for the whole person.

The humanistic teaching method is student-centered.

In contrast, there is such a thing as significant, meaningful, experiential learning. . . .

Why is it that left to his own devices the child learns rapidly, in ways he will not soon forget, and in a manner which has highly practical meaning for him, when all of this can be spoiled if he is "taught" in a way which involves only his intellect?[24]

Passion in the Classroom

One way to promote meaningful learning, as opposed to nonsense learning, is to focus on experience and feelings in the classroom as well as on numbers and words. Some psychologists argue that there are times for passion in the classroom; we must learn to engage the hearts as well as the minds of our children.[52] One great teacher who follows that advice is Sylvia Ashton-Warner, a woman who for years taught the children of the Maori people in New Zealand. "Words,"

she writes, "must have intense meaning for a child. They must be part of his being."[53] To teach children reading, she gets them to select words centered around the emotions of fear and sex; each child develops and learns to read his or her own private vocabulary, one that is intensely meaningful.

Summerhill

Summerhill, a school about one hundred miles from London, is an example of a school following a humanistic approach in education. A. S. Neill, the founder of Summerhill, believed that all children are basically good and show an intrinsic desire to learn when they are not blocked by the conventional school system. Freedom is important at Summerhill. Attendance at classes is not required; all children eventually attend some classes because they want to, to satisfy their natural curiosity. When children come to Summerhill from the conventional school systems they regard classes not as fun, but as punishment, and show what Neill called "lesson aversion"—a tendency to hate classes and lessons. As Neill said:

Children who come to Summerhill as kindergarteners attend lessons from the beginning of their study; but pupils from other schools vow that they will never attend any beastly lessons again at any time. They play and cycle and get in people's way, shy of lessons. This sometimes goes on for months. The recovery time is proportionate to the hatred their last school gave them. Our record case was a girl from a convent. She loafed for three years. The average period of recovery from lesson aversion is three months.[54]

Intellectual development, Neill believed, is not enough. Education must also engage the emotions of the child; the separation of intellect from feeling in modern education should be overcome. Summerhill's focus on emotional development may occur at the expense of intellectual development. A recent survey of fifty Summerhill graduates found that the majority had one major complaint against the school: the lack of academic opportunity and inspired teachers.[55]

No More School

The humanistic approach to teaching is based on the assumptions that human beings are inherently active and that their basic nature is good. Since they are active, they do not need to be prodded into action; since they are good, children's natural development—if not interfered with—will lead them to become good adults. This philosophy of human beings is historically rooted in the writing of Jean Jacques Rousseau, a French philosopher. Rousseau believed that civili-zation corrupted people and interfered with their natural development. The longer children were "educated," the more they lost of their natural goodness. "Look upon every delay as an advantage," Rousseau wrote; "it is gaining a great deal to advance without losing anything." With this view of the nature of human beings, some psychologists and educators believe that the greatest barrier to the natural development of children is the school system itself.

The unhappy truth, according to some educational experts, is that schools block learning rather than promote it. George Dennison, an educator, writes:

Why is it, then, that so many children fail? Let me put it bluntly: it is because our system of public education is a horrendous, life-destroying mess.[56]

Do schools, then, serve a legitimate purpose? Historically, schools have always been important transmitters of culture from adult society to the coming generation. Schools have a homogenizing influence: they promote a single culture among people of diverse origins and different languages. This may or may not be a desirable goal. Even though it may be argued that they could do a better job, schools do serve to train children in certain fundamental skills required of citizens in our society. Although some children might learn reading and writing without schools, other children would not. Schools provide a minimum level of competence for all.

A possible option exists of *no school.* But wouldn't children then be uneducated? Some would argue that they would be unschooled but not uneducated, because learning does not depend upon teaching. Learning is a natural tendency in human beings. To have no more school would put an end to our "age of schooling," but Ivan

Illich believes that this is the task of our generation:

This is a time of crisis in the institution of the school, a crisis which may mark the end of the "age of schooling" in the Western world. I speak of the "age of schooling" in the sense in which we are accustomed to speak of the "feudal age" or of the "Christian era." The "age of schooling" began about two hundred years ago. Gradually the idea grew that schooling was a necessary means of becoming a useful member of society. It is the task of this generation to bury that myth.[57]

How essential do you believe schools are in our society? Would the system collapse if schools were abandoned? Even if we *could* do without schools, it is highly unlikely that we would do so. In the meantime, do we not have the responsibility to ensure as best we can that our schools promote education and foster humanity?

⑤ Humanistic teaching methods are concerned with the experience, emotional life, and goals of students. They are student-centered instead of teacher-centered. Teachers using humanistic approaches believe that students do not have to be motivated by teachers in order to learn; they believe that students have a natural desire to learn and will learn on their own if provided sufficient freedom.

Summary

KEY QUESTIONS

1. What differences among students are important to teachers?
   Students differ in their readiness to learn, in their motivation to learn, and in their style of learning.

2. What differences among teachers are important for students?
   Teachers have different personalities and different methods of teaching; these differences influence the quality of teaching. Good teachers seem to be those who are genuine, accepting, and understanding.

3. How can teachers communicate factual information to their students?
   Using the expository method, teachers provide ideas and information through lectures. Using the discovery method, teachers help students discover principles on their own.

4. How can teachers change the behavior of their students?
   Teachers can change student behavior by reinforcing certain responses. The reinforcement can be explicit—as in giving candy for correct answers—or implicit—as in programmed instruction.

5. How can teachers promote the personal growth of their students?
Humanistic teaching methods promote personal growth by focusing on the experiences and feelings of students and by providing them the freedom to learn.

KEY CONCEPTS

readiness	The level of development or preparation required for learning a particular skill.
motivation	The forces or drive behind a person's action; what causes a person to begin an activity and to follow it through.
achievement motivation	The desire for success.
competence motivation	The desire to master new problems and gain new skills.
learning style	A general consistency or pattern describing how a person learns; a set of preferences and abilities in learning that makes one person different from other people.
reflective style	The learning style of those who take the time to consider and evaluate their alternatives before responding.
impulsive style	The learning style of those who respond quickly, before considering all the alternatives.
analytic style	The learning style of those who break down their experience into its parts, then consider the parts independently.
relational style	The learning style of those who tend to respond to the context and relationships of experience or to experience as a whole.
cognitive teaching method	The teaching method primarily concerned with communicating ideas and factual knowledge.
expository method	A cognitive approach consisting of giving information to students through lecturing and talking.
discovery method	A cognitive method in which teachers provide opportunities for students to learn principles on their own.
behavioral teaching method	A teaching method primarily concerned with changing student behavior; based on operant conditioning.

operant conditioning	A type of simple learning based on the consequences of acts; behavior followed by rewarding consequences is strengthened.
Law of Effect	A principle of learning that states that responses followed by rewarding consequences will tend to be repeated or will be strengthened.
programmed instruction	A teaching method that breaks down the material to be learned into small units, each of which requires a response.
humanistic teaching method	A teaching method primarily concerned with the experiences, emotional life, and goals of students.

Suggested Readings

Introduction to Modern Behaviorism by Howard Rachlin. Second edition. San Francisco: W. H. Freeman, 1976. A clearly written introduction to behavioral psychology. Discusses classical and instrumental conditioning techniques, schedules of reinforcement, and biological limits on conditioning. Ends with an interesting review of the applications of conditioning procedures to human problems.

Human Memory: Structures and Processes by Roberta L. Klatzky. San Francisco: W. H. Freeman, 1975. An up-to-date introduction to research on human memory. Presents the view of memory as continuously active in receiving, modifying, storing, and retrieving information. The last chapter deals with strategies for improving memory.

Thinking and Problem Solving: An Introduction to Human Cognition and Learning by Richard E. Mayer. Glenview, Ill.: Scott, Foresman, 1977. A brief summary of the psychology of thinking. Includes a chapter on "artificial intelligence," the use of computers to study human thinking.

A Clockwork Orange by Anthony Burgess. New York: Norton, 1963. A novel of the future, describing how conditioning principles were applied and how they "backfired." The basis of the movie by the same name.

On Knowing: Essays for the Left Hand by Jerome S. Bruner. New York: Atheneum, 1966. A collection of stimulating essays concerning intuition, creativity, and the act of discovery.

The Technology of Teaching by B. F. Skinner. New York: Appleton-Century-Crofts, 1968. Shows how a behavioral technology based on the principles of operant conditioning can be applied to the problems of teaching. Includes discussions of creativity, discipline problems, and teaching machines.

Teacher by Sylvia Ashton-Warner. New York: Bantam Books, 1963. The personal story of a gifted teacher and her imaginative new method for teaching.

Summerhill: A Radical Approach to Child Rearing by A. S. Neill. New York: Hart Publishing, 1960. A lively and readable description of one of the most unusual schools in the world, and of the unique philosophy on which it was founded.

The Lives of Children: The Story of the First Street School by George Dennison. New York: Random House, 1969. An account of a small school on New York's Lower East Side, which promoted freedom for students and for teachers.

Deschooling Society by Ivan Illich. New York: Harper & Row, 1970. A radical educator calls for the end of the age of schooling.

The Mind of a Mnemonist: A Little Book About a Vast Memory by A. R. Luria, tr. by Lynn Solotaroff. New York: Basic Books, 1968. The true story of S., a remarkable man with a photographic memory.

Behavior Modification: An Overview by William L. Mikulas. New York: Harper & Row, 1972. Operant and classical conditioning applied to human behavior problems and psychotherapy. Excellent survey of the conditioning approach to therapy.

Research Methods III

Measuring Behavior

Are women smarter than men? The answer to this question can be determined empirically by observing the actual intelligence of men and women in the world; but to observe intelligence accurately you must measure it in some fashion. So you would answer the question by measuring the intelligence of men and measuring the intelligence of women and comparing them in some way. When this has been done, it has been found that men and women are equally intelligent.

What Is Measurement?

You **measure** something when, on the basis of some rule, you assign a number to it. One measure of a crowd is a number determined by counting the people; one measure of temperature is a number determined by the reading on a thermometer; one measure of intelligence is the score achieved on an IQ test. Measurement is used extensively in all sciences, including the science of psychology.

Your experience and understanding cannot simply be reduced to a list of numbers resulting from measurement. Measurement is a tool, an aid to the understanding, not the goal of science. Because it is often simpler to think about numbers than it is to think about the complexities of real people in the world, some scientists tend to confuse quantification (how many?) with comprehension (why?). Some of the dangers of paying too much attention to numbers, and not enough to the details of the concrete reality, were described by Mark Twain in *Life on the Mississippi*:

In the space of one hundred and seventy-six years the Lower Mississippi has shortened itself two hundred and forty-two miles. That is an average of a trifle over one mile and a third per year. Therefore, any calm person who is not blind or idiotic, can see that in the Old Oolitic Silurian Period, just a million years ago next November, the Lower Mississippi river was upward of one million three hundred thousand miles long, and stuck out over the Gulf of Mexico like a fishing-rod. . . . There is something fascinating about science. One gets such wholesale returns of conjecture out of such a trifling investment of fact.

Why Measure?

Measurement is a tool scientists use when they want to be precise in describing an individual's behavior, when they want to summarize the characteristics of a large group of people, and when they want to generalize from the few to the many.

Describing Individuals

Psychologists use numbers when they want to describe an individual's behavior precisely. Rather than describe Barbara's intelligence as "a little smarter than average," they will say that her IQ is 105. Rather than describe her reflexes as unusually fast, they might say that her reaction time to a sound is one-eighth of a second. Rather than describe her hearing ability as slightly worse than average, they might say that 60 percent of the people her age can hear better than she can. Barbara's eyesight, her personality, her

reading rate, her achievement level in mathematics, her eye-hand coordination, and numerous other traits and behaviors can be measured. The resulting numbers or measures describe Barbara more precisely than can be achieved with a general verbal description. The numbers, of course, do not tell the whole story of Barbara.

Describing Groups

Psychologists use numbers when they want to summarize the traits or behavior of a group of people. What is the IQ of your class? One way to describe the class IQ is to list the IQ of everybody in class. A shorter way to describe the class IQ is to summarize it with a single representative number—the **average** IQ for the class. There are three kinds of averages: the mean, the mode, and the median. The **mean** is computed by adding up the scores and dividing by the number of scores. The **mode** is the score that occurs most often. The **median** is the middle score, the score above which and below which an equal number of other scores fall.

A test was given to five people and they made the following number of errors: 1, 1, 2, 3, 8. The mean number of errors is 3 (1 + 1 + 2 + 3 + 8 = 15, divided by 5 = 3). The modal number of errors is 1 (more people missed 1 than any other number). The median number of errors is 2 (two scores are higher than 2 and two scores are lower). If you had missed 2 on the above test, you could say that you scored better than average (fewer errors than the mean), exactly the average (the same number as the median), or poorer than average (more errors than the mode). Thus there are three different ways to describe average performance on the test. Performance on the test could also be described by providing the **range** of scores (1 to 8).

Making Inferences

Psychologists use numbers when they want to relate their findings on a small group to a larger population of people. Consider again the question, Are women smarter than men? You cannot measure the intelligence of all women and all men to answer this question; there are too many. You must obtain measures from a limited number—a **sample**—and then estimate what is true for all women and men on the basis of what holds true for your sample. **Inference** is the process of generalizing from the characteristics of a few to the characteristics of many. What is the average IQ of college graduates? You can infer that the average IQ for all graduates is around 120 after you have measured the IQ's of a sample of one hundred representative college graduates and found that their IQ's average 120.

Can People Be Measured?

Many of your characteristics can be measured: height, weight, intelligence, reaction time, eyesight, and personality. This does not mean that your identity can be accurately summarized by a list of numbers. While numbers are relatively precise, they are not rich in detail, nor full of complexity, nor do they carry the subtlety that a picture or long verbal description is capable of. Many aspects of your experience and behavior cannot be summarized by numbers.

When you *can* measure an aspect of behavior, misunderstandings about the definitions of terms can often be avoided. What you mean by a concept determines how you measure it; and indicating to others how you measure it communicates specifically what you mean by a concept.

Operational Definitions

In order to avoid misunderstanding, when scientists talk about something they try to define their terms. Many disagreements result from two people talking about two different things when they think they are talking about the same thing.

Mary: Men are much more aggressive than women. They are more likely to fight, to attack, or to kill each other.

Fred: No, women are more aggressive than men. They are more likely to be sarcastic and cutting and to spread malicious gossip.

Who is right? The issue cannot be resolved until Mary and Fred realize that they are talking about two different things: Mary is talking about physical aggression and Fred is talking about verbal aggression.

Mary: Dogs are much more intelligent than cats. Dogs are quick to learn new tricks and respond to different words and hand signals.

Fred: No, cats are more intelligent than dogs. They have enough sense not to be slaves; they're independent.

Who is right? It depends upon what is meant by *intelligence*. Once again Mary and Fred have got to define their terms before they can clear up their disagreement.

Scientists also have to define their terms, and they do so with special care. They employ what are called **operational definitions.** An operational definition of a term is a description of the operations used in measuring the concept. The operational definition of intelligence might be "the score made on a standard IQ test." The operational definition of "quick reflexes" might be "a reaction time to a tone under one-fifth of a second, measured by a latency clock." One operational definition of aggression might be "the number of times during a one-hour period that the person is observed to strike at, push, or kick another person." Another operational definition of aggression might measure instead verbal attacks.

The Example of Dreaming

What is a dream? Many psychological studies of dreaming have been conducted, and these have required some operational definitions of dreaming. Fifty years ago a study of dreaming used an operational definition of dreaming that was "the verbal report of the subject that a dream occurred." More recently, a study of dreaming used the operational definition of "the verbal report of the subject that a dream occurred, plus confirming evidence from measured brain-wave activity." With new measuring instruments such as the electroencephalogram (EEG), which indicates the electrical activity of the brain, it has become possible to measure the duration and frequency of dreams without waking up the sleeper.

The Example of Psychosis

What is psychosis? The operational definition of psychosis that is most commonly used is that of "confinement in a mental hospital as a diagnosed schizophrenic." Thus the measuring instrument used in defining psychosis is the human being whose expert judgment caused the person to be diagnosed as psychotic. A clinical psychologist or psychiatrist may examine the subject in an interview, read a case history prepared by someone else, give the subject a series of psychological tests, and then, on the basis of all the information, judge the person to be psychotic.

An ESP Test

Do you have "psychic," "sixth-sense," or ESP abilities? You can use the concepts you have just read about in order to find out. ESP (extrasensory perception) is an ability some persons supposedly have to perceive in ways other than by such traditional senses as sight and hearing. On page 186 of this book there is a list of twenty psychic symbols. There are only five different symbols: a star, wavy lines, a circle, a cross, and a square. Test your ESP by trying to "sense" the order of the symbols. See if you can reproduce the list by choosing and writing down a symbol for each blank.

★ ⅲ ○ + □

1. ___	8. ___	15. ___
2. ___	9. ___	16. ___
3. ___	10. ___	17. ___
4. ___	11. ___	18. ___
5. ___	12. ___	19. ___
6. ___	13. ___	20. ___
7. ___	14. ___	

Now turn to the symbols and see how many you got correct. What does your score mean? You would expect to get some correct just by chance, purely a result of guessing. How many? Since there are 5 different symbols, the chance of your one guess being correct on any single trial is 1 out of 5, or 20 percent. With 20 opportunities to guess, you would expect to get about 4 correct (20 percent) just by chance (sometimes a few more, sometimes a few less). If you got as many as 7 correct, you have an unusually high score, one made by fewer than 5 percent of persons trying. If you got as many as 10 correct, you performed better than 999 in a thousand.

A group of seven students recently took the ESP test, and, as a psychologist, I want to describe their performance. One way to tell you how well they did would be to list their scores:

Name	Number Correct
Robert	3
Juan	3
Felicia	3
Ted	4
Viki	5
Zzzy	11
Sue	20
Total	49

I could summarize the performance of this group by telling you that the range of their scores was 3 to 20. Or I could tell you what the average score was (mode = 3, median = 4, mean = 7). If the number expected to be correct by chance is 4, how can we account for the fact that the *mean* performance of this group was as high as 7?

Without further evidence you might conclude that the group showed ESP ability. Sometimes group averages, however, can be misleading; the details of the individuals are often lost. In this particular case, further inquiry revealed that Sue achieved her incredible score by cheating and Zzzy was a foreign exchange student from Mars whose head glowed in the dark and who had not just a "sixth sense," but a seventh and eighth as well. To summarize such a mixed group with a single number, therefore, is not very informative.

Somewhat startled by the group's performance on the ESP test, I decided to test them again to get a second measure of their psychic talents. Below I have listed both sets of scores for comparison:

Name	First Test	Second Test
Robert	3	1
Juan	3	5
Felicia	3	3
Ted	4	3
Viki	5	4
Zzzy	11	10
Sue	20	20

Apparently, Zzzy did his usual and so did Sue. Those who scored relatively low on the first test also scored relatively low on the second test, and the high scorers scored high both times. The two sets of scores are related; if you know students' scores on the first test, you can predict their scores on the second test and not be too far off. Scores that are related in this way are said to be **correlated.**

A major task of science is to discover the relationships among natural events in the world. Measuring these events and examining correlations among them reveals these relationships.

KEY CONCEPTS

measurement   Assigning a number to something on the basis of a rule; for example, assigning a number to the temperature on the basis of a thermometer.

average   That which is typical or representative.

mean	An average computed by adding up the scores and dividing by the number of scores; for example, the mean of 3 and 5 is 4.
mode	An average that is the most frequently occurring score.
median	An average that is the middle score, above which and below which an equal number of scores lie.
range	The distance between the highest and lowest scores.
sample	A subset of a larger group or population.
inference	The process of reaching a general conclusion on the basis of observing only a sample.
operational definitions	A description of the operations used in measuring a concept.
correlation	The tendency of scores to co-vary; if scores are related in this way, one score can be predicted from another; for example, height can be predicted from age, up to a point.

Answers for the ESP test on p. 184:
1. ɯ   2. +   3. ★   4. □   5. ★   6. ○   7. +   8. +   9. ○   10. ○   11. □   12. ɯ
13. ★   14. ɯ   15. ○   16. +   17. □   18. □   19. ɯ   20. ★

IV Experience

10 Consciousness and the Brain

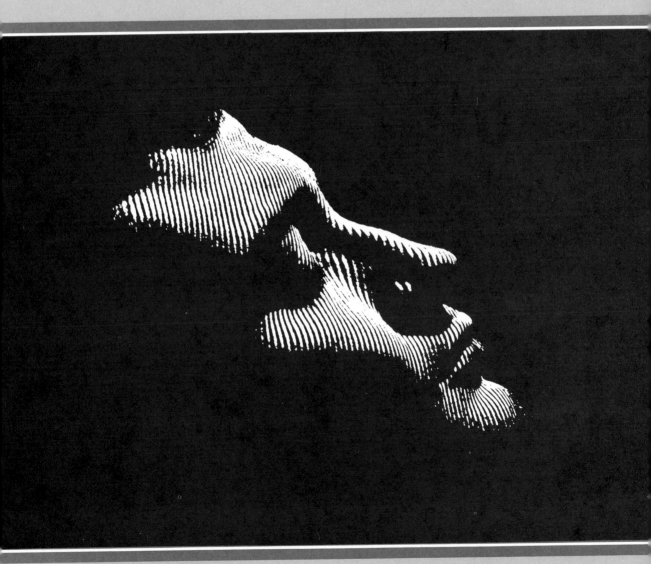

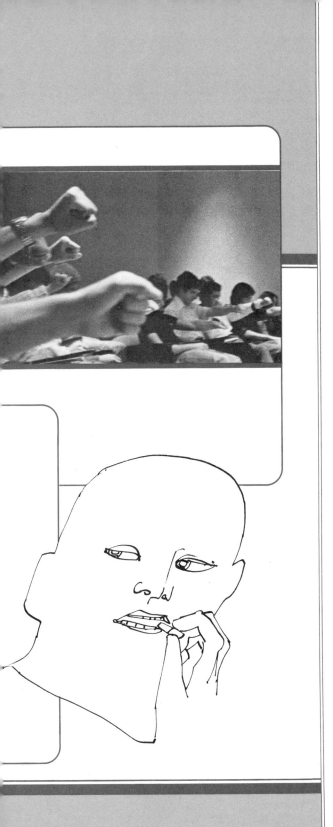

KEY QUESTIONS

1. What is the relation of your mind and body?

2. What is the physical basis of your consciousness?

3. How can altered states of consciousness be produced?

4. What are the effects of drugs on consciousness?

What's on your mind?

What are your thoughts, feelings, and perceptions at this moment? You are aware of this book, the room around you, and your body; you may be aware of feelings of hunger, pleasure, or fatigue; you may be remembering what happened yesterday or planning what you will do tomorrow. Your private awareness of your thoughts, feelings, and perceptions is called your **consciousness.**

Your state of consciousness changes with hypnosis, sleep, meditation, biofeedback, and drugs. These experiences change your consciousness by influencing the physical basis of consciousness in your body. Some of the most exciting recent discoveries in psychology are those revealing the physical basis of consciousness.

Mind and Body

Your mind and body are not separate, independent parts of you. Changes in one are usually accompanied by changes in the other.

Your body affects your mind. Your mental life—your consciousness—is possible because of the activity of your brain and nerves. Your awareness of the world and your self requires that your eyes, ears, nerves, and brain are working properly. Even though your heart may be working normally, you can be declared legally dead, in some states, if your brain has stopped working.

You can lose consciousness with a concussion, a violent blow to the head. One woman fell off her bicycle and struck her head. She lost consciousness and was taken to a hospital. About five days later she began gradually to regain her awareness of the world around her. But it took several weeks for her mind to return to its normal level of consciousness.[1]

Your body affects your mind, but your mind also affects your body. Fear can cause your heart to pound and your hands to tremble. Even when you are not afraid, you can change the rate of your heartbeat simply by thinking different thoughts.[2] Your blood pressure is increased when you are excited and decreased when you are feeling relaxed.[3] Anger, frustration, and anxiety can cause headaches.[4] Prolonged emotional stress can sometimes cause muscle cramps, asthma, heart attacks, and ulcers.

Ulcers result from an excessive flow of digestive juices (hydrochloric acid) in the stomach. Prolonged stress increases the flow of hydrochloric acid in the stomachs of both animals and humans. Psychologists have studied the relation between ulcers and emotional stress in laboratories. Ulcers in rats can be produced experimentally by causing rats to experience psychological conflict.[5] Monkeys trained to make rapid decisions to avoid shock eventually get ulcers, apparently because of the psychological stress involved.[6]

Prolonged psychological stress in humans causes a variety of physical problems. One such problem is a skin disorder called hives. The case of Anna illustrates the consequences of stress for one young woman.

Anna A., a twenty-seven-year-old nurse, was engaged to be married and was somewhat anxious and uncertain about this adventure. A week before her wedding day she developed a severe attack of [hives]: most of her body was covered with raised white, intensely itchy wheals. Two weeks after her marriage, she reappeared at the hospital, radiantly happy and with quite clear skin.[7]

Anna's skin problem probably resulted from anxiety related to her coming marriage. The anxiety affected her skin by causing an allergic reaction to develop, and this led to the skin disorder. Her honeymoon changed her psychological mood and lowered her anxiety, allowing her body to return to normal. Changes in her mind were accompanied by changes in her body. The relation between mind and body depends upon the physical basis of consciousness—namely, the brain and nerves.

S   Your mental life, or private awareness, is called your consciousness. Your consciousness requires a working brain. A brain injury such as a concussion can result in loss of consciousness. Your state of mind can also affect your body. For example, fear and anxiety can result in temporary problems involving heartbeat or blood pressure and also in more lasting problems such as ulcers and hives.

Nervous System

How can you be aware of an itch on your foot? How can an "itch" message from your foot reach your mind? It happens because your body has a communication network, a special system for carrying messages from one place to another, for understanding these messages, and for responding to them. This communication network is called the **nervous system.** Your brain, spinal cord, and nerves are parts of your nervous system.

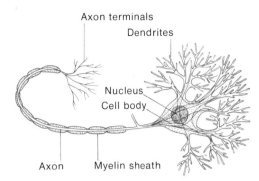

The neuron, or nerve cell.

Nerves and Neurons

Your body is composed of billions of tiny cells. Most of these cells have special functions; they have different jobs to do. There are blood cells, bone cells, skin cells, fat cells, hair cells, muscle cells, and many other kinds of cells. One unique kind of cell is specialized for carrying messages; this is the nerve cell, or **neuron.**

Neurons are the basic units, or components, from which the nervous system is built. Just as the telephone system of a major city is a highly interconnected system of wires and relays, the nervous system of the body is a highly interconnected system of neurons. Telephone lines carry messages in the form of electrical impulses. Neurons also carry messages in the form of electrical impulses; neural impulses, however, are much smaller and are not just electrical—they are also chemical. Telephone lines are often strung together to form cables. Neurons sometimes are also strung together to form a nerve. A **nerve** is like a cord consisting of a bundle of neurons.

Nerves carry messages from one part of your body to another. You are aware of an itch on your foot because a message, in the

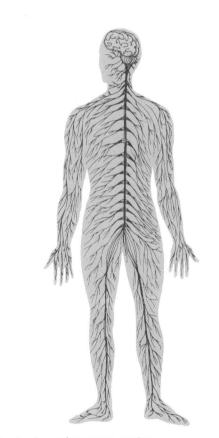

The brain and nervous system.

form of electrical impulses, travels along nerves from your foot to your brain. You are aware of the words on this page because of messages carried by nerves from your eyes to your brain. Your awareness of music on the radio depends upon messages carried by nerves from your ears to your brain. Nerves also carry messages *from* your brain *to* other parts of your body such as muscles and glands. The movement of your hand to scratch your foot is a response to such a message.

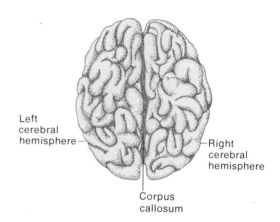

The left and right hemispheres of the brain.

Brain

Your brain, although only about three pounds of pinkish-gray material, is far more complicated than the most advanced computer. It is a control center made up of billions of neurons. Your brain, unlike a computer, will remain active for as long as you are alive; and, unlike a computer, it can sometimes repair itself.

■ *Your Split Brain* Your brain, like a walnut, has two connected halves with wrinkled surfaces. From the back to the front, your brain is divided down the middle; the two sides are called the left and right **cerebral hemispheres.** Each hemisphere controls one side of your body. But they are "crosswired": your left hemisphere controls the right side of your body and your right hemisphere controls the left side of your body. For example, if your right foot itches, the "itch" message is sent initially to your left hemisphere; and if you scratch your foot with your left hand, it is your right hemisphere that directs the left hand to move. If one hemisphere is damaged, the opposite side of the body may have problems. The left side of your body can be paralyzed from damage to the right hemisphere of your brain.

Your left and right cerebral hemispheres are relatively independent; it's almost like having two brains within one skull. The two brains can stay in touch with one another because they are connected by a broad band of nerves called the **corpus callosum.** This nerve pathway permits the "left brain" to know what the "right brain" is doing, and vice versa. On rare occasions, because of an accident or brain operation, individuals have had their corpus callosum sectioned (cut through). The effect of this was to create two separate brains within one skull, each out of touch with the other.

What is it like to have two separate brains? One psychologist studied a number of people with "split brains" and wrote a book about them. He said:

Situated dead center in the middle of the brain is the largest and most mysterious information transmission system in the world—the corpus callosum. With it intact, the two halves of the body have no secrets from one another. With it sectioned, the two halves become two different conscious mental spheres, each with its own experienced base and control system for behavioral operations. [8]

Other scientists have also shown that people with "split brains" (with the corpus callosum cut) have two completely separate minds; each mind is unaware of what is going on in the other.[9]

Since the two hemispheres are "cross-wired," the left hemisphere controls the right hand and the right hemisphere controls the left hand. Normally, information from one hand can be compared with information from the other; the information is exchanged across the corpus callosum. However, when the corpus callosum has been cut, the two hemispheres are out of touch with each other, like the brains of two separate people. If you reached into a sack of fruit with both hands and felt an apple with one hand and a banana with the other, you could tell that they were different; your corpus callosum allows your two hemispheres to "talk" to each other and compare information. However, if your corpus callosum were cut, you would not have known that your two hands held different fruits; your left hand would not know what your right hand was doing or what it was feeling.

Your two brains (your left and right hemispheres) do not have the same abilities. For most people, the left hemisphere is more competent at speech and writing, math, science, and logic. The right hemisphere is generally more competent at art, music, and perception. Thus, the two brains apparently have somewhat different functions.[10]

■ *Localized Functions* Different parts of your brain do different things. To some degree, each ability is located in a different area of the brain; the functions of your brain are said to be partially localized. Not only do your two hemispheres have somewhat different abilities or functions, different parts of each hemisphere also have different functions. In addition, beneath the cerebral hemispheres, at the base and core of the brain, there are also different parts that perform different functions.

Each hemisphere can be divided into four regions, or *lobes.* Each region specializes in certain functions, but is involved in other functions as well. At the very back of each hemisphere is the **occipital lobe,** an area that is important for vision. Damage to the occipital lobe can cause blindness. Just forward of the occipital lobe lies the **parietal lobe,** an area important for skin and body sensations. Perceptions of pain, heat, cold, and touch depend upon the parietal lobe. At the very front of the brain is the **frontal lobe,** an area important for planning, abstract thinking, and problem solving. Damage to the frontal lobe can result in a reduced ability to plan ahead and to deal with complex situations. Along each side of the brain, above the ear, lies the **temporal lobe,** an area important for memory and for hearing. One part of the temporal lobe is responsible for high tones and another for low tones. Damage to the temporal lobe can result in difficulties in understanding speech and in mem-

The lobes of the brain.

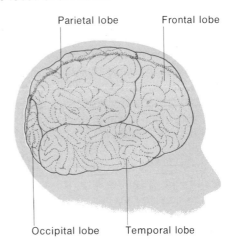

Parietal lobe   Frontal lobe

Occipital lobe   Temporal lobe

ory problems. One patient with a damaged temporal lobe forgot the way to the bathroom and could not relearn it.[11]

■ *Electrical Activity*   The different parts of your brain are made up of billions of tiny nerve cells, or neurons, connected to each other to form complicated networks or circuits. These neural circuits, like the circuits of a computer, work by using electrical impulses. At every moment that you are alive, electrical impulses are traveling along billions of neurons in your brain.

The electrical activity of your brain can be measured from the outside of the skull. Small metal discs are placed on your scalp and wires are run from these discs to a machine called an **EEG** (electroencephalograph). The machine records the brain's electrical signals on a moving roll of paper. Having your brain examined with an EEG involves no pain or discomfort.

Because the level of electrical activity in your brain rises and falls, EEG recordings show waves with peaks and valleys; these "brain waves," like sound waves, have different frequencies. The frequencies of brain waves generally are different in different states of consciousness. For example, a person who is asleep has a characteristic brain wave; the EEG shows when a person is sleeping. When the person begins dreaming, there is a different pattern of brain waves. One type of brain wave that is of particular interest is the **alpha wave.** The alpha wave has a frequency of about ten cycles per second and occurs when the person is relaxed, but awake and alert.

⑤   The neuron, or nerve cell, is the basic unit of the nervous system. Bundles of neurons form cables called nerves. The brain, which is also composed of neurons, has two halves, or cerebral hemispheres. The hemispheres are "cross-wired," so that each controls the opposite side of the body. Between the two hemispheres there is a connecting band of nerves called the corpus callosum. The hemispheres are disconnected and out of touch with each other when the corpus callosum is cut; this results in two separate minds within one skull. Each hemisphere has four regions—the occipital, parietal, frontal, and temporal lobes—that have somewhat different functions. To some degree, vision is localized in the occipital lobe, skin and body sensations in the parietal lobe, planning and abstract thinking in the frontal lobe, and memory and hearing in the temporal lobe. The electrical activity of the brain can be measured with an EEG. EEG recordings show brain waves of different frequencies when the brain is in different states. One type of brain wave is called the alpha wave; it is found when the person is in a state of relaxed awareness.

Altered States of Consciousness

Your state of consciousness at this moment is a normal waking consciousness; you are reasonably alert and aware of yourself and the world around you. But there are other states of consciousness, in which your awareness is either higher or lower than it is now. One of the first American psychologists, William James, put it this way:

Our normal waking consciousness, rational consciousness as we call it, is but one special type of consciousness, whilst all about it, parted from it by the filmiest of screens, there lie potential forms of consciousness entirely different. . . . No account of the universe in its totality can be final which leaves these other forms of consciousness quite disregarded.[12]

These other forms of consciousness—or **altered states of consciousness**—can result from hypnosis, meditation, biofeedback, and drugs. With each of these, your awareness and experience are different from that of normal consciousness. Changes in consciousness are typically accompanied by physical changes in your body. In some cases there are changes in heartbeat, blood pressure, and breathing. EEG recordings show that some states of consciousness are related to different states of the brain. Studies of these altered mental states help us to understand the physical basis of consciousness.

Meditation

Meditation is an ancient practice used for altering consciousness and acquiring inner peace. It involves controlling attention by concentrating the mind fully on one object or event, free from all distractions. Meditation is a way to calm the mind, to make it more aware, relaxed, and receptive. In Yoga meditation (such as "TM," or transcendental meditation), you concentrate on a special word that you repeat silently to yourself over and over again; an example of such a word is "OM." In Zen meditation, you concentrate on your breathing; you think of nothing but the air moving in and out of your body.

One procedure of Zen meditation, used in Japan, involves a special way of concentrating on breathing. You can try a simplified version of Zen meditation by following these instructions. First, sit in a comfortable position and relax your muscles. Rest your hands in your lap and let your head fall forward. Breathe through your nose in a normal way; do not force the air in—let it come in naturally. Then exhale slowly, letting all the air out of your lungs. Each time

Meditation is a way of relaxing.

you exhale, slowly count to yourself—"one," with the first out-breath, then "two," and continue counting for ten breaths. The next time you exhale, begin again at "one." One session of meditation should last twenty or thirty minutes.

This technique of meditation will be accompanied by a physical change in your brain, and with practice may result in an altered state of consciousness. Both Zen and Yoga meditation result in an increase in alpha waves.[13,14,15] Techniques of meditation are effective in promoting relaxation and have been used successfully in psychotherapy, although it is not yet known exactly why meditation is beneficial.[16]

Biofeedback

You are ordinarily unaware of changes in the activity of your brain. These changes can, however, be measured by using an EEG. By observing the EEG records, you can become aware of the pattern of your brain waves. An EEG machine can be connected to turn on a light or a tone whenever your brain produces alpha waves. In this way, you can be given feedback about your brain's electrical activity.

Biofeedback is a technique that measures what is going on in your brain or other parts of your body and provides you with knowledge or feedback of that activity. Feedback about heart rate, blood pressure, muscle tension, and brain waves are examples of biofeedback that have been studied. With biofeedback, people can learn to control these physical responses. Because biofeedback techniques enable people to gain greater control over their inner processes, these techniques have both medical and psychological benefits. For example, biofeedback can promote deep relaxation and has been used as a form of therapy for people with certain neurotic disorders.[14]

Alpha waves have been claimed to reflect a distinct state of consciousness, similar to that of meditation. When your mind is relaxed and alert, it tends to produce alpha waves; but the EEG pattern changes if you begin to worry about something or to concentrate on a problem. During alpha-wave production, people describe their state of consciousness as "relaxed awareness" or "inner peace"; one person described it as "a lovely serene feeling of being in harmony with the universe."[17]

Hypnosis

Hypnosis is an altered state of consciousness in which a person is highly responsive to suggestion. People who are hypnotized seem to be in a dreamlike trance. Their experience of the world and themselves can be easily influenced by the hypnotist; they seem unable to act on their own, following instead the suggestions of someone else. One author described what a hypnotized man would look like:

His eyes are closed, the muscles of his face are rather loose, his entire body is quite relaxed and, if he is sitting in a chair, he often will have slumped down it. The head falls forward on the subject's chest, sometimes far backward or, again, sideways over his shoulder. The arms and hands usually rest limply on a support or hang limply by his sides.[18]

The movement of a hypnotized person has a kind of "slow motion" quality, and the eyes— if they are open—may have an unfocused stare.

Hypnosis can be produced by a variety of methods. Most involve techniques for focusing attention and increasing relaxation. To focus attention, the hypnotist may tell the subject to concentrate on a single object, such as a thumbtack on a wall or a candle on a table. To produce relaxation, the hypnotist may tell the person to relax and suggest that the person is feeling sleepy. Not all people can be hypnotized; those who can, gradually respond to the repeated suggestions and enter a hypnotic trance.

Methods for hypnotizing someone usually begin with a procedure for producing deep relaxation. In a typical procedure, the subject is asked to sit in a comfortable chair and look at a small light. The hypnotist then talks to the subject. The following passage shows examples of some of the things that are typically said in the early stage of this procedure.

Keep your eyes on the light and listen carefully to what I say. Your ability to be hypnotized

Professor Zimbardo demonstrating hypnosis in a psychology class at Stanford University. The students have been told that their left arms are as stiff as iron rods.

*depends entirely on your willingness to coop-
erate. It has nothing to do with your intelligence. As for your will power—if you want to,
you can pay no attention to me and remain
awake all the time. . . . On the other hand, if
you pay close attention to what I say, and
follow what I tell you, you can easily learn to
fall into a hypnotic sleep. . . .*

*Now relax and make yourself entirely com-
fortable. Keep your eyes on that little light.
Keep staring at it all the time. . . .*

*Relax completely. Relax every muscle in your
body. . . . Let yourself be limp. Relax more
and more, more and more. . . .*

*Your legs feel heavy and limp, heavy and
limp. Your arms are heavy, heavy, heavy as
lead. . . . You feel tired and sleepy, tired and
sleepy. . . .*

*Your eyes are tired from staring. . . . The
strain in your eyes is getting greater and
greater, greater and greater. You would like
to close your eyes.*[19]

You may have read stories or seen TV
programs about people who were hypnotized
against their will and turned into human
robots willing to do whatever the hypnotist
ordered. Scientific studies have exposed this
view of hypnosis as a myth. In fact, to be
hypnotized, you must cooperate with the
hypnotist and agree to the procedure. If you
don't want to be hypnotized, you can't be.

A more complicated question is whether
people can be hypnotized and made to do
something harmful, immoral, or criminal.
The answer seems to be yes, but only under
certain special conditions. Studies show that
people who are hypnotized will do harmful
acts when (a) they are given strong, repeated
suggestions to do so, and, in addition, (b) they
are in an experimental or laboratory situation.[19]

In one study that met these two conditions, hypnotized individuals acted in ways
they would normally be unwilling to act.
College students were hypnotized and told to
pick up a poisonous snake with their bare

hands; others were told to throw deadly acid at the experimenter. The results were astonishing: they did what they were told. The hypnotized students reached for the snake but, at the last minute, were prevented from picking it up. Other students threw what they thought was acid at the experimenter (it was, in fact, a harmless liquid). In a later interview, these students reported that they felt they would not be harmed by their actions because it was just an experiment.[20]

Hypnosis, in some ways, resembles sleep; in fact, the word "hypnosis" comes from a Greek word meaning sleep. EEG studies have shown, however, that sleep and hypnosis involve different states of consciousness.[21] The brain waves during sleep and hypnosis are quite different. In terms of brain activity, hypnosis closely resembles waking consciousness. At one time it was thought that the hypnotized brain produced more alpha waves than the brain in normal waking consciousness; more recent studies have shown that there is not an unusual amount of alpha waves produced in hypnosis.[21]

The influence of the mind on the body appears strengthened in hypnosis. Hypnotized subjects have a remarkable capacity to control bodily responses that are typically considered involuntary. For example, hypnotized persons can raise or lower their skin temperature on command. In one experiment subjects were able to cool down one hand and warm up the other so that there was a four degree difference in temperature between them.[22] Heart rate can also be influenced by hypnosis.[22] There is evidence that hypnosis can produce such an insensitivity to pain that surgery can be performed without anesthetic.[23] Hypnosis is a powerful tool for controlling consciousness and behavior, and has been used extensively in psychotherapy.

☒ An altered state of consciousness is one in which your level of awareness is higher or lower than normal. Meditation, biofeedback, hypnosis, and drugs are techniques for producing altered states of consciousness. Meditation is a procedure for controlling attention and making the mind more aware, relaxed, and receptive. Biofeedback is a technique for measuring subtle changes in your body and revealing them to you. With biofeedback you can learn to control responses, such as brain waves, that are normally considered involuntary. Hypnosis is a state of heightened suggestibility. To be hypnotized, a person must cooperate with the hypnotist. Under special conditions, a person can be hypnotized to act in harmful or immoral ways. Meditation and biofeedback can be used to increase the production of EEG alpha waves; hypnosis, however, does not affect the EEG. Meditation, biofeedback, and hypnosis have been successfully used in psychotherapy.

Drugs and Consciousness

This has been called the age of anxiety. It is a time when more and more people are searching for ways to change their consciousness, to find inner peace. The most popular solution has been to turn to drugs, to reach for the instant "high."

Our society apparently believes in chemicals. Each year new chemicals are developed and marketed that can change emotions, perceptions, or personality. Millions of dollars are spent by drug manufacturers to persuade us that their new drugs are the ideal solutions to our problems. Television peddles aspirin as the royal road to psychological health: husbands who cannot cope with their wives, mothers who snap at their children,

Mind-altering drugs are everywhere.

employers who lose their tempers, nervous teachers—all are advised to reach for some brand of aspirin for instant relief. Drugs to make you sleep, drugs to wake you up, drugs to calm you down, all are sold on television through miniature dramas, all ending happily in romance, money, or fame.

Using Drugs

You use drugs.

Coffee and tea contain a drug, caffeine, which is a stimulant. Wine and beer contain alcohol, a sedative drug. Cigarettes, tranquilizers, diet pills, and sleeping pills all contain drugs that affect the mind. Some drugs—LSD, marijuana, and heroin, for example—profoundly change human behavior and consciousness. Some people who use these mind-altering drugs describe them as "increasing awareness," "expanding consciousness," or "providing a different view of reality."

Almost every adult has used drugs, through experiences with cigarettes, coffee, or alcoholic beverages. The use of other drugs is also widespread. In recent years, 6 to 10 percent of all medical prescriptions were for tranquilizers to relieve tension and depression. Close to 50 million prescriptions for barbiturates are filled each year in America.[24] Recent studies show that about 30 percent of high school students and 50 to 75 percent of college students have used marijuana.[25,26,27] More and more college students are using marijuana, although there is some evidence that this trend will not continue.[28]

How do people become users of drugs? Because drugs such as heroin, LSD, and marijuana are illegal, many people do not have these drugs easily available. In order to become a user of illegal drugs, you must have access to them.   Heroin and marijuana also involve a period of learning how to use them; it is not just a matter of taking them and waiting for the effect.   Thus, most people who use illegal drugs have friends who provided the drugs and who taught them how to use them.[29]   For people not now using illegal drugs, the best way to predict whether they will become users is to count the number of friends they have who are users; the more friends who are users, the greater the chance they have of eventually becoming users themselves.[30]

Drugs and the Brain

Mind-altering drugs work by changing the chemistry of the brain.   Whether these drugs are injected, inhaled, or swallowed, they eventually are absorbed into the bloodstream and carried to the brain.   The brain is composed of billions of individual nerve cells (neurons), and the activity of these cells controls behavior and consciousness.   Mind-altering drugs change consciousness by changing the activity of these brain cells.

Your level of arousal ranges from high, when you are excited and alert, to low, when you are drowsy.   During these times the level of activity of your brain is also either high or low.   Certain drugs act, in a sense, to slow down the brain.   For example, alcohol and barbiturates reduce the activity of the brain cells and make you less aware, alert, and active.   These drugs are called **sedative drugs** because they reduce your level of arousal and calm you down.   On the other hand, nicotine, caffeine, and amphetamines speed up the brain and make you more alert and energetic.   These drugs are called **stimulant drugs** because they increase your arousal and energy levels.   The effect of LSD and marijuana is more complicated and not as well understood.   EEG studies show that these drugs alter the activity of only certain brain structures.[31,32]   It is believed that these drugs affect special parts of the brain that are involved in controlling and processing information from the senses; because of this effect, these drugs often result in sensory or perceptual distortions or hallucinations.[33]   LSD and marijuana are called **psychedelic drugs** because of their ability to change consciousness and experience.

Drug Problems

Under certain circumstances drugs can lead to mental disturbance, drugs can induce an uncontrollable craving for more drugs, and drugs can kill.   Because of these real concerns, and some unreal concerns, many drugs are outlawed in this society.   Addiction, mental disturbance, and flashbacks are drug problems of particular psychological interest.

■ *Tolerance and Toxicity*   Any drug can kill you if the dose is high enough.   Why should a person take a dose that high?   The answer is that most drugs produce a **tolerance** for themselves, so that increased doses are necessary in order to obtain the desired psychological effects.   After you have taken the drug for a while, you must begin to take more and more of it in order to experience the same initial effect.   While the amount required to produce the desired effect increases with use, the amount required to kill you does not change.   The **toxicity level**—or the amount producing death—stays the same.   Soon the amount required to produce the desired effect is enough to kill you, and death results from continued usage.

A moderate amount of tolerance develops to continued use of alcohol or barbiturates.   An experienced drinker of alcohol may be able to drink twice as much as a novice before appearing drunk. Heroin, morphine, and codeine require larger and larger doses with continued use. Profound tolerance for these drugs develops, so that in order to ward off withdrawal symptoms the user must take increasing doses. An increased dosage of the amphetamines is required by most people in order to maintain the initial stimulating effect.

The question of tolerance with continued usage of LSD and marijuana is complicated. For LSD, with daily usage, tolerance develops rapidly, so that higher doses are required to produce the same effects.[34] But the tolerance disappears following a few days without using the drug. Thus, LSD does produce tolerance, but it is a temporary effect. Marijuana does not produce much tolerance at low doses (those typical among users in this country).[35] With extremely high doses, however, marked tolerance for marijuana does develop.[36]

■ *Dependence and Addiction* Some people become dependent upon certain drugs so that they feel they need to have them. **Psychological dependence** results in a strong craving for the drug and a feeling of anxiety when it's not available. A psychological dependency results from the continued use of tobacco; a craving, a feeling of urgency, and even a mild panic may develop when cigarettes are withdrawn. Cigarettes contain a stimulant drug, nicotine. Heroin, alcohol, amphetamines, and barbiturates all produce psychological dependence. A regular user of one of these drugs who is denied access to it often becomes quite anxious. Marijuana and LSD do not produce psychological dependence.[37]

Certain drugs produce **physical addiction** so that when the drug is not taken withdrawal symptoms develop in the body. A drug addict, in order to prevent the painful withdrawal symptoms, must continue to take

Alcoholic.

Drug addict.

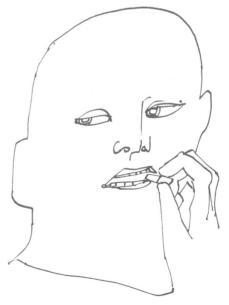

Psychological dependence on drugs and addiction make you a prisoner in a bottle.

the drug. Some heavy drinkers become physically addicted to alcohol. When they stop drinking, they experience severe withdrawal symptoms. Nausea, anxiety, agitation, confusion, tremors, and sweating occur first; then cramps, vomiting, hallucinations, and convulsions develop. Death can occur in the latter stages of severe alcohol or barbiturate withdrawal.[37] Withdrawal from heroin addiction is also painful:

Withdrawal sickness, in one with a well-developed physical dependence, is a shattering experience. . . . About 12 hours after the last heroin dose, the addict begins to grow uneasy. He yawns, shivers, and sweats, while watery discharge pours from inside his nose. . . . For a few hours, he falls into an abnormal restless stupor known among ad-dicts as "yen sleep." On awakening 18 to 24 hours after his last drug dose, the addict enters the lower depths of his personal hell. Yawning may violently dislocate his jaw. More watery mucous pours from his eyes and nose. . . . The hair on his skin stands erect, and his skin shows that typical goose flesh called "cold turkey" in the parlance of the addict. . . . His bowels act with violence. Great waves of contraction pass over the stomach walls, causing explosive vomiting frequently stained with blood. . . . The surface of his abdomen appears corrugated and knotted and abdominal pain is severe.[38]

Alcohol, barbiturates, heroin, morphine, and codeine can all produce physical addiction, a state in which the body itself becomes dependent upon the continued presence of the drug. LSD, marijuana, and the amphetamines do not seem to produce addiction. Physical withdrawal symptoms do not develop from quitting the use of one of these drugs.[37]

■ *Drug Psychosis* Certain drugs can cause a psychotic reaction, a severe mental disturbance. Where a mental disturbance is associated with drug-taking, it is usually found that a history of mental instability existed before the drug experience; in other words, drugs may exaggerate a previous mental condition. The psychotic reaction brought on by drugs is typically characterized by hallucinations (seeing things that aren't there), paranoid delusions (false beliefs that people are out to "get you" and that you are all-powerful), and experiences of nightmarish terror. LSD can cause psychotic reactions lasting months or even years in some individuals,[39] although most investigators believe that such individuals were psychologically disturbed before the drug experience. The exact frequency of psychotic reactions from LSD is unknown, although the evidence indicates that the incidence is less than 1 percent.[40]

Psychotic reactions from marijuana use are also rare: most reports of extreme adverse reactions come from individuals who are inexperienced with the drug, who take a large amount, and who have a history of previous psychological problems.[41,42,43] These psychotic reactions, although frightening, tend to be temporary.

In contrast, psychosis resulting from the heavy use of amphetamines is not rare. The psychotic reaction caused by prolonged and excessive use of amphetamines is indistinguishable from the most common mental illness, schizophrenia. The similarity between amphetamine-produced psychosis and schizophrenia may be due to the fact that individuals who use the drug heavily may be disposed toward schizophrenia before their drug experiences.[44]

■ *Flashbacks* For users of LSD and marijuana, sometimes the drug experience recurs without the drug; this spontaneous recurrence of the drug effect has been called a **flashback.** Flashbacks may happen following the use of LSD as long as a month or even a year after taking the drug.[45] They may happen at any time—walking down the street or driving a car—and they consist of images and illusions resembling those experienced under the influence of LSD. One estimate of the frequency of flashbacks is that one out of twenty regular users of LSD has the flashback experience.[46] One person's LSD flashback involved seeing inanimate objects as weird animals, another consisted of auditory hallucinations.[47] Flashbacks following marijuana use are much rarer, although a few cases have been reported.[48,49]

The problem with flashbacks is that they are not under your control. To have an LSD experience when you want it and plan on it is serious enough; to have an LSD experience when you have not taken the drug and don't expect it, is worse. You do not control the drug experience; the drug controls you.

Psychedelic Drugs

Psychedelic drugs are those drugs which profoundly affect perception and other mental processes; LSD, psilocybin, mescaline, marijuana, and hashish are all psychedelic drugs. These drugs have also been called "mind-expanding." In fact, these drugs do not expand the mind. The ability to think and to solve problems is reduced during an LSD "trip."

LSD, psilocybin, and mescaline differ primarily only in strength (LSD is by far the most potent); in terms of their effects on the

CATALOG OF DRUGS

Amphetamines	A stimulant drug; sometimes called "uppers," "pep pills," "whites," "bennies," or "speed."
Cocaine	A stimulant drug; sometimes called "coke," "gold dust," or "snow."
Caffeine	A stimulant drug found in coffee and tea.
Nicotine	A stimulant drug found in tobacco. Physically addictive.
Alcohol	A sedative drug found in beer, wine, and whiskey. Physically addictive.
Barbiturates	A sedative drug; sometimes called "downers," "reds," "blue heavens," or "yellow jackets." Physically addictive.
Morphine	A narcotic drug made from the opium poppy. Physically addictive.
Heroin	A narcotic drug made from morphine; sometimes called "horse," "junk," or "smack." Physically addictive.
Codeine	A narcotic drug similar to morphine but less potent. Physically addictive.
LSD	A psychedelic drug producing hallucinations; sometimes called "acid."
Marijuana	A psychedelic drug that is smoked or eaten; sometimes called "grass" or "pot." A more concentrated form is hashish or "hash."

mind and body they are essentially identical. Similarly, marijuana and hashish differ in strength (hashish is much more concentrated); the active ingredient in each is the same, a chemical called THC. For these reasons a discussion of LSD and marijuana is a discussion of all common psychedelic drugs.

■ *LSD*   In 1943 a Swiss researcher, Albert Hoffman, accidentally swallowed a tiny amount of LSD, a drug related to the fungus or rust sometimes found on rye or other grains. He described his experience as follows:

In the afternoon of 16 April 1943, when I was working on this problem, I was seized by a peculiar sensation of vertigo and restlessness. Objects, as well as the shape of my associates in the laboratory, appeared to undergo optical change. I was unable to concentrate on my work. In a dreamlike state I left for home,

where an irresistable urge to lie down overcame me. . . . With my eyes closed, fantastic pictures of extraordinary plasticity and intensive color seemed to surge towards me. After two hours this state gradually wore off.[50]

The first acid trip had occurred.

The subjective effects of LSD and related drugs can be described in several categories: (1) *perceptual effects*—colors are intensified, colors and sounds may fuse, illusions may occur in which objects are distorted or begin to shimmer, and hallucinations such as intricate geometrical patterns may appear; (2) *changes in thought*—feelings of great lucid insight and of great intellectual clarity and power develop, although when these "insights" are considered without the influence of the drug they often seem commonplace; (3) *mystical effects*—a feeling of religious awareness, awe, transcendence, or unity develops; (4) *adverse reactions*—psychotic episodes are produced, profound depression or despair occurs, extreme anxiety or panic may develop. Whether the acid trip will be a nightmare or a deeply positive experience is not predictable, although the setting in which the drug is taken makes a difference.

When the experience is a positive one, it can be dramatic and dazzling. One person described the trip as follows:

It was so packed with intensity of feeling, ecstasy, light, color, movement, laughter, tears, and visions that I cannot describe it or remember much more than the overwhelming effect. . . . I was carried, tossed on the creative sea of Being. Love poured through me. . . . Lights dazzled me. Colors spread out in iridescent designs. All was in play, in rhythmic motion. . . . I was penetrated and permeated with the many-splendored beauty of creation.[51]

■ *What LSD Does to Your Mind and Body* LSD increases heart rate and blood pressure and causes the pupils of the eyes to enlarge while the drug is in the system. Nausea, vomiting, and headache are common side effects. Persons on LSD are not able to sleep. It is possible that LSD affects human chromosomes, the structural basis for heredity;[52] however the evidence of chromosomal damage due to LSD intake is not conclusive. Some say yes;[52] some say no.[53] In any case, there is no evidence that women who have taken LSD give birth to malformed babies.[53] The research on the effects of LSD has not progressed far enough for us to know much about the long-term effects of the drug on the human brain.

People on LSD do not do well on tasks requiring attention or concentration; scores on IQ tests are reduced; coordination is poor.[37] In one study, sixteen men between the ages of 20 and 24 were given a battery of tests before and shortly after they were given a small dose of LSD. By comparing scores on the two series of tests, researchers could determine the influence of LSD. The results showed that LSD significantly interfered with memory and abstract thinking.[54] The differences in the scores resembled the differences obtained between the scores of normal subjects and the scores of schizophrenics on these same tests. LSD seems to disrupt most intellectual functions. The psychotic reaction that is sometimes caused by LSD has already been discussed.

LSD, contrary to some claims, does not have an aphrodisiac or sex-stimulating effect. The claim that LSD increases creativity has also not been proven. Some studies indicate that LSD increases creativity[55] and others indicate that it does not.[56] In one study four nationally prominent graphic artists created works of greater aesthetic value (according to a panel of fellow artists) while under the influence of LSD than without the drug.[57]

■ *Marijuana* Marijuana is a mixture of the flowers, leaves, seeds, and stems of the Indian hemp plant. The active drug in the plant, THC, may vary considerably in concentration from one batch of marijuana to another. The most potent concentration of THC is found in the sticky resin secreted by the plant, a substance called hashish (hash).

The effect of marijuana depends upon whether the smoker is naive or experienced with the drug. First-time users often do not feel much affected by the drug.[58] Feeling "high" or "stoned" on marijuana may require learning what aspects of behavior and experience should be attended to; this learning may take more than one experience with the drug. The marijuana "high" involves a feeling of relaxation, a sense of well-being, and an impression that your senses have been sharpened. The experience of time may be changed so that minutes seem like hours. Visual imagery and sensory experience gen-

Marijuana-smoking in Jamaica.

erally seem to be enhanced. The effects of marijuana and hashish are similar; they differ primarily in strength of effect.

■ *What Marijuana Does to Your Mind and Body* Marijuana increases heart rate, reduces muscular coordination, and causes reddened eyes.[58] Dryness of the mouth, nose, and eyes may occur. Appetite is usually increased. There is evidence that marijuana use is associated with lower levels of sex hormones in the body.[59] Contrary to some claims, marijuana does not cause a change in the size of the pupils of the eye; you cannot tell from the size of the pupils whether someone has been smoking marijuana.[58] There is no evidence of bodily harm as a consequence of marijuana use; the possible long-term effects of marijuana use, however, are not known at this time.

Like LSD, marijuana apparently can trigger a temporary psychotic reaction in individuals who are mentally unstable. Although these psychotic reactions usually end within a few days, some have lasted for several months;[60] psychotic reactions from marijuana are extremely rare. The capacity for sustained attention, for intellectual functions, and for estimating the passage of time are impaired under marijuana.[58] Individuals under the influence of marijuana often have difficulty carrying on coherent conversations; they often forget what they are saying and lose their place in their own sentences. This effect can be explained by studies that show the influence of marijuana on short-term memory. Memory of recent events (short-term memory) is significantly worse with marijuana.[61,62]

The facts about the dangers of marijuana are not yet known. There is evidence which suggests, but does not prove, that marijuana can produce personality and behavioral changes in the user. The possible dangers and the present illegality of the drug seem to be good reasons to use caution until the facts are in. The facts about the dangers of alcohol, barbiturates, and amphetamines are conclusive. When used in excess, these drugs cause physical addiction or severe bodily damage.

ⓢ Drugs are a powerful method for altering consciousness. Psychedelic or mind-altering drugs work by changing the level of activity of the brain cells. Sedatives decrease and stimulants increase brain activity. Psychedelic drugs affect parts of the brain involved in controlling and processing sensory information. All drugs have a toxicity level (an amount that will kill), and most drugs produce a tolerance for themselves. Drug tolerance leads to ever-increasing doses, with death resulting when the toxicity level is reached. Continued usage of some drugs leads to either a psychological dependence (a strong craving for the drug when it is not taken) or physical addiction (severe withdrawal symptoms when it is not taken) or both. Drug psychosis and flashbacks are other dangers of drug abuse. LSD and marijuana have profound effects on the mind and body. They distort perception and experience and disrupt most mental activity.

Summary

KEY QUESTIONS

1. What is the relation of your mind and body?
   Mind and body are not separate; changes in one are usually accompanied by changes in the other. Your body affects your mind; you can lose consciousness when your brain is injured. Your mind affects your body; prolonged mental stress can result in ulcers, muscle cramps, heart attacks, and skin disorders.

2. What is the physical basis of your consciousness?
   Your nerves and brain are the basis of your consciousness. The left and right sides of your brain have somewhat different functions; if they were disconnected, you would have two minds in one skull. The electrical activity of your brain generally changes in different states of consciousness.

3. How can altered states of consciousness be produced?
   Meditation, biofeedback, hypnosis, and drugs can produce altered states of consciousness in which your awareness of yourself and the world is changed.

4. What are the effects of drugs on consciousness?
   Drugs change the activity of the brain and, in so doing, change consciousness. Sedatives slow the brain down and stimulants speed it up. Drugs can increase or decrease awareness and can produce distortions in thinking, memory, and perception.

KEY CONCEPTS

consciousness	Mental life; the private awareness of thoughts, feelings, and perceptions.
nervous system	The body's communication system, consisting of the brain, spinal cord, and nerves.
neuron	The nerve cell, the fundamental unit of the nervous system.
nerve	A group of neurons strung together to form a cord.
cerebral hemispheres	The left and right halves of the brain.

corpus callosum	The broad band of nerves that connect the two hemispheres of the brain; when this is cut, a person has a "split brain," with two separate minds.
occipital lobe	A region at the back of each side of the brain that specializes in vision, but also serves other functions.
parietal lobe	A region at the top of each side of the brain that specializes in skin and body sensations, but also serves other functions.
frontal lobe	A region at the front of each side of the brain that specializes in planning, abstract thinking, and problem solving, but also serves other functions.
temporal lobe	A region along the side of each half of the brain that specializes in memory and hearing, but also serves other functions.
EEG	A machine that measures the electrical activity of the brain (brain waves).
alpha wave	A type of brain wave associated with relaxed awareness; it has a frequency of about 10 cycles per second.
altered states of consciousness	A level of awareness that is higher or lower than normal; a state of mind different from normal waking consciousness.
meditation	An ancient procedure for controlling attention and making the mind more aware, relaxed, and receptive.
biofeedback	A technique for measuring subtle changes in the body and revealing them; this technique can be used to provide people with knowledge of their heart rate, blood pressure, and brain waves.
hypnosis	A state of heightened suggestibility in which a person is under the influence of someone else.
sedative drugs	Drugs that reduce the level of arousal.
stimulant drugs	Drugs that increase the level of arousal and make people feel more energetic.
psychedelic drugs	Drugs that change perceptions and consciousness.
tolerance	An effect resulting from some drugs, in which ever-increasing doses are needed to obtain the same impact.
toxicity level	The amount of a drug that will kill.
psychological dependence	An effect produced by some drugs in which—if the drug is not available—there is a strong craving for it and a feeling of anxiety.
physical addiction	An effect produced by some drugs in which—if the drug is not taken—there are physical withdrawal symptoms, such as nausea and sweating.
flashback	A spontaneous recurrence of the drug effect at a time when the drug has not been taken.

11 Dreaming

CHAPTER OUTLINE

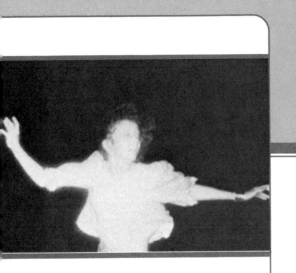

KEY QUESTIONS

1. How can you tell when someone is dreaming?
2. Does everybody dream?
3. What do you dream about?
4. What do your dreams mean?

Once upon a time I dreamt I was a butter-fly. . . . Suddenly I awakened, and there I lay, myself again. Now I do not know whether I was a man dreaming I was a butterfly, or whether I am now a butterfly dreaming I am a man.

Chuang Tzu, Chinese philosopher, 350 B.C.

Dreams are a puzzle and a mystery. They have been a source of wonder and a subject of study for thousands of years. Why do you dream? What do your dreams mean? Some believe that dreams carry important information—either that they are messages you send to yourself or that they are windows into the future.

The ancient Greeks and Egyptians used dreams to predict the future and to diagnose illness; they developed complex systems of dream interpretation.[1] A dream interpretation book written in India in the fourth century A.D. advised that if you dreamed of being swallowed by a fish, surrounded by crows, or of eating salt, then you would become ill or die.[2]

Arguments about the meaning and purpose of dreams have lasted for thousands of years. One reason that these arguments were never resolved was that dreams were private experiences, and because they could not be seen publicly, they were difficult to study. Modern science, however, has developed techniques that have made it possible for one person to study another person's dreaming.

Dream Monitoring with REM

About twenty years ago Aserinsky and Kleitman, two scientists studying sleep, noticed that when people were sleeping their eyes periodically fluttered and twitched. They found that if people were awakened during this period of eye movement, they usually reported that they were in the middle of a dream.[3]

The jerking movements of the eyes during sleep are called **REM (rapid eye movements).** During REM sleep the eyes can be observed moving back and forth beneath the eyelids. Changes in brain waves and in breathing also occur.

If you were wakened during REM sleep, you would probably be interrupted in the middle of a dream. If you were wakened during other periods of sleep, you would probably not be dreaming. This remarkable discovery has made it possible for one person to know fairly accurately when another person is dreaming, without disturbing that person's sleep.

Your eyes are closed when you dream, but they are moving in rapid jerks. Why? No one knows the reason for this activity. One possibility is that your eyes are following the action in your dream, just as they follow action when you are awake. From this point of view a dream is like a private movie, and your eyes move during REM to scan the images. This explanation of REM is called the **scanning hypothesis.**

If the scanning hypothesis is right, it ought to be possible to show a similarity between the direction of the eye movements and the direction of the movement of the dream images. One study showed that persons wakened following periods of vigorous eye movements reported having very active dreams, involving running, searching, or fighting; persons wakened following periods with relatively few eye movements reported inactive dreams, such as watching television or staring at a distant object.[4]

In another experiment electrical recordings (polygraphs) were taken of all eye movements made by subjects during the night. By looking at a written polygraph record, the investigator was able to tell when the eyes began to move and in what direction. At one point in the night one subject began to dream; the eye-movement record showed five equally spaced upward movements followed by a few seconds with only some small horizontal movements right before wakening.[5] The subject reported having the following dream:

Subject: *Right near the end of the dream I was walking up the back stairs of an old house. I was holding a cat in my arms.*

Experimenter: *Were you looking at the cat?*

Subject: *No, I was being followed up the steps by the Spanish dancer Escudero. I was annoyed at him and refused to look back at him or talk to him. I walked up, as a dancer would, holding my head high, and I glanced up at every step I took.*

Experimenter: *How many steps were there?*

Subject: *Five or six.*

In this case and in the majority of 121 other dreams studied by the investigator, eye movements were found to follow action in the dreams. Eye movements during dreams are therefore not random twitches but are sometimes meaningfully related to dream imagery. They allow us to investigate the puzzle of our dreams.

⑤ An important scientific breakthrough occurred when it was found that rapid eye movements (REM) usually accompany dreams. By watching their eyelids, you can tell when other people are dreaming. According to the scanning hypothesis, REM results from watching or scanning dream images.

Who Dreams?

Are you a dreamer? Many people report that they never dream or that they dream only rarely. These reports can now be checked. The new science of dream-monitoring has made it possible to discover who dreams and who does not.

Does Everybody Dream?

Among the hundreds of subjects who have been studied using the REM method, not a single person has been found who does not dream. Everybody dreams, even those who believe that they do not. Furthermore, everybody dreams several times every night. REM periods (and dreams that accompany them) occur about every hour and a half throughout the night. There is a cycle of about four or five REM periods each night. When people are wakened during one of the REM periods, they will almost always report being in the middle of a dream (even those who "never dream").

The Dreams of Children

A psychologist observed his sleeping daughter when she was less than two years old:

I went into her room one morning before she awoke and saw her eyes moving. Suddenly she said, "Pick me! Pick me!" I woke her and she immediately said, "Oh, Daddy, I was a flower."[6]

The REM method of monitoring the occurrence of dreams has been used with infants and children.[7] The results show that newborn infants spend about half of their total sleeping time dreaming (or about 9 hours per day); young children spend about 25 percent of their sleeping time in dreams (or about 2½ hours); adults spend about 20 percent of their sleeping time in dreams (or about 1½ hours); and adults over age fifty spend about 15 percent of their total sleeping time in dreams (or about 1 hour). The proportion of sleeping time each night that is spent in dreaming gradually decreases with age. The psychological basis for this remains unknown.

The Dreams of Animals

You may have watched a dog or cat sleeping quietly and breathing regularly; then suddenly the whiskers twitch, the tongue and paws move, and the eyelids flutter. The animal is dreaming.

All mammals that have been studied show cycles of REM activity during sleep; this includes people as well as the cat, dog, monkey, rat, rabbit, goat, mouse, opossum, and guinea pig.[8] While we know that animals experience REM activity during sleep, we do not know for certain whether they

Both animals and people dream.

experience dreams as we do. There is, however, some evidence that they do dream. One scientist studied the electrical activity in the brains of cats while they were sleeping.[9] He found that the area of the cat's brain responsible for vision was particularly active during REM periods, as if the cats were having visual experiences. Another investigator kept monkeys in a totally dark environment and conditioned them to press a lever near their paw whenever a visual image was presented to them;[10] during REM periods at night the monkeys would sometimes press the lever in their sleep, as if they were having visual experiences.

[S] Though some people never remember dreaming, everybody dreams several times each night. The amount of time spent dreaming declines as you grow older. It is likely that even animals dream.

When You Dream

Did you dream last night? You may not know whether you did or not; dreams are easily forgotten. However, by monitoring REM activity in sleep, it is now possible to know how often you dream and how long your dreams are.

How Often You Dream

How often do you dream? Although we have about four or five REM periods each night, we have more than four or five dreams. During a single REM period we may have several short dreams. The best estimate of the number of dreams ordinarily occurring per night is ten to twenty.[11] Within one REM period the boundary between one dream and the next is marked by body movements. If you observe sleepers and notice that their eyes are twitching, they are probably dreaming; if they then move their body, one dream is probably ending and a new one beginning.

How Long Your Dreams Are

How long are dreams? At one time it was thought that dreams only lasted a few seconds, that the sense of time within the drama of the dream was condensed into a mere moment of real time. We now know that this is false. The REM records suggest that for adults one to two hours are spent dreaming each night if all the REM periods are added together. Since we have several dreams each night, some are apparently short and some longer; some dreams of over thirty minutes have been recorded. These longer dreams tend to occur in the morning before waking.

Remembering Your Dreams

If everybody dreams several times every night, why is it that many people report dreaming only about once a month and other people report that they never dream? One group of persons who reported that they almost never dreamed was studied in a dream-monitoring laboratory.[12] They showed the same REM cycle as other subjects; furthermore, when they were wakened during a REM period they reported being in the middle of a dream. These results and the findings from similar studies[13] indicate that everybody dreams, even those who claim that they don't. The evidence leads to the conclusion that while everybody dreams every night, many dreams are forgotten. There are no nondreamers, but there are people who do not recall their dreams.[14]

A number of studies have found personality differences between people who do and do not recall their dreams.[14] For example, one study[15] found that people who frequently recall their dreams tend to be more sensitive, conservative, shy, stable, and self-assured. People who recalled their dreams less often were found to be more liberal, conscientious, adventurous, and worrying.

⑤ People dream 10 to 20 times each night during four or five REM periods. The passage of time in dreams is not condensed into a moment; most dreams last several minutes. Although everybody dreams, people differ in their ability to remember dreams. The tendency to remember dreams is associated with certain personality characteristics.

What You Dream About

Although each dream is a unique event, there are similarities among the dreams of different people. Certain kinds of dreams are fairly common: dreams of falling, of being attacked, of being chased, of appearing nude in public, of being lost, of getting married, and of making love.[16]

Dream Content

What do people dream about? Thousands of dreams have been analyzed and their contents studied.[17,18] The results of these studies show that most dreams do not take place in bizarre settings; most dream settings are commonplace—a living room, an automobile, a street, a classroom, or a field. The characters in dreams have been found half the time to be either the dreamer or friends and acquaintances of the dreamer; the remainder of the time the characters are strangers. What do people do in their dreams? Passive activities occupy a large part of dreams—talking, sitting, watching, or thinking; strenuous work-related activities are less common. What are the emotions experienced in dreams? The most common type of emotion is fear and anxiety; anger, excitement, and happiness are the next most common emotions felt. Although unpleasant emotions are more common in dreams than pleasant ones, they are usually not intense.

Dreams in Color

I dreamed I was floating in the air, carried by blue, red, and yellow balloons. Then the balloons became large black birds.

Some dreams appear to be in full natural color and others appear to be entirely in black

The dreamer usually awakens before being caught.

and white. Can you recall experiencing a "technicolor" dream? In a study of 3,000 dreams 29 percent were colored or had some color in them.[17] Women reported color in dreams more than men. There seemed to be no experienced difference between the color dreams and the black and white dreams. The relatively low percentage of color dreams may be somewhat surprising; a recent study, however, sheds some light on the puzzle. One researcher, studying dreams from persons wakened in REM periods, found that color was mentioned about 25 percent of the time.[19] Upon further questioning, however, the dreamers revealed that color was experienced in over 80 percent of the dreams. Apparently, color is experienced in most dreams, but is often not reported.

Nightmares

Nightmares often contain frightening events in which the dreamer is the victim of unpreventable psychological or physical harm. Often the dreamer is helpless in the terrible drama but awakens suddenly just before the final danger.[20] Particularly common nightmares are dreams of falling and of being attacked. A survey found that 80 percent of males and 81 percent of females have had both types of nightmares.[16] The following dreams are the nightmares of two young women.[21]

■ *Crazy Woman Dream*
I am in this house. It's a nice house, by a park. I'm alone in the house with this crazy woman. She's acting wild and unreasonable. I don't know exactly like what, something in an insane asylum. It was a very nice house set in a park that was very nice. She was very hostile and at the same time she wanted to hold me. I felt she wanted to hold me, to crush me, to kill me. She hated me very much. I dropped my keys and she wouldn't let me look for them. I found them again and dropped them again, and because I had lost them I had to stay in this house with her. . . . The situation is too horrible. My feelings were great horror, disgust, and fear of this crazy woman.

■ *Tiny Cobra Dream*

There were many tiny cobras. They were about a foot long and sandy colored. This was all in a room, and there were book-shelves. . . . The cobras were concealed everywhere. They came up everywhere I went. They could come out of a book. There were other people around and I was pleading with them not to do it. They had something to do with having these snakes come out. I pleaded with them not to do it because I was so scared of snakes. I didn't kill the snakes. I was too scared to touch them. I was pleading with the people. They were doing it on purpose. They were hiding the snakes. I was tense and scared. I woke up petrified. I kept waking up and I was too frightened to go to sleep again. I kept waking myself up lest I dream about the snakes again.

Sleepwalking

Most sleepwalking occurs in childhood, but it sometimes recurs in later years. The sleepwalker behaves like a robot, moving slowly and with apparent purpose. Most sleepwalking is not remembered upon wakening. This may result from the fact that sleepwalking does not occur during the normal dreaming cycle of sleep, when REM activity is present.[22] Sleepwalkers often will return to bed if gently interrupted, but if abruptly wakened they will experience a period of extreme confusion. An extraordinary case of sleepwalking is described below:

A twenty-two-year-old man was subject to repeated episodes of sleepwalking. One night while asleep he climbed from the window of his apartment, twelve stories above the ground, and walked on a narrow (eighteen-inch wide) outside ledge to another window. He returned to bed without waking.

A horrified roommate awoke in time to watch

the latter part of this performance and his friend's return to the room. He had been afraid to move or to comment for fear of awakening the patient, who might have become startled and fallen to the street below.

When the sleepwalker was awakened, he had no recollection of the incident. He refused to believe it as described, until confronted with his sooty feet and, in the morning, by the clear footprints which he had left on the ledge.[23]

⑤ Most dreams are fairly commonplace, even dull, and involve familiar settings and characters. Although many people do not remember experiencing color in their dreams, studies show that most dreams are in color. Nightmares are far less common than normal dreams, but most people occasionally experience them. Sleepwalking, unlike dreams, does not occur during REM sleep.

Your Need to Dream

If dreams are nothing more than the "confused results of indigestion," as Socrates believed, then it would make little difference whether you dreamed or not; but if dreaming serves an important psychological function, then a certain amount of dreaming may be necessary.

Do you need to dream? Psychologists have studied this question by preventing people from dreaming, then observing the consequences. In one study an attempt was made to prevent subjects from dreaming without interfering with the length of their sleep periods.[24] Each time subjects began to dream, as indicated by REM activity, they were awakened, kept awake for a few minutes, and then allowed to go back to sleep. This procedure for preventing dreaming is called **dream deprivation.** For each of three

Do you need to dream?

to seven consecutive nights subjects were prevented from dreaming, and then for several following nights they were allowed to sleep normally. At a later period the subjects came back to the laboratory and underwent another series of awakenings; this time, however, they were wakened at times when they were not showing REM activity.

What was the effect of dream deprivation? First, on their "recovery" nights following their nights of dream deprivation, they showed a "rebound effect"—the amount of time spent dreaming increased greatly. It was as if the subjects had to make up for the lost dreams by dreaming overtime. This suggests that a certain amount of dreaming is psychologically necessary. Similar results have been shown for animals.[25] A second result of dream deprivation is the stress it imposes on subjects. Some subjects showed anxiety, irritability, and difficulty in concentrating; five subjects developed a substantial increase in appetite during the period of dream deprivation; another subject became agitated and quit the study in a panic. The psychological changes observed in the subjects disappeared as soon as the subjects were allowed to dream.[24]

Why do we need to dream? Why should dream deprivation cause psychological problems? No one knows for sure, but one dream researcher, Charles Fisher, believes that dreaming is the normal person's journey into insanity or psychosis:

The dream is the normal psychosis and dreaming permits each and every one of us to be quietly and safely insane every night of our lives.[26]

Ⓢ Dreaming is psychologically necessary. People prevented from dreaming show anxiety, irritability, and stress; then, when they are permitted to dream, they show a rebound effect by dreaming overtime.

What Your Dreams Mean

Do you believe that your dreams are just scrambled images or do you believe that they are revealing and meaningful? According to the Talmud, "A dream which is not explained is like a letter which has not been read." The idea is that dreams are messages that should be understood. By way of contrast, a famous psychologist of the last century wrote that dreams made no sense and could be compared to the ten fingers of a man who knows nothing about music, wandering over the keys of a piano.

If dreams are meaningful, some basis for interpreting their meaning must be developed; the language of dreams must be studied in order to be understood. The first systematic theory of dreams was developed by Sigmund Freud and published in his book *The Interpretation of Dreams*.[27]

Freudian Theory

In Plato's *Republic* Socrates says that dreams reveal our hidden desires: "In all of us, even in good men, there is a lawless, wild beast nature, which peers out in sleep." That, in essence, is Freud's theory of dreams. According to the **Freudian theory of dreams,** dreams reveal unconscious wishes and these wishes are represented symbolically.

■ *Wish Fulfillment* According to Freud, many of our wishes—particularly those concerning sex and aggression—are inhibited or suppressed. We are unconscious of their existence; their presence in our unconscious is made known only when they "peer out" when we sleep. Freud's principle of **wish fulfillment** states that unconscious wishes are revealed and satisfied in dreams. Dreams, Freud believed, were the "royal road to the unconscious"; by understanding dreams we can know the contents of the unconscious mind. Wishes that we could not imagine acting out in our waking state are played out in the drama of our dreams. It is "safe" to dream our wishes, because in sleep we cannot act on the basis of them. Freud wrote:

No matter what impulses from the normally inhibited unconscious may prance upon the stage, we need feel no concern; they remain harmless since they are unable to set in motion the motor apparatus by which alone they might modify the external world. The state of sleep guarantees the security of the citadel that must be guarded.[27]

Nightmares do not seem to support Freud's wish-fulfillment principle; it is hard to believe that the frightening events of the nightmare express an unconscious wish. Try to recall a nightmare you have had. Do you think you wanted the frightening events actually to happen?

Dreams do not seem to reflect needs or wishes in any clear fashion. Researchers have tested the wish-fulfillment theory. Participants in one psychology experiment reported their dreams on nights following a period of at least twenty-four hours with no intake of fluids whatsoever.[4] The subjects had dry lips and mouths, had difficulty salivating, and were extremely thirsty. In the fifteen dreams that were recorded, there was no instance of a dream involving drinking or an awareness of thirst. These results are not very consistent with Freud's wish-fulfillment principle of dreaming.

■ *Hidden Meanings* Freud believed that a hidden psychic censor prevented unconscious impulses from reaching awareness; this same censor disguised the impulses and wishes revealed in dreams so that they appeared only symbolically. Dreams could

What would Freud say about the latent content of this dream?

be interpreted at two different levels: the **manifest content** of the dream consists of the events of the dream as they were experienced and reported by the dreamer; the **latent content** of the dream is the true meaning that is hidden behind the dream images. The manifest content is the surface content of the dream and the latent content is the hidden meaning of the dream. The same hidden or latent meaning could be represented in many different manifest dreams. Just as, for example, the literary theme of sin and salvation has been represented in many different plays and novels. The underlying theme of these novels (the latent content) is the same, but the actual plots and characters (manifest content) are different.

The following three dreams were experienced by one man in the same night and seem to be united by a common theme.[28] The dreamer was awakened by a bell when his eyes showed REM activity.

Dream One

I was dreaming something about a woman. The last scene was something about some kind of involvement where she's trying to do something about an inheritance and I'm trying to thwart her. I must have thwarted her pretty well, but she still has something she can do, and I'm saying—we're in some kind of dining room—"Let me see your trump card. Let me just look at you." I went over and looked at her in the face and I said, "How can I possibly be afraid of you?" She wouldn't let me look her in the eye. She just kind of turned away a little. And just as the bell went off I was chasing her out and I shouted, "You god damn bitch." The woman was a woman I'd never seen before.

Dream Two

I was watching a guy standing in the street. Suddenly he raised his gun and shot a woman in the back. I'm sure it was a woman. And I

ran. There was a little frame house sitting on the street. Just a few rooms, five or six. I ran in the front door and started running out the back. I was afraid this guy would come out the back door. Somehow I knew he was on my side, yet I was afraid he would come after me. I felt frightened and anxious when I woke up.

Dream Three

This dream started out at a—no, it didn't. Oh, Lord, it started out with Sara Smith (pseudonym). She seduced me. That's how it started. I don't remember how we got undressed or anything, but we got undressed and she was kind of neurotic and I had a queer feeling I was being manipulated. She scorned any way of conventional intercourse. I'd try to do it conventionally and she'd just sneer at me. . . . Finally I got mad and left.

Although the characters and the story line of each dream differ, the underlying attitude of conflict toward women runs through each dream. These dreams therefore could be seen as different ways of expressing the same basic meaning.

■ *Dream Symbols* Since the true meaning of dreams, according to Freud, is expressed symbolically, understanding the language of dreams requires symbolic interpretation. For example, a woman reported a frightening dream of "tiny winged men who wanted to come in through my window." The dream was interpreted, from a Feudian point of view, to have the following latent meaning: "The tiny men as the penis, the wings as the erection, and the window as the female genital are all clear."[29] An object that represents or symbolizes the penis is called a **phallic symbol.** Many objects in dreams Freud interpreted to be phallic symbols representing the penis; for example, the penis may be disguised as a stick, umbrella, gun, plowshare, knife, snake, fish, or any object that is relatively elongated. Freud interpreted any hollow object or container—such as a box, chest, oven, or cave—as a disguised vagina. A young married woman experienced the following dream a few days after she had, for the first time, experienced a completely loving acceptance of the sexual act.

I saw a dark brown fertile field in which a plow was cutting large furrows. Suddenly I myself became the field and the sharp steel plow went easily through the length of my body and cut me into two halves. Although it hurt, it was indescribably beautiful. I experienced myself as the plowed-up field, and the furrow as my own flesh, but it was not bleeding.[30]

Cognitive Theory

An alternative to the Freudian theory of dreams is the **cognitive theory of dreams,** which considers dreams to consist of thoughts and memories similar to mental activity when awake. When we are asleep, information from the environment is not available and action toward the environment is not possible; in this state we periodically construct thoughts and images from stored information and old memories, and these constructions are called dreams. Not all memories are constructed into dreams. Only those memories that have been recently "activated" by emotions are formed into dreams. Excitement, fear, anger, and other emotions bring certain memories to life. From this point of view the connection between the concerns of the day and the dreams of the night can be explained by assuming that memories from the day which have been associated with emotional arousal are those most available for construction into dreams.[31] Calvin Hall, a proponent of the cognitive the-

ory of dreams, characterizes a dream as "a highly private showing of the dreamer's thoughts."[32] Hall writes:

Dreaming is thinking that occurs during sleep. It is a peculiar form of thinking in which the conceptions or ideas are expressed not in the form of words or drawings, as in waking life, but in the form of images, usually visual images. In other words, the abstract and invisible ideas are converted into concrete and visible images. By an odd process which we do not understand, the sleeping person can see his own thoughts embodied in the form of pictures. When he communicates his dream to another person, he is communicating his thoughts, whether he knows it or not.[17]

Evidence for the cognitive theory of dreams comes from the observation that dreams sometimes involve productive mental activity, similar to mental activity when awake. For example, the poem "Kubla Khan" was composed in a dream by Samuel Taylor Coleridge; the plot of the story *Dr. Jekyll and Mr. Hyde* was dreamed by Robert Louis Stevenson; and the structure of the benzene molecule was discovered in a dream by Friedrich Kekulé, a German chemist.[6]

Contact with the Spirit World Through Dreams

A Malaysian people called the Senoi use dreams as tools to understand themselves and to obtain contact with "the powers of the spirit world."[33] Every morning at breakfast the family members share their dreams. Elders analyze the dreams of children and teach the art of dream interpretation. The Senoi believe that the dreamer can actively enter and change a dream while it is in progress. For example, a dream of falling may be changed into a dream of flying. Children are taught that their dreams are their own property and that they control what happens in them.

For the Senoi all dreams have a purpose, and the purpose must be understood. Dreams of falling are believed to be the quickest way to get in contact with the powers of the spirit world. In such dreams the "falling spirits" are attracting you to their spiritual universe, and you should learn from the journey. If a child reports a frightening dream of falling, an elder may answer, "This is wonderful. It is one of the best kinds of dreams. Now, where did you fall and what did you discover?"[33]

[S] Two major viewpoints about dreams are the Freudian theory and the cognitive theory. According to the Freudian theory, dreams are an example of the principle of wish fulfillment; that is, dreams represent unconscious wishes. Freud believed that dreams had two levels of meaning: the manifest content (the dream images as experienced) and the latent content (the hidden meaning of dreams). According to the cognitive theory, dreams are constructed from thoughts and memories that have made an emotional impression on the dreamer; they are similar to waking mental activity.

Summary

KEY QUESTIONS

1. How can you tell when someone is dreaming?

   Until recently, dreaming was private and mysterious and could not easily be studied. Now, however, we know that you can generally tell when other people are dreaming by watching their eyelids during sleep. Dreaming tends to occur when the eyes move rapidly back and forth; this causes the eyelids to flutter and jerk.

2. Does everybody dream?

   Studies have shown that everybody dreams several times each night, although many people do not remember their dreams the next morning.

3. What do you dream about?

Although the content of dreams depends on the person who is dreaming, some kinds of dreams are fairly common. Dreams of falling, of being attacked, of being chased, and of making love are common. Studies have shown that most dreams take place in common settings like in a room, on a street, or in a field.

4. What do your dreams mean?

Two theories have been proposed to explain the content of dreams: the Freudian theory and the cognitive theory. Freud believed that dreams reveal unconscious wishes, but that the wishes are represented symbolically. The cognitive theory considers dreams to be like the thoughts and memories that a person has while awake.

KEY CONCEPTS

rapid eye movements (REM)	Periodic rapid movements of eyes during sleep; usually accompanied by dreams.
scanning hypothesis	The idea that eye movements during dreams result from watching or scanning dream images.
dream deprivation	A condition caused by waking people each time REM begins, so as to prevent dreaming.
Freudian theory of dreams	The theory that dreams reveal unconscious wishes that are expressed symbolically in dream images.
cognitive theory of dreams	The theory that dreams consist of fragments of thoughts and memories that have been associated with emotions.
wish fulfillment	The idea that unconscious wishes are revealed and satisfied in dreams.
manifest content	The events of the dream as they are experienced.
latent content	The hidden "true" meaning of dreams.
phallic symbol	A dream image—such as a pencil or snake—that symbolically represents the penis.

12 Perceiving

CHAPTER OUTLINE

KEY QUESTIONS

1. How do your senses gather information from the world?
2. How is your perceptual world different from your external physical world?
3. How is your perceptual world built?
4. How does your perceptual world differ from the inner experiences of other people?

How can you see through someone else's eyes?

In order for you to understand other people you must be able to understand the world as they experience it. But people experience different perceptual worlds; there are individual and cultural differences in perception.

You see the world differently from other people. Have you ever argued with someone about the size of an object you both saw or about the color of something you were both looking at? Even when you agree with someone about the color of an object, your experience of it may differ. You and a friend may agree that an apple is red—but what does this mean? You and your friend may be using the word "red" differently. For example, people who are color-blind may not be able to tell the difference between the colors red and green. Yet they often describe

229

apples as "red" and leaves as "green." Growing up around persons with normal color vision, they have learned that the words "apple" and "red" go together, as do the words "leaf" and "green." Words do not necessarily reflect experience.

If people experience the world differently, and if language is not always a valid indicator of experience, how can you ever understand the perceptual world of another person? You can start by understanding how the perceptual world is built.

The Human Senses

Aristotle wrote, "Nothing is in the mind which does not pass through the senses." The human senses are the means we have of gathering information about the world we live in and about our own bodies. The senses

What the man sees is not what the camera records.

respond to different aspects of the physical world, allowing us to know the world in many different ways. The eye, ear, nose, tongue, skin, and muscles all contain specialized cells called **sensory receptors;** each receptor is sensitive to a different kind of physical energy, such as light, pressure, or vibration. Sensory receptors react to stimulation by sending electrochemical impulses along nerves to the brain.

These impulses form the raw material of my perceptual experience. If you want to know my perceptual experience, it would help for you to know the physical energy in my environment, to know whether I possessed receptors sensitive to that energy, and to know whether my receptors were in a position to receive that energy. Knowing these things, however, you still would not understand my perceptual experience. Perceptual experience is different from physical energy.

The Perceptual World Is Not the Physical World

The relation between energy and experience is not at all exact. The qualities of the internal perceptual world are not the same as the qualities of the external physical world. For example, to describe your experience of a sound, you might refer to its loudness and its pitch. Sound, pitch, and loudness are characteristics of your experience, however, and not characteristics of the physical world. The primary physical origin of sound is waves of pressure in the air caused by something vibrating. The intensity of pressure is related to the experience of loudness and the frequency of the pressure waves is related to the experience of pitch.

The *psychological* characteristics of light—brightness, hue, and saturation—are primarily determined by the *physical* dimensions of intensity, dominant wavelength, and purity. Color is a characteristic of our experience, not of the physical world. Different physical events can stimulate the same psychological experience. Our perception of the hue "yellow" can arise from light of a particular wavelength uniquely characteristic of yellow, or from the mixture of red and green light, or from pressure on the eyeballs. Obviously, perceptual experience cannot be a copy of physical reality.

Sensitivity and Thresholds

Your eyes, ears, and other senses are extremely sensitive. But there are sounds too quiet and lights too dim for you to detect. You can hear the ticking of your watch when it is close to your ear, but not when it is 50 feet away. Your sensory receptors require a certain minimum amount of physical energy before they can respond. This minimum level of energy is called the **absolute threshold.** A light that is so dim that it cannot be seen is below the absolute threshold; its energy is below the minimum required for the eye to respond.

People differ in their sensitivity. You may be more or less sensitive to sounds than other people; that is, your absolute threshold for sound may be above or below average. Scientists have estimated the average absolute thresholds for the different senses. They estimate that the threshold for vision is the amount of light that would come from a candle 30 miles away on a dark night; the threshold for hearing is the amount of sound from a ticking watch 20 feet away in a quiet room; and the threshold for touch is the amount of pressure felt if the wing of a fly fell on your cheek from a distance of about half an inch.[1]

Tea taster tasting tea.

Sensory Aftereffects

Each perception leaves an aftereffect. A **sensory aftereffect** is a sensory experience that continues its influence after the external stimulation has stopped. The past is with you now and is affecting what you see. To demonstrate this to yourself, place your right hand in a pan of warm water and your left hand in a pan of cool water. After a minute place both hands in a pan of lukewarm water. The water will feel warm to your left hand and cool to your right hand, both at once. Your perception of the water is affected by where each hand was a moment ago, by your immediate past history. The loudness of a particular sound is judged very differently depending upon the loudness of the few sounds immediately preceding it.[2] An object feels heavy after you have recently lifted a

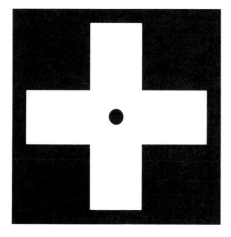

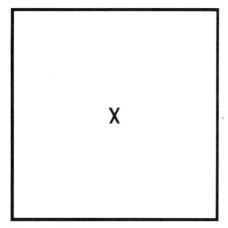

Negative afterimage.

bright. After you have been outside a few minutes, your eyes lose their dark adaptation and you can see the colors around you. What is bright and what is dark obviously depends upon what you have recently seen. Your perceptual experiences occur within the context of your immediate past.

Objects that you have just seen leave their prints on your eyes for a few seconds. You may remember seeing a flashbulb go off when someone took your picture and afterward seeing a black spot wherever you looked. A strong white light leaves an aftereffect that is black, a perception called a **negative afterimage.** Hold this book in bright light and fixate on the dot in the center of the white cross. Focus on the black dot without moving your eyes while you slowly count to fifty. Then look at the *X* in the center of the white square. The negative afterimage, a black cross, should be visible; if it isn't, blink your eyes a time or two. The negative afterimage results from the fact that the pigment in the visual cells on the retina is bleached by light and takes a while to recover. During the recovery period the area that is bleached is less sensitive and gives rise to the perception of a gray image in the shape of the bleached area.

series of light objects, but it feels very light after you have recently lifted a series of heavy objects.[3]

When you walk into a movie theater, you can see very little because you are unaccustomed to the dark—your eyes are not **dark-adapted.** After a few minutes, you begin to be able to see the faces of the people around you as your eyes adapt to the dark. If you walk out of the theater into the afternoon sun, your eyes are dazzled by the light, the colors seem washed out and pale, everything is

The Eye

Your eye is a wonderful device. In some ways it is like an extension of your brain and has a kind of intelligence of its own. It is not simply a passive receiver of light, but is actively involved in seeking and processing information.

■ *The Eye Is Not a Camera* Sometimes we think of our perceptual experiences as if they were pictures inside our heads. You may think that the eye is like a camera; there is some validity to that analogy.

1. Both the eye and the camera collect light and focus it upside-down on a light-sensitive surface. The camera uses film containing a chemical that changes when exposed to light. The back of the eye consists of a coating of small cells, the **retina,** also containing a chemical that changes when exposed to light.

2. The image in a camera can be focused by adjusting the lens. The image in the eye is focused by an adjustment of the **lens** made by small muscles in the eye. Muscles connected to the lens tighten to increase its curvature, causing nearby objects to come into focus. You can feel the tension of these tightened lens muscles by bringing this book close to your eyes.

3. The amount of light entering the camera is controlled by enlarging or contracting a hole behind the lens called the aperture or *f* stop. The amount of light entering the eye is controlled by enlarging or contracting a small hole in front of the lens called the **pupil.** In bright light the pupil is small and looks like a black dot in the center of the eye. In the dark the pupil enlarges to admit more light to the eye. The pupil is surrounded by a muscle called the **iris;** the iris is the part of your eye that makes you blue, brown, or green eyed.

But the eye is not a camera; perceptions are not copies of the external world. You cannot know my perception by knowing only the external world, although that knowledge is a start. Cameras are passive receivers of information; the eye actively searches for information. Cameras record; the perceptual system constructs. The camera registers all, but perception is highly selective. The camera has no memory, but perception learns from the past.

■ *Your Blind Spot* Our perceptual worlds are personal constructions, not copies of the physical world. A simple demonstration of this fact can be made by considering the **blind spot.** Although many people are never aware of it, the field of vision for each eye has a rather large blind area. Because the visual fields of the two eyes overlap somewhat, when we look at the world with both eyes there is not a large area in which we are blind. But looking with only one eye, there is a large "hole" in the perceptual world, an area in which we are absolutely blind. The blind spot results from the fact that there is on the retina of each eye a small spot where the visual nerve **(optic nerve)** from the brain joins the eye. This spot lacks visual receptor cells and is therefore insensitive to light.

The human eye.

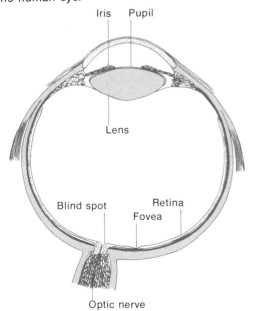

Iris   Pupil

Lens

Blind spot   Retina
Fovea

Optic nerve

X ━━━━━━━━━━━━━━━━━━━━━━━━━━━━●━━━━━━━━━━━━━━━━━━━━━━━━━━━━

Find your blind spot.

You can find your blind spot by looking at the *X* above with your right eye only (close your left eye) from a viewing distance of about ten inches. When you are focused on the *X*, an image of the *X* is projected on the **fovea** of the eye, a part of the retina that is most densely packed with light-sensitive cells. When you have done this, move the book back and forth, closer and farther from your eye, while keeping your eye focused on the *X*. At the right distance from your eye, you will notice that the spot on your right will disappear completely—it will be in your blind area. If the book is brought either closer or farther away from your eye, the spot will reappear as it leaves the blind area. When the spot has disappeared, what do you see in its place? Oddly enough, not a hole in the page, but paper, as if we could see underneath the spot. When the spot has disappeared, many people even see the black line as continuous through the blind area.

If you have a large blind area in your visual field, why is it that you do not see a "hole" in the wall of the room when you look at it with one eye only? If you have a large blind area in your visual field, why is it that you did not see a large "hole" in the page of this book when the spot on the page disappeared? Somehow you "fill in" this void. You repair the hole, in a sense. And the material used for the patch has the same appearance and color as the surrounding field. Apparently, your perceptual world is different from the physical world; it is in part your own construction.

■ *Wiggling Your Eye* The eye is not a camera. If a camera is moved, the image is blurred. The eye is remarkably different.

Your vision fades completely *unless* your eye is moved. Normally, your eyes are continuously in motion, with occasional small jerks and trembling. When the image on the retina is stabilized by using specially designed optical equipment, your visual image disappears rapidly. The movement of your eyes is necessary for vision.

How can you see a world that is still if your eyes are always moving? As your eye jerks and trembles, the image on the retina is in constant motion, yet your perceptual world is stable. You see the words on this page as still, not as moving, in spite of the rapid and continuous movement of your eyes. Somehow from the flux of moving images on the retina of your eye you build stability; you construct an experiential world that is still.

In the building of that stability, mistakes are sometimes made. You can cause your perceptual system to make a mistake quite easily. Close your left eye now, and read this with your right eye only. Place the forefinger of your right hand carefully against the outer corner of your right eye. Apply gentle pressure to this corner rhythmically, nudging your eye by wiggling your finger. By doing this, you are moving your eye back and forth slightly. You will observe that your perceptual world also moves—the page of this book jumps back and forth. Yet when you move your eye back and forth normally, without the use of your finger, your perceptual world is quite stable. In both cases your eye is moving and the image on this page is moving back and forth on your retina as your eye moves. In one case you build a stable percept and in the other case you do not. Why?

One explanation of this difference is that your brain organizes perceptual stability on the basis of information it receives about eye movement.[4] Normally your eye is moved by your eye muscles; when your eye is moved by your finger, your brain is tricked and mistakenly assumes that something in the world is moving.

⑤   The perceptual world is not the same as the physical world. Color and sound are psychological experiences, not physical characteristics. Your sensory receptors, such as those in your eye or ear, respond to the energy in the world; but the energy must be intense enough to be above your absolute threshold in order for you to experience it. Sometimes the effect of stimulation persists, causing a sensory aftereffect such as a negative afterimage. The retina, lens, and pupil of your eye resemble the structures of a camera, but there are major differences in how the eye and the camera function.

Vase or face?

The Organization of Perception

Perception goes beyond the information provided by the senses. We experience a world of objects and people, not a world of points of light and patches of color. We experience a world of structure and relationship, not a world of unconnected surfaces. The raw material given by the senses is used to build the world of our experience. We not only *sense* the physical energy in the world, we struggle to *make sense* of it by organizing it into meaningful experiences.

Principles of Organization

In order to see and make sense of an object, you must first be able to distinguish it as an object; you must be able to separate it from its background. As you look at this book, you see an object separated from the table, wall, or floor that is its background. As you read this page, you see black words standing out against a white background. Perception requires that you separate figures (books, people, words) from their background. You tend to organize what you see into what psychologists call figure and ground. This is the **figure-ground principle** of perception.

How perception is organized was an important issue for psychologists at the turn of the century. Some argued that perception could be understood only by breaking it down into its elements, by analyzing it into its separate parts. Others argued that perception is an organized whole, and is more than the simple sum of its parts. This latter view was stressed by Max Wertheimer, a German psychologist interested in perception.

One day in 1910, while on a train trip, Wertheimer had a sudden insight: if two lights blink on and off in rapid succession, you see continuous movement. Wertheimer got off the train at the next stop, at a city he had not intended to visit, and went in search of a flashing light to test his idea. After two years of experimenting with this illusion, he published a paper describing his discovery. The illusion of movement was called the **phi phenomenon,** and is the foundation of the movie industry: a rapid succession of "still" pictures creates an illusion of continuous movement. For Wertheimer, a gentle man with a walrus moustache, the discovery provided a new framework for psychology—*the whole is different from the sum of the parts.* The parts of a movie consist of a series of frames, each without movement; the sum, however, consists of movement. This insight was the beginning of a new school of psy-

Dot patterns appear to be organized, forming varying subgroups.

chology, the **Gestalt movement,** which stressed the significance of wholes, patterns, and relationships among elements.

The Gestalt movement showed that all perception was organized and patterned. Rather than seeing random and unrelated patches of light, you tend to organize what you see into patterns and relationships. The separate figures that you see are themselves organized and structured. Things that are similar in form or size and things that are close to each other are seen as belonging together. In fact, you tend to see patterns even when no actual patterns exist. Your tendency to organize what you see into patterns or groups is called the **grouping principle** of perception.

The grouping principle was studied in great detail early in this century by the Gestalt psychologists. They observed that ambiguous collections of elements tended spontaneously to form subgroups; this grouping followed certain rules of organization:

Rule of Proximity The term proximity means closeness; the proximity rule of organization is that things that are close together seem to go together or belong together; close things are grouped.

Max Wertheimer

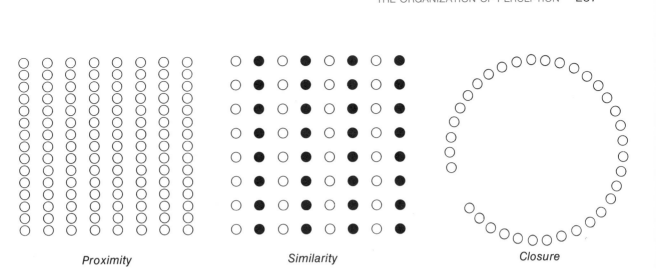

| Proximity | Similarity | Closure |

Rule of Similarity   According to the similarity rule, things are grouped together that resemble each other or are similar; groups or classes tend to be formed of similar elements.

Rule of Closure   The term closure refers to being closed or complete; according to the closure rule, areas tend to be seen as closed or bounded; patterns tend to be seen as complete or closed.   For example, a broken circle that is almost closed—but not quite—will be seen as completely closed and unbroken.

Illusions

Perceptions are organized and go beyond the information given by the senses.   Perceptions are not copies of reality; indeed, perceptions are often distorted interpretations of the external world.   Perceptual distortions are common and are collectively called **illusions.**

In the arrow illusion the two straight lines consisting of the shafts of the arrows are in fact the same length, but they appear to almost everyone as different in length.   The wings of the arrowheads are responsible for causing the illusory difference in length.   In

the railway illusion the two horizontal parallel lines are in fact the same length, but to almost everyone they appear different in length. The slanting lines on each side cause the two lines to appear different in length.

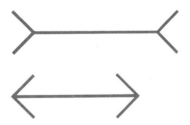

Which arrow shaft is longer?

Which cross piece is longer?

Why are your eyes fooled by these simple line drawings? Psychologists have proposed many different theories over the years to explain the phenomena of illusions, but none is completely satisfactory. Whatever the process is, learning must be involved. Psychologists have found that people living in different cultures experience the illusions differently;[5] for example, people who have not experienced railways are much less likely to experience the railway illusion.[6]

Hallucinations

Sometimes a person's perceptual world is so uniquely individual that it is wholly unrelated to the physical environment. Perceptions that are not related to physical stimulation are called **hallucinations.** All perceptions involve some constructions or distortions but most use as building material the information from the external world obtained by the senses. Hallucinations, however, are built entirely from internal processes; some are clearly related to such internal information as feelings, desires, or memories.[7]

■ *Schizophrenia* Hallucinations can be caused by a variety of conditions; they occur with certain forms of schizophrenia, with injury of the temporal lobe of the brain, and with intoxication by certain drugs. Schizophrenic hallucinations are almost always auditory ("hearing voices") and are typically believed by the patient to be real (not imaginary). When schizophrenic hallucinations are visual, they often involve seeing a nonexistent person or animal in an otherwise normal perceptual world.[8] Persons seen or heard in schizophrenic hallucinations are typically historic or religious figures such as Napoleon, Hitler, Christ, or God.

■ *LSD and Mescaline* In contrast to the hallucinations of schizophrenia, those caused by drugs such as LSD or mescaline are almost always visual and only rarely include perceiving nonexistent persons. For example, the writer Aldous Huxley reports his experiences with the drug mescaline:

Half an hour after swallowing the drug I became aware of a slow dance of golden lights. A little later there were sumptuous red surfaces swelling and expanding from bright nodes of energy that vibrated with a continuously changing, patterned life. At another time the closing of my eyes revealed a complex of grey structures, within which pale bluish spheres kept emerging into intense solidarity and, having emerged, would slide noiselessly upwards, out of sight.[9]

Mescaline and LSD hallucinations often involve perceiving certain abstract visual patterns such as spirals, lattices, or webs. The drug-induced hallucination, in contrast to the hallucination associated with schizophrenia, is rarely believed to be real by the person experiencing it. That is, the person knows that it is a hallucination. In a small but significant percentage of the cases, these drugs cause a psychotic reaction, a continuing "bad trip." Hallucinations are extreme examples demonstrating that the perceptual world is different from the physical world.

S Sensory information is organized into meaningful experience. Two principles of perception are that you organize what you see, first, into figure and ground, and second, into patterns or groups. Illusions and hallucinations demonstrate that perceptual experiences are organized constructions that go beyond the information provided by the senses.

Individual Differences

The world of my experience is a personal construction. While it is usually related to the world of physical energy, sometimes—if I hallucinate—it is not. But if my perceptual world is a personal construction, it is likely to be different from yours. I am a different person, with different feelings, needs, and memories. The fact that there are cultural differences in the experience of certain visual illusions indicates that experiential factors are important in perception. Apparently if you want to understand my perceptual world, you must take into account not only the physical energy in my environment and how my perceptual system changes that energy into experiences but also the extensive effects of my unique past experiences.

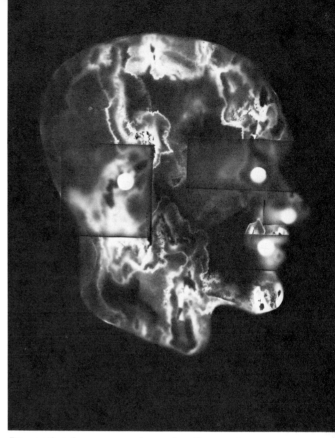

Perception is a personal construction.

The Effect of the Past

The world of our experience is always in the past, since a fraction of a second always passes between an event and our perception of it. But perception is linked to the past in a more significant way. What we see now is always compared with what we have seen. To *recognize* an object or event is to categorize it as something familiar, known, seen before. Thus without the effect of past perception there would be no recognition. Furthermore, your perception of something right now is affected by what you expect to see, in addition to what you have learned to see and what you have just previously seen.

■ *The Red Six of Spades* Research shows that you tend to see what you expect to see.[10] In a perception experiment using a tachistoscope—a machine capable of pre-

senting pictures for just a fraction of a second—people were briefly shown pictures of different playing cards.[11] Some of these playing cards were not true to life. For example in a real deck of cards spades are black, so when individuals were shown a picture of a *red* six of spades, some reported that they saw a black six of spades, some said they saw a red six of hearts, and some said they saw a purple six of spades. Seeing a purple six of spades is a kind of compromise between the reality of the red and the expectancy of the black. If your expectancies are different from mine, your perceptions will be different from mine.

■ *The World Is Upside-down* To some extent what you see is what you learned to see. If you have ever worn cracked eyeglasses for any length of time, you know that initially the crack in the glasses causes a distortion, a wave, in the visual field. With time, however, you adapt to the distortion and the perceptual world seems normal.

Specially made distorting lenses have been worn by some psychologists in an attempt to test the extremes of perceptual adaptation. For example, when they wore prisms over their eyes, shifting the visual field a few degrees to the left, they initially had trouble picking up objects and grasping doorknobs. They kept reaching and missing, grasping for the object to the left of where it really was. Eventually they adapted.

For nine days one man wore special lenses that turned the world completely upside-down.[12] At first it was very difficult for him to move about in the world without bumping into things; everything looked upside-down. When he turned his head up he saw his feet, and when he turned his head down he saw the ceiling. Eventually he adapted so that the world no longer looked upside-down. At the end of nine days when the glasses were removed, he experienced a strange reaction: without the glasses the world looked upside-down. After a time of not wearing the prisms, his perceptual system adapted and the world again looked normal.

Correct . . . vision was achieved by subject M. after wearing the experimental spectacles for nine days. . . . After the spectacles were removed, however, objects appeared to revert to their previous upside-down position—this without any apparatus covering the eyes or in any way obstructing the visual field.

For a few minutes people and furniture seemed suspended from the "ceiling," head downward. . . . Short periods of disorientation and inverted vision occurred for several days after the experiment proper, particularly soon after awakening in the morning.[12]

This ability of human beings to make perceptual adjustments is not possessed by some lower animals. For example, if displacing prism lenses are put on a newborn chick, it will continue to miss when pecking at grain and will not adjust to the prisms.[13]

Paying Attention

How can I understand your unique perceptual world? The experience you construct is only roughly related to physical reality, differing in many ways from mine. Part of this difference depends upon the fact that perception is active and selective. Perception involves processes of actively seeking information from the world—we look, touch, and sniff. The environment around us is full of information, but we are selective in our perception. We look at only part of it; some things we feel, others we do not.

Sometimes we are asked, "Did you see it?" and we reply, "No, I didn't look." Or "Did you hear it?" is answered, "No, I wasn't listening." Looking and listening are perceptual activities which we use selectively when we pay attention. Perception is limited by **selective attention,** your tendency to select out and attend to only part of the physical world. Imagine yourself at a party in a crowded room. There are ten different conversations going on at once. Standing in the middle of the room, you can listen to one of several persons talking. You can listen to the man in front of you or the the woman standing behind you, and you can switch your attention from one person to the other, without moving in any way. However, you probably cannot follow both conversations simultaneously.

A theory of selective attention has been proposed by the psychologist Donald Broadbent. According to this theory, attention acts like a selective filter, allowing only one mes-

You selectively attend to only a small portion of the information available to your senses.

sage at a time to go through to reach consciousness; the others are somehow blocked and are never understood. A common experience at parties shows that this theory needs revision. If you are standing in the middle of the room paying attention to what the man in front of you is saying and the woman behind you mentions your name, you will often hear it (it will not be blocked).[14]

The content of your experience depends upon what you have selected to pay attention to, so if I am to understand your perceptual world, I must discover the focus of your attention.

Your Perceptual Censor

There is some evidence that you have a kind of perceptual censor that edits what you see and blocks out anything that might cause some psychological trauma. One study showed that it took subjects longer to recognize certain "taboo" words like penis and whore than it did to recognize neutral words like apple and stove.[15] It was proposed that a process called **perceptual defense** protects us from seeing certain threatening things. Although there has been considerable controversy raised by this proposal, recent evidence indicates that materials of a highly emotional character do have a negative influence on perceptual processes.[16]

Seeing What You Want to See

Motivation affects perception. Your perceptual world is different from mine because our needs are different and we tend to see what we want to see. Your attention focuses on things related to your needs. When you are hungry you tend to notice food-related items more readily; when you have strong sexual feelings you seem to be perceptually "tuned" to things and people associated with sex. Not only do you attend to things related to your needs but you actually see them differently. When food-related words are flashed briefly on a screen, you tend to recognize them more easily when you are hungry. But the same is not true for words unrelated to food.[17] Your needs bias your perceptions. Coins are judged to be larger by poor children than by rich children.[18] In one experiment a grayish metal slug was shown to children and called either lead, silver, white gold, or platinum. Judgments of size increased regularly with the value of the metals used as labels.[19]

Ⓢ There are individual and cultural differences in perception that involve differences in expectation, learning, attention, and motivation. Your perception is influenced by what you expect to see, what you want to see, and what you have learned to see. In addition, you selectively attend to certain parts of the world, and the process of perceptual defense may block your experience of certain threatening things.

Summary

KEY QUESTIONS

1. How do your senses gather information from the world?

   Your sensory receptors respond to the physical energy in the world by sending neural impulses to your brain. Perception, however, goes beyond the neural information contributed by the senses. Perception involves the active search for information, a selective processing of information, and the organizing and constructing of meaningful and stable experiences.

2. How is your perceptual world different from your external physical world?

   Your perceptual world is different from your physical world because you help to construct it; your choices and your experience make your perceptual world unique. No one else perceives the world exactly as you do.

3. How is your perceptual world built?

   Your perceptual world is a personal construction, influenced by your own needs, memories, and expectations. Your perceptual world depends upon your unique history of experiences. The perceptual world is organized and patterned; you experience a world of objects and people, not a world of points of light and patches of color.

4. How does your perceptual world differ from the inner experiences of other people?

   Because each person's experiences are different, each perceptual world is different. People also selectively attend to only certain parts of the world; the part you select is unique, and your experience is therefore unique. What you expect to see, what you want to see, and what you have learned to see are not always shared by others.

KEY CONCEPTS

sensory receptors	Specialized cells sensitive to various kinds of physical energy, such as light or pressure.
absolute threshold	The minimum amount of stimulation needed for detection.
sensory aftereffect	A sensory experience that persists after the external stimulation is gone.

dark adaptation	An aftereffect of being in the dark, in which the eyes become more sensitive to light; for example, after being in a dark theater.
negative afterimage	A visual aftereffect that appears in the opposite color or shade, such as seeing a black spot after looking at a white light.
retina	A coating of light-sensitive cells on the back of the eye.
lens	The structure in the eye that focuses light.
pupil	The opening in the eye that adjusts to control the amount of light that enters.
iris	The muscle surrounding the pupil that gives color to the eye.
optic nerve	The visual nerve carrying information from the eye to the brain.
fovea	The center of the retina; a small area most densely packed with light-sensitive cells.
blind spot	The blind area in the field of vision resulting from the absence of receptor cells where the visual nerve leaves the eye; also, this insensitive spot in the eye.
figure-ground principle	The rule that perceptual experiences are organized into two parts: objects and their backgrounds.
phi phenomenon	An illusion of movement created by flashing still pictures; the basis of apparent movement in the "movies."
Gestalt movement	A school of psychology that stressed the significance of pattern and organization in perception; founded by Max Wertheimer.
grouping principle	The rule that perceptual experiences are organized into patterns or groups.
rule of proximity	The principle that things that are close together appear to belong together; close things are grouped in perception.
rule of similarity	The principle that things that resemble each other appear to belong together; similar things are grouped in perception.
rule of closure	The principle that areas or figures tend to appear as whole or closed, even if they are incomplete or broken.
illusions	Distorted or incorrect perceptions.
hallucinations	Perceptions unrelated to the physical environment, such as hearing voices when no one is near or seeing a pink elephant on the ceiling.
selective attention	The tendency to notice and perceive only part of the information available in the world.
perceptual defense	A process that censors what we perceive.

Suggested Readings

Licit and Illicit Drugs by Edward M. Brecher & the Editors of Consumers Reports. Boston, Mass.: Little, Brown, 1972. The best available general reference on drugs. Discusses the history, uses, scientific findings, and cultural traditions of all common drugs—including alcohol, nicotine, and caffeine.

Go Ask Alice (author anonymous). New York: Avon Books, 1972. Actual diary of a fifteen-year-old drug user.

Altered States of Consciousness ed. by Charles T. Tart. Garden City, N.Y.: Anchor Books, 1972. Broad survey of altered states of consciousness including yoga, meditation, hypnosis, brain-wave research, dream states.

Hypnosis: A Scientific Approach by Theodore Xenophon Barber. New York: Van Nostrand Reinhold Co., 1969. Survey of scientific investigations into hypnosis. Presents the position that hypnosis does not involve an altered state of consciousness.

The Marihuana Papers by David Solomon. New York: New American Library, 1968. Excellent general collection of older articles on the history, legality, and psychology of marijuana.

Doors of Perception: Heaven and Hell by Aldous Huxley. New York: Harper & Row, 1954. Detailed description of the author's experiences with LSD and peyote.

Eye and Brain by Ronald L. Gregory. New York: McGraw-Hill, 1966. A beautifully illustrated paperback presenting the psychology of visual perception. Has a chapter on art.

Journey to Ixtlan: The Lessons of Don Juan by Carlos Castaneda. New York: Simon & Schuster, 1972. The last and best of three fascinating books by a young American who learns a new way of seeing from a Yaqui Indian "man of knowledge."

A Primer of Psychobiology: Brain and Behavior by Timothy J. Teyler. San Francisco: W. H. Freeman, 1975. Nontechnical introduction to the brain and what is known of its relationship to behavior.

The Machinery of the Brain by Dean E. Wooldridge. New York: McGraw-Hill, 1963. Paperback presenting the story of brain research in humans and animals. Highly readable.

Some Must Watch While Some Must Sleep by William C. Dement. San Francisco: W. H. Freeman, 1974. Entertaining introduction to the field of sleep research. Includes material on dreams, sleep disorders, sleep disturbance and mental illness, and creativity during sleep.

The Interpretation of Dreams by Sigmund Freud. London: Hogarth Press, 1953. Freud's theory of dreams.

Research Methods

IV Laboratory Methods

Psychologists seek to understand human behavior. You might therefore expect to find them studying people in parks, restaurants, college dorms, and other places where people can frequently be found. But most psychologists do not study the behavior of people in the "real world." Instead, they study people in psychological laboratories.

Advantages of Laboratory Studies

Laboratories are not mysterious—they are merely rooms, often with some special equipment in them. There are certain advantages to studying behavior in a laboratory, instead of studying it in a classroom or a park. One advantage is that laboratories are **controlled environments,** places where the researcher determines what happens. Outside of the laboratory, in the "real world," there are all kinds of unexpected noises and changing lights; there are people moving about and fire trucks and airplanes. Unless the psychologist is particularly interested in how people respond to such sounds and lights, these stimuli will be distracting and interfering elements in the study. In a laboratory the researcher can control all unwanted stimuli. All distractions can be removed.

A second advantage of the laboratory is that the researcher can *produce* the stimuli desired. For a study of memory, a slide projector, tape recorder, or memory drum may be used to present words or pictures to people for them to remember. **A memory drum** is an apparatus that presents a sequence of stimuli, one at a time, that have been printed on paper. For a study of perception, a **tachistoscope** may be used; a tachistoscope is a device that flashes very brief images on a screen. Visual perception can be studied with the tachistoscope by varying the duration of stimulus exposure. Using instruments such as these, the psychologist can present exactly the stimuli desired and study the subsequent responses. In this way researchers have determined the answer to such questions as these: What is the absolute threshold for vision or for hearing? What is the visual aftereffect of observing motion? What is the effect of interference on memory for words?

A third advantage of laboratories is that delicate instruments can be used to accurately measure a variety of responses and record them so that they can be studied. For example, a **reaction timer** is a device that measures speed of reaction, in hundredths of a second, and registers or records the result. For example, a reaction timer would be used in a study of the time required to perform mental arithmetic. **A polygraph** is an instrument that records the occurrence and intensity of a variety of biological responses, such as heart rate, blood pressure, or breathing rate. The polygraph has pens that record biological signals on a moving roll of paper. Two especially important responses that are sometimes recorded on a polygraph are the **galvanic skin response (GSR),** which is a measure of the electrical properties of the skin, and **brain waves (EEG),** which reflect the electrical activity of the brain. Instruments such as these require a special electrically insulated room and cannot be carried about outside a laboratory.

A psychological laboratory, then, provides a controlled environment in which behavior can be observed and measured. There are, however, disadvantages to studying behavior in a laboratory. One disadvantage is that most behavior of significance does not occur in a laboratory, but instead occurs in the real world. To move this behavior into the laboratory is to change it in important ways; sometimes the changes are so profound that the resulting study is no longer relevant to the significant "real-world" behavior.

The Animal Laboratory

Many psychologists study animals in psychological laboratories. One reason they do this is because they are quite simply interested in understanding animal behavior. Another reason is that they hope that by studying animal behavior they can understand human behavior. If they hope to understand human behavior, why don't they study human behavior directly? The answer is that humans cannot be treated as animals can.

Learning from Animals

For example, psychologists studying simple learning may deprive a pigeon or rat of food until it is quite hungry, then study the effect of food rewards on learning. Psychologists have attempted to breed a strain of mice especially susceptible to alcoholism. Psychologists have studied the effect of radiation on memory and learning in rats. Psychologists have studied the effect of parental deprivation in monkeys by raising the babies alone. Psychologists have studied the effect of electric shock in the development of fear reactions in dogs. These manipulations could not normally be done with human beings. In each case, however, the psychologist hoped to be able to *apply* the results to people.

What gives psychologists reason to hope that results from animal studies can be applied to people? Partly this hope comes from their assumption that people are not qualitatively distinct among animals, but instead are closely related to the lower animals in many ways. Human brains are similar to monkey brains and, to a lesser degree, even to rat brains. Another reason for having faith that principles of animal behavior can apply to human behavior is that some animal principles have already been applied and have actually worked. For example, the principles of operant conditioning were discovered in the animal laboratory; now, however, they are widely applied to human beings.

The Brains of Animals

Psychologists study the brains and nervous systems of animals in order to further our understanding of our own bodies. These physiological studies are conducted in a variety of ways. Some studies involve measuring the electrical activity of individual circuits or cells in the brain; others involve altering brain chemistry and observing the effects. The oldest method for studying the functions of different parts of the brain involves observing the effects of different kinds of brain damage. Psychologists may experimentally damage the brains of animals as part of a study of the relation of brain and behavior.

The method of **ablation** (the removal of brain tissue) and the method of **lesions** (injury to brain tissue) both involve studying behavior following structural damage; they are based on the assumption that if a part of the brain controls a particular behavior, then damage to that part will result in a change in that behavior.

Ablation and lesions are experimentally performed on animals such as rats and monkeys in order to understand how the brain works. The brains of these animals and the human brain are sufficiently similar so that understanding their brains helps us to understand ours. These experimental procedures have allowed us to discover which parts of the brain are crucial to significant human functions so that damage to these parts can be carefully avoided in brain operations.

The observation of a change in behavior following brain damage in animals or humans does not, however, automatically prove that the area damaged was responsible for controlling the behavior that is affected.

Suppose, for example, that a soldier, suffering a bullet wound damaging a particular area of his brain, is unable to write his name. What can we conclude? There are several possibilities that must be considered: (1) the damaged area contained the memory of his name; (2) the damaged area contained the memory of how to write; (3) the damaged area was a center for the motor control of writing; (4) the damaged area was a sensory center (for example a visual area) required for the performance of the task; (5) the damaged area was part of a motivational or arousal system whose activity was required for the performance of the task. These and other possibilities must be examined within the context of other evidence before a conclusion can be reached about the specific function of the damaged area.

The Dream Laboratory

A laboratory for studying dreams typically consists of a set of rooms with beds and monitoring devices. They are soundproof, temperature-controlled, and, when the lights are off, completely dark. The monitoring devices consist primarily of a polygraph that is recording both brain waves and eye movements. The polygraph reveals when dreaming is occurring because during dreams the EEG and eye-movement patterns are unique.

EEG and REM

EEG waves are recorded by attaching small metal discs (**electrodes**) to the scalp.

These discs pick up tiny electrical charges given off by the brain; the polygraph then amplifies these electrical signals and records them on moving strips of paper. The resulting graph shows the frequency and intensity of the brain's overall electrical activity. Dream periods characteristically show low-voltage but high-frequency waves, similar to the brain waves observed while awake.

Eye movements are detected by electrodes placed near the eyes which pick up electrical activity in the eye muscles. When the eye muscles contract, changes in voltage on the skin can be detected by these electrodes. These signals are then amplified and recorded by the polygraph. Dream periods show **rapid eye movement (REM),** a fluttering or jerking of the eyes.

Dream Deprivation

A psychologist wondered what the function of dreaming was. Is dreaming necessary? To find out, he decided to explore the consequences of dream deprivation by deliberately preventing people from dreaming.[1]

During a series of uninterrupted sleep nights, several participants slept in the dream laboratory while EEG and REM records were kept. This established a normal pattern, or **baseline,** for each participant's cycle of dreaming and sleep. During the next series of nights the participants were awakened and asked to sit up alertly whenever the polygraph showed that they were beginning to dream; this was the dream deprivation procedure. Next, the participants were allowed to sleep undisturbed for a series of nights; this was the "recovery period." For comparison purposes, during another series of nights in the dream laboratory, the participants were awakened during periods when they were not dreaming.

The results showed an increase in dreaming on recovery nights; following periods of dream deprivation, the participants tended to dream more, as if they had to "catch up" on their dreaming. This suggested that people have a need to dream. Furthermore, there were psychological reactions to dream deprivation. Participants were observed to be irritable and anxious during periods of dream deprivation. Weight losses were observed in several of the participants.

KEY CONCEPTS

controlled environment	A place where all stimulation is controlled by the researcher; a laboratory.
memory drum	An apparatus that presents a sequence of stimuli one at a time; used in memory experiments.
tachistoscope	A device that flashes images on a screen very briefly.
reaction timer	A device that measures speed of reaction.
polygraph	An instrument that records the occurrence and intensity of various biological signals.

galvanic skin response (GSR)	A measure of the electrical resistance of the skin; responsive to emotional changes.
brain waves (EEG)	Cyclical changes in the electrical activity of the brain, as measured from the scalp.
ablation	The removal of brain tissue.
lesion	An injury to brain tissue; for example, a cut.
electrode	A metal wire or disc used to conduct electrical signals from the skin or brain to a machine.
rapid eye movement (REM)	The rapid jerking or fluttering of the eyes that accompanies dreaming.
baseline	The normal level or pattern of a response that occurs before an experiment is conducted.

V Sex

13 Male and Female

CHAPTER OUTLINE

KEY QUESTIONS

1. How masculine or feminine are you?
2. How did you develop your masculine or feminine identity?
3. What does it mean to be a homosexual?
4. What causes homosexuality?

How feminine are you? How masculine are you?

The term "masculine" does not mean simply having a male body—it refers to the many, often subtle, qualities and behaviors usually associated with men. Although you might make a few mistakes, you can generally tell a man from a woman without knowing *any* physical characteristics; you can make judgments based on behavior alone, because men tend to behave differently from women. Consider your behavior: Do you ever go shopping in a dress? Do you like to play football? Do you open car doors for your date? Do you sometimes wear lipstick? You can guess a person's sex if you know how the person answers these four questions.

Masculinity-Femininity

Because football is a game more often played by men than by women, playing football is considered a *masculine* activity. It is more characteristic of men than of women. The two sexes differ not only in behavior but also in personality. For example, men tend to be more dominant and aggressive than women. Personality traits like dominance and aggressiveness are therefore considered masculine characteristics.

A Test to Take

Some traits are more characteristic of men; some more of women. A group of 200 college freshmen taking my psychology class checked those adjectives below which best described their personalities. Of the sixteen traits in the list, half were checked significantly more often by men and half by women. Those eight checked more often by men can be called masculine traits and the eight checked more often by women can be called feminine traits. Can you tell the difference? Mark each trait with an M or F to indicate whether you think it is masculine or feminine.

_____ 1. Scientific	_____ 9. Emotional
_____ 2. Romantic	_____ 10. Sensitive
_____ 3. Domestic	_____ 11. Wise
_____ 4. Logical	_____ 12. Mechanical
_____ 5. Competitive	_____ 13. Sincere
_____ 6. Affectionate	_____ 14. Intuitive
_____ 7. Sensible	_____ 15. Brave
_____ 8. Vulgar	_____ 16. Delicate

Those traits checked more often by male students were 1, 4, 5, 7, 8, 11, 12, and 15. The remaining traits were checked more often by females. On the whole, the feminine traits were checked more often than the masculine traits. For example, even though 90 percent of the females considered themselves "sensitive," nearly three-fourths of the males also checked "sensitive." What does it mean if you consider yourself a sincere and sensitive male or a sensible and logical female? You are not alone. Many of the male and female college students in my study described themselves in that way.

"Masculine" and "feminine" are not opposites. A person can have both masculine and feminine traits. One psychologist recently developed a test similar to the one above; it consists of a list of such masculine traits as "aggressive," "competitive," and "dominant" and such feminine traits as "affectionate," "compassionate," and "gentle."[1] The psychologist found that about one-third of the men and women tested scored about equally masculine and feminine; that is, they rated themselves as having about the same number of masculine and feminine traits. Individuals having both masculine and feminine traits are called **androgynous.** Androgynous individuals have a broader range of options and can adapt to a wide range of situations. Unlike people who are exclusively masculine or feminine in their behavior, androgynous individuals can be both sensible and sensitive, both competitive and affectionate.

Human sexuality is expressed in polarity: male and female. Your identification with one of these poles was an important step in your childhood. With that identification came a **sex role**—the requirement to adopt the attitudes, to wear the clothes, and to engage in the behavior appropriate for males or females. Sex roles, however, which once were clearly defined, are now more blurred. Women are demanding more active roles and men are developing more emotional roles than ever before. In some places, men and women are even beginning to look alike; most

Masculinity and femininity are not opposites.

of us have had the experience of passing persons on the street without knowing whether they were male or female.

Three New Guinea Tribes

Ideas of masculinity and femininity are different in different cultures. The anthropologist Margaret Mead, in studying the people of the island of New Guinea, described a remarkable tribe of lake dwellers called the Tchambuli.[2] Tchambuli men, it seems, are emotionally dependent and sexually passive. They like to gossip and spend time decorating their bodies. They are sensitive persons who enjoy painting, music, and drama. On the other hand, Tchambuli women are responsible for obtaining food for the family and are impersonal and business-like. They are more dominant and sexually aggressive than the Tchambuli men. Typical behaviors characterizing many American men and women appear reversed for Tchambuli men and women. That is, typical sex *roles* are reversed. The Tchambuli children learn what is appropriate for their sex *in their culture.* How well would you fit in the Tchambuli culture?

Mead describes two other New Guinea cultures. For one culture, the Mundugumor, both men and women are described as violent, aggressive, and competitive—in other words, characterized by "masculine" traits according to American standards. In a neighboring culture, the Arapesh, both men and women are gentle, loving, and cooperative—what we would call "feminine" traits. Apparently behavior typical of men and of women is not exclusively biologically determined but is highly influenced by cultural norms. The older members of a given culture pass on to the younger members of that culture characteristic patterns of behavior; these patterns are different in different cultures.

The Norm Not the Ideal

It is important for you not to confuse the psychological concepts of masculinity and femininity with other ways in which these words are sometimes used. The concept of **masculinity** in psychology refers to how much a person acts the way men act in their culture or how closely behavior conforms to the norm for men. The concept of **femininity** refers to how much a person acts the way women act or how closely behavior conforms to the norm for women. **Norms** are standards based on the way people do in fact behave in a particular society at a particular time in history.

Psychology uses a **normative model** of masculinity-femininity, a standard based on the norm. There is no implication that people should conform to this model, although you may experience social pressure to do so.

A different meaning of these terms is involved when they are used in a *prescriptive* sense, an attempt to define how you should act. To be masculine—in the sense of a "real man"—refers to conformity, not to a behavioral norm, but to an **idealized model,** a standard based on the ideal. Each society

According to the idealized model, men should pay for the dinner on a date.

has a concept of what the ideal man or the ideal woman should be like, and these concepts differ among different societies. Individuals within a society disagree about what is ideally feminine or ideally masculine. Thus, while some fathers cheat on their income tax, they tell their sons that it is not "manly" to cheat on their school examinations. Some people believe that being ideally masculine includes being sensitive and that being ideally feminine includes being sensible. What are your concepts of being ideally masculine and ideally feminine?

The women's liberation movement is trying to change our concept of what is "feminine"—in the sense of the idealized model. From the women's liberation point of view, the submissiveness, the sexual passivity, and the dependency expected of women lead to a kind of "slavery" that prevents full human development. Unfortunately, the degree to which women are sexually attractive is for

many men dependent upon the degree to which they conform to the feminine idealized model for this society.

Men are also shackled by an idealized model of masculinity that requires them to be decisive, dominant, and aggressive. These idealized models severely limit alternative choices and the unique expression of individuality in both men and women. There is, however, some indication that this is changing as the sex roles blur. Both men and women seem to be experiencing less pressure to conform to narrowly defined ideal models.

⑤ Behavior that is typical of men and women in one culture may be quite different in another culture. The ideals of male and female behavior also differ among cultures. You are called masculine or feminine to the degree that your behavior conforms to what is typical of your culture. However, in American society the pressure for people to conform to these standards seems to be decreasing.

Sex-Role Acquisition

What are the origins of your masculinity or femininity? How did you acquire the attitudes, mannerisms, preferences, and behaviors that are characteristic for persons of your sex? You began to learn at an early age that the behavior appropriate for men was often inappropriate for women and vice versa. Evidence shows that the majority of children by the age of three are aware of their sexual identity and—to some extent—begin to act accordingly.[3] Preference for the masculine or the feminine sex role also begins to emerge early in life, probably by the age of three or four.

In this society the male sex role seems to be more narrowly defined than the female sex role. While girls can engage in activities more appropriate for the male role without being considered abnormal, this is not true for boys. Girls can wear shirts and pants and can play with trucks and guns with little or no social disapproval; boys, however, cannot wear dresses or play with dishes and sewing materials without parental disapproval.

Freudian Theory

You may think that your pattern of sexual behavior began suddenly with adolescence, but it is unlikely that this is so. Most of your behavior has roots in your childhood.

At the beginning of this century Sigmund Freud shocked his contemporaries by asserting that children not only have sexual desires, but they have incestuous sexual desires for their own parents. According to Freud's **principle of infantile sexuality,** sexual gratification is obtained throughout childhood from a variety of sources. Freud thought of personality development in terms of a progression of **psychosexual stages,** periods of

development defined by different sources of sexual pleasure.

■ *Oral Stage* According to Freud's theory, during the first year of life, in the **oral stage,** the infant gains sexual pleasure from sucking and biting. Freud wrote:

The infant's first sexual excitations appear in connection with the other functions important for life. Its chief interest, as you know, is concerned with taking nourishment; as it sinks asleep at the breast, utterly satisifed, it bears a look of perfect content which will come back again later in life after the experience of the sexual orgasm. . . . We perceive that infants wish to repeat, without really getting any nourishment, the action necessary to taking nourishment. . . . The action of sucking is sufficient in itself to give it satisfaction. . . .

Sucking for nourishment becomes the point of departure from which the whole sexual life develops, the unattainable prototype of every later sexual satisfaction, to which in time of need phantasy often enough reverts. . . .

According to Freud, sexual impulses are repressed during the latency stage.

This assessment of the nature of pleasure-sucking has now brought to our notice two of the decisive characteristics of infantile sexuality. It appears in connection with the satisfaction of the great organic needs, and it behaves auto-erotically, that is to say, it seeks and finds its objects in its own person.[4]

■ *Anal Stage* After the oral stage the infant enters a second stage of psychosexual development, the **anal stage.** Freud believed that in this second stage sexual pleasure centers around the eliminative functions, the urinary and bowel habits. Of this stage, Freud wrote:

What is more clearly discernible in regard to the taking of nourishment is to some extent repeated with the process of excretion. We conclude that infants experience pleasure in the evacuation of urine and the contents of the bowels, and that they very soon endeavor to continue these actions so that the accompanying excitation of the membranes in these erotogenic zones may secure them the maximum possible gratification.[4]

■ *Phallic Stage* From ages three to about six, in the **phallic stage,** the source of sexual gratification for the child is masturbation—the manipulation of the penis or the clitoris. Many parents are aware of their child's masturbatory activity that begins during this period.

Toward the end of this stage, a crisis called the **Oedipus complex** develops in which the child experiences conflict because of sexual desire for the parent of the opposite sex. This incestuous desire causes the child to compete for the affection of the parent but also to fear retaliation from the parent's mate. Thus in the case of a boy, Freud assumed that he desired his mother and wished to displace his father. The boy's ambivalent feelings of fear, hostility, and love

for his father that accompany his sexual desire for his mother end with the resolution of the Oedipus complex.

■ *Latency Stage* From Freud's point of view, the resolution of the Oedipus complex was achieved, first, as the boy repressed sexual desire by pushing it from awareness, and, second, as he began identifying with the father. The repression of sexual desire initiates the **latency stage,** a period of little sexual interest which precedes adolescence. During the latency stage sexual thoughts and impulses seem to be forgotten.

■ *Genital Stage* The onset of puberty, at about twelve or thirteen years of age, marks the beginning of the **genital stage** of psychosexual development. This final stage in sexual maturation marks the occurrence of the expression of adult sexuality, in which gratification is found in masturbation and sexual intercourse.

From Freud's viewpoint, the development of sexual identity is the result of passing through a fixed series of stages and successfully resolving the Oedipus complex. The stages are defined in terms of biological processes, such as sucking, urinating, or masturbating. In Freud's theory, the sex role that is finally achieved by the developing child depends upon sex drive and its repression.

STAGES OF PSYCHOSEXUAL DEVELOPMENT

Stage	Age	Source of Sexual Pleasure
Oral	0–1	Sucking, biting
Anal	1–3	Feces expulsion and retention
Phallic	3–6	Masturbation
Latency	6–12	Little or none
Genital	12–	Masturbation and intercourse

Children learn sex roles by observing and imitating adults.

Social-Learning Theory

In contrast to Freud's stage theory of psychosexual development, social-learning theory assumes that sex roles result—not from biological forces—but from learning. **Social-learning theory** is a general theory of behavior that focuses on the relation between behavior and the environment, and emphasizes the influence of other people whose behavior is imitated. Social-learning theory argues that "social learning"—learning by observing and imitating others—begins in infancy and continues throughout life. By contrast, Freud's theory assumes that children identify with their parents primarily at the end of the phallic stage, to resolve the Oedipus complex.

The process of identifying with an adult was especially important for the development of your sexual identity. You needed a **model,** someone to imitate, so that your growth in the area of sexuality, your development as a man or woman, could progress smoothly. From your parent of the same sex you learned what it means to be male or female. **Identification** involves copying the behavior of your parent, incorporating his or her values, attitudes, interests, and mannerisms.

When children perceive their models as exercising power, displaying mastery, and receiving affection, identification takes place more readily because children desire these same experiences and attributes. Children copy success.[5] The extent to which children identify with their parents varies. For example, boys identify with fathers who are nurturant and supportive more than with fathers who are not.[6,7]   For boys without a father, appropriate role models are usually found in older brothers, grandfathers, or friends of the family.   Most children eventually achieve sexual identification with an adult of the same sex but some children do not.

⑤   According to Freud, everyone passes through a fixed set of psychosexual stages, defined by their different sources of sexual pleasure.   These stages are the oral (with sexual pleasure from sucking), anal (from urinary and bowel activities), phallic (from penis or clitoris), latency (from nothing), and genital (from penis or clitoris again).   The Oedipus complex develops toward the end of the phallic stage and, according to Freud, results in the identification with the same-sexed parent.   By contrast, social-learning theory assumes that the process of identifying with others occurs throughout life; from this point of view, the achievement of sexual identity results from observing and imitating others.

Homosexuality

Although encouraged and accepted in ancient Greece, the homosexual in American society has often been treated as an outcast and sometimes suffers the punishment of the law.   In many states homosexual activities are a crime.   The American fear of homosexuality is, by comparison with other nations in the world, extreme.   The charge of homosexuality is sufficient to ruin a person's reputation and career.   Any gesture such as the male embrace that might remotely suggest homosexual interests is carefully avoided. But who is a homosexual?   The answer depends upon what is meant by homosexuality.

Who Is a Homosexual?

If a "homosexual" is defined as someone who has engaged in homosexual activities at some time, then nearly half of the people in this country would be "homosexuals."   Toward the end of the latency stage of psychosexual development, many boys participate in sex play with other boys.   Kinsey, in his *Sexual Behavior in the Human Male* and *Sexual Behavior in the Human Female*, reported that 60 percent of preadolescent boys and 33 percent of preadolescent girls engaged in homosexual activities.[8,9]

I will define a **homosexual** as someone who seeks sexual satisfaction exclusively—or almost exclusively—from members of the same sex.   A **heterosexual** is defined as someone who is attracted to and finds sexual satisfaction primarily from members of the opposite sex.   Not many people are exclusively homosexual.   According to Kinsey's report about 4 percent of American men and less than 2 percent of American women fall into this category; there are only about one-third as many female homosexuals as male homosexuals. Homosexual behavior occurs in all mammals and always is more common in the male of the species than in the female.[8]

Homosexuality refers not to appearance but to sexual preference. Most homosexual men do not appear feminine and most homosexual women, or **lesbians,** do not appear masculine. The "queen"—a feminine, lipstick-type male homosexual—and the "butch"—a masculine, short-haired type female homosexual—are the exceptions rather than the rule.

Until recently, homosexuality was frequently regarded as unhealthy and abnormal. Modern studies have shown, however, that homosexuals are, on the average, as psychologically healthy as heterosexuals.[10,11] Homosexuality is now regarded by most psychologists and psychiatrists as a form of sexual *preference*, not as an illness. In recognition of this modern view, the American Psychiatric Association recently removed homosexuality from its list of psychological disorders.

It is important for you to understand that having a homosexual experience, or even several such experiences, does not make you a homosexual. Almost half the people in the country have such experiences and yet remain heterosexual. Neither do you become a homosexual because you feel attracted to people of your own sex. Furthermore, sexual identity is subject to change, and people can experience changes in their sexual preferences.

Causes of Homosexuality

No one knows for sure what causes homosexuality. There is no single explanation that appropriately applies to all cases. Four different theories of the origin of homosexuality will be presented; the first two explanations are organic (referring to bodily processes) and the last two are psychological.

■ *Genetic Theory* The **genetic theory** considers homosexuality as an inherited condition; according to this theory, homosexuals are "born that way." Sometimes several children in the same family are homosexual. Evidence of homosexuality has on occasion been traced over several generations.[12] Further evidence consistent with this theory comes from twin studies. If one fraternal twin (with different heredity) is homosexual, the other twin has about a 4 percent chance of being a homosexual. This chance is about the same for the general population. But if the co-twin is an identical twin (identical heredity), the chance of both being homosexual rises to about 70 percent.[13]

This evidence suggests a possible genetic basis for homosexuality; however, since identical twins have more similar home environments than fraternal twins, it is difficult to determine whether the increased rate of homosexuality results from the similarity in genes or the similarity in environment. Furthermore, this form of sexual preference may spread by association, which would explain its overrepresentation in some families without the need of referring to a genetic theory.[14] Thus, the evidence for the genetic theory is not very convincing.

■ *Hormone Imbalance Theory* The **hormone imbalance theory** states that male homosexuality results from an excess of female hormones, and female homosexuality results from too much male hormone. Although this possibility has often been raised, there is little evidence supporting it.[15,16] A recent study of thirty male homosexual students found them to have significantly lower levels of male hormones than a comparable group of heterosexual males; however, there was no evidence to show that their sexual preferences were *caused* by their lowered hormone level.[17] Sex hormones seem to affect sexual development and sex drive but

not sex preference. One group of male homosexuals who were administered dosages of male hormones showed increased sexual arousal—but toward their homosexual partners.

■ *Cross-Sex Modeling Theory* The **cross-sex modeling theory** assumes that homosexuality results from a child identifying with the parent of the opposite sex and incorporating the attitudes, mannerisms, and sexual preferences of that parent. From this point of view, sexual preferences are acquired, not inborn, and are based on learning experiences in the environment of the home. Children learn sex roles. Boys are not naturally men, but learn to be men, according to the psychiatrist Andrew Salter:

We must condition our boys to be men. . . . Some boys have no opportunity to learn to become men—they are castrated by their mother's apron strings. And when their fathers are away, or distasteful, or innocuous, their feminization is that much easier.[18]

If the cross-sex modeling theory were true, you might expect that the parents and family backgrounds of homosexuals would be different from heterosexuals. There is some evidence that this is true. Male homosexuals tend to come from families with controlling dominant mothers, who maintain an unusually close and intense relationship with their sons; their fathers tend to be distant, passive, and rejecting.[19,20] According to the cross-sex modeling theory, the son imitates the parent who is successful and powerful (the mother in this case), and adopts the feminine role.[21]

Studies of the families of female homosexuals show a somewhat different pattern.

While parent-child relations in these families were found to be consistently poor,[22] there was particularly intense hostility between fathers and daughters.[23] Female homosexuals report that they were afraid of their fathers and that their fathers were irresponsible, incompetent, and weak.[23] According to the cross-sex modeling theory, girl children should adopt the masculine role and become homosexual only when the father is a more powerful and successful model than the mother. This does not seem to be the case with the fathers of female homosexuals, who tend to be weak and unsuccessful. Thus the cross-sex modeling theory explains male homosexuality fairly well, but not female homosexuality.

Most people who come from families like those described above do not turn out to be homosexual. It is clear that the cross-sex modeling theory is not by itself an adequate answer to explain even male homosexuality.

■ *Seduction Theory*   The **seduction theory** holds that homosexuality results when a child is seduced by a homosexual at an early age. Early sexual experiences clearly are important in developing our sexual preferences; however, in view of the large number of persons having homosexual experiences early in life, there seem to be relatively few homosexuals. Most persons having homosexual experiences are not permanently conditioned by them to become homosexuals. Furthermore, engaging in occasional homosexual acts does not mean that one is a homosexual.

Childhood experiences are important because of the weight precedence carries in the establishment of learning. But the importance of childhood experiences can be overemphasized. . . . No matter how strongly conditioned an older person may have become to a given class of sexual stimuli, and no matter

how strongly conditioned to the avoidance of some other class of sexual stimuli, the acquisition of new tastes remains a possibility. There are instances in which persons who have been exclusively heterosexual for many years have developed homosexual interests, and other instances in which persons who have been exclusively homosexual for many years have developed heterosexual interests.[24]

Restrictions against early homosexual experiences are fairly strict in our society but these experiences do occur. Not so many sanctions are raised against homosexual activity in other cultures. The extent of homosexual activity that occurs is partly determined by the amount of it that is allowed. Some societies freely allow homosexual activity and most members of these societies occasionally practice homosexual activities.[25]

A Case History

Some homosexuals are apparently content with their sexual preferences while others desire to change. Those seen by psychiatrists are unhappy enough with their sexual adjustments to seek help. The following case—a homosexual who came to a psychiatrist for help and subsequently changed his sexual preferences to become heterosexual—should not be considered typical of homosexuals in general.

Patient gives a history of homosexuality of nine years duration. Previous to that time he had what he considered a normal adolescence and young manhood, showing the same interest in girls as his associates. He recalls, however, developing an interest in the male body, particularly the genitalia, and then a fascination for the sexual functions of the male, when he was between the ages of sixteen and twenty years. . . . He never was aggressive in seek-

ing homosexual contacts, but on an average of every two to three months he would put himself in a position to be approached. Between these experiences he would suffer greatly from shame and remorse and would stay strictly away from such localities.

What happened in this case was that the young man had been brought up in a small town. His father was weak and ineffectual, and his mother was over-protective. What sort of masculine attitudes could he absorb?[18]

The psychiatrist interprets this case in terms of a learning or modeling theory, writing that the patient had insufficient opportunity to learn the male role.

Both the cross-sex modeling theory and the seduction theory have considerable validity. Early homosexual experiences may establish sexual preferences for those whose family environment supported cross-sex identification. The evidence indicates that sexual preferences are acquired, not inborn; that such preferences develop through processes of identification and learning in childhood; and that they are even capable of being modified or unlearned through new experiences in adult life.

☒ A homosexual is someone who seeks sexual satisfaction exclusively—or almost exclusively—from members of the same sex. Although many people are at different times attracted to those of the same sex and may even have had a homosexual experience, very few people are exclusively homosexuals. The genetic theory, the hormone imbalance theory, the cross-sex modeling theory, and the seduction theory have all been proposed as possible explanations for the origins of homosexuality; only the last two of these theories seem to have much merit.

Summary

KEY QUESTIONS

1. How masculine or feminine are you?

   The terms "masculinity" or "femininity" refer to how much people conform to behavior that is typical for men and women in their culture. Thus, you are very masculine if your actions, attitudes, interests, and mannerisms are similar to what is most common for men.

2. How did you develop your masculine or feminine identity?

   According to Freud, sexual identity is acquired by the process of identifying with the parent of the same sex. From Freud's point of view this identification occurs at the end of a childhood crisis called the Oedipus complex. Sex roles may also be learned by observing and imitating others.

3. What does it mean to be a homosexual?

The term "homosexual" refers to someone who seeks sexual gratification only from those of the same sex. Thus, it refers to a type of sexual preference, and does not refer to physical appearance at all. Homosexuals are just as normal and psychologically healthy as heterosexuals.

4. What causes homosexuality?

There are several theories of homosexuality, but not enough is known to come to a final conclusion about the origins of homosexual preferences. The genetic theory, the hormone imbalance theory, the cross-sex modeling theory, and the seduction theory have all been proposed to explain the origin of homosexuality. The best available evidence suggests that a combination of factors is responsible and that a single uniform explanation will not apply to everyone.

KEY CONCEPTS

androgyny	Possessing both masculine and feminine traits.
sex role	The style and mannerisms typical of members of one sex.
masculinity	The degree to which an individual conforms to behavior typical of men in a culture.
femininity	The degree to which an individual conforms to behavior typical of women in a culture.
norms	Standards based on the way people typically behave in a particular society.
normative model	A standard of masculinity and femininity based on the norm.
idealized model	A standard of masculinity and femininity based on what is considered perfect or ideal.
principle of infantile sexuality	Freud's idea that sexual gratification is obtained throughout childhood.
psychosexual stages	According to Freud, periods of development in childhood defined by the different sources of sexual pleasure that dominate.
oral stage	The first psychosexual stage during which the infant gains sexual pleasure from sucking and biting.

anal stage	The second psychosexual stage during which the infant gains sexual pleasure from urinary and bowel activities.
phallic stage	The third psychosexual stage during which the child gains sexual pleasure from manipulating his penis or her clitoris.
latency stage	The fourth psychosexual stage during which sexual interests are repressed.
genital stage	The fifth and final psychosexual stage during which sexual pleasure is gained from masturbation and intercourse.
Oedipus complex	A crisis occurring at the end of the phallic stage resulting from a conflict between the child's desire for the parent of the opposite sex and fear of the parent of the same sex.
social learning theory	A general theory of behavior that emphasizes the importance of observing and imitating others as a basis of learning.
model	Someone who is copied or imitated.
identification	The process of copying the attitudes, style, and mannerisms of a model, such as a parent or other older person.
homosexual	A man or woman who seeks sexual satisfaction exclusively—or almost exclusively—from members of the same sex.
heterosexual	A man or woman who seeks sexual satisfaction primarily from members of the opposite sex.
lesbian	A female homosexual.
genetic theory	A theory of homosexuality which assumes that it is inborn, due to heredity.
hormone imbalance theory	A theory of homosexuality which assumes that it is due to an excess of the opposite sex hormone.
cross-sex modeling theory	A theory of homosexuality which assumes that it results from identifying with the parent of the opposite sex.
seduction theory	A theory of homosexuality which assumes that it results from early homosexual experiences.

14 Sexual Arousal

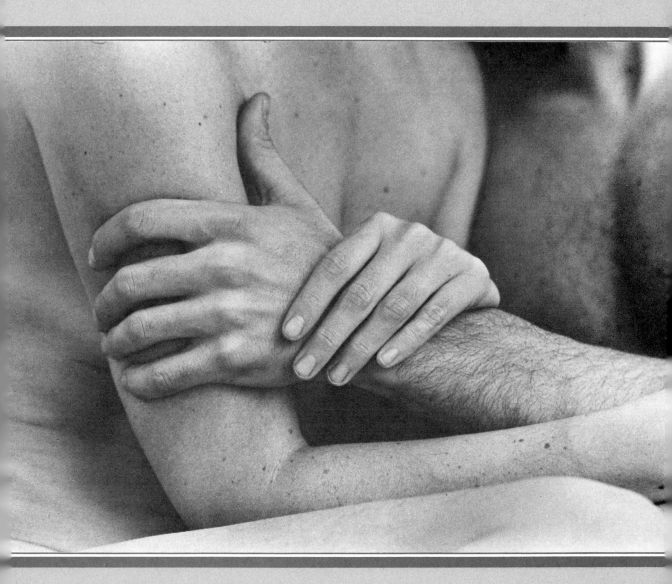

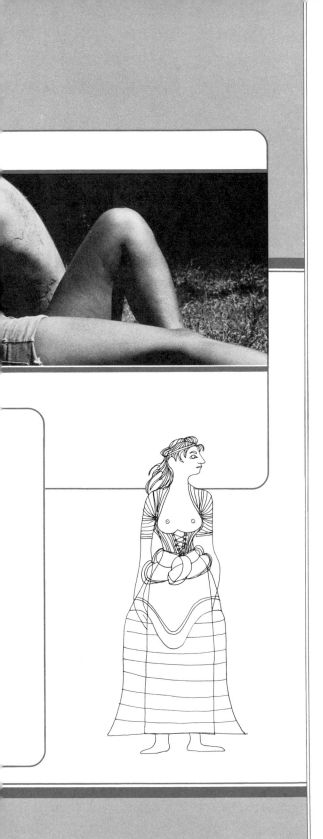

KEY QUESTIONS

1. What are the biological foundations of sexual arousal?
2. How do stimuli become erotic?
3. What are the effects of pornography?
4. How does sex drive differ for men and women?

What arouses you sexually? A nude, a sexually explicit book, fantasies, the caress of someone you love? How does your body respond to sexual excitement? Are you concerned about the intensity of your sex drive? These are personal questions and you might not think they belong in a textbook, but they are neither trivial nor shameful.

Human sexual behavior is central to human life, and the scientific study of human sexuality is a major theme in the history of psychology. Although an understanding of human sexuality is impossible without considering questions of belief, values, and morality, the biological foundations of sex and the relationship between the sexual stimulus and the sexual response can be isolated and studied. Sexual behavior, like other naturally occuring human behavior, can be examined by considering the stimuli that affect it and the form that the response takes.

271

Biological Foundations

The biological basis of sexual arousal consists of the brain, nervous system, hormones, and body surfaces sensitive to touch. Your capacity for sexual arousal depends upon your physical state; for example, fatigue, poor health, and intoxication all reduce the capacity for arousal. This is not to say that your sexual feelings are controlled exclusively by your bodily structures and chemistry; sex is not "just a physical thing"—it's also mental.

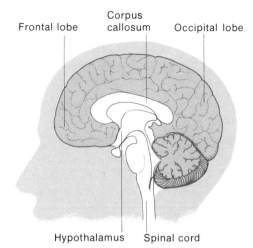

The hypothalamus helps regulate sexual behavior.

The Sexual Control Center of the Brain

The brain is a master control center for regulating behavior—including sexual behavior. Sexual arousal is turned on or turned off by the activity of the brain. Damage to certain areas of the brain have resulted in **hypersexuality** (continuous sexual activity) and in **hyposexuality** (no sexual activity or interest).[1,2] Feelings of sexual pleasure can result from the stimulation of certain brain structures with a tiny current of electricity.[3]

Behavior that is directed toward some goal is called *motivated*, and motivations that serve biological needs are called **drives.** The need for water, food, and sex are three biological drives. These drives energize and instigate behavior. One area of the brain is particularly important in regulating drive level, the **hypothalamus,** a small structure at the base of the brain. Following damage to certain areas of the hypothalamus, some animals no longer show any sexual interest;[4] stimulating other areas of the hypothalamus has been found to produce sexual behavior in animals.[5]

When different parts of the hypothalamus are stimulated with a weak current of electricity, various emotions may result, including rage, fear, and pleasure. Some of these hypothalamic regions have been called **pleasure centers.** If given the opportunity, animals will work to stimulate themselves and will continue until they are exhausted.[6] Another "pleasure center" of the brain is the septal area; like the hypothalamus, the septal area is a small structure deep in the brain. Human patients whose septal areas were stimulated reported that the resulting feeling resembled that preceding a sexual orgasm.[7]

The hypothalamus in rats seems to be similar to the human hypothalamus. An area has been found in the hypothalamus of rats which, when electrically stimulated, causes sexual activity.[8] The sexual behavior of male rats can be turned on and off by turning a switch on and off which controls the electric current reaching their hypothalamus. Studies like this one demonstrate the power of the brain to regulate and control sexual arousal and sexual behavior.

The Autonomic Nervous System

When you run, your heart beats faster; when you are cut, your blood vessels constrict to slow the loss of blood; when you get hot, you sweat. These glands, organs, and blood vessels are controlled by a system of nerves called the **autonomic nervous system.** The autonomic nervous system is a network of nerves connecting the brain to the organs and glands of the body; it is responsible for regulating many automatic functions such as blood pressure and heart rate. The control center for the autonomic nervous system is the hypothalamus, a brain structure that plays an important part in regulating our drives.

■ *Responses in Men and Women* Bodily changes during sexual arousal result from the stimulation of the autonomic nervous system. These changes are remarkably similar for men and women. From observing many different cycles of arousal and orgasm,

Sexual arousal is not just physical.

erogenous zone

Masters and Johnson, the well-known researchers in sexual behavior, have concluded that the basic physiological responses to sexual stimulation in both men and women are twofold: first, tissues become congested with blood, and, second, general muscle tension increases.[9]

Sexual arousal and response in men and women involves many separate components, among which are increases in heart rate and blood pressure; congestion of blood in the sexual organs, causing swelling; deeper breathing; and a generalized body flush. These bodily responses result from the stimulation of the autonomic nervous system.

■ *The Message in the Eyes* One response to sexual stimulation is that the size of the pupil of the eye increases. The **pupil** is the opening in the eye through which light enters. It appears as a round black spot in the center of the eye. In bright light the pupil of the eye constricts and becomes smaller; in the dark it enlarges. By changing size the pupil controls the amount of light reaching the light-sensitive cells at the back of the eye. The pupil is also affected by autonomic arousal.

Sexual arousal as well as other forms of emotional excitement cause the pupil to increase in size. In one study male and female subjects were shown various pictures and the size of their pupils was continuously recorded. Male subjects had larger pupils while looking at pictures of females than while looking at pictures of males. The reverse was true for females. In addition, females had large pupils when looking at pictures of babies. Apparently your pupil increases in size when you are interested or aroused.[10]

Other studies have shown that pupil size increases for heterosexual men while they look at pictures of nude women and for homosexual men while they look at pictures of nude men.[11] In a way the eye is a window into the mind, revealing mental states to the world. The eye also receives information from the world in the form of visual stimuli; sometimes these stimuli are sexually arousing.

■ *The Accelerator and the Brake* The autonomic nervous system has two parts, one of which is like an accelerator and the other is like a brake. The **sympathetic division** of the autonomic nervous system is the part that is like an accelerator; when it is active, it tends to increase heart rate, blood flow, and in general prepare the body for action. The **parasympathetic division** of the autonomic nervous system is the part that is like a brake; when it is active, it tends to decrease heart rate, blood flow, and in general prepare the body for rest. Typically, one of the two parts dominates at one time; to some degree the two parts work against each other.

When you are frightened, the sympathetic division of your autonomic nervous system becomes active; it causes your heart to beat faster, your mouth to become dry, and your muscles to gain blood at the expense of your skin and stomach. When you are resting after a meal, the parasympathetic division of your autonomic nervous system becomes active; it causes your heart to slow, your digestive juices to flow, and your stomach and skin to gain blood at the expense of your muscles.

The two divisions of the autonomic nervous system are both involved in sexual arousal and response. The initial stages of sexual arousal seem to be regulated by the parasympathetic division, while the later stages—including orgasm—seem to be regulated by the sympathetic division. Anxiety, like fright, is associated with the activation of the sympathetic division and actually interferes with the parasympathetic division. It is not surprising, therefore, that high levels of anxiety typically result in sexual problems.

Sex Hormones

What makes the two sexes different? Partly, it's a matter of body chemistry. **Sex hormones** are chemicals released directly into the blood by specialized sex glands—in the male, the *testes*, and in the female, the *ovaries*. Puberty begins with a great increase in the production of these hormones and their subsequent release into the bloodstream. This flood of sex hormones spurs the rapid development of the sexual organs and the so-called secondary sexual characteristics such as body hair. In the male, this change of body chemistry leads to an enlargement of the genitals, and in the female it leads to an enlargement of the ovaries and the onset of menstruation along with the gradual enlargement of the breasts. At the same time that these biological changes are occurring, most adolescents experience increased interest in the opposite sex. Do you remember when you first became interested in the opposite sex?

Stimulation and Stimulants

Sexual arousal is based—most directly—on **tactile stimulation** arising from certain sensitive body areas being touched, and—more indirectly—on sexual thoughts (associations, images, and fantasies). Human beings give and seek this tactile stimulation in a variety of ways, and they use their creative talents to produce books, movies, and paintings that stimulate sexual thoughts.

Someone you love may talk to you, touch you, or send you a letter; this information is received by your senses of hearing, feeling, and seeing. The information begins as physical energy in the world—as air pressure striking our ears, as pressure against our skin, or as patterns of light. Our bodies have special **sensory receptors,** cells that trans-

Sexual arousal and response are affected by the sense of touch.

form these physical energies into nerve impulses. These nerve impulses are electrochemical messages that travel along the nerves to the brain where they are processed and interpreted. The nerve impulses arising from the stimulation of the skin are particularly important for sexual arousal.

The brain, the spinal cord, the nerves, and the sensory receptors of the body are primarily built of individual nerve cells called **neurons.** These nerve cells are unique because their function is to carry messages from one part of the body to another. When one end of a neuron is stimulated—for example, when someone touches you—a neural impulse is generated which travels down the length of the neuron where it will stimulate a muscle or another neuron. If someone sticks your hand with a pin, sensory receptors in and under your skin send neural impulses to your brain; your brain then sends neural impulses down to the muscles of your arm directing it to move.

Your skin responds to pressure, warmth, cold, and pain. The tips of your fingers, the end of your tongue, and your lips are densely packed with pressure-sensitive cells, but your back has many fewer cells. Some skin receptors respond to cold and some to warmth; these same receptors respond to pressure as well. You can find temperature-sensitive cells by very gently touching your skin in different places with the sharp point of a pencil. Here's how to find a cold receptor: Take a pencil and lightly touch different spots on the skin of the underside of your upper arm. The pencil point will feel quite cold when it touches certain of these spots, and it will feel warm when it touches others. Information from the skin receptors as well as information from your ears and eyes travels to your brain where it is organized into experience.

A drug that is supposed to stimulate a desire to participate in sexual activities and to increase sexual capacity is called an **aphrodisiac.** The search for sex stimulants, although very old, has been unsuccessful; in spite of many myths to the contrary, no aphrodisiacs have been found. Alcohol, in small doses, seems to relieve tension and lessen inhibitions; for some people this may lead to an increase in sexual activity. Alcohol, however, has an effect on the body that reduces sexual capacity, particularly in high doses. Marijuana is also not a sex stimulant; there is no evidence that it stimulates a desire to participate in sexual activities or that it increases sexual capacity. Most people report a total lack of sexual interest while on

Is this legitimate advertising?

LSD. The use of heroin and morphine leads to a sharp decrease in sexual interest and capacity. Although many drugs are known to be sex depressants, no drug has been found that is a sex stimulant.

ⓢ The biological foundations of sexual arousal involve various structures in the brain, the autonomic nervous system, sexual hormones, and skin receptors. The hypothalamus is the control center for the autonomic nervous system and its sympathetic and parasympathetic divisions; the autonomic system is involved at all stages of sexual arousal and response. Sex hormones control sexual development and are responsible for the physical changes associated with puberty. Sexual arousal is most immediately dependent upon tactile stimulation; chemical stimulants of sexual arousal—aphrodisiacs—have never been found.

Sexually Arousing Stimuli

The primary source of sexual stimulation is tactile, pressure applied either to the sexual organs themselves or to other **erogenous zones** (sexually sensitive areas) such as the lips, breasts, or thighs. Other sexual stimulation surrounds us; it is less direct but very effective. Cocktail lounges sell drinks by using "topless" or "bottomless" waitresses. Toothpaste is sold on the promise of providing a "sexy" smile. Movies are now more explicitly sexual than ever before. How is it that words on a page, a line drawing, or a picture can be stimulating?

The Role of Learning

Male sexual arousal to a picture of a nude female is clearly a learned, not an inborn, response. What the men of one decade find sexually exciting, the men of another decade may find neutral. The sight of the female ankle used to excite men; today it rarely does. The sexually ideal woman, from the average man's point of view, used to be plump and small-breasted; today she is thin and large-breasted. This change is associated with changes in our society, not with basic biological changes in men; therefore it is a change of learned, not inborn, responses.

What the people of one society find erotic, the people of another may find repulsive. Different cultures endow different bodily features with erotic properties. Black pointed teeth, deformed ears or nose, long swinging breasts, rolls of fat—these are sexually exciting in some cultures but not in ours. The male movie idol in this society looks different from the male movie idol in Japan. Clearly, these cultural preferences are not inborn but are learned.[12]

How does this learning take place? The

process is called **classical conditioning,** an elementary type of learning in which simple emotional responses are acquired. When sexually neutral stimuli (such as pictures) are associated with the occurrence of direct tactile sexual stimulation, these neutral stimuli acquire arousal properties in and of themselves. The sexual response becomes *conditioned* to these other stimuli. For example, many different mammals become sexually aroused when they approach places in which they have had previous sexual experiences; through conditioning the place has acquired the power to produce sexual arousal.

Is there something other than the human body that you find sexually exciting? The odor of certain perfumes or the feel of silken lingerie are conditioned sexual stimuli for some men because they have become associated with sexual arousal and response.

Fetishes

It is believed that sexual fetishes are the result of early learning experiences. A sexual **fetish** is an object that a person comes to associate with sexual activity, objects as unlikely as shoes, underclothing, or furniture. Female underclothing is somewhat erotically arousing to many men; for the fetishist, however, the underclothing itself may be a primary sexual object, having greater sexual significance than the person who wears it.

The first sexual feelings that a thirty-year-old Dutch author reported occurred early in his childhood when he saw a young boy on crutches. Over the years following puberty he masturbated to the fantasy of a lovely woman dressed in furs hobbling on crutches. He made and bought several pairs of crutches, using them at night to walk about his room. He referred to the crutches as his "wives." He eventually married but required his wife, during intercourse, to take a pair of crutches to bed with her.[13]

Egyptian

Etruscan

Greek

Dutch

In each culture costume is used differently for sexual arousal.

Fantasies

Sexual fantasies are a source of sexual arousal and, at the same time, a response to sexual arousal. Erotic fantasies, often resembling miniature dramas, may be more frequent for males than for females. Kinsey's survey of sexual behavior reported that 37 percent of males, as compared with only 22 percent of females, reported definite or frequent fantasies concerning the opposite sex. For those in the survey who masturbated, 72 percent of the males and 50 percent of the females reported that they almost always experienced erotic fantasy during masturbation.[14] A more recent survey of married women found only 7 percent reporting no fantasies during intercourse.[15] The most frequent fantasies involved thoughts of being with another man and of being overpowered.

Pornography

Erotic fantasies are often stimulated by sexy books, magazines, or films; in fact, many sexually explicit novels are erotic fantasies written down. Books, pictures, or films that are intended to be sexually arousing are called **pornography.** The word "pornography" means something different from the word "obscenity," which means material that is offensive or disgusting. There is considerable disagreement about the relationship between these two words. Some people believe that all pornographic material is obscene; other people find some pornography enjoyable. There is also a long history of attempts to legally control the availability of pornography. But in recent years erotic material has been more and more generally available.

What is the effect of exposure to pornography? Most studies report that sexually explicit pictures and films are sexually arousing for both men and women. In one study 200 men and women viewed films of a couple engaging in mouth-genital contact and intercourse.[16] After the films, the audience reported their feelings on a questionnaire. Both men and women reported being sexually aroused, although men reported more arousal than women. Most men reported partial erection while viewing the films. Most women reported varying degrees of genital sensations; some reported breast sensations and vaginal lubrication.

Is pornography obscene?

A concern of many people is the easy availability of pornography to young people. Some argue that these materials will distort impressionable minds and may lead to rape or other forms of sexual deviance. In a followup to the study just discussed, the researcher wanted to find out what effect watching these films had on later sexual activities.[16] He found that there was essentially no effect at all.

If exposure to pornography leads to sex crimes, then it could be assumed that sex criminals have had a greater exposure to pornography than normal individuals. One researcher checked out this idea and found that, contrary to common belief, sex criminals had significantly less exposure to pornography during adolescence than did normal individuals.[17] Conclusions about the long-term effects of exposure to pornography are simply not available; but these effects appear to be less harmful than many people once believed.

ⓢ Sexual arousal is not just physical; it is also mental. Through the process of conditioning, a person associates a variety of stimuli—words, perfume, music—with arousal. These stimuli then become sexually exciting themselves. Thoughts and fantasies are also a source of arousal for both men and women. The intent of pornography is to sexually arouse. Pornographic films, while sexually arousing, have been shown to have little long-term effect.

Your Sex Drive: High or Low?

Your **sex drive** is your interest in, or motivation for, sexual activity; people have different levels of sex drive—some are high and some are low. The extent of your interest in sexual activity is not primarily due to the level of your sex hormones. Learning experiences and recent sexual history also influence your sex drive. Ill health, worry, and anxiety reduce sexual motivation.

The male's capacity to be stimulated sexually is very much a function of age. His capacity shows a dramatic increase with the onset of adolescence; it peaks about three to four years later (at about sixteen to eighteen years of age); it then slowly declines until old age.[14] Male sex drive is partly dependent on sustained sexual involvement, so that sex interest in the elderly is higher for those who have remained continuously sexually active.[9]

The sex drive of women differs from that of men. It is not known whether this difference results from biology or from learning. For men, maximum interest in sexual activity seems to be reached in the late teens. On the average, a woman's maximum sexual motivation is not reached until her late twenties or early thirties—ten or more years after the male peak. Another important difference is that female sex drive does not significantly decline with middle or old age as does male sex drive.[14] Kinsey, in his survey of American sexual behavior, concluded:

In their early adolescent years, when 95 percent of the boys of corresponding age were experiencing orgasm with average frequencies of 2.3 per week, only 22 percent of the girls in the sample were reaching orgasm in any sort of activity, either solitary, heterosexual, or homosexual. In the later teens, when over 99 percent of the males were responding sexually to orgasm with average (median) frequencies of 2.2 per week if they were single, and 3.2 per week if they were married—at a period when the average male was at the peak of his sexual capacity and activity—there was still nearly half (47 percent) of the females who had not had their first orgasm.[14]

Just as individuals vary in their needs for food and sleep, there is an enormous range of individual differences in sex drive. Many persons in their late teens and early twenties experience almost continuous sexual tension with little release. Others rarely feel sexually aroused. Neither is wrong or abnormal. Without a sexual partner your sexual drive can be neither *too high* nor *too low;* it is only within a relationship that there could be a problem with the partners' sex drives. This is a problem of matching. You may be "undersexed" in relation to one sex partner but "oversexed" in relation to another. In other words your sexual drives do not match.

Comparisons between men and women on the number of weekly orgasms may not be particularly meaningful. There are many who suggest that male and female sexuality are quite different. For example, in adolescence there is a great surge of sexual interest in both men and women. In men, however, it seems to be focused on genital pleasure, while in women it seems to be more general, involving awareness of other parts of the body that are changing, such as breasts and hips. With age, the superficial sexuality of adolescence changes to a mature sexuality in adulthood, but the male-female difference remains. Some authors claim that women are more motivated by a desire for love and intimacy than for intercourse,[18] while others argue that women are even more sexually motivated than men. Women, for example, unlike men, have the capacity for multiple orgasms of increasing intensity. In any case, it is generally agreed that male sexuality remains more focused on genital pleasure while female sexuality is more of a wholebody response and involves more of the emotional and psychological aspects.[19]

▣ The strength of your sex drive is the degree of your motivation for sexual activity. The sex drive of both men and women is

influenced by age, but the patterns are different. Male sex drive increases to a maximum at about 16–18 years of age and then begins to decline; female sex drive appears to peak in the late twenties or early thirties and does not decline as much with age. Sex drive is neither too low nor too high in an absolute sense; it is important only in relationship to your sexual partner.

Summary

KEY QUESTIONS

1. What are the biological foundations of sexual arousal?

   The brain, the autonomic nervous system, sexual hormones, and sensory receptors form the basis of the biology of sexual arousal. The master control center for regulating sexual arousal is the brain, particularly a structure called the hypothalamus. The hypothalamus controls the autonomic nervous system which is involved in sexual arousal and response.

2. How do stimuli become erotic?

   The direct source of sexual stimulation is tactile—from the touching of certain erogenous areas. Other erotic stimuli are learned; pictures, words, drawings all gain the power to stimulate sexual arousal through a form of simple learning called conditioning.

3. What are the effects of pornography?

   Studies show that both men and women respond sexually to explicitly sexual films, although men usually respond more than women. In spite of much concern over the effects of exposure to pornography, there is little evidence that it has harmful long-term effects.

4. How does sex drive differ for men and women?

   For men, sex drive appears to increase to a maximum at about age 17, then it gradually declines. For women, sex drive appears to increase until the late twenties or early thirties; it declines with age less than for men. Sexual motivation for men and women may also be qualitatively different. For men, sexuality is more genitally focused; for women, it is less focused and involves more emotional components.

KEY CONCEPTS

hypersexuality	An extremely high level of sexual drive resulting in almost continuous sexual activity.
hyposexuality	An extremely low level of sex drive resulting in little or no sexual activity.
drive	A motivation that serves a biological need, such as the need for food or sex.

hypothalamus	A small brain structure that regulates drives and controls the autonomic nervous system.
pleasure center	A brain area which, when stimulated with electricity, produces satisfaction or pleasure.
septal area	A brain area near the hypothalamus which contains a pleasure center.
autonomic nervous system	The network of nerves connecting the brain to the glands and organs of the body; responsible for regulating automatic functions such as blood pressure.
pupil	The hole in the center of the eye through which light enters.
sympathetic division	The part of the autonomic nervous system that prepares the body for action; the "accelerator."
parasympathetic division	The part of the autonomic nervous system that prepares the body for rest; the "brake."
sex hormones	Chemicals released into the bloodstream by the male and female sex glands, the testes and the ovaries.
tactile stimulation	Sensations resulting from touch or pressure.
sensory receptors	Cells that transform physical energy from the world into nerve impulses; for example, the cells in the eyes, ears, and skin.
neurons	Single nerve cells.
aphrodisiac	A drug supposed to stimulate sexual arousal.
erogenous zones	Sexually sensitive areas of the body, such as lips, breasts, or genitals.
classical conditioning	An elementary type of learning by association in which simple emotional responses are acquired.
fetish	An object that a person associates with sexual activity and requires for sexual gratification; for example, a shoe.
pornography	Sexually stimulating books, pictures, or films.
sex drive	The interest in, or motivation for, sexual activity.

15 Love and Sex

CHAPTER OUTLINE

KEY QUESTIONS

1. What is love?
2. What is sexually normal?
3. How does society regulate sexual behavior?

Remember your first love?

You may think of it now as an infatuation or a silly crush, but it was extremely important at the time, and is important still. The most famous young love is that of Shakespeare's Romeo and Juliet. Romeo says:

Did my heart love, till now?
Forswear it, sight!
For I ne'er saw true beauty
Till this night.

Your first love was a kind of rehearsal and preparation for later more meaningful loves; it was a learning experience in relationship.

Love is often a source of intense delight, and sometimes intense pain, but it is rarely neutral. It is necessary to life in infancy and releases our potential in adulthood. It is the source of much talk and much confusion.

Love

Ashley Montagu wrote a book about love[1] and concluded that love is a general creative principle which must guide our future. In his view, love is a form of behavior that contributes to the healthy growth of both the lover and the loved. Everyone agrees that love is good—but what is love?

Dictionary and Operational Definitions

Much of the poetry, music, literature, and art of the world is concerned with love. "Love" is a common word, a word you use often when you are talking to friends, but what does it mean? The Greeks had more than one word for it: **agape**, spiritual love, or love as giving and caring; and **eros**, erotic or passionate love, represented by Cupid and his arrows. The anonymous author of *The Ladies Dictionary* of 1694 tried to define love, but finally had to give up:

Love, *what is it? Answ. Tis very much like light, a thing that everybody knows, and yet none can tell what to make of it. . . . 'Tis extremely like a sigh.*

Webster's New Collegiate Dictionary of 1974 does considerably better, which suggests some progress:

love: *strong affection for another arising out of kinship or personal ties (maternal love for a child); attraction based on sexual desire; affection based on admiration, benevolence, or common interests; unselfish loyal and benevolent concern for the good of another.*

Yet even this definition somehow is unsatisfactory. Perhaps no set of words on a page can possibly match the quality and intensity of the subjective feeling we all have felt.

Rather than trying to develop a dictionary definition of love, psychologists have tried to define love in terms of behavior. Many psychologists believe that in order to study love scientifically, it must be possible to

measure it. From their point of view, the methods or operations used in measuring love provide the best definition of love. Definitions based on methods of measurement are called **operational definitions.** An advantage of using an operational definition of love is that it avoids confusion about what you mean; if you agree with the operational definition of love, you can objectively determine whether you are or are not in love.

Operational definitions require a method of measurement. But how can love be measured? One approach is by using a "love scale"—a questionnaire asking people to report their behavior and attitudes toward another person. Such a questionnaire consists of a number of items reflecting loving attitudes; the person answering the questionnaire responds to each item by reporting whether or not it correctly describes his or her attitudes. The result is a score that is interpreted as a measure of love. For example, the following items appear on one love scale:[2]

—*You feel he (she) understands you.*

—*You take his (her) suggestions seriously.*

—*You enjoy taking care of him (her).*

—*He (she) is sexually attractive to you.*

—*You feel more secure when you are with him (her).*

The operational definition of love, on the basis of this love scale, would be your total score, reflecting your degree of agreement with each of the items.

You may feel that trying to define love in terms of a score from a love scale is an inappropriate way to understand love. Your score, a single number, just does not seem equal to the depth and complexity of your feeling of love. You may disagree with the validity of the operational definition of love. This is a perfectly reasonable reaction; nevertheless, the development of operational definitions of love has stimulated a great deal of research on love that otherwise would not have been possible.

The Need for Love

Why do psychologists study love? The need for love is deeply rooted in the human psyche. Love is a way of overcoming separateness; and separateness, according to Erich Fromm, is the source of all anxiety. Being separate means being cut off, helpless, unable to use our powers. Fromm says:

The deepest need of man, then, is the need to overcome his separateness, to leave the prison of his aloneness. The absolute failure to achieve this aim means insanity, because the panic of complete isolation can be overcome only by such a radical withdrawal from the world outside that the feeling of separation disappears—because the world outside, from which one is separated, has disappeared.[3]

To overcome separateness you must be known. To be known, to be accepted as you really are, and to be prized for who you are, you must risk being open with another; you must disclose yourself in order to be known. Furthermore, it is in a close relationship with another person that we can best learn about ourselves. The other person, in a sense, acts like a mirror in which we can see ourselves more clearly.

Theories of Love

There are different kinds of love: love can be selfish and possessive or unselfish and giving. In order to understand these differences, theories of love have been developed by psychologists such as Abraham Maslow and Erich Fromm.

Love is a way of overcoming separateness.

■ *Being-Love and Deficiency-Love* Maslow distinguishes between two kinds of love: B-love (**being-love**—love for the being of another person; an unselfish love not dependent upon your needs) and D-love (**deficiency-love**—a selfish possessive love based upon someone's ability to satisfy your needs). B-love does not diminish from being gratified; it is generous and pleasure-giving; it makes possible the truest, most penetrating perception of the other person.

B-love, in a profound but testable sense, creates the partner. It gives him a self-image, it gives him self-acceptance, a feeling of love-worthiness and respect-worthiness, all of which permit him to grow.[4]

D-love is conditional; it depends upon whether personal needs continue to be met. But B-love is unconditional; it depends not upon what you do but upon who you are. And because it depends upon who you are, it is possible only when you allow yourself to be known.

■ *Mature Love and Immature Love*
Fromm also distinguishes between two types of love, **immature love** and **mature love.** Immature love is based on the satisfaction of needs and is similar to Maslow's concept of D-love. An example of immature love is a relationship between two persons, one of whom needs to dominate, command, and exploit the other; the other needs to submit, to be dependent, and to be dominated. The relationship will work only so long as each satisfies the other's needs.

In contrast to immature love, mature love is a relationship that allows individuals to retain their independence, their identity, and their integrity. In mature love people can overcome their sense of separateness yet continue to be themselves. Mature love is not just a pleasant sensation, it is an activity.

Love is an activity, not a passive affect; it is a "standing in," not a "falling for." In the most general way, the active character of love can be described by stating that love is primarily giving, not receiving. . . . Giving is more joyous than receiving, not because it is a deprivation, but because in the act of giving lies the expression of my aliveness.[3]

Erotic Love

Some love involves strong sexual feelings and some does not. Erich Fromm in his book *The Art of Loving* describes some of the varieties of love:

Brotherly love is love among equals; motherly love is love for the helpless. . . . In contrast to both types of love is erotic love; it is the craving for complete fusion, for union with one other person. It is by its very nature exclusive and not universal.[3]

Sex and love are sometimes clearly separable feelings: the love of a mother for a child is a sexless love, and the experience of masturbation can be a loveless sexual activity. When love and sex are joined, in **erotic love,** a high point of human experience is possible, a joy in which the whole is greater than the sum of the separated parts.

One of the best-known lovers of literature, Cyrano de Bergerac, wrote to the woman he loved:

> Love, I love beyond
> Breath, beyond reason, beyond love's own power
> Of loving! Your name is like a golden bell
> Hung in my heart; and when I think of you,
> I tremble, and the bell swings and rings—
> "Roxane!"
> "Roxane!" . . . along my veins, "Roxane!"

Unfortunately, Cyrano was never bold enough to declare his love in person, but his love for Roxane was erotic love, or sexual love, a feeling that combines adoration and tenderness with sexual desire.

Love and sex interact. Love can stimulate sexual desire, and the experience of sex is changed by love. Sexual behavior in erotic love involves freely giving and taking and can be a lusty and wholesome expression of the joy of living. As Maslow wrote:

Sex and love can be, and most often are, very perfectly fused with each other in healthy people. While it is perfectly true that these are separable concepts, . . . still it must be reported that in the life of healthy people they tend to become completely joined and merged with each other.[5]

Even outside of marriage, when intimate sexual behavior such as intercourse occurs, it most often occurs within the context of a loving relationship.[6] A sex survey showed that the overwhelming majority of women who have engaged in premarital intercourse report that they were in love.[7]

Sex is one way for two people in relationship to interact and communicate; as such, it

is profoundly affected by feelings and personal meanings, attitudes, and social and cultural customs, as well as biological urges. This form of love is the foundation of the human family, and of our society built upon the family units.

An understanding of human behavior must include an understanding of sexual behavior. Sexual interests and sexual expression are not only biological processes but are also significant parts of our emotional and spiritual experience. Sex is a major part of life. In a recent survey of college students, over 90 percent reported experiencing urges to engage in sexual activity.[8]

[S] Operational definitions, unlike dictionary definitions, are based on ways of measuring the concept to be defined. An operational definition of love is "the score made on a love scale." Maslow and Fromm observed that there was more than one kind of love; being-love and mature love are terms referring to unselfish love, while deficiency-love and immature love are terms referring to selfish love. Love and sex often interact and are fused in erotic love.

Forms of Sexual Expression

What is normal sexual behavior? Behavior that may be considered to be sexually motivated includes all sorts of human activities, ranging from dancing to sexual intercourse. Some psychologists, notably Freud, have argued that the motivation for most human behavior is sexual—if not explicitly, then in more hidden ways. The discussion here, however, will be confined to direct sexual acts that may culminate in **orgasm,** the climax of sexual feeling, accompanied by intense muscle tension and involuntary contractions. Human sexuality has a variety of outlets to orgasm, and some of the more common forms of expression will be discussed here. Two of these, sex dreams and masturbation, are solitary forms and two others, petting and intercourse, are interpersonal forms. Psychologists consider all of these to be quite normal.

The study of human sexual behavior has only recently become acceptable in our society. The first large-scale sex study was a survey of sexual behavior conducted by Kinsey. Kinsey and his associates interviewed thousands of men and women in different parts of the country and summarized their findings in two books, *Sexual Behavior in the Human Female* and *Sexual Behavior in the Human Male.*[9,10] Many other sex studies have been published since Kinsey's study that reveal how common different kinds of sexual behavior are.

Sex Dreams

Sex dreams, some involving orgasm, are common for both males and females, although more males have these experiences than females. According to Kinsey's sample, 83 percent of males and 37 percent of females have sex dreams to orgasm at some time in their lives. A common explanation of these dreams is the **compensation theory,** which states that orgasms in dreams compensate or make up for a lack of orgasms when awake. If this theory were true, you would expect to find more sex dreams during periods of reduced sexual activity when awake.

Kinsey reports that his survey data do not support this theory, since the frequency of sex dreams is not closely related to the occurrence of orgasms from other sexual outlets.[9] Sex dreams do not increase when other sexual activity decreases.

Masturbation

Masturbation, or self-stimulation, is a widespread sexual practice both in this culture and among other cultures, as well as among other mammals.[11] As such, it can be considered a natural and normal form of sexual expression.

Masturbation typically involves some form of genital manipulation and for both men and women results in orgasms over 90 percent of the time.[9] The "efficiency" of masturbation, however, does not mean that it is the preferred form of sexual expression; masturbation is not only discouraged by some social and religious customs, but as a solitary activity it lacks the profound personal significance and feeling attached to sexual relationships.

According to Kinsey's data, by the age of fifteen 82 percent of males and 20 percent of females have masturbated to orgasm; by the age of twenty these figures have increased to 92 percent for males and 33 percent for females.[9] More recent studies confirm that between 30 and 40 percent of college-age women, and almost all men, masturbate.[8] Eventually, over 90 percent of males masturbate to orgasm, and almost 60 percent of females do so.[9]

For an activity as common as this, there is much ignorance about masturbation. Because of the social controls concerning masturbation, it is a subject rarely talked about; as a consequence, those who practice masturbation often believe that they are strange, different from others, and weak-willed. Many persons suffer unnecessarily because of inappropriate guilt and anxiety associated with their own masturbation activity.

■ Henry: A Case History

Henry, a sophomore, was referred to the college psychiatrist by his counselor after the two had discussed Henry's difficulties with his studies. He reported himself unable to concentrate and to "get down to work." Instead of reading his assignments, he found himself aimlessly leafing through pulp magazines, cheap novels, and the daily paper. He soon began to describe himself as lacking willpower. After considerable hesitation, obvious discomfort, and embarrassment, he revealed that he lacked will-power not only in his studies, but also in controlling his, as he put it, tendency to indulge himself. Finally he admitted that he masturbated from time to time. Henry hastily explained that of course he knew everyone masturbated, but he felt that at his age he should have outgrown the habit and that, even if it was all right to masturbate occasionally, he did it too much. He felt caught in a vicious circle. When unable to concentrate on his work he frequently felt the urge to masturbate, but if he gave in he felt depressed and even less able to work.[12]

It was clear that Henry's problem was not masturbation itself, but rather the way he felt about his practice of masturbating. Henry was plagued by a number of myths about masturbation.

■ *Masturbation Myths* Society and parents are responsible for passing on to children many myths about masturbation. The problem with masturbation is the anxiety and stress caused by these false beliefs, some of which follow:

1. *Teen-agers do it but not adults—it is a habit that is outgrown.* This is false—adults of all ages masturbate, as Kinsey has shown, although the frequency declines with age.[9]

2. *It can be practiced to "excess."* This is false—the only consequence of frequent masturbation is the fatigue lasting for a few minutes.[13]

3. *It causes sexual problems later, such as impotence or frigidity.* This is false—there is no known effect of masturbation on later sexual capacities. In fact, those who suffer least from sexual problems later are those who masturbated in adolescence.[9] (This does not prove a cause-and-effect relationship however.)

4. *It is harmful, either psychologically or physically.* This is false—there is no evidence that masturbation is in any way harmful either psychologically or physically.[14] On the other hand, anxiety and guilt about masturbation can be a problem.

There is an alarming ignorance about masturbation, even among those who should know better. According to one report, half of the graduates of a Philadelphia medical school believed that masturbation frequently causes mental illness (it does not).[15]

Petting

Petting, sexually stimulating another person by touching, is practiced extensively in other cultures and among other mammals.[9] In this society ultimately over 90 percent of both men and women have petting experiences, and over 30 percent have petting experiences to orgasm.[9] The rate of heavy petting—genital stimulation without clothing barriers—apparently is increasing in frequency. While Kinsey reported that about 50 percent of college women experienced heavy petting twenty-five years ago, recent surveys typically obtain a higher percentage, from 60 to 90 percent.[16,17,18] The techniques of petting that are most commonly used are kissing, both simple and deep; breast stimulation, both manual and by mouth; and stimulation of the male and female genitals, both manually and orally. In some cases petting may be preliminary to intercourse.

Intercourse

Premarital intercourse is quite common in most societies in the world. In the majority of primitive societies limited adolescent intercourse is permitted for both males and females. In one study of 158 primitive societies, it was reported that 70 percent did not prohibit premarital intercourse.[6] The majority of persons engage in premarital intercourse in spite of societal prohibitions. Kinsey showed in his survey that about 50 percent of the females and about 70 percent of the males had engaged in premarital intercourse.

The rates of nonvirginity among college students are changing. Twenty-five years ago Kinsey reported that about one in five college women and somewhat over half of the college men had experienced sexual intercourse.[9] A more recent survey of 8,000 college freshmen and juniors found that 29 percent of the freshman women and 36 percent of the junior women were nonvirgin, while 42 percent of the freshman men and 59 percent of the junior men were nonvirgin.[18] Another large survey of university students found 30–40 percent of women and 40–50 percent of men nonvirgin.[19] The findings of a smaller survey of two hundred UCLA students, which showed that 35 percent of the 18–19-year-old women students and 40 percent of the 18–19-year-old men students were nonvirgin, were consistent with the other studies.[20] Thus the change that has taken place in the past twenty-five years or so has been an increase in the proportion of females who engage in premarital intercourse; the rate for males has remained about the same.

⑤ There is great variety in the forms of sexual expression and in the individual patterns of sexual behavior. Sexual behaviors such as sex dreams, petting, masturbation, and intercourse are common and can be considered normal. Premarital intercourse appears to have increased somewhat for women during the past twenty-five years but to have remained about the same for men.

Sex and Personality

In all of the studies of human sexual behavior, the most consistent finding that emerges is that people are different. The variety of people that are sexually stimulating to some persons and the tremendous range in sexual behavior suggests that nobody is alike sexually. To talk about what is the average frequency of some activity or to talk about what is "normal" in sex is practically meaningless because of large individual differences.

Some of the individual differences in sexual behavior are related to other aspects of personality. **Extroverts** (people who are sociable, impulsive, and practical) have been found to be different from **introverts** (people who are shy, thoughtful, and imaginative). One study of college students found that extroverts engaged in a greater frequency of sexual intercourse and had a greater number of different partners than introverts.[21] The extrovert was found to be more likely to endorse a permissive and promiscuous approach to sex, while the introvert was found to be more likely to stress virginity and loyalty to a single partner.

Individuals who are confident, self-assured, or "self-actualized" tend to have a more active sexual life and have fewer sexual problems. A study of married women found that those with high self-esteem were likely to express a positive attitude toward sex, using such descriptive phrases as "very good," "pleasurable," and "something I'm looking forward to," while those with low self-esteem were more likely to express a negative attitude toward sex, using such phrases as "something I've learned to live with," "originally it was distasteful," and "I can take it or leave it."[22]   For psychologically healthy, "self-actualizing" persons in a deep emotional relationship, sex can be a kind of peak experience. As Maslow describes it:

Sexual pleasures are found in their most intense and ecstatic perfection in self-actualizing people. If love is a genuine yearning for the perfect and for complete fusion, then the orgasm as sometimes reported by self-actualizing people becomes the attainment of it. Experiences described in reports that I have obtained have indeed been at so great a level of intensity that I felt it justifiable to record them as mystic experiences.[5]

Few people, however, reach the "ecstatic perfection" that Maslow describes. For most people, sex is a meaningful but not a mystic experience.

The Social Control of Sex

All societies exercise some form of regulation of sexual behavior; our society follows fairly strict social control, even of private sexual acts. Legal controls are imposed not only on sexual activities, such as premarital intercourse or homosexuality, but also on stimuli assumed to be sexually arousing, such as pornography and sex education materials. Most adults have been exposed to one or more of these activities and stimuli. According to one report, nine out of every ten Americans is a sex criminal, having violated some sex law.[23] Sexual "crimes," however, are rarely punished.

Sexual Standards

How should you behave? Just because a practice is common or normal does not necessarily mean that it is proper or right. What is proper? Schools, churches, and parents

are all responsible for communicating the forms of socially acceptable behavior; children are socialized by these agents of society and given standards of behavior. People who do not conform to these social norms suffer punishing consequences. They may be jailed, ostracized, or labeled "promiscuous," "slut," "prude," or "queer."

Children begin to learn sexual standards when very young. The following is a case history of a young woman whose parents were harsh and punishing in their attempt to make her conform to their concept of proper sexual behavior.

At about age four I was accused of playing with myself and was slapped with a metal spatula and made to stand up against a wall. . . . When I was in high school all hell broke loose when I began dating boys. Suddenly there seemed to be no other topic in the minds of my parents but sex. It was a constant flow of accusations. And the situation became worse each year. I was called every name, but the favorite was slut. When I was 16 I was accused of being pregnant and hounded about it, although no attempt was made to take me to a doctor. Every boy I dated was insulted by my father and accusing and insinuating remarks were made to them. Finally during the summer before I was married my mother informed me that I had no right to wear white on my wedding day, that red would be more appropriate for me. I was a virgin at the time.[24]

There are differences among people in the types of standards for premarital sex they accept. One common sexual standard is **abstinence**—intercourse is acceptable only after marriage. **Permissiveness** is the sexual standard stating that intercourse is acceptable between those who are deeply in love or engaged to be married. A third standard, the **double standard,** states that women must be virgin at marriage but not men. According to recent studies, the majority of young men and women consider premarital intercourse as acceptable if the participants are seriously in love or engaged.[25,26] The double standard is still operating, since both men and women place less value on male virginity than on female virginity at marriage.[8] Have you observed different attitudes held by men and women regarding their sexual behavior?

The Generation Gap and the Sexual Revolution

The area of sexual conduct is a great source of conflict between adolescents and their parents, particularly for daughters. The standard of sexual behavior upheld by parents is typically much more conservative than that held by their college-age children.[27]

Are children today more sexually permissive and promiscuous than their parents? The evidence shows that the change that has occurred is primarily a change in *attitudes,* not behavior; there is less hypocrisy today since attitudes and actual behavior are more consistent. There is less of a difference between how young people act and what they say they believe. As one researcher concluded after surveying the sexual attitudes and behavior of thousands of young people:

The popular notion that America is undergoing a sexual "revolution" is a myth. The belief that our more permissive sexual code is a sign of a general breakdown of morality is also a myth. These two myths have arisen in part because we have so little reliable information about American sexual behavior. . . .

What has been happening recently is that our young people have been assuming more responsibility for their own sexual standards and behavior. The influence of their parents has been progressively declining.[7]

A sign of the more permissive attitude toward sex in this country is the liberalization of the views of some church groups. The control of sexual behavior has not only been legal and parental in nature but also theological. Attitudes of some churches are changing however. This new point of view is evident in a report prepared by a committee of leading Presbyterians. Although the report does not represent official church policy, it is an example of the increasing liberalization of the attitudes of religious leaders in this country; they take issue with the view that sex is shameful.[28]

Sex Education. *We consider it a matter of the highest importance in the Christian formation of children that they be equipped with a realistic understanding and appreciation of their own and others' sexuality.*

Masturbation. *We find no evidence for any theological, psychological or medical strictures against masturbation per se. . . . There is nearly unanimous medical opinion that no physical harm to the body is produced even by frequent masturbation. There is even some argument for the positive value of masturbation in relieving sexual tension.*

Homosexuality. *The essentially negative attitudes of church and society toward the phenomenon of homosexuality has often resulted in aggravated suffering and grievous injustice for homosexual persons. Laws against private homosexual acts between consenting adults should be repealed.*

Premarital Intercourse. *Sexual expression with the goal of developing a caring relationship is an important aspect of personal existence and cannot be confined to the married and the about-to-be-married. . . . We question whether society has the right to impose celibacy or celibate standards on those who do not choose them.*

All societies regulate sexual conduct.

The Individual's Response

Guilt is a common feeling resulting from violating a behavior standard of your group or society. Since the majority of people in our society violate the stated sexual standard, most experience feelings of guilt in varying degrees. Guilt over sexual activities, however, typically diminishes as the sexual activities continue; one study showed that over three-fourths of those studied were not in any way restrained from sexual activities by feelings of guilt.[7] Most people begin their active sexual lives with some minor behavior such as masturbation or kissing and then gradually advance through stages to sexual intercourse. As each new stage of intimacy is reached for the first time, guilt feelings occur, then may diminish with continued experience. A study of the sexual behavior and feelings of college women revealed that, among those students who had engaged in intercourse (22 percent), the predominant attitude present was one of enjoyment and satisfaction.[29] This was particularly true for those experiencing sex within the context of a deep emotional relationship.

Many people, however, refrain from sex before marriage, preferring to maintain a sexual standard prohibiting premarital intercourse. Such standards are often based in moral or religious principles. For some persons, violation of these principles could lead to prolonged feelings of anxiety and guilt. Thus the choice of limiting sex to marriage is a way of avoiding these unpleasant consequences.

S　The most common standard of sexual behavior held by young people today is permissiveness, the attitude that intercourse is acceptable between those who are deeply in love, even though they are not married. Attitudes are still, however, influenced by the double standard. There has been a great change in sexual attitudes but little change in sexual behavior.

Summary

KEY QUESTIONS

1. What is love?

   The dictionary defines love in a variety of ways, including "unselfish loyal and benevolent concern for the good of another" and "attraction based on sexual desire." Instead of dictionary definitions, psychologists tend to use operational definitions, which are based on using a method of measurement. An operational definition of love is "the score made on a love scale." A variety of types of love have been described; Maslow and Fromm stress the difference between love that is selfish, dependent, and conditional and love that is unselfish, unconditional, and based on giving.

2. What is sexually normal?

   Surveys of people's sexual behavior show clearly that many forms of sexual expression are common and therefore normal. Sex dreams to orgasm occur in the lives of about 80% of men and 40% of women. Masturbation is practiced by over 90% of men and over 30% of women. Petting to orgasm is practiced by about 60–90% of men and women, and about 30–40% of college women and 40–50% of college men have engaged in premarital intercourse.

3. How does society regulate sexual behavior?

Each society regulates sexual behavior by establishing and enforcing standards for what is proper. Schools, churches, and parents all communicate these standards to the young. The most common sexual standard endorsed by young people today is permissiveness, which states that intercourse is acceptable between two people who love each other deeply. When people violate society's standards, they feel guilt; guilt about sexual behavior, however, does not seem to restrain people for very long.

KEY CONCEPTS

agape	The Greek word for spiritual love; love as giving and caring.
eros	The Greek word for erotic or passionate love.
operational definition	A definition of a concept based on a description of the method of measuring it.
being-love (B-love)	Maslow's term for an unselfish love; the person does not require the satisfaction of his or her own needs.
deficiency-love (D-love)	Maslow's term for a selfish possessive love; the person's love is conditional upon the satisfaction of his or her own needs.
immature love	Fromm's term for a selfish love that lasts only as long as needs are satisfied.
mature love	Fromm's term for love based primarily on giving; an unselfish love that allows people in relationship to maintain their independent identities.
erotic love	A feeling that combines adoration and tenderness with sexual desire.
orgasm	The climax of sexual feeling, associated with high levels of muscle tension and contraction.
compensation theory	The theory that orgasms in sex dreams make up for a lack of sexual activity while awake.
extroverts	A personality type; people who are sociable, impulsive, and practical.

introverts	A personality type; people who are shy, thoughtful, and imaginative.
abstinence	A standard of sexual behavior stating that intercourse is acceptable only after marriage.
permissiveness	A standard of sexual behavior stating that intercourse is acceptable between those who are deeply in love or engaged to be married.
double standard	A standard of sexual behavior stating that premarital intercourse is acceptable for men but not for women.

Suggested Readings

The Development of Sex Differences ed. by Eleanor E. Maccoby. Stanford, Calif.: Stanford University Press, 1966. A collection of important papers reviewing research on sexual development. Includes a lengthy annotated bibliography.

Learning to Love by Harry Harlow. New York: Ballantine Books, 1971. Presents Harlow's classic studies of love among the monkeys. Five forms of love are distinguished. Applications to human beings are suggested.

The Art of Loving by Eric Fromm. New York: Harper & Row, 1956. A beautiful book about the psychology of love.

Sexual Behavior in the Human Female by Alfred C. Kinsey *et. al.* Philadelphia: W. B. Saunders, 1953. A comprehensive attempt to discover and to report what people do sexually, and what the social significance of sexual behavior may be. Results of interviews with thousands of men and women, with the findings reported in many statistical tables.

Human Sexual Response by William H. Masters & Virginia E. Johnson. Boston: Little, Brown, 1966. Highly technical account of the anatomy and physiology of the human sexual response. Dispels many myths. Very difficult reading.

The Sexual Wilderness by Vance Packard. New York: McKay, 1968. A popular account of contemporary sexual behavior and attitudes. Includes results from a large-scale survey.

The City and the Pillar by Gore Vidal. New York: New American Library, 1965. A description of homosexuality and the homosexual life-style.

A General Introduction to Psychoanalysis by Sigmund Freud. New York: Washington Square Press, 1952. Description of the theory, methods, and results of psychoanalysis. Of special relevance to this section is Freud's analysis of the sexual life of children and his stages of psychosexual development.

Sexual Behavior and Personality Characteristics ed. by Manfred F. De Martino. New York: Grove Press, 1963. Interesting collection of articles on sexual behavior and sexual problems.

Research Methods

V Case Studies

A case study is an intensive study of one person. Rather than attempting to understand the behavior of a whole population, the researcher attempts to understand in depth the behavior of a single individual. Great novels are, in a way, fictionalized case studies; they are often intensive explorations of a single character.

The Case-Study Method

Each person is unique and has unique talents and problems. Understanding uniqueness is the special contribution of the case-study method. Case studies are careful descriptions of individuals, and as such they preserve the facts about cases for others to study. For example, a famous case study is the book entitled *The Three Faces of Eve*. This book is a study of a young woman named Eve White who displayed three separate personalities. She was one of the rare cases of multiple personality, and her history is preserved in this popular book. Eve White was a shy and gentle woman who was seeing a therapist because of her severe headaches and black-outs. Nothing unusual occurred until one day when she suddenly switched personalities:

As if seized by sudden pain, she put both hands to her head. After a tense moment of silence, both hands dropped. There was a quick, reckless smile, and, in a bright voice that sparkled, she said "Hi there, doc!" . . . This new and apparently carefree girl spoke casually of Eve White and her problems, always using she *or* her *in every reference, always respecting the strict bounds of separate identity. . . . When asked her name, she immediately replied "Oh, I'm Eve Black."*[1]

299

Like other case histories, the case of Eve White reveals a great depth of understanding on the part of the researcher. How is this understanding achieved?

Interviews, Records, and Tests

Suppose you were a psychologist and you wanted to understand in depth an emotionally disturbed client. How might you proceed? If you were to take a scientific approach, you would seek an empirical understanding; you would observe and collect facts. But what kind of facts?

Information about the nature and source of psychological problems might come from a variety of sources. One source is the interview. By asking questions and listening carefully, the researcher can learn a great deal about what the person thinks, feels, and wants, about the early home life, and about other significant people who may be involved. A second source of information is psychological tests, which are useful in assessing personality and intelligence. Most tests yield scores that permit an individual to be compared with others on a variety of traits. A third source of information for case studies is existing records; an individual's life history is sometimes apparent from public legal records or medical records.

On the basis of interviews, tests, and other information the psychologist puts together a picture of the individual as a whole. Often the facts lead the psychologist to a conclusion or inference about the nature of the problem. For example, on the basis of information from interviews and from certain psychological tests, a psychologist may infer that a psychotic person has a brain disorder and may recommend treatment accordingly. Such an inference, although supported by empirical evidence, is more in the nature of an informed guess than of a definite

fact. The psychologist cannot see the actual condition of the person's brain. The clinician must often rely on intuition when drawing a conclusion from insufficient evidence.

The Case of Michael Boland

The following case study shows how information is gathered and conclusions are reached in intensive studies of single individuals. It reports the case history of a young man named Michael Boland who came to a clinic for help.

Michael Boland was 21 years old when he phoned for an appointment at a local guidance clinic. His problem, as he stated it on the phone, was that he tended to attract and be attracted to members of his own sex. He also felt that he was too shy and anxious.

Michael looked younger than 21 years of age. His tall, slim appearance, with wavy hair, long lashes, and even features, gave him an air of prettiness. Michael wore conspicuously stylish clothes and jewelry, with every article carefully matched.

Michael described his mother as a sweet, kind, and sensitive person, and said that he had been very close to her. He said that his mother had always been very protective in her relationship with him, and he missed not having guidance and concern that his mother had continuously provided.

Whenever Michael went out in the evening, his mother stayed awake until he got home and she expressed relief that he had returned without any mishaps befalling him. Michael would then feel extremely guilty because his mother was ill, and she had been kept awake because of worry and apprehension about his welfare.

Michael characterized his relationship with his father as one of coolness and distance, rather than open conflict. He said that he had never felt a deep emotional bond with his father, and they rarely had any extended conversations.

[After graduation from high school] Michael began to frequent homosexual bars at irregular intervals, but his mother did not allow him to spend every evening out of the house. He stated that many of the men he met at the bars were physically attracted to him, and this was a very enjoyable experience. Michael also said that he derived a great deal of physical pleasure from homosexual activity.

Michael reported that he often felt greatly troubled by the rights and wrongs of his sexual behavior and thought he was committing a sin.

Michael was seen by a female psychologist, Dr. T. The client appeared to be quite anxious during the first interview, and he tended to speak in a quavering and barely audible tone of voice. He found it difficult to maintain eye contact with the examiner, and often looked to one side or down at his hands.

The client completed a general personality inventory, the MMPI. He was asked to give stories to a number of cards from the Thematic Apperception Test (TAT), in order to gain more information about social relationships and interaction patterns.

There was evidence on the test material of anxiety, depression, and repetitive and bothersome thoughts. The client, however, was not overwhelmed by his personal difficulties.

The client's responses to the test material suggested an uncertainty about sexual identification. Some of the figures on the TAT cards were initially labeled as female, and then as male. He tended to view females his own age as physically unattractive and artificial. The client responded in a very negative manner to concepts about his own body. He also indicated that he sometimes wished that he were a girl.

In general, the test results confirmed the information about the client that had been gained from the interview.

Therapy was recommended in order to help Michael deal with his inner turmoil and guilt feelings about his sexual orientation, and to aid him in modifying his shy and dependent behavior. The goal of therapy was to enable the client to make future decisions, including the selection of a sexual partner, on the basis of a more open choice, rather than because of poor interpersonal skills.[2]

The passage above illustrates some of the techniques used in a case study to help the clinician and the client get a better understanding of the problem at hand. The client was asked to complete a series of tests solely for this purpose. One of these tests was the **Thematic Apperception Test (TAT),** for which the client was shown a series of pictures and asked to make up stories about them. Then the clinician could evaluate the stories in terms of the problem being considered. Another test that was given was the **Minnesota Multiphasic Personality Inventory (MMPI).** The MMPI is a general personality test, consisting of around 600 questions, each of which is answered "yes" or "no." It is designed to detect abnormal personality traits.

Clinical Intuition

As you have seen from the case study just presented, individuals reveal much information in clinical interviews. Some of this information is explicit and verbal and some of it is implicit and nonverbal. Gestures, facial expressions, and intonations of the voice are often cues that an experienced clinician is able to use to come to a conclusion about the person being interviewed.

The ability to come to a conclusion without having explicit evidence is called **intuition.** Psychologists who spend a lot of time interviewing people often develop a highly refined clinical intuition. In a book called *Listening with the Third Ear*, Theodore Reik—a well-known therapist—described an instance of his clinical intuition during a therapy session with one of his patients:

One session at this time took the following course. After a few sentences about the uneventful day, the patient fell into a long silence. She assured me that nothing was in her thoughts. Silence from me. After many minutes she complained about a toothache. She told me that she had been to the dentist yesterday. He had given her an injection and then had pulled a wisdom tooth. The spot was hurting again. New and longer silence. She pointed to my bookcase in the corner and said, "There's a book standing on its head." Without the slightest hesitation and in a reproachful voice I said, "But why did you not tell me that you had had an abortion?" [3]

How was Reik able to reach this remarkable (and correct) conclusion? From Reik's point of view, the patient's silence during the interview indicated that she was resisting making her thoughts known and therefore something significant was on her mind. Reik regarded the idea of tooth extraction as a symbol of birth, and the remark about the upside-down book gave Reik an image of a fetus in the womb. Thus Reik came to the concept of an abortion on the basis of a number of cues evident during the course of the interview. While this intuition was correct in this case, not all clinical intuition hits the mark so clearly; intuition is often wrong.

Sampling Situations or People

Much of psychological research involves the study of groups of people. A sample is taken from the whole population of people, the sample is studied, and a **generalization** is made about the nature of the population on the basis of the information obtained from the sample. To the extent that all people resemble the sample of people studied, the generalization about all people will be valid.

Generalization Across Situations

The case study, however, is an intensive study of only one person. Instead of sampling numerous people, the case study samples numerous situations from the life of one person. On the basis of information obtained from the sample of situations from the life of the individual, a generalization is made about all situations in the life of the person. For example, the person might be observed in several social situations and found to be withdrawn and shy in each. On the basis of that information, the generalization might be made that the person is shy in all situations. To the extent that the sampled situations resemble all situations in the person's life, the generalization will be valid. In a series of interviews a man might describe events in his life that he found particularly frightening. The interviewer might note that each of the described events involved a situation in which he was dependent upon a woman; the interviewer might then postulate that the man being studied is—in general—frightened of dependency on women.

Nomothetic or Ideographic

The two kinds of psychological studies that have just been compared—sampling people or sampling situations—are examples of two general approaches in scientific research. The **nomothetic approach** strives to establish general laws that apply to all people on the basis of studying a selected sample of people. The **ideographic approach** strives for an in-depth understanding of an individual, on the basis of studying a selected sample of events from the life of that individual. The case-study method is an ideographic approach to research, emphasizing the uniqueness of the individual case.

Proponents of the ideographic approach call it dynamic, holistic, deep, and sensitive; opponents of the approach call it vague, subjective, unscientific, and uncontrolled. Proponents of the nomothetic approach call it public, objective, reliable, and rigorous; opponents of the method call it mechanical, artificial, incomplete, and superficial. Nevertheless, both types of research have contributed to the science of psychology. Each approach is more suitable for investigating one particular type of question. The nomothetic approach often asks how you are like other people. The ideographic approach often asks how you are different from other people.

Observer Bias

Case studies involve intuitive interpretations of test results and information obtained from interviews. Because this kind of information is often subjective, the case-study method is especially vulnerable to the problem of **observer bias.** Each observer has a particular way of viewing the world. A particular fact, as seen from different points of view, supports different conclusions. The interpretation placed on the facts depends upon the theory of human behavior that you subscribe to. For example, an interviewer with psychoanalytic leanings might see a patient's silence as "resistance," while an interviewer with different theoretical beliefs might see the silence as a sign that the patient is able to relax in the therapeutic relationship.

Another problem is the biasing effect of **selective attention,** the tendency to attend to and perceive only part of the information available. Since there are more facts available than can be meaningfully understood, observers must make some selection from the total. Different observers select different subsets of facts as having significance. The particular subset that is selected is a function of the observer's expectations, beliefs, and history.

Being aware of their vulnerability to observer bias, case-study interviewers take special precautions to make their studies as objective as possible. They learn to prolong the stage of data collection and put off conclusions until adequate facts emerge. Interviewers learn to check and recheck their observations. They learn to be receptive and open to details, even those that are unexpected.

KEY CONCEPTS

case study	An intensive study of one person.
Thematic Apperception Test (TAT)	A personality test that involves making up stories about pictures.

Minnesota Multiphasic Personality Inventory (MMPI)	A general personality inventory consisting of hundreds of questions; it is designed to test for a variety of abnormal personality traits.
intuition	The ability to come to a conclusion without having explicit evidence.
generalization	A conclusion about the nature of a population based on evidence from a sample.
nomothetic approach	A scientific approach based on studying groups of people, aimed at establishing general laws.
ideographic approach	A scientific approach based on studying a single individual, aimed at an in-depth understanding of the individual.
observer bias	The tendency for observations to be distorted by different interpretations, opinions, expectancies, or beliefs.
selective attention	The tendency to attend to and perceive only a small part of the information available.

VI Growth

16 Personality

CHAPTER OUTLINE

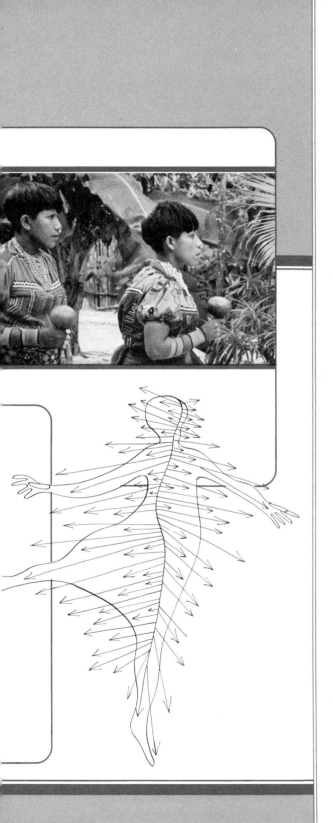

1. What is personality?
2. How can you describe your personality?
3. What are theories of personality?
4. Are you normal?

Who are you?

You will spend most of your life, one way or another, trying to answer this simple question. Each day you learn more and more about yourself; you have a growing understanding of what you are like, where you are going, and why you do the things you do. An important goal of this book is to add to this understanding.

Your concern for who you are is a search for your *self*. Awareness of self is learned early in life; a baby girl discovers the boundaries of her body, what is and what is not *self*, by playing endlessly with her hands and feet. She learns where she stops and where the world begins. But learning about your self does not stop with the discovery of the boundaries of your body; it continues throughout life, focusing on understanding your particular pattern of thinking and acting—the discovery of your psychological self, your *personality*.

What Is Personality?

Who are you? You could answer this question by describing your typical pattern of behavior in the world—perhaps you are a person who is "aggressive," "lazy," "intelligent," or "cheerful." You would be describing your personality.

The word "personality" comes from the Latin word *persona*, which meant the mask worn by actors to signify their role in the drama. Today however the word refers to more enduring personal qualities, the personality or self. Your **personality** is your typical way of reacting to the world and relating to the people around you. To say that you are "cheerful" means that in many different situations and at many different times you express joy or optimism rather than gloom or pessimism. The "you" of today here in this room is similar in certain ways to the "you" of yesterday somewhere else; both were "cheerful."

Personality characteristics describe consistencies both at different times and in different situations. Although there are differences between your behavior today and your behavior last month, there are similarities and consistencies, too. Although there are differences between your relationship to your mother and your relationship to other women, there are also similarities. These similarities and consistencies in your way of behaving are what characterize your personality.

Seeming and Being

Appearances are not always what they seem; seeming and being are different. The "self" that we present to the world is often false, a personal construction behind which we hide our real selves.

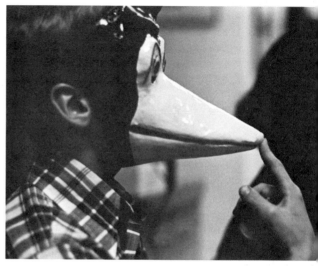

Seeming and being are different.

A choice that confronts every one of us at every moment is this: Shall we permit our fellow men to know us as we now are, or shall we seek instead to remain an enigma, an uncertain quantity, wishing to be seen as something we are not?

This choice has always been available to us, but throughout history we have chosen to conceal our authentic being behind various masks. . . . We conceal and camouflage our true being before others to foster a sense of safety, to protect ourselves against unwanted but expected criticism, hurt, or rejection. This protection is purchased at a steep price. When we are not truly known by the other people in our lives, we are misunderstood. When we are not known, even by family and friends, we join the all too numerous "lonely crowd."[1]

The way we *act* and the way we *are* often are different. We may present different selves to different people: the self we present at home may not be the self we present to close friends. Think of yourself as having three different faces: a social face, a personal face, and a real face.

■ *Social Face*   Your **social face** represents how you act in public. Like a wig, this face may have several interchangeable styles, depending upon whom you wish to impress. Imagine yourself making an appearance at a party where there are many strangers in the room. As you enter the room, you strive to appear unconcerned, cheerful, and "cool"; you strive to hide your nervousness and inexperience.

You strive to create good first impressions. In public, you wear a kind of false face—a mask—in order to present yourself at your best. You have learned that people often judge you on the basis of your physical appearance, clothes, voice, cosmetics, and mannerisms. You use these superficial aspects to create for yourself a public image, a social face.

■ *Personal Face*   Your **personal face** represents your **self-concept,** or the way you see yourself. Your personal face is the person you think you are. This private vision could be a grandiose idea or a rather harsh judgment and may or may not correspond to reality. The feelings you have about yourself are reflected in this private vision.

Your self-concept can be positive or negative. If you have a positive self-concept, you may think of yourself as competent, worthy, likable, and intelligent. If you have a negative self-concept, you may think of yourself as inadequate, inferior, and worthless. What is your self-concept? In the following table, which of the statements do you feel best describe you?[2] Check the ones that fit you best.

What kind of a personal face do you have? How positive is your self-concept? Your idea of yourself and the impressions others have of you are often different; your personal face and social face are rarely the same. You can discover this difference by asking a friend to check the statements below that correspond to the image others have of you.

Positive Self-Concept	Negative Self-Concept
☐ I am intelligent	☐ I feel hopeless
☐ I am self-reliant	☐ I am worthless
☐ I am satisfied with myself	☐ I am insecure within myself
☐ I am tolerant	☐ I just don't respect myself
☐ I am sexually attractive	☐ I am shy
☐ I am optimistic	☐ I don't trust my emotions
☐ I usually like other people	☐ I am a hostile person
☐ I am a responsible person	☐ I often feel humiliated
☐ I am emotionally mature	☐ I have few values and standards of my own

How do you see yourself?

■ *Real Face* Your **real face** represents what you are in reality. This is how you would appear if you could see yourself clearly. This is the self referred to in the poet's line "To thine own self be true." If you could be peeled like an onion, with your outer shell of pretense and pride removed, your naked core—your real self—would be exposed. This is not a rigid plaster mask but is changing, becoming, as you grow. If you are on a journey in search of your self, this is the reality awaiting you at the end of your trip.

A Test to Take

If I were to ask you who you are, how would you describe yourself? Which mask would you wear? Would you pretend to be something that you are not? Which of the following characteristics describe you the way you really are? Which describe the impression you try to create at parties? Check off the alternative for each number below that corresponds to your real self. Are your social face and real face ever the same?

1. ☐ I am sometimes careless and impulsive
   ☐ I am always self-controlled

2. ☐ I am sometimes very depressed
   ☐ I am always cheerful

3. ☐ I am sometimes lonely
   ☐ I am never lonely

4. ☐ I am sometimes selfish
   ☐ I am always generous

5. ☐ I am sometimes shy
   ☐ I am always friendly and sociable

6. ☐ I am sometimes nervous and anxious
   ☐ I am always cool and calm

7. ☐ I am sometimes naive and ignorant
   ☐ I am always experienced and knowledgeable

8. ☐ I am sometimes embarrassed
   ☐ I am never embarrassed

9. ☐ I am sometimes dumb
   ☐ I am always intelligent

10. ☐ I am sometimes angry
    ☐ I am never really angry

How well do you know your friends? Which of the above characteristics describe your best friend? Do you think you know the "real face" of your best friend?

⑤ The word "personality" comes from the Latin word for "mask" and refers to your typical way of reacting to the world and the people around you. You have aspects to your personality, or three "faces": a social face, a personal face, and a real face. Your social face is your public self; your personal face is your private image of yourself, or your self-concept; your real face is what you are in reality.

Describing Your Personality

Carl Jung

What kind of a person are you? How would you describe yourself? Are you friendly, shy, nervous, idealistic, talkative, selfish, cheerful, dominant, suspicious, reserved, jealous, intelligent, lazy, considerate, inquisitive, forgetful, creative, modest, sensitive, enthusiastic, moody? How many different words can you think of that accurately describe who you are? We have developed thousands of words to describe ourselves. Trying to understand ourselves, trying to understand others, and trying to communicate this understanding are among the most significant of human activities. Psychologists have over the years developed many systematic ways to describe personality.

Personality Types

What type of person are you? Do you think that people can be classified into different personality types? It is certainly possible to classify people. Just as trees or cats can be classified into different types, people can also be classified into different types. A **personality type** is a set of personality characteristics that one group of people has in common that makes them different from another group.

Carl Jung, an early disciple of Freud, developed a theory of personality types. Jung was born in 1875 in a small country town in Switzerland and was the son of a Protestant clergyman. Early in his studies Jung showed an interest in religion, ancient languages, and archaeology, but after a dream he had while in college, he abruptly switched to natural science and worked for an M.D. degree.

Jung was a close friend and follower of Freud, but broke with the founder of psychoanalysis after criticizing Freud's emphasis on sex. Jung viewed the motivating force for people not as primarily sexual, as Freud did, but as a creative energy, shared by all.

Jung introduced his book *Psychological Types*[3] by contrasting the opposing natures of Plato and Aristotle. Plato was a poetic visionary and mystic for whom ideas were more real than the world of objects. Aristotle

Are you an introvert?

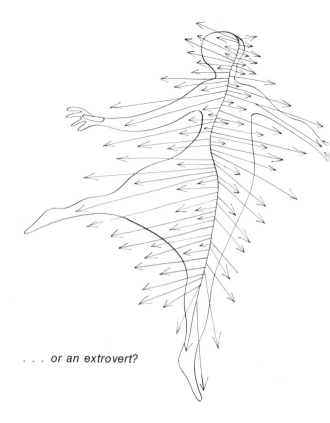

. . . or an extrovert?

was a scientist, concerned with studying and classifying the forms and events of the external world. According to Jung, Plato and Aristotle represent two fundamentally different tendencies in the human personality: Plato, concerned with the inner world, was an introvert and Aristotle, focusing his energies on the outer world, was an extrovert.

Introverts turn inward, seek isolation, and tend to withdraw from social engagements. They are reflective and introspective, absorbed with self-searching thoughts. They are self-critical and self-controlled, giving an outwardly cold appearance. They prefer to change the world rather than to adjust to it. **Extroverts** seek social contacts and are outgoing and accommodating. They appear friendly and outspoken and make friends easily. They are tolerant of others but relatively insensitive to the motivations and moods of their friends. They prefer to experience things rather than to read about them. Can you apply one of Jung's two personality types to yourself? How do you appear to others, as an introvert or an extrovert?

Most people are a mixture of introvert and extrovert, being neither wholly one nor the other. This is one of the problems of classifying people into types. Unlike rocks, few people can be easily sorted into boxes according to type. We are just not that simple; each of us has the potential for behaving in different ways in different circumstances.

Personality Traits

An alternative way of describing your personality is to think of yourself—not as a type—but as a collection of traits. **A personality trait** is a relatively permanent personality dimension or characteristic that makes you different from someone else. For example, "aggressiveness" is a personality trait; you can have varying degrees of this trait, from extremely aggressive to only slightly aggressive. Your personality can be described by listing the degree to which you have each of many different personality traits.

Dominance is another trait; it is characteristic of both humans and animals. Some individuals tend to be very dominant; they seem confident, independent, are often argumentative, and they seek leadership positions that enable them to direct and control the activities of others. The dominant person finds it easy to initiate interactions with others and to resist pressures to conform. The opposite of dominance is **submissiveness.** The submissive person tends to be timid, dependent, and conforming. Such a person suppresses personal dissatisfactions and follows the lead of others.

Animals show this personality trait as well as humans. Groups of chickens that have been together for some time establish a "pecking order" among themselves; a pecking order is also known as a **dominance hierarchy.** At the top of this hierarchy is a bird that can peck at and dominate all the rest without getting pecked back. The second bird in the pecking order can peck at all those below it on the hierarchy, but is pecked at by the most dominant bird. The unfortunate bird on the bottom is pecked by all the others and can peck none in return.[4]

In human groups there are dominance hierarchies too. Individuals are dominant with some people and submissive with others. That is, in the human "pecking order," some people are above us (they dominate us) and some people are below us on the hierarchy (we dominate them). Where are you in the human pecking order? Do you tend to be dominant or submissive in most of your relationships? How do you act in a group of your peers? Do you usually lead or follow? What if a woman is dominant and a man submissive? What if a child is dominant and a parent submissive? Is it "natural" for certain kinds of people to be dominant and "natural" for others to be submissive?

Security is another important personality trait. Secure people have a firm sense of their own identities. They relate easily to other people, and in their involvement with them generally feel accepted. They are usually optimistic, seeing other people as friendly and having good intentions; they are adventurous, striking out on their own and expecting the best.

Insecurity is the opposite of security. Insecure people may lack an overriding sense of personal identity. The ordinary events of living often threaten their feeling of security or safety, and they are preoccupied with preserving themselves. Such people often feel isolated, unloved, and discontent. Insecure people are generally pessimistic, seeing other people as hostile and rejecting. They often feel discouraged and expect the worst from the world, as if some disaster were always about to happen. Few individuals are wholly secure or wholly insecure; most of us are somewhere between the two extremes. How would you describe yourself? How do you pretend to be?

Some individuals, like this woman executive, tend to be dominant.

Situational Differences

The idea of personality types and traits suggests that people have relatively permanent and consistent ways of behaving in different situations and at different times. But recent studies of personality have questioned this idea.[5] How consistently do you behave? You are not the same at school and at home. You are not the same alone and with friends. You are not the same with your parents and with strangers. You behave differently in different situations.

This does not mean that the concept of personality traits is useless. It does mean that, in considering your personality traits, you should take into account different situations and how you behave in them. You may be consistently outgoing in certain types of situations and consistently shy in others. You may be dominant in some circumstances and submissive in others. To describe your personality accurately, these situational differences must be considered.

[s] Personality can be described in many different ways. One way is by classifying people into types, such as introvert or extrovert. A second way is to think of people as having different dimensions or traits, such as dominance or insecurity. A problem with both the type and trait descriptions is that they assume that people behave consistently over time and in different circumstances; but in fact there are important situational differences in personality.

Theories of Personality

A theory of personality is a comprehensive explanation that describes how some individuals are different from others. Personality theories typically identify the important ways in which personalities vary and may offer an explanation of how these personality differences originate. Different theories view personality differently. Three major views of personality are represented in the psychoanalytic, social-learning, and humanistic theories of personality.

Psychoanalytic Theory

Sigmund Freud, the founder of psychoanalysis, believed that people could be understood only by understanding their inner thoughts and feelings. Some thoughts and feelings are conscious while others are unconscious. According to Freud's psychoanalytic theory, certain memories and impulses are repressed—pushed into the unconscious—and we are thereafter unaware of them. Painful thoughts and feelings are repressed in order to avoid anxiety; if we are unaware of them, we can't be frightened by them. These unconscious ideas and memories, though we are unaware of them, continue to influence our behavior. Individual differences in personality, according to psychoanalytic theory, result from differences in the content of the unconscious mind and from differences in coping with these unconscious feelings and ideas.

Freud conceived the total personality to consist of three systems which, in the healthy person, work together cooperatively. The totally unconscious **id** consists of basic biological drives—the avoidance of thirst and hunger, the need for sex—and operates according to the **pleasure principle.** The sole aim of the id is to seek the gratification of pleasure and avoid pain, thereby reducing bodily tension

The second system, according to Freud, is the **ego,** the executive of the personality, responsible for voluntary processes such as perceiving, thinking, and remembering. The

People around you are models whose behavior you observe and copy.

ego takes into account the reality of the world as well as the demands of the id and tries to devise constructive ways to achieve satisfaction.

The third system is the **superego,** the moral area of the personality. Initially, children depend upon the guidance of their parents for determinations of good and bad, for what is moral and what is sinful. As children become older, they adopt their parents' ethical standards as their own; they assimilate or "internalize" this moral code. The superego is this internalized moral code. Eventually children no longer need their parents for moral judgments; they are controlled by their superegos. At this time the child is said to have a conscience. The id is full of "wants"; the superego is full of "shoulds"; the ego is the "me" that seeks the compromise between the "wants" and the "shoulds." How do you see yourself in terms of these personality concepts? Do you have struggles between the impulsive demands for instant pleasure coming from your id and the moral judgments of conscience coming from your superego?

Social-Learning Theory

A second major theory of personality is the social-learning approach. The social-learning theory of personality stresses the ways in which patterns of behavior are learned through interaction with other people and with the environment. As you grow up your personality is shaped and molded by the experiences you have. You learn to behave differently under different conditions. From this point of view, individual differences in personality result from different histories of learning experiences.

You learn by doing and also by observing. When you were young, you struck another and then were punished for it. This is an example of **direct learning,** or learning by doing. Many of your actions as a child resulted in rewards or punishments, approval or disapproval. You learned to do things leading to rewards and approval and you learned to avoid doing things leading to punishment and disapproval.

Much of your learning, however, resulted not from doing but from observing others.

When you were young, you learned to play certain games by watching others play. This is an example of **observational learning,** or learning by watching and imitating others. People around you—your parents, an older brother, or your friends—were models whose behavior you observed and copied. Because observational learning is so effective, many people are concerned with the aggression and violence shown on TV. By watching others display violence, children may learn to become more violent themselves. Are there parts of your personality that you acquired by observing and copying your parents?

Humanistic Theory

The psychoanalytic theory of the personality focuses on unconscious memories and impulses, while the social-learning theory focuses on learned behavior. Both of these theories conceive of your personality as determined by the past—either by old memories that are now repressed or by your past history of learning. In contrast, humanistic theory focuses on your view of yourself and on your growth toward fulfillment. From this point of view, individual differences in personality result from differences in the perception of self and the world.

According to the humanistic theory of personality, people are oriented toward the future; they plan, strive for goals, and seek fulfillment. Personality can be understood as a process of growth or becoming, rather than as something determined by the past. Carl Rogers and Abraham Maslow, two humanistic theorists, stressed the way people viewed themselves and their world, and explored the conditions of personal growth. Both believed that openness to experience and self-acceptance fostered growth and led to fulfillment. How clearly can you see yourself? How aware are you of your feelings in most situations? Can you accept your feelings? Or do they make you feel guilty or upset?

⑤ A personality theory attempts to give a complete explanation for why people behave as they do. The psychoanalytic theory of personality focuses on how unconscious impulses and memories influence behavior. The personality is assumed to consist of three parts: the id, ego, and superego. The social-learning theory of personality stresses the influence of learning on behavior. From this point of view, your typical way of behaving is the result of both direct and observational learning. The humanistic theory of personality focuses on how people experience themselves and their worlds. According to this view. people are oriented toward the future and seek fulfillment.

Carl Rogers

Being Different

No two people are alike. Even twins from the same egg, with identical genetic structures, are different as a consequence of differences in their experiences. In the English language there are over 1,000 words to describe individual differences in personality. The number of combinations possible of those thousand words, according to one estimate, exceeds by far the total number of atoms in the universe! The possible varieties of personality are equally numerous.

What does being different mean for you? Your body, your needs, your memories, your thoughts, your personality—all are unique. There has never been someone like you, there is no one quite like you now in the world, and there never will be. Your individuality does not make you worse or better than anyone else: everybody is in the same boat.

Try *feeling* your difference. Imagine that your eyes were orange and you had green spots on your nose and you were the tallest person in the world. How would you feel at a party?

Why does being different, or even the thought of being different, cause so much worry? Imagine looking the way you look right now in a world where everybody else was eight feet tall with orange eyes and green spots on their noses. You might feel like painting green spots on your nose to hide your difference. Even now, at this moment, you are trying not to be different. The clothes you wear, to some extent, follow the fads or fashion of the day for your age group. Why, in fact, are you wearing clothes at all? We seem to have a basic desire not to stand out in the crowd, not to be very different. There is security in joining the crowd, but there is something lost too: the possibility to be truly yourself, to be entirely free. Suppose you did not try to cover up the ways you were different from other people; suppose you did not hide your differences in body, feelings, desires, thoughts, and personality. Would you still be normal?

Are You Normal?

Have you ever wondered whether certain of your thoughts, feelings, or behaviors were normal or not?

Perhaps you have feared that in some ways you are not normal. Deciding whether you or someone else is normal is not at all easy to do. Here is a personality description of an individual written by a psychologist. Would you say that the person described here is normal or abnormal?

You have a strong need for other people to like you and for them to admire you. You have a tendency to be critical of yourself. . . . Your sexual adjustment has presented some problems for you. Disciplined and controlled on the outside, you tend to be worrisome and insecure inside. At times you have serious doubts as to whether you have made the right decision or done the right thing. . . . You have found it unwise to be too frank in revealing yourself to others. At times you are extroverted, affable, sociable, while at other times you are introverted, wary, and reserved. Some of your aspirations tend to be pretty unrealistic.[6]

What kind of person has just been described? Is it possible for a person who has those kinds of problems to be a *normal person?* The description was invented by a psychologist, then given to college students. Surprisingly, a survey showed that over 90 percent of the college students rated the personality description given as a "good" or "excellent" interpretation of their own indi-

"Normal" behavior differs among cultures. This is a purification ceremony at a child's funeral in East Nepal, where the people believe in reincarnation.

vidual personalities.[6] Some of the comments made by the students were: "I agree with almost all your statements and think they answer the problems I may have"; "On the nose! True without a doubt"; "This interpretation applies to me individually"; "Unbelievably close to the truth." Almost all of the students accepted the *same* statement as a description of themselves.

Normal Problems

"Normal" does not mean "having no problems." Everybody has problems that worry them to some extent. The typical student in high school or college has doubts and worries about physical attractiveness, ability to love and be loved, the control of anger, the sex drive, and sexual behavior. The secret fears we all have are, remarkably enough, very similar; what you fear and what

I fear are not that different. Many of the weaknesses you see in yourself are felt by almost everyone else; your feelings of guilt or shame about the things you have done are felt by almost everyone, for almost everyone has done the things you have done.

What is the normal person like? Psychologists who have tried to study the normal person can't agree among themselves. One psychologist, after studying seventy young persons selected because of their normality, concluded: "The vast majority of our subjects exhibit some anxiety about sexual role function. . . . Our subjects demonstrate specific struggles with anxiety, depression, shame, and guilt."[7] Another psychologist selected fifty men from over 1,900 men on the basis of their being "most normal." His testing of them showed that over 50 percent of them had neurotic symptoms, although the disorders were mild.[8] The elected student councils from three colleges were tested in another study.[9] One college president commented, "It is as normal a group as you'll ever get." The psychologist found that some of the "normal" students had alarming problems, such as extreme depression, withdrawal, coldness, sadism, and other symptoms of neurosis. He concluded that 57 percent could benefit from mental health services and 14 percent urgently needed psychiatric care. Obviously, being normal does not mean being without problems.

Normality Is a Value Judgment

What does it mean to be normal? The word **normal** is used in more than one way; sometimes it means good and sometimes it means typical or average. It is used both evaluatively and descriptively. When it is used *evaluatively*, a value judgment is made; in this sense "normal behavior" means "good behavior," what you ought to do, what is acceptable or desirable. "Abnormal behavior," then, means what is bad, undesirable, immoral, or bizarre. Thus certain sexual practices are referred to by some people as "abnormal acts," even though the majority of people have participated in them. Masturbation is one such sexual act. What people mean when they call masturbation abnormal is that in their opinion it is not good or desirable. You are justified in asking what are the criteria, standards, values, and hidden assumptions behind the use of the words "normal" and "abnormal."

Cultural Differences

What is "good" and "acceptable" behavior in one culture may not be "good" in another culture. The Tchambuli tribe of New Guinea has different standards of normality than we do. A businesslike and sexually aggressive Tchambuli man or an emotionally dependent and sexually passive Tchambuli woman would be considered "abnormal" in their society.

■ *Being Kind Is Being Crazy* The anthropologist Ruth Benedict cites an extreme example of cultural differences:

The most spectacular illustrations of the extent to which normality may be culturally defined are those cultures where an abnormality of our culture is the cornerstone of their social structure. . . . A recent study of an island of northwest Melanesia describes a society built upon traits which we regard as beyond the border of paranoia. . . . Their preoccupation with poisoning is constant; no woman ever leaves her cooking pot for a moment untended. . . . Fear and distrust pervade the culture. . . . They have even rigorous religiously enforced customs that forbid the sharing of seed even in one family group.[10]

In this island society where suspicion, mistrust, and fear were "normal," where no one could work with another or share food with another, there was one man who was regarded by all his fellows as crazy.

He was not one of those who periodically ran amok and, beside himself and frothing at the mouth, fell with a knife upon anyone he could reach. . . . But there was one man of sunny, kindly disposition who liked work and liked to be helpful. Men and women never spoke of him without laughing; he was silly and simple and definitely crazy (according to the people of his island society).[10]

The point is that what is normal is normal *for some group*. For some comparisons, the group is an entire culture. There can also be great differences within a given culture.

■ *The Case of the Ozark Preacher* As you move from place to place within our country, you encounter differences in what is socially acceptable behavior.

In an isolated rural area of the Ozark Mountains a man received a revelation from God, and a "call" to preach that revelation to his neighbors. He did so successfully. Later he was "called" to preach in the neighboring communities, and with equal success. He soon achieved great prestige in the area as a highly respected charismatic leader. But then he received a "call" to go to the city. Soon after arriving in St. Louis he was arrested for preaching on the street in the business district during the rush hour. Subsequently he was diagnosed by a psychiatrist as a paranoid schizophrenic, because he had delusions of grandeur and hallucinations. Here a man who conforms to a rural, lower-class subculture seems to be a deviant from the point of view of an urban, middle-class subculture.[11]

What does it mean to be normal? For Kuna Indian women from the San Blas Islands off Panama, it means wearing leg bands and nose rings.

Normal Means Typical

One of the ways the word "normal" is used is evaluatively, referring to behavior that is acceptable. The second way that "normal" is used is *descriptively*. From this perspective an act is "normal" if it is typical of a group, if it is conventional or ordinary for that group. An act is abnormal if it is unusual or unconventional for that group. Defining "normal" in this way, it is correct to say that masturbation is normal, since it is typical for this culture. From this point of view, a person who has an IQ of 130 is just as unusual, and therefore abnormal, as a person who has an IQ of 70; both are equally far away from the average IQ of 100.

It is not necessarily undesirable to be deviant; being different from what is typical can be either good or bad. All people of unusual talent or intelligence are "abnormal"

in the sense of being different from the usual. Are you normal? Many things that you do, many thoughts and feelings that you have, many fears and fantasies you dwell on are normal—in many ways you are not that different from other people. But you are unique; no one else is quite like you, and because you are different in some ways from all other people, you are in these ways "abnormal."

⑤ Being normal does not mean being without problems. The word "normal" is used in different ways. Sometimes it is used evaluatively, to refer to behavior that is regarded as good. Other times it is used descriptively, to refer to behavior that is typical or average for a culture.

Summary

KEY QUESTIONS

---

1. What is personality?

   Your personality is your typical way of relating to people and reacting to the world; it is what makes you different from other people. The concept of personality refers to your enduring personal characteristics or consistencies in your behavior in different situations or at different times.

2. How can you describe your personality?

   Personality can be described by classifying people into different types, such as introvert or extrovert, or by identifying different personality traits, such as dominance or insecurity. Since people behave differently in different circumstances, situational differences must also be taken into account when describing personality.

3. What are theories of personality?

   A theory of personality is a general explanation that accounts for the nature and origin of differences in personality. The psychoanalytic, social-learning, and humanistic theories are different ways of viewing personality.

4. Are you normal?

   The word "normal" is used to refer both to good behavior and to typical behavior. To be normal does not mean to have no problems. Most of what you do and feel are done and felt by most other people; because of this, in most ways you are normal (or typical). But in some ways you are different from everyone else—you are unique—so you are to some degree "abnormal."

KEY CONCEPTS

---

personality	An individual's typical way of relating to people and reacting to the world.
social face	A public image; the false front that is presented to other people.
personal face	A private image; an individual's self-concept.
real face	The true self; what an individual is in reality.

self-concept	A private image of oneself; an individual's personal face.
personality type	A set of personality characteristics that one group of people has in common that makes them different from other groups.
introvert	A personality type that turns inward, withdraws from social engagements, is introspective, self-controlled, and reflective.
extrovert	A personality type that turns outward, seeks social contacts, is friendly, outspoken, and tolerant.
personality trait	A characteristic or dimension of personality that each person possesses in varying degrees, such as aggressiveness, dominance, or insecurity.
dominance	A personality trait describing the tendency to be confident, independent, and controlling.
submissiveness	The opposite of dominance; refers to the tendency to be timid, dependent, and conforming.
dominance hierarchy	A group that can be ordered from most dominant to most submissive; an individual in this group dominates those below and is dominated by those above; a "pecking order."
security	A personality trait describing the tendency to relate easily to other people, to feel accepted, to be optimistic and self-confident; individuals with this trait have a firm sense of their own identities.
insecurity	The opposite of security; refers to the tendency to feel threatened by living, unloved, pessimistic, and discontented.
id	According to Freud, that part of the personality that is the unconscious storehouse of basic biological drives.
ego	According to Freud, that part of the personality that deals with reality and is responsible for voluntary processes of thinking, perceiving, and remembering.
superego	According to Freud, that part of the personality that is the internalized moral code or conscience.
pleasure principle	The principle that governs the operation of the id, namely, the seeking of pleasure and the avoiding of pain.
direct learning	Learning by doing.
observational learning	Learning by watching and imitating others.
normal	Refers to behavior that is either good or is typical for a culture.

17 Relationships

CHAPTER OUTLINE

KEY QUESTIONS

1. What is the basis of friendship?
2. What are the forms of interpersonal communication?
3. What is nonverbal communication?
4. What are the characteristics of good and bad relationships?

We need other people. We need close personal relationships. Without others we are lost, confused, lonely.

A prisoner who had been placed in solitary confinement wrote, "Gradually the loneliness sets in. Later I was to experience situations that amounted almost to physical torture, but even that seemed preferable to absolute isolation."[1]

You spend a lot of time with other people, talking with them, working with them, or simply being together. Most of your behavior is social—it occurs in interaction with others. The way you act in the presence of others is different from the way you act when you are alone; what you do is modified and influenced by what others do. In turn, you affect the behavior of persons you are with.

Many of our personal problems are actually *interpersonal*—they stem from our difficulties in relating to other people. Understanding the nature of interpersonal relationship is a step toward social growth.

Friendship

Will Rogers once said, "I never met a man I didn't like." Most of us, however, like some people and dislike others. You have met a lot of people in your life, but only a few of them became your friends. Why did those particular people become your friends and not others? How do you feel about them?

A Friendship Scale

Can friendship be measured? One psychologist has developed what he calls a "liking scale," a way of measuring how well one person likes another.[1] Think of a good friend of yours and check the items below that reflect your attitudes toward that person.

☐ When I am with this person, we are almost always in the same mood.

☐ I think that this person is unusually well adjusted.

☐ I would highly recommend this person for a responsible job.

☐ In my opinion, this person is an exceptionally mature person.

☐ I have great confidence in this person's good judgment.

☐ Most people would react very favorably to this person after a brief acquaintance.

☐ I think that this person and I are quite similar to each other.

☐ I would vote for this person in a class or group election.

☐ I think that this person is one of those people who quickly wins respect.

☐ I feel that this person is an extremely intelligent person.

☐ This person is one of the most likable people I know.

☐ This person is the sort of person I myself would like to be.

☐ It seems to me that it is very easy for this person to gain admiration.

The items in the "liking scale" reflect three aspects of liking: respect for the other person, a positive evaluation of the other person, and the perception that the other person is similar to you. Do these correspond to what it means to you to like someone?

Similarity and Complementarity

Think about yourself and your friends, then try to decide which of the following is true:

1. Birds of a feather flock together.
2. Opposites attract.

Are you and your friends similar or are you opposite in many ways? When you think about it, you will realize that you and your friends are similar in some ways and different in others, so neither of these general rules is probably totally true for you.

■ *Birds of a Feather* In certain ways, you and your friends are similar. According to the **principle of similarity,** birds of a feather should flock together; people who are similar ("of a feather") should be friendly ("flock together").

Who your friends are depends in part on which people you meet, since you cannot make friends with people you never see. But the people you meet are often similar to you in various ways: they are similar geographically, since they probably live in the same general area; they are often similar economically and similar in age. One study of engaged couples found similarities in many

value a person who needs to be submissive. A person who is dependent may be attracted to a person who tends to take charge. This theory would be supported by evidence showing that people who like each other have personality characteristics that are opposite. Although some studies have found a tendency toward opposing personalities between friends,[8] most studies find couples to have similar, not opposite, personalities.[9,10,11] Thus, while there is some evidence that opposites attract, most of the evidence supports the idea that birds of a feather flock together.

Reinforcement and Exchange Theories

Our relationships are a source of rewards and punishments for us. Some relationships are highly rewarding, others are punishing, and still others are rather mixed. According to the **reinforcement theory of friendship,** we tend to like those people who reward or reinforce us; the more they reward us, the better we like them.[12] There are many potential rewards in relationships: praise, approval, agreement, and validation are all rewarding. This idea was expressed by a character in one of Disraeli's novels when he said, "My idea of an agreeable person is a person who agrees with me."

The best-selling book by Dale Carnegie, *How to Win Friends and Influence People,*[13] argues that people like to be appreciated and they tend to like those who express this appreciation. Many psychological studies have confirmed that people like those who reward them through praise or other positive evaluations.[14,15,16]

An alternative view of how people become close is the **exchange theory of friendship.**[17] According to this theory, there is an "interpersonal marketplace" and each person has a "market value." Physical attrac-

background dimensions, including religious affiliation, income and social status of parents, and the type of family relationship in which they were raised.[2] Persons tend to select marriage partners of similar intelligence level[3] and of similar educational attainment.[4] A series of studies has shown that the degree of interpersonal liking is related to the proportion of agreement in attitudes and beliefs between couples.[5,6]

Why should we be attracted to persons who are similar to us in attitude and belief? One possibility is that we respond to those who support us when they express agreement with our ideas, and this validation is a rewarding experience.

■ *Opposites Attract* A common theory of friendship and love is that "opposites attract." This is called the **principle of complementarity.** If you and a friend are *complementary,* you are opposite but each supplies what the other lacks. The idea is that you like people who are mirror images of yourself—their strengths are your weaknesses or their needs and your needs are opposite and therefore do not compete.[7] For example, a socially awkward person may particularly value a person who is socially at ease. A person who needs to dominate may

to look extremely attractive or quite plain. The men who had been told that they did well on the IQ test were more likely to make romantic advances to the attractive woman; the men who had been told that they did poorly were more likely to make advances to the plain woman. The faked IQ results apparently had raised or lowered the estimates the men had of their own social desirability, or market value, and this—in turn—influenced their subsequent selection of a romantic partner with a high or low market value.

To think of friendship in terms of reinforcement and market values is to have, it seems to me, a particularly limited and pessimistic view of friendship. While there is certainly some truth in these two theories, most of us have experienced close friendships that cannot adequately be described in these economic terms. What do these theories leave out? They fail to discuss commitment, loyalty, and sensitive understanding, and these, I believe, are more important than the reinforcement we provide each other. What do you think?

Ⓢ Why do two people become friends? One possibility is that people like those who are similar to them (principle of similarity); a second possibility is that people like those with opposite needs (principle of complementarity). Most available evidence supports the principle of similarity. Two theories to account for the formation of friendships are the reinforcement theory and the exchange theory. According to the reinforcement theory, we like those people who reward us with praise, agreement, or validation. People who are similar to us are more likely to be agreeable and therefore more likely to be reinforcing. According to the exchange theory, we estimate our own "market value," then try to sell ourselves to those of equal or higher value.

tiveness, high status, wealth, wit, and other characteristics add to our market value. Those with high market values have high capacities for rewarding others. We estimate our own desirability, then try to "sell" ourselves to those with equal or greater value. If we overestimate our value, we risk rejection. People who are extremely attractive, according to this theory, tend to associate with others who are extremely attractive (or wealthy) because they are after the best deal they can get in the "marketplace."

One experiment manipulated the estimations people had of their own value.[18] The experimenter gave a group of men an IQ test, then told half of them that they had done exceptionally well and told the remaining half that they had done exceptionally poorly. These results, of course, were faked; what the men were told was unrelated to how they actually scored on the test. The subjects of the experiment were then placed in contact with a young woman who was either made up

Communication

Friendship requires communication. You spend a lot of time trying to communicate to your friends how you feel. Sometimes you are understood and sometimes not. Have you ever felt when talking to a friend that the two of you were "on the same wavelength"?

Can you remember the last conversation you had with someone? What was it about? Were real feelings and ideas exchanged or did you talk about the weather? Perhaps you communicated something with your facial expressions instead of just your words—communication can be both verbal and nonverbal. Verbal communication uses words. But if information or feelings are to be transmitted from one mind to another, both talk and listening are required. Sometimes we communicate when we talk and sometimes not.

Parallaction

Parallaction is pseudo-interaction in which two or more people *appear* to be having an exchange but there is no real involvement with each other.[19] It is termed parallaction because the action is going on in parallel, independently, with no intersection. Parallaction occurs in our ritual greetings to each other. These rituals serve the function of a nod of recognition but their form is verbal. They consist of words but they have no meaning—they are a form of noncommunication.

John: Hello! How are you?

Sue: Fine, thanks. How are you?

John: Just great.

Sue: Nice day, huh?

John: Sure is.

Sue: Warm enough for you?

John: You bet. Think it'll rain?

Sue: I don't know—maybe.

John: Well, see you later.

Sue: Okay, don't work too hard.

John: Yeah, be good now.

Sue: Be seeing you.

John: Bye bye.

Sue: So long.

This parallaction is a greeting ritual in which neither information nor feelings are exchanged. There is no intention of conveying information, only of recognizing the presence of each other.

Another common form of parallaction occurs when two persons are talking but neither person is listening. Joe talks, and while he is talking Ellen is thinking only of what she will say when he is through; when Joe finishes, Ellen talks, and Joe starts thinking about what he is going to say when she is through. Rather than listening to each other,

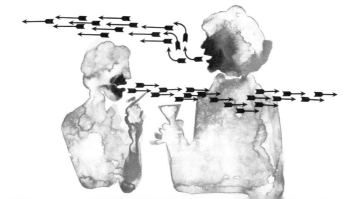

Parallaction.

they act independently; they are having a pseudo-interaction.

> *Joe:* I got a letter from my father today. All he seems to care about is whether my grades are up and how much money I'm spending.
>
> *Ellen:* I got the craziest letter you ever saw today! Came from Susie, my friend who is in Europe. She writes hysterical letters.
>
> *Joe:* So my father sends me ten dollars in the letter and says to spend it on good books and not the movies.
>
> *Ellen:* Susie says that the movies over there are just terrible. She just can't wait to come home so she can see the ones she's missed.

Mystification

While parallaction is *non*communication, mystification is *mis*communication. **Mystification** occurs when two people are talking but one or both are hiding or falsifying their true feelings or intentions. Sometimes we mystify people because we do not want to hurt their feelings.

> *Jim:* Hello, Laurie. I've been wanting to see you. I tried to phone you. Did you get the message to return my call?
>
> *Laurie:* Yes, and I was just about to call you.
>
> *Jim:* But I left a message every day this week.
>
> *Laurie:* Gee, I've been real busy.
>
> *Jim:* Are you mad at me or something?
>
> *Laurie:* Oh, no. I've been real busy.
>
> *Jim:* How about a movie tomorrow night?
>
> *Laurie:* I'm sorry Jim. I'm real busy tomorrow night.

Sometimes we mystify people in order to manipulate them for our own selfish reasons. A man comes to the door and asks you to participate in a survey that he is taking; in fact, he is a salesman and is trying to sell you magazine subscriptions.

Our sexual interactions often involve mystification. A man asks a woman out with the excuse that there is a good movie playing. His real motivation, however, is sexual not aesthetic. The woman of course is well aware of his real intention, and if she shares his sexual interests, she may go along with the game.

Games People Play

Games are another example of pseudo-interaction. Sometimes two people appear to be communicating when in fact they are having a ritualized stereotyped encounter, the object of which is to win, not to exchange information or feelings. Games in social interaction are basically dishonest, because each player has an ulterior motive in playing. According to one theory, each of us has three selves internalized within: a parent, an adult, and a child. The parent, the adult, or the child within us can each be a player in a game.[20] In the game entitled "Why don't you—Yes but," one player (Bill) takes the role of parent and the other player (Mary) takes the role of child.[20]

> *Mary:* My husband always insists on doing his own repairs, and he never builds anything right.
>
> *Bill:* Why doesn't he take a course in carpentry?
>
> *Mary:* Yes, but he doesn't have the time.
>
> *Bill:* Why don't you buy him some good tools?
>
> *Mary:* Yes, but he doesn't know how to use them.
>
> *Bill:* Why don't you have your building done by a carpenter?

Mary: Yes, but that would cost too much.

Bill: Why don't you accept what he does the way he does it?

Mary: Yes, but the whole thing might fall down.

In this game, Mary will win if she can hold off every solution with a "Yes, but . . ." response. The game ends in silence when all suggestions have been rejected as inadequate. Mary's reward for winning the game is the feeling that it is the other person who is inadequate, not she. The other person is regarded as inadequate because he has tried to think of an acceptable solution to Mary's problem but has failed.

Authentic Communication

Not all meetings end in parallaction, mystification, or games; some involve a true exchange of feelings and information. **Authentic communication** is occurring, not ritual. It is not easy for two people to talk to each other and communicate. In order to communicate you must be open with your thoughts and feelings and that is difficult and sometimes scarey. To reveal yourself to other people gives them the power to hurt you if they want to do so; but it also makes it possible for them to know you and to like you. If you do not communicate and therefore do not allow yourself to be known by another, you have little chance of developing fulfilling relationships.

There is much evidence that indicates that healthy relationships are based on self-disclosure. If you hide how you are reacting to the other person, your concealment can sicken the relationship. . . . Being silent is not being strong; strength is the willingness to take risks in the relationship, to disclose yourself with the intention of building a better relationship.[21]

If you do communicate, if you do disclose who you are to another, you will find in most cases that your disclosure is reciprocated. If you trust me enough to reveal yourself to me, I will trust you enough to reveal myself to you. This reciprocation of self-disclosure is called the **dyadic effect.**

It is not easy to communicate things that are truly meaningful to you. That is why so much of our conversation amounts to nothing more than parallaction or mystification. It is also often more difficult to talk about the present than the past. The order of disclosures, from least difficult to most difficult, appears below:

I tell you how Jane felt about John, neither person being present.

I tell you how Jane feels about John, neither person being present.

Communication involves a true exchange of feelings and information.

I tell you my past feelings about Sam, who is not present.

I tell you my present feelings about Sam, who is not present.

I tell you my past feelings about you.

I tell you my present feelings about you.[21]

Why is it so difficult for you to tell me how you feel about me? One reason is that you fear that I will hurt you by using the information against you, or by rejecting you, or by not understanding you. But if you don't tell me how you feel, I may never know you in any depth. Although disclosure is necessary for a truly close relationship, it does not guarantee one. Sometimes disclosure to unsympathetic people can cause you great hurt. While it is necessary to take risks to be close, it is also necessary to use common sense in self-disclosure.

⑤   Friendship is based on communication. Authentic communication, involving a true exchange of feelings and information, is difficult. It requires that you are open and honest and have the courage to disclose yourself. A consequence of openness is the dyadic effect, or reciprocation of self-disclosure. Parallaction (noncommunication), mystification (miscommunication), and games (communication with ulterior motives) are common types of interaction. When these are present, the possibility for true communication is remote.

Body Talk

Hands talk and smiles talk. Communication consists of more than words. You communicate with your facial expression, with the clothes you choose to wear, with the inflection and loudness of your speech, with your posture, and with your body movements. This type of communication is called **nonverbal communication.** In two-way conversations words have been estimated to carry less than 35 percent of the total meaning communicated.[22] You already know how to read the language of the body fairly well, but you can learn how to read it better. The body is like a book and each part of the body communicates information. The meaning of the message that is sent is sometimes the feelings or intentions of the sender. Sometimes body talk consists of signals or regulators used for controlling the pacing of conversations.

Regulators

Regulators are body signals sent between two people when they are talking that signify that communication and comprehension are occurring.[23] In a two-way conversation the speaker signals the listener to indicate when it is permissible to answer by using tonal variations and pauses in speech and by moving head and eyes in certain ways. An upward tonal inflection (as in a question) or a downward tonal inflection (as in a declarative sentence), when accompanied by an extended pause, is a signal that the speaker is temporarily finished and that it is now permissible for the listener to respond. However, if the extended pause is accompanied by the speaker moving eyes upward, then the signal is different: the listener should not interrupt, because the speaker wishes to continue.[24] The listener also uses body signals to communicate with the speaker.

1. The listener maintains eye contact with the speaker and slowly nods the head up and down. This is a signal that the listener understands what is being said and that the speaker may continue.

2. The listener maintains a quizzical or blank look, sometimes accompanied by a slight frown. This is a signal that the listener is not understanding the message and that the speaker should repeat it in different words.

3. The listener moves the eyes upward without speaking. This is a signal that the speaker should stop talking so that the listener can respond.

4. The listener raises the eyebrows or frowns. This is a signal that the listener disagrees with or is skeptical about what is being said. The speaker then usually elaborates on the point or strengthens the case with additional evidence.

5. The listener extends a hand, palm forward, toward the speaker. This is a signal that the speaker should stop abruptly so that the listener can respond.

Messages

There are many meaningful messages that can be sent with the body. Unlike regulators, **body messages** convey actual information. In effect, these body messages replace words and sentences; sometimes words cannot communicate the subtle feeling carried by a facial expression or the complex information about size or direction carried by appropriate hand gestures.

■ *Talking Without Words* The body language is often used to communicate direction, distance, and size. The hands point, the arms stretch out, or the thumb and forefinger are held a certain distance apart—all of these gestures carry important meanings. The hitchhiker's thumb tells drivers that a ride is wanted. I use my hand to say "Come," "Go," "Look," or "Good-bye." I cup my hand behind my ear to ask you to speak louder; I put my forefinger in front of my lips to ask you to be quieter.   I rub my hand in a circling motion on my stomach to tell you that your food tastes good.   I hold my nose to say "You stink!"

■ *Feelings You Cannot Hide*   Body language is particularly useful in communicating emotion.   Words often fail when it comes to expressing feelings, but the body talks clearly, sometimes saying more than we want it to.   The face is ever changing, with the muscles around the mouth and eyes communicating subtle feelings.   People all over the world smile when happy and frown when sad.   Charles Darwin suggested that the facial expression of emotion was an inborn signal, and presented as evidence the similarities between the facial expressions of people and other animals, such as monkeys.   While there are clearly differences among societies in the details of emotional expression, there are great similarities also.   Research shows that observers in the United States, Brazil, Japan, New Guinea, and Borneo all showed remarkable agreement about the emotion being expressed in photographs of faces.[25]

Posture, too, expresses emotion.   When you are slumped forward, head down, with your arms tightly crossed in front of you, you communicate depression and withdrawal.   When you are interested in someone, you will often turn your body toward them and may lean forward.   The hands also express feelings.   You cover your face with your hands to express shame.   When you are angry, your fists are clenched.   You hunch your shoulders and turn your palms up to express puzzlement.   You may strike your palm against your forehead to express surprise or forgetfulness.   How you move your hands—slowly or rapidly—communicates how you are feeling.

What you say with words can be controlled fairly well.   You can tell the truth or

you can lie or you can choose not to talk.   It is much harder to control body language.   Often your body will communicate how you are feeling when you choose not to reveal your feelings with words.   Sometimes your words will say one thing and your body another.   We have learned to trust body language more than word language because it is harder to lie with the body.   A person may say "I like you" with words but say "Stay away" with the body; a person may say "I feel fine" with words but say "I feel terrible" with the body.   These contradictory messages are sometimes the result of insincerity (deliberate deceit) and sometimes the consequence of not knowing how you feel.

Most information in conversations is exchanged nonverbally, in "body talk." Two types of nonverbal communication are regulators and body messages. Regulators are nonverbal signals that indicate that communication and comprehension are occurring. They regulate the flow of the conversation. Body messages convey actual information; for example, facial expressions send body messages about emotion.

Interpersonal Relationships

We are social creatures; much of life consists of relating to others. We have interpersonal relationships with family, friends, lovers, and others in our society with whom we come in frequent contact. The quality of these relationships significantly contributes to the quality of life. Persons who are psychologically healthy have the capacity to develop deep and satisfying relationships with others. This does not mean that your health is measured by the number of your friends. Quite the contrary is true; studies of particularly healthy individuals have shown that they tend to have only a few intense relationships. Thus, the quality, not the quantity, of human relationships is the key factor.

Relationships that Promote or Block Growth

Human relationships are opportunities for growth. Good relationships foster self-understanding, self-confidence, and self-acceptance; they provide us the chance to exercise our most positive human traits—love, commitment, and trust.

Martin Buber has described two forms of interpersonal relationship.[26] The **I-Thou relationship** is a relationship between the being of one and the being of another; it is a relationship in which each person *confirms* the other by recognizing, validating, and accepting the other's nature. By contrast, the **I-it relationship** occurs between an observer and an object; one person is treated as a thing, not a unique being. Perhaps in some relationship you have felt treated as an object, a thing to be manipulated, instead of a separate being with your own feelings, needs, and perceptions. I-Thou relationships promote growth, but I-it relationships block growth.

Test Yourself

Think about the different interpersonal relationships in which you are involved. You have relationships with members of your family, with neighbors, with friends in school, and with peers of the opposite sex. What is the quality of these relationships? Good interpersonal relationships have special characteristics, some of which are listed below. You can test each of your relationships against this list to judge its quality.

☐ *Is it honest?*

Each of you can risk being honest with the other. You are not afraid to tell the other person what you are thinking and how you feel.

☐ *Is it supportive?*

You are mutually supportive and accepting of the other. You express your approval, praise, and appreciation of the other. You accept and value the other person just the way he or she is.

☐ *Is it deep?*

The relationship is between two "real" selves, not between the social or public impressions you try to create. Each of you feels you really know and understand the other in a personal, not superficial, way.

☐ *Is it meaningful?*

The relationship is a significant part of your life. What happens to the other and how he or she feels are matters of concern for you.

☐ *Is it transcendent?*

Each of you is involved with the life of the other in an unselfish way. You are not self-centered or egocentric in the relationship; you are not in it for what you can get out of it. The relationship transcends, or goes beyond, your selfish needs.

Sources of Difficulty

Few interpersonal relationships have all of the ideal features just listed. Healthy relationships do not just happen but have to be actively built. It takes commitment and work on the part of both people. Why are your relationships not ideal? Some of the sources of difficulty in interpersonal relationships are presented here for you to consider.[27] Which are your stumbling blocks?

☐ *Egocentricity*

A concern with one's own interests to the extent of being insensitive to the welfare and rights of others.

☐ *Deceitfulness*

A tendency, often accompanying egocentricity, to take an exploitative approach to interpersonal relationships. Sometimes deceit extends to outright lying and stealing, but more commonly it shows itself in the efforts of an "operator" to manipulate people and situations to his or her own advantage.

☐ *Overdependency*

A tendency to lean excessively upon others for either material aid or emotional support and to rely upon them for making decisions.

☐ *Hostility*

A tendency to be antagonistic and suspicious toward other people.

☐ *Inferior feelings*

A basic lack of self-confidence or self-esteem which may be expressed either in oversensitivity to "threat" or in exaggerated efforts to prove one's own adequacy and worth by such techniques as boasting, showing off, and being hypercritical of other people.

☐ *Emotional insulation*

An inability to make the necessary emotional investment in a relationship, for fear of being hurt.

⑤ Some relationships promote personal growth while others do not. Buber's I-Thou relationship promotes growth because participants confirm and validate each other. By contrast, the I-it relationship blocks growth because one person treats the other as an object to be manipulated.

Summary

KEY QUESTIONS

1. What is the basis of friendship?

   The old saying, "Birds of a feather flock together," is often true. You tend to like those who are similar to you. This may be because you like those who reward you with validation or praise. People with similar values are more likely to reward each other.

2. What are the forms of interpersonal communication?

   Authentic communication between two people is relatively rare. Pseudo-communication, miscommunication, and "games" are common forms of interaction that are not authentic.

3. What is nonverbal communication?

   Nonverbal communication is communication through facial expression, posture, speech inflection, and body movements. This form of communication serves the purposes of regulating the flow of conversations and exchanging information.

4. What are the characteristics of good and bad relationships?

   Good relationships promote growth because each person confirms the other and is supportive and honest. Bad relationships interfere with growth and involve hostility, deceitfulness, dependency, or emotional insulation.

KEY CONCEPTS

principle of similarity   The idea that people like others who are similar to themselves in values, beliefs, and background; in other words, that "birds of a feather flock together."

principle of complementarity	The idea that people like others who are unlike themselves, and that one looks for someone to supply what the other lacks; in other words, that "opposites attract."
reinforcement theory of friendship	The theory that you like those people who reward you.
exchange theory of friendship	The theory that you form friendships by estimating your "market value," then selling yourself to those with equal or higher value.
parallaction	A pseudo-interaction, without real involvement, in which each participant acts independently and does not exchange information.
mystification	A form of miscommunication in which the participants are hiding their real feelings or intentions.
games	Stereotyped interactions in which the hidden motive is to win, not to exchange information or feelings.
authentic communication	A true exchange of information and feelings involving openness and self-disclosure.
dyadic effect	The tendency for self-disclosure to be reciprocated; when one person is open and honest in a relationship, this encourages the other person to be open and honest in return.
nonverbal communication	Communication through facial expression, posture, speech inflection, and body movements; that is, communication that does not depend upon the meaning of words.
regulators	Body signals sent between two people that indicate whether comprehension is occurring and that control the flow of the conversation.
body messages	Nonverbal communications, such as hand gestures or emotional expressions, that convey actual information.
I-Thou relationship	A relationship in which each person confirms the other by recognizing, validating, and accepting the other's nature.
I-it relationship	A relationship in which one person is treated as an object, a thing to be manipulated, instead of as a unique being.

18 Potential

CHAPTER OUTLINE

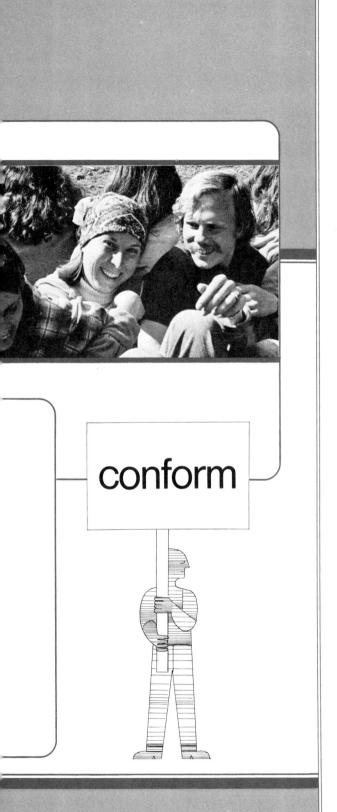

conform

KEY QUESTIONS

1. What are intelligence and creativity and how are they measured?
2. What is psychological health?
3. What is your stage of growth?
4. What is psychotherapy?

What is your potential for growth? Can you improve your personality and the quality of your relationships? You *can* change; you can become more healthy than you are. Human personality and human behavior are not fixed. They are flexible, modifiable; they hold the potential for growth. This potential for growth is one of the most important differences between human beings and the lower animals. The behavior of an ant is rigidly fixed by a genetic program, but you can change yourself and grow. The intention or desire for growth is an important ingredient for the process of growth itself; your decision to change is itself a step toward growth.

Human Potential

The limits of human potential are unexplored. A number of psychologists have claimed that we use only 10 percent of our capacity and that the challenge of our time is to release the vast, unused potential that we have.[1] At present, this claim cannot be confirmed because we just don't know the limit of our powers. If you could, how would you choose to grow? Which of your present capacities would you choose to expand? Perhaps you would strive to increase your intelligence and creativity.

Intelligence

Your **intelligence** is your ability to learn and solve problems. Your abilities to reason, to remember, to read, and to work with numbers all reflect your level of intelligence. Tests have been developed in an attempt to measure intelligence. These intelligence tests take many forms, but they all have in common the production of a quantitative measurement of intelligence, a number called the IQ. **IQ,** or **intelligence quotient,** is a score computed from the answers on an intelligence test. For children, it reflects the relationship of "chronological" age (age in years) to "mental" age (age of a child of equal intelligence). An IQ of 100 means that you are of average intelligence; an IQ of 50 means that your intelligence is much lower than average; an IQ of 150 means that your intelligence is much higher than average. For children IQ can be obtained from the following formula:

$$IQ = \frac{\text{Mental Age}}{\text{Chronological Age}} \times 100.$$

Because mental capacity ceases to increase much beyond the middle teens, the concept of "mental age" is not meaningful applied to adults. For the sake of convenience, tables have been developed so that the IQ score can be found directly, without computing the ratio of mental age to chronological age.

If your IQ is 100, you would expect that about 500 people out of 1,000 would have IQ's higher than yours. If your IQ is 110, you would expect that about 270 people out of 1,000 would have IQ's higher than yours. If your IQ is 120, you would expect about 110 people out of 1,000 would have IQ's higher than yours. If your IQ is 140, you would expect about 7 people out of 1,000 would have IQ's higher than yours.

Pesons whose IQ's are below 70 are called **mentally retarded,** and persons with IQ's above 130 are called **mentally gifted.** Slightly over 2 percent of the population are mentally retarded and about the same percentage are mentally gifted. Retarded adults with an IQ between 53 and 69 are classified as "mild." These individuals typically are able to take care of themselves and can develop skills in reading and arithmetic to a third- to sixth-grade level. Retarded adults with an IQ between 36 and 52 are classified as "moderate." They typically cannot care for themselves, although they are able to perform simple manual tasks; they can learn to communicate verbally, but usually cannot read. Individuals with IQ's below 35 are classified "severe" to "profound." They typically require continual direction and supervision in a protective environment, such as a special home or institution.

■ *Genius* It has been estimated that John Stuart Mill (1806–1873) had an IQ of about 190.[2] An IQ that high is so rare that in the entire population of the United States, you might expect to find only one or two persons with an IQ of 190. John Stuart Mill began hard intellectual work before the age of three, by which time he had learned to read some Greek. By the age of eight Mill had read extensively in philosophy and history, written both in English and Greek, and had begun the study of Latin, algebra, and geometry. Mill was educated exclusively by his

HIGH IQ

one capsule before each final exam

father, a strict disciplinarian who taught Mill to be skeptical and to think for himself. A study of the early life of John Stuart Mill suggests that an important part of being a genius is extremely hard work.

■ *Heredity and Environment* Differences in intelligence are due to a variety of sources. It can be shown that part of the difference among individuals in intelligence is due to inherited characteristics. Studies show, for example, that the more similar two persons are genetically, the more similar they tend to be in intelligence.[3] Brothers are more similar in intelligence than cousins, and cousins are more similar in intelligence than persons not genetically related. Identical twins are not only extremely similar in their physical features but are also extremely similar in intelligence level.

Environment also contributes to differences in intelligence. An extreme case is the individual who has been deprived of the opportunity to learn to read and write the language; such a person would make a low score on a written IQ test. The more opportunity children have for learning in the home and the more encouragement they are given for intellectual accomplishment, the higher their IQ's tend to be.[4]

Teachers can influence the IQ's of students through their expectations. In one study elementary school teachers were led to believe that certain students would be "bloomers"; that is, that they would experience rapid gains in IQ during the year.[5] In fact, the children designated as "bloomers" were chosen at random, but the teachers did not know this. Over the period of a school year, the students showed a significant increase in IQ, apparently caused by the expectations of their teachers.

■ *IQ Is Not Intelligence* IQ does not *equal* intelligence. IQ is only one measure of intelligence. Although it may be the best measure we have, in some ways it is a relatively poor one. First, different IQ tests yield different IQ scores for the same individual. According to one IQ test score, a person may be categorized as below normal in intelligence, whereas a second test may categorize the person as above normal. If yardsticks were like that, you wouldn't trust them very much. Furthermore, the same IQ test given at different times yields different scores. In one study of two hundred children who were tested twice, 85 percent of the group changed up or down 10 or more points from the first IQ test to the second, and 10 percent changed 30 or more points in IQ.[6]

IQ tests may not measure the ability we think of as "intelligence." When we call a woman *intelligent* what do we mean? We do not mean simply that her English vocabulary is large, that she is familiar with mathematical thinking, and that she can analyze and solve problems that might be encountered in the lives of white middle-class American people—yet these skills are primarily those which IQ tests measure. On the basis of an IQ test, some intelligent students from Spanish-speaking homes have been classified as "retarded," because of their unfamiliarity with the language used in the IQ test. The available IQ tests are probably inappropriate measures of the intelligence of black Americans, since the average black person grows up in an environment with substantial differences in language and culture as compared to the average white person. Since the items on IQ tests were largely developed and standardized on white middle-class children, the tests are biased against Chicano and black children.[7]

The IQ test is a useful predictor of grades in school. Many studies have shown that students with high IQ's make better grades,[8] because IQ tests and classroom tests require similar kinds of skills.[9] But neither IQ[10] nor school grades[11] are useful predictors of non-academic achievement. Success in life is not related to success in school or to success on IQ tests, except insofar as certain jobs require academic degrees. David McClelland, a Harvard University researcher, has recently proposed that the term "intelligence" be dropped from IQ tests and that they be named to reflect what they are: scholastic achievement tests.[9]

Creativity

One of the most highly valued human characteristics is creativity. All of us are creative. We are creative to the degree that we behave or respond creatively. What is a creative response? There is general agreement that a creative response has two impor-

tant features: (1) uniqueness or unconventionality; and (2) appropriateness or fit. The garbled language of the schizophrenic and the language of the poet are similar in that both are unconventional; they are different in that the language of the poet seems appropriate, while the language of the schizophrenic is simply confused. Thus, **creativity** is the ability to respond uniquely and appropriately.

■ *How Creative Are You?* You are creative. You have original ideas; you sometimes come up with unusual solutions to problems. Perhaps you have some talent in creative writing, painting, crafts, or music. But how much creativity do you have? The measurement of creativity is very difficult, and many different tests have been developed. One test, the "Uses Test," requires people to think of unusual uses for common objects like bricks or paper clips. "Building a fireplace" would be a common use for a brick; "as a paperweight" would be an uncommon, and therefore creative, use for a brick. Another test that has been used to identify creative individuals requires people to choose which designs they like best.

Psychologists have found that artists and other creative persons prefer designs that are highly complex, asymmetrical, free-hand rather than ruled, and restless and moving in their general effect.[12] Preference for complexity seems to go along with artistic interests, unconventionality, and creativity. Do you prefer complex asymmetrical designs or simple ruled ones?

What are the characteristics of the creative person? The creative person is not necessarily extremely intelligent. Although a minimal level of intelligence is necessary for a person to be creative, many highly intelligent persons are not particularly creative. Studies have shown that the relationship between measured creativity and measured intelli-

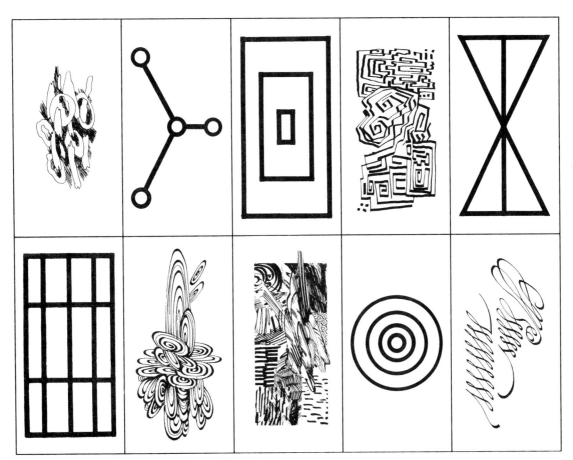

Creativity test. Which designs do you like best?

gence is rather small.[13,14] Apparently the capacity to get the conventionally "correct" answer to a problem, on the one hand, and the capacity to devise a unique but fitting solution, on the other hand, are two different capacities. A person can have one of these talents without the other or the person might have both.

What kind of people are creative people? One psychologist compared a group of highly creative architects with a group of average architects in order to discover how the creative individuals were different.[15] The relatively uncreative architects tended to see themselves as responsible, sincere, reliable, sociable, and cooperative. By contrast, the creative architects tended to see themselves as imaginative, independent, individualistic,

sensitive, and committed. Personality studies of creative architects,[15] creative writers,[16] and creative research scientists[17] agree that creative individuals tend to be highly independent, self-accepting, and spontaneous or impulsive. Creative people are more independent both in their attitudes and in their social behavior; they are more introverted, more open to experience, more self-accepting, more flexible, and more intuitive.[18]

■ *Creativity and Conformity* Creative persons are more healthy, psychologically, than uncreative persons. Contrary to the folk myth of the "mad genius," creativity is inhibited and reduced by neurosis or madness. Current investigators of creativity tend to agree that creativity is an expression of the

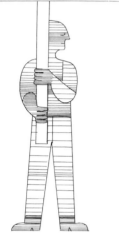

psychologically healthy person.[19]   Creative persons are more open to experience[18] and are less anxious.[20]

Creative people are not afraid of being themselves; they have courage.

The courage of the creative person . . . is the courage to be oneself in the fullest sense, to grow in great measure into the person one is capable of becoming, developing one's abilities and actualizing one's self. Since the creative person is not preoccupied with the impression he makes on others, and is not overly concerned with their opinion of him, he is freer than most to be himself. . . .

Creative persons are not conformists in the realm of greatest importance to them, the area of their creative striving, but on the other hand they are not deliberate nonconformists, either. Instead, they are genuinely independent.[15]

It takes courage to be creative in the face of all the pressures toward conformity that we encounter at every turn. Teachers in the school system tend to reward intelligence and conformity, but not creativity.[12] To be the same—same clothes, same goals, same thoughts—is safe. To be the same means not to be singled out; to go along with the crowd means to be safe. But every person is unique; you are different from every other human being on earth. To be most truly yourself is to make the most of your uniqueness. You cannot actualize yourself and also conform to the crowd. Clark Moustakas compared the creative and the conforming person:

To be creative means to experience life in one's own way, to perceive from one's own person, to draw upon one's own resources, capacities, roots. It means facing life directly and honestly. . . .

When a person's involvement in a situation is based on appearances, expectations, or the standards of others; when he acts in a conventional manner, or according to prescribed roles and functions, when he is concerned with status and approval; his growth as a creative self is impaired. When the individual is conforming, following, imitating, being like others, he moves increasingly in the direction of self-alienation. . . . Gradually the conforming person loses touch with himself, with his own real feelings.[21]

■ *Conditions Fostering Creativity* What does it take to be in touch with yourself, to face life directly and honestly, to be a creative person? Certainly, conditions that promote conformity tend to interfere with creativity. Several important conditions that foster creativity have been identified by Carl Rogers.[22] Rogers described three conditions in the person (inner conditions) and three conditions in the person's environment (outer conditions) that tend to increase creativity.

According to Rogers, the inner conditions fostering creativity are openness to experience, internal standards, and the ability to "toy" with ideas. A person who is open to experience is sensitive to things as they really are, and does not jump to conclusions based on prior expectations. A person who is open to experience is not quick to label people or events, but postpones conclusions until all evidence is in. A person with internal standards strives to satisfy personal goals and expectations rather than someone else's. A person with internal standards decides what is good or bad on the basis of an internal standard of evaluation rather than on the basis of external standards established by others. A person with the ability to "toy" with ideas enjoys exploring new combinations of concepts and can see problems in fresh ways.

The outer conditions fostering creativity are unconditional acceptance, absence of external evaluation, and empathetic understanding. Unconditional acceptance fosters creativity; people who are valued by those around them and accepted without reservations are more likely to be creative. The absence of external evaluation fosters creativity by permitting people to develop their own internal standards. Empathetic understanding fosters creativity; when people are truly understood by those around them, they are encouraged to be fully themselves.

⑤ Your intelligence is your ability to learn and to solve problems. Tests of intelligence yield a score—the IQ or intelligence quotient. A score of 100 reflects average intelligence, while a score below 70 indicates that the person is mentally retarded and a score above 130 indicates that the person is mentally gifted. Both heredity and environment contribute to intelligence.

Your creativity is your ability to respond uniquely and appropriately to problems. Although a minimal level of intelligence is required to be creative, high intelligence is not related to creativity. Creative people have been found to be more independent, more self-accepting, more spontaneous, more introverted, more open to experience, and more intuitive. According to Carl Rogers, creativity can be promoted by fostering certain inner and outer conditions.

Psychological Health

Are you psychologically healthy? How can you tell? It depends upon what is meant by "psychological health." There is no absolute, objective definition of "health," just as there is no absolute definition of "good" or "beautiful." Different cultures and different individuals have different views of what is "good," "beautiful," and "healthy." The definition of health, in other words, involves human values, and different groups have different values. Generally speaking, those aspects of behavior and experience which are positively valued are considered "healthy."[23]

Healthy Personalities

At one time many people considered mental health to be equivalent to "good social adjustment." Individuals were regarded as "mentally healthy" if they were well-adjusted in their society. To adjust to your society, you must conform to the expectations of that society. However, today we recognize that adjustment to many aspects of our society is disease-producing. Social pressures contribute to ulcers, anxiety, and mental illness.

Being healthy is not the same as being "normal." The normal person is not a person who has no problems, who is perfectly healthy. The normal person is instead a person who is more or less average—average in the number of colds suffered per year and average in the severity of emotional problems.

Psychological health has often been defined negatively, in terms of the absence of disease. This tendency has led psychology to focus on human deficiency instead of human potential. Many of the concepts used in describing the normal personality are derived from symptoms of the mentally ill. The psychological description of a normal person, in effect, specifies how similar the individual is to a mentally ill person rather than to a mentally healthy person. But psychologists recently have begun to use concepts based on human potential rather than on human disease. A positive view of mental health can be developed by considering those aspects of human behavior and experience which we highly value and toward which we want to grow. Try to imagine an ideal person, one who is perfectly healthy psychologically. What kind of abilities and traits would such a person possess?

Being psychologically healthy is similar to being physically healthy: both involve the capacity to function well and both involve a feeling of well-being. Feeling well and functioning well are positively valued. The details of this ideal concept of health have been described by the psychologists Rogers[22] and Maslow.[24]

Rogers: The Fully Functioning Person

Carl Rogers describes the healthy person as a **fully functioning person,** one who is happy, creative, and socially effective. An important aspect of the fully functioning person, according to Rogers, is **congruence.**

Incongruence.

A person is congruent if inner feelings, awareness of those feelings, and outward expression of feelings all correspond, or are congruent with one another. Most of us lack congruence in some way. We may lack congruence because we do not express the feelings we are aware of, or we may lack congruence because we are not entirely aware of the feelings we have. A friend, noticing your abrupt manner and scowling face, asks, "What are you so mad about?" You reply, "Who, me? I'm not mad about anything!" But you are angry; sometimes you know it at the time and just don't want to admit it, and sometimes you are not aware that you were angry until later. Your inner feelings were not congruent with the feelings you expressed.

Maslow: The Self-Actualized Person

Abraham Maslow described the ideally healthy person as a **self-actualized person,** one whose basic needs are satisfied and whose potential is fulfilled. From Maslow's point of view, self-actualization cannot take place until fundamental human needs have been met: basic needs of belongingness, affection, respect, and self-esteem; freedom from pain, fear, and hunger; being safe and secure.[25] Persons who are self-actualized, Maslow discovered, are better able to experience life fully, vividly, with full concentration and total absorption, and without self-consciousness; they are able to take risks and to be spontaneous; they have the courage to be honest and to be different, even if that means being unpopular.[26] All the self-actualized persons whom Maslow studied were devoted to some task, call, vocation, or beloved work— a cause "outside" themselves in which they found meaning and satisfaction.

According to several studies,[27,28] people who are more self-actualized are more likely to agree with the following statements. Check the ones you agree with.

- ☐ I can like people without having to approve of them.
- ☐ People are basically good.
- ☐ The truly spiritual person is sometimes sensual.
- ☐ My moral values are self-determined.
- ☐ I trust the decisions I make spontaneously.
- ☐ I am able to risk being myself.
- ☐ For me, work and play are the same.
- ☐ I enjoy detachment and privacy.
- ☐ I have had an experience where life seemed just perfect.
- ☐ I am self-sufficient.

All people have *moments* of self-actualization in their lives during which this state of ideal health is briefly achieved. These moments Maslow calls **peak experiences.** Peak experiences are moments of great joy, wonder, or awe when a person seems to surrender to a great experience; fears and inhibitions are replaced by a feeling of great power and well-being. In some peak experiences, of a mystical or religious nature, the world is felt as a great unity, while in other peak experiences, particularly the love experience or the aesthetic experience, one small part of the world and one moment in time are experienced as all of reality.[24]

Can you remember a peak experience you have had in your life? When have you felt moments of ecstasy or wonder? Can you remember moments of intense well-being when everything felt vividly real? Perhaps it was when you fell in love, one day when you looked at the ocean or a sunset, or when you fulfilled some great ambition. These peak experiences are moments of self-actualization. These are the times that you are most healthy.

Being Healthy: A Checklist

The psychologically healthy person is one who has many positively valued behaviors and experiences and has few negatively valued behaviors and experiences. Following is a list of positively valued traits, based primarily on the writings of Rogers and Maslow. Look at the list and check off each item that is generally true for you. How many can you check? Few persons are honestly able to check all of these. In fact, if you are able to check even half of these "ideal" traits, you are probably healthy.

You feel good; most of the time you have a feeling of well-being.

- ☐ You feel secure and safe; you are rarely anxious.
- ☐ You have feelings of belongingness and rootedness; you do not usually feel outcast and isolated.
- ☐ You feel loved and love-worthy; you rarely feel rejected, worthless, unlovable, or inferior.
- ☐ You feel competent; you are relatively self-confident about your own abilities; you have self-esteem and self-respect.
- ☐ You trust and you are open to your own feelings; you are immediately aware of your feelings and can act on them; you can be spontaneous.
- ☐ You have "peak experiences"—ecstatic, intensely satisfying moments when all seems vividly real.

You can do things; you function well.

- ☐ You can do most of the things you want to do; you can take care of yourself.
- ☐ You are committed to and intensely involved in some work or cause "outside of your own skin."
- ☐ You can accept yourself and others; you can disclose yourself to others.

- ☐ You can experience fully, without self-consciousness.
- ☐ You can show spontaneity and also self-control.
- ☐ You have the capacity for forming and maintaining intimate interpersonal relationships; you can love.
- ☐ You can be self-directed; you are relatively independent from the expectations of others.
- ☐ You are creative.

ⓢ Psychological health refers to those aspects of behavior and experience that are positively valued and toward which we want to grow. According to Carl Rogers, the psychologically healthy person can be described as "fully functioning." One characteristic of fully functioning people is that they are congruent—that is, they are aware of their feelings and express them accurately. According to Abraham Maslow, the ideally healthy person can be described as "self-actualized." Self-actualized people have met their basic needs and fulfilled their potentials. While few of us are completely self-actualized, most of us have occasionally experienced that state in moments of great joy, wonder, or awe. Maslow calls these moments peak experiences.

What Is Your Stage of Growth?

Few persons can truly be described as ideally healthy, as self-actualized or fully functioning. Most of us are at some stage of development below the ideal. What stage are you at?

Stage One
You are unwilling to talk about yourself; you talk only about externals—about facts, not feelings. You don't recognize your own feelings; you lack congruence. You see yourself

as static, constant, unchanging. Close personal relationships with others you find dangerous and threatening. You maintain personal distance and tend to see others as objects. You live by external rules, values, and expectations; you are a conformist. You don't believe you have any problems.

Stage Two
You talk about yourself, but you see your *self* as an object, as separate from you. You are able to talk about personally meaningful feelings and experiences but always in the past or future, never in the present; you cannot communicate how you are feeling right now. You recognize your feelings, but you don't accept them; you tend to see your feelings as shameful or abnormal. You begin, with great

self-consciousness, to risk relationships with others. You begin to search for your own internal rules and values, but you still basically conform; you don't trust yourself yet. You recognize that you have problems, but you don't feel responsible for them.

Stage Three
You can communicate your feelings and experiences in the present; your feelings seem to "bubble up" in spite of your still-remaining fears and distrusts. Although you have these immediate experiences of feelings, you are often surprised and frightened by them, rather than pleased. You begin to have lengthy periods of selfless absorption, of unselfconsciousness. You experiment with being nonconforming. You feel greater ef-

fectiveness in handling problems and in making choices. You recognize the central importance of close personal relationships and can identify the problems you have in this area. You accept greater responsibility for your own problems.

Stage Four

You can communicate your feelings and experiences freely, both verbally and nonverbally, at the time they are happening. You are very aware of your own feelings; you accept them as being you. You trust your own impulses. You live very much in the present, experiencing what *is*, not trying to interpret and explain what is in terms of the past. You see yourself as changing, as growing. Close, open relationships with other persons are highly valued. You can be independent even at the risk of being unpopular. You have strong feelings of competence and well-being and participate fully in the richness of life.

Stage Four is equivalent to being self-actualized or to being a fully functioning person. Few people have achieved this stage of growth, although you will recognize aspects of yourself there; at moments you have been at this stage, when you have had peak experiences. Most of us are at Stages One, Two, or Three most of the time.

How can you move from Stage One to Stage Two? How can you grow and eventually become fully functioning? How can you achieve that ideal stage of psychological health? You cannot be healthy simply by trying to be healthy; you cannot be happy simply by deciding to be happy.

The pleasure principle is self-defeating. The more one aims at pleasure, the more his aim is missed. In other words, the very "pursuit of happiness" is what thwarts it. . . . This is due to the fact that pleasure, rather than being a goal in itself, is and must remain a side-effect, or by-product, of attaining a goal. Attaining a goal . . . is the reason why I am happy. This is why it is not necessary to pursue happiness. [23]

Pleasure, happiness, and self-actualization cannot be effectively *pursued;* instead, they *ensue,* or automatically result, from your having satisfied a need, attained a goal, or grown toward health. Your deciding to be happy will not make you happy; happiness follows from what you *do.*

You have unpleasant feelings sometimes and this is quite natural. But if your unpleasant feelings are severe, unending, and tend to color your whole emotional life, then you want to stop feeling so bad. We are all sometimes blue, but if you are blue most of the time, then you want to change. As you grow toward health, you tend to experience fewer and fewer persistent unpleasant feelings.

What you do and what happens to you are under your control. You are in charge. And what you do will determine whether you grow toward health or whether you stay as you are now. While you cannot attain psychological health by pursuing it directly, you can grow in the direction of health through certain kinds of experiences and these experiences are under your control. Some experiences move you toward health; some move you away from health. To learn about yourself and others, to love and be loved, and to live actively and productively—all are growth-producing experiences.

⑤   Early stages of psychological growth are characterized by conformity, failure to recognize your own feelings, fear of close relationships with others, and the tendency to live by external standards. Later stages of growth are characterized by recognition and acceptance of your own feelings, trust of your impulses, living in the present, and a tendency to see yourself as changing and growing, not static. Learning about yourself and others, loving and being loved, and living actively and productively are all growth-producing experiences.

Psychotherapy

Many people, at some time in their lives, ask professionals to help them move toward health. **Psychotherapy** is a special kind of help provided by a person trained to help people overcome their problems and fulfill their potential.

The professionals providing this help are called psychotherapists. There are several types of psychotherapists. A **clinical psychologist** has a postgraduate academic degree, an M.A. or a Ph.D. in psychology, plus specialized training in personality theory, mental testing, psychological research, and therapeutic techniques. A clinical psychologist does not have a medical degree and cannot administer drugs.

A **psychiatrist** is a licensed physician who in addition to regular medical training took a residency in psychiatry. Besides being qualified in verbal psychotherapy, the psychiatrist can administer drugs and other medical therapy.

A **psychoanalyst** is a psychotherapist, usually a medical doctor, who has had extensive psychoanalytic training. Psychoanalysis is a particular theory of therapy that assumes that personality problems arise from unconscious conflicts.

From ancient times there have been attempts to help people solve their problems. In Egypt, three thousand years before Christ, a psychiatrist named Imhotep warded off the evil spirits believed to be causing mental disorders by using magical amulets, opium, and olive oil.[29] Later, physicians healed by using mystical words of an ancient language,

such as Greek or Hebrew, together with charms and amulets. Still later, words and phrases were used by themselves to drive off evil and restore mental health.

Today modern psychotherapy is almost exclusively verbal. The process of psychotherapy is a learning process for the clients. Over a period of time certain aspects of the clients' behavior are changed. They may learn, for example, new and more satisfactory modes of interacting with others. The form of the client-therapist interaction varies with the type of psychotherapy practiced.

Do You Need Professional Help?

The question of whether you, in particular, need psychotherapy cannot adequately be answered by a book, but part of that answer can be given here. In the first place, it is important to understand the difference between psychotherapy and conventional medical care. If you *need* a doctor and you don't see one, you may very well die; however most people do see doctors about complaints that if unattended would not cause their death. The job of a medical doctor is to cure organic, or bodily, diseases. A psychotherapist, on the other hand, is often not consulted to cure a "mental disease," but to help a normal person grow toward better health. If you do not see a psychotherapist, you will not die, but you won't be helped to grow. Psychotherapeutic interactions are intensive learning experiences, in which a client learns new ways of feeling, experiencing, and acting. A psychotherapist is like a teacher to whom people go when they want to learn to grow.

Do you *need* a French teacher? Answer: Yes, if not knowing French interferes with your work or your human relationships, and if this makes you unhappy, and if you want to learn French. Otherwise, no. Do you *need* a

psychotherapist? Answer: Yes, if your present way of feeling, experiencing, and behaving interferes with your work or with your human relationships, and if this makes you unhappy. Otherwise, no.

If you decide that you want psychotherapy, whom should you see? The past fifty years have produced a bewildering variety of different types of psychotherapies. There is not general agreement on which type is best. It is likely that certain types of psychotherapy are more effective for some people and other types for other people. Some of the more important types are described in the sections that follow.

Psychoanalysis

Psychoanalysis is the method of psychotherapy developed by Freud. The method is based on Freud's concepts of personality and personality development. Two concepts particularly important in psychoanalysis are the principles of unconscious motivation and early determinism.

Freud believed that our own needs, motives, and impulses are often unknown to us; that is, we are not conscious of them. The principle of **unconscious motivation** states that we are often unaware of our needs and impulses. Certain impulses—particularly sexual and aggressive ones—are taboo in our society. Because our parents and the rules of this society prohibit us from expressing these impulses freely, we repress them; we banish them to our unconscious. But even though they are unconscious, they nevertheless continue to affect our behavior in various ways. The primary goal of psychoanalysis is to make these unconscious motivations fully conscious.

Freud believed that early childhood experience is responsible for shaping the adult personality. The principle of **early determinism** states that the characteristics of the adult personality are controlled or determined by early childhood experience. It was at this time that significant feelings, impulses, and memories were repressed. One of the goals of psychoanalysis is to give clients insight into the historical causes of their behavior; that is, to help them to discover what aspects of their early experiences are responsible for their present attitudes, feelings, and actions.

Freud believed that we use up "psychic energy" in keeping impulses and conflicts out of awareness; when in the course of psycho-analysis unconscious material becomes conscious, psychic energy is freed and the influence of these unconscious impulses and conflicts on the personality is reduced.

There are two major methods used in psychoanalysis to get at unconscious material. The first method is called **free association;** the client is told to lie down and relax and then to say anything that comes to mind. This idea is to freely reveal the contents of your mind, with no censorship, regardless of how shocking or insignificant the thought may seem. It is difficult to do this without censoring your own thoughts and words; but if you can do it, according to Freud, you will reveal without meaning to do so unconscious impulses and conflicts.

The second method used in psychoanalysis to get at unconscious material is called **dream analysis.** The dream, Freud believed, is a kind of window into the unconscious; the contents of dreams express unconscious impulses and conflicts in a symbolic or disguised fashion. The content of the dream that you remember and report is called the **manifest content;** the true meaning of the dream—the unconscious meaning—is called the **latent content.** The goal of the psychoanalyst is to interpret the symbols in the manifest content of the dream in order to reveal the unconscious material in the latent dream content.

Psychoanalysis is a very time-consuming therapy; an individual may spend one hour a day, five days a week, for several years in the process of psychoanalysis. Because there are relatively few trained psychoanalysts and a lengthy period is required for its completion, it is an opportunity for growth available to very few individuals. It is also extremely expensive, limiting it to those who are relatively wealthy. One survey of persons who completed psychoanalysis found that only 60 percent could be considered as cured or

greatly improved. In this survey, for each person who was rated as markedly improved, more than 600 hours of psychoanalysis were required.[30] This finding implies that psycho-analysis may be an appropriate form of therapy for only a limited number of people.

Behavior Therapy

Behavior therapy focuses on the symptoms, not on the supposed underlying causes, of a psychological problem. The behavior therapist assumes that what has to be treated is what the client actually *does;* no consideration is given to such ideas as unconscious impulses, underlying conflicts, insight, or dream analysis. "If a person has a fear of cats, eliminate the fear rather than look for subconscious conflicts which produce the fear. If a person is an alcoholic, stop the drinking behavior rather than look for underlying causes."[31] What a person does is primarily what that person has learned to do. Many persons learn bad habits, just as a cat in the laboratory can be taught to be neurotic.

An explicit assumption of the behavior therapist is that human behavior is subject to causal determination no less than that of billiard balls or ocean currents. . . . The general attitude of the behavior therapist to his patients is in accord with this deterministic outlook. He regards the patient as a joint product of his physical endowment and of the molding influence of the succession of environments through which he—an organism—has passed. Each environment, each exposure to stimulation, has modified, through learning, the character of the organism to a greater or lesser extent.

Since the patient has had no choice in becoming what he is, it is incongruous to blame him for having gone awry, or to disparage him for maintaining his unhappy state. . . . The behavior therapist schools the patient to realize that his unpleasant reactions are due to emotional habits that he cannot help; that they have nothing to do with moral fibre or an unwillingness to get well; that similar reactions are easily induced in animals, who remain neurotic for just as long as the experimenter chooses. . . . So the overcoming of a human neurosis is within the control of the therapist through techniques quite similar to those used in the laboratory.[32]

The goal of the behavior therapist, then, is to modify the behavior of the client; that is, the goal is to change what the client does. The methods of behavior therapy were developed in the laboratory by experimental psychologists and are based on simple principles of learning. With these methods the therapist helps the client unlearn old habits that are maladaptive and learn new habits that work better.

One technique of behavior therapy is called **desensitization.** The fear of snakes can be desensitized by repeatedly exposing clients to snakes in a special set of circumstances. Clients are first taught how to relax; they then relax as they are exposed to snakes in a mild and nonthreatening way. For example, clients may relax as they *imagine* a small garter snake enclosed in a glass jar across the room. According to the theory on which desensitization is based, these repetitive exposures cause the *fear* response to snakes to be replaced by a *relaxation* response to snakes. Thus, an old emotional habit is unlearned and a new emotional habit is learned.

The procedures of behavior therapy seem to be highly effective for certain kinds of psychological problems. Behavior therapy is often very brief and is therefore available to more people than is psychoanalysis. Many

psychologists, however, believe that the course of psychological growth consists not in the acquisition of better habits (a change in doing), but rather in an evolution of consciousness (a change in being). This point of view is reflected in the third type of therapy presented here.

Client-Centered Therapy

Psychoanalysis and behavior therapy attempt to "cure" their clients; they are concerned with getting rid of sickness or bad habits—a kind of rehabilitation of the mind. In contrast to these forms of therapy, **client-centered therapy** focuses on psychological health and is oriented toward positive growth rather than the curing of sickness.

According to client-centered therapy, the person in therapy (the client) has a drive toward health and will grow in a positive way if the right circumstances are available. The goal of the therapist is to create the conditions for growth; the clients, however, are responsible for changing themselves. The therapist attempts to create a therapeutic relationship with the client; within the context of a warm and accepting relationship, positive growth spontaneously occurs.

According to Carl Rogers, founder of client-centered therapy, the following conditions are necessary for positive changes in personality: (1) unconditional positive regard for the other; (2) empathetic understanding of how the other feels; and (3) genuineness or congruence.[33] Client-centered therapists are uncritically accepting, warm and understanding, and honest and open with their feelings; they rarely interpret or give advice. They focus on the present feelings of the clients, rather than on symptoms, dreams, or early childhood experience. Within the context of a warm and accepting relationship, the clients begin to explore and to clarify their

own feelings. In this way clients grow from Stage One to Stage Four.

Group Therapies

Psychoanalysis, behavior therapy, and client-centered therapy typically involve only two people—a therapist and a client. In contrast, **group therapy** is a form of psychotherapy involving a therapist and 8 to 12 clients meeting together. Many personal problems stem from difficulties in communicating and relating to other people; individuals in group therapy have the opportunity to work with these problems by relating to each other.

One form of group therapy is the **encounter group** (sometimes called a sensitivity group or a T-group). The general purpose of encounter groups is to increase sensitivity to yourself and to others. The specific goals of these groups include increasing your awareness of your own feelings and the feelings of others, increasing your ability to understand other people and to communicate with them,

becoming more authentic in the presentation of yourself to others, and developing openness and trust in interpersonal relations.[34]

The methods used by encounter groups are based on the assumption that openness in emotional expression broadens and deepens your experience of yourself. Attention is focused continually on current experiences. The discussion of feelings and memories of the past and the possible historical roots of present difficulties is discouraged. Dialogue is maintained at a level of feeling, not fact. Constant feedback is provided. This feedback is most often accepting and warm, so that a feeling of trust and togetherness develops in which masks and pretense can be dropped.[35] The openness that is achieved during the group session may not carry over into everyday life. The impersonal atmosphere of the school, factory, or office often does not support openness and trust.

The experience of the encounter group session is often deep and intense. Members may be profoundly moved and occasionally wind up weeping or hugging each other, or both at once. The effect can also be harmful to unstable participants when it is not guided by someone who is experienced.[36]   Most often, however, participants leave the group with a feeling of joy.

A second type of group psychotherapy is **Gestalt therapy.**   Founded by the late Fritz Perls, Gestalt therapy focuses on the "here and now" of experience.   Awareness of body and behavior is often blocked by distortion and insensitivity; the Gestalt therapist strives to remove these blocks in the group sessions. One technique is to ask the group members to focus their attention on different parts of their bodies.   The Gestalt approach emphasizes the value of spontaneity, sensory awareness, emotional responsiveness, and closeness and flexibility in relating to others.

A third type of group psychotherapy is **transactional analysis,** or **TA.**   According to transactional analysis, the personality has three parts, or "ego states"; these parts are called "Parent," "Adult," and "Child."   Your "Parent" represents your perception of how your parents acted when you were a child. You can get in touch with your inner "Parent" by thinking now of something your parents told you when you were young that you still obey or fight against.   Your "Adult" represents your capacity for objectively and realistically dealing with the world; you are at this moment (I hope) in your "Adult" state.   Your "Child" is that part of your personality that thinks, feels, and acts as you did when you were actually a child.

According to transactional analysis, interpersonal relationships involve transactions between one part of your personality and one part of someone else's.   For example, sometimes your relationships involve "Adult-Adult" transactions and sometimes "Child-Parent" transactions.   By getting to know the parts of your personality and by analyzing your transactions with other people, you can become more aware of how you relate to people and can explore new ways of relating.

Ⓢ   Psychotherapy is a special kind of help for people who want to overcome their problems and to grow.   Psychotherapists include clinical psychologists, psychiatrists, and psychoanalysts; only psychiatrists are legally permitted to administer drugs.

Psychoanalysis is a form of psychotherapy that strives to make unconscious material conscious, using the techniques of free association and dream analysis.   According to Freud, the founder of psychoanalysis, the adult personality was shaped in childhood; this idea is called the principle of early determinism.   During childhood, significant feelings, impulses, and memories were repressed and made unconscious; according to the principle of unconscious motivation, these feelings continue to influence our behavior.

Behavior therapy is a form of psychotherapy that focuses on what people actually do, not on unconscious or underlying problems.   According to this view, our problems were learned and can be unlearned.   One technique of behavior therapy is desensitization, a procedure for replacing fear responses with relaxation responses.   By contrast, client-centered therapy assumes that people will change and grow naturally if they are provided with the right conditions; according to Rogers, these conditions are a special kind of warm and accepting relationship.

In group therapies people meet in groups of 8 to 12 with a psychotherapist.   Encounter groups, Gestalt therapy, and transactional analysis are examples of different types of group therapy.

Helping Others to Grow

You do not need to be a professional therapist in order to help others grow—any close and open relationship with another can be health-producing.   Because you control the kind of relationships you have, you can

Close relationships promote growth.

choose to have relationships that promote growth or ones that inhibit growth. If you have a high positive regard for others, if you really understand how others feel, if you are genuine and honest yourself, then you are a therapeutic person who is promoting growth in your friends.

Other persons encourage you to grow toward health too. You can probably remember a friend, a parent, or a teacher who has served this important function in your life. Remember one time when someone encouraged you to act exactly the way you felt? That was a growth experience. Remember when someone encouraged you to express your feelings—to talk about your fears, doubts, hopes? That was a growth experience. Remember when someone told you very frankly exactly how he or she felt about you? That was a growth experience. Remember when someone accepted you and loved you just the way you were? That was a growth experience. You can help others toward health by encouraging them to be "real," by helping them to know and to experience their feelings, by accepting them the way they are, and by prizing them.

Summary

KEY QUESTIONS

1. What are intelligence and creativity and how are they measured?

Your intelligence is your ability to learn and solve problems. Both your heredity and environment are important in determining your level of intelligence. IQ tests measure intelligence but are not very satisfactory measures. Your creativity is your ability to respond in unique and appropriate ways. One test of creativity asks you to think of unusual uses for common objects like bricks.

2. What is psychological health?

Psychological health consists of those aspects of behavior and experience that are positively valued and toward which we want to grow. Psychologically healthy people have been described as "fully functioning" or "self-actualized."

3. What is your stage of growth?
Growth toward health moves from conformity to independence, from living in the past to living in the present, from inability to recognize your feelings to full awareness and acceptance of your feelings.

4. What is psychotherapy?
Psychotherapy is a special kind of help aimed at assisting people to overcome their problems and to grow toward psychological health. Many different kinds of psychotherapy have been developed. Psychoanalysis has the goal of making unconscious motivations conscious. Behavior therapy has the goal of modifying behavior, of changing habits. Client-centered therapy has the goal of creating a warm and accepting relationship in which growth can occur.

KEY CONCEPTS

intelligence	The ability to learn and to solve problems.
intelligence quotient (IQ)	A score on an intelligence test that reflects a person's level of intelligence compared to others of the same age.
mentally retarded	People with IQ's below 70.
mentally gifted	People with IQ's above 130.
creativity	The ability to respond uniquely and appropriately.
fully functioning person	Rogers' term for the psychologically healthy person; one who is happy, creative, and socially effective.
congruence	A condition in which inner feelings, awareness of feelings, and outward expression of feelings correspond.
self-actualized person	Maslow's term for the ideally healthy person; one whose basic needs have been met and whose potential is fulfilled.
peak experiences	Moments of great joy, wonder, or awe; moments of self-actualization.
psychotherapy	A special kind of help provided by a trained professional and aimed at assisting people to overcome their problems and to grow.
clinical psychologist	A psychotherapist with a postgraduate degree in psychology; cannot administer drugs.
psychiatrist	A psychotherapist with a medical degree; can administer drugs.

psychoanalyst	A psychotherapist with extensive training in psychoanalysis.
psychoanalysis	The method of psychotherapy developed by Freud; its major aim is to make unconscious material conscious.
unconscious motivation	Needs and impulses that have been repressed so that a person is unaware of them.
early determinism	The view that adult personality is determined by early childhood experiences.
free association	The procedure of saying anything that comes to mind, without censorship.
dream analysis	The technique of analyzing and interpreting dreams in order to reveal unconscious material.
manifest content	The content of a dream as the dreamer describes it.
latent content	The "true" meaning of a dream, as revealed by dream analysis.
behavior therapy	A form of psychotherapy based on principles of learning that focuses on the symptoms of a psychological problem, not on underlying causes.
desensitization	A technique of behavior therapy that replaces fear responses with relaxation responses.
client-centered therapy	A form of psychotherapy that assumes that a warm and accepting relationship will promote spontaneous growth.
group therapy	Psychotherapy conducted with a group of 8 to 12 people at once.
encounter group	A group psychotherapy that focuses on sensitivity and awareness of feelings, authentic communication, and interpersonal trust.
Gestalt therapy	A group psychotherapy that focuses on sensory awareness, body awareness, and "here and now" experience.
transactional analysis	A group psychotherapy that assumes the personality to have three parts—"Parent," "Adult," and "Child"; transactions with other people are analyzed in terms of these three parts of the personality.

Suggested Readings

Let's Talk: An Introduction to Interpersonal Communication by Freda S. Sathre, Ray W. Olson, & Clarissa I. Whitney. (Second edition.) Glenview, Ill.: Scott, Foresman, 1977. Clear interesting discussion of interpersonal communication skills. Clever illustrations. Includes chapters on conflict reduction and intercultural communication.

Reaching Out: Interpersonal Effectiveness and Self-Actualization by David W. Johnson. Englewood Cliffs, N.J.: Prentice-Hall, 1972. An attempt to provide both a theory of interpersonal effectiveness and means of increasing actual skills in relating to others.

Games People Play: The Psychology of Human Relationships by Eric Berne. New York: Grove Press, 1964. A humorous and insightful description of the gamelike nature of many human interactions. Over a hundred different games are described and analyzed.

The Transparent Self by Sidney M. Jourard. (Rev. ed). Princeton, N.J.: D. Van Nostrand Co., 1971. A passionate plea for openness, disclosure, and honesty in interpersonal relationships. The author argues that self-disclosure is fundamental to psychological health.

Toward a Psychology of Being by Abraham H. Maslow. Princeton, N.J.: D. Van Nostrand Co., 1962. An inquiry into human potential. Rather than focusing on psychological disorder, Maslow focuses on people's highest values and aspirations. A study of self-actualized and psychologically healthy people.

On Becoming a Person: A Therapist's View of Psychotherapy by Carl R. Rogers. Boston: Houghton Mifflin, 1961. Rogers' theory of personality and psychotherapy. Of special interest are his stages of growth in the process of becoming a fully functioning person.

The Fifty-Minute Hour by Robert M. Lindner. New York: Bantam Books. Fascinating account of several case histories of individuals in psychoanalysis.

Behavior Therapy Techniques: A Guide to the Treatment of Neuroses by J. Wolpe & A. A. Lazarus. New York: Pergamon Press, 1966. Presents the view that neuroses are learned habits of reaction and can be removed by a conditioning procedure, as described in the book.

The New Psychotherapies by Robert A. Harper. Englewood Cliffs, N.J.: Prentice-Hall, 1975. A brief explanation of types of psychotherapy available today, including family therapies, group therapies, and behavior therapies.

First Impressions: The Psychology of Encountering Others by Chris L. Kleinke. Englewood Cliffs, N.J.: Prentice-Hall, 1975. A fascinating account of what happens when people come face to face for the first time. Discusses the effect of eyes, body language, and voice on first impressions.

Why Am I Afraid to Tell You Who I Am? by John Powell. Chicago: Argus Communications, 1969. Discusses the role of disclosure in interpersonal relationships and describes how to improve communication. Offers insights on self-awareness and personal growth.

The Human Personality by Dean Diggins & Jack Huber. Boston, Mass.: Little, Brown, 1976. An excellent, highly readable introduction to the psychology of personality. Discusses personality research and theory, personality problems, and personality change.

Liking and Loving: An Invitation to Social Psychology by Zick Rubin. New York: Holt, Rinehart and Winston, 1973. Reviews research on interpersonal attraction. Summarizes what is known about how we select friends and mates. This book is both authoritative and fun to read.

Research Methods

VI Tests and Surveys

You are unique. But how can your uniqueness be described? The ways in which your personality and abilities differ from other people's could be listed and verbally described; or, to characterize you more precisely, these differences could be measured. Can the dimensions of your mind be measured? To some extent, yes; psychological tests are "rulers" attempting just that. **Psychological tests** are intended to measure some psychological trait; for example, an IQ test measures intelligence.

By contrast, the goal of a **survey** is to measure some aspect of the behavior of a group of people. This is accomplished by asking them what they believe, prefer, or do. For example, before each presidential election, surveys estimate the voting intention of American voters. Often, as is the case with voters, the group in whose behavior you are interested is so numerous that you cannot talk with each person. In such cases you must sample.

Sample and Population

A **sample** is a subset of, or selection from, the population as a whole. The term **population** refers to the entire group in which you are interested. A good sample is both large enough and representative enough to "stand in" for the whole population, so that the results obtained from surveying the sample may be assumed to hold for the population as well. When you come to a conclusion about a population (all students or all voters) on the basis of evidence from a sample (some students or some voters), you are **generalizing.** To generalize is sometimes warranted and sometimes not.

After meeting one person from New York with red hair, you may mistakenly conclude that everybody from New York has red hair.

365

Your *sample* (one red-haired person) from the *population* (New York residents) was neither large enough nor representative enough to warrant your *generalization* that all New Yorkers have red hair.

Suppose you wanted to estimate the proportion of Americans who have consulted a psychiatrist or clinical psychologist. You conduct a survey of patients in a nearby mental hospital, finding that all have received psychological help, and conclude that everybody in the country has received psychological help. Your *sample* (patients in the hospital) was not representative of the population (all Americans); it was therefore a *biased sample.* It was biased because not all people live in hospitals and those who do may be different in some way from the general population. A **biased sample** is an unrepresentative sample.

A representative sample of American adults is sometimes formed by selecting persons from many different geographic regions, races, occupations, and economic and educational levels. The characteristics and opinions of such a sample are assumed to reflect the characteristics and opinions of the population as a whole.

A psychological test is a method of obtaining a selected sample of a person's behavior. On the basis of that sample a psychologist may generalize and draw a conclusion about *all* of the person's behavior. On the basis of a paper-and-pencil test of intelligence (a one-hour sample of behavior), a psychologist is able to reach a conclusion about the person's intelligence in general.

Such a test serves *descriptive, diagnostic,* and *predictive* purposes. A test is descriptive insofar as it helps to precisely characterize the ability or personality of an individual. ("Joan has an IQ of 60.") A test is used diagnostically when a psychologist **diagnoses,** or classifies, an individual's psychological problem on the basis of test results. ("Joan is mentally retarded.") A test is pre-

dictive when it is used to predict, or forecast, future behavior. ("Joan can be expected to have serious academic difficulties in school.") Research concerning individual differences in ability or personality often relies upon the descriptive, diagnostic, and predictive functions of psychological tests.

Reliability and Validity

Any ruler or other measuring device is useful only to the degree that it yields dependable results and to the degree that it actually measures what it claims to measure. **Reliability** means consistency or dependability; useful psychological tests and surveys are reliable in that they yield consistent results on repeated measurements. A rubber ruler is an unreliable measure of height; each time I measure your height I would obtain a different figure. Similarly, if a psychological test given on one day shows that you are a genius and on the next day shows that you are a moron, the test is unreliable or inconsistent.

Validity refers to how well a test or survey measures what it is supposed to measure; useful psychological tests and surveys are valid in that they are appropriate and effective instruments for describing or predicting some aspect of behavior. A ruler is a valid measure of height but an invalid measure of time; different marks on the ruler are just not related to different amounts of time.

If you invent a new test of intelligence that proves to be of no value in predicting academic success, reading comprehension, mathematic ability, or competence in the world, your test of intelligence will be called invalid; it does not seem to measure what it claims to measure. If your final exam in psychology class consisted exclusively of a series of questions about Latin or geology, the test would be invalid, since it would not measure the amount learned in psychology. To check on the validity of a test, first you must know exactly what it is supposed to measure.

Types of Tests

There are many varieties of psychological tests, each designed to serve different descriptive, diagnostic, or predictive purposes. Important decisions are made on the basis of results from these tests. You may be hired or fired on the basis of a test; you may pass or fail a class on the basis of a test; you may become a lawyer or a doctor on the basis of a test. Four important types of tests are those measuring ability, achievement, personality, and interests.

Ability Tests

An example of an ability test is the **Scholastic Aptitude Test** given by the College Entrance Examination Board. The test is designed to measure general academic ability and to predict grades in college. Many colleges consider SAT scores when deciding whether to admit a student who applies. A second example of an ability test is a standard IQ test, such as the Otis, the WAIS, or the Stanford-Binet. These tests yield a measure of intelligence called the IQ or intelligence quotient. If your IQ falls between 90 and 110, you are considered to be of average intelligence.

Achievement Tests

An example of an achievement test is the final exam given in a high school or college class. Such a test is designed to measure what has been learned in a particular area. It may consist of objective items, such as true-false or multiple-choice questions, or of subjective items, such as essay questions.

Personality Tests

Psychologists have developed many types of personality tests, designed to describe individual differences in personality. These tests do not have right or wrong answers; instead, the way you answer is used to characterize your personality. The **Rorschach** inkblot test consists of ten cards, each with a picture of a different inkblot. Persons taking the test are asked to look at each card and describe what they see. The way subjects respond to a card is used to describe and to diagnose their personality. The test is very controversial, and its usefulness has been seriously questioned by many psychologists who consider it unscientific.

A second example of a personality test is the Minnesota Multiphasic Personality Inventory **(MMPI).** The MMPI was developed to measure those traits which commonly characterize psychological disorders, but it has often been used to describe the personalities of normal people. The test consists of hundreds of true-false questions concerning various subjects such as physical health, sexual adjustment, religious and political attitudes, fears, fantasies, delusions, and hallucinations. The MMPI is an objective test in that the answers have standard interpretations based on empirical evidence. This test can be scored by a computer. Below are some examples of questions similar to those asked on the MMPI; each consists of a statement that is related as either "true," "false," or "cannot say."

☐ There are people who are plotting against me.

☐ I am frequently troubled by unusual feelings in the pit of my stomach.

☐ My hands shake most of the time.

☐ Love is only for persons who are weak.

☐ I am afraid to step on cracks in the sidewalk.

☐ Nobody could possibly like someone like me.

☐ I always do what I want no matter what happens.

☐ I am afraid of losing my mind.

☐ Someone has control over my mind.

☐ Most of the time I wish I were dead.

☐ Almost every day something happens to frighten me.

☐ I am a special agent of God.

☐ It is safer to trust nobody.

Interest Tests

Vocational interest tests are used to advise individuals about career and educational choices. The **Strong Vocational Interest Blank** is a test consisting of 400 items measuring interest in or preference for various occupations, school subjects, people, and activities. The test is scored in such a way as to show the similarities between your pattern of interests and those of people working in dozens of different occupations.

Problems with Tests and Surveys

The use of tests and surveys is sometimes controversial. Surveys attempting to forecast voting behavior are on rare occasions wrong. Tests are occasionally charged with being racially biased. Tests and surveys share a common feature that makes them vulnerable to criticism: both attempt to come to conclusions about a whole person or a whole group of people on the basis of a limited sample.

Controversies over Tests

The attempt to measure psychological traits using tests involves certain difficulties. In interpreting your responses on a personality test, for example, a psychologist must assume that you are answering honestly. But what if you were faking your answers, trying to appear as an especially well-adjusted individual? All personality tests depend to some extent on the basic honesty of the people who are taking them, but some tests have special protections against faking. For example, the MMPI has a special, built-in "lie-scale," a way of scoring certain items that detects an attempt to fake answers.

A second problem with tests is whether psychologists have the right to ask highly personal questions. Some personality tests include questions about political, religious, and sexual attitudes. The charge has been made that such tests constitute an "invasion of privacy." Tests, like knives, are tools that can be used for good or for ill. Although the issue has not yet been perfectly resolved, psychologists take their responsibility very seriously and follow a strict code of ethics designed to prevent the misuse of test results.

A third problem arising from the use of tests is the issue of cultural and racial bias in tests. IQ tests, for example, although designed to measure general intelligence, in fact consist of verbal questions having specific content. The subject matter of some questions concerns food, clothing, or housing habits more common to some members of our society than to others. Persons from different subgroups in our society have different familiarity with the items discussed in certain IQ questions; the experience of middle-class white America is not shared by all citizens. Test items referring to that experience are biased against other groups. Additionally, different subgroups of people use different languages or dialects; tests written in standard English are often biased against students from Spanish-speaking homes. The problem of cultural and racial bias in tests has been of great concern to psychologists in recent years, and much effort has been devoted to the development of tests that are less biased.

Whom Do You Believe?

Surveys work by asking people questions. But can you believe what they say? Sometimes people misrepresent themselves. Other times what a person remembers may not conform to what actually happened. In one survey of 920 adults, about one-third falsely claimed to have contributed to a community charity.[1] In this case it was possible to check the truthfulness of the answers because independent records were kept; in many cases it is not possible. Then there may be no better source than the people themselves. Psychologists sometimes go to great lengths to avoid relying on the verbal reports of people; often, however, these are probably closer to the truth than any other source. As Gordon Allport wrote:

If we want to know how people feel: what they experience and what they remember, what their emotions and motives are like, and the reasons for acting as they do—why not ask them?[2]

The problems of relying on personal reports can be seen in the examples of sex surveys and mental health surveys.

■ **The Example of Sex** Kinsey and his associates at the Institute for Sex Research at Indiana University conducted personal interviews with nearly 6,000 women and with over 5,000 men. Kinsey's study was the first large-scale survey attempting to determine the sexual behavior and experiences of American men and women.

The task of surveying sexual behavior by means of interviews raised some particularly difficult issues. Would people tell the truth or would they lie a little to create a better impression? Because sexual behavior occurs privately, there is no way to check for honesty. Kinsey was able to show, however, that his findings agreed fairly well with the find-

ings of other investigators. Furthermore, Kinsey compared the reports of spouses interviewed separately and found that these reports were very similar. For these reasons, Kinsey expressed confidence that his results were fairly accurate.[3]

A second problem of the sex survey was that of obtaining a representative sample of people to interview. On the basis of past experience, Kinsey believed that the traditional methods of obtaining a representative sample would not work for a sex survey; if he just went knocking on doors, a substantial percentage of people would not agree to be interviewed. And those that would agree to an interview might not be representative; for example, they might be more sexually liberal than the average person. For these reasons Kinsey decided to create a sample by asking whole groups to participate. Clubs and other organizations with a diversity of occupational, religious, and geographical backgrounds were asked to cooperate in the scientific study; because groups volunteered as a unit, there were few individual refusals. This method of choosing a sample has been severely criticized by other scientists; they claim that it was not a representative sample. For example, it is biased against those who are poorly educated; they do not appear in proportion to their numbers in the whole population. In spite of these difficulties, Kinsey's survey results have generally been confirmed by other studies that have followed it.

■ **The Example of Psychosis** Surveys of the "mental health" of the nation obtain different results, depending upon the sample surveyed. One survey asked a sample of about three thousand adults: "Have you ever felt that you were going to have a nervous breakdown?"[4] About 25 percent of the women and about 12 percent of the men said yes. What does this difference between men and women mean? One possibility is that more women tend to come close to a nervous breakdown than do men. A second possibility is that women are more likely to confess their emotional instability than are men (maybe men lie more about how they feel). A third possibility is that women are more likely to interpret extreme emotions as "coming close to a nervous breakdown"; perhaps women put a different meaning on the question. A fourth possibility is that women are more likely to remember their periods of extreme emotionality than are men. Thus, the obtained difference between the reports of men and women does not necessarily mean that women are less stable than men; there are alternative possibilities that must be considered.

KEY CONCEPTS

psychological test	A standard instrument intended to measure individual differences in a psychological trait; for example, an IQ test measures individual differences in intelligence.
survey	A poll or questionnaire consisting of questions addressed to a group of people; its purpose is to measure some aspect of the behavior of a group.
sample	A subset or selection from a larger group.
population	An entire group; the set being sampled.
generalization	Reasoning from evidence obtained from a sample to a conclusion about a population.
biased sample	An unrepresentative sample; a sample with characteristics systematically different from its population.
diagnosis	The classification, or labeling, of a problem.
reliability	Consistency or dependability.
validity	The degree to which an instrument actually measures what it is supposed to measure.
Scholastic Aptitude Test	A test designed to measure general academic ability and to predict college grades; given by the College Entrance Examination Board.
Rorschach	A test of personality using "inkblots" on cards.
MMPI	A personality test, consisting of hundreds of true-false questions, designed to measure abnormal personality traits.
Strong Vocational Interest Blank	A test measuring interest or preference in various occupations.

VII Conflict

19 Anxiety

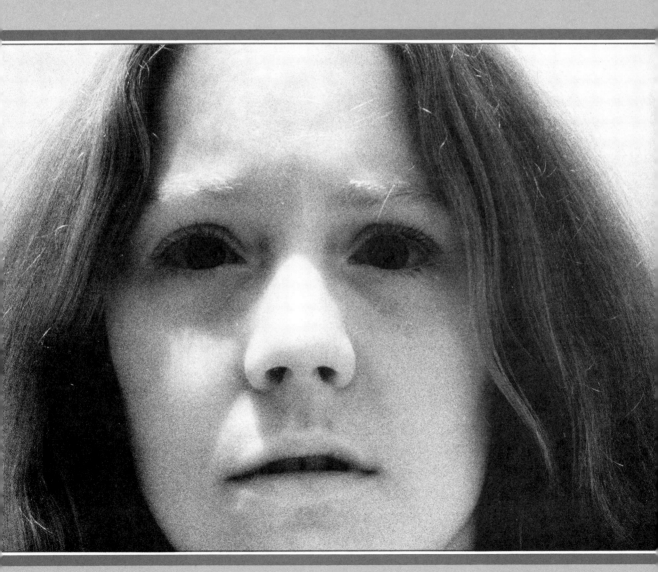

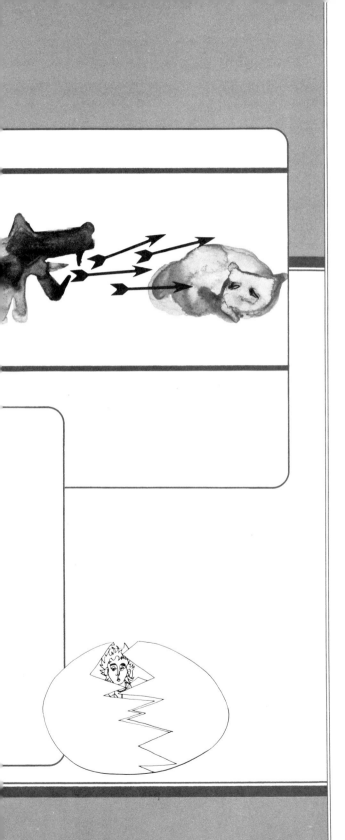

1. What is anxiety?
2. What causes anxiety?
3. How do you react to anxiety?
4. What's good about anxiety?

Have you been feeling nervous, worried, and unhappy?

At this moment you may feel emotionally upset and unable to concentrate; you may feel frustrated because you have been unable to satisfy some of your needs; you may feel anxious and depressed when you think about the days or years ahead. What are you worried about?

☐ Parents	☐ Being independent
☐ Friends	☐ Grades
☐ Ability to love	☐ Health
☐ Physical appearance	☐ Sex
☐ Feeling inferior	☐ Money

Unhappiness, worry, and frustration often arise from underlying conflicts; you are being pulled in different directions at once, and you may not even be fully aware of the forces pulling you. A **conflict** is a struggle between opposing wishes, needs, or forces.

375

What can you do about the unpleasant feelings that so often result from conflicts? Awareness of your conflicts is a first step.

Conflict

What are your conflicts? What are the forces pulling you in different directions? You have many different wants and needs. Sometimes one need you have is opposed to another need you or someone else may have; you cannot satisfy both needs, so you have a *conflict.* When you have two opposing needs within yourself, you have an **internal conflict.** When you have a need that is opposed to the need of someone else or of society, you have a **social conflict.** Both internal conflicts and social conflicts are sources of much human suffering.

Fly the nest.

Social Conflict

You live with other people and you are sometimes in conflict with them. Even if your family and your society are democratic, you cannot always have your own way; what you want and what the group wants are sometimes opposed. Social conflict can arise between individuals as well as between an individual and a group. I may want you to be or to act in a particular way, and you may want to be or to act in another way: this puts us in conflict.

■ *Parents* Do you remember the last conflict you had with your parents? Try to remember a time when your wants and their wants were opposed.

Your father and mother have many expectations, some realistic and some unrealistic, about the way you live your life. Some of these expectations are clearly stated, others are unspoken. You wanted to be free but your parents did not want you to be free: this put you in conflict with them. Your parents wanted you to conform but you did not want to conform: this put you in conflict with them. Your choice of clothes, hair style, language, and other aspects of your personal life have probably resulted in a variety of conflicts between you and your parents.

How are such conflicts resolved? The most typical response is a combination of three approaches: (1) The parents eventually feel that the children are old enough to be responsible for their own behavior and therefore no longer need parental guidance. (2) As the children grow older they begin to act more like their parents, thus reducing the possibility of conflict between them. (3) The children don't tell their parents how they are acting, thinking, and believing, thus avoiding conflict over what the parents would find objectionable.

Become a chip off the old block.

Retreat into a shell.

■ *Couples* Another type of social conflict is the conflict that occurs between the sexes. You may have had the experience of feeling that you loved someone who did not love you. Your desires and needs involved the other person, because without the participation of the other person, your needs could not be satisfied. If the other person did not love you, a frustrating conflict resulted. Even two persons who are romantically attracted to each other are often in conflict.

The needs of one person may conflict with the needs of the other. One person may want strong personal commitment; the other may want to be more free and less involved. One person may want sexual intimacy; the other may not be ready for that kind of relationship. How are these conflicts resolved? What typically happens is that individuals with similar needs pair off. This does not avoid conflict but it reduces it.

■ *Society* A third type of social conflict exists between you and the society in which you live. Each society has a set of agreed-upon rules, laws, customs, and values, which the individual member of society is expected to follow. Each society expects its members to think, act, and believe in certain "socially acceptable" ways. These ways are unique for a particular society; the expectations of the American society are different from the expectations of other societies. But each individual within a society is also unique; for some the rules and expectations fit better than for others. Consider this example: what would happen if everyone had to wear the same size shoes? For some they would be too tight, for others too loose, and on some people they would fit very well. How well do the rules and expectations of this society fit you?

Conflicts arise between what you want and what your society wants. As you grew up within this culture, however, you gradually learned to want what your society wants, at least most of the time. Not all individuals grow up within the major American culture; some move here from other countries and others grow up in minority subcultures within this country with a somewhat different set of rules and expectations. Individuals who are in transition from one society (with its values and expectations) to another society (with different values and expectations) face especially serious social conflicts. The

Can you retain your own beliefs and values?

children of immigrants to this country often must choose between the beliefs and values of their parents and the beliefs and values of their peers in this country. The harmful effects of this conflict are seen in the high rates of delinquency, crime, divorce, and insecurity among second-generation Americans.[1,2]

Minority persons in this society often suffer conflicts between the expectations and values of their subculture and the expectations and values of the majority culture. People living in an area not primarily populated by their own ethnic group show higher rates of mental disorder than members of the majority group.[3] Minority people who retain their own minority beliefs and values suffer fewer psychological problems than those people who give them up.[4] The central dis-

tricts of large cities are areas characterized by greater cultural conflict than the suburbs. The likelihood of crime, suicide, and mental illness increases as one approaches the center of a large city.[5] How are these conflicts resolved? (1) Individuals become "socialized"; that is, they change and accept the expectations and values of the majority culture. (2) The expectations and values of the majority culture also change to adapt to the individuals, although this change is very slow.

Internal Conflict

When one of your needs is incompatible with another one of your needs, you have an internal conflict. You want to be able to speak French, but you don't want to learn it:

you have a conflict. You want to be slim, but you also want to eat sweets: you have a conflict. You want to go out with the opposite sex, but you shrink away when you have the opportunity: you have a conflict. Other examples are numerous: you want to pass the test, but you want to watch TV instead of studying; you want to be entirely independent of your parents, but you don't want to support yourself; you want to be sexually satisfied, but you cannot at this time without violating your beliefs about morality. Which of these are *your* conflicts?

■ *Approach or Avoid* Internal conflict can be classified into three categories: approach-approach conflict, avoidance-avoidance conflict, and approach-avoidance conflict. The term "approach" refers to a positive reaction toward something or a liking of it; the term "avoidance" refers to a negative reaction toward something or a tendency to dislike it. You have an **approach-approach conflict** when you like two different things but can only have one. It's time to order dessert—will you have ice cream or pie? It's time to go to college—will you go to this one or to that one? It's time to choose a career—will you be a teacher or a lawyer? There are moments in life, "choice points," when different paths can be taken, when decisions can be made about different possible futures, or, on a smaller scale, when decisions must be made about what to do in the next few minutes. When both alternatives that you must choose from are attractive and desirable, you are in conflict (an approach-approach conflict).

Sometimes the alternatives from which you must choose are negative, unwanted, and undesirable, and you are placed in an **avoidance-avoidance conflict.** You don't like either choice, but you must choose anyway. Do you pay taxes or go to jail? Do you study all weekend or do you flunk the final?

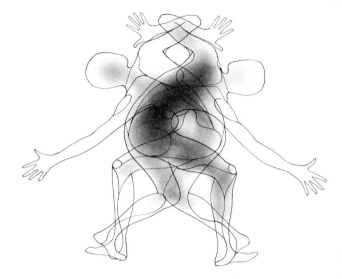

Do you go to the dentist or do you continue to have toothaches? When you try to avoid one of these undesirable alternatives, you find that you must accept the other undesirable alternative; you cannot avoid both. You are thus in a dilemma and experience a conflict.

Sometimes the same choice is both desirable and undesirable; it has both attractive and unattractive aspects. When these two tendencies operate at the same time, you have an **approach-avoidance conflict.** You want it, but you don't want it. Another piece of pie would taste very good, but it might give you a stomachache—should you have a second helping? You think that being a doctor would be very satisfying, but you fear you might fail some of the difficult academic courses that are required—should you try to become a doctor? You want very much to receive the attention and affection of a certain person of the opposite sex, but you fear that you would not make a favorable impression and would be humiliated or rejected—should you try to go out with that person? An example of an approach-avoidance conflict is the young man who sat in the telephone booth for an hour. He wanted to call a particular woman to whom he was very attracted, but the prospect of talking to her made him nervous. Fearing that he would be rejected, he finally left without calling. The conflict was resolved in favor of fear. Approach-avoidance conflicts like this have been studied experimentally with animals.

■ *How to Drive Your Cat Crazy* Approach-avoidance conflicts sometimes have serious psychological consequences. Psychologists have known for many years how to induce mental disturbances in animals such as rats,[6] dogs,[7] and cats.[8] The experimenters who work with these animals are not cruel; they feel that the study of abnormal behavior in animals might contribute to our understanding of psychological problems in humans. If we can understand how animals become neurotic and how to treat them, then we might be able to develop treatments for human problems. An experimental technique used in many of these studies with animals involves presenting the animal with an approach-avoidance conflict and observing the consequences of the conflict on the animal.

In one study,[8] several cats were first taught to open the hinged lid of a food box in order to eat. Each cat gradually learned to get at the food by lifting the lid with its head or paws and eagerly worked for its food in this way for several months. One day without warning each cat was given a mild blast of air at the moment of feeding. The physically harmless air blast was delivered to the cat's head just as it was about to eat. This mild stimulus had very strong effects. The typical reaction of a cat was to rush to the far side of the cage and crouch in fear, making no further attempt to feed in spite of its hunger. The next day, hungrier than ever, a few cats tried again to feed and received another air blast. For almost every cat one or two such

experiences were enough to cause them to refuse to eat, regardless of extreme hunger. In order to be kept alive they had to be forcibly tube-fed.

The cats experienced an approach-avoidance conflict. On the one hand they were hungry and food was readily available; on the other hand they feared the mild air blast. In almost every cat this conflict produced a general "mental breakdown," which, because it was produced in the laboratory, has been called **experimental neurosis.** For months afterward, previously quiet cats treated in this way tended to be tense and nervous, trembling frequently, with sweating, raised blood pressure, and irregular breathing. Other cats seemed to lose their tameness, becoming vicious and aggressive and attacking other cats in their cage. One cat put its head inside the food box and remained fixed in this position without eating, despite extreme hunger from several days of starvation. These "neurotic" cats were treated with a variety of procedures in an attempt to make them well again. Prolonged rest away from the food box, reassurance by stroking and petting, and watching other normal cats eat all proved to be somewhat effective procedures in getting the cats to eat again on their own.

ⓢ A social conflict results when your wishes or needs oppose those of other people or of your society. An internal conflict results from two opposing wishes or needs within yourself. Three types of internal conflict are approach-approach conflicts, in which you must choose between two desirable alternatives, avoidance-avoidance conflicts, in which you must choose between two undesirable alternatives, and approach-avoidance conflicts, in which the same choice is both desirable and undesirable. Approach-avoidance conflicts can produce experimental neurosis, a type of mental disturbance in animals.

What Is Anxiety?

Conflicts produce tension; when the conflicts are severe, the state of tension may be prolonged and experienced as an unspecified but unpleasant feeling called **anxiety.**

Anxiety is a feeling similar to fear, an experience of alarm, as if something unpleasant were about to happen. Although you are consciously aware of the unpleasant feeling, you are often unable to identify its source; you know you feel worried, nervous, moody, and tense, but you don't know why.[9]

When anxiety is severe, your body reacts: increased heart rate, fast and shallow breathing, perspiration, muscular tension (especially in the back of the neck), and muscle tremor. Additional physical reactions are sometimes continuous fatigue, stomach upsets, and constipation or diarrhea. These physical symptoms resemble those found in the "neurotic" cats after they had been presented with a severe approach-avoidance conflict.

Just as pain serves as a signal of a bodily problem, anxiety serves as a signal of a psychological problem. A severe pain in your foot indicates to you that your foot is in trouble and should be moved. A feeling of anxiety signals a kind of psychological danger. Anxiety can serve as a signal that you have an internal conflict that needs to be resolved. You may then take action to reduce the danger and anxiety. Often when an important internal conflict is resolved, the feeling of anxiety is greatly reduced. Think of when you solved a personal problem or resolved an internal conflict. Did you then feel more relaxed and less tense?

Anxiety Reactions

The experience of intense anxiety, with all of its bodily reactions, can interfere drastically with normal functioning. Thought and judgment deteriorate, self-control becomes increasingly difficult, concentration is impossible, and the mind is overwhelmed by unpleasant feelings of despair and alarm. You have experienced anxiety and you know how it makes you feel. Occasionally a feeling of intense anxiety will come on suddenly, as in the case of the young woman who described her experience as follows:

It was just like I was petrified with fear. If I were to meet a lion face-to-face, I couldn't be more scared. Everything got black and I felt I would faint, but I didn't. My heart was beating so hard and fast it would jump out and hit my hand. . . . My hands got icy, and my feet stung. My head felt tight, like someone had pulled the skin down too tight, and I wanted to pull it away. . . . I couldn't breathe. I was short of breath. . . . I don't know what I'll do. . . . I can go along real calmly for a while. Then, without any warning, this happens. I just blow my top.[10]

This woman experiences **acute anxiety reactions,** feelings of extreme anxiety that come quite suddenly and then disappear.

Anxiety can also be experienced almost continuously, rather than suddenly coming and going. A continuous feeling of intense anxiety is called a **chronic anxiety reaction** and can interfere seriously with everyday life, as the following example shows. A man describes the way he feels:

I feel tense and fearful much of the time. I don't know what it is. I can't put my finger on it. I am frightened, but don't know what I fear. I keep expecting something bad to happen. I just get all nervous inside. . . . I fear I might go all to pieces, maybe become hysterical.[10]

Can you recall the last time you felt anxious? Did you experience a physical reaction?

What was happening at the time? What did you do about it?

Basic Anxiety

According to psychiatrist Karen Horney, there is a basic anxiety, developed in childhood, that underlies a variety of adult anxieties. She believes that when children grow up under threatening or hostile conditions they feel isolated and helpless in a threatening world. The conditions producing basic anxiety are disturbed interpersonal relations between children and adults, as evidenced by excessive domination, indifference, overindulgence, erratic behavior, lack of reliable warmth, or overprotection.

Horney proposes that children, in trying to cope with these unfavorable conditions, will follow one or more of these three strategies: (1) moving *toward* people—they accept their own helplessness and become submissive and dependent, thereby gaining a feeling of belonging that makes them feel less weak and less isolated; (2) moving *against* people—they accept the hostility around them and determine to fight for their own protection; (3) moving *away from* people—they accept their isolation and distrust and build up a world of their own. Conflicts occur in adults when they use combinations of two strategies. The combination of strategies (1) and (2), for example, results in a conflict between being helpless and dependent on others, on the one hand, and being hostile, defiant, and angry, on the other hand. Hostility and dependency don't work well together.

$\boxed{\text{S}}$ Anxiety is an unpleasant feeling of tension and worry, typically accompanied by a variety of physical reactions. Intense anxiety can appear suddenly (acute anxiety reaction) or can be felt continuously (chronic anxiety reaction). According to Karen Horney, adult anxiety begins in childhood as basic anxiety, caused by disturbed interpersonal relations in the family. The child reacts by adopting a strategy of moving toward, against, or away from people.

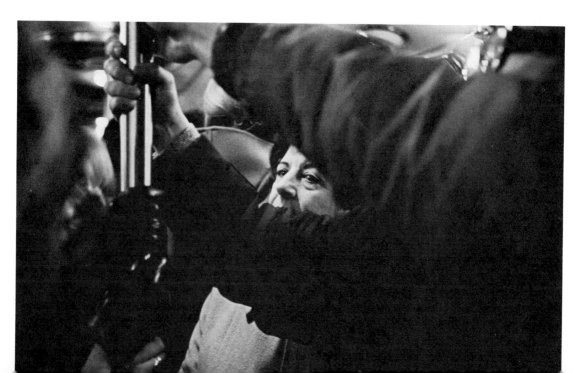

DEFENSE AGAINST ANXIETY 383

Defense Against Anxiety

The experience of anxiety is extremely unpleasant, and we avoid it when we can.
According to Freud, the self is relatively
fragile and must be protected from excessive
anxiety. We use various strategies for defending the self from anxiety, and these are
called **defense mechanisms**. Defense mechanisms typically operate unconsciously to
ward off anxiety; we usually are not aware
that we are using a defense. Here is a list of
some defense mechanisms. Do you recognize any that you might have used today?

Repression

*"I can't remember ever having a sinful
thought"*

Repression, or selective forgetting, is the
most fundamental defense against the
anxiety resulting from emotional conflict.
Thoughts, impulses, and experiences that
produce severe anxiety are "forgotten" or
pushed from awareness, so that the anxiety
that accompanies them will not occur. In
our society sexual and aggressive impulses
are responsible for the most common internal
conflicts and are most subject to repression.
People in conflict have two opposing tendencies; if they repress one or both of them, the
conflict is temporarily resolved.

To be successful as a defensive strategy
for guarding against anxiety, repression must
be continuous and complete. This as a matter of fact is rarely possible. People who
have been punished severely for the expression of anger may become extremely anxious
whenever they begin to get angry. They may
repress their anger in order to avoid conflict
and anxiety. But repression of anger might
fail in extreme circumstances, and as their
anger threatens to become conscious their

anxiety will increase. People who have repressed sexual impulses will feel anxious
whenever sexually tempted, due to the increased difficulty of keeping sexual feelings
from awareness.

Reaction Formation

"I've never been afraid of anything" (trem-
bling)

Reaction formation is a defense mechanism
that consists both of repressing how you
actually feel and insisting that you feel the
opposite way. Suppose for a moment that
you hate your father. To accept these hostile
feelings may produce too much threat and
anxiety; therefore you repress them and insist
that just the opposite is true: you dearly love
your father, he is the best father in the world.

Reaction formation is suspected to underlie many forms of extreme behavior.
Psychologists have proposed, for example,
that men who always display extreme stereotyped "masculine" behaviors may be reacting
against underlying repressed homosexual
impulses. Some mothers have a conflict
between the social expectation that they
should love their child and the simple fact
that they do not. A mother who feels hostile
toward her child may be made so anxious by
this feeling that she not only "forgets" it but
also insists that she loves the child intensely,
continually demonstrating this "affection" in
an exaggerated fashion.

Projection

"Nobody at this school likes me"

Projection is a defense against anxiety by
which you attribute to others certain
thoughts, feelings, or impulses that you have
but can't admit. In order to guard against
anxiety, you may repress feelings of anger

Displacement.

and hostility toward other people and "project" these unacceptable feelings onto them, so that you come to believe that *they* feel angry and hostile toward *you*. People with repressed homosexual impulses may "project" these feelings onto others believing that the persons around them are making subtle homosexual advances toward them. People who feel that everybody dislikes them may simply be projecting their own hostility, which, if they admitted, might give them intolerable anxiety.

Rationalization

"The teacher flunked me because I'm a . . ."
(woman, black, athlete, radical)

Rationalization is a defense against the anxiety that results from personal failures or disappointments. Anxiety can be reduced if the failure can be made acceptable, if it can be explained away so that our self-esteem is not damaged. We rationalize a failure by inventing a logical, but fictitious, excuse for it.

Suppose you failed a test because you had not mastered the material; you rationalize your failure by saying that the teacher had a grudge against you. You didn't win the class election because you didn't get enough votes; you rationalize your failure by saying that you really didn't want to be elected anyway. You weren't accepted at the college of your choice; you rationalize your failure by saying that the college probably isn't any good anyway. College students are very good at rationalization and can usually figure out an explanation for almost any failure. How did you rationalize the last bad grade you made?

Displacement

Father spanks son, who kicks the dog, who chases the cat

Displacement is the shifting of a response from one object to another. The boss has yelled at the father; the father is angry at the boss but can't express it safely, so he displaces his anger to his son and spanks him. The son is angry at his father but can't express it safely, so he displaces his anger to the dog and kicks it. The dog is "angry" at the son but can't express it safely, so he displaces his "anger" to the cat and chases it. In displacement, a feeling is displaced to a safer substitute. The displacement of aggression is as well known among animals as it is among people. One psychologist trained two rats to attack each other. Then he removed one of the rats and replaced it with a rubber baby doll. The doll was viciously attacked by the rat in a displacement of aggression.[11]

Scapegoating is a kind of displacement of negative feelings in which a person or group of people is unfairly blamed for a problem. The number of lynchings in this country was high during economic depressions and was low during more prosperous times. Blacks in the South may have served as "scapegoats," convenient substitutes toward which society could vent its frustrations.

Robert: A Case History

We all use defense mechanisms. The following case shows a college student whose underlying conflicts were so severe that he experienced intense anxiety in spite of his use of several defense mechanisms.

Robert went to his college counselor for help. He had been having increasing difficulty sleeping and would awaken in the middle of the night with acute anxiety reactions. During these anxiety attacks he would have a terrible fear that he was going insane. He would wake up trembling and fearful, with his heart beating rapidly. His counselor eventually discovered that when Robert was about five his mother, trying to stop his frequent masturbation, told him that it would make him insane. This threat caused Robert to suffer a severe conflict between his increasing biological urges and his fear of insanity. Robert was now a college freshman, and was afraid to masturbate; his sole sexual outlet consisted of wet dreams from which he awakened in acute anxiety. Robert's reaction to this conflict was complex: (1) He renounced sex in all its forms, emphasizing the "wholesome cleanness" of his feelings toward his friends; (2) he did not remember ever having masturbated as a child; (3) he was irritated because he felt that a couple of his female classmates kept watching and following him and had nothing on their minds but sex; (4) he said that he had thought about getting married and having a family, but that his chosen profession required that he give up sex and dedicate himself to his work.

Each of Robert's four reactions represents a defense mechanism. Can you identify which reaction corresponds to which defense? (The correct answers appear at the end of the chapter.)

⑤ Freud proposed that we develop strategies for protecting ourselves against the experience of anxiety, unconscious strategies called defense mechanisms. In repression, the fundamental defense mechanism, thoughts and impulses that threaten to produce anxiety are pushed from awareness and forgotten. Reaction formation involves repressing how you actually feel and then insisting that you feel the opposite way. Projection consists of attributing to others certain thoughts or impulses you have but cannot admit. Rationalization is the attempt to explain away failure so as to protect your self-esteem. Displacement involves shifting a reaction from one person to a safer substitute.

Positive Anxiety

Anxiety can be a source of great suffering and pain but it has a positive side as well. Not all anxiety is bad. Some anxiety is a normal and even necessary part of life. As the anthropologist Margaret Mead wrote:

It is clear that we have developed a society which depends on having the right amount of anxiety to make it work. . . . People who are anxious enough keep their car insurance up, have the brakes checked, don't take a second drink when they have to drive, are careful where they go and with whom they drive on holidays. People who are too anxious either refuse to go into cars at all—and so complicate the ordinary course of life— or drive so tensely and overcautiously that they help cause accidents. People who aren't anxious enough take chance after chance, which increases the terrible death toll of the roads.[12]

Anxiety is a fact of life in the modern world. Moderate levels of anxiety energize behavior, motivating us to act, plan, and take care of ourselves.

Anxiety is a sign of conflict and stress. But conflict means the opportunity for choice, and choice is necessary for growth. Your anxiety may be a sign that you are extending yourself, reaching out, becoming more independent. Each new stage of life is typically accompanied by anxiety: the first day at a new school, your first date, your first job, leaving home, graduation, or marriage. To face conflict and confront anxiety is to engage life and promote personal growth and self-understanding. The poet Kahlil Gibran described this feeling when he wrote, "Your pain is the breaking of the shell that enclosed your understanding."

Summary

KEY QUESTIONS

1. What is anxiety?
   Anxiety is an experience of tension, worry, and alarm—as if something very unpleasant were about to happen. It is a feeling similar to fear, but you are generally unable to specify its source.

2. What causes anxiety?
   Feelings of anxiety signal a psychological conflict; forces seem to be pulling you in different directions. One source of anxiety is an internal conflict, produced by two opposing needs within yourself. A second source of anxiety is a social conflict, when your needs oppose those of someone else or of society.

3. How do you react to anxiety?
   Your reaction to anxiety may include a variety of unconscious defense

mechanisms, such as repression or projection. Your body reacts with increased heart rate and blood pressure, fast and shallow breathing, perspiration, and muscular tension.

4. What's good about anxiety?

While the experience of anxiety is unpleasant, it is a normal and necessary part of life and is sometimes a sign of personal growth. Your anxiety may be a sign that you are extending yourself, risking new roles, and becoming more independent.

KEY CONCEPTS

conflict	A struggle between opposing wishes, needs, or forces.
internal conflict	A struggle between two opposing wishes or needs within an individual.
social conflict	A struggle between the needs of one person and the opposing needs of someone else or of society.
approach-approach conflict	A conflict involving a choice between two desirable alternatives.
avoidance-avoidance conflict	A conflict involving a choice between two undesirable alternatives.
approach-avoidance conflict	A conflict involving a choice that is both desirable and undesirable.
experimental neurosis	A mental disorder in laboratory animals caused by an approach-avoidance conflict.
anxiety	A feeling of tension, worry, and alarm.
acute anxiety reaction	A feeling of intense anxiety that comes on suddenly and then disappears.
chronic anxiety reaction	A feeling of intense anxiety that is continuous.
defense mechanism	An unconscious strategy for protecting ourselves against the experience of anxiety.
repression	A defense mechanism in which thoughts and impulses that threaten to produce anxiety are pushed from consciousness and forgotten.

reaction formation	The repression of a feeling and the insistence that its opposite is true.
projection	Attributing to others certain thoughts or impulses an individual may have but cannot admit.
rationalization	The attempt to explain away failure so as to protect self-esteem.
displacement	Shifting a reaction from one person to a safer substitute.
scapegoating	A displacement of negative feelings in which a person or group of people is unfairly blamed for a problem.

Answers to question about defense mechanisms (p. 385):   (1) reaction formation;   (2) repression;   (3) projection;   (4) rationalization.

20 Neurosis

KEY QUESTIONS

1. What is neurosis?
2. What are the types of neurosis?
3. What causes neurosis?
4. Are you neurotic?

When she saw her husband kissing another woman, Rose suddenly became blind. The anxiety of seeing them together was too much, so she gave up her sight. A soldier, about to be sent on a dangerous mission to the front lines, suddenly became paralyzed; he would not have to fight if he could not walk. An eight-year-old girl washed her hands 20 to 30 times every day; if she was prevented from doing this, she panicked. A man was so terrified of germs that he could not leave his house without wearing rubber gloves. Giving up the ability to see or walk is a huge price to pay for avoiding the experience of anxiety. Having to wash your hands or wear gloves all the time are terribly awkward ways of dealing with fear.

Some strategies for coping with anxiety are extreme; they prevent a person from living a normal life, and they are unsuccessful in solving the problems of stress and anxiety. Such a strategy is called a neurotic reaction, or a **neurosis.**

Normal or Neurotic?

The difference between a normal person and a neurotic person is often not entirely clear. Both normal persons and neurotic persons defend themselves against anxiety. The difference between the normal defense mechanism and a neurotic reaction is a matter of degree: one, the normal defense mechanism, is a reasonably flexible response to anxiety, may be modified if the situation changes, and does not seriously interfere with living; the other, the neurotic reaction, is an inflexible response to anxiety, continues to be repeated even when the situation changes, and interferes with living.

Self-Defeating Behavior

Neurosis is not adaptive; that is, the underlying conflicts producing the anxiety are not resolved by the neurotic strategy. Instead the neurotic behavior protects the person against the experience of anxiety while the conflicts continue to be present. Becoming blind or paralyzed may reduce anxiety but does not solve the problems causing the anxiety. Because the conflicts continue to be present, the neurotic person is continually threatened by them. By allowing people not to face their conflicts, neurotic reactions interfere with new learning experiences which might in time solve the problem. In this way neurotic reactions retard growth and change; a neurosis promotes rigid and inflexible behavior. Behavior that is neurotic tends to be repeated over and over again, regardless of how useful or appropriate it is. Although the neurotic behavior defends the person against pain, it is self-defeating in the long run. The woman who became blind rather than see something painful does not have the oppor-

tunity to learn that her husband's behavior has changed.

Neurotic Trends

Sometimes people show a relatively consistent way of behaving; they have a consistent style or mode of reaction. Such a pattern or mode is identified as *neurotic* when it serves as a defense against anxiety and when it interferes with living. These neurotic patterns of behavior have been called "overdriven strivings"[1] and **neurotic trends.**[2]

Can you think of friends who seem to have an inflexible style in relating to others? Their style is probably important in making them feel safe and free from anxiety. Certain neurotic patterns have been shown to be fairly common. A **neurotic compliant trend** is shown by individuals who strive in an exaggerated manner to win the affection and esteem of everyone around them so that they can depend upon them for support. The term "compliant" means yielding and submissive. A **neurotic aggressive trend** is shown by individuals who strive in an exaggerated manner to defeat and put down everyone around them. A **neurotic detached trend** is shown by individuals who consistently move away from all people, isolating themselves from others so as to avoid the threats of human relationships.

A neurotic trend has three important qualities: (1) It is *indiscriminate*. The term "indiscriminate" refers to a failure to distinguish between different situations. In a neurotic trend the same reaction is shown in essentially all circumstances even when it is clearly inappropriate. It may be inappropriate to try desperately to win the affection of your grocery clerk; it may be inappropriate to consistently strive to defeat and put down your husband or wife. (2) A neurotic trend is *insatiable.* The term "insatiable" means incapable of being satisfied. For example, the neurotic striving for affection is never satisfied; no amount of affection is ever enough. (3) It is *overreactive* to failure. When the neurotic pattern fails, there is an exaggerated reaction. Blocking the reaction gives rise to exaggerated despair and anxiety. A neurotic aggressive person who has not successfully defeated someone feels very anxious and depressed. A neurotic compliant person who has been striving for affection reacts extremely to even the slightest rejection and feels great despair.

⬚ The difference between normal and neurotic behavior is a matter of degree. Neurotic behavior is more rigid, inflexible, and self-defeating; it interferes with new learning and growth. Some people show a neurotic trend or consistent neurotic pattern of being excessively compliant, aggressive, or detached.

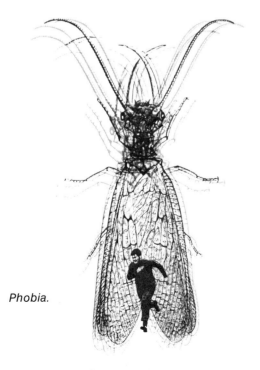

Phobia.

Types of Neurosis

Along with the consistent trends or patterns of behavior, a neurotic often develops specific behaviors or reactions. These repetitive and rigid responses work for the neurotic in that they serve as a defense against anxiety. The woman who became blind upon seeing her husband with another woman developed such a neurotic reaction. It is important to realize that all neurotic reactions differ from normal behavior only in *degree;* that is, neurotic reactions are simply exaggerated reactions common in normal individuals. A description of different types of neurotic reactions appears below.

Phobic Reactions

Sometimes a person shows great fear of something that is relatively harmless; this neurotic reaction is called a **phobia.** A person with a phobia will make a great effort to avoid the object or situation that is feared. Many persons have mild phobias of some sort; you may have unreasonable fears of elevators, garden snakes, or small spiders. Sometimes, however, these fears are extreme and interfere with living.

■ *Unreasonable Fears* One man, a chemist, was terribly afraid of flowers. This phobia interfered with his work because certain chemicals that smelled like flowers also made him very anxious.

The sight or smell of flowers, particularly bouquets, sprays, and cut flowers, brought on intense fear, dread, and anxiety. This might be even more intense if the flowers were beginning to wither. Flowers had become for him an external threatening object which had to be avoided at all costs.[3]

Persons have developed phobic reactions to many different kinds of objects and situations. Some of the different phobias have been named. Following is a list of some of these names:

Acrophobia—fear of heights
Agoraphobia—fear of open spaces
Arachnophobia—fear of spiders
Brontophobia—fear of thunder
Claustrophobia—fear of closed spaces
Cynophobia—fear of dogs
Nyctophobia—fear of the dark
Ophidiophobia—fear of snakes

What are you afraid of? Are these fears realistic or are they phobic?

■ *The Case of the Wife and the Red-Headed Woman* A forty-five-year-old woman visited her husband one Sunday morning in his hospital room where he was recovering from an illness.[3] When she walked in she found her husband with a young red-headed woman. The husband admitted that he had been intimate with the woman for the past two years. The wife then developed a phobic reaction to things associated with her painful experience: (1) every Sunday morning she woke up in a panic; (2) she became very anxious whenever she approached the hospital and avoided it whenever possible; (3) the clothes that she wore that day made her anxious and she had to throw them away.

Obsessive-Compulsive Reactions

An **obsession** is an idea or desire that intrudes, unwanted, into your mind over and over again. We all experience some minor obsessions. When we leave on a trip we may be obsessed with the thought that we have forgotten to pack something or that we have left the door unlocked. In neurotic obsessions, however, unwanted and recurrent thoughts force themselves into the person's mind and interfere with normal thinking.

A **compulsion** is an irrational repetitive act over which you seem to have little control. Compulsions, like obsessions, intrude, unwanted, into a person's life. We also all experience some minor compulsions. As children many of us compulsively avoided stepping on cracks in the sidewalk, and as adults we have particular set ways of dressing in the morning or taking baths. These compulsive rituals do not interfere with living; but in neurotic compulsions, unwanted acts occur over and over again and prevent the person from doing other things.

■ *Hand-Washing* One man had obsessive thoughts about cleanliness; he kept thinking about germs on his body. He also had a compulsion to wash his hands.

His hands were reddened and sensitive from the thorough scrubbing received on a daily average of twenty-five times or more. Occasionally when his level of anxiety or internal pressure became quite high, even this frequency of washing greatly increased. . . . He could not stand to brush against another person, and if this happened, dry-cleaning of his garments was often a necessity. . . . He usually had to wear a special pair of gloves when dressing or undressing.[3]

Clearly, this man's neurotic reaction handicapped him in his attempts to live a satisfying life.

■ *Peter and His Lucky Numbers* Both obsession and compulsion can be seen in the following case. Peter's home life was intolerable; he had contempt for his timid and frightened mother and was terrified of his angry father. The grandfather gave Peter

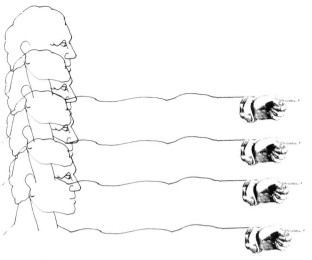

Compulsion.

attention and love and became increasingly important to the young boy. But Peter was obsessed by thoughts that the old man might die.

Peter began to be visited by anxious thoughts which seemed to force themselves into his mind. He had images of the house catching fire; he was afraid it would be struck by lightning or shattered in a high wind. He thought of various ways in which harm might come to his grandfather, and then he began to develop symptoms which had the character of magical acts designed to prevent this catastrophe. If the thought crossed his mind that the house might burn, he felt compelled to touch something in order to avert the danger. If he had such a thought while stepping on a crack, he had to step on the crack again to cancel the thought. Soon he needed to perform extra touchings for good measure, and sometimes he would spend nearly an hour going through one of these operations. When people began to notice his peculiar behavior, he developed a technique for discharging all the unlucky thoughts of the day in the privacy of his bedroom at night. If he pointed four times (a lucky number) to the southwest (a lucky direction), he could counteract the danger. But he never felt satisfied. He had to point 4 × 4 × 4

× 4 times, 256 times, and this took half an hour. He invented short cuts like stamping his foot to stand for groups of numbers, but in the end no time was saved. If the ritual could not be completed, he felt absolutely miserable. He was at the mercy of obsessive thoughts *and* compulsive actions.[1]

Notice the difference between the mild obsessions and compulsions that we experience in our normal behavior and the severe neurotic reaction of Peter, a reaction that seriously interfered with his life.

Depressive Reactions

Depression is the feeling of despair, worthlessness, and sadness that often occurs in response to actual or imagined loss, failure, or misfortune. **Neurotic depression** is different from normal depression. It is much more intense and lasts longer. The person who is neurotically depressed feels persistently sad, worthless, unlovable, inadequate, and lonely. Eating and sleeping habits are often changed; at times the person will sleep excessively, at other times there will be difficulty sleeping. Fatigue and apathy become continual facts of life. Sometimes the person will consider suicide as the only way to end the misery.

■ *Lack of Interest and Energy* Neurotic depression varies greatly in intensity. The following case shows a relatively mild neurotic reaction, as described by the person experiencing the depression.

I don't have very much interest in my work. . . . I'm tired. Don't seem to have as much energy as usual. . . . I just don't feel very well. My appetite isn't very good, and sometimes I'm restless. . . . I'm not very happy these days. My sleeping isn't very

frequent crying spells, which had not lessened over the past two months. Angela found it hard to concentrate on her job, had great difficulty falling asleep at night, and had a poor appetite. She said her depression had begun after she and her boyfriend Jerry broke up two months previously. . . . It became difficult for her to initiate a conversation with others, and many times her lips felt as if they were stiff, and she had to make an effort to move them in order to speak. . . . She felt constantly tired, and loud noises, including conversation or the television, bothered her. She preferred to lie in bed rather than be with anyone, and she often cried when alone.[4]

Although each of us has felt depressed at different times, a person suffering from a neurotic depression finds constant difficulty in life, love, and work. Great sadness, feelings of worthlessness, and lack of self-esteem make it difficult to live a satisfying life.

Dissociative Reactions

Dissociation means separation or splitting apart. In a **dissociative reaction,** one aspect of the personality is isolated from the remainder, resulting in a loss of memory and personal identity. People forget who they are and even where they live. Two types of dissociative reactions are amnesia and multiple personality.

■ *Loss of Memory* **Amnesia** is a loss of memory for certain parts of your past life. In many cases individuals do not know their own name, work, family, or home; they lose all memory for personal identity. Amnesia is often associated with psychological stress or trauma, and can be considered as a way to escape from unbearable emotional conflict. Here is a case history showing the background of an amnesia victim:

good. I wake up early and worry about a lot of things. . . . I don't feel I've accomplished very much in life. I don't think I'm a very worthwhile person. . . . If I could just get back some interest and ambition.[3]

■ *Angela's Crying Spells* Sometimes the neurotic reaction is much more severe, as in the following case of a woman who was severely depressed after she and her boyfriend stopped seeing each other.

Angela Savanti was 22 years old, lived at home with her mother, and was employed as a secretary in a large insurance company. She stated that she had had passing periods of "the blues" before, but her present feelings of despondency were of much greater proportions. She was troubled by a severe depression and

Donald G. was 22 and attended college at night while working in the daytime to support himself and his mother. Donald had a girlfriend whom he wanted to marry, but his mother disliked her. It was clear that he could not support himself, a wife, and his mother while going to college. Finally his girlfriend told him that he must make a choice between her and his mother, giving him one month to decide. One week before the decision was due, Donald disappeared. Two weeks later he was discovered in another state, and could remember neither his name nor his home. Amnesia had solved his problem; he no longer had to make a choice.[5]

Donald G.'s personal identity was lost over the conflict. This seems to be an unreasonably large price to pay for avoiding the anxiety associated with the decision and certainly did not lead to a satisfactory resolution of the problem. The response of amnesia is therefore a neurotic reaction and is self-defeating.

■ *The Three Faces of Eve*   In the case of **multiple personality,** individuals seem to have two or more distinct personalities and identities, only one of which is present at a time. Individuals with this rare disorder change from one personality to another, as in the case of "Dr. Jekyll and Mr. Hyde." People with such a "split personality" may be in conflict over two opposing patterns of behavior. They solve the problem by essentially becoming two people. At one time they are person A, at another time they are person B. Multiple personality is a rare condition, but certain dramatic cases have been reported.

One of the best-known cases of multiple personality was reported in a book and movie entitled *The Three Faces of Eve,* based on the life of a real person.[6] Eve White was a twenty-five-year-old woman who suffered from severe headaches followed by black-outs. During one therapy session Eve suddenly changed her pattern of behavior and introduced herself to the doctor as "Eve Black." While Eve White was quiet, sweet, and industrious, Eve Black was mischievous, vivacious, and irresponsible. Eve White's blackouts were actually periods in which Eve Black was in control. Eve White was not aware of Eve Black's existence, although they shared the same mind. After months of therapy a third personality emerged—Jane—who was mature and competent.

Conversion Reactions

An individual with a **conversion reaction** has sensory or muscular problems without a physical cause. A woman became blind upon seeing her husband with another woman; a soldier became paralyzed when ordered to the front lines. These persons

Conversion reaction.

have, in a sense, converted their mental conflicts into the bodily symptoms of blindness and paralysis. In addition to blindness and paralysis, conversion reactions may include deafness, inability to taste or smell, inability to speak, visceral problems such as hiccups, vomiting or diarrhea, seizures, anesthesia, and even the physical conditions of a pregnancy. These symptoms are real. Victims are not faking but suffer from them as much as if they had a physical basis.

Problems with a physical basis and problems resulting from a conversion reaction may differ in that conversion reactions often do not make sense in terms of what we know about the anatomy and physiology of the body. For example, a conversion reaction resulting in a loss of feeling in an arm or leg may affect an area of the skin that might be covered by a glove or stocking; nerve damage, however, would affect a very different area because of the way the nerves are distributed. Because of their psychological nature, conversion reactions may be cured by a treatment such as psychotherapy.

■ *A Paralyzed Arm Cannot Murder*   In the following case a woman could not tolerate her own hostile feelings, so she "converted" them into a partial paralysis of her right arm.

A twenty-six-year-old married mother sought treatment because of a tremendous dragging weakness of her right arm. This was severe enough to result in an inability to do her housework adequately, or properly to care for her eight-month-old daughter. She also reported being so anxious when in the kitchen that she could not bear to remain there long. . . .

She had been so deprived of love and affection herself that the needs of her child in this direction had become an intolerable burden to her. This resulted in a rejecting attitude to-

ward the child. . . . The response of the child in turn was to become restless, tense, and anxious, and to develop poor sleeping habits and digestive upsets. All of this resulted in an added drain on the mother. Her resentment and hostility toward the child were increased, setting up a vicious circle. The weak arm developed as a final safeguard against conscious awareness of her overwhelming rage. . . . The anxiety about the kitchen was found to relate to the kitchen knives (potential murder weapons) which were kept there. One cannot easily wield a knife with a paralyzed arm.[3]

The mother escaped her conflict by developing a physical symptom, a partially paralyzed right arm. In the course of psychotherapy this woman's conversion reaction gradually disappeared.

■ *Secondary Gains*   The physical problems of a conversion reaction often seem to have two types of benefits: first, the problem allows people to escape their conflicts, thus reducing their anxiety; second, people often receive sympathy and attention because of the problem. The second benefit is called a **secondary gain** and can serve the function of encouraging the problem to continue once it occurs. The conversion reaction results in a secondary gain for a person to the extent that other persons are stimulated to respond with sympathy, affection, and attention. The following case illustrates a secondary gain brought about by a neurotic conversion reaction:

A middle-aged married woman had to nurse her mother-in-law, who was paralyzed in both legs. Her husband forced her to do this, and seemed to become concerned only with his mother, forgetting his wife. One day the wife took a walk, feeling rebellious, but at the same time very anxious as she became dimly aware of angry wishes that the old lady would die. She felt faint and sat down on a park bench. A moment later she tried to rise, only to discover that both her legs were paralyzed and that she now needed as much of her husband's attention as did his mother.[1]

Traumatic Reactions

Everyone has a breaking point. Under conditions of extreme shock or injury, an emotional collapse may occur. A trauma is a physical or psychological injury or shock and a **traumatic reaction** is a neurotic disorder resulting from such a shock. This reaction may involve intense anxiety, phobias, dissociation, depression, or other types of neurotic problems. Traumatic reactions can result from any kind of overwhelming stress, such as war, accidents, or natural disasters.

■ *A War Trauma* Soldiers in combat face extreme stress and some may break down. Continued exposure to rifle fire, mines, and bombing had both immediate and long-term psychological consequences for soldiers who had fought in Vietnam. After returning from the war, many veterans suffered from recurrent nightmares, jumpiness, and depression, and experienced great difficulties in interpersonal relations.[7]

One soldier had been pinned down by enemy fire for 12 hours and had seen most of his platoon killed. He had a temporary traumatic reaction and was flown directly from the battlefield to a hospital.

No information accompanied him, he had no identifying tags on his uniform, and he was so completely covered with mud that a physical description of his features was not possible. His hands had been tied behind him for the flight, and he had a wild, wide-eyed look as he cowered in a corner of the emergency room,

glancing furtively to all sides, cringing and startling at the least noise. He was mute, although once he forced out a whispered "VC" and tried to mouth other words without success. He seemed terrified. . . . His hands were untied, after which he would hold an imaginary rifle in readiness whenever he heard a helicopter overhead or an unexpected noise. . . .

Soon after his arrival at the hospital the patient was given tranquilizers to calm him and keep him asleep for approximately 40 hours. When he was allowed to wake, the medication was discontinued. Although he appeared somewhat dazed and subdued, his response to ward activities was dramatic. Within 72 hours after his admission to the hospital, the patient was alert, oriented, responsive, and active. Although still a little tense, he was ready to return to duty. He was sent back to his combat unit on his third hospital day.[8]

■ *Disaster at Buffalo Creek* Tornadoes, hurricanes, fires, floods, and earthquakes are natural disasters resulting in extraordinary psychological stress. They injure the mind as well as physical structures. For example, one year after a tornado struck San Angelo, Texas, about 50 percent of the townspeople who were examined reported they still suffered from emotional problems caused by the storm.[9] While the immediate psychological response to disaster is shock and confusion, there may be long-term, and even permanent, traumatic reactions. These problems have been observed in the residents of a mountain valley in West Virginia.

The Buffalo Creek valley in West Virginia had 14 small towns with a population of four to five thousand people. On February 26, 1972, disaster struck. An enormous dam broke and released a tidal wave of water and mud which destroyed everything in its path. Over 100 people were killed and 4,000 were

Emotional problems commonly result from natural disasters, such as floods.

left homeless. Two years after the disaster, over 90 percent of the survivors who were examined showed anxiety, depression, nightmares, phobias, and other psychological problems.[10] Many of these were diagnosed as showing a traumatic neurosis. The survivors sued the company that owned the dam and received $6 million for psychological damages.[11]

⑤ Neurotic reactions appear in a variety of forms: an unreasonable fear (phobia); recurring, unwanted ideas (obsessions); irrational repetitive actions (compulsions); a splitting apart of the personality (dissociation) resulting in loss of memory (amnesia) or alternating distinct personalities (multiple personality); sensory or muscular problems without a physical cause (conversion reaction); and a neurotic reaction to a physical or psychological shock (traumatic reaction). Each of these forms of neurosis is a self-defeating, inflexible reaction to intense anxiety.

The Function of Neurosis

The different neurotic reactions just discussed are similar in that each is a reaction to intense anxiety. Although they serve the function of avoiding the unpleasant experience of anxiety, they also handicap people in their attempts to live a satisfying life. Rather than dealing with the source of the anxiety—the underlying conflicts—people follow rigid and inflexible modes of behavior that actively prevent the confrontation with and understanding of the source of their problems.

People with phobic reactions in a sense displace their anxiety from their internal conflicts to an external object or event; this object can be avoided, and so the experience of anxiety is avoided. They do not have to deal with their problems; they are simply avoided. People with a dissociative reaction escape their conflicts by losing their identity; they become someone else, not the person with the conflict. People with obsessive-compulsive reactions deny that their thoughts and acts are their own; they are forced upon them. If they have no control over their thoughts and acts, they cannot be responsible for them and cannot be expected to deal with them. People with depressive reactions insist that they are completely helpless and incapable of attending to their own problems. Because they lack the energy to cope with them, they simply bear the weight of them as helpless victims. People with conversion reactions escape conflicts by converting them into physical problems. They do not have to deal with the problems because they can deny responsibility for them. In these varied ways neurotic reactions promote the continuation of problems by allowing individuals to avoid facing their conflicts and solving them.

Causes of Neurosis

Each neurotic person shows a unique pattern of self-defeating behavior. The variety of different neurotic patterns suggests that there is no unique, single cause of neurosis. Different theories of the causes of neurosis reflect different points of view about which particular influence is most important in understanding this disorder. Three of these theories are described below.

Psychoanalytic Model

According to Freud's psychoanalytic theory, neurosis results from a distorted or exaggerated use of repression, projection, and other defense mechanisms. As unconscious conflicts, primarily originating in childhood, threaten to become conscious, intense anxiety is produced. While most people are able to control anxiety by using ordinary defense mechanisms, the neurotic is not able to do this effectively. In the neurotic, the pressure of unconscious conflicts distorts and exag-

gerates the defense mechanism. These distortions result in the neurotic pattern of behavior. For example, neurotic amnesia may result from the distorted use of repression as a defense mechanism, and phobia may result from the distorted use of displacement as a defense mechanism.

Behavioral Model

According to the behavioral theory, neurotic reactions are "bad habits" that have been learned. The principles of operant and classical conditioning are used to explain how a particular "bad habit" could have been learned. For example, a spider phobia could be explained by the principle of classical conditioning; an intense fear of spiders is regarded as a conditioned response, resulting from the repeated association of spiders (conditioned stimulus) and the pain of their bites (unconditioned response). One author uses the principle of operant conditioning to explain a case of blindness that was a conversion reaction.[12] The man's life was so miserable that blindness was, from his point of view, an improvement. As a result of his blindness, he received a pension, did not have to work, and spent his time at home listening to music. In effect, there were rewarding consequences to his blindness.

Interpersonal Model

According to the interpersonal model, neurosis results from a pattern of distorted interpersonal relations in the family. The relationships of mother to child, father to child, and mother to father are crucial learning experiences for the child. From these experiences the child learns how to relate to other people and how to cope with personal

Professionals can help people deal with their anxiety and self-defeating behaviors.

and interpersonal conflict. When these relationships are distorted, the child may learn distorted or neurotic patterns of behavior. Through these relationships neurotic parents may pass on neurotic patterns to their children. Studies show that neurotic children tend to come from families with great conflict between the parents.[13] Parents who are confused, frightened, and unstable cannot provide their children with healthy models for responding to the stresses of life.

[S] Three theories explain the origin of neurosis. The psychoanalytic model proposes that neurosis results from distorted ways of defending against the anxiety produced by unconscious childhood conflicts. The behavioral model proposes that neurotic reactions are "bad habits" which are learned according to the principles of conditioning. The interpersonal model proposes that neurosis originates in disturbed family patterns in which children learn neurotic ways of reacting to stress and relating to people.

Are You Neurotic?

When you read about neurotic reactions, you may notice that your own behavior in some ways resembles neurotic behavior. You recognize *yourself* in some of these descriptions of neurotic persons. Does this mean that you are neurotic?

We are all very similar; you, me, a neurotic person. To classify people as neurotic is not to claim that they are extremely different from normal persons. Your behavior and the behavior of neurotics differ mainly in degree. You are different from obsessive-compulsive neurotics not because they have recurring obsessive thoughts and you do not but because they are more bothered by obsessive thoughts than you are. In fact, they are so bothered that they have grave difficulties functioning in life. You are different from depressive neurotics not because they have periods of depression and you do not but because their depressions are severe and persistent and yours are not. Their depressions are so severe that they interfere with their ability to function in life. You are different from phobic neurotics not because they have unreasonable fears and you do not but because their fears interfere seriously with their life and yours do not. If, despite your problems, you are able to function fairly well in life, you are probably not neurotic. If you have further questions about yourself that you want answered, you should see your teacher, a counselor, or a psychologist.

Summary

KEY QUESTIONS

1. What is neurosis?
   Neurosis involves self-defeating, rigid, and repetitive ways of avoiding anxiety. Neurotic reactions handicap people in living a normal life and interfere with solving problems and adapting to changing circumstances.

2. What are the types of neurosis?
   Neurotic reactions include exaggerated feelings of depression or fear; recurring, irrational actions or ideas; the splitting of the personality into two or more parts; and sensory or muscular problems without a physical cause.

3. What causes neurosis?
   The causes of neurosis are not definitely known; there is probably not a single cause of neurosis, but instead many different causes. The psychoanalytic, behavioral, and interpersonal models are three theories that explain possible causes of neurosis.

4. Are you neurotic?
   Normal and neurotic behaviors differ mainly in degree; behavior that is neurotic is more self-defeating and interferes more with normal living. Since you are able to function fairly well in life, you are probably not neurotic.

KEY CONCEPTS

neurosis A rigid and self-defeating pattern of reaction to intense anxiety.

neurotic trend A consistent style of neurotic reaction.

neurotic compliant trend A neurotic style shown by individuals who seek, in an exaggerated and inappropriate manner, the affection of everyone around them.

neurotic aggressive trend A neurotic style shown by individuals who seek, in an exaggerated and inappropriate manner, to defeat and belittle everyone around them.

neurotic detached trend A neurotic style shown by individuals who, in an exaggerated and inappropriate manner, isolate themselves from everyone around them.

phobia An intense, unreasonable fear of an object or event.

obsession A recurring unwanted idea or impulse.

compulsion An irrational, repetitive, involuntary act.

depression Feelings of despair, dejection, and worthlessness.

neurotic depression Intense and lasting depression.

dissociative reaction A splitting apart of the personality into two or more relatively independent parts.

anmesia A dissociative reaction involving a loss of memory for personal identity or past events.

multiple personality A dissociative reaction in which two or more distinct identities appear to alternate within the same individual.

conversion reaction Sensory or muscular problems that exist without a physical cause.

secondary gain An incidental benefit of a neurotic reaction in which individuals receive attention or sympathy for their problems.

traumatic reaction A neurotic reaction to overwhelming psychological or physical shock or injury.

21 Psychosis

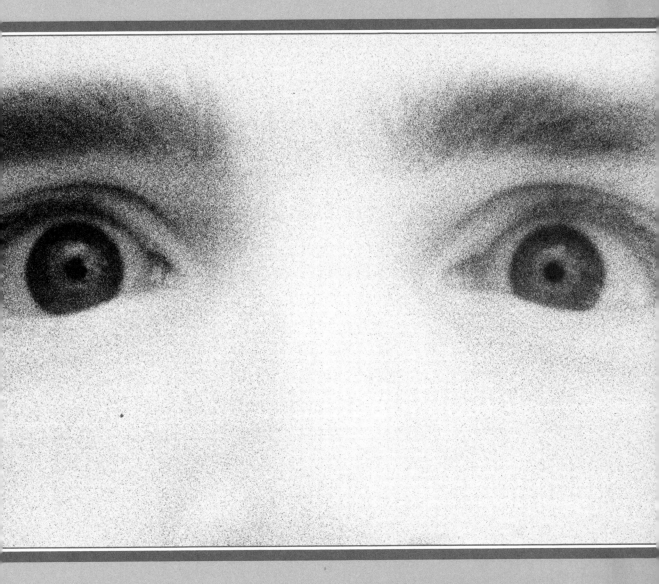

CHAPTER OUTLINE

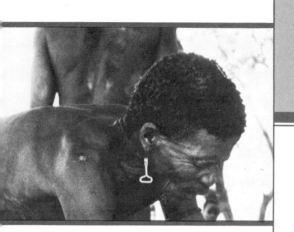

KEY QUESTIONS

1. How is psychosis different from neurosis?
2. What are the symptoms of psychosis?
3. What are the types of psychosis?
4. What causes psychosis?

Have you ever wondered what it is like to be insane? Madness, or—to use the technical term—**psychosis,** is a major psychological disturbance that affects hundreds of thousands of persons in this country. More than half of all the hospital beds in America are occupied by persons who are suffering from psychosis.

What is it like to be psychotic? One psychotic person described his own experience:

I call attention to a great crime, which has hardly its equal in history. . . . A conspiracy was inaugurated against me, unparalleled by anything heard of before. . . . Now, wherever I go, these diabolical agents are following me. They not only injure me in business, but are molesting everyone who may come in contact with me. They place chemical odors in every room where I may be. The effects of these odors upon my system are as numerous as they are painful. Now and then I lose, almost, my consciousness, and only with the utmost efforts can keep my eyes open. Often, again, I experience a feeling as if my whole body was pierced with needles. At night especially these merciless agents pour such chemical odors or gases into my room that I have a choking sensation, and I am unable to breathe. Pain seems to squeeze my eyes out of the sockets, and visions arise before me.[1]

This individual was forced to leave one job after another because of his continuing problems, and he finally wrote a letter to the district attorney, demanding police protection from the "evil agents" he believed to be following him.

People who are psychotic are rarely a danger to others; they are instead people who have problems coping with the stressful requirements of their everyday life. They may be so disturbed that they are incapable of carrying on everyday activities, such as eating and going to the bathroom. They are often withdrawn and isolated and find it impossible to communicate with others and to relate to them emotionally. Psychotics are out of contact with the reality of the world and other people. They are unable to deal with it effectively or to communicate about it.

Psychosis and Neurosis

How can you tell whether a person with disturbed behavior is neurotic or psychotic? Neurotic people are those whose attempts to defend against their own anxiety interfere with their daily life. Neurotics typically lack self-confidence, are basically unhappy, and are painfully insecure; but they are able to care for themselves, to work, and to relate to people, although often only with considerable difficulty. A neurotic's ability to function in life is only mildly disturbed.

A neurotic commonly experiences depression, anxiety, and numerous bodily complaints, but has no bizarre disturbances in perception and thinking. Neurotics typically have some understanding of their own problems; they may know what they are, but not know what to do about them.

The behavior of the psychotic is more bizarre than the behavior of the neurotic. Psychotic individuals are out of contact with reality; they cannot effectively operate in the world and their ability to communicate with and relate to other people is severely disturbed. Sometimes psychotics are unable to care for themselves and may be hospitalized for their own protection. They may hear strange voices or see people when there is no one there. Other bizarre behavior may occur such as jumbled language, inappropriate weeping and giggling, and unusual postures. These severe problems seriously interfere with the ability to meet the demands of life. Psychotics, however, typically have no insight into their problems. They often do not know what their problems are and are out of contact with the reality of themselves and the environment around them. They are, in a sense, living in another world. It is an unreal world created by the psychotic mind, a place of confusion and terror.

Psychotic Symptoms

When you see psychotic people, you may see them acting or talking in strange and bizarre ways. These bizarre ways of talking and acting are *symptoms* of psychosis. A **symptom** is a sign or indication of a disorder. Psychotics may have one or a combination of several types of disordered behavior or symptoms, among which are disturbances in perception, in ideas, in emotions, and in the movement of the body. Disturbances in perception and ideas are common psychotic symptoms.

Hallucinations

Disturbances in perception are called **hallucinations.** A person who hallucinates sees or hears something in the absence of any external physical source. A hallucination resembles a waking dream in which you experience something that is not there but that seems very real to you. Sometimes these hallucinations take the form of seeing a dead relative or religious figure such as the Virgin Mary or Jesus Christ; sometimes they take the form of smelling nonexistent odors or hearing voices.

■ *Voices from Another World* Hearing voices is a more common form of hallucination than seeing something that is not there. One man described his hallucinations as follows:

The "voices" manifest themselves in me as nervous impulses, and always have the character of soft lisping noises *sounding like distinct human words. . . . For about seven years—except during sleep—I have never had a single moment in which I did not hear voices. They accompany me to every place and at all times; they continue to sound even when I am in conversation with other people.*[2]

■ *Strange Visions* Another man, hospitalized because of his psychosis, had come to believe that his hospital attendant was in reality Jesus Christ. One day while walking around the hospital grounds he experienced the following visual hallucination:

I became aware of something remarkable happening in the air only a very short distance

Hallucinations resemble waking dreams.

in front of me. It seemed to me that there had been some big air waves, and then through them the well-known form of [my attendant] appeared, facing me, and coming towards me. I thought for a second that he had been rendered invisible by ordinary heat waves that had happened to be between us, and that he had just walked through them. As soon as I thought this, he seemed to disappear for a second; once again he became clearly visible, firm, and solid, all but his feet, which seemed lost in vibrating air; an instant afterwards they became visible, and I heard the gravel crunch under his tread as he took four or five paces up to me.[3]

■ *Poisons Sent from God* A third man believed that he was in constant "nerve contact" with God and that the lines of communication between him and God were rays or filaments. These rays, he believed, were the carriers not only of voices but also of poisons sent from God. He wrote:

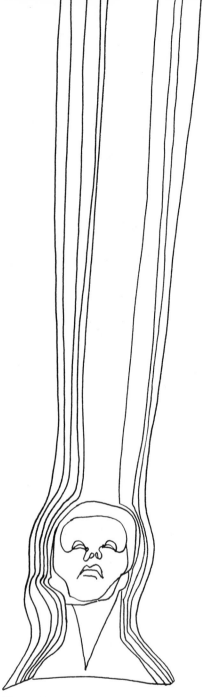

The poisoned filaments.

as long drawn out filaments approaching my head from some vast distant spot on the horizon. I can see them only with my mind's eye when my eyes are closed by miracles or when I close them voluntarily, that is to say they are then reflected on my inner nervous system as long filaments stretching towards my head.[2]

Delusions

Disturbances in ideas are called **delusions.** Not all false ideas are delusions; we all sometimes have false ideas, but people with delusions have bizarre irrational ideas of what is going on around them in the world, and no amount of evidence will persuade them that they are wrong. If you insist that you are Napoleon, you have a delusion. Common types of delusions are **delusions of grandeur** (in which people believe themselves to be a famous person or one who has magical powers), **delusions of persecution** (in which people believe that various people or organizations are "out to get them" by killing or torturing them), and **delusions of reference** (in which people believe that random events occurring around them are all concerned with them in some way—for example, the belief that people are always whispering about them on the bus).

■ *My Weird Powers* One psychotic patient was obsessed with feelings of guilt and with a belief in his own personal power. He had delusions of grandeur.

I am causing a lot of people to become insane, accidentally, by reason of the power that leaves me and comes back. . . . This power causes railroad accidents, which is awful. My presence in the world is injurious to many people—I don't understand how. . . . People's voices change when talking; sometimes they appear pale and drowsy, again peppy and

With my mind's eye I see the rays which are both the carriers of the voices and of the poison of corpses to be unloaded on my body, full of life, and it seems to me that I am the medium of all that; it seems that I exercise some involuntary control over them. . . . I imagine people losing their teeth; babies are dwarfed; people have nervous breakdowns, etc.,—all on my account. . . . I can't see how I could be such a freak of nature as to have these powers.[6]

■ *Plots Against Me* One man wrote a book about his psychosis in which he described his delusion of persecution. He believed that individuals in the mental hospital around him were in a vast plot against him.

None of my food had its usual flavor. This soon led to that common delusion that some of it contained poison—not a deadly poison, for I knew that my enemies hated me too much to allow me the boon of death, but a poison sufficient to aggravate my discomfort. . . . Although I was not entirely unaware that something was ailing with my mind, . . . all these horrors I took for the work of detectives, who sat up nights racking their brains in order to rack and utterly wreck my own with a cruel and unfair "Third Degree."[4]

■ *Talk About Me* A woman had the delusion that she was rotting away, that she had an offensive body odor, and that everywhere she went people talked about her unfavorably. She had a delusion of reference.

Everything which occurred around me I imagined was related to me. I would sit in a classroom and overhear a fragment of conversation and my sick mind would fasten upon a word or two that I thought referred to me. . . . If I heard the word "smell" I suffered tortures, knowing that it referred to the odor of corruption which, I was convinced, still clung to me. My hair had become coarse and dead, having something the appearance of

dried seaweed and whenever I heard the word "hair" I knew that mine was being discussed.[5]

⑤ The various strange behaviors seen in psychotic individuals are the symptoms of psychosis. Psychotic symptoms include disturbances in perception, in ideas, in emotions, and in the movement of the body. Psychotic hallucinations are like waking dreams and may involve hearing voices or seeing people who are not present. Psychotic delusions are bizarre and irrational ideas. Common types of delusions are delusions of grandeur (*I am the King of France*), delusions of persecution (*They are out to get me*), and delusions of reference (*Everybody is talking about me*).

Diagnosis

A person may be classified as psychotic on the basis of such symptoms as hallucinations and delusions. **Diagnosis** involves identifying or classifying a problem on the basis of the symptoms. Diagnosing a person as having a cold is based on the symptoms of a sore throat, a cough, and a runny nose. Diagnosing a person as psychotic or as a particular type of psychotic is not, however, so simple. A person who is classified or diagnosed as psychotic is judged to be out of contact with reality. But what is reality?

Disease or Misbehavior?

Reality is to some degree socially or culturally defined, and it therefore depends on where you live. Reality in one culture may include ghosts; reality in another may exclude ghosts. A person who hears the voice of God may be "out of contact with reality" in Los Angeles, California, but in contact with reality in rural Brazil.

Reality is, to some degree, culturally defined.

psychotic in most other countries in the world. Their uniquely individual realities, their own private worlds, would most likely not correspond to the "reality" defined by any of the world's peoples.

Vague Descriptions

Cultural differences in the definition of reality and in the rules for socially acceptable behavior are not the only difficulties in diagnosing a person as psychotic. There are disagreements among the professionals. They agree on the broad diagnostic classifications such as neurosis or psychosis, but there are major differences in point of view regarding the meaning of the particular forms of psychosis. The consequence of this is that a person may be diagnosed differently by two different people.[10,11] The existing diagnostic classifications of the forms of psychosis are somewhat vague and should not be taken as more than rough descriptive categories.

People diagnosed as psychotic behave in ways unacceptable to their society. They do not have a "disease" that they have "caught"; it is just that their behavior does not conform to the rules and reality of their culture.[7,8] There is a sense in which the meaning of "reality" is defined by the general agreement of the population. From this point of view people are psychotic if they have lost contact with the views of their culture and are thereby unable to communicate with persons around them. In fact, psychosis has been defined as the failure to develop a refined system of generally accepted interpretations of reality.[9]

However, people are enough alike, whatever the culture, so that the concept of "reality" is not always different in each culture; thus, most people labeled as psychotic in this country would also probably be considered

⑤ Diagnosing a person as psychotic means classifying or labeling the person as psychotic or as a particular kind of psychotic. This sort of diagnosis involves more complex problems than the diagnosis of a physical disease. One problem is that a psychotic is considered out of contact with reality, but reality is to some degree defined differently in different cultures. Another problem with diagnosis is that the existing classifications are somewhat vague, and even professionals sometimes disagree on their definitions.

Types of Psychoses

The varieties of psychotic reactions have traditionally been grouped into two broad classes: **organic psychoses** (those with known physical causes) and **functional psychoses** (those without known physical causes). An example of a psychosis with a known physical cause (an organic psychosis) is **senile psychosis,** a gradual psychological deterioration that sometimes occurs in elderly persons. An inadequate blood supply to the brain results in symptoms of depression, loss of memory, suspicion, restlessness, and general confusion. Most psychotic reactions, however, are of the functional type with no known physical cause. The two most common types of functional psychoses are affective psychosis and schizophrenia.

Affective Psychosis

Some psychotic persons have severely disturbed affective behavior. The term *affective* refers to emotions or moods. In **affective psychosis,** the mood is extremely high, extremely low, or alternates between these two extremes.

■ *The One-Hundred-Foot Letter* **Mania** is an affective psychosis in which people seem joyous, deliriously happy, and wildly energetic; people in a manic state talk a great deal, jumping from one idea to another, and feel extremely confident, making grandiose plans that are never carried out. They move about constantly, running back and forth, jumping up and down, doing exercises, and shouting and singing. One man who was hospitalized for mania wrote letters on long rolls of wrapping paper and later described his experience:

More than once letters twenty or thirty feet long were written, and on one occasion the accumulation of two or three days of excessive productivity, when spread upon the floor, reached from one end of the corridor to the other—a distance of about one hundred feet.

My hourly output was something like twelve feet. . . . Under the pressure of elation one takes pride in doing everything in record time.[4]

■ *The Weeping Man* A different type of affective psychosis is **psychotic depression.** Psychotic depression resembles the way you feel when you are discouraged and depressed, but in psychosis the mood is tremendously exaggerated. A person suffering from psychotic depression may sit motionless for days, brooding, refusing to see anyone, feeling utterly hopeless and worthless. The following case is an example of this type of affective psychosis.

Mr. T. S. . . . would spend most of his time sitting on a chair by the side of his bed, moaning and wringing his hands. His facial

expression was one of the deepest dejection, and his eyes were reddened from weeping. . . . As a rule, Mr. S. would not speak unless spoken to, but occasionally he would address another patient or a member of the ward staff. At such times he would usually blame himself in the harshest terms for having "ruined his family," saying that he did not deserve to live.[12]

■ *The Alternating Woman* Just as you experience changes of mood from joy to discouragement, some psychotic persons swing from one extreme (mania) to the other extreme (depression). The cycle from mania to depression, and back again to mania, may take place over a period of just a few days, or it may take years to complete.

One woman was brought to the hospital after she had already gone through two periods of mania and two periods of depression. During her depressed periods she seems full of sorrow, acts dejected, is inactive, and speaks almost entirely in monosyllables. When she is asked a question, she may take a minute or two to answer, and then replies in a dismal tone with a single word. She typically sits quite still, with her head bowed, her brow wrinkled, and her hands clasped in her lap. By contast, in her manic phase it is impossible for her to remain still even for a moment. She runs about the hospital singing, dancing, slapping patients and nurses on the back, and throwing things about. She tears off her clothes and throws her arms around any man who happens to appear.[13]

Schizophrenia

Schizophrenia is the most common form of psychosis; about half of all the patients in the mental hospitals in this country are diagnosed as schizophrenic.[14] "Schizo" means split, and "phrenia" means *mind;* **schizophrenia** may be thought of as a disorder in which the mind is split off, or separated, from reality.

The term "schizophrenia" is often used incorrectly in magazines and on TV to refer to people with split personalities, those who at one time seem to be one kind of person and at another time seem to be another kind of person. Such people are not schizophrenics.

Rather, schizophrenics escape from reality to their own private world. Their thoughts are often irrational, disorganized, and bizarre; their feelings may appear totally absent or entirely inappropriate to the circumstances in the world around them; their language may be illogical, disconnected, and twisted; and they may experience hallucinations and delusions. Schizophrenics often have difficulty communicating with others and sharing their experiences. They live inside shells that nobody can penetrate. There are several varieties of schizophrenia.

■ *Barbara* One variety of the disorder is called **simple schizophrenia** and is characterized mainly by symptoms of apathy and withdrawal from social contact, as shown in the case of Barbara. Barbara, a girl of fifteen, came from an unhappy home; her alcoholic father and her cold bitter mother paid little attention to her. Barbara developed severe conflicts with the onset of menstruation (for which she was not prepared) and with the increase in her sexual feelings and thoughts (which she regarded as sinful). Now, during the first year of high school, she dropped all social contacts and would not see her friends or talk to them on the telephone. She spent hours alone in her room and was very withdrawn at home, becoming increasingly apathetic, moody, and irritable. Finally she stopped going to school and spent all her time alone in her room, sitting quietly by her window.

simplis christianus pueris de

■ *L. Percy King* Another variety of schizophrenia is called **paranoid schizophrenia.** Persons with this disorder have delusions of grandeur and persecution; that is, they believe themselves to be some great person or historical figure, and they believe that others are against them or out to get them. L. Percy King was a patient in a state hospital who believed that he had made the greatest discoveries in the history of the world (delusion of grandeur) and that he was the object of a group of pursuers who had been after him for thirty years (delusion of persecution). King heard these evil pursuers talk to him by way of what he called "radio voices" (hallucination).

Among these pursuers, I was gradually to discover by deduction, were evidently some brothers and sisters who inherited from one of their parents some astounding, unheard of, utterly unbelievable occult powers. Believe it or not, some of them, besides being able to tell a person's thoughts, are also able to project

their magnetic voices—commonly called "radio voices" around here—a distance of a few miles without talking loud and without apparent effort. . . . Thus, in connection with their mind-reading ability, they are able to carry on a conversation with a person over a mile away and out of sight, by ascertaining the person's unspoken thoughts, and then by means of their so-called "radio voices," answer these thoughts aloud audibly to the person. An uninitiated person would probably be very much startled by such phenomena. For example, what would you think if you were on a level desolate tract of land without any vegetation or places of concealment upon it, and without a human being within miles, when you heard a mysterious seemingly unearthly voice answer a question you were just thinking about?[15]

■ *The Three Christs* Persons with paranoid schizophrenia take great pains to maintain their delusions and to justify their irrational beliefs, which often concern their own identity. Psychologist Milton Rokeach studied three men—a farmer, a clerk, and an electrician—in the state mental hospital at Ypsilanti, Michigan.[16] Suffering from schizophrenia, each of the three men denied his real identity and claimed to be Jesus Christ. At one remarkable meeting Dr. Rokeach brought the three men together in a small room and asked them to introduce themselves. Their real names were Joseph, Clyde, and Leon.

Joseph was fifty-eight and had been hospitalized for almost two decades. Of medium height and build, bald, and with half his front teeth missing, he somehow gave the impression of impishness . . .

"My name is Joseph Cassel."
Joseph, is there anything else you want to tell us?
"Yes, I'm God."

Clyde introduced himself next. He was seventy and had been hospitalized for seventeen years. Clyde was over six feet tall and, despite the fact that he was all but toothless, stated, whenever asked, that he was in excellent health—and he was. He spoke indistinctly, in a low, rumbling, resonant voice. He was very hard to understand.

"My name is Clyde Benson. That's my name straight."
Do you have any other names?
"Well, I have other names, but that's my vital side and I made God five and Jesus six."
Does that mean you're God?
"I made God, yes. I made it seventy years old a year ago. Hell! I passed seventy years old."

Leon was the last to introduce himself. Of the three, he looked the most like Christ. He was thirty-eight and had been committed five years before. . . . Leon denied his real name vigorously, referring to it as his "dupe" name, and refusing to co-operate or have anything to

do with anyone who used it in addressing him. We all called him Rex.

"Sir, it so happens that my birth certificate says that I am Dr. Domino Dominorum et Rex Rexarum, Simplis Christianus Pueris Mentalis Doktor. . . . *It also states on my birth certificate that I am the reincarnation of Jesus Christ of Nazareth . . . and it so happens that I was railroaded into this place because of prejudice and jealousy and duping that started before I was born. . . . I do not consent to their misuse of the frequency of my life."*
Who are "they" that you are talking about?
"Those unsound individuals who practice the electronic imposition and duping."[16]

[S] Psychotic reactions are called organic when they have a known physical cause and functional when they do not. Two major types of functional psychosis are the affective psychoses and schizophrenia. Mania is a form of affective psychosis in which the person is wildly energetic, confident, and talkative. Psychotic depression is an affective psychosis in which the person is extremely dejected and inactive. Schizophrenia is a form of functional psychosis characterized by hallucinations, delusions, social withdrawal, and emotional reactions that are either inappropriate or absent. Two types of schizophrenia are simple schizophrenia, characterized by apathy and withdrawal, and paranoid schizophrenia, characterized by delusions of grandeur and persecution.

Causes of Psychosis

The origins of affective psychosis and of schizophrenia are still a mystery, in spite of years of scientific research devoted to investigating the problem. The research suggests a number of promising leads, but shows that there is not just one cause of the disorder. Many different theories have been developed to account for the cause of schizophrenia, the most common psychosis, and some of these are mentioned here so that you can see how scientists have gone about studying this disorder.

Regression Model

One point of view toward the origin of schizophrenia comes from Freud and his theory of psychoanalysis. Freud argued that schizophrenia represented a **regression**—a return to childish ways of thinking and acting—as a result of a complete breakdown of psychological defenses. According to psychoanalytic theory, a schizophrenic person has "regressed" to an earlier stage of personality development, one that was appropriate in infancy. This view can be called the *regression model* for the cause of schizophrenia.

For the schizophrenic, life is full of fear, people are dangerous, and a retreat to infancy provides a measure of security. Schizophrenics, like infants, often cannot provide for their own physical needs and must be cared for; some psychologists believe there is a similarity between infants intently playing with finger paints and regressed schizophrenics, some of whom watch with fascination as they smear their feces on the wall.

Interpersonal Model

Another point of view is that the origins of schizophrenia can be found in disturbed interpersonal relationships within the family. This view can be called the *interpersonal model*. The families of schizophrenics have been studied by psychologists, and the family members have been found to have more interpersonal conflict than do normal families.[17] The members of schizophrenics' families also tend not to listen to each other.[18] Communications between parents of schizophrenics and their children have been found to be wandering, disruptive, and illogical.[19] A pattern of disturbed relationships within the family could be either a *cause* of schizophrenia in the children or a *response* to the problem of having a schizophrenic child in the family. Since many recent studies show that the family abnormality exists before the onset of schizophrenia in the child, there is good evidence that disturbed families are a cause of schizophrenia, not simply a response to it.[19] The whole pattern of relationships in such a family is often disturbed and may be directly responsible in producing schizophrenia.[20]

Genetic Model

A third point of view on the cause of schizophrenia is that it is an inherited neurological disease.[21] This view can be called the *genetic model* for the origin of schizophrenia. There is substantial evidence that a tendency toward schizophrenia runs in families. When two individuals have identical genes (identical twins), the chances are very high that the second twin will be schizophrenic if the first one is. The evidence is virtually conclusive that a tendency toward schizophrenia is inherited.[22,23] This implies that there should be physical differences between schizophrenics and normals; and, indeed, there is evidence that the nervous systems of schizophrenics and normals are different.[24,25] While the tendency for schizophrenia may be inherited, it is clear that other factors are also very important; the amount of psychological stress in people's early lives, the pattern of interpersonal relationships in their families, and the quality of parental care and loving they have received, all contribute significantly to their behavior in the world.

ⓢ   Three theories that account for the cause of schizophrenia are the regression model, the interpersonal model, and the genetic model. According to the regression model, schizophrenics retreat or regress to childlike ways of behaving in order to gain a sense of security in a world they experience as threatening. According to the interpersonal model, disturbed patterns of communication within the family cause the disorder. According to the genetic model, the tendency toward schizophrenia is inherited.

Summary

KEY QUESTIONS

1. How is psychosis different from neurosis?

   While neurotics can typically function in life in spite of their symptoms, psychotics are so disturbed that they often cannot care for themselves, cannot work, and cannot relate to other people. Psychosis is more severe and more disabling than neurosis.

2. What are the symptoms of psychosis?

   The psychotic person is out of contact with the socially-agreed-upon reality of the external world and cannot deal with it or communicate about it effectively. Psychotics may show such symptoms as delusions, hallucinations, and inappropriate emotional reactions.

3. What are the types of psychosis?

   Affective psychosis and schizophrenia are two broad classes of psychosis, each having several types. A person with affective psychosis has extremes of mood, ranging from wild elation to utter dejection. A person with schizophrenia may display delusions, hallucinations, and social withdrawal.

4. What causes psychosis?

   The causes of psychosis are not known with certainty. Three theories of the cause of schizophrenia are the regression, interpersonal, and genetic models. According to the regression theory, schizophrenia represents a return to childish ways of thinking and acting as a result of a breakdown in psychological defenses. According to the interpersonal theory, schizophrenia results from a pattern of disturbed communication within the family. According to the genetic theory, schizophrenia is an inherited disease.

KEY CONCEPTS

psychosis	A severe mental disorder characterized by loss of contact with reality, accompanied by disturbances in emotions, ideas, or perceptions.
symptom	A sign or indication of disorder; for example, hallucinations are an indication of psychosis.
hallucination	A disturbance in perception in which something is seen, heard, or felt which does not exist.
delusion	A false belief that is bizarre and irrational and is held in spite of contrary evidence; for example, the belief that one is Napoleon.
delusion of grandeur	A false belief that one is a great or powerful person; for example, the belief that one controls the world.
delusion of persecution	A false belief that one is being victimized; for example, a man may believe that others are out to get him.
delusion of reference	A false belief that unrelated events are personally directed; for example, a man may have the belief that everybody is talking about him.
diagnosis	Classifying or identifying a problem on the basis of its symptoms; for example, classifying a person as psychotic on the basis of the person's delusions.
organic psychosis	A psychosis with a known physical cause; for example, senile psychosis.
functional psychosis	A psychosis with no known physical cause.
senile psychosis	A psychosis resulting from an inadequate blood supply to the brain, typically in an elderly person.
affective psychosis	A psychosis characterized by moods that are extremely high or extremely low.
mania	An affective psychosis in which people are wildly energetic, confident, and talkative.
psychotic depression	An affective psychosis in which people are extremely inactive and dejected.
schizophrenia	A functional psychosis characterized by social withdrawal and disturbances in perception and ideas.
simple schizophrenia	A type of schizophrenia characterized by apathy and social withdrawal.
paranoid schizophrenia	A type of schizophrenia characterized by delusions of grandeur and persecution.
regression	A return or retreat to an earlier stage of personality development; for example, a return to infantile behavior.

Suggested Readings

Autobiography of a Schizophrenic Girl, anonymous, with intrepretation by Marguerite Sechehaye. New York: New American Library, 1970. The moving, true story of a girl named Renee who became schizophrenic and later was successfully treated. The author describes her thoughts, perceptions, and emotions as she becomes schizophrenic.

The Experience of Anxiety by Michael Goldstein & James O. Palmer. (Second edition.) New York: Oxford University Press, 1975. Presents case histories of children and adults with psychological problems, including a description of diagnosis and treatment.

Helplessness: On Depression, Development, and Death by Martin E. P. Seligman. San Francisco: W. H. Freeman, 1975. Presents the theory that depression and anxiety result from helplessness that is learned and can be unlearned. Includes examples from old age homes, hospitals, POW camps, and zoos showing helplessness can even result in unexpected death.

The Myth of Mental Illness by Thomas S. Szasz. New York: Hoeber, 1961. The author takes the controversial position that there is no such thing as "mental illness." What has been called "mental illness" are actually only examples of problems in living and should be faced as such.

I Never Promised You a Rose Garden by Hannah Green. New York: New American Library, 1964. A novel about a sixteen-year-old psychotic girl and her three years in a mental hospital. One of the best novels ever written about a psychotic person.

Dibs in Search of Self by Virginia M. Axline. New York: Ballantine Books, 1964. The true story of a disturbed child and his search of self through the process of client-centered therapy. A favorite book of many students.

The Three Faces of Eve by Corbett H. Thigpen & Hervey M. Cleckley. New York: McGraw-Hill, 1957. A famous study of a woman with multiple personality. The basis of a movie by the same name.

The Three Christs of Ypsilanti by Milton Rokeach. New York: Vintage Books, 1964. Study of three men in a state mental hospital, each of whom believed he was Jesus Christ. Rokeach brought them together in one room and asked each of them to introduce himself.

The Divided Self: An Existential Study in Sanity and Madness by Ronald D. Laing. Baltimore, Md.: Penguin Books, 1965. An existential study of schizophrenia, including theory and case histories. An attempt to make "going mad" comprehensible.

Research Methods VII Correlational Studies

In earlier chapters it was pointed out that schizophrenics tend to come from families with disturbed relationships, that men tend to act more aggressively than women, that adults spend less time dreaming than children, and that highly prejudiced persons tend to come from families in which severe discipline is used. These are observations of relationships, of things in the world that are associated. The term **correlation** describes such relationships or associations.

Variables and Variation

Psychologists are interested in finding relationships between concepts. A concept having different values is called a **variable.** "Intelligence" is a variable, having many different values such as very low, average, or high; "height" is a variable, having different values such as 5 feet, 6 feet, and 7 feet; "sex" is a variable, having the two values male and female; "age" is a variable, having many different values such as 16 years, 17 years, or 96 years; "frequency of dreaming" is a variable, having values ranging from never to, say, 30 times a day.

Sometimes the values of two variables tend to go together. For example, people who are young in age tend also to be short in height. When variables are related in the way that age and height are related, the variables are said to be *correlated*. The values of one variable tend to go together with the values of a second variable. Variation in one variable is somewhat predictable from variation in the second variable; for example, knowing age helps you to predict height.

Consider the example of aggression. "Aggressiveness" is a variable, since people differ in the level of their aggressiveness. If the variable "aggressiveness" were correlated with the variable "sex," then their relationship would enable you to predict values of one if you knew the values of the other (although you might make some mistakes); knowledge of a person's aggressiveness would help you to guess the person's sex. For example, if you knew that a person was highly aggressive, you would guess that the person was a male, and you would be right more often than wrong. Knowing the level of aggressiveness helps you to predict sex.

Correlation Coefficient

Variables can be highly related or only slightly related. A measure of the degree of relationship between two variables is the **correlation coefficient.** The correlation coefficient is a number that ranges from minus one to plus one (all values between -1 and $+1$ are possible).

If two variables are not correlated, their correlation coefficient is zero. If two variables are perfectly correlated (one is perfectly predictable from the other), their correlation coefficient is either plus one or minus one. A positive (plus) correlation coefficient indicates that the relation is such that high values of one variable tend to go together with high values of the second variable, and low values of one tend to go together with low values of the other. For example, there is a positive correlation between height and age in children: the higher your age is, the higher your height is. A negative (minus) correlation coefficient indicates a relation in which high values of one variable tend to go together with low values of the second variable, and vice versa. For example, there tends to be a negative correlation between education and prejudice: the more education you get, the less prejudiced you tend to be.

An example of a perfect *positive* correlation (correlation coefficient of $+1.00$) can be seen in the following (imaginary) data. Each person in my psychology class has two scores, one for each of two variables. The first variable is the amount of time spent studying for the midterm (measured in hours); the second variable is the performance on the midterm (measured as the number of questions answered correctly out of 30).

Notice that the variables co-vary; that is, they vary together. The higher the number of hours of study, the higher the number of questions correct. The lower the number of

	# Hours of Study	# Questions Correct
Mary	40	28
Rafael	35	26
Pat	30	23
Caryn	25	22
Le Roy	20	20
Earl	10	19
Kathy	1	5

hours of study, the lower the number of questions correct. Because the two variables are related in this way, they are *correlated.* Notice also that they vary together perfectly; that is, the person with the highest score on one variable is also the person with the highest score on the second variable. In fact, each person is ranked the same on each variable. Because of this, the correlation coefficient for these data is $+1.00$.

Suppose that the measure of performance on the psychology midterm was the number of questions missed, instead of the number correct. Then the results would look like this:

	# Hours of Study	# Questions Missed
Mary	40	2
Rafael	35	4
Pat	30	7
Caryn	25	8
Le Roy	20	10
Earl	10	11
Kathy	1	25

Notice that the two variables still co-vary, but now they vary inversely; that is, the higher one score is, the lower the other score is. The higher the hours of study, the lower the number of questions missed. Variables related in this inverse way are *negatively* correlated. The correlation coefficient describing the relationship would be -1.00.

Causation

Certain variables are said to show **causation,** to be causally related; one variable is believed to cause the other. Consider the two variables "amount of alcohol drunk in the past thirty minutes" and "degree of intoxication." Observation at parties and elsewhere would indicate that the two variables are correlated; further, we have reason to believe that one causes, or produces, the other. Science attempts to discover such causal relationships, but the discovery of causes is often very difficult.

The idea of causation implies not only that two variables are correlated, but also that (1) changes in one precede changes in the other, and that (2) other possible causes have been ruled out of consideration. First, if two variables are causally related, one of them (the cause) must come before the other (the effect). The effect cannot precede the cause. Second, in order to claim that two variables are causally related, you must be able to demonstrate that the correlation between them is not a result of some other factor. To claim that alcohol causes intoxication, you must show that the intoxication was not a result of some other factor, such as the olives in the martini.

Correlation Is Not Always Causation

A common mistake people make is to regard evidence for correlation as sufficient evidence of causation. As we have just seen, in order to claim that a causal relationship exists between two variables, you need to have not only evidence of correlation but also additional evidence concerning such questions as the order of the variables (the cause must precede the effect).

A psychologist interested in the relationship between *religious attitudes* and *criminal tendencies* might visit fifty cities and obtain from each a measure of religious belief and a measure of criminal tendencies. The measure of religious attitudes might be the number of churches that the city supports, and the measure of criminal tendencies, the average daily number of serious crimes committed. When the data are examined, a correlation coefficient is computed and the psychologist is surprised to discover that there is a high positive correlation between the two variables: the greater the number of churches, the greater the average number of crimes per day.

Does this mean that religion causes crime? There are two important reasons why this evidence for correlation cannot be regarded as evidence for causation. The psychologist is not justified in concluding that religion causes crime because (1) there is no evidence that changes in religious belief preceded changes in the crime rate—perhaps the heavy crime rate caused an upsurge in religious interest; and (2) there is no reason to exclude other possible causes—perhaps the high population in some cities leads to both a high number of churches and a high number of crimes, compared to cities of low population. Since the third variable, population, could be responsible for the variations in the number of churches in a city and for the variations in the number of crimes in a city, the relation between the number of churches and the number of crimes cannot be regarded as causal.

The Example of Psychosis

Is psychosis more common among the rich or among the poor?

Hollingshead and Redlich[1] wanted to find out if there is a correlation between social class (rich or poor) and mental health (psychotic or not psychotic). To test this relationship, they chose the small community of New Haven, New York. By studying the census and psychiatric records, the investigators could find the incidence of psychosis among individuals of different social classes.

The variable of psychosis and the variable of social class were negatively correlated. They found that lower-class individuals made up the majority of the community's psychiatric patients. They also found that psychotherapy tended to be reserved for the wealthier class while the lower class tended to receive no treatment.

Correlation does not always mean causation; the fact that psychosis and social class are correlated does not necessarily mean that one causes the other. There are several alternatives that are possible.

One possibility is that psychosis is caused by the conditions of the lower social class. According to the **stress hypothesis,** psychosis results from stresses and pressures in the environment; and the environment of poor people is significantly more stressful. Thus, lower-class life may produce psychosis.

A second possibility is that lower social class is caused by psychosis. According to the **drift hypothesis,** mental disturbance leads to poorer ability to function and to make money; this leads to a downward drift in social position. This does not mean that all lower-class people are psychotic. It means, instead, that most psychotic people are lower class because they cannot function at a higher level.

A third possibility is that psychosis and social class are not causally related at all; instead, a third factor independently influences them both. According to the **genetic hypothesis,** both social class and psychosis result from inherited traits. For example, it is possible that psychosis is an inherited biochemical disorder, and that social class results from an individual's intelligence, which is primarily an inherited characteristic. Some of these possibilities are not very convincing; they are mentioned here to make the point that all alternatives should be considered. Pause to consider the possibilities before you jump to the conclusion that one variable causes or produces another.

The Example of Dreaming

In the chapter on dreaming you read that dreams are typically accompanied by a kind of eye twitch called rapid eye movement (REM). Another way to express this finding is to say that there is a correlation between the presence of dreaming and the presence of rapid eye movement; when one occurs the other also tends to occur. You would not want to conclude, however, that rapid eye movement causes dreaming or that dreaming itself causes rapid eye movement. We have reason to believe that both are caused by some third factor, for example, a cyclical bodily condition or brain state. If we could independently cause eye movement during sleep, we might determine for sure whether eye movement causes dreaming; we would produce our artificial eye movement, and then wake the sleeper to find out whether dreaming had occurred. The possibility is so unlikely that no one has tried it as yet.

KEY CONCEPTS

correlation The degree to which two variables co-vary, or vary together.

variable A concept having different values; "intelligence" is a variable, having many different values.

correlation coefficient A measure of the degree of correlation that ranges in value from -1.00 to $+1.00$; both extremes (-1.00 and $+1.00$) reflect perfect correlation.

causation The degree to which one variable produces, influences, or modifies the other.

stress hypothesis The view that psychosis is produced by the pressures of lower-class life and the difficulties present in poor living conditions.

drift hypothesis The view that psychosis leads to poverty because psychotic individuals have difficulty earning a living.

genetic hypothesis The view that psychosis and social class are influenced by heredity.

VIII Groups

22 Conformity

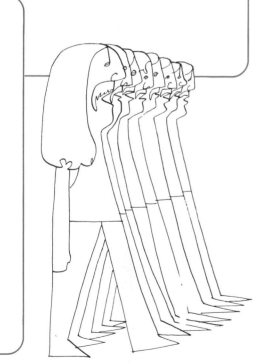

KEY QUESTIONS

1. What are fads, fashions, and social norms?
2. What is the difference between conformists, anticonformists, and independents?
3. Why do you conform?
4. What conditions lead you to accept authority?

The following is from an interview with a twelve-year-old girl:

A. *I like Superman better than the others because they can't do everything Superman can do. Batman can't fly and this is very important.*

Q. *Would you like to be able to fly?*

A. *I would like to be able to fly if everybody else did, but otherwise it would be kind of conspicuous.*[1]

Being conspicuous used to be a lot easier. "Rugged individualism" was at one time an important social value, but it has now been replaced by "togetherness." David Riesman has argued that Americans of past generations were more **inner-directed**—making decisions on the basis of their own personal, internalized values—whereas present-day

431

Americans are more **other-directed**—depending upon the opinion of others to tell them what is right and wrong.[2] According to Riesman, the children of an earlier era were trained for independence, whereas modern children are trained for conformity.

While conforming and joining the crowd carries with it a feeling of safety, the safety is brought at a considerable cost: the loss of freedom and the loss of self. Is it possible to "go along with the crowd" and still keep in touch with yourself? Can you conform and still be free? To a certain degree everybody goes along with the crowd; for example, we tend to eat the same kind of food and to wear the same general kind of clothes.

Fads, Fashions, and Social Norms

Members of a group tend to be alike in some ways. The members of one club tend to be different from the members of another club; persons from the same country tend to have more in common than persons from different countries. Most groups have a shared belief system, a set of similar ideas and attitudes about the world. Groups have sets of common beliefs for several reasons; individuals tend to join only those groups with which they generally agree; the group often has shared experiences which give rise to similarity in attitudes among the members; and groups reward members who agree and punish members who disagree with group beliefs. Fads, fashions, and social norms are all different aspects of these shared beliefs among group members.

Fads and Fashions

Fads are short-lived practices or customs that sweep the country periodically. For a brief time practically everybody is dancing the twist—and then it fades from popularity. Yo-yos or hula-hoops are seen everywhere for a while—then they disappear.

Fashions are more enduring social customs. When you do not behave according to the current fashion, you may be ridiculed or ostracized. There are fashions of dress (remember the miniskirt?) that change every year or so; there are fashions in architecture (Victorian), painting (pop-art), and books (sex manuals). There are fashions in raising and teaching children (progressive education).

When a fashion has been introduced and has become common, our eye is formed to it, and no one looks right or stylish who does not conform. We also know that after the fashion has changed, things in the discarded fashion look dowdy and rustic. No one can resist these temptations, try as he may.[3]

Hair style, cosmetics, and clothes seem particularly influenced by fashions that change every few years. The consequences for not being "in fashion" can often be quite severe. Lack of conformity to current fashions can result in reduced opportunity for social relationships, in dismissal from school (because of hair style or clothes), or in being fired from a job. Have you ever been out of style because of your hair or clothes? How did other people respond to you? How do you feel about conformity to fashion?

Social Norms

A more permanent fad or fashion is called a **social norm.** Social norms are rules for behavior; they specify what is socially proper and what is improper. Each society develops its own set of social norms, so that social norms differ from one culture to another. In this country it is the norm to eat three meals a day; in other countries two or four meals a day may be eaten. Social norms govern appropriate forms of greeting, social interactions, manners while eating, attitudes toward the sick and disadvantaged, and codes of conduct at significant times in human life such as birth and death. It is not clear why social norms arise in the first place. Uniformity of belief and behavior may come from the need of individuals to have their behavior approved or validated by their peers. People validate others who are like themselves.

It is rare to have the opportunity to observe the origins of a social norm. One researcher had that chance with a group of Japanese monkeys. In order to control their movements and thus be able to observe this particular troop of monkeys, a Japanese scientist began placing sweet potatoes on the beach for the monkeys to eat. The monkeys stayed around the beach to eat the sweet potatoes. For some time the monkeys ate the potatoes without incident. Then one monkey did something different:

In 1953 a young female in the Ko-shima troop began to wash in the sea the potatoes that we set out on the beach. Little by little the habit spread to other monkeys in the troop, until today a full two-thirds of all the individuals in the group invariably wash their potatoes before eating them, and the practice is more or less completely established as an element in the troop's cultural life. The washing of the sweet potatoes spread gradually, to the first young female's playmates, to her brothers and sister, then to their particularly intimate associates.[4]

A new social norm had been started. Sweet potatoes were to be washed. The sweet potatoes must be carried to the sea in order to wash them, and this occupied both hands. In order to get to the water with the potatoes, the monkeys must walk on their hind legs. Thus the potato-washing custom required the monkeys to begin walking upright. The new social norm produced entirely new behavior. Various human behaviors may have had similar beginnings.

[S]   All groups tend to evolve shared behaviors and shared belief systems—similar ways of acting and seeing the world. Fads, fashions, and social norms are examples of conformity to these belief systems. Everybody conforms to one degree or another; we live socially and influence each other—so the question of conformity is a question of degree.

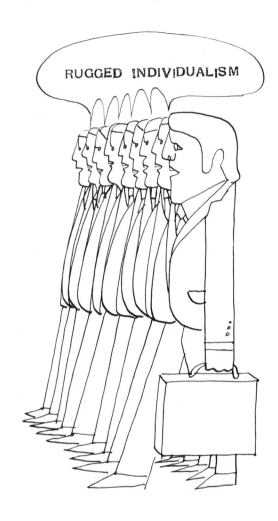

Do You Conform?

You belong to several social groups: your family, neighborhood, school, club, or country. Each of these groups has developed rules for behavior—that is, social norms. Sometimes in order to conform to the beliefs and behavior of those around you you must say or do things in which you do not believe. Thus there is often a conflict between your personal beliefs and the pressures to conform to the beliefs of others. Do you yield to those pressures easily?

The Conformist

The word **conformity** means to go along with the group, to change your beliefs or behavior so that they are consistent with the expectations of others. A *conformist* is a person who conforms by yielding to group pressure. Not all uniformity in behavior among members of a group is the result of group pressure. For example, the fact that you sneeze when you smell pepper is not an example of conformity; it is not a case of your yielding to group pressure.

The character Stepan Arkadyevitch in Tolstoy's *Anna Karenina* provides a case study in conformity:

Stepan Arkadyevitch took in and read a liberal newspaper, not an extreme one, but one advocating the views held by the majority. And in spite of the fact that science, art, and politics had no special interest for him, he firmly held those views on all subjects which were held by the majority and by his paper, and he only changed them when the majority changed them—or, more strictly speaking, he did not change them, but they imperceptively changed of themselves within him.

Stepan Arkadyevitch had not chosen his political opinions or his views; these political opinions and views had come to him of themselves, just as he did not choose the shapes of his hats or coats, but simply took those that were being worn. And for him, living in a certain society—owing to the need, ordinarily developed at years of discretion, for some degree of mental activity—to have views was just as indispensable as to have a hat. If there was a reason for his preferring liberal to conservative views, which were held also by many of his circle, it arose not from his considering liberalism more rational, but from its being in closer accord with his manner of life. . . . And so liberalism had become a habit of Stepan Arkadyevitch's, and he liked his newspaper, as he did his cigar after dinner, for the slight fog it diffused in his brain.

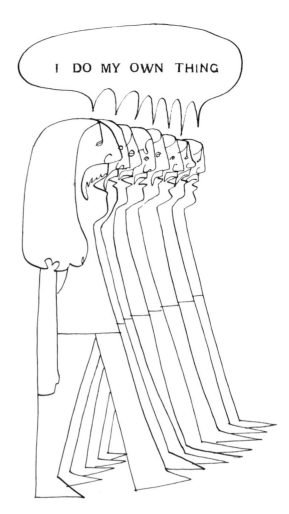

The Nonconformist

There are two types of nonconformity, and these are called independence and anticonformity.[5] **Anticonformity** is behavior that goes directly against the social norm. One of the ways you can choose what to do is simply to choose what others say is the right thing to do; a second way you can choose what to do is always to do the opposite of what others say is right. The first is the way of conformity; the second is the way of anticonformity. If you decide to wear long hair just because your parents want you to wear short hair, you are an anticonformist. An anticonformist is just as dependent upon the crowd as a conformist is; neither is independent.

Independence is the expression of private belief in the face of group pressure to conform. Independent people are able to resist group pressure to conform; in choosing what to do independent people do not use the social norm as a guide. Independent people maintain their private opinions and beliefs in spite of pressure to go along with the crowd. Conformists go along with the social norm; anticonformists go against the social norm; and independents go their own ways. Most people are a combination of each. How do you respond to group pressure? Are you a conformist, an anticonformist, or an independent?

John F. Kennedy's book *Profiles in Courage*[6] provides numerous examples of independent people who had the courage to resist pressure to conform. One of these people, Senator Edmund Ross, was pressured by members of his political party in 1868 to vote with them in favor of the impeachment of President Andrew Johnson. The Republicans needed exactly 36 votes and they had 35. Ross's vote would be decisive. The Senator's political career was at stake; he was pressured by his colleagues, by the voters, and by the newspapers to go against his beliefs and vote "guilty." But his answer was "not gulity."

[S] Each society develops its own set of standards of behavior, or social norms; individual members of society are pressured to accept these standards and to conform to them. A person who is a conformist yields to this pressure by giving up private beliefs or values. A person who is an anticonformist chooses to go directly against the social norm by doing the opposite. A person who is independent is able to maintain private beliefs in spite of pressure to go along with the crowd.

Group Pressure

Each of us experiences pressure to conform. There are rewards for conforming and punishments for not conforming. If you conform, you feel that you belong and you are accepted by the other members of the group; if you do not conform, you are rejected or ostracized, and you may even lose your membership in the group.

Who sets the standards that you conform to? When you are young, you conform more to your parents' beliefs and behavior; when you are older, you begin to conform more to the standards set by your peers—those individuals closer to your own age. In a study that showed this, children were asked to

make choices between the advice given by parents and the advice given by children.[7] The children who participated in the study ranged in age from three to eleven. The results showed that as the children got older the relative influence of their peers increased and the influence of their parents diminished. We all experience continual group pressure to conform; the identity of the group to which we conform, however, changes as we grow older.

Sherif's Experiment

You can easily imagine that choices related to aesthetics and values might be highly influenced by group pressure; your attitudes toward lipstick, beards, bras, or long hair are affected by social norms. But what about your perception? Can you believe your eyes, or is what you see also influenced by the expectations of others?

In the 1930's Muzafer Sherif[8] recruited a number of participants for a psychology experiment and seated them in a completely dark room. At the end of the room there was a small stationary point of light. Without a reference or context, a small point of light in a dark room appears to move; this is called the **autokinetic illusion.** Sherif's participants were asked to indicate the distance that they saw the light move in the dark. If these judgments were made privately, the amount of movement specified by each subject varied greatly, from a few inches to several feet. But when the group members made public judgments, the guesses tended to converge toward a common range of numbers; in other words a group norm emerged.

In a similar experiment a male participant was put into a room with three persons who were secretly working for the experimenter and who had been told what to say. These individuals are called "confederates."

The participant assumed that the confederates of the experimenter were other participants like himself.[9] While the participant's private estimates of the movement of the light averaged a little less than 4 inches, he radically changed his estimates when exposed to the judgments of the other "participants." The confederates of the experimenter stated that they thought the light was moving about 15 inches; the participant then changed his estimate from 4 to 14 inches. He had given up his own judgment in order to conform to the group.

Asch's Experiment

In the 1950's Solomon Asch conducted an experiment to find out what people would do when there was a conflict between the opinion of the group and the evidence of their own eyes.[10] Would people believe their own eyes, even though their perceptions went against the unanimous judgment of others?

The experimental task required participants to match line lengths. They were shown a straight line of a certain length, say 10 inches, and three additional comparison lines, say 8, 10, and 12 inches. The participants had to choose the one of the three comparison lines that was the same length as the first line. With no group pressure operating, participants almost never made a mistake in this task; the task was very easy. With groups of eight male participants, when the first seven (all secret confederates of the experimenter) named the wrong line, then the last participant had the choice of going along with the error of the group or of believing the evidence of his own eyes. About one-third of the participants conformed fairly consistently to the incorrect majority opinion, while about one-fourth consistently followed their own independent judgment and always chose the correct line.

The remaining participants sometimes conformed and sometimes did not.

These experiments show the power that others hold over you. It is not surprising that you conform to the fads and fashions of the day in order to be accepted by the groups to which you belong. These experiments show that a substantial proportion of people find the opinion of others so compelling that they are willing to base their judgments on the group's judgment rather than to believe the evidence of their own eyes.

Enforcing Conformity

How do groups exert pressure on individuals to conform to their social norms? Group pressure works because groups have great powers of reward and punishment. Some groups have formal arrangements for rewarding members who conform: schools have honor rolls, industries have bonus payments, and cities have good citizenship awards. These awards are given to those group members who are judged to be "ideal" group members, because they comply with the group's set of rules for proper behavior. All groups have informal rewards for members who conform. Conforming members are given the group's approval and acceptance.

Members who deviate from the social norms of their groups suffer **negative sanctions** (punishments) for not conforming. Some of these negative sanctions are formalized in jail sentences or fines. Most often a group applies informal pressure at first in order to get deviant members to "mend their ways" and begin conforming to the group's standards. If members refuse to comply, then the group may reject them so that they are no longer members.

A group has a potent punishment for a member who persists in his deviancy despite pressures on him to shift: it may redefine its boundaries so as to exclude the deviant, thereby protecting uniformity among members. Rejection of a deviant can be accomplished in various ways. He may be set apart so that no one talks or listens to him, he may be dropped from activities of the group, or he may be expelled.[11]

⑤ Groups apply pressure to members in order to get them to conform, and members who deviate from the group norms are punished (suffer negative sanctions). The experiments by Sherif and Asch showed that a substantial proportion of people find the opinion of others so compelling that they are willing to ignore the evidence before their own eyes.

Blind Obedience

When you were a child you did what you were told—most of the time. Adults also are often asked to obey. You are asked to obey teachers, policemen, the President, or an army sergeant. A soldier is ordered to kill and must obey or suffer punishment. During the Second World War German soldiers were ordered to burn thousands of Jews. They obeyed.

What would you be willing to do under orders?

Following Orders

Psychologists have searched for tasks that persons would be unwilling to do under orders but have had difficulty finding one. One psychologist asked college students to sort garbage; they did, with little objection.[12] Other students were asked to pick up a poisonous snake; they obeyed (and were stopped just in time).[13] Students obeyed when they were asked to put their hands into a container of nitric acid (they were not permitted to do so), and they even obeyed when they were asked to throw acid into someone's face (but the experimenter did not allow them to do it).[13]

Why do people obey? What leads them to accept authority? Studies show that authority is accepted as legitimate and is obeyed when one of three conditions is met: (1) the authority is seen as beneficial to groups or values to which the individual is committed; (2) the authority is seen as trustworthy; and (3) the authority is seen as having the support of the majority of the people.[14] Psychology experimenters are often seen as having these three characteristics and so are obeyed by most people, even when they ask them to do absurd or dangerous tasks.

Milgram's Study of Obedience

Suppose you were told to electrocute someone. What would your reaction be? Would you obey and follow the orders? Stanley Milgram designed an elaborate experiment to find out the answer to that question.[15] People who volunteered for the experiment were told that they were participating in an experiment on the effects of punishment on learning. Their job was to administer a painful electric shock to a man—the "learner"—whenever he made a mistake and forgot one of the words he was supposed to memorize. Those who were to administer the electric shocks were actually the only ones studied, because the "learner" was a male actor who was working for the experimenter. The machinery was rigged so that no electric shock was actually given, although the participants believed that they were shocking people.

The participants observed the "learner" being strapped down in a chair and electrodes being attached to his arm. At this point the "learner" expressed some concern about the experiment and revealed that he had a heart condition. The "teachers" then went into another room, and the learning task proceeded. The "learner," of course, made many mistakes (as he had been instructed to do); at each mistake the "teachers" were

and 100-volt shocks, and at 120 volts the victim shouts to the experimenter that the shocks are becoming painful. Painful groans are heard on administration of the 135-volt shock, and at 150 volts the victim cries out, "Experimenter, get me out of here! I won't be in the experiment any more! I refuse to go on!" Cries of this type continue with generally rising intensity, so that at 180 volts the victim cries out, "I can't stand the pain," and by 270 volts his response to the shock is definitely an agonized scream. Throughout, he insists that he be let out of the experiment. At 300 volts the victim shouts in desperation that he will no longer provide answers to the memory test; and at 315 volts, after a violent scream, he reaffirms with vehemence that he is no longer a participant. From this point on, he provides no answers, but shrieks in agony whenever a shock is administered; this continues through 450 volts.[15]

Milgram showed that, under some circumstances, people are willing to commit dangerous acts just because they are ordered to do so. Why did they obey such orders? An important reason is that they were able to yield all responsibility for their actions to an "authority"—in this case a researcher in a white coat. The participants in Milgram's study did not feel completely responsible for the "electrocution"; the responsibility was spread, or diffused, among two or more people. Thus, one condition that makes this kind of mindless obedience possible is **diffusion of responsibility**—a sharing or spreading of the responsibility for actions.

A second reason for the obedience shown in Milgram's study is that the participants were not treated in a personal manner, as individuals. There was a degree of anonymity—the participants knew that their names would not be disclosed publicly. The "teachers" and their "victim" were located in two different rooms during the study and had

supposed to press a switch that they believed would deliver an electric shock to the "learner." Every time the "learner" made a mistake, the "teachers" were supposed to increase the voltage of the shock. Participants faced a board with a row of switches on it, labeled from 15 to 450 volts, and had to pick one switch each time. Milgram wanted to find out how strong a shock people would be willing to administer.

He was surprised and dismayed by what he found. Over 60 percent of the participants were willing to give the highest level of shock to the "learner," even though the "learner" at lower levels screamed in pain and begged for mercy (this was all part of the actor's script).

The victim indicates no discomfort until the 75-volt shock is administered, at which time there is a slight grunt in response to the punishment. Similar reactions follow the 90-

no personal contact. The participants could punish the victim by pulling a switch and did not have to face him directly. These conditions lead to what is called **deindividuation**—feeling anonymous, one of the crowd, without a unique identity.

Blind obedience, resulting from diffusion of responsibility and deindividuation, occurs other places than the psychology laboratory. For example, members of any large organization—an army or a corporation—may experience these conditions.

Milgram also found, in his study of obedience, that if there is a group of subjects in the room all at once, a single dissenter gives the others the courage to disobey and to use their own judgment.[16] This shows that it is easier to think for yourself when you have social support for doing so. It also shows that, by refusing to obey, you can have a strong effect on others.

[S] Individuals under some circumstances are willing to yield responsibility to an "authority" and obey orders without question. Milgram showed that people will even obey an order to deliver a dangerous electric shock to another person. A single dissenter from blind obedience, however, gives others the courage to disobey orders contrary to their own values. Deindividuation and diffusion of responsibility are conditions that promote blind obedience.

Summary

KEY QUESTIONS

1. What are fads, fashions, and social norms?

   Fads are short-lived practices that last for a brief period and then fade from popularity. Fashions are more enduring social customs. Social norms are more permanent rules for behavior that specify what is socially proper and improper; these vary from culture to culture.

2. What is the difference between conformists, anticonformists, and independents?

   A conformist yields to group pressure. The anticonformist goes directly against group pressure. A person who is an anticonformist will do the exact opposite of what the group wants. The independent expresses private beliefs in the face of group pressure to conform.

3. Why do you conform?

   Everyone feels pressure to conform. You conform to group norms because groups have powers of reward and of punishment. Conforming members of groups receive approval and acceptance from other members. Members who deviate from the group's rules suffer more pressure or rejection from the other members.

4. What conditions lead you to accept authority?

You accept authority when you see it as beneficial to your values, when it seems to be trustworthy, and when it seems to have the support of the majority of people around you. Blind obedience is more common in a situation where you are relatively anonymous and do not feel totally responsible for your actions.

KEY CONCEPTS

inner-directed	Making decisions on the basis of personal values.
other-directed	Depending upon the opinions of others to make choices.
fads	Short-lived practices that sweep the country periodically as social customs.
fashions	Enduring social customs; for example, styles of dress.
social norm	A behavior standard of a particular group or society; a rule for behavior that specifies what is proper.
conformity	Going along with group standards or expectations and going against private beliefs.
anticonformity	Doing the opposite of what the social norm dictates.
independence	The expression of private beliefs in the face of group pressure to conform.
autokinetic illusion	An illusion in which a stationary point of light in a dark room appears to move.
negative sanctions	Punishment or threat of punishment for not conforming.
diffusion of responsibility	A sharing or spreading of the responsibility for actions.
deindividuation	Feeling anonymous, one of the crowd, without a unique personal identity.

23 Prejudice

CHAPTER OUTLINE

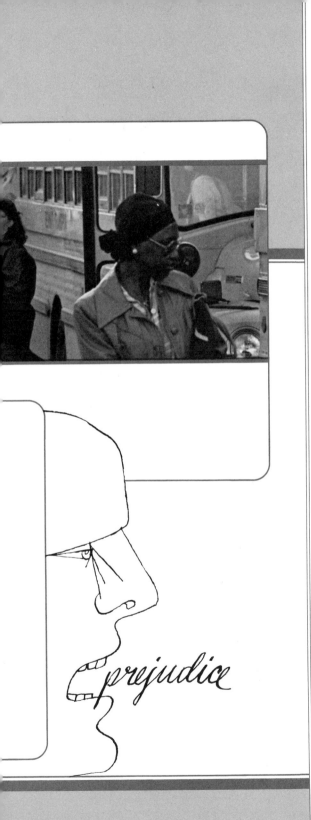

prejudice

KEY QUESTIONS

1. What is prejudice?
2. What causes prejudice?
3. What are the effects of prejudice?
4. How can prejudice be reduced?

Think of the perfect person.

Try to imagine an ideal human being standing before you. What is your ideal person like? What is your image of human perfection? For many people, the image is blond, blue-eyed, pink-skinned, and male. Yet few of us look like that. We cannot live up to that image. Because we are not pink males, we are judged inferior and are the victims of prejudice.

What Is Prejudice?

"A woman's place is in the home."

"All Jews care about is money."

"Children should be seen and not heard."

"Some of my best friends are blacks, but I wouldn't want my sister to marry one."

You have heard remarks like these before. What is similar about them? First, each statement groups people of a particular

445

type together; it regards them all as the same even though each individual is unique. This tendency to see all members of a group as the same is called **overgeneralization.** Second, each statement reflects a negative attitude toward the people who have been grouped together: women are seen as incapable of acting productively in the world; Jews are seen as having selfish motives; children are seen as stupid; and blacks are seen as undesirable mates. Regarding members of groups as having such negative characteristics is called **devaluation.** When you deny the value or worth of people, you devalue them.

Prejudice is a preconceived and unfavorable attitude toward an entire group; it consists of a combination of overgeneralization and devaluation. For example, a person who is prejudiced against women sees all women as similar in having certain traits.

You are an individual but sometimes people see you as a category instead of a person. When people respond only to your group category of black, white, male, or female, you lose your individuality. You have become stereotyped. A **stereotype** is a set of fixed ideas about a person that is based on group membership. It is the consequence of categorizing first and observing second. It is the product of prejudice.

About forty years ago one hundred college students were asked to describe the personalities of persons from various national and ethnic groups.[1] These students showed definite stereotypes about the typical personalities of each of ten groups. "Americans" were most commonly rated as hardworking, intelligent, materialistic, ambitious, and progressive. "Italians" were rated as artistic, impulsive, passionate, quick-tempered, and musical. "Jews" were rated as shrewd, greedy, hard-working, and intelligent. "Negroes" were rated as superstitious, lazy, happy-go-lucky, ignorant, and musical.

Few of us look like the "perfect person."

These students had fixed ideas about what black Americans were like, ideas that contrasted sharply with their view of themselves as "Americans." Of course these students were white.

Stereotypes of blacks have changed somewhat in the past forty years since this study was completed. The evidence of several studies shows that the stereotype of blacks is less negative than it was, although it is still negative.[2,3] Fixed ideas about racial and ethnic groups are remarkably resistant to change; they tend to be learned early in life and to last over the years.

What are your stereotypes? Do you have fixed ideas about the personality of another person you have not met? Do you tend to categorize first and observe later?

People can be divided into many different groups, and each group has its subgroups. Prejudice is commonly reflected in our attitudes toward these subgroups. Recently attention has been drawn to prejudice against blacks, Chicanos, Jews, and women. Prejudice against Irish, Catholics, Asians, and

American Indians has also been a serious problem. The prejudice shown against children and men has been, for the most part, entirely ignored. Yet children have no equality before the law, are often treated as property, and are clearly "second-class citizens." Prejudice against men takes the form of a prejudgment that any particular man will show his "masculinity" by being insensitive, vulgar, unexpressive, materialistic, and violent.

⑤ Prejudice is a preconceived and unfavorable attitude toward an entire group of people; it consists of a combination of overgeneralization (seeing all members of a group as the same) and devaluation (regarding them as inferior). One product of prejudice is a stereotype, a set of fixed ideas about members of a group. Stereotypes come from categorizing first and observing second.

Causes of Prejudice

Why is there prejudice? Why does this kind of intergroup hostility exist so commonly in the world today? Certainly the causes of prejudice are not simple; scientists have been studying prejudice for decades and we do not yet know how to prevent it. From the many studies of prejudice three important theories have developed to explain it: (1) competition, (2) belief differences, and (3) scapegoating. Each of these three theories has some merit, but no single theory seems to explain all prejudice.

Competition

When two groups are in competition, they tend to develop negative attitudes toward each other. In order to demonstrate this idea one psychologist studied boys attending a summer camp. He selected 22 twelve-year-old boys who did not know each other and formed them into two equal groups.[4] The two groups were then made to compete with each other through a series of contests. As the competition developed, the members of each group began to devalue the members of the other group; this devaluation took the form of expressions of hostility, name-calling, and unwillingness to associate with members of the other group. In just a few days two groups of strangers who were competing against each other showed intergroup prejudice.

Anti-Chinese feeling in California became strong following the completion of the transcontinental railroad when large numbers of Chinese laborers began to compete on the open labor market with whites.[5] Anti-Japanese feelings increased suddenly with the increase in Japanese immigration during the 1890's when the Japanese began to be used as a source of cheap labor.[5]

Prejudice against blacks increases when whites feel that their jobs are threatened by blacks. When white unions began to feel the pressure of black labor, prejudice against blacks increased. During periods of economic depression in this country, the number of lynchings of blacks increased, while during periods of prosperity the number of lynchings decreased, although this relationship is not very strong.[6] When there is not enough to go around, groups compete with each other for scarce resources. This competition stimulates hostility and prejudice.

Belief Differences

A second theory of prejudice holds that prejudice results from the perceived differences of belief systems.[7] According to this theory, whites are prejudiced against blacks

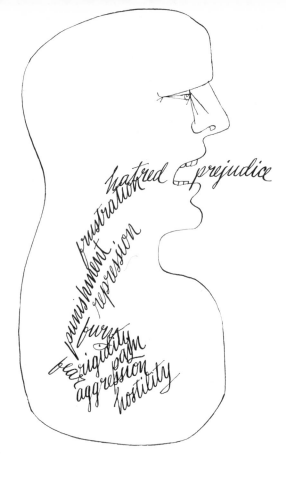

hatred prejudice
frustration
punishment
repression
bury
fear rigidity pain
aggression hostility

color are more obvious than differences in beliefs. Skin color can easily be seen, but beliefs are private and are often unknown. When beliefs are unknown, we make assumptions about them based on skin color.

Apparently skin color is a cue that signals information about a person's beliefs; and if skin color is different, the person's beliefs are assumed to be different also. If I automatically assume that your beliefs are different from mine because of your different skin color, I may dislike you and choose not to associate with you; and if I do not associate with you, I will not have the opportunity to discover what your beliefs really are.

Scapegoating

A **scapegoat** is a target for redirected or **displaced aggression.** If you punish your dog, the dog may react with aggression against your cat. The dog's hostile reaction was displaced from you to the cat. In this situation, the cat is a scapegoat.

The third theory of prejudice holds that prejudice is a form of displaced aggression and that certain subgroups of society such as the blacks serve as scapegoats for this aggression. Four steps are involved in this theory: (1) A person is frustrated or threatened; (2) the person reacts with aggressive impulses to this frustration; (3) either the source of the frustration is unknown (such as frustration resulting from economic depression) or the source of the frustration is seen as dangerous (such as frustration caused by one's father or one's boss); in either case, the aggressive impulses must be blocked or inhibited; (4) a safe target (a scapegoat) for the anger and aggression is found, and the aggression is displaced (redirected from the original target that was the source of the frustration to another target).[12] Prejudice, then, is displaced aggression directed toward

not because of the racial differences, but because they believe that blacks have different beliefs; and people are suspicious of those with different beliefs.

Studies show that we tend to like people whose beliefs are similar to ours and dislike people whose beliefs are different.[8] The greater the difference in beliefs, the greater the prejudice.[9]

One study compared prejudice because of beliefs with prejudice because of race. Whites were asked to choose between blacks whose beliefs were similar to theirs and whites whose beliefs were different. The whites preferred, as friends, blacks with similar beliefs to whites with different beliefs.[10] The experiment was repeated using Southern whites as subjects and obtained the same results.[11] This study showed that differences in beliefs were more important than differences in skin color. But differences in skin a group, such as blacks, that serves as a scapegoat. These four steps can be summarized as follows:

Frustration

   ↘ *Aggression*

      ↘ *Inhibition*

         ↘ *Displaced Aggression*

One study that supports the scapegoating theory involved boys at a summer camp.[13] One night the boys were expecting to see a movie but were deliberately kept waiting for a long time; this was an attempt to make them frustrated. Following this, measures of their attitudes toward Japanese and Mexicans were taken and compared with similar measures taken before the frustrating wait. The results showed a less favorable attitude after the long wait. Apparently even the small frustrations of day-to-day life affect your prejudice toward people of other subgroups. Of the numerous studies stimulated by the scapegoating theory, some have supported the idea of scapegoating and some have not. The theory probably works only in certain circumstances.

S   Three theories have been proposed to explain the causes of prejudice. The competition theory focuses on the prejudice and hostility that result when different groups compete for scarce resources. The belief difference theory argues that prejudice results from perceived differences in beliefs. The scapegoat theory assumes that prejudice is a type of displaced aggression and that the victims of prejudice are scapegoats.

The Development of Prejudice

Some people are extremely prejudiced and others are not. What causes these differences? Studies show that some parents and schools distort the minds of children and teach them prejudice.

Learning How to Hate

Children learn what attitudes and beliefs they are expected to hold. For the most part, children learn their prejudices from other people with whom they interact: parents, friends, and teachers. Studies show that there is a strong relationship between the extent of a child's prejudice and the extent of the parents' prejudice.[14] If parents are prejudiced, their child tends to be prejudiced also. In one study a psychologist invented a groups of persons called the "Piraneans." Slides of people supposedly of this group were shown to 180 elementary school children; then their attitudes toward these people were measured and compared with their parents' attitudes toward blacks, Jews, and other subgroups. It was found that the attitudes of the children toward the imaginary group resembled the attitudes of their parents toward real groups; when the parents were prejudiced, the children were too. These children had learned to be prejudiced—not toward a particular group—but in general.[15]

The learning of prejudice by children most likely takes place through the processes of modeling and identification. Children tend to imitate the behavior and beliefs of their parents and other significant adults. Furthermore, as children grow up they typically identify with the parent of the same sex and adopt the attitudes and mannerisms of that parent. In this way, children can learn to hate from their parents.

Parents are not the only teachers of hate. Children adopt the attitudes of society that they experience around them. Until very recently, magazines, movies, and television consistently portrayed all persons except white Americans as inferior. The characters

displayed to children conformed more to stereotypes than to reality. All blacks were shown in menial jobs; all Mexicans were shown as lazy. Recently, the representation of minorities in the media has improved, but it is still true that the hero of most stories is white and male and most TV servants are black and female.

Schools have taught a biased history. It has been, and to some degree still is, a history from the white person's point of view; it neglects important contributions made by nonwhites. Some school counselors still advise blacks and Chicanos to pursue careers as laborers and to take courses in school to prepare for menial jobs.

Schoolteachers speak for their culture; their attitudes and values reflect the attitudes and values of the rest of society. But the attitudes held by teachers and taught by teachers are often prejudiced. One New York City schoolteacher classified a number of her Puerto Rican students as mutes, unable to speak. When questioned about this, she reported that they had not spoken a word to her in six months. When asked if they talked to one another, she replied, "Sure, they cackle to each other in Spanish all day!"[16] The school system, for the most part, is staffed by white English-speaking persons and reflects the values and beliefs of white English-speaking persons. In a speech before the U.S. Senate, Dr. David Sanchez reported:

Equal education has been a fraud. How can there be equal education if some of the students are looked on as defective. The injuries of the Latin American child have been inflicted by those who claim to teach and motivate him, who have in reality alienated him and destroyed his identity through subtle rejection of his language which nobody speaks, his culture which nobody understands and ultimately him whom nobody values.[17]

Prejudiced Personalities

How can a person be prejudiced against a group that does not exist? It cannot come from the experience of interacting with the people involved, since they are imaginary; such a prejudice cannot be learned, since no opportunity for learning was possible. Yet studies have shown that many people are prejudiced against groups that do not exist, and these are the same people who are prejudiced against real groups.[15] People who are prejudiced against one minority group tend to be prejudiced against other minority groups as well.[18] Findings such as these have led to the idea that prejudice has more to do with the personality of the person who is prejudiced than with present social conditions. Prejudiced people may simply be different psychologically from other people. From this point of view, the personality of the person who is prejudiced should differ from the personalities of others.

The personality pattern characterizing highly prejudiced people has been called the **authoritarian personality.** An individual with this type of personality keeps feelings under great control, is extremely conventional and resistant to change, and shows a dependence on and admiration of authority figures.

A massive study of the personalities of prejudiced people was undertaken during and immediately following the Second World War, and a report of this study was later published in a book entitled *The Authoritarian Personality.*[18] For this study, about two thousand people took tests designed to measure prejudice, political beliefs, and personality. One of the most important parts of the test was a set of questions called the **F scale,** designed to measure basic personality traits that were assumed to support prejudice. High agreement with the items of this scale was supposed to reflect fascistic, authoritar-

ian, or antidemocratic tendencies. Some of the items from the F scale appear below; check the ones that you agree with.

☐ Obedience and respect for authority are the most important virtues children should learn.

☐ Sex crimes, such as rape and attacks on children, deserve more than mere imprisonment; such criminals ought to be publicly whipped, or worse.

☐ When a person has a problem or worry, it is best for him not to think about it, but to keep busy with more cheerful things.

☐ People can be divided into two distinct classes: the weak and the strong.

☐ Nowadays when so many different kinds of people move around and mix together so much, a person has to protect himself especially carefully against catching an infection or disease from them.

☐ A person who has bad manners, habits, and breeding can hardly expect to get along with decent people.

☐ Young people sometimes get rebellious ideas, but as they grow up they ought to get over them and settle down.

Prejudiced people tend to agree more with these items than nonprejudiced people.[19] The results of this test and more intensive studies of prejudiced persons supported the idea that highly prejudiced people tend to have a particular personality pattern. They tend to have unquestioning admiration for authorities and to hold in contempt persons they believe to have a status position lower than themselves. Interpersonal relationships for these people tend to be based on power and status. Highly prejudiced people show rigidity in their personality and thinking; they have little tolerance for unclear situations and prefer definite pat solutions to problems.[18]

What causes the prejudiced personality? One approach to this problem is to assume that prejudice is a form of displaced aggression and that the person who is prejudiced is scapegoating. According to the scapegoating theory, the prejudiced person has been frustrated or threatened by someone against whom retaliation was not safe; the impulse to fight back was inhibited because such action would be dangerous; and the aggression was therefore displaced or redirected to a relatively safe target, a minority group. The highly prejudiced person, then, should be someone who has been severely threatened or frustrated by someone against whom retaliation was dangerous or impossible.

Studies have shown that highly prejudiced persons tend to have aggressive and punishing parents.[18] The punishment they experienced as children was often arbitrary and violent. Whippings and beatings were commonly used punishments. One prejudiced person described her parents' disciplinary methods as follows:

. . . mother had a way of punishing me—lock me in a closet—or threaten to give me to a neighborhood woman who she said was a witch. . . . I think that's why I was afraid of the dark. . . .

Father picked upon things and threatened to put me in an orphanage.[18]

It is easy to believe that such punishment might provide a source of frustration that would later cause a prejudiced personality. The reactions of anger, hostility, and aggression that are inhibited in the child emerge later in the authoritarian adult as prejudice.

⑤ Research has shown that prejudice is learned and that certain personalities are more likely to be prejudiced than others. Some children learn prejudiced attitudes from their parents, peers, or teachers. In addition, children with aggressive and punishing parents tend to develop prejudiced personalities. People with authoritarian personalities are highly prejudiced and tend to have unquestioning admiration for authorities. The F scale is a test measuring the authoritarian personality.

Racism

Racism is prejudice against a person primarily because of skin color. Since racial prejudice has not yet been eliminated from the American scene, you probably have either directly experienced racism or at least witnessed examples of it. Racism can affect blacks, Chicanos, Puerto Ricans, Asians, Indians—anyone who seems "different" from the white Anglo majority in this country.

Racism involves overgeneralization— all persons of a particular skin color are regarded as the same, in spite of clear individual differences. Racism also involves devaluation—members of the other race are all seen as possessing undesirable traits. Studies show that whites tend to have antiblack attitudes, although this is *less* true for younger white people.[20] Blacks tend to have anti-white attitudes, and this is *more* true for younger black people.[21] Racism appears at its worst in prejudice against black Americans and has too often been expressed violently.

Violence

Violence and prejudice seem to go together. Violence against blacks is an ugly but significant part of the history of this country and is all too common even now. Racial prejudice that leads to murder can be viewed as an expression of complete devaluation.

For the crime of killing a white man's cow, William Carr, a Negro, was killed at Planquemies, Louisiana. The lynching was conducted in a most orderly manner, Carr being taken from the sheriff without resistance by a mob of thirty masked men, hurried to the nearest railroad bridge and hanged without ceremony.[22]

When this lynching took place, around the turn of the century, an average of two black persons were lynched each week in this country. More recently, there was violence against black Americans during the period of school desegregation in the South. Dick Gregory, who was there, wrote that in order to understand that violence you would have to experience it yourself.

Maybe you got to feel what it feels like to be walking down that street with that little black kid's hand in the palm of your hand and your hand is soaking wet—from your sweat because you know what's going to happen but the kid don't. And as you approach those steps to that school, not only are you attacked by the white mob but also by the sheriff and the police.

Next thing you know you're knocked down in the gutter with that cracker's foot in your chest and a double barrel shot-gun in your throat saying "move, nigger, and I'll blow your brains out." . . .

Maybe you have to lay in that gutter, knowing it's your *time now, baby, and then you look across the street, laying down in the gutter, from the gutter position, and see the FBI standing across the street taking pictures. . . . And then as you lay there in that gutter, man, it finally dawns on you that that little five-year-old kid's hand is not in the palm of your hand anymore. And that really scares you . . . and you look around trying to find the kid and you find him just in time to see a*

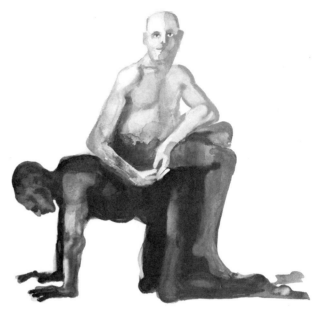

Historically, white people have kept black people down.

brick hit him right in the mouth. Man, you wouldn't believe it until you see a brick hit a five-year-old kid in the mouth.[22]

Other groups, such as religious minorities, have also felt the violence in prejudice. It is difficult, however, for the person who has never experienced prejudice to fully understand its cruelty. This may contribute to the persistence of unexamined stereotypes in our culture.

Effects of Racism

The consequences of racial prejudice affect both whites and blacks in this country. Have you felt it, or can you imagine what it would be like to suffer from discrimination all of your life; to be denied the promise of society; to be seen as mentally crippled or dirty because of your color; to be feared as something unknown; to be labeled as "culturally disadvantaged"? How would you react?

■ *Anger*   A common reaction is anger: *All blacks are angry. White Americans seem not to recognize it. They seem to think that all the trouble is caused by only a few "extremists." . . . The emerging rage now threatens to shatter this nation.*[23]

These remarks, from the book *Black Rage,* convey one response to racial prejudice—anger. When you are aggressed against, the natural reaction is to hit back, and this is how many blacks are now feeling. They have suffered from white aggression for several generations and they now feel like hitting back. The urban riots of the 1960's made clear the depth of anger the black community was feeling. When the participants of the Detroit uprising were asked why they were rioting, the typical response was, "Fighting back against white racism."[24] The recent riots in South Africa are a further example of a black community reacting with anger to white prejudice.

The National Advisory Commission on Civil Disorders, following an extensive study of racial disorders in American cities, reported:

This is our basic conclusion: Our Nation is moving toward two societies, one black, one white—separate and unequal. . . . Segregation and poverty have created in the racial ghetto a destructive environment totally unknown to most white Americans. What white Americans have never fully understood—but what the Negro can never forget—is that white society is deeply implicated in the ghetto. White institutions created it, white institutions maintain it, and white society condones it. . . . Racial prejudice has shaped our history decisively; it now threatens to affect our future.

*White racism is essentially responsible for the explosive mixture which has been accumulat-*ing *in our cities since the end of World War II.*[25]

■ *"Passing"*   Another possible reaction to racism is for the victim to identify with the aggressor. "If you can't beat them, join them," the saying goes, and some blacks follow this saying by identifying with whites. The term "passing" refers to the attempt by light-skinned black people to "pass" for white and be accepted by white society without prejudice. While this practice is not as common today as it used to be, minor versions of passing are still common. One variety of passing is seen among blacks who try to look "white" by using skin bleaches. Preference for light skin among black people has been common since plantation days. Parents still tend to favor a light-skinned child.[26] Among black college students, there is still a tendency for light-skinned persons to be preferred as dates.[27]

A second form of passing is adopted by some blacks who identify with the aggressor. They do not go so far as to try to appear like a white person, but they turn away from the black community and identify with the interests of the white community. Such a person is described in the book *Black Rage:*

His characteristics seem so connected to employment that we call it "the postal-clerk syndrome." This man is always described as "nice" by white people. In whatever integrated setting he works, he is the standard against whom other blacks are measured. "If they were all only like him, everything would be so much better." He is passive, nonassertive, and nonaggressive. He has made a virtue of identification with the aggressor, and he has adopted an ingratiating and compliant manner. In public his thoughts and feelings are consciously shaped in the direction he thinks white people want them to be. The pattern begins in childhood when the mother may actually say: "You must be this way because this is the only way you will get along with Mr. Charlie."[23]

■ *Acceptance*   A third reaction to racial prejudice is to accept the negative judgment of society as true. To accept the racist view is to agree that you are inferior, dirty, and lazy. There is evidence that some black children by the age of four have been so influenced by their prejudiced society that they believe the racial stereotype about themselves. Black children in these studies tended to look down on blacks.

In one classic older study, 253 black children between the ages of two and seven were shown two dolls, one black and one white. The psychologists asked the children, "Which doll looks nice?", "Which doll looks bad?", and "Which doll is a nice color?" Most of the black children picked the white doll as the one that looked nice and had a nice color, and picked the black doll as the one that looked bad.[28] Another study found that 60 percent of black children, but only 10 percent of white children, preferred to play with children of the other race.[29]

Robert Coles is a child psychiatrist who studied the effects of school desegregation in the South. One technique he used was to have weekly interviews with children of both races who attended newly integrated schools. Rather than ask these children to talk about their experiences, Coles asked them to draw and paint whatever they wished. In this way the children's feelings and experiences were communicated to the psychiatrist. Coles described one black child named Ruby:

The first Southern child to put my crayons and paints to use was Ruby. She and I started talking, playing and drawing together when she was six years old, and braving daily mobs to attend an almost empty school building. . . .

For a long time—four months, in fact—Ruby never used brown or black except to indicate soil or the ground; even then she always made

On the left if Ruby's drawing of a white girl and on the right is her drawing of herself. Both were done by Ruby at age 6, originally in colored crayon. Note the difference in size and detail.

sure they were covered by a solid covering of green grass. It was not simply on my account that she abstained from these colors; her school drawings showed a similar pattern. She did, however, distinguish between white and Negro people. She drew white people larger and more lifelike. Negroes were smaller, their bodies less intact. A white girl we both knew to be her own size appeared several times taller. While Ruby's own face lacked an eye in one drawing, an ear in another, the white girl never lacked any features.[30]

Ruby's drawings of herself and other black people showed her feelings of inferiority and her lack of pride and self-esteem. To some extent, she had accepted the attitude of white society toward her.

Black Is Beautiful

The times are changing. Feelings of black pride and racial identity are stronger now than ever before. "Black Is Beautiful" is a slogan that is gaining wider acceptance among blacks. Black leaders are emerging who are calling for "Black Power" and black control of black communities. The emergence of African nations has led to a rediscovery of "Black Culture" and "Black Heritage." Blacks are rejecting the prejudiced attitudes of white society and developing a higher sense of self-esteem.

Two black psychiatrists, William Grier and Price Cobbs, explain that blacks who embrace blackness and feel pride in their racial identity feel a sudden lifting of the spirit. Blacks who prize their blackness are freed from feelings of fear and inferiority that are the result of white racism.

The psychological realities of black life took shape under the pressure of white hatred.

Black men were moved by the passions that move all men and faced life with the mixtures of courage and cowardice that all men have mustered—except with the difference that the complete range of life was lived under the press of American bigotry.

[Pride in] blackness has the effect of penetrating and shattering the pressure bearing down on and distorting black lives. It allows blacks to cleanse themselves of fear, and, in one act, remove not only the intimidation of immediate hostility, but also all ceilings, permitting freedom to move as far and as fast as one's wits will allow.

Freedom from fear is strong wine![31]

⑤ Racism is prejudice against a person on the basis of skin color. It involves overgeneralization and devaluation, and has all too often been expressed in violence. Three reactions to racism are anger, "passing," and acceptance. Those who can take pride in their racial identity can be free of the feelings of fear and inferiority caused by racism.

Sexism

What's wrong with this story?

A father and his son were driving home when they had a terrible accident. The father was killed instantly and his son was severely injured. The son was taken to the hospital and rushed into the Emergency Room. The surgeon came in and said, "I can't treat this patient. *He's my son!*" Another doctor was called and the boy eventually recovered.

Since the child did not have two fathers, how can this story be explained? If this story sounds impossible to you, your thinking has been prejudiced by your sexist culture. You have been trained to think of women as housewives, secretaries, and maids, and not as professionals. In the case of the story above, the doctor was the boy's mother; the story seems impossible only because you failed to see this possibility. Prejudice against a person on the basis of sex is called **sexism.** Attitudes toward and assumptions about women commonly reflect this kind of prejudice.

"Male Chauvinist Pigs"

Western society is now and for centuries has been completely dominated by white males. A selection of historical quotations about women shows us the roots of present attitudes:

Wives, submit yourselves unto your husbands . . . for the husband is the head of the wife, even as Christ is the head of the church.

—Ephesians 5:23–24

Most women have no characters at all.

—Alexander Pope

Nature intended women to be our slaves . . . they are our property; we are not theirs. They belong to us, just as a tree that bears fruit belongs to a gardener. What a mad idea to demand equality for women! . . . Women are nothing but machines for producing children.

—Napoleon Bonaparte

Regard the society of women as a necessary unpleasantness of social life, and avoid it as much as possible.

—Count Leo Tolstoy

A male chauvinist is a man who displays a strong belief in the superiority of men over women. The quotations you have just read all reflect male chauvinism. These sexist attitudes are varieties of prejudice. Overgeneralization is one part of sexual prejudice: all women are seen as alike, possessing certain standard personality characteristics. Categorization (by sex) comes first; observation comes second. The tremendous differences among women are ignored in the process of overgeneralization. Devaluation is another part of sexual prejudice. Women are regarded as inferior beings who are acceptable only so long as they "stay in their place."

Sexist attitudes are learned early and are deeply held. Even psychologists sometimes show traces of sexism. In one recent study, practicing clinical psychologists were asked to describe a mentally healthy (a) man, (b) woman, and (c) adult, sex unspecified. The psychologists' descriptions of mentally healthy men and women were different. The important finding, however, was that their descriptions of mental health in general (a healthy "adult") resembled their descriptions of mentally healthy men, but not women.[32] The psychologists' attitudes were consistent with the assumption of the natural inferiority of women. Women who conformed to the ideal model of adult health were not considered mentally healthy. According to these psychologists, adult mental health is reflected in how healthy men behave, but not in how women behave.

Conflicting Roles

In 1792 a writer described the role of woman as follows:

She was created to be the toy of man, his rattle, and it must jingle in his ears whenever, dismissing reason, he chooses to be amused.[33]

The stereotype of the "ideal woman" is not much different today. Germaine Greer in her book *The Female Eunuch* described the female stereotype as follows:

The stereotype is the Eternal Feminine. She is the Sexual Object sought by all men, and by all women. . . . She need achieve nothing, for she is the reward of achievement. . . . Her glossy lips and mat complexion, her unfocused eyes and flawless fingers, her extraordinary hair all floating and shining, curling and gleaming, reveal the inhuman triumph of cosmetics. . . . She sleeps unruffled, her lips red and juicy and closed, her eyes as crisp and black as if new painted, and her false eyelashes immaculately curled. Even when she washes her face with a new and creamier toilet soap her expression is as tranquil and vacant and her paint as flawless as ever. . . . For she is a doll: weeping, pouting or smiling, running or reclining, she is a doll.[33]

A man's woman?

Few women can live up to this stereotype but many try. The image of the beautiful and desirable woman is held out before them continuously as they grow up. Magazine advertisements and movies manufacture the unreal but ideal woman. In the struggle to be the stereotype, a woman must give up herself. Greer writes that she is sick of that struggle.

So what is the beef? Maybe I couldn't make it. Maybe I don't have a pretty smile, good teeth, nice tits, long legs, a cheeky arse, a sexy voice. Maybe I don't know how to handle men and increase my market value, so that the rewards due to the feminine will accrue to me. Then again, maybe I'm sick of the masquerade. I'm sick of pretending eternal youth. I'm sick of belying my own intelligence, my own will, my own sex. I'm sick of peering at the world through false eyelashes, so everything I see is mixed with a shadow of bought hairs; I'm sick of weighting my head with a dead mane, unable to move my neck freely, terrified of rain, of wind, of dancing too vigorously in case I sweat into my lacquered curls. I'm sick of the Powder Room. I'm sick of pretending that some fatuous male's self-important pronouncements are the objects of my undivided attention, I'm sick of going to films and plays when someone else wants to, and sick of having no opinions of my own about either.[33]

Thoroughly opposed to the stereotype of the "Eternal Feminine" is individual achievement, self-reliance, intelligence, and competitive spirit. Yet these qualities are also held out before women as desirable. Women in schools and colleges particularly are encouraged to strive to develop their intellectual potential to the fullest, but this would conflict with the stereotyped sex roles. Thus, women are expected to move in two directions at once. They are pressured to fulfill the feminine role and be passive, dependent, and ignorant; and they are pressured to fulfill the achievement role and be active, independent, and intelligent. Women in this society have a **role conflict;** they are asked to live up to opposing sets of expectations. A successful woman is tolerated only if she also satisfies the feminine stereotype; but the roles are conflicting. One author expressed it this way:

Nobody objects to a woman's being a good writer or sculptor or geneticist if, at the same time, she manages to be a good wife, a good mother, good-looking, good-tempered, well-dressed, well-groomed, and un*aggressive.*[34]

Sex Discrimination

After struggling through four years of college, a twenty-four-year-old female secretary wrote:

I have a bachelor's degree in French literature. The smartest thing I ever did, however, was to take a typing course my junior year in high school; without it I would never be able to find a job.[35]

Her experience is not unusual. Nearly one out of every five employed women with a college degree is working as a clerical worker, sales worker, or service worker of some type.[36] These women are clearly working below their potential. The most common occupations for women are secretary, saleswoman, private household worker, teacher in elementary school, bookkeeper, waitress, and professional nurse.[37] Most of these jobs are poorly paid. Furthermore, the proportion of women working in less skilled and lower paid service occupations is increasing, while the proportion working in the leading professions is declining.[36] Only about 9 percent of the scientists, 7 percent of the physicians, and 3 percent of the lawyers are women.

A major recent study of sex discrimination in employment sampled 539 women and 993 men nationwide.[38] Only full-time regular workers were included in the final analysis. The results showed that the average woman earned $3,458 less than the average man with the same type of job and similar background. The annual incomes of about 95 percent of the women were less than comparable men. The average woman's annual income was less than 60 percent of a comparable man's income. The study concluded that about 95 percent of women workers suffer from sex discrimination in employment. A more recent study shows that the gap between the pay rates for men and women is growing larger each year.[39]

Putting Women in Their Place

There is a striking parallel between the roles of women and blacks in America. Women are regarded as irrational and incompetent just as blacks used to be. Women are expected to be submissive and nonaggressive, otherwise they will be seen as "pushy" or "uppity" just as blacks used to be. The "place" of women (and they should know their place) is in the home as unpaid

servants or in poorly paid service jobs else-where; blacks compete with women for these positions. From early infancy women are trained to know their "place" and to be satisfied with it; blacks used to be similarly trained. The black woman suffers two kinds of discrimination: one because she is black and one because she is a woman.

But blacks in some ways have made greater progress toward freedom than have women. Attention has been so focused on racist attitudes that you tend to be aware of them when they exist. But prejudice against women is often a **nonconscious ideology**—an ideology (set of assumptions and beliefs) that you are not conscious of having. This is made clear in the following example:

Consider an analogy. Suppose that a white male college student decided to room or set up a bachelor apartment with a black male friend. Surely the typical white student would not blithely assume that his black roommate was to handle all the domestic chores. Nor would his conscience allow him to do so even in the unlikely event that his roommate would say: "No, that's okay. I like doing house-work. I'd be happy to do it." We suspect that the typical white student would still not be comfortable if he took advantage of this offer, if he took advantage of the fact that his roommate had been socialized to be "happy" with such an arrangement. But change this hypothetical black roommate to a female marriage partner, and somehow the student's conscience goes to sleep. At most it is quickly tranquilized by the thought that "she is hap-piest when she is ironing for her loved one." Such is the power of a nonconscious ideology.

Of course, it may well be that she is *happiest when she is ironing for her loved one.*

Such, indeed, is the power of a nonconscious ideology![40]

The ideology, or set of assumptions and beliefs, underlying the oppression of blacks has recently been made conscious by focus-ing the attention of society on it, and it has been rejected. Or, at least, it is in the process of being rejected. But the ideology underly-ing the oppression of women has not been made conscious yet. One of the purposes of the women's liberation movement is to make that ideology conscious, just as the civil rights movement made conscious the ideology sup-porting racial discrimination.

The attitudes toward women, including the attitudes women have toward themselves, are learned. Women are socialized into the roles they fill in society. Parents teach their little girls to be passive and nonassertive, that is, to be "feminine." Parents actively dis-courage girls from being interested in science or mathematics and provide them with sew-ing lessons instead. Girls also learn their place from advertising on TV and in maga-zines.

Blacks at one time were consistently por-trayed in films and on TV as stupid and lazy. Fortunately, this has changed, but the repre-sentation of women in the media has not improved very much. What is the effect of girls being exposed to ads such as this one from Parker Pens:

You might as well give her a gorgeous pen to keep her checkbook unbalanced with. A sleek and shining pen will make her feel prettier. Which is more important to any girl than solving mathematical mysteries.[41]

The image of women on television teaches little girls to know their place. Women in TV ads are shown as anxiously concerned about the adequacy of their laundry, cleaning, and cooking efforts. They are shown as endlessly devoted to the task of modifying their appearance so as to please men. They are rarely shown as independent and intellectual persons working in one of the professions.

Advertising did not create these images about women, but it is a powerful force for their reinforcement. It legitimizes the idealized, stereotyped roles of woman as temptress, wife, mother, and sex object, and portrays women as less intelligent and more dependent than men. It makes women believe that their chief role is to please men and that their fulfillment will be as wives, mothers, and homemakers. It makes women feel unfeminine if they are not pretty enough. . . . It creates false, unreal images of women that reflect male fantasies rather than flesh and blood human beings.[40]

Men's Liberation

Women are not the only victims of sexual prejudice. Men, too, must live up to impossible images of the ideal; they must be tall, strong, aggressive, decisive, and unemotional. When they are growing up, boys are taught over and over again that they must "act like a man." They are told that expressing emotions is not "manly." There is, however, a growing resistance to this sexist stereotype. One man said, "The overriding characteristic of men in this society is emotional constipation."[42] Another said, "We don't cry. We are machines. And we have been made that way by society because machines are better for production."[43] Some psychologists now believe that the price men pay for struggling to conform to society's image of masculinity is the high rate shown by men of ulcers and heart attacks. The men's liberation movement is an attempt to liberate men from the male stereotype.

The issue, for both men and women, is the right of individuality and choice. Sexist attitudes narrow the range of acceptable choices; for example, women are judged badly if they are aggressive and men if they are passive. Yet some men are by nature less aggressive than some women. Men and women alike are pressured to conform to preconceived models of "masculine" and "feminine." These models may fit some people but they do not fit everyone. Thus, these models restrict choices and individuality. The problem of sexism is that it denies people the right to be different, to be individual.

[S] Sexism is prejudice against a person on the basis of sex. A male chauvinist is a man who has a strong belief in the superiority of men over women. Sexist attitudes in society cause role conflicts in women; women experience opposing pressures to be both feminine and independent. A consequence of sexism is sex discrimination in employment; women are denied equal pay and equal opportunity. Men are also victims of sexual prejudice; men are expected to feel and behave in particular ways that correspond to the male stereotype. Combating sexual prejudice is particularly difficult because sexist attitudes involve a nonconscious ideology, a set of beliefs that you are not aware of having.

Reducing Prejudice

The world is becoming crowded. We must learn to live together, and this requires the reduction of prejudice. What can be done to reduce prejudice? One approach is to attack the cause of prejudice.

Prejudice might be caused by competition, by the perceived differences of beliefs, and by scapegoating. Prejudice from competition might be reduced if everyone could have a satisfactory job so that fears of unemployment could be eliminated; or social legislation might provide an adequate guaranteed annual income so that economic fears are reduced. When there is enough to go around, we do not have to fight for what we get. Prejudice arising from the perceived differences of beliefs might be reduced by education or experience. Contact between ethnic groups, for example, typically results in reduced prejudice.[44] This is particularly true when the contact is relatively intimate and is between individuals of equal status. Prejudice from scapegoating, since it involves fundamental aspects of the personality, might be reduced through some form of psychotherapy. Several studies have shown that therapy does reduce racial prejudice.[45,46] Since scapegoating is considered to originate in punishing child-rearing practices, a change to more permissive discipline should also be effective in preventing prejudice.

Finally, for those men and women who have been socialized into accepting the racist or sexist views of themselves, some form of reeducation is necessary. The ideology that supports racism and sexism must be revealed, made conscious, and rejected.

We must learn to live together.

Summary

KEY QUESTIONS

1. What is prejudice?
   Prejudice consists of seeing all members of a group as alike in having undesirable traits. Overgeneralization involves seeing all members of a group as alike; devaluation involves seeing all members of a group as having undesirable traits. Racism and sexism are two types of prejudice.

2. What causes prejudice?
   Prejudice begins in childhood, when children learn from their parents and society what beliefs they are expected to hold. Adult prejudice may result from economic competition, belief differences, and scapegoating. Prejudice is more likely to develop in certain types of personalities than in others.

3. What are the effects of prejudice?
   Three reactions to prejudice are anger, "passing," and acceptance. As individuals begin to develop pride in their own identities, "passing" and acceptance become less likely.

4. How can prejudice be reduced?
   Prejudice can be reduced by changing the social and economic conditions of society, by increasing intergroup contact and education, and by changing child-rearing practices of parents to be less punishing.

KEY CONCEPTS

prejudice	A preconceived and unfavorable attitude toward an entire group.
overgeneralization	The tendency to see all members of a group as the same; for example, to see all men as aggressive.
devaluation	The tendency to regard some people as inferior or worthless.
stereotype	A set of fixed ideas about a person based on categorizing the person as a member of a group.
scapegoat	A target for displaced aggression.

displaced aggression	Hostile feelings directed—not against what provoked them—but against a safe substitute.
authoritarian personality	A personality type characterized by resistance to change, admiration for authority figures, contempt for persons of lower status, and extreme prejudice.
F scale	A test measuring the authoritarian personality.
racism	Prejudice against a person on the basis of skin color.
sexism	Prejudice against a person on the basis of sex.
male chauvinist	A man who strongly believes in male superiority.
role conflict	A problem resulting from having two opposing sets of expectations for how to behave; for example, college women are expected to be "feminine" (i.e., passive and dependent) but also are expected to be independent, successful, and intelligent.
nonconscious ideology	A set of assumptions and beliefs that one has but is not aware of.

24 Aggression and War

CHAPTER OUTLINE

How Aggressive Are You?

The Causes of Aggression
  The Instinct Theory of Aggression
    Murder, Murder Everywhere
    Your Violent Brain
  The Reaction Theory of Aggression
    Reflexive Fighting
    The Frustration-Aggression Hypothesis
  The Learning Theory of Aggression
    Imitating Models
    Observing Film and TV Violence
    Reinforcement

Some Causes of War
  The Biological Theory of War
  The Emotional Theory of War
  The Cognitive Theory of War

Alternatives to War

Summary

KEY QUESTIONS

1. What are the causes of aggression?
2. What are some causes of war?
3. What can be done to prevent war?

Americans have been called an aggressive and violent people. Crimes such as murder, rape, child abuse, assault, and assassination have been occurring in this country with increasing frequency. A few years ago the news was full of massacres in Vietnam and murder cults in California. Now we hear of bombings, beatings, and riots.

A recent survey showed that 12 percent of American adults have punched or beaten another person and 17 percent have slapped or kicked someone. About 32 percent report that they were spanked frequently as children. Almost 70 percent of those surveyed agreed with this statement: "When a boy is growing up, it is very important for him to have a few fist-fights."[1] Do you agree?

The term **aggression** refers to fighting or attacking behavior. It is a form of interaction, since it occurs between people, and it has the purpose or intent of hurt and injury. **Anger** is the feeling or emotion that accompanies aggression. Physical aggression, resulting in physical injury, is only one type of aggression; verbal aggression, where words are weapons, is another form of attack.

467

How Aggressive Are You?

People vary in the extent of their aggressiveness. Some react with aggression to the slightest irritation; others almost never react aggressively. To find out how aggressive you are, take the aggression test that is presented below.[2] Think about each of the statements carefully, and then check the statements that are true for you.

☐ 1. Once in a while I cannot control my urge to harm others.

☐ 2. I can think of no good reason for ever hitting anyone.

☐ 3. If somebody hits me first, I let the person have it.

☐ 4. Whoever insults me or my family is asking for a fight.

☐ 5. People who continually pester you are asking for a punch in the nose.

☐ 6. I seldom strike back, even if someone hits me first.

☐ 7. When I really lose my temper, I am capable of slapping someone.

☐ 8. I get into fights about as often as the next person.

☐ 9. If I have to resort to physical violence to defend my rights, I will.

☐ 10. I have known people who pushed me so far that we came to blows.

☐ 11. When I disapprove of my friends' behavior, I let them know it.

☐ 12. I often find myself disagreeing with people.

☐ 13. I can't help getting into arguments when people disagree with me.

☐ 14. I demand that people respect my rights.

☐ 15. Even when my anger is aroused, I don't use "strong language."

☐ 16. If people annoy me, I am apt to tell them what I think of them.

☐ 17. When people yell at me, I yell back.

☐ 18. When I get mad, I say nasty things.

☐ 19. I could not put other people in their place, even if they needed it.

☐ 20. I often make threats I don't really mean to carry out.

Is it possible to measure aggressiveness with a true-false test? Your score on this brief test undoubtedly is influenced by many things, including how aware you are of your own behavior. Your score, therefore, is only a crude indication of your level of relative aggressiveness. Your score is a number that has meaning only when it is compared to the scores made on the test by many other people.

Your aggression score consists of points added up for certain items that you checked and for other items that you did not check. To score the aggression test, give yourself one point for each of the following items that you *did not* check: 2, 6, 15, 19. Give yourself one point for each of the remaining items that you *did* check. The sum of your points is your "aggression score."

Men and women score differently on this test. The average for men is about 10 points and the average for women is 8 points. A score of 1 to 4 could be interpreted as showing low aggression, a score of 5 to 16 moderate aggression, and a score of 17 to 20 high aggression. You might compare your score on the first 10 questions to your score on the remaining 10 questions. The first 10 items were designed to measure physical aggression and the remaining 10 items were designed to measure verbal aggression. Are you more aggressive physically or verbally?

The Causes of Aggression

If we can understand our violence, perhaps we can control it. Why do people strike one another? Are we born killers? Psychologists studying aggression have identified three factors associated with aggression: heredity, environmental events, and learning.

Suppose a wife kills her husband. To understand this killing, we can ask (1) Is the woman a killer by instinct—was she born a killer? (2) Was the killing a reaction to frustration or to some other environmental event? (3) Was the woman rewarded in the past for her aggression—did she learn to kill?

The Instinct Theory of Aggression

Two great minds of this century, Einstein and Freud, believed people were born killers. Einstein wrote that human beings had an inborn lust for hatred and destruction. Freud believed that "the tendency to aggression is an innate, independent instinctual disposition in man."[3] Freud proposed that people have a universal death instinct, **Thanatos,** which turns into aggression when directed toward others. According to the **instinct theory of aggression,** aggression is an inborn tendency and people have "killer instincts."

A recent statement of the idea of aggression as an instinct appears in the book *On Aggression* by Konrad Lorenz.[4] Lorenz is an **ethologist,** a scientist who studies the behavior of animals in natural settings. Lorenz's study of animals has led him to believe that both animals and human beings have inborn compulsions to be aggressive, and that this biological need, like sex, requires periodic outlets.

What is an **instinct?** The term refers to complex behavior that is inherited; a genetically determined, not learned, pattern of behaving. It is a specific response pattern that is triggered by particular stimuli. Nest-building in birds has been called an instinct; there is a unique type of nest for different species of birds and no learning seems to be required for successful nest-building. Fighting behavior in rats is also an instinct. For example, in the Norway rat, the sequence of fighting behavior is highly determined; when two rats fight, they follow the same rigid pattern, even if they were raised in the laboratory and had no opportunity to learn how to fight.[5]

Aggression exists in people as well as animals. The question is, Is that aggression instinctual or learned? If it is instinctual, it should be universally present and should have a distinct biological basis.

■ *Murder, Murder Everywhere* Aggression seems to be universally present in animal and human life. Most animals display aggression in the competition over food, mates, and territory. Some animals, such as caribou, elephants, and sea otters do not stake out territories; they have no space that they will fight to protect.[6] Even animals that do fight over mates or territory rarely cause each other injury.[5] The combatants follow very strict "rules of the game" that prevent the death of the loser. An example is the male oryx antelope; he has rapier-shaped horns, but he does not gore his rival in battle. The "rules" provide that the only acceptable moves are pushing and clashing of forehead against forehead. Although threats are common among animals, violent aggressive acts are rare.[7] Human aggression is not like that. We don't follow the rules.[8]

To generalize from animals to people may not be valid. What is true for one may not be true for both. The case of human aggression will have to be considered separately from that of the animals. Some believe that people are killers by nature, and that the beast in us peers out whenever civilization fails to control our aggressiveness.

The situation relative to human aggression can be briefly stated under three headings. First, man has been a predator for a long time and his nature is such that he easily learns to enjoy killing other animals. Hunting is still considered a sport, and millions of dollars are spent annually to provide birds, mammals, and fish

to be killed for the amusement of sportsmen. In many cultures animals are killed for the amusement of human observers (in bullfighting, cockfighting, bear baiting, and so forth). Second, man easily learns to enjoy torturing and killing other human beings. Whether one considers the Roman arena, public tortures and executions, or the sport of boxing, it is clear that humans have developed means to enjoy the sight of others being subjected to punishment. Third, war has been regarded as glorious and, whether one considers recent data from tribes in New Guinea or the behavior of the most civilized nations, until very recently war was a normal instrument of national policy and there was no revulsion from the events of victorious warfare, no matter how destructive. . . . Man's nature evolved under these conditions. . . . The consequence of this evolutionary history is that large-scale human destruction may appear at any time social controls break down; recent examples are Nazi Germany, Algeria, the Congo, Vietnam.[9]

Other scientists believe that human aggressiveness is not due to the beasts from which human beings evolved, but is the result of our unique culture and technology. Human aggression is different from animal aggression. Animals rarely harm others of the same species; they threaten but do not kill. If the animals from which we evolved are less violent than we are, then it seems unlikely that aggression is a biological necessity in humans. It is more likely that the culture and technology that sets humans apart from the lower animals is responsible for aggression and war.

■ *Your Violent Brain* Your brain plays a key role in the aggressive response. Thought, movement, and feeling originate in the human brain as tiny electrical impulses. Some scientists, in an attempt to control epileptic seizures, have tried to influence behavior by stimulating the brain with elec-

trical impulses from wires. One patient, normally a mild-mannered woman, became extremely aggressive, verbally hostile, and threatened to strike the experimenter when electric current was provided to a particular region of her brain. When the current was turned off, she immediately returned to her peaceful and quiet condition.[10] Can you imagine what it would be like for someone else to turn your violence on and off by pressing a switch?

The outer wrinkled surface of the brain—the **cortex**—is the area most responsible for thought, problem solving, and other intellectual activities. The brain centers for aggression are deep beneath this surface but are kept in control (usually) by the action of the cortex. What would happen if the cortex did not restrain the aggression centers? Scientists have surgically removed the cortex from certain animals, thus releasing the aggression centers for cortical control. They found that the animals responded aggressively to almost anything, even gentle petting. Because the aggressive reaction was so intense, yet seemed to lack all emotional involvement, it was called **sham rage.**

Technology acts as a buffer between aggressors and victims.

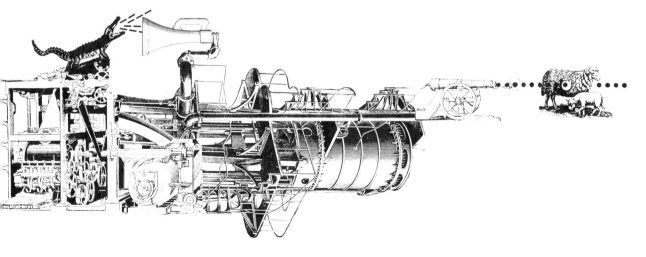

Numerous studies demonstrate that the brain system responsible for aggressive reactions to irritation or annoyance is separate from the brain system responsible for aggressive reactions to fear.[11] One study showed that a friendly cat will either attack a nearby rat or will attack the experimenter, depending upon which region of the brain is electrically stimulated. The cat could be controlled by turning a switch.[12]

A few persons, confined to mental hospitals, have uncontrollable rages, making them a threat to themselves and to those around them. Constant physical restraint is sometimes necessary for such persons. This form of superaggression has been found to be caused in many cases by brain tumors in a particular area of the brain. Following corrective brain surgery, these violent individuals typically become calm and passive.[13] It is clear that the brain has innate organized systems for the control of aggressive behavior and that these systems sometimes do not function properly.

Aggression involves the whole body, not just the brain. The heart rate and blood pressure increase; sugar is released into the bloodstream to be available as fuel to the muscles; breathing is faster; blood is diverted from the internal organs to the muscles (suddenly digestion is not as important as hitting or running). In both animals and people, the teeth are bared when rage is intense, and gutteral noises are made. The similarity of the rage reactions of animals and people suggests that the rage reaction is inborn and not learned.

There is no doubt that people have an inborn aggressive response system, involving the brain and the body. An aggressive response, however, is not automatically elicited or triggered by a specific external stimulus. There is great variability among people in what makes them angry and aggressive. The stimulus that elicits the aggressive response

also changes with age and education. Although the aggressive response is innate, its relation to events in the environment is learned. Insults did not produce an aggressive reaction in me at birth; I could not even comprehend the language. The stimuli that produce aggression in people are learned.

The manner in which the aggressive response is expressed is also learned. There is a standard pattern to certain aspects of bodily reaction in aggression (blood pressure, heart rate, and so forth), but how we aggress against one another depends upon history and learning. People have invented wondrous machines for aggression, and their children learn from them how to use these machines.

Just as you have innate bodily structures that make it possible for you to talk, you have innate bodily structures in the brain and body that make it possible for you to express aggression. But what you say when you talk and what makes you aggressive and how you express your anger—these must be learned. Are people born killers? People are born with the capacity to kill, but there is no evidence that they have an inborn compulsion to use that capacity. Killing is something that is learned.

Ⓢ The instinct theory of aggression proposes that people have inborn aggressive tendencies. In support of this theory, it is argued that aggression is universally present in human and animal life and that there is a distinct biological basis for aggression in certain brain structures. Animals, however, rarely kill members of their own species; unlike human beings, animals follow strict rules that prevent them from harming each other. If we are basically beasts, born killers, it is surprising that animals from which we evolved are less aggressive than we are. Furthermore, although we have innate biological structures that make aggression possible, these structures do not determine the direction or the form of the aggressive acts. It is clear that learning must be involved.

The Reaction Theory of Aggression

According to the **reaction theory of aggression,** aggression occurs in response to external stimulation; it is a reaction to, and a way of coping with, events in the environment.

■ *Reflexive Fighting*   Attack is often followed by counterattack, in both animals and humans. If I stick a pin in you, you might hit me. Several studies have shown that animals respond similarly. Aggression seems to be an automatic reaction to pain, so long as there is something nearby to attack. Reflexive fighting in response to pain has been demonstrated for mice, hamsters, cats, rats, and monkeys.[14] Electric shock was used to cause animals pain in the studies. The animals themselves were not responsible for the occurrence of the shock, but when in pain they would attack each other anyway.

The scientists who perform such experiments are not sadistic or unfeeling; they believe that they are making important contributions to the body of knowledge about aggression and that understanding aggression is important for human survival. My own view is that the potential value of the knowledge gained from such studies does not warrant the methods used. How do you feel about this question?

■ *The Frustration-Aggression Hypothesis*   Aggressive human behavior occurs in certain specific situations and not in others. An early attempt to characterize what situations might lead to aggression is the **frustration-aggression hypothesis.**[15] This proposal is simply that aggression is always a con-

sequence of frustration; that is, the stimulus for aggressive responses is frustration. One psychologist decided to study this hypothesis with pigeons. But how do you frustrate a pigeon? He reasoned that if a pigeon became used to being rewarded every time it made the correct response, it would be frustrated when the reward suddenly stopped. This would be like failing to receive your paycheck on time. The experiment was done using two pigeons in the same box. When the reward suddenly stopped, one pigeon became enraged and viciously attacked the other pigeon in the box.[16] The human analog might be that after a man misses his paycheck he goes home and yells at his wife.

It is clear from these studies that aggression often follows frustration, but this is not always the case.[2] Aggression seems to occur at times when no frustrating event precedes it, and some things that appear frustrating are not followed by aggression. The frustration-aggression hypothesis will work for those cases only if "frustration" is *defined* as any event that precedes aggression and "aggression" is defined to include unobservable internal processes. In this way, whenever a clearly frustrating event is observed that is not followed by an observable aggressive response, it is possible to claim that there was an aggressive reaction but it was internal and therefore not observable. Furthermore, whenever a clearly aggressive act occurs that is not preceded by an observable frustrating event, it is possible to claim that since aggression occurred, frustration must have occurred but was invisible. This kind of reasoning is circular and tends to go nowhere. Although the frustration-aggression hypothesis stimulated a lot of research, the circularity that developed from the vagueness of the definitions limited the usefulness of the idea.[17]

The reaction theory of aggression has consequently been more useful in accounting

Aggression sometimes follows frustration.

for aggressive behavior in animals than for human behavior.

ⓢ The reaction theory of aggression assumes that aggression is a response to external stimuli. For example, pain seems to elicit automatic attack reactions in many animals. In human beings, the frustration-aggression hypothesis proposes that aggression is always a reaction to frustrating events. This hypothesis, however, has not been very well supported. Human aggression appears not to be a simple reaction to outside stimuli; it is far more complex than a reflex.

The Learning Theory of Aggression

Certain forms of aggression are explicitly taught. The army trains its recruits to kill.

High schools and colleges teach young people to be aggressive in football, boxing, and other sports. Parents expect male children to be physically aggressive and reward their sons with praise when they conform to these expectations. For the most part, however, aggression is not taught in the same way as arithmetic; instead the child learns violence by imitating violent individuals, by observing our violent society, and by being rewarded for aggressive acts. According to the **learning theory of aggression,** aggression results from imitation and reinforcement.

■ *Imitating Models* Children learn through imitating adults. The adults serve as models for the child to copy. In one experiment Albert Bandura compared the behavior of three groups of children: one group witnessed an adult behaving aggressively; a second group witnessed an adult behaving nonaggressively; and the third group saw no adult model.[18] The aggressive adult model was observed attacking a large inflated doll with a mallet, then kicking the doll around the room. The nonaggressive adult model was observed quietly playing with Tinker Toys. Following their exposure to the adult models, the children were given some attractive toys to play with, and then the toys were taken away. The removal of the toys was an attempt on the part of the experimenter to make the children angry and frustrated. Finally, the children were allowed to play by themselves in the room with the large doll, the Tinker Toys, and other toys while they were secretly observed through a one-way mirror.

The children who had been exposed to the aggressive adult model played much more aggressively with the large doll than either the children exposed to the nonaggressive model or the children exposed to no model. The children tended to imitate the adult model they had witnessed, either by sitting quietly and playing or by attacking and beating the large doll, depending upon which adult model they had seen.

Children imitate their parents, and parents are often aggressive. Parents aggress against children when they use physical punishment. Physically punishing a child for being aggressive seems to be contradictory: the parent aggresses the child in the attempt to teach the child not to be aggressive. The effect of parental aggression is that children copy it.[19] The best predictor of aggressiveness in children is aggressiveness in their parents; the child who has a history of severe physical punishment at home, including punishment for aggression, tends to be the child who will behave most aggressively.[20]

■ *Observing Film and TV Violence* We are exposed to more violence today than ever before—on films, television, and in books and magazines. Should the "impressionable minds" of children be protected from this violence? Are the minds of children "impressionable"? A study by Bandura showed that children are influenced by violence portrayed on film. After watching either a realistic film or a cartoon film showing aggressive acts, children engaged in more aggressive behavior themselves. Watching aggressive films made the children act more aggressively.[21] Several studies show that young adults are similarly affected by witnessing violence in films. A typical finding is that after watching a violent film, college students are more willing to administer painful electric shocks to another person in a psychology experiment. Apparently viewing the film increased their aggressiveness.[22,23]

Experimental studies of the effects of film violence can be criticized. The laboratory situation in which these studies occurred, for example, is not at all like real life. The film strips children watch in these experiments are short and out of context. The question of what effect the observation of violence has remains without a definite answer; there is, however, enough evidence to warrant a strong suspicion that watching film and TV violence increases aggressiveness in viewers under some circumstances. Apparently people imitate not only "real-life" models, but also models shown in films or on TV.

■ *Reinforcement* Children learn that aggression "pays"; it is often rewarded, or reinforced. Male children may be punished for being a "sissy" and praised for fighting. When people are in conflict, often the more aggressive individual wins. Observations of nursery-school children show that aggressive acts are usually rewarded—the victim runs away or gives up a toy or candy to the aggressor; children who begin nursery school

After being spanked herself, child spanks her doll.

relatively unaggressive learn rather quickly to become more aggressive.[24] In a laboratory study, children were provided the opportunity to attack a large doll; each time they struck the doll they were rewarded with a marble. Later they were observed while playing games with other children. It was found that the children who were rewarded previously for attacking the doll were consistently more aggressive toward the other children.[25] We not only learn aggression by observing and imitating others but we also learn it because it has rewarding consequences.

[s] The learning theory of aggression proposes that aggression is learned through imitation and reinforcement. Children learn by imitating adults, whether the adults appear in "real life" or in films or TV. Children exposed to aggressive adult models will themselves act more aggressively. In addition, children learn aggression because aggressive acts are rewarded; reinforcement for aggression is provided both by parents and by peers.

Some Causes of War

War is aggression on a national scale. The world has never lived in peace for long; the history of this century is a history of aggressive acts of enormous destruction. In the past 5,000 years there have been fewer than 300 years of peace. Over 14,000 wars have been recorded in which millions of persons have been killed.[26] The Vietnam war was brought into the living room of almost every family in America because of the television coverage. The agony of that involvement led many people to ask, "Can we ever live in peace?"

If science can help us understand the causes of war, then the prevention of war becomes a possibility. Clearly, there is no single cause for war; political, economic, and social factors are important, but psychological factors make their contribution also. Furthermore, the effect of a particular condition depends upon the pattern of other conditions forming its context, and the context for international behavior is extremely complex.[27] But international behavior is human behavior, so an understanding of the causes of war must include an understanding of the behavior of people. Psychologists have proposed biological, emotional, and cognitive determinants to explain the existence of aggressive wars among human beings.

The Biological Theory of War

Perhaps we are doomed to live forever in a state of war. Some believe that the history of the world compels us to conclude that war is part of human *nature* (or at least a part of the nature of nations). According to the **biological theory of war,** we have an inborn urge for destruction. If we are born killers and live in tribes that we call countries, then war is inevitable. If war is in our genes, it may be pointless to struggle for peace. Perhaps we cannot escape our genetic destiny. However, the idea that we have killer instincts is an idea that may lead to the abandonment of the search for peace.

The Emotional Theory of War

A second possible cause of war is emotional, not biological. The course of events is often influenced by individual personalities, some of whom may be neurotic or mad. With our present technology of mass destruction, the mind of a single person—the mind behind the finger on the button—may hold the future of the world. According to the **emotional theory of war,** war results from such personality factors as frustration and conflict.

Nations in some ways are like individual people. What causes a person to react aggressively may cause a nation to react aggressively.

A stimulus for individual aggression is frustration. There is some evidence that frustration is also a stimulus for international aggression. One study defined the frustrations of a nation in terms of the gaps between the expectations of the population and their achievement.[28] On the basis of this definition of social frustration, 84 nations were classified according to their level of frustration. These same nations were classified according to the extent of their participation in international acts of hostility during a recent six-year period. The second classification, on the basis of international hostility, did not take into account whether a nation initiated an attack or was reacting to an attack; the history of the action was not considered. Of the nations studied, only Finland did not participate in a single aggressive act; the four most aggressive on this scale were (in order) the U.S.S.R., U.S.A., the United Arab Republic, and Israel. The results showed that there was a tendency for frustrated nations to be aggressive and satisfied nations to be peaceful. When these results were combined with other measures, a consistent picture began to emerge: the nonaggressive country was one with a relatively permissive political regime, a low rate of economic change, and relatively little social frustration; the aggressive country was one with a relatively authoritarian government, a high rate of economic change, and a high level of social frustration.[28]

The Cognitive Theory of War

A third possible cause of war is cognitive. Biological causes of war are rooted in the mechanisms of the body; emotional causes of war are based on the feelings and personality dynamics in people's minds; cognitive causes of war depend upon thought: our systems of rationality and belief. According to the **cognitive theory of war,** war results from our beliefs and expectations.

One cognitive cause of war may be our belief that war is inevitable. In a study of attitudes toward war, it was shown that the belief that atomic war would occur was increased by reading materials about the construction of bomb shelters.[29] If people expect and prepare for war, the chance that war will actually occur may increase. Gor-

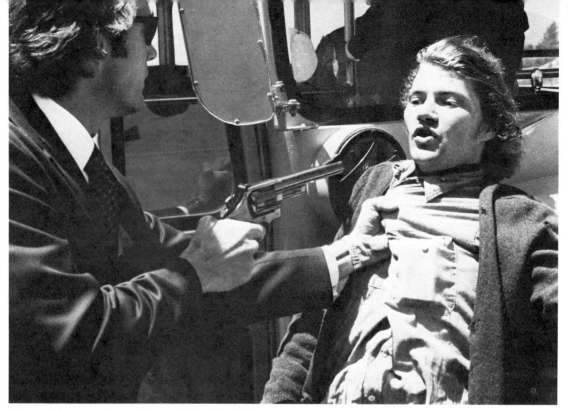

Entertainment at the movies: "Dirty Harry" (Clint Eastwood) gets his man.

don Allport has proposed that expectations of war cause war:

When people's minds have become habituated to accepting a designated enemy as a menace, the next step is to set the final expectation that will lead to war.[30]

This belief is a direct contradiction of the idea that adequate preparation is a deterrent to war.

When persons with different systems of belief and different ways of thinking try to solve a problem, it is likely that they will develop two different solutions. Different systems of belief may lead to conflict. Different cognitive systems, some psychologists believe, will be the prime source of future international conflicts.

My principle guess about the future is this: the prime source of war in the future is likely to lie in cognitive differences concerning the means as to how common ends may be best achieved. First priority should therefore be assigned to the necessity for learning how cognitive differences can be resolved. . . . Unhappily, cognitive conflict provides as large a potential for violence and destruction as does traditional conflict over power and gold. The long and bitter religious wars, some of which are still with us, are evidence of this fact.[31]

Differences in beliefs and ways of thinking make communication particularly difficult, and communication appears to be necessary for peace.[32]

⑤ Possible psychological causes of war are proposed by the biological, emotional, and cognitive theories of war. The biological theory assumes that we have an inborn urge for destruction; the emotional theory assumes the problem to originate in the human personality; the cognitive theory assumes that our beliefs and expectations lead to wars.

Alternatives to War

What if the biological theory of war is correct? If aggression is an innate biological urge, is it pointless to struggle for peace? Can we work against our own nature, our evolutionary past, and provide alternatives to war? One possibility is to find safe outlets for our aggression, outlets that do no harm. Competitive sports are believed by some to be a socially acceptable channel for expressing aggression. Playing football may relieve aggressive impulses so that they do not have to be discharged in fighting. Nations could invest much more energy in the development of international games like the Olympics, with the hope that the aggression of citizens could be safely discharged on the sportsfield instead of the battlefield. A second alternative to war is to create new people designed for peace in a new world. Brain surgeons are now experimenting with removing parts of the brain in order to make people passive, and biochemists are studying "peace drugs," tasteless chemicals that reduce hostility and aggression.[33]

What if the emotional theory of war is correct? If war is the result of the human personality and people's reactions to frustration and pain, then the number of wars could be reduced through therapy—both for individuals and for social systems or nations. Therapeutic interventions into social systems are already quite common in this country. The attempts to reduce prejudice through legislation and the social provisions for the welfare and health of citizens are examples of interventions at a systems level. Such interventions have the result of reducing the frustration of the population, thereby reducing its aggressivness. Individual psychotherapy is another approach to preventing wars by working toward psychological health.

What if the cognitive theory of war is correct? If war is the consequence of cognitive conflict, then we must struggle to understand each other. Communication is essential for that understanding. But communication may be impossible without education; if I cannot learn about your belief system and your way of thinking about problems, I cannot communicate with you. I can learn about you effectively only through interaction with you. Contact between individuals with different cognitive systems promotes understanding through communication and education. Thus what must be worked for is *community*, a sense of togetherness, in which different systems are integrated and interdependent. Within a community, obstructive differences in cognitive systems diminish through peaceful interaction.[27]

Aggressive people are heroes.

OUR HERO   OUR HERO

Summary

KEY QUESTIONS

1. What are the causes of aggression?

We are born with the capacity for aggression. An aggressive response is automatic when certain brain structures are stimulated. External situations or events can also produce an aggressive reaction. However, most aggressive acts seem to be the result of learning. We are not born killers; we learn to kill.

2. What are some causes of war?

One theory holds that the problem lies in our genes—we have an inborn urge for destruction. A second theory holds that the problem lies in our personality—as individuals or as nations we need psychotherapy. A third theory holds that the problem lies in the way we think—we have different belief systems and inadequate communication.

3. What can be done to prevent war?

A range of possibilities exists, depending upon your view of the causes of war. Psychotherapy and "peace drugs" may be used to pacify the brain. Both individuals and social systems could be provided psychotherapy in order to reduce aggressiveness. Education, contact, and communication may be increased to help people understand each other and integrate differing belief systems.

KEY CONCEPTS

aggression	Fighting or attacking behavior; actions having the intent of hurting others.
anger	The feeling of emotion that accompanies aggression.
Thanatos	Freud's term for a universal death instinct.
ethology	The study of animals in their natural settings.
instinct	A complex behavior that is inherited; for example, nest-building in certain birds.
cortex	The outer wrinkled surface of the brain; an area especially important for human perception and intelligence.
sham rage	Intense aggressive behavior observed in animals lacking a cortex.

frustration-aggression hypothesis	The proposal that aggression is always a consequence of frustration.
instinct theory of aggression	The theory that aggression is an inborn tendency; that we are born with "killer instincts."
reaction theory of aggression	The theory that aggression occurs in response to external stimulation.
learning theory of aggression	The theory that aggression results from learning through imitation and reinforcement.
biological theory of war	The theory that war results from our inborn urge for destruction.
emotional theory of war	The theory that war results from frustration, conflict, and other personality problems.
cognitive theory of war	The theory that war results from our systems of belief and ways of thinking.

Suggested Readings

The Social Animal by Elliot Aronson. San Francisco: W. H. Freeman, 1972. Highly readable application of social psychological research to issues of prejudice, propaganda, conformity, alienation, aggression, and political upheaval.

Profiles in Courage by John F. Kennedy. New York: Harper, 1955. Accounts of several individuals who were able to withstand the pressures to conform and to abandon their principles.

Pain and Promise: The Chicano Today ed. by Edward Simmen. New York: New American Library, 1972. A series of essays discussing the Chicano movement from many different points of view. Shows the rise of group awareness and the increase in ethnic pride and power among Chicanos.

Prejudice and Racism by James M. Jones. Reading, Mass.: Addison-Wesley, 1972. The psychology, sociology, and history of racism are summarized. Discusses individual, institutional, and cultural racism.

Black Rage by William H. Grier & Price M. Cobbs. New York: Basic Books, 1968. The authors, two black psychiatrists, argue that all blacks are angry, and their rage threatens to shatter the nation.

Autobiography of Malcolm X by Malcolm X & Alex Haley. New York: Grove Press, 1966. The story of one man's courageous struggle for personal identity in a hostile environment.

Black Skin, White Masks by Frantz Fanon. New York: Grove Press, 1967. A powerful and poetic book concerning the achievement of self-identity among blacks.

Woman in Sexist Society ed. by Vivian Gornick & Barbara K. Moran. New York: Signet Books, 1972. A collection of readings attacking our "sexist" society. Examines the role of woman in love, marriage, mothering, education, and work.

The Female Eunuch by Germaine Greer. New York: Bantam Books, 1971. An attack on male-dominated society and an appeal for women's liberation.

Half the Human Experience: The Psychology of Women by Janet S. Hyde & B. G. Rosenberg. Lexington, Mass.: D. C. Heath, 1976. An introduction to the psychology of women for both men and women readers. Discusses the biological influences on female behavior as well as the psychological and cultural influences.

Human Aggression and Conflict: Interdisciplinary Perspectives by Klaus R. Schere, Ronald P. Abeles, & Claude S. Fischer. Englewood Cliffs, N.J.: Prentice-Hall, 1975. A comprehensive introduction to the psychology of aggression and conflict. This highly readable book presents theories, research, and real-life examples to clarify concepts of aggression.

On Aggression by Konrad Lorenz. New York: Bantam Books, 1966. An argument for the biological basis of aggression supported by many descriptions of animal aggression. Claims that we have a killer instinct, which, like the sexual urge, demands periodic release.

Research Methods VIII

Controlled Experiments

What is the effect of motivation on learning? Do you learn more when you are highly motivated? Correlational studies have shown that people with high motivation score higher on learning tests than people with lower motivation; that is, there is a positive correlation between motivation and learning. But this correlation does not prove that motivation influences or causes learning. There are several possibilities: (1) making high scores on learning tests may cause you to be highly motivated; (2) being highly motivated may cause you to make high scores on learning tests; and (3) some third factor, such as genetic endowment, may cause both, but motivation and learning have no effect on each other. Combinations of these alterna-

tives are also possible. How can you decide among the alternatives?

Experiments

To discover which alternative is the best requires an **experiment**—a method of observing behavior systematically under carefully controlled conditions. In the experimental method, as opposed to the correlational method, researchers control what happens. Because they control what happens, the experimenters are able to investigate the causes of behavior. They are able to produce changes in one variable, keeping other variables constant, and observe the effects on behavior.

A Sample Experiment

To experimentally discover the effect of motivation on learning, an experimenter would have to manipulate levels of motivation and then observe the consequences in behavior. One way to do this would be to attempt to produce different levels of motivation in different groups of students. For example, a large psychology class might be divided in half by randomly assigning students to one of two groups. One group, called the **experimental group,** is given some kind of special treatment in an attempt to increase their motivation to learn; the second group, called the **control group,** is treated as usual, with no special treatment. The second group is a kind of comparison group.

Because the class is large and is divided randomly, it is extremely unlikely that the two groups differ systematically before the experiment is conducted. For example, it is unlikely that one group would be all male and the other all female; it is unlikely that one group would be significantly more intelligent than the other group. With a large number of participants, and with random assignment to groups, it turns out that differences between groups average out. At the beginning of the experiment, then, the experimental and control groups can be regarded as equivalent.

Students in both groups are asked to learn the same list of twenty psychology terms. Before the lists are presented, students in the experimental group are offered $.50 for every term learned correctly, while students in the control group are offered no reward. At the end of the experiment, if the two groups are significantly different in the number of terms they learn, the difference can be attributed to the difference in monetary reward (and, by assumption, in motivation), since in all other respects the two groups are believed to be equivalent.

In order to claim that changes in motivation *cause* changes in learning, you must demonstrate that (1) changes in motivation are correlated with changes in learning; (2) changes in motivation precede changes in learning; and (3) possible alternative explanations, such as differences in genetic endowment, can be ruled out.

Correlation would be shown if the "high motivation" group (experimental group)

learned more than the "low motivation" group (control group); the variables of motivation and learning would be positively correlated.

Precedence of motivational changes can be assumed; the changes in motivation would have preceded the changes in learning, since motivational differences were produced by the experimenter before the learning task was presented (the experimenter offered to pay one group but not the other).

Alternative explanations of differences in learning between the two groups can be ruled out because the students were randomly assigned to one of the two groups and because the experimenter produced the motivational differences. Thus, it could not be claimed that the difference in learning between the two groups was due to a genetic difference, since it is extremely unlikely that two large randomly selected groups would be systematically different in genetic structure. It is therefore possible in an experiment of this sort to come to a conclusion about the effect of motivation on learning.

Independent and Dependent Variables

In the experiment described above, the experimenter is interested in examining the possible relationship between two variables: (1) motivation level and (2) the amount learned. If the two variables are found to be correlated—for example, if people learn more if motivated, then the experimenter will assume that there is probably a causal relation between the two variables; namely, that high motivation *causes* increased learning.

The variable that the experimenter manipulates or varies (in this case level of motivation) is called the **independent variable.** The independent variable is often considered as a cause of behavior. The variable that the experimenter does not manipulate directly is called the **dependent variable;** the dependent variable (amount learned) is affected by (depends upon) the independent variable. The values of the independent variable are called the "conditions" or the "treatments" of the experiment. The learning experiment just described had two conditions (two values of the independent variable): (1) high motivation and (2) normal motivation.

Experimental Design

The **experimental design** is a plan for research. Different experimental designs describe different ways of manipulating the independent variable and different ways of assigning participants to the conditions of the experiment. A common design involves the assignment of one group of people to one experimental condition and a second group to another condition. After the conditions of the experiment are experienced by the groups, the behavior of the groups is measured and compared.

In one experimental study of observational learning, 84 children were randomly divided into three groups.[1] One group observed an adult model express opinions contrary to the children's beliefs and observed the adult receive rewards for doing so. Children in a second group were themselves induced to express opinions contrary to their true beliefs and were rewarded directly for doing so. A third group experienced both of the above conditions of "direct" and "vicarious" reward. Which group of children would be more likely to change their beliefs? The results showed that both groups observing adult models reversed a large number of their beliefs, but that children in the group without the opportunity for observational learning did not change many of their beliefs. You can conclude from these results that adult "modeling" behavior *causes*

changes in children's expressions of their beliefs.

Experimental Analogs

Many psychology experiments study significant human behavior in an indirect way. Psychologists may study rats instead of people, even though they wish ultimately to apply what they learn to people. Rats are simpler, more convenient, and less expensive. Psychologists may study college students in their experiments, even though they wish to apply what they learn to schizophrenics. College students are available and cooperative. The hope is that there is a similarity or *analogy* that holds between the subjects who are actually studied and the population to which the results will eventually be applied.

A second type of study uses independent variable analogs: a psychologist interested in the effects of stress on behavior may employ a form of stress in an experiment that is unknown in the real world—for example, electric shock applied to the forefinger. Shock is convenient and easily controlled. The hope is that there is a similarity or analogy that holds between the experimental manipulations of shock (values of the independent variable) and the conditions of stress in the world that concern the psychologist.

A third type of study involves dependent variable analogs: a psychologist interested in the effects of stress on meaningful behavior may study the effects of stress on forms of behavior unknown in the real world—for example, nonsense-syllable learning. The hope is that there is an analogy between the dependent variable measured in the experiment (nonsense-syllable learning) and the real-life behavior in which the psychologist is interested (for example, classroom learning).

Whether the psychologist is justified in generalizing from restricted experimental conditions employing some type of analog to conditions in the world is an empirical question; the question can be answered by ascertaining the accuracy of predictions about real-world events made from the experimental analog; applying experimental results in the world sometimes seems to work and sometimes does not.

Sources of Problems

Experiments, as methods of discovering causal relations in the world, are open to many errors of inference and design. Some of the more common problems that experimenters face in designing experiments include order effects, placebo effects, and selection errors.

Order Effects

Sometimes behavior is measured both before and after an experimental manipulation; the assumption is that a difference between the first and the second measurements will be due to the experimental condition. A researcher might, for example, give you one creativity test, then give you a cup of coffee (the experimental treatment), and then measure your creativity again with a second test. An increase in your creativity score could not be attributed exclusively to the effect of the coffee; the increase might be due to an **order effect.** That is, you might have done better on the second test because it was second—you had learned something from the first test that helped you the second time around.

Placebo Effects

Psychologists studying the effects of a particular drug on behavior must be concerned with the manner of administering the drug. Pills have effects beyond the effects of the chemical they contain; pills containing only inactive substances, such as sugar pills, are known to produce improvement in feelings of well-being, for example. Medically inactive pills ("placebos") are given by many doctors to patients whom they cannot help in other ways. If a person is given a pill containing a drug and subsequently feels better or performs better, you do not know whether the improvement in mood or performance is due to the drug or to the **placebo effect**—the psychological effect of a treatment such as taking a pill. The true effects of a drug can be determined by giving one group of people pills containing the drug and giving a second group of people identical-looking pills that do not contain the drug. Differences between the two groups can be then attributed to the effects of the drug alone.

Selection Errors

If an experimenter uses two groups of participants, each experiencing a different experimental condition, it is necessary that the two groups be equivalent in all ways except for the differences in experimental treatment. Thus, if the results show that behavior of the two groups is different, the experimenter would like to be able to attribute the difference in behavior to the difference in experimental conditions, not to other differences. **A selection error** occurs if the participants selected for groups are unequal to start with.

In order to test the effects of sleep on memory, you might have a group of fourth-graders learn a list of words just before going to sleep, then test them in the morning; then have a group of high school seniors learn a list of words in the morning, and test them after eight hours. If the two groups showed a difference in the amount of material remembered, you would not be able to attribute that difference to the experimental condition of sleep or wakefulness, since there were other significant differences between the two groups (age) that could have caused the differences in memory.

In order to avoid selection errors of this sort, the experimenter is careful to randomly assign participants to the experimental conditions, or to match the people in one group with the people in the other group. The aim is to make the groups equal in all ways except for the difference resulting from the experimental condition.

What's Wrong with This Experiment?

Professor Z. believed that vitamin C had the capacity to prop up tired minds and that aspirin also had a mysterious power to make students more clever. To test this idea, he decided to give vitamin C pills to his psychology class and to give aspirin tablets to his advanced calculus class. All students were given a standard IQ test, then they took a pill, and then they took the IQ test over again. Professor Z.'s hypothesis was that both classes would show a significant increase in IQ between the first and second tests as a consequence of the magic chemicals.

The results of the experiment were as follows: the average IQ for the thirty students in his psychology class was 115 on the first test; after the vitamin C pills, their average IQ increased to 135. The average IQ for the thirty students in the advanced calculus class was 117 on the first test; after the aspirin tablets, their IQ increased to 122. Thus, average IQ in the psychology class increased 20 points after taking vitamin C and the average IQ in the calculus class increased 5 points after taking aspirin.

Professor Z. called a press conference and triumphantly announced his conclusion: vitamin C and aspirin both increase IQ, but vitamin C increases it more. Other scientists severely criticized this conclusion, saying that his experiment had at least three serious defects. What are they? (Check your answers on the next page.)

KEY CONCEPTS

experiment	A form of controlled observation in which the researcher manipulates one thing and then observes the consequence.
experimental group	In an experiment, the group receiving the special treatment.
control group	In an experiment, the group receiving no special treatment; the comparison group.
independent variable	In an experiment, the variable manipulated by the experimenter.
dependent variable	In an experiment, the variable influenced by the independent variable.

experimental design   A plan for conducting an experiment, consisting of a method for manipulating the independent variable and observing the dependent variable and a method of assigning participants to conditions.

order effect   A change in behavior that may be due to repeating the conditions of measurement; for example, the second time that a test is given you may do better merely because you are more familiar with the test.

placebo effect   A change in behavior due to taking a pill or other treatment, independent of the content of the pill; for example, some people may feel better after taking a medically inactive sugar pill.

selection error   A difference in behavior between groups that results from the groups being unequal to start with; an error resulting from bias in assigning participants to experimental conditions.

Answers to "What's Wrong with This Experiment?"

1. For both classes, the improvement in IQ may have resulted from having the opportunity to take the IQ test a second time; that is, the *order effect* may have operated.
2. For both classes, the improvement in IQ may have resulted from the psychological effect of taking a pill—any pill; that is, the *placebo effect* may have influenced the results.
3. There were at least two differences between the two classes: (a) one group got aspirin, the other vitamin C; and (b) one group elected to take psychology, the other, advanced calculus. Differences in IQ gain between the two classes could be due to (a) or to (b) or to both. Since the two classes were not initially equivalent, a *selection error* was made.

IX Ecology

25 Environment

KEY QUESTIONS

1. What is an ecosystem?
2. How do you adapt to stress and what is the cost of adaptation?
3. How do your surroundings affect your behavior?
4. What is the psychological effect of living in cities?

The world is interactive. Each molecule, mountain, child, or king exists in relationship to many things.

Nothing exists in perfect isolation; the different people and things in the world are continually being influenced and changed by each other. The earthworms and I have an important interaction that centers around my garden: I keep the soil moist and rich in organic material for them, and they work the soil for me so that it stays loose and oxygen can reach the roots of my vegetables. Everything I do affects my environment, and my environment in many different ways affects me.

The Ecosystem

Ecology is a science emphasizing interaction. It is the study of the great web of life, the relationships and interdependence of organisms to each other and to the environment. Because people are dependent on their environment, they have reason to be concerned about such ecological problems as air and water pollution. People pollute the air and water, then consume their own pollutants. People affect their environment and in turn are affected by it.

Closed and Open Systems

The **ecosystem** is the network of relationships existing among organisms and environments. A pond is an ecosystem, consisting of various forms of animal and plant life, water, earth, and atmosphere forming a complex system of relationships and dependencies. The earth itself is a larger ecosystem, of which people are an important part. Because such systems are highly interactive, changes in one part of the ecosystem cause changes in other parts. Human survival may depend upon our ability to understand our ecosystem and become aware of the consequences of our present course of behavior.[1]

The focus here is on **systems,** as opposed to isolated parts or pieces of things. The idea of a system emphasizes relationship, structure, and interdependence, rather than individual objects isolated from their context. It stresses wholes rather than parts. Ecology is one of several fields of science that have successfully applied the concept of systems.[2]

Two kinds of systems can be differentiated: **closed systems** and **open systems.** A closed system is a set of interacting parts that is independent of external forces; an open system is vulnerable to the forces in its environment and is affected by them. Science has frequently regarded people as existing in a closed system, relatively independent from environmental forces. Recently we have become increasingly aware that we live in an

We live in an open system.

open system; not only do we change our environment but the environment changes us.

Our Unique Power

Our place in the ecosystem is unique because we alone have the power to destroy it. People have already destroyed many other forms of life in their ecosystem, and some believe that the great web of life is itself threatened. Our power enables us to change our environment so rapidly that the consequences—the side effects—are often not known until it is too late.[3]

Man is damaging the earth in various ways, not the least of which is through environmental pollution. Products of erosion, sewage, and industrial wastes have been polluting environments for a long time, but the problem has become more acute as the population pressure increases. Agriculture has recently embraced the theory that the way to avoid damage from pest organisms is to make the environment poisonous. . . . Some pesticides, notably DDT, have become virtually a normal constituent of the world environment and have turned up even in the fat of penguins from Antarctica. . . . The frightening thing is that man brought this about in just a few years with an irresponsible disregard for possible effects on ecosystems.[1]

⑤ The ecosystem is the network of relationships existing among organisms and their environments. The idea of a system focuses on relationship, structure, and interdependence rather than on individual objects isolated from their context. Of the two types of systems, the closed system is independent of external forces while the open system is vulnerable to them. It is now believed that we live in an open system in which we change our environment and it changes us.

Adaptation and Stress

Adjustment to the changes in your environment is called **adaptation.** Adaptation reflects the vulnerability of people to the forces in their environment; people adapt because they live in an open system.

You have a great capacity to adapt to your environment; you can learn to survive in climates as different as the jungle, the desert, the arctic, and the Los Angeles smog. Under different climatic conditions, the environment acts on you to provide you with information about the appropriateness of your behavior.[4] For example, if the weather turns cold, you feel chilled and put on a sweater; your chill is information indicating that you need to do something. The atmosphere in Los Angeles is polluted and provides the residents with information feedback about the fact in the form of eye irritation and bronchial disease. Busy freeways, particularly freeway on-ramps, cause bodily reactions of anxiety and stress.[5] Often the action of the environment on people is threatening or stressful; under these conditions adaptation is a means of coping with stress, learning either to avoid it or to live with it.

General Adaptation Syndrome

Many physical and emotional problems result from stress.[6] Physical and psychological stress have been shown to precede heart disease, arthritis, ulcers, infections, and skin disease.[7] Illness often follows the stress associated with important changes in life, such as a death in the family, the birth of a child, moving, or divorce.[8,9] Stress also diminishes sexual activity both in animals and in people.[6]

The body reacts to environmental stress in certain standard ways. The pattern of response to prolonged extreme stress has been labeled the **general adaptation syndrome.**[6] The general adaptation syndrome consists of three stages. The first stage is the **alarm reaction,** during which heart rate increases, blood is directed to the skeletal muscles to prepare for a "fight or flight" reaction, and other bodily changes occur. The second stage is **resistance,** during which the body seems to return to normal and all the bodily resources are consumed adapting to the stress. The third stage is **exhaustion,** when the body is unable to continue resisting the stress. If the stress continues, the bodily reactions of the alarm stage may recur and death is likely.

Cost of Adapting

Most of us live in chronic mild stress. The pace of modern life, the cars on the busy streets, the pollutants in the air we breathe are with us daily and we adapt to them. What is the consequence of this adaptation?

According to René Dubos in his book *Man Adapting,*[10] the problem is not whether we can adapt to the changing environment, but rather what the cost will be of our adapting to continual stress.

The aspect of the problem of adaptation that is probably the most disturbing is paradoxically the very fact that human beings are so adaptable. This very adaptability enables them to become adjusted to conditions and habits which will eventually destroy the values most characteristic of human life.

Millions upon millions of human beings are so well adjusted to the urban and industrial environment that they no longer mind the stench of automobile exhausts, or the ugliness generated by the urban sprawl; they regard it as normal to be trapped in automobile traffic, to spend much of a sunny afternoon on concrete highways among the dreariness of anonymous and amorphous streams of motor cars. Life in the modern

Most of us live in chronic stress.

city has become a symbol of the fact that we can become adapted to starless skies, treeless avenues, shapeless buildings, tasteless bread, joyless celebrations, spiritless pleasures—to a life without reverences for the past, love for the present, or hope for the future.

Man is so adaptable that he could survive and multiply in underground shelters, even though his regimented subterranean existence left him unaware of the robin's song in the spring, the whirl of dead leaves in the fall, and the moods of the wind—even though indeed all his ethical and esthetic values should wither. It is disheartening to learn that today in the United States schools are being built underground, with the justification that the rooms are easier to clean and the children's attention not distracted by the outdoors![10]

We can adapt, but there is a price for that adaptation. If we do not want to be transformed, through adaptation, into creatures alien to our traditions, we must understand our relationship to the environment, what we do to it, and what it does to us.

But what is so bad about starless skies and what is so good about the wind or a robin's song? We do not know whether our response to the beauty of the natural world is culturally conditioned or whether it has an innate basis, perhaps as inborn categories formed through human evolution in the natural world. If cultural, our aesthetic response can be modified to suit our new world of concrete and steel; if innate, our aesthetic response may serve biological needs which, in the artificial world, will remain unfulfilled.

⑤ Adaptation is a method of adjustment to changes in the environment that are stressful. The patterned response to prolonged stress is called the general adaptation syndrome. The syndrome consists of three stages aimed at coping with environmental

stress. One problem with adaptation is that sometimes it takes a heavy cost if we make drastic changes from our normal traditions.

Natural Environments

The context for behavior is the natural world: the system of air, water, land, plants, and animals in which people live. People act on the natural world and change it; polluted streams, air-conditioned buildings, vanishing species of animals, and paved landscapes are evidence of the ability we have to modify our own environment. But our behavior is also modified by the environment.

Climate

Some scientists believe that climate has shaped the pattern of human history; weather can be shown to be related to social conditions, health, crime rates, mental activity, and personality.[11] Although the evidence that climate *causes* these behavioral effects is weak, there is strong evidence that climate affects people in important ways. The bodily reaction to heat and cold reveals a variety of ways available for maintaining an acceptable bodily temperature. When the body is exposed to heat, there is increased blood flow through the capillaries and an increase in sweating, both resulting in greater heat loss; when the body is exposed to cold, there is constriction of certain blood vessels and an increased metabolic rate, both resulting in reduced heat loss.[10]

Temperatures considered to be comfortable throughout the world are fairly standard; while there are some differences among cultures, the upper limit of comfort is typically in the middle seventies.[12] Although people can adapt to temperature extremes, a sudden increase in temperature causes a stress reaction. Rapid changes in climate seem to have greater effects than stable climates.

A variety of psychological functions suffer at high temperatures: sleep is more disturbed,[12] certain motor skills are poorer,[13] productivity and efficiency are less,[14] test scores are lower,[15] and eyesight is poorer.[16] Rates of suicides, homicides, and admissions to mental hospitals all show a relation to climate, increasing as the temperature rises.[17] There are seasonal changes in the rate of birth of mentally retarded children, which suggests that high summer temperatures somehow affect unborn babies in certain cases.[18] No one knows whether the higher rate of retardation is due to stress reactions in the mothers caused by high temperatures or is due to inadequate diets on the part of the mothers during the hot months. In any case, the temperature of the environment has important effects on human behavior.

Wildness

As more and more of the natural world is transformed into highways and cities, we increasingly value what remains untouched. We now know that the wilderness is a national resource that must be preserved. The significance of wildness to human life is shown by Henry David Thoreau in his famous book, *Walden:*

We need the tonic of wildness, to wade sometimes in marshes where the bittern and the meadow-hen lurk, and hear the booming of the snipe; to smell the whispering sedge where only some wilder and more solitary fowl builds her nest, and the mink crawls with its belly close to the ground. At the same time that we are earnest to explore and learn all things, we require that all things be mysterious and un-
explorable, that land and sea be infinitely wild, unsurveyed and unfathomed by us because unfathomable. We can never have enough of nature. We must be refreshed by the sight of inexhaustible vigor, vast and titanic features, the sea-coast with its wrecks, the wilderness with its living and its decaying trees, the thunder cloud, and the rain which lasts three weeks and produces freshets. We need to witness our own limits transgressed, and some life pasturing freely where we never wander.[19]

John Muir, naturalist, conservationist, and founder of the Sierra Club, described his favorite wilderness, Yosemite Valley in California:

But no temple made with hands can compare with Yosemite. Every rock in its walls seems to glow with life. Some lean back in majestic repose; others, absolutely sheer or nearly so for thousands of feet, advance beyond their companions in thoughtful attitudes, giving welcome to storms and calms alike, seemingly aware, yet heedless, of everything going on about them. Awful in stern, immovable majesty, how softly these rocks are adorned, and how fine and reassuring the company they keep: their feet among beautiful groves and meadows, their brows in the sky, a thousand flowers leaning confidingly against their feet, bathed in floods of water, floods of light, while the snow and waterfalls, the winds and avalanches and clouds shine and sing and wreathe about them as the years go by, and myriads of small winged creatures—birds, bees, butterflies—give glad animation and help them make all the air into music.[20]

National parks like Yosemite are becoming increasingly crowded. The rate of increase in the use of these recreation sites has been about four times the rate of increase in population during the past two decades.[21]

Why are so many people leaving the cities

and going to the wilderness? In a recent survey about half of the respondents said that they were there for the emotional experience of it and about one-third said they were there for the aesthetic experience of it.[22] Those who were interviewed in this study, hikers in the Northeast, reported emotional experiences associated with the splash of a leaping trout, building a campfire, or seeing a large game animal such as a deer. Outdoor recreation also provides the opportunity to escape from the stresses of civilization: wilderness is a "tonic" for the problems experienced in the city.[23]

The physical environment affects your mood. Think of how you might feel standing on a sidewalk in a large city, or driving on a freeway in heavy traffic, and compare that with how you might feel among the pines in the mountains, or on the beach watching the waves crash. It is important to preserve wildness in order to preserve the feelings caused by wildness. In a recent study I asked one hundred college students to report their moods in twenty different environments.[24] The students said they felt most tense, most threatened, and most depressed in the following places: freeways, elevators, large cities, sidewalks, and classrooms. The students felt most relaxed, most safe, and most happy in the following places: at the ocean, mountains, and farms, on the grass, and among the trees. These findings support the idea that wilderness is a tonic and civilization a stress. Where do you feel most happy?

ⓢ You are affected by the natural world around you. The climate in which you live affects you both physically and psychologically. More and more people are leaving the cities for the wilderness to escape the stress of civilization. The wilderness seems to provide a "tonic" for people while urban life produces stress.

Constructed Environments

The wind, the rain, the snow, the heat, and the cold are only rarely experienced by most of us: we live in artificial, constructed environments. Shopping centers are being built that are enclosed completely in shells with controlled light, temperature, and humidity; the cities of the future may be enclosed in artificial environments.

We seem to enjoy controlling our environment, yet, paradoxically, we drive for greater and greater distances in search of natural environments when we escape the city. Even some animals seem to find it rewarding to control their environments. Wild rats and mice that are brought into the laboratory will work to turn off a light or an activity wheel that has been turned *on* by the experimenter, and will work to turn on a light or an activity wheel that has been turned *off* by the experimenter.[25] Apparently these animals prefer to be in charge of their own world.

Aerospace and Hydrospace

The control of the environment is sometimes necessary for survival. For example, the natural environment of outer space is deadly, so aerospace projects require carefully constructed artificial environments if people are to survive. Spaceships must not only contain the essential elements to sustain physical life but also must be designed to support people working efficiently and feeling well. These special requirements of people in aerospace are similar to the needs of people in hydrospace, living and working in artificial environments under the sea. The study of people in completely artificial environments is probably essential to understanding the person of the future, and psychology will make an important contribution to that understanding.[26,27,28]

Buildings

Buildings affect our behavior. Novelists place horror stories in large dark castles or mansions; they place depressing stories in single bare rooms or shacks; and they place humorous or happy stories in unusual older houses with cluttered rooms. These buildings form behavioral settings, contexts that affect the behavior and feelings of the persons in them.

Any new physical environment, whether a bungalow, school, office building or jail, can have significant immediate and perhaps long-range effects upon the behavior of its occupants. Nowhere may such influences be more readily observed than within the walls of a total institution such as a mental hospital and within other large but less pervasive settings such as general hospitals, schools, universities, offices, apartment complexes, and new towns.[29]

■ *Color and Beauty*   The color of rooms in buildings affects behavior. Red is experienced as exciting and stimulating, blue as secure, and green as peaceful.[30] Red and other warm colors seem to induce a state of arousal and disruption, although no biological basis for this effect has been established.[31]

The beauty of buildings affects behavior. Buildings that are aesthetically pleasing support feelings of expansiveness and well-being. One study compared behavior in three types of rooms: beautiful, average, and ugly.[32] Participants were asked to rate each of ten pictures of persons as to how much

Bradbury building, Los Angeles.

fatigue and displeasure each person showed. Although the pictures were the same, the judges in beautiful rooms tended to perceive people as less fatigued and as showing less displeasure than the judges in the average or ugly rooms. The only difference among the experimental conditions was the environment in which the judgments occurred. In another study, problem-solving ability was compared in an ugly attic room and in an orderly pleasant room.[33] The number of problems solved was significantly fewer in the ugly attic room. Again, the surrounding building made the difference.

■ *Form* The form of buildings affects behavior. Doors and walls channel movement; furniture is designed for certain postures and not others; the way rooms are connected determines the sequence of activities most likely to occur. Certain kinds of building designs cause illusions and perceptual distortions in normal persons, similar to those experienced in some forms of mental illness.[29] Illusion-inducing buildings would clearly be inappropriate as mental hospitals, yet some older mental hospitals are of this type.

The size of rooms[34] and the arrangement of furniture in rooms[35] has been shown to influence behavior, particularly the degree of social interaction. The constructed environment controls social interaction by blocking certain relationships and allowing others; if your door and my door both open to the same courtyard, we are more likely to be friends than if they don't. Proximity, or more specifically, physical accessibility, has been shown to determine friendship patterns in a variety of settings: housing developments, military barracks, and university dormitories.[36] Certain buildings are designed so that the formation of stable human relationships is prevented or discouraged; examples of such buildings are train stations, jails, mental

hospitals, and hotels. Other buildings encourage and foster the development of human relationships; many private dwellings are of this type. Such buildings promote face-to-face contact in small groups of people.[37]

Cities

Coming into a large city from a small town or rural area can be quite a shock:

When I first came to New York it seemed like a nightmare. As soon as I got off the train at Grand Central I was caught up in pushing, shoving crowds on 42nd Street. Sometimes people bumped into me without apology; what really frightened me was to see two people literally engaged in combat for possession of a cab. Why were they so rushed? Even drunks on the street were bypassed without a glance. People didn't seem to care about each other at all.[38]

■ *Alien Worlds* If the present rate of world population growth continues, the entire usable surface of the earth will be covered in a vast city. There would be no forests left, no meadows, no wilderness, no new areas to explore.

Imagine that the growth of population and the evolution of technology have urbanized the entire globe — that a single world city covers the usable surface of the earth. The prospect is a nightmare. One instantly has a vision of being trapped in endless rows of tenements or little suburban houses, of no escape from the continual presence and pressure of other people. The city would be monotonous, faceless, bewildering. It would be abstract, out of contact with nature. . . . The air would be foul, the water murky, the streets crowded and dangerous. Billboards and loudspeakers would force

Are cities alien to people?

their attentions on everyone. One could be at home in a sealed room, but how could one farm or hunt or explore? . . . Would not this world, entirely man-made be utterly alien to every man?[39]

The rate of population growth will probably not continue, and such a future although possible is unlikely. But the image of the world-city clarifies our vision of our present cities: Are they not also alien to people?

With all their problems cities are also stimulating, vital, exciting, and full of resources for human health and development. Cities are full of diversity and change. Interesting people, music, films, restaurants, libraries, and theaters are all easily accessible. There is always something to do in a city. What does the city mean to you?

■ *City People* Cities are composed of strangers. Both the benefits and problems of cities derive from this fact. Because you are anonymous in a city, you have less pressure to conform; no one knows who you are and no one much cares what you do. Cities are more tolerant of deviance and independence. The streets and sidewalks of the city carry strangers back and forth, but also serve other purposes: they are playgrounds for children, places for adults to meet without intimate contact, and guardians of the safety of the citizens.

Streets and their sidewalks, the main public places of a city, are its most vital organs. . . . Sidewalks, their bordering uses, and their users, are active participants in the drama of civilization versus barbarism in cities. To keep the city safe is a fundamental task of a city's streets and its sidewalks.[40]

Streets that are safe have "eyes on the street"; children play under the watchful eyes of the shopkeepers and shoppers. Streets with too few small shops opening onto the street are typically unsafe in a large city.

People living in cities and people living in small towns or rural areas seem to be quite different. To a certain extent, different kinds of people choose to live in different settings but it may also be that the environment changes the people. In the ecosystem of the city the person and the city interact and both change. Several studies have compared people in cities with people in small towns. In one study student experimenters rang doorbells of residents in a city and in several small towns asking to use the phone. Three to four times as many small-town residents cooperated as did city residents.[38] Another study showed that small-town residents were more likely to help strangers calling on the telephone than were city residents.[38] Apparently, city people are less trusting than rural or small-town people.

Cities can offer excitement and stimulation.

■ *City as Zoo* People are controlled by the environment they construct. City freeways and sidewalks replace an open plain; these become channels for human movement. Just as pipes control the passage of water, freeways and sidewalks control the passage of persons. Our constructed environment limits our freedom.

Buildings also limit freedom. For example, consider classrooms in schools and colleges. Because of the form of the room and the orientation of the seats, all persons look in the same general direction and sit equally spaced throughout the room.

Because the constructed environment limits drastically the alternatives of behavior, our behavior in the artificial world tends to become standardized and stereotyped. Animals in a zoo experience the extreme controls of an artificial constructed environment, and sometimes they develop stereotyped patterns of movement within their cages. I remember one hyena I once watched which

paced back and forth in its small cage in such a highly ritualized, invariable pattern that the concrete on the floor of the cage was worn into a permanent valley that marked its path. Perhaps we are building our own cages.

Cities are not yet zoos; they may limit choices, but they also provide freedom from snow and rain. Freeways provide freedom to travel great distances. Urban technology provides freedom from the necessity of continuous labor in order to eat. These urban freedoms, of course, are gained at a price. The question is, Are they worth it?

People can adapt to almost any ecosystem. The price of that adaptation, however, may destroy the life-style and human values we have evolved. Although cities are tolerant, vital, and stimulating, people in that environment seem to suffer from health, safety, and interpersonal problems more than people in rural environments. Perhaps as we live in more and more crowded conditions and in more and more artificial environments, our environment becomes more stressful and more limiting. The cities of the future must expand freedom rather than limit it.

We must learn how to plan and build our cities in such a way as to give all of us the maximum choices. Since our cities restrict because of their structure, the total number of our choices . . . we must study the type of structure that eliminates the smallest number of alternatives. To achieve this we must conceive the best type of life and then build the structure that allows the best function in the sense of a maximum of choices.[41]

Ⓢ   People seem to enjoy being in control of their environment. Sometimes a controlled environment is vital for survival as with the aerospace and hydrospace environments. It has been shown that many aspects of our environment such as colors, sizes, and shapes of buildings affect our behavior. Cities seem to provide a sort of anonymity for their inhabitants and this has certain advantages; but they also impose both physical and psychological stress.

Summary

KEY QUESTIONS

1. What is an ecosystem?

   An ecosystem is a network of relationships existing among organisms and their environments. It is a highly interactive system in which each part affects the others. Your environment is an ecosystem; you change your environment and it in turn changes you.

2. How do you adapt to stress and what is the cost of adaptation?

   You live with mild continuing stress, and you have learned to adapt to it. Extreme stress may result in a patterned response called the general adaptation syndrome. A danger to adaptation is that you may change so drastically that you lose your values and your traditions.

3. How do your surroundings affect your behavior?

   The weather can affect your personality, mood, health, and mental activity. As compared to the city, wilderness makes people feel less anxious. In the city, the shapes of buildings and the colors of rooms also affect your behavior.

4. What is the psychological effect of living in cities?

   Cities are controlled environments and limit behavioral alternatives. Cities promote tolerance and anonymity but are highly stressful for many people. The crowding, noise, and fast pace of life in cities provide psychological stress. Change itself is stressful, and cities promote change. Cities limit certain kinds of freedom and enhance others.

KEY CONCEPTS

ecology	The study of the relationships and interdependence of organisms to each other and to the environment.
ecosystem	The network of relationships existing among organisms and environments; for example, a pond or the earth itself.
systems	Parts in relationship, having structure and interdependence.
closed system	A set of interacting parts that are independent of external forces.
open system	A set of interacting parts that are vulnerable to the forces in the environment and are affected by them.
adaptation	Adjustment to changes in the environment.
general adaptation syndrome	A patterned response to prolonged extreme stress in the environment.
alarm reaction	First stage of the general adaptation syndrome in which heart rate increases to prepare for a "fight or flight" response.
resistance	Second stage of the general adaptation syndrome in which bodily resources are consumed adapting to the stress.
exhaustion	Third stage of the general adaptation syndrome in which the body is unable to continue resisting the stress.

26 Social Space

CHAPTER OUTLINE

KEY QUESTIONS

1. What is your personal space and what happens when it is violated?
2. What is the effect of social isolation?
3. What is the effect of crowding?

How can we live together? The nineteenth-century philosopher Arthur Schopenhauer answered this question with a parable:

A company of porcupines crowded themselves very close together one cold winter's day so to profit by one another's warmth and so save themselves from being frozen to death. But soon they felt one another's quills, which induced them to separate again. And now, when the need for warmth brought them nearer together again, the second evil arose once more. So that they were driven backward and forward from one trouble to the other, until they had discovered a mean distance at which they could most tolerably exist.

You may not always think so, but other people are more important than anything else in your environment. Sometimes the problem is: How can you live with them? Other times the problem is: How can you live without them? Actually, you haven't much choice. You live in a small world and the world is full of people. You have to live with

509

them. In fact, studies of human behavior indicate that you need to live with them; being able to interact with at least a few people is necessary for your well-being.

As our world becomes more and more populated, the number of people that you will encounter in your immediate environment will increase. Your behavior will become more and more controlled by the presence and behavior of other people. Your social space will become increasingly crowded. As greater numbers of people share the limited physical space that is available to us, each individual's personal share diminishes.

Territories

Many animals, including humans, seem to have **territories**—geographical areas in which they live and which they defend against the intrusion of strangers. In many species of birds the males claim an area surrounding the nest and attack members of their species that intrude into this territory. Dogs and cats have territories with specific boundaries.

Some territories are **fixed,** having a definite geographical location, and some are **portable,** moving with the animal.[1] Your front yard may define your dog's fixed territory, and it will attack any other dogs that attempt to enter. In addition, your dog has a portable territory—a space that surrounds its body. A strange dog intruding into this portable territory will also be attacked.

Some social scientists have claimed that people, too, have fixed and portable territories that they defend against intrusion. On a small scale your home can be seen as a fixed territory that you defend. More and more people are building fences around their homes, apparently to defend their territory.[2] There is also a zone around your body—a portable territory—that you prevent strang-

ers from entering. If someone comes too close, you move away. Sometimes the boundaries of these territories are clearly marked and sometimes they are ambiguous.

Wolf Territory

The territory defended by a family of wolves in Canada may include more than a hundred square miles. A biologist who was sent to study the behavior of wolves in the wild had to camp within the territory of a particular wolf family, close enough to their den to observe their habits.[3] He found that once a week the family made the rounds of their territory boundaries, marking them with urine. (You have seen dogs making their rounds in the neighborhood, similarly marking their territory with urine on trees and fences.) The biologist studying the Canadian wolves decided to claim his own territory and to mark its boundary with his urine as the wolves did. He wrote:

Wolves are territorial.

One evening, after they had gone off for their regular nightly hunt, I staked out a property claim of my own, embracing perhaps three acres, with the tent at the middle, and including a hundred-yard long section of the wolves' path.

Staking the land turned out to be rather more difficult than I had anticipated. In order to ensure that my claim would not be overlooked, I felt obliged to make a property mark on stones, clumps of moss, and patches of vegetation at intervals of not more than fifteen feet around the circumference of my claim. This took most of the night and required frequent returns to the tent to consume copious quantities of tea; but before dawn brought the hunters home the task was done, and I retired, somewhat exhausted, to observe results.

I had not long to wait. At 0814 hours, according to my wolf log, the leading male of the clan appeared over the ridge behind me, padding homeward with his usual air of preoccupation. As usual he did not deign to glance at the tent; but when he reached the point where my property line intersected the trail, he stopped as abruptly as if he had run into an invisible wall. . . . His attitude of fatigue vanished and was replaced by a look of bewilderment.[3]

The wolves would not cross the newly marked boundary line, but they proceeded to place their own markings around the edges of the biologist's territory.

Your Territory

You have a portable territory, a zone around your body called your **personal space.** Your personal space is like an imaginary bubble surrounding you that keeps you at a distance from others. You can locate the boundary of your personal space

Maintaining interpersonal distance.

by asking someone to stand still, then walking closer and closer until you begin to feel uncomfortable. Imagine yourself walking up to someone and standing only one foot away; you would feel distinctly uneasy and would have a strong desire to back off. This is because the other person has violated your personal space.

It is also possible for you to stand too far away. Imagine yourself walking up to someone in order to talk and stopping about fifteen feet away. Interacting at that distance just would not feel comfortable. Thus, it is possible to be either too close or too far away from someone else. There is an intermediate distance that is most comfortable; this optimal distance is called the **optimal interpersonal distance.** The optimal interpersonal distance is the distance that two people typically maintain between themselves; it is the distance that violates neither person's personal space yet is also close enough for comfort.

How is the optimal interpersonal distance maintained? You can test this by the following methods. The next time you are talking with someone, take a step forward and observe what happens; later take a step backward and notice the consequences. When you step forward, the other person will probably step back in order to regain the best interpersonal distance; when you step back, the other person will probably step forward. People are motivated to maintain a comfortable interpersonal distance.

■ *In Elevators* A convenient place for observing the effect of interpersonal distance on human behavior is in an elevator. You will observe that people tend to space themselves in the limited area available so as to maximize interpersonal distance. Two people in an elevator often will stand in opposite corners; four people usually arrange themselves near each of the four corners; with five people, one person has to stand in the middle. As people enter or leave the elevator, those remaining re-arrange themselves so as to keep as far apart as possible.

Because people in an elevator are already too close for comfort (they have violated each other's personal space), rituals are developed for reducing the effect of the intrusion. One of these rituals concerns rules for looking: you can look at your shoes, you can look at the lights indicating the floors, you can look at the elevator door, or you can look at your fingernails, but you cannot look at the other people in the elevator. If eye contact occurs between you and another person in an elevator, you quickly look away, pretending that it was an accident.

■ *In Different Cultures* The interpersonal distance that is most comfortable differs among cultures. For example, the English maintain a greater distance between themselves than do the French; because of this, the English may consider the French

Interpersonal distance varies among cultures.

intrusive; the French may consider the English unfriendly.

Laying claim to a territory and maintaining a certain distance from one's fellows are probably as real biological needs in man as they are in animals, but their expressions are culturally conditioned. The proper distance between persons in a group varies from culture to culture. People reared in cultures where the proper distance is short appear "pushy" to those coming from social groups where propriety demands greater physical separation. In contrast, the latter will appear to the former as behaving in a cold, aloof, withdrawn, and standoffish manner.[4]

Ⓢ Territories are geographical areas that are defended against invasion. Fixed territories have definite locations while portable territories move with the individual. You have a kind of portable territory surrounding you which is called your personal space. The optimal interpersonal distance is the physical distance between two people at which they feel most comfortable; this distance varies among different cultures.

Social Isolation

As our world becomes more crowded, concerns about privacy multiply. We experience increasing invasion of our privacy by others. We often feel surrounded. It is becoming harder to get away and be alone.

Being Alone

The term **social isolation** refers to being alone, without human companionship. Sometimes we seek isolation and sometimes it is imposed on us. One response to the need for privacy is the construction of buildings and fences to create a degree of social isolation. Sometimes we withdraw from society in order to prevent invasions of privacy. But there are consequences of withdrawal; the sense of being alone in a crowd or isolated in the big city is more and more common.

Solitary confinement is enforced social isolation. The fact that solitary confinement is effectively used as punishment demonstrates the significance that human companionship has for us. We need other people; without them we feel punished.

Effects of Isolation

Because we are "social animals," we seek companionship. What happens when a person is alone for a prolonged period of time? To study this problem, researchers experimented with monkeys. They found that monkeys raised in social isolation become psychologically abnormal. Compared to their group-raised peers, the socially deprived monkeys do not play and explore their environments; they do not develop normal grooming habits; they do not form social relationships with other monkeys when they have the opportunity; and they do not mate.[5]

Studies of humans who have been socially isolated report similar results. There have been a few extreme cases of social isolation reported where an infant has been abandoned by its parents and left in the wilderness. There have also been reports of older children who have supposedly wandered into the wilderness and survived without any human assistance. These individuals have been called **feral children.** Similar to these stories are reports of children who were isolated and confined to small rooms or closets by their parents until found by authorities. In these well-documented cases, the children showed poor psychological growth and abnormal human functioning. Studies of these cases have shown that lack of sufficient social stimulation from other people may interfere with normal intellectual growth.

Isolated Groups

Small groups, isolated from other people in remote Antarctic stations, or confined together in prisons or on long sea voyages, report that boredom, apathy, and irritation are common results of the experience.[6,7] Socially isolated groups cannot solve their problems by escaping from each other or by changing from one group to another; they must stay together and live with the tensions that arise. One result is that members of such groups tend to keep a tight lid on their emotions, and they tend to develop more rigid rules for relating. One experimental study of socially isolated pairs of men found that during isolation signs of stress, emotional symptoms, and interpersonal conflicts increased, and task performance decreased.[8]

Reality Check

Studies of people who have been in extreme social isolation show us how much we need each other. When deprived of human companionship for long periods of time, people may suffer severe psychological problems. Other people not only help keep us from feeling lonely, but they provide important feedback for us.

You respond to me, most often by providing feedback that validates my observations, thoughts, and feelings. Sometimes, though, I make a mistake, and you correct me. Your feedback tells me whether or not you see and hear more or less what I see and hear. When you are with me, you serve as a **reality check** for my observations and thoughts. You check what I do and say, correcting my mistakes and misapprehensions; I, in turn, correct yours.

But if I am alone, then I have no "reality check" and it is easier for me to develop grossly mistaken ideas about reality. When I am alone at night and hear a rustling noise outside the window, I may become convinced that there are intruders snooping about the house. If you were with me, you could tell me that the noise came from the trees moving in the wind. It's easy to develop fears based on false ideas when you are alone, without feedback from others. Sometimes persons who suffer from **delusions**—false ideas about reality—have a history of relative social isolation that has prevented them from receiving the normal corrective feedback from others that most of us receive.

S Social isolation refers to being alone, without human companionship. Sometimes social isolation is sought and sometimes it is imposed. It may be sought to fulfill our growing need for privacy in this crowded world. The effects of isolation can be extreme, as in the cases of abandoned children. Studies have shown that we need each other to serve as a "reality check" for our thoughts.

Crowding

The population of the world is growing at an alarming rate. By 1850 there were about one billion people on earth; 80 years later, in 1930, the population had doubled to two billion. At the present rate of increase, the world's population will double about every 37 years. If this rate of increase were to continue for the next 900 years, there would be one hundred persons for every square yard of the earth's surface, land or sea.[9] The problem of crowding in the modern world has not approached that degree of severity, but in certain parts of the world today crowding is a serious problem.

What does it mean to be crowded? Crowding can limit your freedom of choice: when the number of people you are in contact with is so great that you are unable to do things you would like to do, then you are experiencing crowding.[10] A few annoying and intrusive people may make you feel more crowded than a greater number of close friends. However, for the purposes of studying the psychological effects of crowding, **crowding** is defined simply in terms of an excessive number of people around you.

In cities there are two ways to think about crowding: (1) a high density of persons in a neighborhood and (2) a high density of persons in a dwelling.[11] Although an urban ghetto is crowded by either definition, small rural farm dwellings are crowded on the inside while neighborhoods full of luxury apartments are only crowded on the outside—that is, in terms of the density of population in the neighborhood. In either case, the psychological effects of crowding come from human interaction and the consequences of that interaction on behavior and experience.

Crowding and Arousal

As the world becomes more crowded, you encounter more people. You have learned to attend to people: they are your major sources of pleasure and pain. Encounters with people are personally meaningful and are a powerful source of stimulation.

Every encounter you have with another person tends to increase your level of arousal.[12] Your **arousal level** is your degree of activation. At low levels of arousal you feel drowsy; at very high levels of arousal you feel overstimulated and anxious.

The brain mechanisms involved in this arousal process become highly active under crowded conditions.[13] In animals these parts of the brain show abnormalities as a consequence of high population density.[14] Animals or humans exposed to high arousal levels for extended periods of time show physical and emotional signs of severe stress. You might expect persons living in crowded conditions to attempt to cope with crowding by reducing their arousal level. Alcohol and barbiturates reduce arousal; their use may be one way that people cope with the excessive stimulation and crowding so common in our cities.

Amphetamines excite the brain, increasing arousal levels. If crowding has its psychological effect through increasing arousal, amphetamines plus crowding should have a double effect. The combination of amphetamines and crowding has been studied with animals. The dosage of amphetamine required to produce death from overstimulation in mice is lower for crowded mice; the more the mice are crowded, the less the dosage of amphetamine needed to produce death.[15] Even mild stimulants like caffeine (found in coffee) can overstimulate crowded mice and produce death.[15]

Crowding and Health

Crowding increases arousal level, sometimes to the point of stress. Prolonged stress from overstimulation creates physiological changes in the brain and the body, particularly in the glands in the endocrine system. The endocrine glands (pituitary, adrenal, and thyroid) help regulate metabolism, growth, and sexual development. In animal populations that are crowded over an extended period of time, growth is stunted and the death rate increases. There is some evidence that the rate of heart attack in animals is increased as a result of crowding.[4] These deaths are believed to result from the stress resulting from unavoidable and excessive social interactions.

In any social system individuals develop different amounts of power and status. In a crowded social system individuals high on the social hierarchy have more social space (luxury apartment versus crowded tenement) and are less threatened by social interaction because they have power. In animal populations that are crowded, it is the low-ranking individuals who tend to die off; they are much more affected by the stresses of crowding than are high-ranking individuals.[16]

Crowding stresses have harmful effects on human health and social organization. There is reason to believe that some of the unfortunate effects of concentration camps on human health may have resulted from the crowded conditions that prevailed.

There is indirect evidence that inmates of concentration camps experienced acute forms of the stress syndrome that may have accounted for many deaths. Concentration camps are more appropriately compared with highly congested animal populations than are city slums, since even in very crowded cities, *the poor do have some mobility. They can escape from their immediate congestion on streets and associate with other segments of the population. The incidence of street gangs and juvenile delinquency is especially characteristic of overcrowded city areas and constitutes a form of social pathology. Several studies have also indicated a higher incidence of schizophrenia and other psychotic and neurotic behavior in congested urban areas than in more spacious environments, but other factors may be involved here.*[17]

In general, the rate of mental disturbance is higher in crowded areas and lower in more sparsely populated areas.[11] There is a decreasing incidence of diagnosed psychosis as you move from the center of a city outward to the suburbs. There is a similar relation between crowding and the rate of suicide, the rate being higher in more densely populated areas. Crowding stresses in the inner city may be responsible for the increase in psychological problems that are observed. There is considerable evidence that some forms of schizophrenia resemble reactions to excessively high arousal; there is some similarity between schizophrenics and normal individuals under excessive stimulation.[18]

Of course, just because the rate of psychosis is high where crowding is intense does not necessarily mean that crowding causes psychosis. It is possible that both crowding and psychosis result from the same social problems and that neither causes the other. For example, the likelihood of both crowding and psychosis may be increased by inadequate economic opportunity. It is also possible that people less prone to develop psychosis move away from the central city. Additionally, people in the suburbs may be less likely to be labeled psychotic—regardless of their mental condition—than people in the central city.

The Rat Sink

Crowding occurs when the population increases and the living space does not. The effects of crowding have been difficult to study because human population density cannot be manipulated for the purpose of scientific investigation; but animal populations can and have been controlled for this purpose.

In a series of important experiments, John Calhoun[19,20,21] created an experimental rat universe—an enclosed and separate world for rats, with abundant food, water, and nesting material. The idea was to create an originally ideal environment for rats, and then study their behavior as the rat population increased.

Calhoun soon found that as crowded conditions developed, the stress accompanying unavoidable social interaction caused severe behavioral problems. Calhoun describes his first rat universe:

Dr. John B. Calhoun studying the effects of overcrowding on mice.

I confined a population of wild Norway rats in a quarter-acre enclosure. With an abundance of food and places to live and with predation and disease eliminated or minimized, only the animals' behavior with respect to one another remained as a factor that might affect the increase in their number. There could be no escape from the behavioral consequences of rising population density. By the end of 27 months the population had become stabilized at 150 adults. Yet adult mortality was so low that 5,000 adults might have been expected from the observed reproductive rate. The reason this larger population did not materialize was that infant mortality was extremely high. Even with only 150 adults in the enclosure, stress from social interaction led to such disruption of maternal behavior that few young survived.[20]

■ *Crowding and Cannibalism* Calhoun next observed rats under controlled indoor conditions. They were confined to rooms provided with everything needed to maintain life and were studied as their population density increased. Calhoun found that crowded conditions caused rats to behave strangely. Females became progressively poorer at maternal functions such as nest-building and caring for the young; eventually females stopped building nests altogether. Crowded females began to abandon their litters and to allow the young to starve to death. Cannibalism became increasingly common. Courtship and mating became rare. Some males seemed to go berserk, attacking females viciously and biting juvenile and infant rats. Other males became very passive and withdrawn, ignoring other rats of both sexes and not participating at all in the social structure of the rat colony. A third type of crowded male became hyperactive and hypersexual, but did not seem to be able to tell the difference between male and female partners. As crowding increasingly disrupted their normal social behavior, the rat population stopped growing and even began to decline. Thus, rat populations seem to have a built-in population control that prevents them from becoming permanently crowded and overpopulated.

■ *Togetherness* A peculiar condition developed within the crowded rat universes that Calhoun called the "rat sink."[19] Although food was continuously available to the rats, they would eat only at certain times—when other rats were also eating—so that the feeding area became extremely crowded at certain periods of the day. Eating became a social habit; rats would eat only in the presence of other rats. Furthermore, only certain of the several feeding stations were used. Calhoun concluded that, as crowding increased, it became more likely that other rats would be present during eating. The accidental presence of other rats during eating had a conditioning effect. Eating food became associated with the presence of other rats. Because of this association, the presence of other rats eventually became rewarding or reinforcing, and then rats began to seek the company of others. This created an extremely crowded area within the rat colony that Calhoun referred to as the **rat sink.** In colonies in which rat sinks developed, the disruptive effects of crowding were particularly severe.

Although humans have a lot of space in which to live in this world, we tend to congregate in extremely crowded cities, cities in which the effects of crowding seem to be particularly severe. The presence of other people, because of past associations, apparently has become rewarding and we pursue those rewards. The problems of our cities resemble the problems of the rat sink.

Coping with Crowding

When an animal's personal space is invaded, it may either attack the intruder (fight) or withdraw so as to preserve interpersonal distance (flight). This response to crowding is called the **fight-or-flight reaction.** Either strategy has the effect of reducing the experience of crowding by lowering the level of social stimulation. People also tend to react to crowding with either an aggressive or withdrawal response. People have a fight-or-flight reaction.

■ *Fight* An effective means of blocking intrusions into your social space is to become more aggressive and fight back. Evidence shows that aggressive reactions increase under crowded conditions. One study related the average number of persons per room to various behavior patterns observed among occupants. It was found that arousal levels, withdrawal reactions, and eruptions of violence all increased as crowding increased.[22] An experimental study of the effects of crowding varied the number of young children in a room and observed their aggressive tendencies and their social interactions.[23] As the number of children in the room was increased from six to twelve, individuals tended to become more aggressive (fighting, snatching toys) and more withdrawn from social interactions. These results are consistent with the point of view that crowding increases arousal and that two strategies for coping with crowding stress are "fight" and "flight," both of which tend to keep people away.

■ *Flight* There seem to be signs of increasing withdrawal ("flight") in our society, some of which may be a consequence of our increasingly crowded landscape. An American visitor to England was told, "Forgive us our seemingly cold indifference. This is a small and crowded island. We can exist only by ignoring each other."[2]

Studies of the relationship of organizational size to behavior show that as size increases, absence rates and lateness increase and worker morale decreases.[24] Apparently one reaction to being a member of a large group or company is to withdraw. A study of 218 high schools showed that there is a relationship between population density and withdrawal from participation in school activities; the larger the school, the fewer activities an individual student was likely to become involved in.[25] The excessive use of drugs in our society may also be a type of withdrawal or "flight."

Our cities, organizations, and schools are increasing in size each year. There are probably optimal sizes for our groups, in terms not only of productivity but also of human health and happiness. These optimal sizes have been surpassed, but a recognition of the effect of crowding on human behavior may help reverse the trend toward bigness.

⑤ One effect of crowding is arousal. Crowded conditions activate arousal systems in the brain. Constant arousal causes psychological stress which can cause physical problems. "Fight or flight" are two strategies for coping with stress by keeping people away.

Summary

KEY QUESTIONS

1. What is your personal space and what happens when it is violated?
   You have an imaginary bubble surrounding your body, an area that you try to keep free from intruders. This area is your personal space. When somebody comes too close to you, you back off in order to keep your space from being violated. The interpersonal distance that is comfortable for you may not be comfortable for people from other cultures.

2. What is the effect of social isolation?
   We need other people—we are "social animals." Individuals and small groups that have been socially isolated for prolonged periods show signs of stress and may not function normally. Other people provide important feedback for us, and without it we may develop false ideas about ourselves or about the world.

3. What is the effect of crowding?

Crowding produces excessively high arousal levels; if crowding is prolonged, physical and psychological harm may result. The severe stress resulting from crowding creates physiological changes in the brain and body, particularly in the endocrine system. There is also evidence that crowding is associated with higher levels of mental disturbance and aggression.

KEY CONCEPTS

territory	Geographical area that a person or animal lives in and defends against invasions.
fixed territory	A territory having a definite geographical location.
portable territory	A territory having no definite location but which moves with the individual.
personal space	The immediate area surrounding the body that a person defends from invasion; the person's portable territory.
optimal interpersonal distance	The physical distance between two people at which they feel most comfortable; close enough for comfort, but far enough away so that personal spaces are not violated.
social isolation	The state of being alone, without human companionship.
solitary confinement	Enforced social isolation used for punishment.
feral children	Refers to cases of children who were abandoned by their parents and who survived in the wilderness without human company; reports of such children have not been absolutely substantiated.
reality check	Feedback about reality provided by other people.
delusion	A false idea about reality.
crowding	An excessive number of people.
arousal level	Level of activation or stimulation.
rat sink	In a rat colony, an extremely crowded area resulting from the social reinforcement provided by other animals.
fight-or-flight reaction	The tendency to attack or withdraw from an intruder when personal space has been violated.

27 Sensory Pollution

CHAPTER OUTLINE

KEY QUESTIONS

1. What is an optimal level of stimulation?
2. What is sensory deprivation and how can it affect you?
3. What is sensory overload and how can it affect you?

The environment is full of the wastes created by people. The water we drink and the air we breathe frequently contain harmful chemical pollutants. Pollution is an unwanted consequence of human action on our environment.

The Los Angeles smog attacks rubber and makes it brittle. Nylon stockings have been known to pop and run during warm humid days in Richmond, Virginia, in Jacksonville, Florida, and in many other places, apparently as a result of high concentrations of sulfur oxides in the air. Damage to growing plants is reported everywhere, and there are lawsuits for livestock poisoning, especially by fluorides in the air.[1]

There have been several smog disasters in the past twenty years, resulting in the deaths of thousands of persons, and we must expect more in the future.[1] In a 1970 survey, 70 percent of the respondents in certain large cities reported that air pollution was a problem around their homes.[2] Noise pollution, too, is becoming more and more of a national problem.

It is unlikely that the pollution of the air, water, and sensory environments will kill us all; we can learn to survive in almost any environment because of our adaptability. We can adjust to almost anything. But there is a cost of adjusting to a polluted world. As one author wrote:

I am sure that we can adapt to the dirt, pollution and noise of New York City or Chicago. That is the real tragedy—we can adapt to it. As we become adapted we accept worse and worse conditions without realizing that a child born and raised in this environment has no chance of developing his total physical and mental potential. It is essential that we commit ourselves to such problems as a society and as a nation, not because we are threatened with extinction, but because, if we do not understand what the environment is doing to us, something worse than extinction will take place—a progressive degradation of the quality of human life.[3]

What do you think: Is there something worse than extinction?

Sensory Pollution in the Ecosystem

Human beings act on the environment and the environment in turn acts on them. One of the ways that the environment "talks back" to people is through the chemical pollutants in the air and water around us; another way is through the pollution of the sensory world—the visual and auditory environment in which we live. When meadows are transformed into asphalt-covered parking lots, the visual environment has been changed; when sonic booms from jet aircraft replace bird songs, the auditory environment has been changed. Since these sensory changes are undesirable side effects of our technological intervention in the environment, they are termed **sensory pollution.**

Sensation and Information

The effect of sensory pollution is worsening each year. More and more of the natural world is being paved over and the noise level in the cities is rising to a painful roar.

Normally, sensation brings information from the world, information that is vital to human survival and comfort. Thunder, for example, tells us that rain may be coming. The new artificial world, however, is often empty of information, a monotonous world protected by heating and air conditioning from the changes of the seasons. On the other hand, the constructed world can also be quite the opposite: a chaos of sounds and images carrying signals at an ever-increasing pace. At this pace, the excess of information cannot be responded to and so it becomes valueless.

Human beings have challenged nature and may have won. But the winning brings with it consequences that were unplanned: pollution in the ecosystem, an artificial world of overstimulation or understimulation that may alter the quality of human life.

Optimal Level of Stimulation

Imagine that you are blind and deaf. No information from sights or sounds would be available to you. How would you feel? Imagine that you are on a busy freeway at rush hour driving very fast. A jet aircraft passes overhead and a loud ambulance siren is close by. Your senses are bombarded with stimulation. How would you feel?

Some psychologists believe that people

need an intermediate level of stimulation, not too much and not too little, and that we avoid both extremes if we can. According to one scientist, we have a drive or strong motivation to maintain an **optimal level of stimulation**[4,5]—an amount of stimulation that is best for human functioning. When the environment is not stimulating enough, we begin to explore, to investigate, or to manipulate it in order to increase the variation of stimulation reaching our brains.

Some psychologists propose that a mechanism at the base of the brain, the **ascending reticular activating system (ARAS),** controls the amount of information reaching the brain.[6] Both very high and very low levels of stimulation fail to activate the ARAS sufficiently and so these extremes are not dealt with as well as moderate levels of stimulation. Performance suffers when an organism is underactivated and also when it is overactivated. When the amount of stimulation and information becomes too high or too low, an individual begins to function poorly and to show signs of stress.[7]

Preference is also affected by the level of stimulation. In a variety of studies, people have been offered the choice of looking at pictures of low, intermediate, or high complexity. Pictures of intermediate complexity are experienced as more pleasant than those of low or high complexity.[8,9] Apparently, pictures of intermediate complexity provide a preferred level of stimulation.

⬚ The term "sensory pollution" refers to undesirable sensory side effects of the changes we have brought about in our environment. These side effects are mainly experienced as increases or decreases in the typical level of stimulation; we tend to live more and more in a monotonous world of understimulation or a chaotic world of overstimulation. But we prefer and function best at an intermediate level of stimulation, which for us is optimal.

Sensory Deprivation

The constructed world is at times monotonous and dull, the variation of nature having been shut out or carefully controlled. In such places people are deprived of normal stimulation from the environment. The extreme reduction of stimulation is called **sensory deprivation.** Super highways and hospitals have been identified as two environments offering little stimulus change; people in these environments may experience sensory deprivation.[10]

Sensory Deprivation in the Hospital: A Case Study

Have you ever been confined to bed for several days? The experience is notably unpleasant. You feel bored and irritable and may feel disoriented and weak.

Psychologists studied hospital patients confined to bed for long periods of time and found a number of them who developed unusual symptoms of anxiety, delusions, and hallucinations. These symptoms vanished when the patients were allowed to experience a varied sensory environment.[10] One woman was in the hospital waiting for an operation on her eyes. Before she was hospitalized, she behaved quite normally, but then she began acting strangely.

She was one of five patients remaining on a ward that had been largely evacuated for redecorating. The patient's bed was some distance from the other remaining patients, and was surrounded by screens. Both of her eyes were covered with bandages. She was noted to be quite restless, her hands and face in constant movement. Her thought processes were confused and rambling. Her voice was whiney and childish. She complained that her medication was poisoned, and that she was

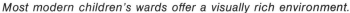

Most modern children's wards offer a visually rich environment.

being smothered. She told of seeing a "funny little man" like a cartoon, and said she was unable to tell whether she had been dreaming or awake at the time.

The patient was operated on the following day, after which only one eye was bandaged and she was brought into closer contact with other patients and staff. The psychotic aspects cleared almost at once and the patient was discharged a week after surgery, free from mental abnormality.[11]

The woman apparently suffered from sensory deprivation; she was not receiving adequate stimulation, and her bizarre symptoms were consequences of that fact. When she could see again and was placed in closer contact with other patients, her sensory environment became more complex and the symptoms disappeared.

Children in certain hospital nurseries suffer from sensory deprivation also. In one study, patterned sheets and a movable toy were added to the otherwise monotonous white environment of the nursery for some infants. Those children with the added visual stimulation showed faster development of certain motor skills.[12] Children in an orphanage with white walls and reduced light level were also found to suffer from sensory deprivation; many of them could not walk by the age of four, although they were not physically confined in any way.[13] Adequate stimulation is apparently necessary for normal development.

Bored Monkeys and Rats

Monkeys and rats also prefer a varied sensory environment. In one study, a monkey was confined to an enclosed box, with a small window that could be opened by the animal. The monkey quickly learned to open

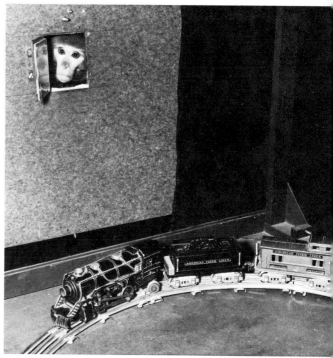

A curious monkey.

the window in order to look outside. The experimenter then rigged the window so that it would open only after many separate attempts to open it; still the monkey was willing to work hard for a peek outside.[14] Apparently the opportunity to look outside was rewarding.

Other studies with monkeys show that stimulation is not only rewarding to animals—it is necessary. One experimenter deprived chimpanzees of all visual stimulation from birth on. Later examination revealed that the optic nerve fibers leading from the eyes to the brain shriveled and became useless. Some stimulation is necessary for the continued functioning of nerves and cells in the sensory system.

Given a choice, rats demonstrate a preference for more complex environments rather than environments with little sensory variation.[15] Rats growing up in less complex environments show poorer abilities at solving problems,[16] which suggests that an environment lacking sensory stimulation may reduce thinking capacity. Rats growing up in less complex environments have also been shown to have smaller (lighter) brains than rats growing up in more stimulating environments.[17] What is a stimulating environment for a rat? In the above study the rats were provided with little toys, such as ladders, wheels, boxes, and platforms; in addition they were allowed to explore a larger cage with novel patterns of barriers on the floor each day.

The Understimulated Mind

"Bored to tears," "bored to death," "bored out of your mind"—how do you react to boredom? How do you feel when your world is very dull? Without normal environmental stimulation, you may tend to feel that your mind is slow, confused, or "fuzzy."

■ *Stimulation and Thought* Without continual stimulation, thinking is more difficult. Laboratory experiments have shown that sensory deprivation interferes with human thought. College students volunteered as subjects in most of these experiments and were shut off from most stimulation for periods of hours or days. A common procedure used to isolate subjects from environmental stimulation was to place them in a dark quiet room on a soft bed; earplugs and blackened goggles were worn to further block sounds and light.

In one experiment subjects were tested before isolation, after two, twenty-four, and forty-eight hours of isolation, and then on the two days following isolation.[18] The battery of tests consisted of problems in simple arithmetic, number series, and anagrams. The subjects who experienced sensory deprivation showed poor performance on all tests, as compared to another group of students who took the same tests without sensory deprivation. Tasks involving logical reasoning seem to be particularly affected by an environment that is not stimulating.[19] Other studies show that memory,[20] attention,[21] and concentration[22,23] are all poorer for persons experiencing inadequate stimulation.

■ *Stimulation and Anxiety* A lack of sufficient stimulation from the environment not only is boring and mind-dulling, it also is stressful. The subjects in sensory-deprivation experiments commonly express feelings of fear, anxiety, and even panic as the period of isolation continues.[24]

In one study ten subjects were isolated in small individual cubicles where each sat in silence and darkness for two hours.[25] For some time after leaving the sensory deprivation condition, the subjects' speech was slurred, their facial expressions were bizarre, they appeared confused and disorganized, and they expressed various fears and anxieties. In another experiment twenty subjects were isolated in sensory deprivation for as long as each subject could stand it.[26] The average length of time that they were willing to endure sensory deprivation was 29 hours for men and 49 hours for women. One subject became severely depressed and began crying. Many others experienced panic attacks. The experimenters reported:

At first most volunteers show a tendency to sleep, some for an unduly long time. Then follows a period of growing agitation, tension, and restlessness. Disturbed thinking, particularly obsessional, occurs about this stage; and most subjects experience panic which makes them leave the room. But some of our volunteers, even when perspiring profusely, with trembling limbs, dry mouth, and [rapid heart beat], still cling to the conventional dislike of "anything psychological" and maintained that their reason for giving up had been backache, headache, or some other "socially approved" symptom.[26]

■ *Stimulation and Hallucinations* In a dim twilight world shadows play tricks on the mind. With a prolonged lack of environmental stimulation, both illusions and hallucinations may develop. **Illusions** are distortions of reality. One person reported (after six days of sensory deprivation), "the wall bulged toward me and then went back . . . the whole room is undulating, swirling."[27] **Hallucinations** are perceptual experiences of things that are not there. Hallucinations are a common experience arising from lengthy sensory deprivation experiments. Sometimes these hallucinations resemble those induced by certain drugs, such as LSD and mescaline.

In one study each of eight subjects was required to lie on a bed in a quiet room for eight hours; the subjects wore goggles with a frosted glass so that light was admitted but no forms could be discriminated.[28] In addition they wore cotton gloves to reduce stimulation of the hands. Several of these subjects reported hearing music, buzz saws, voices, or the chirping of birds. Several visual hallucinations were also reported, including the following:

The herd of elephants. Oh, that was pretty. That came very spontaneously. It was just sort of elephants in black, with pink and blue and purple. . . . They were moving.[28]

When there is little to see in the world, it seems that the mind makes up things to see.

⑤ When you are deprived of adequate sensory experience (sensory deprivation), you are not only bored, but your mind does not work normally. You may feel fuzzy-minded and anxious or experience illusions or hallucinations. Experiments have shown that sensory deprivation makes thinking more difficult and also can cause anxiety and fear.

Sensory Overload

The opposite of sensory deprivation—sensory overload—also disturbs the functions of the mind.

If you stand on a crowded downtown street-corner at five o'clock in the evening, you receive a lot of sensory information. There is a chaos of intense sounds and images, more than you could possibly respond to. Although we have created wastelands with little stimulation in certain parts of the artificial world, we have also created an excess of stimulation in other parts. Our technology has made possible the development of multicolored flashing lights, pictures of all sorts, and noises and sounds of greater and greater intensity. We manufacture our own stimulation. **Sensory overload** is an excess of stimulation, far greater than the optimal level of stimulation. What is the effect of sensory overload from the environment?

Effects of Overload

According to one scientist our society suffers from an excess of stimulation, and as a consequence, "Overstimulated and bewildered parents bring up overstimulated and bewildered offspring unable to cope with overstimulation."[29]

Bombarded with rapidly changing sights and sounds from the environment, individuals may be confused by the abundance of choices for responding; this creates a kind of conflict, which may result in stress. Studies have shown that as information multiplies and mental load increases, a variety of emotional and bodily changes occur: the rate of blinking decreases[30] and blood pressure increases.[31]

One important study compared the effects of eight hours of sensory deprivation with the effects of eight hours of sensory overload.[32] The sensory deprivation consisted of silence and darkness and the sensory overload was provided by strobe lights going off at random intervals, two tape recorders playing simultaneously, a filmstrip projector showing random scenes, and two slide projectors. The results showed that both overload and deprivation increased hostility and certain physiological measures of stress and anxiety. In addition the sensory overload condition increased both the heart rate and the breathing rate.

Another investigator created an overload condition by requiring subjects to work at an unnaturally rapid pace on certain psychological tests.[33] Subjects in the overload condition performed more poorly than subjects who worked at a normal speed; moreover the type of errors they made resembled the type of errors made by patients that were mentally disturbed. An experiment using a short exposure to sensory overload (twenty minutes) showed essentially no effects of overload.[34] These studies confirm that prolonged exposure to sensory overload has similar effects to prolonged exposure to sensory deprivation: overload disturbs thought processes and creates anxiety and stress.

Noise Pollution

Listen to the noises of modern civilization: the jet airplane overhead, an ambulance siren, a jackhammer, the screech of chalk on a blackboard, a gum-chewing neighbor, amplified rock music, a motorcycle speeding by. Noise, especially in cities, is reaching such an intensity that scientists and politicians talk about **noise pollution** in our environment. Noise pollution is an excess of unwanted noise and is a special case of sensory overload.

■ *The Sonic Environment* We live in a world of sounds, a **sonic environment.** Some of these sounds are wanted; they communicate important information, they are related to your activities, and they are under your control. Some are not, and they are often called *noise.* They are the undesired residue of people living closely together in a machine age; they are the pollutants of the sonic environment.

Noise is annoying. Loud sounds, high-pitched sounds, discordant sounds, unpredictable or uncontrollable sounds, and sounds associated with danger, pain, or fear— these sounds are particularly bothersome. The intensity of noise increases each year because we invent larger and more powerful machines while we live closer and closer together. A recent survey of residents of Detroit and Los Angeles revealed that about 25 percent of the women and about 33 percent of the men were regularly annoyed by noise at home or at work.[35] Residents near airports or under paths of supersonic flights are often particularly annoyed by noise; their houses rattle, their sleep is interrupted, and their attempts to communicate with other people are often blocked.[36]

Citizens are responding to the threat of noise pollution. Besides regulating the maximum amount of noise that vehicles can make many local and state laws require noise mufflers.[37] New York City has prohibited construction in Manhattan between 6 P.M. and 7 A.M. and placed strict limitations on noise from air compressors, air conditioners, motor vehicles, sirens, and auto horns.[38] Property owners near airports suffer a loss in the value of their houses as the noise level increases; a group of Los Angeles property owners sued the city because of the airport noise and were awarded $740,000 as compensation for their losses.[39] Millions of dollars worth of court actions over noise are still pending. The federal government will probably take some action on noise pollution in the near future.

■ *The Effects of Noise*   Noise does more than annoy; it causes stress reactions, it interferes with memory and attention, and it can damage the ear itself. Persons briefly exposed to loud noise suffer a temporary reduction in the ability to hear; if the noise exposure is prolonged, permanent damage to the ear and permanent loss of hearing can result. Airport workers exposed to the loud noise of jet aircraft become increasingly deaf over the years.[36] Performers of rock music and their audience suffer hearing losses.[36] The loss of hearing can be regarded as a kind of adaptation to the noise:

Noise is another aspect of environmental pollution that certain human beings come to tolerate, but at great cost. People adapt to continuous exposure to loud and painful noise by shutting out the objectionable sounds from perception. This, however, does not prevent destructive anatomical effects from taking place. There may be an impairment of hearing—a permanent inability to hear certain frequencies. The cost of adaptation to noise is therefore a loss in the enjoyment of music and of the more subtle qualities of the human voice.[40]

The evidence for the effects of noise on thinking is unclear. Some studies find that noise interferes with memory,[41] and others find that it has little effect.[42] Noise does seem to interfere with attention and concentration.[43] Whereas unpredictable loud noises

How does noise affect you?

probably interrupt thinking briefly, most tasks do not suffer from brief time-outs from thinking; most tasks therefore are not interfered with by noise. The more complex the task, the more likely that it would be interfered with by loud noise.

Noise causes stress reactions. When a sudden noise strikes your ear, your heart starts beating more rapidly, your blood pressure increases, your muscles are tensed, your skin turns pale due to constricting blood vessels, your pupils get larger, and you experience other stress reactions.[36,44] Persons who are exposed to loud noises experience frequent stress reactions. A variety of other physical and psychological problems soon follows. Prolonged exposure to noise has been linked with chronic fatigue;[45] headaches;[46] physical illnesses;[36] and irritability, frustration, and emotional upsets.[47,48] People living near noisy airports have a significantly higher rate of admission to mental hospitals than people living in quieter residential areas.[49] Since our whole society is becoming noisier, these problems will probably increase.

Coping with Sensory Overload

What can you do about sensory overload? If you decide that you do not want to surrender passively to the superstimulation of your environment and the physical and psychological stresses that it causes, what action can you take? Chances are you have already developed adaptive strategies for dealing with overload, but you may not recognize them. Some of the strategies used to cope with sensory overload are *queuing, filtering, simplifying, escaping,* and *reforming.*[50,51]

■ *Queuing* The word *queuing* means placing in a line. **Queuing** is one strategy for coping with sensory overload by delaying the responses to the many environmental demands so that they can be dealt with one at a time. In other words, when you get overloaded, you put things off. During the frenzy of exams you may postpone social interactions, then resume them later. A problem with queuing as a strategy for dealing with sensory overload is that you are not acting spontaneously in the present; by the time you get around to responding to the things you have put off, the world and your feelings may have changed.

■ *Filtering*   The strategy of **filtering** involves responding selectively to the environment; there is so much stimulation and information that you cannot deal with it all so you deal only with part of it. You ignore all but the most urgent demands. During exams you may read only the most important material, filtering out less urgent readings. When you are experiencing a sensory or information overload, you may respond to stoplights and to police sirens, but not to flowers and bird songs. A problem with the strategy of filtering for dealing with sensory overload is a diminished perception of subtle aesthetic properties of the environment. With such a strategy you can afford to be sensitive only to the grosser, more intense sights and sounds in your environment.

■ *Simplifying*   The strategy of **simplifying** involves responding in a general way to a lot of things, but in a specific way to nothing. The categories of discrimination are broadened, so that all trees are seen as alike, all policemen are seen as alike, or all cars are seen as alike. During exams when sensory overload is intense, you may respond in a general way to all of your friends, rather than treating each of them as unique. A problem with the strategy of simplifying for dealing with sensory overload is that you tend to lack an appreciation of the great differences among people and among things. Things are classified together that have important differences; you tend not to experience the uniqueness of things in the world.

■ *Escaping*   The strategy of **escaping** involves withdrawing from the excess of stimulation in the environment. You check out or tune out, either temporarily or permanently, from the bombardment of environmental stimulation. Some people have used this strategy fairly successfully in abandoning the overload of civilization and turning to a simpler life-style. The search for the simple life away from the city can be seen as an application of this strategy. During exams you may escape into fantasy, escape through drugs, or escape through excessive sleep: all are different ways to withdraw from the overload in your environment. A problem with the strategy of escaping is that you must withdraw from the reality of the world, and you often must do so indiscriminately, abandoning the good as well as the bad aspects of your environment.

■ *Reforming*   Another strategy for dealing with sensory overload is **reforming.** This is the difficult task of using human intelligence to design the environment so that it is suitable for human survival. This task requires the reconstruction of much of the artificial world so that it is compatible with human needs and life-styles. Designing the environment of the future depends upon an understanding of the individual's relationships to the environment, but this is an undertaking that has only just begun.

Ⓢ   When exposed to an excessive level of stimulation (sensory overload), you may feel confused and fearful. Your heart rate, breathing rate, and blood pressure may increase as the environment becomes stressful. Noise pollution is a special case of sensory overload. Noise disrupts attention, causes stress reactions, and can cause permanent damage to the ears. We can cope with sensory overload by using certain adaptive strategies to reduce the amount of stimulation.

Summary

KEY QUESTIONS

1. What is an optimal level of stimulation?

   An intermediate level of stimulation—neither too high nor too low—is best for us. It is, however, increasingly difficult to find this optimal level in our artificial world; more and more we seem to live in a world of understimulation or overstimulation.

2. What is sensory deprivation and how can it affect you?

   Sensory deprivation is an extreme reduction in stimulation to a level much less than the optimal level of stimulation at which we function best. Sensory deprivation can cause you to feel disoriented, confused, and anxious. If prolonged, it can even cause you to experience perceptual illusions and hallucinations.

3. What is sensory overload and how can it affect you?

   Sensory overload is an extreme excess of stimulation, far more than the optimal level. It, too, can cause disorientation and confusion. The stress resulting from sensory overload causes a variety of physical changes in your body. Noise pollution is a special case of sensory overload and is an increasing social problem. Various strategies are commonly used to cope with the stress of sensory overload.

KEY CONCEPTS

sensory pollution	Sensory changes that are the undesirable side effects of our technological intervention in the environment.
optimal level of stimulation	The best or ideal level of stimulation for human beings, neither too high nor too low.
ascending reticular activating system (ARAS)	A structure at the base of the brain that controls the amount of information reaching the brain.
sensory deprivation	The extreme reduction of stimulation.
illusions	Perceptual distortions.

hallucinations Perceptual experiences of things that are not there; perceptions not based on an external source.

sensory overload An extreme excess of stimulation.

noise pollution An excess of unwanted sound.

sonic environment The world of sounds.

queuing Delaying the response to the many environmental demands so that they can be dealt with one at a time.

filtering Responding selectively to the environmental demands.

simplifying Responding in a general way to a lot of things, rather than responding in unique ways to individual things.

escaping Withdrawing from the excess of stimulation in the environment.

reforming Using human intelligence to design the environment so that it is suitable for human survival.

Suggested Readings

Psychology and America's Urban Dilemmas by Richard D. Ashmore & John B. McConahay. New York: McGraw-Hill, 1975. Discusses what psychologists or psychology students can do about the urban problems of crowding, pollution, and violence. Suggests that psychology can be applied to the tasks of changing both individuals and systems.

Living in Cities: Psychology and the Urban Environment by Charles Mercer. Middlesex, England: Penguin Books, 1975. Shows how people change the environment and the environment, in turn, changes people. Emphasizes the psychological study of physical space in cities.

Man Adapting by René Dubos. New Haven: Yale University Press, 1965. A far-ranging discussion of the relation of people to their environment. The effects of environmental stress and pollution on health and disease.

The Death and Life of Great American Cities by Jane Jacobs. New York: Vintage Books, 1961. A stimulating study of the problems of cities, showing how behavior is influenced by the structure of neighborhoods and cities.

The Territorial Imperative by Robert Ardrey. New York: Dell, 1966. A discussion of the relation of aggression to territories in people and animals. Human territorial behavior may be seen on the football field and on the battleground, according to Ardrey.

Never Cry Wolf by Farley Mowat.   New York: Dell, 1963.   A delightful true story of one man's adventures with a family of wolves in the Canadian wilderness.   The descriptions of the wolves' territorial behavior are of special interest.

The Hidden Dimension by Edward T. Hall.   Garden City, N.Y.: Doubleday, 1969. Examines crowding, animal territoriality, and human use of space.   A highly readable paperback.

Personal Space: The Behavioral Basis of Design by Robert Sommer.   Englewood Cliffs, N.J.: Prentice-Hall, 1969.   A discussion of the relation of behavior and the spatial environment.   Shows how the design of the physical setting affects our behavior.

Research Methods IX

Beyond the Laboratory

Much of psychology is concerned with the relation between environment and behavior. The relation between a person's *past* environment and *present* behavior is examined, for example, by studies in the development of personality, in the origins of prejudice, or in the growth of learning. The relation between a person's *present* environment and *present* behavior is examined by studies in perception or environmental psychology.

    Environmental psychology, studying the effects of the physical and social environment as a whole, has required the development of new, more holistic methods of psychological research. The effects of a natural environment cannot effectively be studied in the laboratory.

Laboratory Research in Psychology

Research in psychology oftentimes is conducted in a laboratory: a set of rooms in which the conditions of stimulation (light, temperature, sounds, and so forth) can be carefully controlled and the responses of subjects (heartbeat, brainwave activity, verbal expressions, and button-pushings) can be accurately recorded and measured.

    There are many advantages to laboratory research. Without the complex instruments of the laboratory, control of stimulation and measurement of behavior would be less convenient and less accurate. In a service station, school, park, or other natural setting certain psychological responses, such as EEG, cannot be recorded. In a laboratory all distracting stimulation can be eliminated. On the street there are birds, trucks, and sirens; these events are not under the experimenter's control in natural settings so that if a change in heartbeat occurs, the psychologist has no effective way of determining which of several environmental events was the cause. Laboratories, then, are places where conditions can be carefully controlled and this is a definite asset in many studies.

In a typical laboratory experiment a psychologist might be interested in determining the sensitivity of the human eye to red light. The experiment requires that light intensity and hue be carefully controlled and that no stray light be allowed to enter the experimental chambers. Such an experiment clearly could not be conducted in a natural setting; laboratory equipment and controls are essential.

Ecological Research in Psychology

Because laboratories are very convenient for studying certain psychological problems, laboratory research has become very popular in psychology. Some university psychology departments focus exclusively on laboratory research. There are, however, problems which do not lend themselves to laboratory study and which require a different approach. According to one psychologist, these problems may require new methods and a new breed of researchers.

Unfortunately, it has become orthodox policy in many university circles that the laboratory is supreme, that investigation without experimental manipulation of treatments and testing of hypotheses is unworthy of the term research, and that laboratory environments are preferable to natural settings.

Acceptance of ecological principles . . . has a number of profound implications for the scientific methods of psychology. In the first place, methods are required that are adapted to the circumstances of the real world in which behavior occurs naturally rather than for the convenience of the scientist. A new generation of field-oriented workers in psychology

will be needed to go forth into the world as it is.[1]

Naturalistic Methods

Naturalistic methods are methods of psychological research that take place in natural settings in the real world. They are not confined to the laboratory. Naturalistic methods are ways of studying natural ongoing systems in the world.

Naturalistic observation is the simplest of these methods, consisting of observing and recording behavior as it occurs in the world as it is; with this method the observer remains unobtrusive and does not disrupt the flow of ongoing behavior.

A second method is **participant observation,** a more complex method in which the observer both records and participates in the behavioral events; for example, in order to study the social system operating in a prison, the researchers might temporarily become prisoners so that they can both observe and participate in the social system.

A third method, the **field experiment,** requires the experimenter to manipulate certain conditions in a natural setting and observe the results. Examples of field experiments are studies in which the seating arrangements in libraries and airport waiting rooms have been systematically altered in order to observe the effect on how people interact in public places.

Rich, Molar, and Relevant

Studies in natural settings are typically less precise than laboratory studies, but they are richer in that they yield a variety of information about a wide variety of variables rather than information about a single variable. Studies in natural settings are typically less molecular or reductionistic and more molar or holistic; the analysis and isolation of each constituent part of an act or situation is more appropriately attacked by laboratory studies than by naturalistic studies. Studies in natural settings are usually more immediately relevant than laboratory studies (more often directly applicable to real-world problems) but less rigorous (less adherence to controlled scientific methods). It is likely that the requirements of the new environment psychology will foster the development and application of new molar, rich, and relevant methods in psychology.

Zimbardo's Field Experiment

Suppose that you are walking down the street and you come upon an old abandoned car; it looks as if it has no owner—the license plates are missing and the hood is up. As you are walking away from the car, two people come up and take the battery out, then some teen-agers start breaking the windows and headlights. What do you do?

Zimbardo conducted a field experiment to study this situation and found that what people did depended upon the size of the city in which they lived.[2] He placed a car on the street in the Bronx, New York, and another on the street in Palo Alto, California. The hoods of the cars were raised and the license plates removed. Both cars were observed for 64 hours.

In New York, within the first ten minutes, two people began to strip the car of all parts. By the 35th hour, random destruction had left the car a worthless hunk of metal. The car in Palo Alto was virtually untouched except by one passerby who stopped to lower the hood of the car. Zimbardo concluded from this field experiment that the crowded conditions of New York produce a kind of anonymity which makes destructive violence possible.

The Observational Unit

Any type of psychological research must specify the **observational unit:** the way in which behavior and environment are classified and recorded. Laboratory psychology developed molecular units of observation called "stimuli" and "responses." From this point of view the environment was considered to consist of combinations of elementary stimuli and behavior to consist of combinations of responses. A stimulus in the laboratory may be a flash of light lasting for a fraction of a second and a response may be a button-push.

Naturalistic studies have evolved different units of observation. For example, Barker, an environmental psychologist, has developed a unit for observing behavior called the "behavior episode" and a unit for observing the environment called the "behavior setting." A **behavior episode** is a natural behavior unit, a thing people commonly do in the world.[3] This is not a molecular "response" such as a button-push in the laboratory or a change in heart rate, but it is a large, molar act, such as "entering the drugstore," "reading a comic book," or "watching a friend eat ice cream." A **behavior setting** is a part of the environment in which behavior occurs, such as an American Legion dinner, a high school basketball game, or a drugstore.[4] Observing and recording the behavior episodes as they occur in behavior settings is the objective of Barker's ecological approach.

Barker has studied the relation between population density and participation in behavior settings. His results show that when population density is low, there are pressures toward increased participation in activities; for example, when few people are around, a nine-year-old's baseball game might include a four-year-old or even a mother. When population density is high, there is competition for the right to participate, and persons who are not acceptable are vetoed out of the game.[4] A related finding is that students in small high schools are more likely to be participants in activities, whereas students in large high schools are more likely to be spectators.[5]

KEY CONCEPTS

naturalistic observation	Observing and recording behavior as it occurs in the world, without interfering or manipulating.
participant observation	A research method in which the observer both records and participates in the behavior studied.
field experiment	An experiment conducted in a natural setting.
observational unit	The way in which behavior and environment are classified and recorded.
behavior episode	Natural behavior units; whole, meaningful acts in the world.
behavior setting	A part of the environment in which behavior occurs.

X Freedom

28 Mind Control

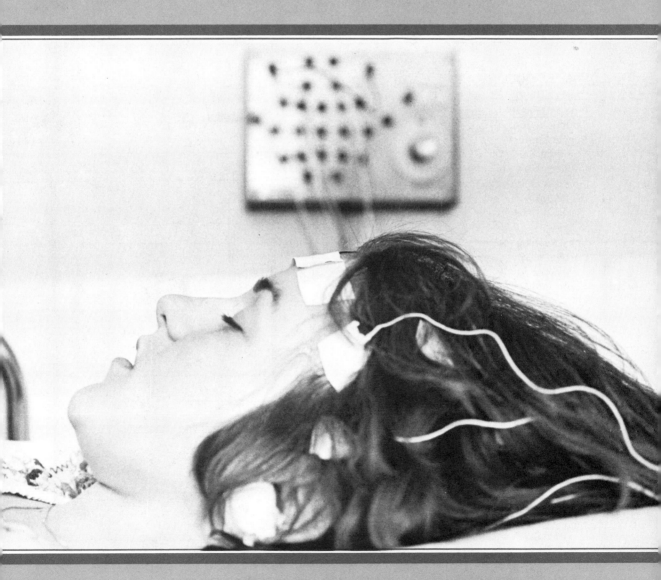

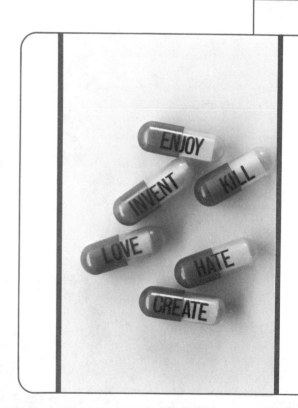

CHAPTER OUTLINE

1. What are some physical means for controlling the mind and behavior?
2. What are some psychological means for controlling the mind and behavior?
3. Is mind control good or bad?

Your mind can be partially controlled by others. Psychology has developed methods for manipulating your behavior and experience.

Speculations about controlling the minds and behavior of others have been common themes in the science fiction of the past—for example, Orwell's *1984* and Huxley's *Brave New World*. These novels are about future societies that completely control the minds of their citizens. But science fiction tends to become science fact; psychology is now developing the tools to enable us to make Orwell's vision a reality. In his book *Behavior Control*, Perry London writes:

Behavior control is the ability to get someone to do one's bidding. From antiquity until almost now, the only common means for doing this have been coercion by force and threat of force and persuasion by inspiration and education, but these techniques have been mostly gross or tedious in their application and clumsy or unsure in their effects.

All this is changing now, and means are being found . . . that will soon make possible precise control over much of people's individual actions, thoughts, emotions, moods, and wills. Never in human history has this occurred before, except as fantasy. . . .

As 1984 draws near, it appears that George Orwell's fears for Western democracy may have been too pessimistic, or at least premature, but it is also clear that his concepts of the technology by which tyranny could impress its will upon men's minds were much too modest. By that time, the means at hand will be more sophisticated and efficient than Orwell ever dreamed.[1]

Do we have the means at hand to totally control people's minds? Can a tyrannical politician or evil psychologist turn us into robots?

The answer clearly is no.

The technology of mind control at present is not powerful enough to be used in this way. The methods of mind control are becoming increasingly efficient and sophisticated, but these methods are not now effective enough to turn us into robots. Your mind and behavior can be influenced or shaped by the tools of psychology, but not totally controlled.

The Physical Control of the Mind

A technique for partially controlling the mind is to physically alter the brain itself. There are a variety of ways to do this. Certain drugs alter brain chemistry; this changes your experience of reality and your behavior. Surgery can be used to change the brain by cutting it or by removing parts of it, and behavior can thereby be changed. Direct

electrical stimulation of certain parts of the brain excites or inhibits those brain circuits which control different behaviors such as those involved in sex or aggression.

Chemical Control

Within the past twenty-five years there has been a psychopharmacological revolution. **Psychopharmacology,** the study of mind-affecting drugs, has provided new and powerful tools for the control of behavior.

One hot August evening in 1955, Helen Burney sat listlessly on her bed in the violent ward of the large Texas hospital where she had been confined for the past four months. During most of that unhappy time, Helen had been highly vocal, abusive, and overactive. Only the day before she had tried to strike a ward aide, but immediately several burly attendants had grabbed her, roughly tying her into a straitjacket and pinioning her arms against her chest. But today Helen's behavior was very different. Her incessant talking and shouting had stopped; all day long she spoke only when spoken to; most of the time she lay on her bed with her eyes closed, moving little, and looking rather pale. However, she was unusually cooperative with the nursing personnel, got out of bed when told to, and went to the dining room without resisting. What had happened to bring about this remarkable change?

That morning she had received an injection of a new synthetic drug, chlorpromazine, which had been discovered a few years earlier in France. . . . The era of clinical psychopharmacology had begun.[2]

Today drugs are used extensively in the treatment of the mentally disturbed. Many individuals previously had to be confined to a mental hospital because of their bizarre or self-destructive behavior or because they were not able to take care of themselves in the world. Most of these persons are now able to live at home and to work as a result of taking the new mind drugs.

There are drugs for the treatment of many psychological disorders. Most of these drugs fall into three major categories: minor tranquilizers, major tranquilizers, and antidepressants. **Minor tranquilizers** are drugs used to reduce mild anxiety states. These drugs are usually prescribed for persons diagnosed as having psychosomatic disorders or persistent anxiety. **Major tranquilizers,** such as chlorpromazine, are sometimes referred to as antipsychotic drugs because they are used primarily for treating schizophrenic patients. The **antidepressant** drugs are used to reduce severe depression. People who use these drugs show an elevation in mood within a short period of time.

The use of drugs to control the behavior of patients in mental hospitals has been a very controversial issue for many years. Some people say that drugged patients in mental hospitals become "formula robots." There is no doubt that drugs are used extensively in mental hospitals and sometimes too extensively; but to some it does seem preferable to use a tranquilizer rather than a straightjacket to restrain an uncontrollable patient. Current studies are being done to determine the long-term effects of drugs on hospitalized people.

There are also drugs for the control of many normal everyday behaviors. There are drugs to make you sleep (barbiturates) and drugs to wake you up (caffeine or amphetamines); there are drugs to increase your hunger (marijuana) and drugs to decrease your hunger (amphetamines); there are drugs that give you psychotic symptoms (LSD) and drugs that take away psychotic symptoms (chlorpromazine). If people continue to dose themselves, the pill of the future may be

Are your feelings chemical?

a multilayered compound that you would take upon waking up in the morning. The outside, and first-acting layer, would consist of amphetamine (a pep pill) to wake you up quickly and make you alert; amphetamine, however, has the side effects of making you high strung and eliminating your appetite. The next layer, therefore, would consist of THC, the active ingredient in marijuana, which would combat the effects of the previous layer by increasing your appetite and relaxing you; marijuana, however, has the side effect of making you drowsy, which won't do in the middle of the day. The next layer, therefore, would consist of another amphetamine to make you alert and energetic; as the amphetamine wears off, however, depression and tension often set in. The next layer would consist of a tranquilizer to combat the effects of the amphetamine. Since the tranquilizer probably would not be sufficient to allow you to sleep that night (after two doses of pep pills in the daytime), the final layer—the core—of the pill of the future would consist of barbiturates to make you sleep. Thus, every day, in every way, friendly chemicals would be your help and guide. Programmed by chemicals, you would be a formula robot.

Psychosurgery

Since the brain is the great coordinator of behavior, when the brain is damaged behavior often changes. Most bodily functions can be eliminated by destroying the appropriate part of the brain; paralysis of the left or right side of the body, lack of speech, blindness or deafness, or death can result from brain injury. Suppose the function you wanted to eliminate was psychotic behavior; it is possible, although extremely unlikely, that you could find a particular part of the brain which was responsible for the psychotic behavior and which, when destroyed, would eliminate it. Brain surgery for psychosis has been attempted, but the results are not very promising. **Psychosurgery** is the term given to surgery performed on the brain in order to change a certain behavior.

For many years a psychosurgery technique called **prefrontal lobotomy** was used to treat uncontrollable patients. For this operation a burr hole was drilled in each temple and a knife was introduced into the brain through each hole and was then moved back and forth. This cut the connections between the frontal lobes and the hypothalamic region of the brain.[3] The operation was performed to calm down uncontrollable psychotic patients. Unfortunately, there were also negative side effects; the brain-damaged patients lacked initiative, had impaired planning ability and reduced foresight, and were impulsive, unreliable, and socially inept.[4] Since psychosurgery cannot be undone, other methods, primarily drugs, have tended to replace brain operations as methods of controlling the behavior of the mentally disturbed.

Electrical Control

The work of the brain is carried on electrically. The individual cells (neurons) that make up the brain send and receive tiny electrical impulses; they form brain circuits for processing information and controlling the movements of the body. These circuits can also be made to operate by stimulating the brain with electricity from an external source. This technique is called **ESB,** the **electrical stimulation of the brain.** A fine wire, or *electrode,* carrying an electrical charge can be touched to various brain structures to produce changes in mood, perception, or movements.

Sometimes these wire electrodes are permanently implanted in the brain and rigged so that electrical current can be turned on and off by remote control. One psychologist described, with some exaggeration, what might be possible with ESB:

Docility, fearful withdrawal, and panicked efforts at escape can be made to alternate with fury and ferocity of such degree that its subject can as readily destroy himself by exhaustion from his consuming rage as he can the object of it, whom he attacks, heedless of both danger and opportunity. Eating, drinking, sleeping, moving of bowels or limbs or organs of sensation, gracefully or in spastic comedy, can all be managed on electrical demand by puppeteers whose flawless strings are pulled from miles away by the unseen call of radio.[1]

■ *Happy Rats and Angry Bulls* A well-known study of electrical stimulation of the brain was done by James Olds in 1953. Olds was conducting experiments on electrical stimulation of the reticular formation of a rat's brain. He found that he could implant electrodes in this area of the brain and not interfere with the rat's normal health. One electrode was mistakenly implanted near the

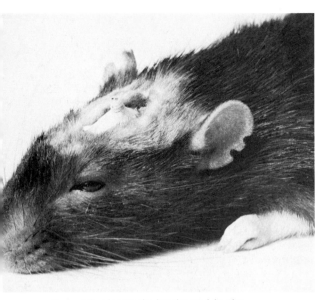

Rat with electrode implanted in the hypothalamic region of its brain.

hypothalamic region of the rat's brain. Olds found, by accident, that when he sent a mild current of electricity through this electrode the rat acted as if it enjoyed the feeling. It continually returned to that area of the cage where it had been stimulated. Olds concluded that the rat found the stimulation rewarding or pleasurable. He then concluded that there must be **pleasure centers** in the brain which, when electrically stimulated, produce a rewarding and pleasurable experience.

A pioneer in the study of the electrical stimulation of the brain, José Delgado, implanted electrodes in the brain of a bull and connected the electrodes to a miniature radio receiver. Later the enraged bull charged Delgado but was stopped abruptly when Delgado pressed a button on a small radio transmitter he carried; Delgado had communicated with the bull's brain by radio wave.[5]

■ *"Your Electricity Is Stronger Than My Will"* In an attempt to treat certain brain disorders, Delgado has operated on and implanted electrodes in the brains of many individuals. Because so little is known about

the brain, what happens when these electrodes are stimulated is often a surprise. Sometimes the brain stimulation causes body movement, which the patients believe they are causing themselves or which they report they have no control over.

In one of our patients, electrical stimulation of [one part of the brain] produced head turning and slow displacement of the body to either side with a well-oriented and apparently normal sequence, as if the patient were looking for something. This stimulation was repeated six times on two different days with comparable results. The interesting fact was that the patient considered the evoked activity spontaneous and always offered a reasonable explanation for it. When asked "What are you doing?" the answers were, "I am looking for my slippers," "I heard a noise," "I am restless," and "I was looking under the bed." . . .

In one of our patients, stimulation of [another part of the brain] through implanted electrodes evoked a flexion of the right hand starting with contraction of the first two fingers and continuing with flexion of the other fingers. The closed fist was then maintained for the rest of the 5-second stimulation. This effect was not unpleasant or disturbing, and it developed without interrupting ongoing behavior or spontaneous conversation. The patient was aware that his hand had moved involuntarily but he was not afraid. . . . When the patient was warned of the oncoming stimulation and was asked to try to keep his fingers extended, he could not prevent the evoked movement and commented, "I guess, Doctor, that your electricity is stronger than my will."[5]

■ *Electric Sex* Stimulation of certain areas of the brain produces feelings of intense pleasure, sometimes sexual pleasure. Two patients were fitted with brain electrodes

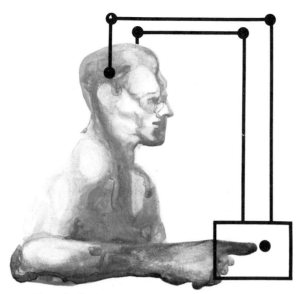

Electrical stimulation of the brain.

and were each given a box with buttons with which they could stimulate themselves in different areas of the brain.

The patient, in explaining why he pressed [one] button with such frequency, stated that the feeling was "good"; it was as if he were building up to a sexual orgasm. He reported that he was unable to achieve the orgiastic end point, however, explaining that his frequent, sometimes frantic, pushing of the button was an attempt to reach the end point. This futile effort was frustrating at times.[6]

The second patient was also able to stimulate himself. One of the effects of brain stimulation for him was to alter the subject matter of his conversation, so that he would begin making sexual remarks.

The actual content [of his conversation] varied considerably, but regardless of his baseline emotional state and the subject under discussion in the room, the stimulation was accompanied by the patient's introduction of a sexual subject, usually with a broad grin. When questioned about this, he would say, "I don't know why that came to mind—I just happened to think of it."[6]

Delgado reports the case of a thirty-six-year-old woman who had electrodes implanted in her brain in an attempt to control a brain disorder.

Electrodes were implanted in her right temporal lobe and upon stimulation of a contact . . . , the patient reported a pleasant tingling sensation in the left side of her body "from my face down to the bottom of my legs." She started giggling and making funny comments, stating that she enjoyed the sensation "very much." Repetition of these stimulations made the patient more communicative and flirtatious, and she ended by openly expressing her desire to marry the therapist.[5]

Both before and after the electrical stimulation of her brain, the patient behaved very properly and was not excessively friendly or familiar.

S Psychology has developed an impressive technology of mind control consisting of methods and tools that others can use to partially control your mind. Psychopharmacology, psychosurgery, and electrical stimulation are now being used to change the brain directly and thereby alter behavior.

The Psychological Control of the Mind

Physical control requires some kind of contact between the person who is controlled and the person who is controlling, at least initially. Psychological control, however, can work completely at a distance. You can be controlled through brainwashing, through conditioning, or through hypnosis without being touched. Psychological methods for the control of the mind offer both more promise and more danger than physical methods. With psychological methods millions can be controlled at once through television or other advertising media; with psychological methods the victims of mind control are most often unaware that their minds are being influenced and therefore offer no resistance.

Brainwashing

Brainwashing, as I will use the term, refers to the variety of psychological ways in which, without choice, attitudes and beliefs are changed. You have little choice in the formation of beliefs that are established either unconsciously or by force. Advertising is a form of indoctrination that seeks attitude change without awareness. The political brainwashing that has been used in war attempts to force a radical change in belief. All brainwashing techniques depend for their effectiveness on psychological principles.

■ *Advertising* Advertising techniques are part of the technology of mind control. The psychological principles of association, identification, and vicarious learning are the foundation for most advertising tricks. **Association** is the process that links together two ideas or events that have occurred; when two stimuli occur together, they tend to become associated, so that the presentation of one gives rise to the responses natural to the other. This is a form of classical conditioning. Because of association you think of "sex appeal" when you see brand X toothpaste. **Identification** is the process of observing and imitating others. It enables us to imagine that we are like a character on TV; I identify with the man in the mouthwash ad and I consequently feel his worries and his pleasures. If he worries about bad breath, I may also. **Vicarious learning** is learning that occurs through observation of someone else's experience; you may learn about hot stoves by watching another person touch one.

Modern advertisements use these psychological principles in order to create a need for their product, to identify their product as a solution to this need, and to strengthen a buying habit for that product. A product need may be created by TV dramas whose characters (with whom we can identify) suffer punishment because of a particular "problem." For example, a woman is shown being ignored because of "bad breath" or a man is shown being passed over for promotion because of his gray hair. Identification and vicarious learning cause us to feel punished when we see these people being punished for their "problems"; thereafter the thought of the so-called problem causes us to feel discomfort and anxiety, and we are motivated to do something about it. Advertising has created a need.

The second step is to identify a solution to the created problem. Advertising accomplishes this through repetition and association. A particular brand name is repeated over and over again; research has shown that *liking* increases with the familiarity resulting from repetition.[7] But the brand name is not simply repeated: it is associated with images of famous people, wealth or power, and sex. The responses to these images—respect, admiration, or attraction—are thus conditioned to the product that is being advertised. The repeated image of a sexually attractive person leaning against a new car transfers your feelings toward the person to the image of the car; thus the car should become more attractive and your chances of buying it should increase. Advertising has presented a solution to the problem in the form of an attractive product.

The third step that advertising must make is to strengthen buying habits. Advertising accomplishes this by creating dramas whose characters are strongly rewarded for buying

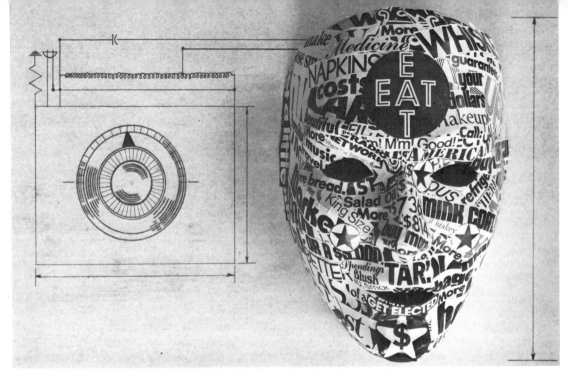

Are you controlled by advertisements?

the product being advertised. If I buy the mouthwash, I will be loved; if I dye my hair black, I will be promoted; my husband will stop making rude remarks about my coffee if I buy brand X. Because we identify with the characters in the advertisements, the effect of their receiving rewards is similar to the effect of our receiving rewards. The advertising formula can be summarized as follows: punish people for a problem, condition positive associations to a particular brand that will solve that problem, and reward people for buying that particular brand. Can you identify this kind of reasoning in ads you have seen recently for aspirin, toothpaste, coffee, or detergent?

■ *Political Brainwashing* Why did American soldiers captured by the Chinese during the Korean war "confess" to many bizarre crimes that they did not commit? They were persuaded by the Chinese to confess. The procedure for persuading the prisoners to confess came to be called

"brainwashing." The typical experience of the prisoner of war consisted of two stages. During the first stage, lasting several months, the prisoners were marched to the north of Korea; the stresses of the marches were very severe, with many suffering from inadequate food, clothing, and medical care. During the second stage, lasting two or more years, the men were housed in a prisoner of war camp where they were under constant pressure to collaborate.[8]

One man who experienced Chinese brainwashing later described it. He was brought before an interrogator who accused him of "crimes against the people." When he protested his innocence, he was told, "The government never arrests an innocent man." He was confined in a small empty cell, handcuffed and chained, and had to eat like a dog, with only his mouth and teeth. They continually told him that if he confessed all he would be treated better. On the third night without sleep the prisoner began to confess all his conversations with his associates in the past few months, but this was not enough for his captors. After eight days without sleep, living in chains, suffering almost constant interrogation, he gave up resisting and began inventing crimes. But the crimes were not believable enough and had to be related to the facts so that his confession would gain acceptance. After three and one-half years of brainwashing in the "reeducation center," his confession was deemed acceptable. A news conference was called and he confessed before the cameras. By this time he had come to partially believe that he truly was a criminal and had committed the crimes to which he confessed.[9]

The psychological condition that the Chinese brainwashers attempted to induce in the prisoners is called the **DDD syndrome.** The three D's stand for the three essential elements of the brainwashing procedure: debility (being extremely weak), dependency (relying on others for help), and dread (having fear and anxiety).

Debility *was induced by semi-starvation, fatigue and disease. Chronic physical pain was a common feature. Loss of energy and inability to resist minor abuse, combined with the lack of proper facilities for the maintenance of personal hygiene, led to . . . a sense of terrible weariness and weakness.*

Dependency, *produced by the prolonged deprivation of many of the factors, such as sleep and food, needed to maintain sanity and life itself, was made more poignant by occasional unpredictable brief respites, reminding the prisoner that it was possible for the captor to relieve the misery if he wished.*

Dread *is the most expressive term to indicate the chronic fear the Communists attempted to induce. Fear of death, fear of pain, fear of nonrepatriation, fear of deformity or permanent disability through neglect or inadequate*

medical treatment . . . these and many other nagging despairs constituted the final component of the DDD syndrome.[10]

■ *The Patty Hearst Case* The trial of Patty Hearst brought the concept of brainwashing to the attention of many people. After having been kidnapped by a terrorist organization—the SLA—the newspaper heiress became a participant in a series of crimes. Was she a criminal or a victim? At her trial she claimed she was brainwashed by her captors and was therefore not responsible for her actions.

Using Patty Hearst's defense arguments, we can reconstruct how the brainwashing might have been accomplished. The SLA members apparently tried to create the DDD syndrome. They first attempted to weaken or debilitate her by blindfolding her and tying her hands; she was then locked in a small closet where she was forced to stay for some sixty days, at times without bathroom privileges. She was also starved for short periods of time.

The next phase of the brainwashing procedure was to make her dependent upon her captors. She learned early that her well-being and survival depended completely upon the SLA. Many times during her experiences she was treated fairly well. She was often allowed bathroom privileges so that she could maintain some sense of decency. But as soon as she thought that things were getting better, all privileges would be revoked and she would then be treated worse than before. By alternately giving and taking away privileges, the SLA emphasized her dependency.

The last phase of the brainwashing procedure was to induce fear or dread. While Patty Hearst was in the closet, the SLA members frequently threatened her with her life. She was repeatedly touched, shoved, and confronted with cocked guns. She was told

Was Patty Hearst brainwashed?

that if she did not conform to their ideas, she would die.

The SLA thus created the three essential conditions for brainwashing—debility, dependency, and dread. Was the brainwashing procedure effective, or was her conversion to a revolutionary a voluntary act? There is no way of deciding this. But at her trial the jury decided that she was responsible for what she did.

Manipulation Through Conditioning

Conditioning by association (classical conditioning) and conditioning by consequences (operant conditioning) have profound effects on human behavior. If you have control over the rewards and punishments operating in someone's life, you have control over much of that person's behavior.

The behavior of people can be conditioned even without their knowledge or per-

mission. For example, it has been shown that the content of a person's conversation can be controlled by the listener applying verbal rewards selectively. If a listener says "uh-huh" whenever a talker says a particular type of word, the talker will say that type of word more often. In one experiment students from a large introductory psychology class at the University of Illinois were asked to recall events from their early childhood. For half of them, whenever they reported a memory concerned with their family, the experimenter replied "uh-huh" in a flat, noncommittal tone. The effect of this "reward" was that those students increased the frequency of reporting family memories. In other words the Law of Effect operated. According to the **Law of Effect**, responses that are reinforced (rewarded) tend to be repeated. Of all the students in the experiment, only one was aware of the relationship between the memory report and the verbal "reward"; most students were manipulated without their knowledge.[11]

Classical conditioning, which works by association, can also be used to manipulate behavior. Through classical conditioning an association is formed between a stimulus and a response; for example, with this procedure a dog can be taught to salivate when it hears a bell ring.

A special type of classical conditioning is called **aversive counterconditioning.** It is called *aversive* because it uses aversive (unpleasant) stimuli in the conditioning procedure. It is called *counter*conditioning because its purpose is to substitute one reaction for another opposing reaction. For example, an experimental treatment of alcoholism involves a drug, antabuse, which when combined with small amounts of alcohol, causes nausea and vomiting. After several experiences with drinking alcohol after having taken antabuse, a negative or unpleasant reaction is conditioned to alcohol. After aversive counterconditioning with antabuse, feelings of nausea accompany even the thought of drinking alcohol. If you have ever been sick following an overindulgence in a particular kind of food or beverage, you have had a counterconditioning experience; while before this experience you had a positive reaction to the food or beverage, afterwards even the thought of it made you ill.

All kinds of behavior can be controlled by the use of conditioning methods, either conditioning by association or conditioning by consequences. As Perry London writes, in his book *Behavior Control:*

A large body of scientific literature shows plainly that conditioning methods can be used to control several types of voluntary and involuntary activity, affecting thinking, language, imagination, emotion, motivation, habits, and skills. People can be conditioned to blush or otherwise react emotionally to meaningless words or phrases; to respond impassively to outrageous epithets; to hallucinate to signals; to feel fear, revulsion, embarrassment, or arousal upon demand; to feel cold when they are being warmed or warm when being chilled; to become ill when lights are flashed; to narrow or enlarge their blood vessels or the pupils of their eyes; to feel like urinating with an empty bladder or not feel the need with a full one; to establish habits and mannerisms they had never known before; and to break free forever from lifelong patterns of activity they thought could never be forgotten.[1]

Hypnosis

In February of 1778 Friedrich Mesmer claimed to have discovered the secret fluid of life, a universal curative force he called **animal magnetism.** He began treating the sick with iron filings, his own brand of "magnetized" water, and magnetic steel instruments. The treatment became so popular that Mesmer began to accommodate large numbers of patients at once.

Mesmer, wearing a coat of lilac silk, walked up and down amid this palpitating crowd. Mesmer carried a long iron wand, with which he touched the bodies of the patients, and especially those parts which were diseased; often, laying aside the wand, he magnetized them with his eyes, fixing his gaze upon theirs, or applying his hands.[12]

Eventually it was discovered that iron filings and steel rods were not needed to produce the effect of "animal magnetism." Today "animal magnetism"—or hypnotism as we now call it—remains controversial and somewhat mysterious in spite of thousands of scientific studies that have been conducted on the subject.

Hypnosis is a state of heightened suggestibility in which a person is under the influence of someone else.

How is the hypnotic trance induced today? There are many varieties of methods used, but most depend upon techniques for narrowing the attention of the person who is to be hypnotized. Hypnotists may ask their patients to stare at a thumbtack stuck into the wall slightly above eye level. Then the patients are told that their eyelids are becoming heavy and that they should think of nothing but sleep. These instructions are repeated monotonously over and over again as the patient stares fixedly at the spot on the wall. Soon the eyes close and the patient is hypnotized.

Under hypnosis people are highly suggestible. It has been reported, for example, that temporary blindness and deafness can be induced by suggestions from the hypnotist.[13] However, the pupil of the eye responds to light, even for a person with hypnotic blindness,[14] and a person who is

Hypnosis is a state of heightened suggestibility.

hypnotically deaf responds to the spoken words "Now you can hear again." Thus, there are probably no sensory problems caused by hypnosis, even though individuals may *act as if* they were blind and deaf.

Although hypnosis has been widely used for the control of behavior for therapeutic purposes—quitting smoking, lessening chronic pain, improving ulcers, promoting painless childbirth, and so forth—the reason why hypnosis works is not really understood. Some researchers maintain that hypnosis is not particularly different from other waking states; hypnotized persons have simply been motivated to act as if they were hypnotized, according to this viewpoint.[15] Hypnotized persons behave like normal persons who have been strongly motivated to cooperate.

S Psychological methods for mind control—such as brainwashing, conditioning, and hypnosis—work at a distance. In some cases, victims of psychological mind control are unaware that their minds are being influenced and therefore offer no resistance.

The Ethics of Mind Control

Is mind control good or bad? Some argue that behavioral technology is a tool, just as a knife is a tool, and that good or evil is a result of the manner of its use, not of the instrument itself. New tools, however, mean new possibilities, new alternatives for action, and new power. The refinement of scientific techniques for the control of human beings introduces vast new sources of power for those desiring power.

Control means power. Behavior control means power over people. In times past, it meant power over life and death and some visible activities in between. Now, it is coming to mean power over all the details of people's lives—of attitudes, actions, thoughts, and feelings, of public postures and the secrets of the heart. . . . The moral problem of behavior control is the problem of how to use power justly. This is no new question, but critical questions in human experience rarely are.[1]

How will the power be used? Who will use the power? And to what ends? Our future rests upon the answers to these difficult questions. As Carl Rogers has said:

To hope that the power which is being made available by the behavioral sciences will be exercised by the scientists, or by a benevolent group, seems to me a hope little supported by either recent or distant history. . . . If behavioral scientists are concerned solely with advancing their science, it seems most probably that they will serve the purposes of whatever individual or group has the power.[16]

Rogers contends that we should celebrate our creative powers rather than our manipulative powers, and that instead of seeking an improved technology for mind control, we should seek self-actualization.

B. F. Skinner disagrees. He writes, "What we need is more control, not less, and this is itself an engineering problem of the first importance."[17] Skinner believes that we cannot avoid controls, and that therefore our problem is to design a society with good controls rather than bad ones. He says:

What is needed is a new conception of human behavior which is compatible with the implications of a scientific analysis. All men control and are controlled. The question of government in the broadest possible sense is not how freedom is to be preserved but what kinds of control are to be used and to what ends.[16]

If, as Skinner believes, we are all controlled by external environmental forces, then there is no freedom. Freedom is only an illusion we have, resulting from our ignorance of the forces that control us. If we are all controlled, then we should discover the forces controlling us—the rewards and punishments that we receive from society—and identify the ways in which our behavior is influenced. At least we would then be conscious robots. If there is no freedom, then we must learn how to use controls more deliberately, with greater regard for our values; we should design good controls and try to eliminate bad controls.

The idea that freedom is an illusion may be a self-fulfilling prophecy: a declaration that, even if it is not true now, soon will be if we act as if it were.

S The technology of mind control leads to new possibilities for the future, some promising and some dangerous. Who will use the power? Carl Rogers believes that the state will use psychological power for its own ends and that we should celebrate human freedom rather than exploit mind control. B. F. Skinner argues that we must learn to design a society with good controls rather than bad ones, because control itself is inevitable.

Summary

KEY QUESTIONS

1. What are some physical means for controlling the mind and behavior?
   Drugs have been used extensively for treating and controlling mentally disturbed patients. Psychosurgery is another direct means of changing behavior. Since the brain controls behavior, behavior can be controlled when parts of the brain are physically altered. Behavior can also be controlled by using electrical stimulation of the brain.

2. What are some psychological means for controlling the mind and behavior?
   Psychological methods for behavioral control work indirectly or at a distance. Hypnosis, brainwashing, and conditioning techniques are examples of methods for psychological manipulation.

3. Is mind control good or bad?
   People have different views of the ethics of mind control. Carl Rogers believes that we should not exploit the technology of mind control, but

should instead celebrate our freedoms and creative powers. B. F. Skinner argues that we need more control, not less; since control itself is inevitable, all we can hope for is that the control be good.

KEY CONCEPTS

psycho-pharmacology	The study of mind-affecting drugs.
minor tranquilizers	Drugs used to reduce mild anxiety and tension.
major tranquilizers	Drugs used to control psychotic behavior.
antidepressants	Drugs used to reduce severe depression.
psychosurgery	Surgery performed on the brain in order to change behavior.
prefrontal lobotomy	A type of psychosurgery in which connections between the frontal lobes and the hypothalamic area of the brain are cut.
ESB (electrical stimulation of the brain)	A technique in which a weak electrical current is sent through a part of the brain.
pleasure center	An area of the brain that produces an enjoyable experience when it is stimulated with electricity.
brainwashing	A psychological means of forcefully changing attitudes and beliefs.
association	The process that links two ideas or events that have occurred together.
identification	A process of observing and imitating others.
vicarious learning	Learning that occurs by observing someone else.
DDD syndrome	A psychological condition supposedly necessary for political brainwashing to occur; consists of debility, dependency, and dread.
Law of Effect	The principle stating that responses which are reinforced tend to be repeated.
aversive counter-conditioning	A classical conditioning technique in which a negative reaction is substituted for a previously positive reaction.
hypnosis	A state of heightened suggestibility in which a person is under the influence of someone else.
animal magnetism	An early name for hypnosis; claimed by Mesmer to be the "secret fluid of life."

29 Self Control

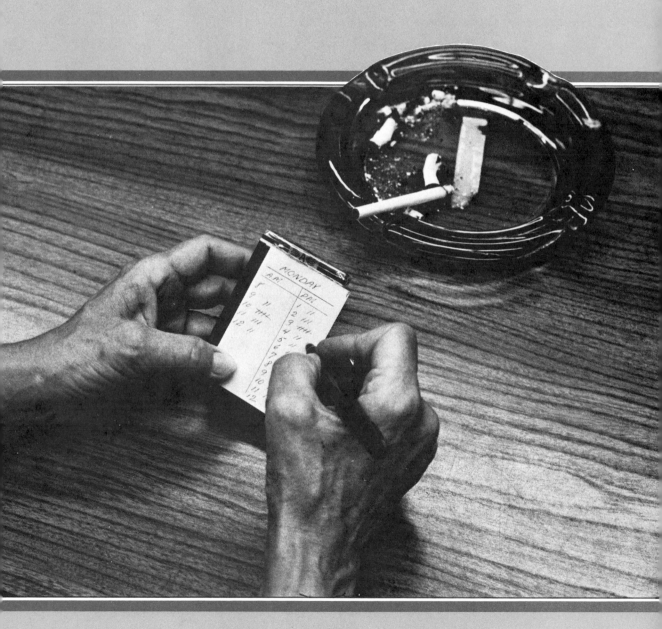

CHAPTER OUTLINE

1. How can you change your habits?

2. How can you control your emotional reactions?

3. How can you improve your relationships?

The more control you have over your own life, the less control other people can have over you. Psychology provides tools others can use to control your mind and behavior; it also provides tools you can use to control your self. What does it mean to have "self control"? It means to take charge of your own destiny, to stop being a passenger and get into the driver's seat of your life. It means freedom.

Sometimes the term "self control" is used differently, to refer to the absence of emotional expression, the absence of spontaneity, or a tendency to avoid pleasurable activities. That is not the way I am using the term in this chapter. By **self control** I mean the ability to manage your habits and emotional reactions so that you are free to do what you want to do.

You have the power to run your life. Use it.

Freedom

What does it mean to be free? Erich Fromm distinguished two types of freedom: freedom *from* and freedom *to*. Freedom from restrictions, freedom from poverty and disease, freedom from injustice, freedom from pain—this is one type of freedom. Freedom to vote, freedom to say what you want, freedom to dress as you please, freedom to read and learn—this is another kind of freedom.

Freud was concerned primarily with the first type of freedom; he emphasized the limitations imposed by unconscious controls. For Skinner, the concept of freedom is an illusion; all that can be hoped for is to be relatively free *from* aversive (unpleasant) consequences. By contrast, Maslow and Rogers emphasized the significance of the freedom *to* act and feel; in their view, psychologically healthy people have more freedom to act consistently with their feelings, to be authentic, and to make free choices.

Unfree People

Freedom is not something that you either have or do not have. Some people are more free than others; and sometimes you feel more free than at other times. There are degrees of freedom.

Certain people are regarded as relatively unfree. For example, when people are drunk or intoxicated with drugs, they and others feel that they are not responsible for what they may do; they are not in control of themselves and are therefore not free. An individual who is hypnotized is not in control and is therefore not free. Obsessive-compulsive neurosis limits freedom; individuals suffering from this problem feel a loss of voluntary control. For example, a man may feel a compulsion to wash his hands over and over

Self control leads to greater freedom of choice in ways of dressing and behaving.

again; he does not want to do it and tries to resist doing it, but is not successful. Certain types of compulsive actions are called **irresistible impulses,** because they suddenly appear and have the force of commands. For example, **kleptomania** is a compulsion to steal. Individuals with this disorder steal repetitively, often taking small or useless items, and feel unable to resist their impulses. Other types of compulsive impulses are **pyromania,** a compulsion to set fires, and **exhibitionism,** a compulsion to expose the sexual organs. Each of these disorders involves a great loss of voluntary control over behavior; individuals feel that they simply cannot help what they do.

Free People

Whom do you regard as relatively free? Chances are, you regard most *other* people as freer than you are. Imagine yourself in an argument with your mother. If she does something you don't like, you may get angry with her because you think that she can control herself and stop doing it. By contrast, if *you* do something that *she* doesn't like, you feel that you can't help yourself and therefore she should not be mad. For exam-

ple, if while you are talking with her she repeatedly interrupts you, you may feel that she is acting by choice; however, if you repeatedly interrupt her, you may feel that you were too excited to control yourself. To consider another example, if someone else is overweight, you may feel that the person lacks "willpower"; but if *you* are overweight, you may feel that the situation is beyond your control—you cannot control yourself.

Why do you regard other people as having more freedom? One reason is that you see yourself "from the inside" and you see them "from the outside." You are aware of the forces influencing your own behavior, but you are relatively ignorant of the pressures operating on other people. You therefore assume that their choices are freer from pressure and influence. You assume that they have more voluntary control.

When do you feel most free?

Your Freedom

When do you personally feel most free?
Sometimes your behavior is relatively automatic. You may be walking or driving without really being aware of what you are doing. You may brush your teeth in the morning without even remembering later whether you have done it. One author describes his automatic behavior as an "inner robot":

I am writing this on an electric typewriter. When I learned to type, I had to do it painfully and with much nervous wear and tear. But at a certain stage a miracle occurred, and this complicated operation was "learned" by a useful robot whom I conceal in my subconscious mind. Now I only have to think about what I want to say; my robot secretary does the typing. He is really very useful.[1]

When you are behaving automatically, you don't feel free; you don't feel that you are making free choices.

You feel free when you are aware of what you are doing, when you are fully conscious and "in touch" with your feelings. Freedom requires awareness. But you must also be able to do what you want to do. You must feel relatively free from external controls; you must feel under internal rather than external control. How can you be more self-determined? How can you gain more voluntary control of your behavior? The answer does not depend upon "willpower," but instead depends upon what you do.

Managing Your Actions

What is the relation between what you want to do and what you actually do? If you are in control, managing your actions, then what

you do and what you want to do are about the same. Sometimes, however, you may do things that you do not want to do. You may bite your fingernails, smoke, or overeat, and feel that these behaviors are beyond your power to control. Other times you may want to do certain things, but you do not do them. You may want to exercise or study more and yet have great difficulty in settling down and doing these things. How can you gain control over your actions so that you are able to do what you want to do and you are able to stop doing what you do not want to do?

Analyzing Your Behavior

The first step toward self control is self-understanding. To change your behavior, you must first understand clearly what you are now doing, when you are doing it, and—if possible—why. In effect, you must become a scientist observing your own behavior.

What about yourself would you like to be able to change? Do you have a bad habit you would like to eliminate? In analyzing your behavior, your first problem will be to specify a problem behavior precisely, to state exactly what it is, with concrete examples. Rather than stating something general ("I'm too shy" or "I'm too lazy"), try to state the problem in terms of actual examples ("I want to be able to initiate more conversations with members of the opposite sex" or "I want to spend more time studying and less watching TV").

Once you have stated precisely the behavior you want to change, the next step is to observe the behavior very carefully in order to find out what exactly you are now doing. In most cases, this careful observation requires counting your behavior. For several days, count the number of times the behavior occurs. This record of the frequency of occurrence of the problem behavior is called the **baseline.** The baseline record should be portable, so that you can carry it about with you during the day and record the problem behavior immediately after it occurs. In the following example a student used a 3 × 5 card for recording baseline behavior:

One of our very bright students reported that he had the bad habit of being rude to his friends. He seemed to insult them and to do it often. He began record keeping by carrying in his pocket a 3 × 5 card with two columns on it, labeled, "Did insult" and "Did not insult." As soon as he had finished some conversation with a friend or acquaintance, he would take out the card and make a check in one of the two columns. For example, he might run into a buddy on campus and stop to talk for a few minutes, then the two would go their separate ways. Our student would immediately make an entry in one of his columns.[2]

Keeping a record of your problem behavior is possible if you are aware of your behavior, but what if you are not conscious of what you are doing? You may bite your fingernails or crack your knuckles without being fully aware of your actions. You may have a cigarette half-smoked and be unaware of having put it in your mouth. Some of your "bad habits" are actions that you are not aware of doing deliberately. A procedure for increasing your awareness of your problem behaviors is **negative practice.** Negative practice consists of deliberately doing what you do not want to do; that is, of voluntarily practicing the bad habit. By repeating the habit on purpose, you gain more awareness of it and more control over it.

A man came to a psychologist complaining about headaches, fatigue, and anxiety.[3] An interview with the young man and his wife revealed that he had a bad habit of banging his head into his pillow while asleep. This not only interrupted his sleep but also caused pain in his neck, head, and shoulders. Furthermore, he had apparently been doing this since he was one year old. The man was instructed to use negative practice; each night just before going to sleep he pounded his head into the pillow on purpose until he was tired. After four nights of negative practice his head-banging habit stopped and he was able to sleep soundly. And so was his wife.

Antecedents and Consequences

In analyzing your behavior, you will want to study not only what you do but also when, and in what circumstances, you do it. Your behavior does not occur in isolation, out of context, independent from the world you live in. There are events that precede and events that follow your actions. Events that precede your behavior are called **antecedents.** For example, what are the antecedents of nail-biting behavior? If you have a nail-biting habit, you will find that there are certain situations in which you will bite your nails and others in which you won't. The antecedent situations preceding nail biting may be those situations causing tension or nervousness—for example, a midterm exam.

Events that follow behavior are called **consequences.** According to the **Law of Effect,** behavior with good or favorable consequences tends to be repeated. This can sometimes be a problem for bad habits; a behavior may have favorable short-term consequences but unfavorable long-term consequences. Habits of this sort are very difficult to change because the behavior is being rewarded. For example, what is the consequence of eating a banana split? The short-term consequence is good—a satisfying feeling—but the long-term consequences are less favorable—excess weight. To take an extreme example, the short-term consequences of smoking a cigarette may be favorable—good taste—but the long-term consequences may be unfavorable—cancer.

Think of a bad habit you have. What are its antecedents? What are its short-term and long-term consequences?

Breaking Bad Habits

Once you have analyzed your behavior so that you know what you are doing, how often, and in what circumstances, you are ready to try to change your behavior.

Changing your behavior requires gaining control over the antecedents and consequences of it. To some degree a habit is controlled by its antecedents, but there are ways for you to weaken that control and gain more self control. One way to weaken antecedent control is to avoid the antecedents; that is, avoid the circumstances in which it is likely that the bad habit will occur. For example, what are the antecedents of excessive eating, drinking, and smoking? One circumstance is the presence of other people who are eating, drinking, or smoking. If you want to limit your behavior of this type, you can avoid the social situations that are its antecedents. Eventually the power of the social situations to tempt you into your bad habit will decrease. A second way to weaken antecedent control is to perform an **incompatible behavior**—that is, to do something that would interfere with the bad habit. For example, to some degree, chewing gum is incompatible with smoking; so if you chew gum after meals, you will be less tempted to smoke after meals. If, during periods of tension, you put your hands into your pockets, you will be less likely to bite your nails. By becoming aware of the antecedents of your bad habits and by weakening the control of these antecedents over your behavior, you can increase your self control.

Habits are also controlled by their con-

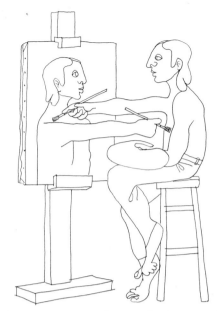

You have more control over who you are than you think.

sequences. If the short-term consequences of an act are rewarding, the act may become a habit. You can gain more control over your behavior by managing the consequences. For example, if you want to be able to study more, you must make the short-term consequences of studying more favorable. But what is a favorable consequence? What is rewarding to you? You can best answer this question by noting what you like to do. What makes you feel good, what are your interests, what are the things you frequently do but are not forced to do? These are potential rewards for you; when you make one of these the short-term consequence of some behavior, the frequency of that behavior should increase. If you arrange your study schedule so that after every two hours of study you get to read a chapter in your favorite novel or watch a half hour of TV, then the frequency of studying should increase.

A young woman wanted to exercise more but was unable to do it. She decided that one of the things that she liked to do and that was important to her was the opportunity to take a hot shower. In order to increase the frequency of her exercise, she made taking a shower the short-term consequence of exercising. She established a rule that she could not shower until she had exercised 15 minutes.[2]

⑤ To change your behavior, you must know what you do, how often, and in what circumstances. You can begin by keeping a record of the frequency of occurrence of the problem behavior to establish a baseline. Events that precede (antecedents) and events that follow (consequences) all help support and maintain your behavior. Changing behavior requires gaining control over these antecedents and consequences. Negative practice may be of use to increase your awareness of your habit and may even help eliminate it.

Managing Your Reactions

You have many emotional reactions to other people and the world around you. You may feel fear in the presence of a spider or snake, tension and anxiety when speaking before a class, relaxation and pleasure while listening to your favorite record. These reactions are learned; you were not born with your present fears and joys.

Gaining self control requires fewer irrational automatic fears and anxieties. You may have a strong fear of public speaking or final examinations; you do not want to have these reactions because they are self-destructive—they not only make you feel bad, they also make you perform poorly. When you are anxious, your body reacts with sweating, a pounding heart, muscular tension, cold hands and feet, stomach upsets, and headaches. You have difficulty thinking clearly and concentrating, and you cannot perform well on examinations. These are learned reactions. If you want to change your behavior, they can be unlearned.

Relaxation

You can learn to relax. The anxiety and nervousness that you feel can produce tension in the body, muscular tension; by relaxing your muscles, you can change your mental state.

A method called **progressive relaxation** is used by psychologists who treat clients with extreme tension and anxiety; progressive relaxation induces deep muscular relaxation by contracting and relaxing the muscles of the body in a step-by-step fashion. When a muscle is contracted or tightened, you feel a **tension sensation.** The object of the progressive-relaxation method is to become highly sensitive to your tension sensations, to become aware of all the bodily tensions you may have, then to relax them.

By alternately tightening and relaxing the muscles in your body, you can become completely relaxed. Try it now. Sit in a quiet and comfortable place. Tighten the muscles in your feet and the calves of your legs; then relax them. Notice the difference between the way the muscles feel tensed or relaxed. Tighten the muscles in your thighs; then relax them. Tighten the muscles in your stomach, noticing the tension sensations; then relax them. Continue to tighten and relax the muscles in your body in a step-by-step fashion.

When you are through, relax everywhere, breathing slowly and deeply, letting your body feel loose and heavy. Imagine the tension flowing down your body and out your toes. Focus on finding tension spots and relaxing them.

This method of relaxation is somewhat similar to the practice of meditation.[4] In **Zen meditation** the individual sits in a quiet and comfortable place and breathes in an effortless way; the person focuses intently on an internal sensation—that accompanying breathing—while relaxing. A goal is to ob-

You can control your body.

serve yourself without reaction or evaluation. The technique of progressive relaxation developed by psychologists during this century differs little from meditation techniques used for thousand of years.

Self-Desensitization

To manage your emotional reactions, you need to learn to relax in the presence of what has been upsetting you; you need to learn to relax while taking a test or while observing a spider; you need to relax while giving a speech or asking someone for a date; you need to relax in thunderstorms or in the dark; you need to relax while driving in traffic or traveling in an airplane. A technique for learning to relax in such situations is desensitization. **Desensitization** involves systematically pairing the feared situation with relaxation.

Fear can be overcome by degrees much better than all at once. A person who is afraid of the water should not be thrown suddenly into the lake, but rather gradually exposed to small amounts of water under nonthreatening conditions. Repeated grad-

ual exposure is the basis of the method of desensitization.

How can you use desensitization yourself? First, think of an irrational fear you have—for example, fear of public speaking. Next, think of a number of examples of the fear. Some examples should be ones that elicit only minor anxiety, and others should be ones that elicit stronger fears. The example situations (10–20 of them) should then be arranged in order of their ability to elicit fear—from ones that are only slightly feared to ones that are very feared. This arrangement of situations, ranked from the least to the most threatening, is called an **anxiety hierarchy.**

The process of desensitization consists of imagining, as vividly as possible, the first situation (least feared) while relaxing. The method of progressive relaxation can be used to maintain complete relaxation while imagining a situation from the hierarchy. The tension aroused by imagining the feared situation should be released by the relaxation procedure; by pairing an image of the feared object or event with the relaxation response, you increase your ability to relax in the presence of the real object or event. There is

568

a transfer of the ability to relax from the imagination to reality. A basic principle of desensitization is that progress up the hierarchy (toward imagining more threatening situations) is made only after complete success at earlier levels of the hierarchy; you don't move on to a second feared situation until you are able to imagine the first situation while remaining completely relaxed.

Meditation has been found effective in reducing fear and anxiety.[5,6] The effectiveness of meditation may come from its resemblance to desensitization.[4] Both methods involve systematic relaxation, focusing on an internal event, and repeatedly maintaining relaxation while imagining or thinking of worries or fears.

⑤ You can gain greater control over yourself. You can learn how to relax and how to get rid of irrational fears. Progressive relaxation is a method of deep muscular relaxation that helps you control bodily tension. Control over irrational fears involves first learning how to relax, then using desensitization to reduce the fear. Desensitization is a method of reducing fear that involves pairing relaxation with the feared object or stimulus. The process of desensitization begins with imagining a slightly threatening situation while remaining relaxed.

Managing Your Interactions

Your relationships with other people are potentially the most rewarding and the most punishing part of your life. When an important relationship is not going well, you feel miserable, worthless, or depressed; when a relationship is going well, you feel optimistic, powerful, and happy. Of course, because these interactions involve two people, by definition what happens is not just up to you,

You can control
your emotional reactions.

but you can strongly influence your relationships to make them better for you. Managing your interactions involves identifying certain problems and then changing your behavior.

Identifying Problems

Sometimes you know that things are not going right, but you don't know why. It is helpful to be able to analyze your relationship to determine the source of the difficulty. A problem with some relationships is that they are not open. In an open relationship, the individuals are willing to reveal themselves— their hopes, fears, likes, dislikes—and to interact in an honest fashion. In relationships that are not open, the individuals hide their true feelings and try at all times to be socially acceptable; they put on false faces and do not let you see the real person underneath. A second major problem with some relationships is that they are not supportive. In a supportive relationship, the individuals seek ways to show approval, validation, and caring. In relationships that are not supportive, the individuals put each other down and undermine each other's position; they are very involved with themselves but not each other; each would rather be right than loving. A third major problem is that some relationships are not trusting. In a trusting relationship, the individuals are willing to be vulnerable; each trusts the other to be loving, not hurtful. In relationships without trust, the individuals must be on guard at all times; they are afraid of appearing stupid or unattractive; they are jealous of each other's time and interest.

Changing Behavior

The key to changing relationships is communication. Most people don't listen very well; when someone else is talking, we often just wait until the person is through so we can get our turn. Furthermore, little communication takes place, for most talk in relationships is superficial, not about feelings or deeply held beliefs.

The act of listening is not passive; it involves more than having ears directed toward the sound. Listening is active, involving attending, paraphrasing, and clarifying. When you attend to someone, you establish contact—by looking at the person with interest and by occasionally nodding to indicate that you are attending to what is being said. By repeating what is said, but in your own words, you let the speaker know what you are hearing. This allows the speaker the opportunity to correct you if you have misunderstood. By clarifying, the listener tries to bring the message into focus; by asking clarifying questions or asking for elaboration, the listener makes sure that the speaker's message is conveyed. This kind of listening is an active task and guarantees that communication will occur.

In addition to listening, communication requires telling the truth. Many people are afraid to reveal how they feel; they are afraid that they will be hurt or laughed at. But to maintain a close relationship you must take the risk of being known, of revealing who you are to someone else. As one author wrote:

If you and I can honestly tell each other who we are, that is, what we think, judge, feel, value, love, honor and esteem, hate, fear, desire, hope for, believe in and are committed to, then and then only can each of us grow. Then and then alone can each of us be what he really is, say what he really thinks, tell what he really feels, express what he really loves. This is the real meaning of authenticity as a person, that my exterior truly reflects my interior.[7]

How can you reveal your feelings to someone else? One way is to increase your use of what have been called "I messages."[8] An **I message** is simply a sentence that tells how you feel in a direct way. For example, "I like you" or "I am upset because you didn't call me." You can improve your relationships by listening more actively and by being willing to reveal your feelings through "I messages."

⑤   Three basic problems affecting some relationships is that they are not open, supportive, and trusting. Relationships can be improved by improving communication; this involves listening more actively and being willing to reveal who you are.

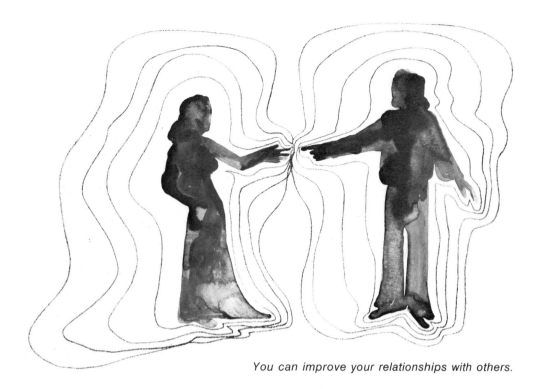

You can improve your relationships with others.

Summary

KEY QUESTIONS

1. How can you change your habits?

   One way to change your habits is by controlling the environmental context in which the behaviors occur—namely, what comes before and what comes after them in the world. Once you know what you do, how often, and under what circumstances you do it, you can weaken the environmental control over the habit.

2. How can you control your emotional reactions?

   Since you cannot be frightened and relaxed at the same time, you can control your irrational fears by learning to relax. Progressive relaxation is a special method for producing deep relaxation and eliminating muscular tensions. By repeatedly and gradually exposing yourself to the situations you fear while relaxing, you can learn to relax and unlearn fear.

3. How can you improve your relationships?

   Relationships can be improved by making them more open, supportive, and trusting. This can be achieved through improved communication; improving communication depends upon your willingness to actively listen and to reveal who you are.

KEY CONCEPTS

self control	An individual's ability to manage his or her habits and emotional reactions.
irresistible impulse	A sudden strong compulsion to do something, usually something socially unacceptable or unlawful.
kleptomania	A compulsion to steal.
pyromania	A compulsion to set fires.
exhibitionism	A compulsion for bodily exposure, usually exposure of the sexual organs.
baseline	A record of the frequency of occurrence of a behavior before attempts are made to change it.
negative practice	A technique of deliberately practicing a bad habit in order to gain increased voluntary control over it; for example, by practicing knuckle-cracking at regular intervals each day, the habit may be controlled.
antecedents	Events that regularly precede an action.
consequences	Events that follow an action; for example, rewards.
Law of Effect	The principle that actions followed by favorable consequences tend to be repeated.
incompatible behavior	Behavior that would interfere with another action.
progressive relaxation	A method of producing deep muscular relaxation by alternately tightening and relaxing sets of muscles.
tension sensation	The feeling associated with a tightened muscle.
Zen meditation	A practice that involves sitting in a comfortable place and focusing on breathing.
desensitization	A technique for reducing fear by pairing relaxation with the feared situation.
anxiety hierarchy	An arrangement of feared situations, ranked from the least to the most threatening.
I message	A direct statement of feeling that uses the word "I"; for example, "I love you."

30 Revolution

CHAPTER OUTLINE

KEY QUESTIONS

1. What are the radical changes under way in our society?
2. What kind of people are rebels and why do they rebel?
3. How will young adults shape the future society?

Make no mistake: the upheavals of the moment are but a mild foretaste of what is to come. That which is now upon us in America reaches beyond disorder, riot or insurrection. Beyond revolution, beyond classification; what is now unfolding is no less than the transformation of all things.[1]

Whether freedom will be enhanced or diminished by the transformations that are under way depends upon the nature of our participation. Change itself is value free; it can be for the better or for the worse.

Recently the rate of change has accelerated in America. There are revolutions now in progress in this country—for example, the revolutions in values and in technological power—with which we must cope. When the rate of change is too fast, when the future intrudes into our lives before we have learned to cope with the present, then we experience confusion and distress. Alvin Toffler, author of the book *Future Shock*,[2] describes the state as "the dizzying disorientation brought on by the premature arrival of the future."

Signs of Change

The future is intruding into the present. Everywhere there are signs of change: there are changes in values, or consciousness, changes in schools, and changes in life-styles.

New Consciousness

Charles Reich, in his best-selling book *The Greening of America,*[3] describes three value systems (Consciousness I, Consciousness II, and Consciousness III) that are found in America. **Consciousness I** was the predominant value system before the Second World War; **Consciousness II** is the value system predominant today; and **Consciousness III** is the value system of the future which is, according to Reich, presently sweeping the country, especially among the young.

Chances are, your grandfather's values conformed fairly well to Consciousness I—a kind of rugged individualism—while your father's values may conform fairly well to Consciousness II—organization and social reform. You, or someone you know, may have adopted Consciousness III—a radically new way of thinking. Reich describes Consciousness III as a revolutionary change in consciousness.

There is a revolution coming. It will not be like revolutions of the past. It will originate with the individual and with culture, and it will change the political structure only as its final act. It will not require violence to succeed, and it cannot be successfully resisted by vio-

Consciousness I: Rugged individualism.

Consciousness II: Regulated bureaucracy.

lence. It is now spreading with amazing rapidity, and already our laws, institutions and social structure are changing in consequence. It promises a higher reason, a more human community, and a new and liberated individual. Its ultimate creation will be a new and enduring wholeness and beauty—a renewed relationship of man to himself, to other men, to society, to nature, and to the land.

This is the revolution of the new generation. . . . At the heart of everything is what we shall call a change of consciousness. This means a "new head"—a new way of living—a new man. This is what the new generation has been searching for, and what it has started achieving.[3]

Reich's optimistic vision of the future cultural benefits of the youth movement has been criticized as being naive and simplistic,

as it may well be. Kenneth Keniston has a more sober view of the youth movement:

The counter culture may replace the barbecue pit with the hippie pad, family togetherness with the encounter group, and the suburban coffee hour with the commune, but the focus is still on the private world instead of on the social and political scene where it should be.[4]

It is worth noting that this criticism of today's youth for having a subjective orientation (toward the private world) rather than a political orientation (toward social reform) is based on a value system consistent with Consciousness II. Achieving social reform through political organization is a value of Consciousness II but not of Consciousness III.

Consciousness I, II, and III are summarized in the table following.

Consciousness III: Cooperation.

	Consciousness I	Consciousness II
Cause of Social Problems	Social problems are due to bad character.	Social problems are due to aspects of society that can be changed through reform.
How to Solve Problems	Struggle and competition; survival of the fittest.	Organize; create a bureaucracy with a hierarchy of status and power.
Duties of a Citizen	Very few. Life is a harsh pursuit of individual self-interest	Commitment to public interest; sacrifice to common good. Work for your country, not yourself.
Way to Success	Success equals hard work, character, and self-denial.	Success equals dedication to goals beyond self—the common good.
Freedom	Each person has the right to pursue opportunities where they can be found.	Business and individuals have a social responsibility; this is ensured through government regulation.

	Consciousness III
Cause of Social Problems	Social problems result from competition, judgment, and classification; from the system of authority and hierarchy; from giant technology and an increasing distance from nature; and from self-alienation which follows from the evils of the present system.
How to Solve Problems	Problems can be solved by abandoning the present corrupt system; and then by cooperating in the creation of true community, a new form of interpersonal relationships with no hierarchy.
Duties of a Citizen	The task for citizens is to work to preserve themselves from being destroyed by the state.
Way to Success	Live fully at each moment; remain open to self and experience; work for self-understanding and self-development.
Freedom	Freedom based on personal responsibility and honesty; personal moral code transcends all law; individuals should strive to be liberated from the imperatives of society.

New Schools

Following is the dedication written at the beginning of a book on how to start your own free school:[5]

To the millions of children still
in prison in the United States
and
to the handful of adults trying
to spring them

What is a **free school?** It is a school that promotes freedom; it is not a school that charges no tuition. Free schools offer a radical alternative to the public school system. According to one survey, the number of free schools in America increased from about twenty-five in 1967 to over six hundred in 1972.[6] The survey found these alternative schools in thirty-nine states, but most were concentrated in California and New York.

At the base of the free school movement is the belief in individual freedom. A. S. Neill's *Summerhill*[7] describes an example of a free school that has been operating successfully for many years in England. Free schools are oriented toward the growth of the whole person rather than the narrow focus on intellectual skills. A principle assumption of free schools is that growth occurs most naturally within the context of meaningful human relationships. This means that free schools need very small classes, rather than the large classes of the public school system. They need a flexible curriculum dependent upon student interest, rather than a standardized, state-directed series of courses. They need teachers who are participants in the learning process, rather than teachers who dictate and supervise experiences. They need programs focused on feeling rather than on obedience. They need a cooperative, nonevaluative educational environment, rather than a judgmental climate.

Have free schools been successful in their effort to promote freedom? According to some critics, they have failed. Jonathan Kozol, in his book *Free Schools*,[8] argues that students in these schools are deceived into believing that they have more freedom than students in more traditional schools. In fact, they may simply have different but equally restricted choices; there may be no more freedom involved in the choice between pottery and painting found in the free school than in the choice between algebra and Latin found in the more traditional school. Adults dictate the available options in both cases.

There are several types of free schools. Some operate out of private homes, some out of farms, and some out of stores or warehouses. Free schools are available for individuals from preschool age up to college age. One variety of free school is an attempt to develop a self-sufficient and therapeutic community, as separated as little as possible from everyday living. An example of this kind of school is Mulberry Farm School:

We are on 370 acres in the Ozarks. We have children from ages 6 through 18.

We see that children are often subjected to pressures and influences which cause them to react with fear, hostility, unhappiness, and reduced ability to learn. We assert that we can reverse these negative reactions by (1) association with adults who are warm, supportive, interested, capable and motivating, (2) individual progress in learning, (3) use of innovative, stimulating materials and equipment, (4) real work—participation in farming, care of animals, cooking, gardening, building, maintenance and the like, (5) good diet, (6) facilities for recreational learning—plenty of space, two creeks, two ponds stocked with fish, woods, horses, camping, swimming, boating, trips in our bus.[9]

Free schools are often started by people with high hopes and ideals, but they are sometimes short on realistic judgment and basic skills. Free schools have been criticized as havens for adults who do not want the responsibility of making decisions and for children who reject learning. In fact, there is a great diversity in motives and in ability among participants in free schools. It is possible that there will emerge from this diversity a revolutionary change in our school systems.

New Life-styles

Young people are creating a radically different life-style—a whole new way of living that is separated from mainstream American life. According to Theodore Roszak:

Most of what is presently happening that is new, provocative and engaging in politics, education, the arts, social relations (love, courtship, family, community) is the creation either of youth, who are profoundly, even fanatically, alienated from the parental generation, or of those who address themselves primarily to the young.[10]

The new life-style is partly a reaction against what the young consider to be corrupt aspects of our present society. The interest in *naturalness* in food and clothes may be a reaction against what some consider the extreme artificiality of formal fashions and pre-packaged foods. The interest in *handicrafts* may be a reaction against a supertechnology that has alienated us from the products of our own labor. The interest in *primitive rural living* may be a reaction against life in our polluted urban centers. The interest in *community* may be a reaction against a society founded on economic relationships and competitive individualism.

Making adobe bricks at the Morning Star Commune, New Mexico.

However, what has emerged from these reactions is a new life-style with a philosophy and integrity of its own. One of the forms in which the new life-style is expressed is intentional communities, or **communes.** A commune is a group of people who choose to live together for the purpose of sharing. Occasionally these collectives share sexually, as well as in other ways, and form what are called **group marriages.** Harrad West, a group marriage commune living in California, consists of six adults and three children.[11] In most communes, however, couples pair off as they do in conventional society.

According to a recent estimate, there are in excess of 1,000 rural and 2,000 urban communes in North America.[12] A member of a rural farm commune wrote a book about his experiences and described the commune as follows:

Chestnut Hill, a dirt road cuts across it like a scar that never healed properly. The road runs east to west, the bottom part of the hill drops sharply and comes to an abrupt halt at land's edge. Then a narrow river forms its natural border. . . .

Almost all of Chestnut Hill was settled by the Ripley family who built this great house and several others around here. But the Ripley children and their children moved away, and the farm, the house and this sixty-acre piece of land were sold after old Lucian Ripley, who lived here all alone, died of a stroke. The children went to the cities in search of homes heated with the flick of a switch, looking for middle-class security that their farmer parents were never quite able to guarantee. And we, who are the children of the secure, find ourselves reclaiming that land, desirous of the poverty that helps keep us free.[13]

The life-style of some of the young in America—and possibly the life-style of the future—resembles the life-style of the past. Back to nature, back to simplicity, and back to handicraft, is in some ways back to the last century. But after living with pollution and freeways and machines, we may see simplicity with new eyes.

Communes are social experiments. Most of these experiments do not survive for long; the problems of living and working together are not solved easily. But new social forms are being invented and tried out. Old forms are being brought back to life and tested. If we seek to build a new society, and if we trust experience more than guesswork, then the results of experiments with these miniature societies should be particularly relevant to the design of the future.

⬜ Everywhere there are signs of change. Changes in consciousness, schools, and life-styles are particularly significant because they may forecast a revolutionary change in our whole culture. Consciousness III, with its values of sharing, openness, and freedom, supports recent changes in schools and life-styles that are more open and free.

The Present Revolutions

Perhaps change itself is the only constant. Every day seems to bring new and baffling changes in values, knowledge, and technology. Finding ways to live with change may be the challenge of the future. When the old is completely overturned, when a change is essentially total, we call that change **revolution.** Revolutions are now under way in social and political values, in sexual attitudes, in technology, and in psychology.

Social Revolution

The peace and civil rights movements have profoundly changed the social fabric of the country. Individuals who protested the Vietnam war and the military draft were bent on completely changing the direction of American military policy. Those fighting for civil rights have pressured society to grant equal rights to blacks, Chicanos, American Indians, women, homosexuals, and children. Leaders from each of these subgroups of society have attempted to create moral and political forces for radical changes in laws and in attitudes.

Sexual Revolution

The sexual revolution is a revolution in *attitudes* toward sex. While sexual behavior has changed to become somewhat more permissive, surveys show that the changes in behavior are not so great as many believe. Sexual attitudes, however, have changed radically. Books are openly published and sold today that would have been burned a generation ago. More couples are openly living together without marriage today. Modern clothes reveal, rather than hide, the human body. Parties of "swingers" are plainly advertised in some newspapers.

Technological Revolution

Technology—"that great, growling engine of change"[2]—has been growing at a rapidly accelerating pace. Every major advance in invention or application creates a new power for human use and new problems for human adaptation. Rapid transportation systems have radically changed the effective "size" of the earth; people who used to be strangers in far-off lands are now neighbors who can be visited over the weekend. Television and computer technology have created an explosion of information. The work that people used to do is now increasingly done by machines. What is the role of people in the coming era of machines?

Man is becoming mechanistic, both physically and mentally. Machines, on the other hand, are becoming more humanlike in their appearance, their structure, and in the way they perform their tasks. . . . Objectively, I cannot help feeling that, relatively, man is declining and machines are growing. . . . Man has created new kinds of machines. Now machines are creating a new kind of man.[14]

Psychological Revolution

The power of machines to change human beings, however, cannot match the power of people to change themselves. As the influence of psychology grows and as the power of psychological tools expands, the ability of people to control each other through technical manipulation increases. According to some, we may evolve into a **psytocracy**, a

form of society where everything—including people—is controlled through technical manipulation.

A psytocracy is a form of tyranny, but not in the classical sense of the word. The slaves and the masters are indistinguishable. Each person is so conditioned to social norms and values that he eagerly performs whatever the social machine demands. . . . In a psytocracy there is no dissent because everyone defines freedom in the same terms, for example, the freedom to do gleefully what is expected of him.[15]

What is the role of psychology in the future? General interest in psychology seems to be increasing throughout the country. The newsstands are full of popular best-selling books on psychology; television and movie plots seem to focus increasingly on psychological problems instead of physical dangers; the psychology departments in colleges and universities often have the most heavily enrolled courses on campus. The increased interest in psychology offers both a promise and a threat; and both arise from the same source—the increased power to control human behavior. Will the power be used for good or evil? That is a question only the future will answer.

Aldous Huxley, author of two novels about the psychology of the future, *Brave New World* and *Island*, had a gloomy view of what the future will bring:

We have had religious revolutions, we have had political, industrial, economic, and nationalistic revolutions. All of them, as our descendants will discover, were but ripples in an ocean of conservatism—trivial by comparison with the psychological revolution toward which we are so rapidly moving. That will really be a revolution. When it is over, the human race will give no further trouble.[16]

Change Agents

The revolutionary changes in this country are not so much happening to us as they are made by us; these changes are the results of changes in human attitudes and behavior. Certain people can be called **change agents**— individuals who make changes happen. A psychotherapist is a change agent who helps unhappy clients to change; an inspired teacher is a change agent who promotes growth in students; and a rebel is a change agent who triggers a change in society.

What is a **rebel?** According to Camus, the French writer and philosopher, a rebel is a person who says *no.*[17]

America was born in revolution, when the early founders of the country rebelled against the English. Rebels are people who resist authority and fight for a new social structure. They are deviants in their own society, violating the standards of belief and behavior that are the norm for their peers; they fight to establish a new society, with new standards of belief and behavior. They seek radical change.

Three Rebels: King, Seale, and Berrigan

Martin Luther King, Jr., expressed his philosophy of nonviolent resistance in an essay written from his jail cell in Birmingham, Alabama. He had been arrested for his participation in an illegal demonstration against segregation, and he had broken the law deliberately. He wrote:

One who breaks an unjust law must do it openly, lovingly . . . , and with a willingness to accept the penalty. I submit that an individual who breaks a law that conscience tells

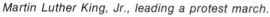

Martin Luther King, Jr., leading a protest march.

him is unjust, and willingly accepts the penalty by staying in jail to arouse the conscience of the community over its injustice, is in reality expressing the very highest respect for law.[18]

King was successful in changing federal law, but within five years the civil rights movement had changed and many leaders were rejecting King's nonviolent approach. Bobby Seale, one of the founders of the Black Panther party, described this new point of view in 1968 when he wrote:

We aren't hungry for violence; we don't want violence. Violence is ugly, guns are ugly. But we understand that there are two kinds of violence: the violence that is perpetuated against our people by the fascist aggression of the power structure; and self-defense—a form of violence used to defend ourselves from the unjust violence that's inflicted upon us.[19]

Another rebel, a Jesuit priest named Daniel Berrigan, destroyed some draft records in Catonsville, Ohio, in an act of protest against the Vietnam war; he then went into hiding to escape arrest, moving secretly from place to place. By not willingly accepting the penalty, he too broke with King's vision of civil disobedience. While on the run the fugitive priest wrote a book explaining his act, in which he described the crisis facing the youth of America:

The time is here (is at hand) when middle America will choose between its property and its sons. Is at hand. And the choice, when the chips are down, is already made: the renunciation of the bloodline in favor of possessions. Helicopters over Berkeley, Weathermen hunted down, resisters in jail or exile. Case of one resister: his father sat stonily on the draft board which rejected his plea for C.O. (being accepted as a conscientious objector). The father urged in fact, secretly, the severest prosecution of his son.[20]

When your society demands conformity to policies or laws that you believe to be evil, what should you do? What are the acceptable forms of protest? Some believe that a person has an obligation to deliberately violate a law or social norm that their conscience tells them is unjust. Others believe that a person should work for change within the system without violating the law.

In 1972 Bobby Seale announced his candidacy for mayor of the city of Oakland, California. Rejecting the past rhetoric of violence, he expressed the intention of working for change within the established political system.

What do you think is the proper response to bring about change in society?

The Mind of the Rebel

Who are the rebels who are calling for radical change in America? How should we understand them—in terms of their politics, their personalities, their family origins? Are they different from you or me?

Why do men rebel? . . . What could possibly be so wrong with so many of the world's men and women that they should fight so hard to stay outside the Eden we think we are offering them.

I make three assumptions. First, everyone who is now a rebel became a rebel; he was once upon a time a child who spoke no politics. The rebel is someone who has changed.

Second, men do not imperil their own and others' lives for unimpressive reasons. . . . When they do something dangerous, they have been convinced that not to do it was more dangerous. . . .

Third, I assume that the rebel is much like myself, someone whom I can understand. He is politically extraordinary. That does not mean that he is psychologically so.[21]

If these assumptions are right, the activist should be found to be psychologically normal. Several studies have confirmed this prediction.[22,23] One study found that campus demonstrators had higher self-regard, higher self-acceptance, and were more spontaneous and more self-actualized than non-demonstrators.[23] In general, studies show that activists were psychologically mature and well-adjusted individuals.

Because activists openly violate social norms, people often consider them psychologically abnormal. Criticism and dissent are sometimes regarded as symptoms of mental disorder. The civil rights workers in the South in 1964 and later in Appalachia were often called crazy and self-destructive.[24]

All societies have ways of dealing with those members who violate social standards for acceptable belief and behavior; both jails and mental hospitals in this country contain persons who deviate markedly from social norms. Political dissenters in Russia, according to some reports, are systematically placed in mental hospitals. Our society however is more tolerant of political deviation than many others. Because American psychologists follow a strict professional code of ethics, political dissent alone would not result in a professional diagnosis of mental disturbance, although nonprofessionals might describe the political protester as "crazy." Political protesters—because they publicly violate the standards of society—are prime candidates for the label "criminal" or "crazy," and people study them for the purpose of explaining the origins of their mental "problems."

Political rebels are change agents, and their "mental problems" help to bring about changes in society. Sometimes these changes are constructive and sometimes destructive. Hitler was a political rebel too.

Student Activists

Since the late 1950's, when Northern students joined Southern students in an effort to eliminate segregation in the South, students on campuses all over the country have occasionally joined together in active protest. By the thousands, student activists confronted their communities with their moral outrage.

Even at the height of the Vietnam war protests during the late 1960's, the activists comprised only a small proportion of the total student body. Who were these campus radicals? They were not students fighting against the conservative values of their parents; a notable fact about these students is that their parents were often politically liberal and economically fairly well-off.[25,26] Both student radicals and their parents shared a humanistic value system. These values consist of a humanitarian concern for the social conditions of others, as well as a concern with individual development and self-expression. The discrepancy between their values and the state of their society led them to rebel.

A Theory of Revolution

The **discrepancy theory of revolution** emphasizes the difference between expectancy and reality, and states that revolutions result when this difference is large. The perception of injustice is intensified in a society with a large discrepancy between expectation and reality. Starvation and malnutrition still exist in this overfed nation; there is an increasing difference between the educational and economic opportunities of the nation's poor and the nation's rich. The Vietnam war, Watergate, and recent political and corporate corruption were, for many people, violations of basic and accepted values. The discrepancy between belief and action, between expectation and reality, has been accentuated by the television camera, from which few can hide. The war in Vietnam and the civil rights protests in the South were brought into the living rooms of most Americans. Revolution depends upon the perception of injustice, and the perception of injustice depends upon the communication of existing discrepancies.

S   Revolutions are currently under way in this country—vast changes in social and political values, in sexual attitudes, in technology, and in the power and use of psychology. These changes are not so much happening to us as made by us; some people, however, are more powerful change agents than others. Rebels are people who resist authority and fight for a new social structure. Studies have found that most rebels are psychologically normal, although their society often tends to regard them as abnormal. According to the discrepancy theory of revolution, rebellion results from a large discrepancy between expectancies and reality.

Is there a generation gap?

The Generation Gap and the Future Society

The world is changing rapidly and we are changing with it. Our values, opinions, beliefs, and attitudes today are different from those of yesterday. There have been radical changes in our attitudes toward drugs, sex, the role of women, the environment, and our life-style.

The Youth Culture and the Generation Gap

Rapidly changing attitudes may be responsible for the so-called **generation gap**— the differences between parents and their children in values, opinions, and beliefs. Adolescents and young adults are typically more liberal than their parents, and the resulting generation gap results in frequent conflicts. According to Roszak,[10] young people today have formed a **counterculture,** a way of life and a set of values quite different from the mainstream life-style. This youth counterculture values peace, love, freedom, cooperation and sharing, openness and honesty, self-expression, naturalness, and humanism.

The anthropologist Margaret Mead argues that there is now a great gulf, a permanent division, between the younger and older generations.[27] From Mead's point of view, however, the generation gap is not necessarily bad; she sees in this division between parent and child a guide to the future, a future composed of a new form of culture. Mead identifies three kinds of culture: **postfigurative,** in which children learn primarily from their parents; **cofigurative,** in which children and adults learn from their peers; and **prefigurative,** in which adults learn from their children. Mead finds that we are changing into a prefigurative culture, in which children will serve as scouts, explor-

In a prefigurative culture, young adults explore the frontiers and their parents follow.

ing the frontiers of knowledge and experimenting with new life-styles.

Why should we be moving toward a prefigurative culture? It may be the natural result of having a highly industrialized, technological society. Advanced industrialization has been accompanied by urban migration, as the place of work shifted from the farm or shop to the office or factory. In the city families work together less often, so family ties have been weakened. Industrialization has also brought an increased need for professional and technical labor; the specialized training necessary to support this work has required prolonged schooling, and this has further weakened family ties. As the youth have tended to be isolated from their families, they have depended more on their peers and less on their parents for guidance. The increased freedom from parental traditions has made it possible for young adults to experiment and innovate with forms of dress, music, and life-styles, which the older generation increasingly has begun to adopt. Thus, children become the "scouts" exploring the frontiers, and their parents follow.

Psychology and the Good Life

Young adults will play an increasingly important role in shaping the future of this society; they will control the velocity and guide the direction of the continuing revolutions propelling us into the future. But what will be their tools to shape the future? Where will they get a map pointing the way to the good life?

They may turn to psychology for answers. The use of psychological principles to manipulate our society as a whole has, as George Miller has written,

implications for every aspect of society [which] would make brave men tremble. . . .

Scientific psychology is potentially one of the most revolutionary intellectual enterprises ever conceived by the mind of man.[28]

Scientific psychology offers power, and the power can be used for good or evil.

Some believe that the development of a humanistic science of psychology—one concerned with human growth and development instead of manipulation—may provide the guidance that is urgently needed in shaping our future. As Abraham Maslow wrote:

And to those of good will who want to help make a better world, I recommend strongly that they consider science—humanistic science—as a way of doing this, a very good and necessary way, perhaps even the best way of all.

We simply do not have available today enough reliable knowledge to construct the One Good World. We do not even have enough knowledge to teach individuals how to love each other—at least not with any certainty. The best answer, I am convinced, is in the advancement of knowledge. The life of science can also be a life of passion, of beauty, of hope for mankind, and of revelation of values.[29]

The technical manipulation of society through behavioral principles will become increasingly possible with the growth of psychological knowledge. A new and promising opposing trend, particularly evident among young people, is grounded in their concep-tions of themselves as people and in their life-styles. Consistent with the humanistic psychology of Carl Rogers or Abraham Maslow, the new value system is oriented toward honesty, openness to experience, and self-development.

The new consciousness, the new schools, and the new life-styles may lead ultimately to a new society. This future society may be designed as a community formed deliberately to promote a better life. There is every reason to believe that psychology could play a significant role in that design.

S   The generation gap is the difference between parents and children in values and beliefs; in recent years this difference has become so marked that adolescents and young adults may have developed their own unique culture, a counterculture opposed in many ways to the majority culture. According to Margaret Mead, we are moving toward a prefigurative culture, in which adults will follow the lead of youth. But where will the youth lead and where will they find the answers necessary to shape the good life? A humanistic science of psychology may offer guidance.

Summary

KEY QUESTIONS

1. What are the radical changes under way in our society?

   We are witnessing social, sexual, technological, and psychological revolutions in this country. The pace of change is accelerating. Even our basic value system is changing to offer less support for competitive individualism and more support for openness and sharing.

2. What kind of people are rebels and why do they rebel?

   Rebels are change agents, fighting for a new social structure. Because they violate social norms, they may be judged as deviant or abnormal;

but studies show that they are in fact psychologically normal. According to one theory of revolution, people rebel because of the large discrepancy between expectancy and reality. When you expect health, wealth, and justice but perceive instead disease, poverty, and injustice, you are motivated to rebel.

3. How will young adults shape the future society?

The technological revolution in this country has led to the development of a youth counterculture which, according to Margaret Mead, the older generation will increasingly copy. Young people will be the "scouts" and their parents will follow. The science of psychology may help by providing a map for that journey.

KEY CONCEPTS

Consciousness I	The value system that was most common before the Second World War, based on a preference for rugged individualism.
Consciousness II	The value system most common today, based on a preference for reform through bureaucratic programs.
Consciousness III	A value system held by some young adults today and which is predicted to be more common in the future; based on preference for community, openness to experience, and personal—rather than absolute—moral codes.
free school	A nontraditional school emphasizing freedom and personal growth.
commune	A group of people choosing to live together for the purpose of sharing.
group marriage	A group of three or more people living together and sharing sexual experiences.
revolution	A radical change so that the old is completely overturned and replaced with the new.
psytocracy	A society whose members have been conditioned for their roles and are controlled through technical manipulation.
change agent	An individual who makes change happen—for example, a teacher or a rebel.
rebel	A person who resists authority and fights for a new social structure.
discrepancy theory of revolution	The theory stating that revolution results from large differences between expectancy and reality.

generation gap   The difference between parents and their children in values, opinions, and beliefs.

counterculture   A way of life and set of values opposed to the majority culture; for example, the youth counterculture.

postfigurative culture   A culture in which children learn primarily from their parents.

cofigurative culture   A culture in which children and adults learn from their peers.

prefigurative culture   A culture in which parents learn from their children.

Suggested Readings

Behavior Control by Perry London. New York: Harper & Row, 1969. Discusses the danger and promise of mind control, with descriptions of hypnotism, psychosurgery, drugs, conditioning, and other tools of our psychotechnology.

Using Psychology: Principles of Behavior and Your Life by Morris K. Holland. Boston, Mass.: Little, Brown, 1975. Applications of the principles of psychology explained in an easy, step-by-step manner. Describes how students can use psychology to study more effectively, to improve memory, to break bad habits, to improve personal relationships, and to gain better control of their own lives.

Behavioral Self-Control by Carl E. Thoresen & Michael J. Mahoney. New York: Holt, Rinehart and Winston, 1974. Principles and methods of self-control, presented in a brief, readable book. Discusses self-observation techniques, self-reward, and self-punishment.

Beyond Freedom and Dignity by B. F. Skinner. New York: Alfred A. Knopf, 1971. Argues that behavior is determined, controlled by the environmental consequence, and that therefore the idea of human freedom is an illusion.

Future Shock by Alvin Toffler. New York: Random House, 1970. Discusses our "collision with tomorrow." The rate of change in information, institutions, and values presents serious problems for our society. Individuals are overstimulated and society suffers from "future shock."

The Making of a Counter Culture by Theodore Roszak, Garden City, N.Y.: Anchor Books, 1969. A study of contemporary youth culture. Asserts that most of what is new, provocative, and engaging in life is the product of alienated youth or of their spokesmen.

Research Methods

X

Science and Human Values

Values and Scientific Questions

Values and Scientific Methods

Values and Scientific Facts

Values and Applied Science

A fact is something that is believed to be true or probably true; a **value** is what is believed to be good or is preferred. Facts describe what actually occurs; values describe what should be. The scientific method is a set of rules for deciding what the facts are; it cannot resolve value questions. For example, the scientific method can help answer the factual question, "What are the differences in beliefs between this generation and the previous generations?"; but the scientific method cannot answer the value question, "Which generation is better?"

Although the scientific method is not appropriate for answering questions concerning values, this does not mean that science is not affected by values. Science, just like all other human activities, is highly affected by human values. Our values influence the questions that science asks; our values affect the methods we apply in trying to answer

those questons; our values affect the facts yielded by those methods; and our values affect the ways in which those facts are applied in the world.

Values and Scientific Questions

Here are some questions that have been asked by scientists: What is unique in the family backgrounds of individuals who are highly creative? Does watching violence on TV increase or decrease a child's aggressiveness? What are the effects of marijuana on perception and thinking? Which is the more effective method for reducing psychotic behaviors: psychoanalysis or desensitization therapy?

Where did these questions come from? In each case the question arose from the interests, concerns, and values of the scientist. A scientist would probably not think of asking the question, "What is unique in the family backgrounds of individuals who are highly creative?", if the scientist did not *value* creativity. A scientist would probably not think to ask the question, "Does watching violence on TV increase or decrease a child's aggressiveness?", if the scientist did not *value* nonaggressiveness. It is not true that all scientific questions can be directly related to the values of the scientist who asks them, but values clearly influence many of the problems studied.

The world is full of information, and scientists—like all of us—can pay attention only to a part. What part is of interest and worthy of observation? What questions are worth asking and answering? To some degree, the theory that a scientist believes in will determine the questions asked. As one psychologist wrote:

Theories determine facts, not vice versa. Indeed, there would be no data at all without prior theoretical speculation of what, in the flux of experience, constitutes significant observation. Facts, far from being the data base upon which theory rests, are the end products of theory.[1]

Theories, values, and beliefs are guides to observation. They illuminate sensations with meaning. They tell us what questions are worth asking and answering.

Values and Scientific Methods

The scientific method itself arises from certain specific values: the value of truth, objectivity, rationality, skepticism, creativity, curiosity, accuracy, order, and understanding. The pursuit of science can be viewed as the pursuit of these values as goals. Science is but one way of knowing; other ways of deciding what is true arise from other systems of values. For example, "intuition" as a way of knowing arises from the value of subjectivity, rather than objectivity. Intuitive people trust their own reactions and judgments more than those objectively agreed upon by others. "Acceptance of authority" as a way of knowing arises from the value of compliance, of skepticism. The knowers trust experts more than themselves. Science is supported by values different from these.

The way the scientific method is used is also based on questions of human values. In any science, at one particular time in history, there is often one generally accepted conceptual framework or belief system with which almost all studies are consistent. Kuhn has called these systems of techniques, values, and beliefs **paradigms**.[2] Paradigms limit the type of theories and explanations that are proposed. For example, there was for many years in psychology an "S-R" paradigm; almost all theories and explanations were consistent with the reduction of environment and behavior to "stimulus" and "response." The S-R paradigm in psychology derived from the value of reductionism, elementism, and mechanism in the study of people. Within the S-R paradigm, attempts were made to reduce complex behavior to elementary stimulus-response connections. Today more complex paradigms are emerging using cognitive processes as their basis rather than simple conditioning.

Often the application of the scientific method in psychology involves special questions of ethics and human values. When does psychological study threaten the invasion of privacy? Under what circumstances can scientists experiment on human beings? Whom should the psychologist serve, the individual or the state? How should psychologists treat animals in their experiments? These questions are by no means resolved, but the professional association of psychologists, the American Psychological Association, has formulated careful rules to guide psychologists in their activities relating to each of these questions. Rules for the treatment of human and animal subjects, for example, have been developed to safeguard subjects from danger or exploitation. The development of a common standard of ethics for psychologists was possible because most psychologists share a common value system.

Values and Scientific Facts

The scientific method, as it is used in psychology, always includes a scientist: a person who has designed the research, who has developed the experimental conditions, who has observed and recorded the behavior of subjects in these conditions, and who has analyzed the results. This person has values, beliefs, and expectations.

Studies have recently shown that the values of the experimenter can determine the way an experiment turns out.[3] If experimenters expect one kind of result, they are slightly more likely to obtain that result. This effect is called **experimenter bias.** Observers are often biased in favor of their own beliefs and values; they tend to see selectively and to remember selectively what agrees with their value system. Furthermore, experimenters are apparently able unconsciously to influence the subject they are studying to conform to their expectations, through subtle bodily and facial cues. Unless precautions are taken, the "scientific facts" that emerge from the application of the scientific method are influenced by the value system of the experimenters.

Values and Applied Science

Values influence the type of question asked, the type of method used to answer the question, the facts yielded by the method, and also the ways in which the facts are applied. Science is a tool, just as a knife is a tool; how science or a knife is used can be for good or for ill. The application of the facts of science and the use of the knife are both strongly affected by human values.

The science of psychology has helped develop a technology of behavior control; those who master that technology can partially control human minds. Human values will determine the ends served by that technology. There is no doubt that the tools will be used; the only question remaining unanswered is how. There are revolutions under way in our society, revolutions both in the power of applied psychology and in human values and consciousness. If advances in behavioral technology are not met with advances in thoughtful concern about the ends to be served by that technology, then our future may be shaped by **mechanistic values** (efficiency, speed, production, standardization) rather than **humanistic values** (individual worth, equality, compassion, freedom).

As scientific psychology increases its power to modify human beings, the design of a new human and a new society will be undertaken, for tools once developed are always used. But used to what ends? What will that future person be like? We have only values to guide us in the choices that we face.

KEY CONCEPTS

fact	That which is believed to be true.
value	That which is preferred or believed to be good.
paradigm	A generally accepted conceptual framework or belief system that dominates a science at one time in history.
experimenter bias	The tendency for the results of an experiment to conform to the expectations of the experimenter.
mechanistic values	The value of efficiency, speed, production, and standardization.
humanistic values	The value of individual worth, equality, freedom, and compassion.

References

Chapter 1: The Nature of Psychology

1. *Los Angeles Times,* January 20, 1975.
2. *Los Angeles Times,* January 20, 1975.
3. *Los Angeles Times,* March 28, 1975.
4. DeKoninck, J. M., & Koulack, D. Dream content and adaptation to a stressful situation. *Journal of Abnormal Psychology,* 1975, *84,* 250–260.
5. Fromkin, V., *et al.* The development of language in Genie: A case of language acquisition beyond the "critical period." *Brain and Language,* 1974, *1,* 81–107.
6. Laughlin, H. P. *The neuroses.* Washington, D.C.: Butterworth, 1967.
7. Russell, R. K., & Sipich, J. F. Treatment of test anxiety by cue-controlled relaxation. *Behavior Therapy,* 1974, *5,* 673–676.
8. McKeachie, W. P. A tale of a teacher. In T. S. Krawiec (Ed.), *The psychologists.* New York: Oxford University Press, 1972.
9. Boneau, C. A., Golann, S. E., & Johnson, M. M. *A career in psychology.* Washington, D.C.: American Psychological Association, 1970.

Chapter 2: The Science of Psychology

1. Jones, A. D. Cannabis and alcohol usage among the Plateau Tonga: An observational report of the effects of cultural expectation. *Psychological Record,* 1975, *25,* 329–332.
2. Finnel, W. S., & Jones, J. D. Marijuana, alcohol, and academic performance. *Journal of Drug Education,* 1975, *5,* 13–21.
3. Stillman, R. C., *et al.*

State-dependent (dissociative) effects of marijuana on human memory. *Archives of General Psychiatry,* 1974, *31,* 81–85.
4. Kagan, J. A psychologist's account at mid-career. In T. S. Krawiec (Ed.), *The psychologists.* New York: Oxford University Press, 1972.
5. Rogers, C. R. *On becoming a person.* Boston: Houghton Mifflin, 1961.

Chapter 3: Learning Psychology

1. Miller, G. A. *Psychology: The science of mental life.* New York: Harper & Row, 1962.
2. Jones, E. *The life and work of Sigmund Freud.* New York: Basic Books, 1961.
3. Maslow, A. H. Neurosis as a failure of personal growth. *Humanitas,* 1967, *3,* 153–170.
4. Coles, R. *Erik H. Erikson: The growth of his work.* Boston: Little, Brown, 1970.

Chapter 4: Heredity

1. Beach, F. A. The descent of instinct. *Psychological Review,* 1955, *62,* 401–410.
2. Lack, D. *Darwin's finches.* New York: Harper & Row, 1961.
3. Marshall, A. J. *Bower birds.* London: Oxford University Press, 1954.
4. McNemar, Q. Twin resemblance in motor skills, and the effect of practice thereon. *Journal of Genetic Psychology,* 1933, *42,* 70–97.
5. Lennox, W. G., Gibbs, E. L., & Gibbs, F. A. The brain wave pattern, an heredity trait: Evidence from 74 "normal" pairs of twins. *Journal of Heredity,* 1945, *36,* 233–243.
6. Conrad, H. S., & Jones, H. E. A second study of familial

resemblance in intelligence. *39th Yearbook, Part II, National Society for the Study of Education.* Chicago: University of Chicago Press, 1940.
7. Leahy, A. M. Nature-nurture and intelligence. *Genetic Psychology Monographs,* 1935, *17,* 235–308.
8. Erlenmeyer-Kimling, L., & Jarvik, L. F. Genetics and intelligence: A review. *Science,* 1963, *142,* 1477–1479.
9. Vandenberg, S. G., & Johnson, R. C. Further evidence on the relation between age of separation and similarity in I.Q. among pairs of separated identical twins. In S. G. Vandenberg (Ed.), *Progress in human behavior genetics.* Baltimore: Johns Hopkins Press, 1968.
10. Thompson, W. R. The inheritance and development of intelligence. *Proceedings of the Association for Research in Nervous and Mental Disease,* 1954, *33,* 209–231.
11. Wender, P. H. The role of genetics in the etiology of the schizophrenias. *American Journal of Orthopsychiatry,* 1969, *39,* 447–458.
12. Kallman, F. J. *Heredity in health and mental disorder.* New York: Norton, 1953.
13. Abe, K. The morbidity rate and environmental influence in monozygotic co-twins of schizophrenics. *British Journal of Psychiatry,* 1969, *115,* 519–531.
14. Wilson, R. P. A study of twins with special reference to heredity as a factor determining differences in environment. *Human Biology,* 1934, *6,* 324–354.
15. Jones, H. E. Perceived differences among twins. *Eugenics Quarterly,* 1955, *2,* 98–102.
16. Smith, R. T. A comparison of

socioenvironmental factors in monozygotic and dizygotic twins, testing an assumption. In S. G. Vandenberg (Ed.), *Methods and goals in human behavior genetics*. New York: Academic Press, 1965.

17. Kallman, F. J. *The genetics of schizophrenia*. New York: Augustin, 1938.

18. Bridger, W. H. Individual differences in behavior and autonomic activity in newborn infants. *American Journal of Public Health*, 1965, *55*, 1899.

19. Schaffer, H. E., & Emerson, P. E. Patterns of response to physical contact in early human development. *Journal of Child Psychology and Psychiatry*, 1964, *5*, 1–13.

20. Rogers, D., & McClearn, G. E. Alcohol preference of mice. In E. Bliss (Ed.), *Roots of behavior*. New York: Harper & Row, 1962.

21. Nichols, J. R. Addiction liability of albino rats: Breeding for quantitative differences in morphine drinking. *Science*, 1967, *157*, 561–563.

22. Scott, J. P., & Fuller, J. L. *Genetics and social behavior of the dog*. Chicago: University of Chicago Press, 1965.

23. James, W. T. Social organization among dogs of different temperaments: Terriers and beagles raised together. *Journal of Comparative and Physiological Psychology*, 1951, *44*, 71–77.

24. Newman, H. H., Freeman, F. N., & Holzinger, K. J. *Twins: A study of heredity and environment*. Chicago: University of Chicago Press, 1937.

25. Freedman, D. An etiological approach to the genetical study of human behavior. In S. G. Vandenberg (Ed.), *Methods and goals in human behavior genetics*. New York: Academic Press, 1965.

26. Gottesman, I. I. Heritability of personality: A demonstration. *Psychological Monographs*, 1963, *77* (9, Whole No. 572).

27. Eysenck, H. J., & Prell, D. B. The inheritance of neuroticism: An experimental study. *Journal of Mental Science*, 1951, *97*, 441–465.

Chapter 5: Childhood

1. Dennis, W. *The Hopi child*. New York: Appleton-Century-Crofts, 1940.

2. Hilgard, E. R. Learning and maturation in preschool children. *Journal of Genetic Psychology*, 1932, *41*, 35–56.

3. Gibson, E. J., & Walk, R. D. The "visual cliff." *Scientific American*, 1960, *202*, 67–71.

4. Campos, T. J., Langer, A., & Krowitz, A. Cardiac responses on the visual cliff in prelocomotor infants. *Science*, 1970, *170*, 196.

5. Kaplan, E. L., & Kaplan, G. A. Is there such a thing as a prelinguistic child? In J. Eliot (Ed.), *Human development and cognitive processes*. New York: Holt, Rinehart and Winston, 1970.

6. Chomsky, N. Language and the mind. *Readings in psychology today*. Del Mar Calif.: CRM Books, 1969.

7. Milne, A. A. *Now we are six*. New York: E. P. Dutton and Company, 1955.

8. Bloom, B. S. *Stability and change in human characteristics*. New York: Wiley, 1964.

9. Sears, R. R., Maccoby, E. E., & Levin, H. *Patterns of child rearing*. Evanston, Ill.: Row, Peterson, 1957.

10. Wittenborn, J. R. A study of adoptive children. *Psychological Monographs*, 1956, *70*, 1–115.

11. Macfarlane, J. W., Allen, L., & Honzik, M. P. A developmental study of the behavior problems of normal children between twenty-one months and fourteen years. *University of California Publications in Child Development*, Vol. *II*. Berkeley: University of California Press, 1954.

12. Despert, J. L. Urinary control and enuresis. *Psychosomatic Medicine*, 1944, *6*, 294–307.

13. Huschka, M. The child's response to coercive bowel training. *Psychosomatic Medicine*, 1942, *4*, 301–308.

14. Beloff, H. The structure and origin of the anal character. *Genetic Psychology Monographs*, 1957, *55*, 141–172.

15. Erikson, E. H. *Childhood and society*. New York: Norton, 1963.

16. Mischel, W. *Introduction to personality*. New York: Holt, Rinehart and Winston, 1971.

17. Brown, D. G. Masculinity-femininity development in children. *Journal of Consulting Psychology*, 1957, *21*, 197–202.

18. Whiting, J. W. M. Resource mediation and learning by identification. In I. Iscoe & H. W. Stevenson (Eds.), *Personality development in children*. Austin: University of Texas Press, 1960.

19. Mussen, P. Early socialization: Learning and identification. In G. Mandler *et al.* (Eds.), *New directions in psychology III*. New York: Holt, Rinehart and Winston, 1967.

Chapter 6: The Family

1. Davis, K. Final note on a case of extreme isolation. *American Journal of Sociology*, 1947, *52*, 554–565.

2. Koluchová, J. Severe deprivation in twins: A case study. *Journal of Child Psychology and Psychiatry*, 1972, *13*, 107–144.

3. Fromkin, V., *et al.* The development of language in Genie: A case of language acquisition beyond the "critical period." *Brain and Language*, 1974, *1*, 81–107.

4. Spitz, R. A. Motherless infants. *Child Development*, 1949, *20*, 145–155.

5. Spitz, R. A. Hospitalism: A follow-up report. In A. Freud, W. Hoffer, & E. Glover (Eds.), *The psychoanalytic study of the child*. Vol. *II*. New York: International Universities Press, 1946.

6. Bettelheim, B. *Truants from life*. New York: The Free Press, 1955.

7. Harlow, H. F., & Zimmerman, R. R. Affectional responses in the infant monkey. *Science*, 1959, *130*, 421–432.

8. Harlow, H. F. The nature of love. *The American Psychologist*, 1958,*13*, 673–685.

9. Harlow, H. F., & Harlow, M. K. Learning to love. *American Scientist*, 1966, *54*, 244–272.

10. Flint, B. M. *The child and the institution: A study of deprivation and recovery.* Toronto: University of Toronto Press, 1966.

11. Taylor, A. Deprived infants: Potential for affective adjustment. *American Journal of Orthopsychiatry*, 1968, *38*, 835–845.

12. Stendler-Lavatelli, C. B. Environmental intervention in infancy and early childhood. In M. Deutsch, I. Katz, & A. R. Jensen (Eds.), *Social class, race and psychological development.* New York: Holt, Rinehart and Winston, 1968.

13. Skeels, H. M. & Dye, H. B. A study of the effects of differential stimulation on mentally retarded children. *Proceedings of the American Association of Mental Deficiency*, 1939, *44*, 114–136.

14. Rheingold, H. L. The modification of social responsiveness in institutional babies. *Monograph of the Society for Research in Child Development*, 1956, *21* (2), Series No. 63.

15. Frank, L. K. *On the importance of infancy.* New York: Random House, 1966.

16. Aberle, D. The psycho-social analysis of a Hopi life history. In Y. A. Cohen (Ed.), *Social structure and personality.* New York: Holt, Rinehart and Winston, 1951.

17. Aldrich, C. K. Thief! *Psychology Today*, 1971, *4*, 67.

18. Douvan, E., & Adelson, J. *The adolescent experience.* New York: Wiley, 1966.

19. Winterbottom, M. R. The relation of need for achievement to learning experience in independence and mastery. In J. W. Atkinson (Ed.), *Motives in fantasy, action, and society.* Princeton, N. J.: D. Van Nostrand, 1958.

20. Adorno, T. W., Frenkel-Brunswik, E., Levinson, D. J., & Sanford, N. R. *The authoritarian personality.* New York: Harper & Row, 1950.

21. Sears, R. R., Maccoby, E. E., & Levin, H. *Patterns of child rearing.* Evanston, Ill.: Row, Peterson, 1957.

22. Glueck, S., & Glueck, E. *Unraveling juvenile delinquency.* New York: Commonwealth Fund, 1950.

23. Harper, L. V. The scope of offspring effects: From caregiver to culture. *Psychological Bulletin*, 1975, *82*, 784–801.

24. Gruenberg, E. M. On the psychosomatics of the not-so-perfect fetal parasite. In S. A. Richardson & A. F. Guttmacher (Eds.), *Childbearing: Its social and psychological aspects.* Baltimore, Md.: Williams & Wilkins, 1967.

25. Chess, S. Temperament in the normal infant. In J. Hellmuth (Ed.), *The exceptional infant (Volume I: The Normal Infant).* New York: Brunner/Mazel, 1967.

26. Farber, B. Types of family organization: Child-oriented, home-oriented, and parent-oriented. In A. M. Rose (Ed.), *Human behavior and social processes.* Boston: Houghton Mifflin, 1962.

27. Lane, R. C., & Singer, J. L. Familial attitudes in paranoid schizophrenics and normals from two socioeconomic classes. *Journal of Abnormal and Social Psychology*, 1959, *59*, 328–339.

28. Lidz, T., Fleck, S., & Cornelison, A. R. *Schizophrenia and the family.* New York: International Universities Press, 1965.

29. Fleck, S. Family dynamics and origin of schizophrenia. *Psychosomatic Medicine*, 1960, *22*, 333–343.

30. Frank, L. K. *On the importance of infancy.* New York: Random House, 1966.

31. McCurdy, H. G. The childhood pattern of genius. *Journal of the Elisha Mitchell Scientific Society*, 1957, *73*, 448–462.

32. Baldwin, A. L., Kalhorn, J., & Breese, F. H. Patterns of parent behavior. *Psychological Monographs*, 1945, *58*, No. 268.

33. Rosenberg, M. *Society and the adolescent self-image.* Princeton, N.J.: Princeton University Press, 1965.

34. Coopersmith, S. Studies in self-esteem. *Scientific American*, 1968, *218*, 96–107.

35. Bacon, M. K., Child, I. L., & Barry, H. A cross-cultural study of correlates of crime. *Journal of Abnormal and Social Psychology*, 1963, *66*, 291–300.

36. Mead, M. Future family. *Trans-action*, 1970, *8*, 50–53.

Research Methods II: Observing Behavior

1. Elkind, D. Giant in the nursery—Jean Piaget. *New York Times Magazine*, May 26, 1968, 25–80.

2. Piaget, J. *The construction of reality in the child.* New York: Basic Books, 1954.

3. Bales, R. F. *Interaction process analysis: A method for the study of small groups.* Cambridge, Mass.: Addison-Wesley, 1950.

4. Miller, A. G. Role of physical attractiveness in impression formation. *Psychonomic Science*, 1970, *19*, 241–243.

5. Rosenthal, R., & Jacobson, L. *Pygmalion in the classroom.* New York: Holt, Rinehart and Winston, 1968.

6. Münsterberg, H. *On the witness stand: Essays on psychology and crime.* Clark Boardman, 1908.

Chapter 7: Learning

1. Frankenburg, W. K., & Dodds, J. B. The Denver developmental screening test. *Journal of Pediatrics*, 1967, *71*, 181–191.

2. Aldrich, C. A., & Norval, M. A. A developmental graph for the first year of life. *Journal of Pediatrics*, 1946, *29*, 304–308.

3. Orlansky, H. Infant care and personality. *Psychological Bulletin*, 1949, *46*, 1–48.

4. Dennis, W., & Dennis, M. G. The effect of cradling practices

upon the onset of walking in Hopi children. *Journal of Genetic Psychology*, 1940, *56*, 77–86.

5. Gardner, R. A., & Gardner, B. T. Teaching sign language to a chimpanzee. *Science*, 1969, *165*, 664–672.

6. Bandura, A., & Walters, R. H. *Social learning and personality development.* New York: Holt, Rinehart and Winston, 1963.

7. Holland, M. K., & Swiryn, M. Improvement following the imaginary practice of a perceptual-motor skill. Unpublished manuscript, 1973.

8. Harlow, H. F. The information of learning sets. *Psychological Review*, 1949, *56*, 51–65.

9. Bruner, J. S. *The process of education.* New York: Vintage Books, 1960, p. 16.

10. Levinson, B., & Reese, H. W. Patterns of discrimination learning set in pre-school children, fifth graders, college freshmen, and the aged. *Monographs of the Society for Research in Child Development*, *32*, 1967 (Whole No. 115).

11. Warren, J. M., & Baron, A. The formation of learning sets by cats. *Journal of Comparative and Physiological Psychology*, 1956, *49*, 227–231.

12. Koronakos, C., & Arnold, W. J. The formation of learning sets in rats. *Journal of Comparative and Physiological Psychology*, 1957, *50*, 11–14.

13. Miller, G. A. *Psychology: The science of mental life.* New York: Harper & Row, 1962.

14. Pavlov, I. P. *Conditioned reflexes.* New York: Oxford University Press, 1927.

15. Watson, J. B., & Rayner, R. Conditioned emotional reactions. *Journal of Experimental Psychology*, 1920, *3*, 1–12.

16. Rice, B. Skinner: The most important influence in psychology? In M. Merbaum & G. Stricker (Eds.), *Search for human understanding.* New York: Holt, Rinehart and Winston, 1968.

17. Breland, K., & Breland, M. A field of applied animal psychology. *American Psychologist*, 1951, *6*, 202–204.

18. Boneau, C. A., Holland, M. K., & Baker, W. M. Color-discrimination performance of pigeons: Effects of reward. *Science*, 1965, *149*, 1113–1114.

19. Holland, M. K., & Baker, W. M. Spectral generalization testing with pigeons using brief discrete trials. *Psychonomic Science*, 1968, *10*, 1–2.

20. Skinner, B. F. "Superstition" in the pigeon. *Journal of Experimental Psychology*, 1948, *38*, 168–172.

21. Williams, C. D. The elimination of tantrum behavior by extinction procedures. *Journal of Abnormal and Social Psychology*, 1954, *59*, 269.

22. Azrin, N. H., & Powell, J. R. Behavioral engineering: The reduction of smoking behavior by a conditioning apparatus and procedure. *Journal of Applied Behavior Analysis*, 1968, *1*, 193–200.

23. Keutzer, C. S., Lichenstein, E., & Mees, H. L. Modification of smoking behavior: A review. *Psychological Bulletin*, 1968, *70*, 520–533.

24. Stuart, R. B. Situational versus self control of problematic behaviors. In R. D. Rubin (Ed.), *Advances in behavior therapy, 1970.* New York: Academic Press, 1970.

Chapter 8: Memory

1. Halacy, D. S. *Man and memory.* New York: Harper & Row, 1970, p. 88.

2. Sperling, G. The information available in brief visual presentations. *Psychological Monographs*, 1960, *74*, Whole No. 498.

3. Conrad, R. Acoustic confusions in immediate memory. *British Journal of Psychology*, 1964, *55*, 75–83.

4. Conrad, R., & Hull, A. J. Information, acoustic confusion and memory span. *British Journal of Psychology*, 1964, *55*, 429–432.

5. Baddeley, A. D., & Dale, H. C. A. The effect of semantic similarity on retroactive interference in long- and short-term memory. *Journal of Verbal Learning and Verbal Behavior*, 1966, *5*, 417–420.

6. Bousfield, W. A. The occurrence of clustering in the recall of randomly arranged associates. *Journal of General Psychology*, 1953, *49*, 229–240.

7. Wickelgren, W. A. Size of rehearsal groups and short-term memory. *Journal of Experimental Psychology*, 1964, *68*, 413–419.

8. Miller, G. A. The magical number seven, plus or minus two: Some limits on our capacity for processing information. *Psychological Review*, 1956, *63*, 81–97.

9. Mandler, G. Organization and memory. In K. W. Spence & J. T. Spence (Eds.), *The psychology of learning and motivation*, Vol. II. New York: Academic Press, 1968.

10. Brown, R., & McNeill, D. The "tip of the tongue" phenomenon. *Journal of Verbal Learning and Verbal Behavior*, 1966, *5*, 325–337.

11. Earhard, M. The facilitation of memorization by alphabetic instructions. *Canadian Journal of Psychology*, 1967, *21*, 15–24.

12. Haber, R. N., & Haber, R. B. Eidetic imagery: I. Frequency. *Perceptual and Motor Skills*, 1964, *19*, 131–138.

13. Holt, R. R. Imagery: The return of the ostracized. *American Psychologist*, 1964, *19*, 254–264.

14. Stromeyer, C. F., III. Eidetikers. *Psychology Today*, 1970, *4*, 76–80.

15. Luria, A. R. *The mind of a mnemonist.* New York: Basic Books, 1968.

16. Jenkins, J. J. Remember that old theory of memory? Well forget it! *American Psychologist*, 1974, *29*, 785–795.

17. Bransford, J. D., & Franks, J. J. The abstraction of linguistic ideas. *Cognitive Psychology*, 1971, *2*, 331–350.

18. Lashley, K. S. *Brain mechanisms and intelligence.* Chicago: University of Chicago Press, 1929.
19. Brierley, J. B. The neuropathology of amnesic states. In C. W. M. Whitty & O. L. Zangwill (Eds.), *Amnesia.* Washington: Butterworth, 1966.
20. Smith, A., & Burklund, C. W. Dominant hemispherectomy: Preliminary report on neuropsychological sequelae. *Science,* 1966, *153,* 1280–1282.
21. Deutsch, J. A. The physiological basis of memory. *Annual Review of Psychology,* 1969, *20,* 85–104.
22. Davis, R. E., Bright, P. J., & Agranoff, B. W. Effect of ECS and puromycin on memory in fish. *Journal of Comparative and Physiological Psychology,* 1965, *60,* 162–166.
23. Zemp, J. W., Wilson, J. E., Schlesinger, K., Boggan, W. O., & Glassman, E. Brain function and macro-molecules, I. Incorporation of uridine into RNA of mouse brain during short-term training experience. *Proceedings of the National Academy of Science,* 1966, *55,* 1423–1431.
24. Penfield, W. The interpretive cortex. *Science,* 1959, *129,* 1719–1725.
25. Gomulicki, B. R. The development and present status of the trace theory of memory. *British Journal of Psychology, Monograph Supplement,* 1953, No. 29.
26. Guttman, N., & Julesz, B. Lower limits of auditory periodicity analysis. *Journal of the Acoustical Society of America,* 1963, *35,* 610.
27. Underwood, B. J. Interference and forgetting. *Psychological Review,* 1957, *64,* 49–60.
28. Anon. *I lost my memory: The case as the patient saw it.* London: Faber & Faber Ltd, 1932.
29. Williams, M. *Brain damage and the mind.* Baltimore, Md.: Penguin Books, 1970.
30. Williams, M., & Zangwill, O. L. Retrograde memory disturbances. *Journal of Neurology, Neurosurgery, and Psychiatry,* 1952, *15,* 54.
31. Milner, B. Amnesia following operation on the temporal lobe. In C. W. M. Whitty & O. L. Zangwill (Eds.), *Amnesia.* Washington: Butterworth, 1966.
32. Laughlin, H. P. *The neuroses.* Washington: Butterworth, 1967.
33. Yates, F. A. *The art of memory.* London: Routledge & Kegan Paul, 1966.
34. Hunter, I. M. L. *Memory.* Baltimore, Md.: Penguin Books, 1957.

Chapter 9: Teaching

1. Havighurst, R. *Developmental tasks and education.* New York: Longmans, Green, 1952.
2. Elkind, D. Giant in the nursery—Jean Piaget. *New York Times Magazine,* May 26, 1968, 25–80.
3. Bruner, J. S. *Toward a theory of instruction.* Cambridge, Mass.: Harvard University Press, 1966.
4. Bruner, J. S. *The process of education.* Cambridge, Mass.: Harvard University Press, 1960.
5. Winterbottom, M. R. The relation of childhood training in independence to achievement motivation. In D. McClelland *et al.* (Eds.), *The achievement motive.* New York: Appleton-Century-Crofts, 1953.
6. Singer, R. D., & Singer, A. *Psychological development in children.* Philadelphia: W. B. Saunders, 1969.
7. Harlow, H. F. Mice, monkeys, men and motives. *Psychological Review,* 1953, *60,* 23–32.
8. White, R. W. Competence and the psychosexual stages of development. In M. R. Jones (Ed.), *Nebraska symposium on motivation.* Lincoln: University of Nebraska Press, 1960.
9. Maslow, A. H. *Toward a psychology of being,* 2nd ed. Princeton, N. J.: Van Nostrand, 1968.
10. Coopersmith, S. *The antecedents of self esteem.* San Francisco: W. H. Freeman, 1967.
11. Carlsmith, L. Effect of early father-absence on scholastic aptitude. *Harvard Educational Review,* 1964, *34,* 3–21.
12. Kagan, J., Moss, H. A., & Sigel, I. E. The psychological significance of styles of conceptualization. *Monographs of the Society for Research in Child Development,* 1963, *28,* 73–112.
13. Kagan, J., & Kogan, N. Individual variation in cognitive processes. In P. Mussen (Ed.), *Carmichael's manual of child psychology,* Vol. 1. New York: Wiley, 1970.
14. Coyle, P. J. Differences in reflection-impulsivity as a function of race, sex, and socio-economic class. *Dissertation Abstracts,* 1967, *27* (12-B), 4549.
15. Eska, B., & Black, K. N. Conceptual tempo in young grade-school children. *Child Development,* 1971, *42,* 505–516.
16. Lee, L. C., Kagan, J., & Rubson, A. Influence of a preference for analytic categorization upon concept acquisition. *Child Development,* 1963, *34,* 433–442.
17. Cohen, R. Conceptual styles, culture conflict, and nonverbal tests of intelligence. *American Anthropologist,* 1969, *71,* 828–856.
18. Holland, V. Social and physiological correlates of information processing systems. Unpublished manuscript, 1972.
19. Rosenthal, R., & Jacobson, L. *Pygmalion in the classroom: Teacher expectation and pupils' intellectual development.* New York: Holt, Rinehart and Winston, 1968.
20. Getzels, J. W., & Jackson, P. W. The teacher's personality and characteristics. In N. L. Gage (Ed.), *Handbook of research on teaching.* Chicago: Rand McNally, 1963.
21. Ryans, D. G. Some relationships between pupil behavior and certain teacher characteristics. *Journal of Educational Psychology,* 1961, *52,* 82–90.

22. Konnin, J. S., & Gump, P. V. The comparative influence of punitive and nonpunitive teachers upon children's concepts of school misconduct. *Journal of Educational Psychology*, 1961, *52*, 44–49.

23. Thistlethewaite, D. L. *College press and changes in study plans of talented students.* Evanston, Ill.: National Merit Scholarship Corp., 1960.

24. Rogers, C. R. *Freedom to learn.* Columbus, Ohio: Charles E. Merrill, 1969.

25. Freire, P. *Pedagogy of the oppressed.* New York: Herder and Herder, 1972.

26. McKeachie, W. J. Research on teaching at the college and university level. In N. L. Gage (Ed.), *Handbook of research on teaching.* Chicago: Rand McNally, 1967.

27. Caro, P. W., Jr. The effect of class attendance and "time structured" content on achievement in general psychology. *Journal of Educational Psychology*, 1962, *53*, 76–80.

28. Jensen, B. T. A comparison of student achievement and non-attendance. *College and University*, 1951, *26*, 399–404.

29. Greene, E. B. Relative effectiveness of lecture and individual reading as methods of college teaching. *Genetic Psychology Monographs*, 1928, *4*, 457–563.

30. Holland, M. K. Teaching structures. Unpublished manuscript, 1972.

31. Eglash, A. A group discussion method of teaching psychology. *Journal of Educational Psychology*, 1954, *45*, 257–267.

32. Husband, R. W. A statistical comparison of the efficacy of large lecture vs. smaller recitation sections upon achievement in general psychology. *Journal of Psychology*, 1951, *31*, 297–300.

33. Barnard, J. D. The lecture-demonstration versus the problem-solving method of teaching a college science course. *Science Education*, 1942, *26*, 121–132.

34. Ausubel, D. P., & Robinson, F. G. *School learning: An introduction to educational psychology.* New York: Holt, Rinehart and Winston, 1969.

35. Bruner, J. S. The act of discovery. *Harvard Educational Review*, 1961, *31*, 21–32.

36. Bruner, J. S. *Toward a theory of instruction.* Cambridge, Mass.: Harvard University Press, 1966.

37. Bruner, J. S. *On knowing: Essays for the left hand.* New York: Atheneum, 1966.

38. Kersh, B. V. The motivating effect of learning by directed discovery. *Journal of Educational Psychology*, 1962, *53*, 65–71.

39. Gagné, R. M. & Brown, L. T. Some factors in the programming of conceptual learning. *Journal of Experimental Psychology*, 1961, *62*, 313–321.

40. Skinner, B. F. *The technology of teaching.* New York: Appleton-Century-Crofts, 1968.

41. Watson, J. B. *Behaviorism.* New York: W. W. Norton, 1930.

42. Keller, F. S. "Good-bye, teacher . . ." *Journal of Applied Behavioral Analysis*, 1968, *1*, 79–89.

43. Risley, Tod. Learning and lollipops. In J. P. DeCecco (Ed.), *Readings in educational psychology today.* Del Mar, Calif.: CRM Books, 1967, pp. 129–138.

44. Schramm, W. *The research on programmed instruction: An annotated bibliography.* Washington, D.C.: U.S. Office of Education, 1964.

45. Krumboltz, J. D., & Weisman, R. G. The effect of overt versus covert responding to programmed instruction on immediate and delayed retention. *Journal of Educational Psychology*, 1962, *53*, 89–92.

46. Crist, R. L. Overt versus covert responding and retention by sixth-grade students. *Journal of Educational Psychology*, 1966, *57*, 99–101.

47. Goldbeck, A. & Campbell, V. N. The effects of response mode and response difficulty on programmed instruction. *Journal of Educational Psychology*, 1962, *53*, 110–118.

48. Uttal, W. R. Teaching and machines. In J. P. DeCecco (Ed.), *Readings in educational psychology today.* Del Mar, Calif.: CRM Books, 1967.

49. Faw, V. D. A psychotherapeutic method of teaching psychology. *American Psychologist*, 1949, *4*, 104–109.

50. McKeachie, W. J. *Teaching tips: A guidebook for the beginning college teacher.* Boston: D. C. Heath, 1969.

51. Bills, R. E. Investigation of student centered teaching. *Journal of Educational Research*, 1952, *46*, 313–319.

52. Jones, R. M. *Fantasy and feeling in education.* New York: New York University Press, 1968.

53. Ashton-Warner, S. *Teacher.* New York: Bantam Books, 1963.

54. Neill, A. S. *Summerhill: A radical approach to child rearing.* New York: Hart Publishing, 1960.

55. Bernstein, E. What does a Summerhill old school tie look like? *Psychology Today*, 1968, *2*, 37–70.

56. Dennison, G. *The lives of children: The story of the First Street School.* New York: Random House, 1969.

57. Illich, I. D. *Celebration of awareness: A call for institutional revolution.* Garden City, N.Y.: Doubleday, 1970.

Chapter 10: Consciousness and the Brain

1. Williams, M. *Brain damage and the mind.* Middlesex, England: Penguin Books, 1970.

2. Schwartz, G. E. Cardiac responses to self-induced thoughts. *Psychotherapy*, 1971, *8*, 462–466.

3. Schaefer, H. Psychosomatic problems of vegetative

regulatory functions. In J. C. Eccles (Ed.), *Brain and conscious experience.* New York: Springer-Verlag, 1966.

4. Bakal, D. A. Headache: A biopsychological perspective. *Psychological Bulletin,* 1975, *82,* 369–382.

5. Sawrey, W. L., Conger, J. J., & Turrell, E. S. An experimental investigation of the role of psychological factors in the production of gastric ulcers in rats. *Journal of Comparative and Physiological Psychology,* 1956, *49,* 457–461.

6. Brady, J. V. Behavioral stress and physiological change: A comparative approach to the experimental analysis of some psychosomatic problems. *Transactions of the New York Academy of Science,* 1964, *26,* 483–496.

7. Treisman, M. Mind, body, and behavior: Control systems and their disturbance. In P. London & D. Rosenhan (Eds.), *Foundations of abnormal psychology.* New York: Holt, Rinehart and Winston, 1968.

8. Gazzaniga, M. S. *The bisected brain.* New York: Appleton-Century-Crofts, 1970.

9. Sperry, R. W. Brain bisection and mechanisms of consciousness. In J. C. Eccles (Ed.), *Brain and conscious experience.* New York: Springer-Verlag, 1966.

10. Ornstein, R. E. *The psychology of consciousness.* San Francisco: W. H. Freeman, 1972.

11. Milner, B. Amnesia following operation on the temporal lobes. In C. W. Whitty & O. L. Zangwill (Eds.), *Amnesia.* London: Butterworth, 1966.

12. James, W. *The varieties of religious experience.* New York: New American Library, 1958.

13. Wallace, R. K. Physiological effects of transcendental meditation. *Science,* 1970, *167,* 1751–1754.

14. Glueck, B. C., & Stroebel, C. F. Biofeedback and meditation in the treatment of psychiatric illnesses. *Comprehensive Psychiatry,* 1975, *16,* 303–321.

15. Anand, B. K., Chhina, G. S., & Singh, B. B. Some aspects of EEG studies in Yogis. *Electroencephalography and Clinical Neurophysiology,* 1961, *13,* 452–456.

16. Smith, J. C. Meditation as psychotherapy: A review of the literature. *Psychological Bulletin,* 1975, *82,* 558–564.

17. Hoover, E. L. Alpha: The first step to a new level of reality. *Human Behavior,* 1972, May–June.

18. Weitzenhoffer, A. M. *General techniques of hypnotism.* New York: Grune and Stratton, 1957.

19. Barber, T. X. *Hypnosis: A scientific approach.* New York: Van Nostrand Reinhold, 1969.

20. Orne, M. T., & Evans, F. J. Social control in the psychological experiment: Antisocial behavior and hypnosis. *Journal of Personality and Social Psychology,* 1965, *1,* 189–200.

21. Evans, F. J. Hypnosis and sleep: Techniques for exploring cognitive activity during sleep. In E. Fromm & R. E. Shor (Eds.), *Hypnosis: Research developments and perspectives.* Chicago: Aldine Publishing, 1972.

22. Zimbardo, P., Maslach, C., & Marshall, G. Hypnosis and the psychology of cognitive and behavioral control. In E. Fromm & R. E. Shor (Eds.), *Hypnosis: Research developments and perspectives.* Chicago: Aldine Publishing, 1972.

23. Taugher, V. J. Hypno-anesthesia. *Wisconsin Medical Journal,* 1958, *57,* 95–96.

24. Blum, R. H., & Funkhouser-Balbaky, M. L. Mind-altering drugs and dangerous behavior: Dangerous drugs. Annotations and Consultants' Papers, Task Force on Narcotics and Drug Abuse, President's Commission on Law Enforcement and Administration of Justice, 1967.

25. Corder. B. W., *et al.* An analysis of trends in drug use behavior at five American universities. *Journal of School Health,* 1974, *44,* 386–389.

26. Single, E., Kandel, D., & Faust, R. Patterns of multiple drug use in high school. *Journal of Health and Social Behavior,* 1974, *15,* 344–357.

27. Wogan, M. Illicit drug use among college students. *College Student Journal,* 1974, *8,* 56–62.

28. Goldstein, J. W., Gleason, T. C., & Korn, J. H. Whither the epidemic? Psychoactive drug use career patterns of college students. *Journal of Applied Social Psychology,* 1975, *5,* 16–33.

29. Becker, H. Becoming a marijuana user. *American Journal of Sociology,* 1953, *59,* 235–242.

30. Blum, R. H., *et al. Students and drugs.* San Francisco: Jossey-Bass, 1969.

31. Tassinari, C. A., Peraita-Adrados, M. R., Ambrosetto, G., & Gastaut, H. Effects of marijuana and delta-9-THC at high doses in man: A polygraphic study. *Electroencephalography and Clinical Neurophysiology,* 1974, *36,* 94.

32. Klonoff, H., & Low, M. D. Psychological and neurophysiological effects of marijuana in man: An interaction model. In L. Miller (Ed.), *Marijuana: Effects on human behavior.* New York: Academic Press, 1974.

33. Winters, W. D., & Wallach, M. B. Drug-induced states of CNS excitation: A theory of hallucinosis. In D. H. Efron (Ed.), *Psychotomometic drugs.* New York: Raven Press, 1970.

34. Ray, O. S. *Drugs, society, and human behavior.* St. Louis: C. V. Mosby, 1972.

35. Perez-Reyes, M., Timmons, M. C., & Wall, M. E. Long-term use of marijuana and the development of tolerance or sensitivity to delta-9-tetrahydrocannabinol. *Archives of General Psychiatry,* 1974, *31,* 89–91.

36. Jones, R. T., & Benowitz, N. The 30-day trip: Clinical studies of cannabis tolerance and dependence. In S. Szara & M. Braude (Eds.), *Pharmacology of*

marijuana. New York: Raven Press, 1975.

37. Canadian Government's Commission of Inquiry, *The non-medical use of drugs.* Middlesex, England: Penguin, 1971.

38. DeRopp, R. S. *Drugs and the mind.* New York: Grove Press, 1964.

39. Cohen, S., & Ditman, K. S. Complications associated with lysergic acid diethylamide (LSD-25). *Journal of the American Medical Association,* 1962, *189,* 181–182.

40. Cohen, S. Lysergic acid diethylamide: Side effects and complications. *Journal of Nervous and Mental Disease,* 1960, *130,* 30–40.

41. National Commission on Marihuana and Drug Abuse, *Marihuana: A signal of misunderstanding.* New York: New American Library, 1972.

42. Unwin, J. R. Non-medical use of drugs with particular reference to youth. *Canadian Medical Association Journal,* 1969, *101,* 72–88.

43. Smith, D. E. Acute and chronic toxicity of marijuana. *Journal of Psychedelic Drugs,* 1968, *2,* 37–47.

44. Hekimian, L. J., & Gershon, S. Characteristics of drug abusers admitted to a psychiatric hospital. *Journal of the American Medical Association,* 1968, *205,* 124–130.

45. Rosenthal, S. H. Persistent hallucinosis following repeated administration of hallucinogenic drugs. *American Journal of Psychiatry,* 1964, *121,* 238–244.

46. Horowitz, M. J. Flashbacks: Recurrent intrusive images after the use of LSD. *American Journal of Psychiatry,* 1969, *126,* 147–151.

47. McGlothlin, W. H., & Arnold, D. O. LSD revisited: A ten-year follow-up of medical LSD use. *Archives of General Psychiatry,* 1971, *24,* 35–49.

48. Keeler, M. H. Adverse reactions to marijuana. *American Journal of Psychiatry,* 1967, *124,* 128–131.

49. Keeler, M. H., Rifler, C. B., & Liptzin, M. B. Spontaneous recurrence of marijuana effect. *American Journal of Psychiatry,* 1968, *125,* 384–386.

50. Hoffman, A. Psychotomimetic drugs: Chemical and pharmacological aspects. *Acta Physiologica et Pharmacologic Nederlandica,* 1959, *8,* 240–258.

51. Alpert, R., Cohen, S., & Schiller, L. *LSD.* New York: New American Library, 1966.

52. Cohen, M., Marinello, M., & Bach, N. Chromosomal damage in human leukocytes by lysergic acid diethylamide. *Science,* 1967, *155,* 1417–1419.

53. Dishotsky, N. I., Longhman, W. D., Mogar, R. E., & Lipscomb, W. R. LSD and genetic damage. *Science,* 1971, *172,* 431–440.

54. Silverstine, A. B., & Klee, G. D. Effects of lysergic acid diethylamide (LSD-25) on intellectual functions. *American Medical Association Archives of Neurology and Psychiatry,* 1958, *80,* 477–480.

55. Zegans, L. S., Pollard, J. C., & Brown, D. The effects of LSD-25 on creativity and tolerance to regression. *Archives of General Psychiatry,* 1967, *16,* 740–749.

56. Cohen, S. A quarter century of research with LSD. In J. Ungerleider (Ed.), *The problems and prospects of LSD.* Springfield, Ill.: Charles C. Thomas, 1968.

57. Berlin, L., Gutherie, T., Weider, A., Goddell, H. K., & Wolff, H. G. Studies in human cerebral function: The effects of mescaline and lysergic acid on cerebral processes pertinent to creative activity. *Journal of Nervous and Mental Disease,* 1955, *122,* 487–491.

58. Weil, A. T., Zinberg, N. E., & Nelson, J. M. Clinical and psychological effects of marijuana in man. *Science,* 1968, 1234–1242.

59. Kolodny, R. C. Research issues in the study of marijuana and male reproductive physiology in humans. In J. R. Tinklenberg (Ed.), *Marijuana and health hazards: Methodological issues in current research.* New York: Academic Press, 1975.

60. McGlothlin, W. H. Cannabis: A reference. In D. Solomon (Ed.), *The marijuana papers.* New York: New American Library, 1966.

61. Dornbush, R. L., Fink, M., & Freedman, A. M. Marijuana, memory and perception. *American Journal of Psychiatry,* 1971, *128,* 194–197.

62. Finkleberg, J. R., Melges, F. T., Hollister, L. E., & Gillespie, H. K. Marijuana and immediate memory. *Nature,* 1970, *20,* 226.

Chapter 11: Dreaming

1. Bromberg, W. *The mind of màn: A history of psychotherapy and psychoanalysis.* New York: Harper & Row, 1959.

2. Von Grunebaum, G. E., & Caillois, R. *The dream and human societies.* Berkeley: University of California Press, 1966.

3. Aserinsky, E., & Kleitman, N. Regularly occurring periods of eye motility, and concomitant phenomena during sleep. *Science,* 1953, *118,* 273–274.

4. Dement, W., & Wolpert, E. The relation of eye movements, body motility, and external stimuli to dream content. *Journal of Experimental Psychology,* 1958, *55,* 543–553.

5. Roffwarg, H., Dement, W., Muzio, J., & Fisher, C. Dream imagery: Relationship to rapid eye movements of sleep. *Archives of General Psychiatry,* 1962, *1,* 235–258.

6. Dement, W. C. *Some must watch while some must sleep.* San Francisco: W. H. Freeman, 1972.

7. Hartman, E. *The biology of dreaming.* Springfield, Ill.: Charles C. Thomas, 1967.

8. Snyder, F. The physiology of dreaming. In M. Kramer (Ed.), *Dream psychology and the new biology of dreaming.* Springfield, Ill.: Charles C. Thomas, 1969.

9. Evarts, E. Activity of neurosis in visual cortex of cat during sleep with low voltage fast EEG activity. *Journal of Neurophysiology,* 1962, *25,* 812–816.

10. Vaughn, C. J. Behavioral evidence for dreaming in rhesus monkeys. *Physiologist,* 1964, *1,* 275.

11. Dement, W. C. An essay on dreams: The role of physiology in understanding their nature. In T. M. Newcomb (Ed.), *New directions in psychology II.* New York: Holt, Rinehart and Winston, 1965.

12. Goodenough, D., Shapiro, A., Holden, M., & Steinschriber, L. A comparison of "dreamers" and "nondreamers": Eye movements, electroencephalograms, and the recall of dreams. *Journal of Abnormal and Social Psychology,* 1959, *59,* 295–302.

13. Antrobus, J., Dement, W., & Fisher, C. Patterns of dreaming and dream recall: An EEG study. *Journal of Abnormal and Social Psychology,* 1964, *69,* 341–344.

14. Cohen, D. B. Current research on the frequency of dream recall. *Psychological Bulletin,* 1970, *73,* 433–440.

15. Hill, A. B. Personality correlates of dream recall. *Journal of Consulting and Clinical Psychology,* 1974, *42,* 766–773.

16. Hall, C. S. The significance of the dream of being attacked. *Journal of Personality,* 1955, *24,* 168–180.

17. Hall, C. S. What people dream about. *Scientific American,* 1951, *184,* 60–63.

18. Snyder, F. The phenomenology of dreaming. In L. Madow & L. H. Snow (Eds.), *The psycho-dynamic implications of the physiological studies on dreams.* Springfield, Ill.: Charles C. Thomas, 1970.

19. Kahn, E., Dement, W., Fisher, C., & Barmack, J. Incidence of color in immediately recalled dreams. *Science,* 1962, *137,* 1054–1055.

20. Feldman, M. J., & Hyman, E. Content analysis of nightmare reports. *Psychophysiology,* 1968, *5,* 221.

21. Bonime, W. *The clinical use of dreams.* New York: Basic Books, 1962.

22. Jacobson, A., & Kales, A. Somnambulism: All-night EEG and related studies. In S. S. Kety, E. V. Evarts, & H. L. Williams (Eds.), *Sleep and altered states of consciousness.* Baltimore, Md.: Williams & Wilkins, 1967.

23. Laughlin, H. P. *The neuroses.* Washington, D.C.: Butterworth, 1967.

24. Dement, W. The effect of dream deprivation. *Science,* 1960, *131,* 1705–1707.

25. Jouvet, M. Paradoxical sleep—A study of its nature and mechanisms. In K. Akert, C. Bally, & J. Schade (Eds.), *Sleep mechanisms.* Amsterdam, 1965.

26. Kleitman, N. Patterns of dreaming. *Scientific American,* November 1960.

27. Freud, S. *The interpretation of dreams.* London: Hogarth Press, 1953.

28. Dement, W., & Wolpert, E. Relationships in the manifest content of dreams occurring on the same night. *Journal of Nervous and Mental Disease,* 1958, *126,* 568–578.

29. Garma, A. *The psychoanalysis of dreams.* London: Pall Mall Press, 1966.

30. Boss, M. *The analysis of dreams.* New York: Philosophical Library, 1958.

31. Breger, L., Hunter, I., & Lane, R. W. The effect of stress on dreams. *Psychological Issues,* 1971, *7,* Monograph 27.

32. Hall, C. S. A cognitive theory of dreams. *Journal of General Psychology,* 1953, *49,* 273–282.

33. Stewart, K. Dream theory in Malaya. In C. T. Tart (Ed.), *Altered states of consciousness.* New York: Wiley, 1969.

Chapter 12: Perceiving

1. Galanter, E. Contemporary psychophysics. In R. Brown *et al.* (Eds.), *New directions in psychology.* New York: Holt, Rinehart and Winston, 1962.

2. Holland, M. K., & Lockhead, G. R. Sequential effects in absolute judgments of loudness. *Perception and Psychophysics,* 1968, *3,* 409–414.

3. Helson, H. Adaptation level theory. In S. Koch (Ed.), *Psychology: A study of science,* Vol. I. New York: McGraw-Hill, 1959.

4. Von Holts, E. Relations between the central nervous system and the peripheral organs. *British Journal of Animal Behavior,* 1954, *2,* 89–94.

5. Kilbride, P. L. Factors affecting the magnitude of the Ponzo perspective illusion among the Baganda. *Perception and Psychophysics,* 1975, *17,* 543–548.

6. Segall, M. H., Campbell, D. T., & Herskovitz, M. J. Cultural differences in the perception of geometrical illusions. *Science,* 1963, *139,* 769–770.

7. Horowitz, M. J. A cognitive model of hallucinations. *American Journal of Psychiatry,* 1975, *132,* 789–795.

8. Feinberg, I. A comparison of the visual hallucinations in schizophrenia with those induced by mescaline and LSD-25. In L. J. West (Ed.), *Hallucinations.* New York: Grune & Stratton, 1962.

9. Huxley, A. *The doors of perception and heaven and hell.* Middlesex, England: Penguin, 1959.

10. Haber, R. N. Nature of the effect of set on perception. *Psychological Review,* 1966, *73,* 335–351.

11. Bruner, J. S., & Postman, L. On the perception of incongruity. *Journal of Personality,* 1949, *18,* 206–223.

12. Kohler, I. The formation and transformation of the visual world. *Psychological Issues,* 1964, *3,* 28–46.

13. Hess, E. H. Space perception in the chick. *Scientific American,* 1956, *195,* 71–80.

14. Treisman, A. M. Selective

attention in man. *British Medical Bulletin*, 1964, *20*, 12–16.

15. McGinnies, E. Emotionality and perceptual defense. *Psychological Review*, 1949, *56*, 244–251.

16. Natsoulas, T. Converging operations for perceptual defense. *Psychological Bulletin*, 1965, *64*, 393–401.

17. Wispe, L. G., & Drambarean, N. C. Physiological need, word frequency, and visual duration thresholds. *Journal of Experimental Psychology*, 1953, *46*, 25–31.

18. Bruner, J. S., & Goodman, C. C. Value and need as organizing factors in perception. *Journal of Abnormal and Social Psychology*, 1947, *42*, 33–44.

19. Ashley, W. R., Harper, R. S., & Runyon, D. L. The perceived size of coins in normal and hypnotically induced economic states. *American Journal of Psychology*, 1951, *64*, 564–572.

Research Methods IV: Laboratory Methods

1. Dement, W. C. The effects of dream deprivation. *Journal of Nervous and Mental Disease*, 1955, *122*, 263.

Chapter 13: Male and Female

1. Bem, S. L. The measurement of psychological androgyny. *Journal of Consulting and Clinical Psychology*,1974, *42*, 155–162.

2. Mead, M. *Sex and temperament in three primitive societies.* New York: William Morrow, 1935.

3. Brown, D. G. Sex-role development in a changing culture. *Psychological Bulletin*, 1958, *55*, 232–242.

4. Freud, S. *A general introduction to psychoanalysis.* New York: Washington Square Press, 1952.

5. Kagan, J. The concept of identification. *Psychological Review*, 1958, *65*, 296–305.

6. Mussen, P. H., & Distler, L. Masculinity, identification, and father-son relationships. *Journal of Abnormal and Social Psychology*, 1959, *59*, 350–356.

7. Payne, D. E., & Mussen, P. H. Parent-child relations and father-identification among adolescent boys. *Journal of Abnormal and Social Psychology*, 1956, *52*, 358–362.

8. Kinsey, A. C., Pomeroy, W. B., Martin, C. E., & Gebhard, P. H. *Sexual behavior in the human female.* Philadelphia: W. B. Saunders, 1953.

9. Kinsey, A. C., Pomeroy, W. B., & Martin, C. E. *Sexual behavior in the human male.* Philadelphia: W. B. Saunders, 1948.

10. Rosen, D. H. *Lesbianism: A study of female homosexuality.* Springfield, Ill.: Charles C. Thomas, 1974.

11. Acosta, F. X. Etiology and treatment of homosexuality: A review. *Archives of Sexual Behavior*, 1975, *4*, 9–29.

12. Raybin, J. B. Homosexual incest. *Journal of Nervous and Mental Disease*, 1969, *148*, 104–110.

13. Kallman, F. J. Comparative twin study on the genetic aspects of male homosexuality. *Journal of Nervous and Mental Disease*, 1952, *115*, 283–298.

14. West, D. J. *Homosexuality.* London: Gerald Duckworth, 1955.

15. Myerson, A., & Neustadt, R. Bisexuality and male homosexuality. *Clinics*, 1942, *1*, 932–957.

16. Moore, T. V. The pathogenesis and treatment of homosexual disorders: A digest of some pertinent evidence. *Journal of Personality*, 1945, *14*, 47–83.

17. Kolodny, R. C., Masters, W. H., Hendryx, J., & Toro, G. Plasma testosterone and semen analysis in male homosexuals. *New England Journal of Medicine*, 1971, *285*, 1170–1174.

18. Salter, A. *Conditioned reflex therapy.* New York: Capricorn Books, 1961.

19. Snortum, J. R., Gillespie, J. F., Marshall, J. E., McLaughlin, J. P., & Mosberg, L. Family dynamics and homosexuality. *Psychological Reports*, 1969, *24*, 763–770.

20. Hooker, E. Parental relations and male homosexuality in patient and nonpatient samples. *Journal of Consulting and Clinical Psychology*, 1969, *33*, 140–142.

21. Bieber, I. (Ed.) *Homosexuality: A psychoanalytic study.* New York: Basic Books, 1962.

22. Kenyon, F. E. Studies in female homosexuality. *British Journal of Psychiatry*, 1968, *114*, 1337–1350.

23. Bene, E. On the genesis of female homosexuality. *British Journal of Psychiatry*, 1965, *111*, 815–821.

24. Churchill, W. *Homosexual behavior among males.* New York: Hawthorn Books, 1967.

25. Ford, C. S., & Beach, F. A. *Patterns of sexual behavior.* New York: Harper & Row, 1951.

Chapter 14: Sexual Arousal

1. Scoville, W. B. The limbic lobe in man. *Journal of Neurosurgery*, 1954, *11*, 64–66.

2. Blumer, D., & Walker, E. Sexual behavior in temporal lobe epilepsy. *Archives of Neurology*, 1967, *16*, 37–43.

3. Delgado, J. M. R. *Physical control of the mind.* New York: Harper & Row, 1969.

4. Sawyer, C. H. Reproductive behavior. In J. Field (Ed.), *Handbook of physiology.* Vol. II. Washington: American Physiology Society, 1960, 1225–1240.

5. Caggiula, A. R., & Hoebel, B. G. "Copulation-reward site" in the posterior hypothalamus. *Science*, 1966, *153*, 1284–1285.

6. Olds, J. Hypothalamic substrates of reward. *Physiology Review*, 1962, *42*, 554–604.

7. Heath, R. G. Electrical self-stimulation of the brain in man. *American Journal of Psychiatry*, 1963, *120*, 571–577.

8. Vaughan, E., & Fisher, A. E. Male sexual behavior induced

by intracranial electrical stimulation. *Science*, 1962, *137*, 758–760.

9. Masters, W. H., & Johnson, V. E. *Human sexual response.* Boston: Little, Brown, 1966.

10. Hess, E. H., & Polt, J. M. Pupil size as related to interest values of visual stimuli. *Science*, 1960, *132*, 349–350.

11. Hess, E. H., Seltzer, A. L., & Shlien, J. M. Pupil response of hetero- and homosexual males to pictures of men and women: A pilot study. *Journal of Abnormal Psychology*, 1965, *70*, 165–168.

12. Bandura, A. A social learning interpretation of psychological dysfunctions. In P. London & D. Rosenhan (Eds.), *Foundations of abnormal psychology.* New York: Holt, Rinehart and Winston, 1968.

13. Stekel, W. *Sexual aberrations: The phenomena of fetishism in relation to sex.* Vol. II. New York: Liveright, 1930.

14. Kinsey, A. C., Pomeroy, W. B., Martin, C. E., & Gebhard, P. H. *Sexual behavior in the human female.* Philadelphia: W. B. Saunders, 1953.

15. Hariton, E. B. The sexual fantasies of women. *Psychology Today*, 1973, *6*, 39–44.

16. Mosher, D. L. Sex differences, sex experiences, sex guilt, and explicitly sexual films. *Journal of Social Issues*, 1973, *29*, 95–112.

17. Goldstein, M. J. Exposure to erotic stimuli and sexual deviance. *Journal of Social Issues*, 1973, *29*, 197–220.

18. Bardwick, J. M. *Psychology of women: A study of bio-cultural conflicts.* New York: Harper & Row, 1971.

19. Hyde, J. A., & Rosenberg, B. G. *The psychology of women: Half the human experience.* Lexington, Mass.: D. C. Heath, 1976.

Chapter 15: Love and Sex

1. Montagu, A. *The practice of love.* Englewood Cliffs, N.J.: Prentice-Hall, 1975.

2. Pam, A., Plutchik, R., & Conte, H. R. Love: A psychometric approach. *Psychological Reports*, 1975, *37*, 83–88.

3. Fromm, E. *The art of loving.* New York: Harper & Brothers, 1956.

4. Maslow, A. H. *Toward a psychology of being.* Princeton, N.J.: D. Van Nostrand, 1962.

5. Maslow, A. H. *Motivation and personality.* New York: Harper & Brothers, 1954.

6. Ehrmann, W. *Premarital dating behavior.* New York: Holt, Rinehart and Winston, 1959.

7. Reiss, I. L. How and why America's sex standards are changing. *Trans-action*, 1960, *5*, 26–32.

8. Kaats, G. R., & Davis, K. E. The dynamics of sexual behavior of college students. *Journal of Marriage and the Family.* 1970, *32*, 390–399.

9. Kinsey, A. C., Pomeroy, W. B., Martin C. E., & Gebhard, P. H. *Sexual behavior in the human female.* Philadelphia: W. B. Saunders, 1953.

10. Kinsey, A. C., Pomeroy, W. B., & Martin, C. E. *Sexual behavior in the human male.* Philadelphia: W. B. Saunders, 1948.

11. Ford, C. S., & Beach, F. A. *Patterns of sexual behavior.* New York: Harper & Row, 1951.

12. Group for the Advancement of Psychiatry. *Sex and the college student.* New York: Atheneum, 1966.

13. Ellis, A. Masturbation. In M. F. De Martino (Ed.), *Sexual behavior and personality characteristics.* New York: Grove Press, 1963.

14. Masters, W. H., & Johnson, V. E. *Human sexual response.* Boston: Little, Brown, 1966.

15. Sheppe, W. M., & Hain, J. D. Sex and the medical student. *Journal of Medical Education*, 1966, *41*, 457–464.

16. Packard, V. *The sexual wilderness.* New York: McKay, 1968.

17. Luckey, E., & Nass, G. D. A comparison of sexual attitudes and behavior in an international sample. *Journal of Marriage and the Family*, 1969, *31*, 364–379.

18. Groves, W. E., Rossi, P. H., & Grafstein, D. Study of life styles and campus communities. A preliminary report to students who participated. Department of Social Relations, Johns Hopkins University, 1970.

19. Christensen, H. T., & Gregg, C. F. Changing sex norms in America and Scandinavia. *Journal of Marriage and the Family*, 1970, *32*, 616–627.

20. Holland, M. K. Sexual behavior and attitudes among UCLA students. Unpublished manuscript, 1972.

21. Eysenck, H. J. Introverts, extroverts and sex. *Psychology Today*, 1971, *4*, 49.

22. De Martino, M. F. Dominance-feeling, security-insecurity, and sexuality in women. In M. F. De Martino (Ed.), *Sexual behavior and personality characteristics.* New York: Grove Press, 1963.

23. Pilpel, H. F. Sex vs. the law: A study in hypocrisy. In A. Shiloh (Ed.), *Studies in human sexual behavior: The American scene.* Springfield, Ill.: Charles C. Thomas, 1970.

24. Athanasiou, R., Shaver, P., & Tavris, C. Sex. *Psychology Today*, 1970, *4*, 37.

25. Reiss, I. *The social context of premarital sexual permissiveness.* New York: Holt, Rinehart and Winston, 1967.

26. Freeman, H. A., & Freeman, R. S. Senior college women: Their sexual standards and activity. *Journal of the National Association of Women Deans and Counselors*, 1966, *29*, 136–143.

27. Bell, R. R., & Buerkle, J. V. Mother and daughter attitudes to premarital sexual behavior. In A. Shiloh (Ed.), *Studies in human sexual behavior: The American scene.* Springfield, Ill.: Charles C. Thomas, 1970.

28. Star, J. The Presbyterian

debate over sex. *Look*, August 8, 1970, 54.

29. Freedman, M. B. The sexual behavior of American college women: An empirical study and an historical survey. In A. Shiloh (Ed.), *Studies in human sexual behavior: The American scene.* Springfield, Ill.: Charles C. Thomas, 1970.

Research Methods V: Case Studies

1. Thigpen, C. H., & Cleckley, H. A. *The three faces of Eve.* New York: McGraw-Hill, 1957.

2. Leon, G. R. *Case histories of deviant behavior: A social learning analysis.* Boston: Holbrook Press, 1974.

3. Reik, T. *Listening with the third ear.* New York: Farrar, Straus, 1948.

Chapter 16: Personality

1. Jourard, S. M. *The transparent self: Self-disclosure and well-being.* Princeton, N.J.: D. Van Nostrand, 1964.

2. Dymond, R. F. Adjustment changes over therapy from self-sorts. In C. R. Rogers & R. F. Dymond (Eds.), *Psychotherapy and personality change.* Chicago: University of Chicago Press, 1954.

3. In De Laszlo, V. (Ed.) *The basic writings of C. G. Jung.* New York: The Modern Library, 1959.

4. Schjelderup-Ebbe, T. Social behavior of birds. In C. Murchison (Ed.), *Handbook of social psychology.* Worcester, Mass.: Clark University Press, 1935.

5. Mischel, W. *Personality and assessment.* New York: Wiley, 1968.

6. Ulrich, R. E., Stachnik, T. J., & Stainton, N. R. Student acceptance of generalized personality interpretations. *Psychological Reports*, 1963, *13*, 831–834.

7. Offer, D. Studies of normal adolescents. *Adolescence*, 1966, *1*, 305–320.

8. Golden J., Mandel, N., Glueck, B. C., & Feder, Z. A summary description of fifty "normal" white males. *American Journal of Psychiatry*, 1962, *119*, 48–56.

9. Bond, E. D. The student council study. *American Journal of Psychiatry*, 1952, *109*, 11–16.

10. Benedict, R. Anthropology and the abnormal. *Journal of General Psychology*, 1934, *10*, 59–80.

11. Slotkin, J. S. Culture and psychopathology. *Journal of Abnormal and Social Psychology*, 1955, *51*, 269–275.

Chapter 17: Relationships

1. Rubin, Z. *Liking and loving.* New York: Holt, Rinehart and Winston, 1973.

2. Burgess, E. W., & Wallin, P. Homogamy in social characteristics. *American Journal of Sociology*, 1943, *49*, 109–124.

3. Reed, E. W., & Reed, S. C. *Mental retardation: A family study.* Philadelphia: W. B. Saunders, 1965.

4. Garrison, R. J., Anderson, V. E., & Reed, S. C. Assortative marriage. *Eugenics Quarterly*, 1968, *15*, 113–127.

5. Byrne, D., & Nelson, D. Attraction as a linear function of proportion of positive reinforcements. *Journal of Personality and Social Psychology*, 1965, *1*, 659–663.

6. Byrne, D., & Griffitt, W. A developmental investigation of the law of attraction. *Journal of Personality and Social Psychology*, 1966, *4*, 699–703.

7. Winch, R. F., Ktsanes, T., & Ktsanes, V. The theory of complementary needs in mate selection: An analytic and descriptive study. *American Sociologists Review*, 1954, *19*, 241–249.

8. Izard, C. E. Personality similarity and friendship. *Journal of Abnormal and Social Psychology*, 1960, *61*, 47–51.

9. Miller, N., Campbell, D. T., Twedt, H., & O'Connell, E. J. Similarity, contrast and complementarity in friendship choice. *Journal of Personality and Social Psychology*, 1966, *3*, 3–12.

10. Becker, G. The complementary-need hypothesis: Authoritarianism, dominance and other Edwards Personality Preference Schedule scores. *Journal of Personality and Social Psychology*, 1964, *32*, 45–56.

11. Banta, T. J., & Hetherington, M. Relations between needs of friends and fiancées. *Journal of Abnormal and Social Psychology*, 1963, *66*, 401–404.

12. Byrne, D., & Clore, G. L. A reinforcement model of evaluative responses. *Personality: An International Journal*, 1970, *1*, 103–128.

13. Carnegie, D. *How to win friends and influence people.* New York: Simon & Schuster, 1936.

14. Aronson, E., & Worchel, P. Similarity vs. liking as determinants of interpersonal attractiveness. *Psychonomic Science*, 1966, *5*, 157–158.

15. Shraugher, J. S., & Jones, S. C. Social validation and interpersonal evaluations. *Journal of Experimental Social Psychology*, 1968, *4*, 315–323.

16. Jacobs, L., Berscheid, E., & Walster, E. Self esteem and attraction. *Journal of Personality and Social Psychology*, 1971, *17*, 84–91.

17. Homans, G. *Social behavior.* New York: Harcourt, Brace and World, 1961.

18. Kiesler, S. B., & Barol, R. L. The search for a romantic partner: The effects of self-esteem and physical attractiveness on romantic behavior. In K. J. Gerger & D. Marlowe (Eds.), *Personality and social behavior.* Reading, Mass.: Addison-Wesley, 1970.

19. Luft, J. *Of human interaction.* Palo Alto, Calif.: National Press Books, 1969.

20. Berne, E. *Games people play: The psychology of human relationships.* New York: Grove Press, 1964.

21. Johnson, D. W. *Reaching out: Interpersonal effectiveness and self-actualization.* Englewood Cliffs, N.J.: Prentice-Hall, 1972.

22. McCroskey, J. C., Larson, C. E., & Knapp, M. L. *Introduction to interpersonal communication.* Englewood Cliffs, N.J.: Prentice-Hall, 1971.

23. Scheflen, A. E. Communication and regulation in psychotherapy. *Psychiatry*, 1964, *27*, 126–136.

24. Wiener, M., Devoe, S., Rubinow, S., & Geller, J. Nonverbal behavior and nonverbal communication. *Psychological Review*, 1972, *79*, 185–214.

25. Ekman, P., Sorenson, E. R., & Friesen, W. V. Pan-cultural elements in facial displays of emotion. *Science*, 1969, *164*, 86–88.

26. Buber, M. *I and thou.* New York: Scribner's, 1970.

27. Coleman, J. C. *Personality dynamics and effective behavior.* Chicago: Scott, Foresman, 1960.

Chapter 18: Potential

1. Otto, H. A. *Human potentialities: The challenge and the promise.* St. Louis, Mo.: Warren H. Green, 1968.

2. Cox, C. M. The early mental traits of three hundred geniuses: II. In L. M. Terman (Ed.), *Genetic studies of genius.* Stanford, Calif.: Stanford University Press, 1926.

3. Erlenmeyer-Kimling, L., & Jarvik, L. F. Genetics and intelligence: A review. *Science*, 1963, *142*, 1477–1479.

4. Wolf, R. M. The identification and measurement of environmental process variables related to intelligence. Unpublished Ph.D. dissertation, University of Chicago, 1963.

5. Rosenthal, R., & Jacobson, L. *Pygmalion in the classroom: Teacher expectation and pupils' intellectual development.* New York: Holt, Rinehart and Winston, 1968.

6. Honzik, M. P., Macfarlane, J. W., & Allen, L. The stability of mental test performance between two and eighteen years. *Journal of Experimental Education*, 1948, *17*, 309–324.

7. Albee, G. W., *et al.* Statement by SPSSI on current IQ controversy: Heredity versus environment. *American Psychologist*, 1969, *24*, 1039–1040.

8. McNemar, Q. Lost: Our intelligence? Why? *American Psychologist*, 1964, *19*, 871–882.

9. McClelland, D. C. Testing for competence rather than for "intelligence." *American Psychologist*, 1973, *28*, 1–14.

10. Elton, C. F., & Shevel, L. R. *Who is talented? An analysis of achievement.* Iowa City, Ia.: American College Testing Program, 1969.

11. Berg, I. *Education and jobs: The great training robbery.* New York: Praeger, 1970.

12. Barron, F. The psychology of creativity. In T. Newcomb (Ed.), *New directions in Psychology II*, New York: Holt, Rinehart and Winston, 1965.

13. Getzels, J. W., & Jackson, P. W. *Creativity and intelligence.* New York: Wiley, 1962.

14. Wallach, M. A., & Kogan, N. *Modes of thinking in young children: A study of the creativity-intelligence distinction.* New York: Holt, Rinehart and Winston, 1965.

15. MacKinnon, D. W. The study of creative persons: A method and some results. In J. Kagan (Ed.), *Creativity and learning.* Boston: Beacon Press, 1967.

16. Barron, F. *Creativity and psychological health.* Princeton, N.J.: D. Van Nostrand, 1963.

17. Gough, H. G. Techniques for identifying the creative research scientist. In *Conference on the creative person.* Berkeley: University of California, Institute of Personality Assessment and Research, 1961.

18. Dellas, M., & Gaier, E. L. Identification of creativity: The individual. *Psychological Bulletin*, 1970, *73*, 55–73.

19. Anderson, H. H. Creativity in perspective. In H. H. Anderson (Ed.), *Creativity and its cultivation.* New York: Harper & Brothers, 1959.

20. Reid, J. B., King, F. J., & Wickwire, P. Cognitive and other personality characteristics of creative children. *Psychological Reports*, 1959, *5*, 729–737.

21. Moustakas, C. *Creativity and conformity.* Princeton, N.J.: D. Van Nostrand, 1967.

22. Rogers, C. R. *On becoming a person: A therapist's view of psychotherapy.* Boston: Houghton Mifflin, 1961.

23. Jourard, S. M. *The transparent self: Self-disclosure and well-being.* Princeton, N.J.: D. Van Nostrand, 1964.

24. Maslow, A. H. *Toward a psychology of being.* Princeton, N.J.: D. Van Nostrand, 1962.

25. Maslow, A. H. A theory of metamotivation: The biological rooting of the value-life. *Journal of Humanistic Psychology*, 1967, *7*, 93–127.

26. Maslow, A. H. Self-actualization and beyond. In J. F. T. Bugental (Ed.), *Challenges of humanistic psychology.* New York: McGraw-Hill, 1967.

27. Shostrum. E. L. An inventory for the measurement of self-actualization. *Educational and Psychological Measurement*, 1964, *24*, 207–218.

28. McClain, E. W. Further validation of the personal orientation inventory. *Journal of Consulting and Clinical Psychology*, 1970, *35*, 20–22.

29. Bromberg, W. *The mind of man: A history of psychotherapy and psychoanalysis.* New York: Harper Colophon Books, 1963.

30. Masserman, J. H. Ethology, comparative biodynamics, and psychoanalytic research. In J. Scher (Ed.), *Theories of the mind.* New York: The Free Press, 1963.

31. Mikulas, W. L. *Behavior modification: An overview.* New·York: Harper & Row, 1972.

32. Wolpe, J., & Lazarus, A. A. *Behavior therapy techniques: A guide to the treatment of neuroses.* New York: Pergamon Press, 1966.

33. Rogers, C. R. The necessary and sufficient conditions for personality change. *Journal of Consulting Psychology*, 1957, *21*, 95–103.

34. Bradford, L. P., Gibb, J. R., & Benne, K. D. *T-group theory*

and laboratory method. New York: Wiley, 1964.

35. Rogers, C. R. Process of the basic encounter group. In J. F. T. Bugental (Ed.), Challenges of humanistic psychology. New York: McGraw-Hill, 1967.

36. Yalom, I., & Lieberman, M. A study of encounter group casualties. Archives of General Psychiatry, 1971, 25, 16–30.

Research Methods VI: Tests and Surveys

1. Parry, H. J., & Crossley, H. M. Validity of responses to survey questions. Public Opinion Quarterly, 1950, 14, 61–80.

2. Allport, G. W. The trend in motivational theory. American Journal of Orthopsychiatry, 1953, 23, 107–119.

3. Kinsey, A. C., Pomeroy, W. B., Martin, C. E., & Gebhard, P. H. Sexual behavior in the human female. Philadelphia: W. B. Saunders, 1953.

4. Gurin, G., Veroff, J., & Feld, S. Americans view their mental health: A nationwide interview survey. New York: Basic Books, 1960.

Chapter 19: Anxiety

1. Thomas, W. I., & Zaniecki, F. The Polish peasant in Europe and America. New York: Alfred A. Knopf, 1958.

2. Lemert, E. M. Exploratory study of mental disorders in a rural problem area. Rural Sociology, 1948, 48, 13.

3. Durham, H. W. Social structures and mental disorder: Competency hypothesis of explanation. Milbank Memorial Fund Quarterly, 1961, 39, 257–311.

4. Kerckoff, A. C. Anomie and achievement motivation: A study of personality development within cultural disorganization. Social Forces, 1959, 37, 196–202.

5. Gerard, D. L., & Houston, L. G. Family setting and the social ecology of schizophrenia. Psychiatric Quarterly, 1953, 27, 90–101.

6. Maier, N. R. F. Studies of abnormal behavior in the rat. New York: Harper & Row, 1939.

7. Pavlov, I. P. Conditioned reflexes. London: Oxford University Press, 1927.

8. Masserman, J. Behavior and neurosis: An experimental psychoanalytic approach to psychobiologic principles. Chicago: University of Chicago Press, 1943.

9. Basowitz, H., Persky, H. Korchin, S. J., & Grinker, R. R. Anxiety and stress. New York: McGraw-Hill, 1955.

10. Laughlin, H. P. The neuroses. Washington, D.C.: Butterworth, 1967.

11. Miller, N. E. Studies of fear as an acquirable drive. I. Fear as motivation and fear reduction as reinforcement in the learning of new responses. Journal of Experimental Psychology, 1948, 38, 89–101.

12. Mead, M. One vote for this age of anxiety. New York Times Magazine, May 20, 1956, p. 13.

Chapter 20: Neurosis

1. White, R. W. The abnormal personality. New York: The Ronald Press, 1956.

2. Horney, K. Our inner conflicts: A constructive theory of neurosis. New York: W. W. Norton & Co., 1945.

3. Laughlin, H. P. The neuroses. Washington, D.C.: Butterworth, 1967.

4. Leon, G. R. Case histories of deviant behavior. Boston: Holbrook Press, 1974.

5. Thorpe, L. P., Katz, B., & Lewis, R. T. The psychology of abnormal behavior: A dynamic approach. New York: The Ronald Press, 1961.

6. Thigpen, C. H., & Cleckley, H. A. The three faces of Eve. New York: McGraw-Hill, 1957.

7. De Fazio, V. J. The Vietnam era veteran: Psychological problems. Journal of Contemporary Psychotherapy, 1975, 7, 9–15.

8. Bloch, H. S. Army clinical psychiatry in the combat zone, 1967–1968. American Journal of

Psychiatry, 1969, 126, 289–298. Copyright 1969, the American Psychiatric Association. Reprinted by permission.

9. Moore, H. E. Some emotional concomitants of disaster. Mental Hygiene, 1958, 42, 45.

10. Titchener, J. L., & Kapp, F. T. Family and character change at Buffalo Creek. American Journal of Psychiatry, 1976, 133, 295–299.

11. Stern, G. M. From chaos to responsibility. American Journal of Psychiatry, 1976, 133, 300–301.

12. Brady, J. P., & Lind, D. L. Experimental analysis of hysterical blindness: Operant conditioning techniques. Archives of General Psychiatry, 1961, 4, 331–339.

13. Gassner, S., & Murray, E. J. Dissonance and conflict in the interactions between parents and normal and neurotic children. Journal of Abnormal Psychology, 1969, 74, 33–41.

Chapter 21: Psychosis

1. Courtney, J. E. Dangerous paranoiacs: With autobiography of one. Alienist & Neurologist, 1901, 22, 139–149.

2. Schreber, D. P., in Memoirs of my nervous illness, ed. and trans. by I. Macalpine & R. A. Hunter. London: Dawson, 1955.

3. Davidson, D. Remembrances of a religio-maniac. Stratford-on-Avon, England: Shakespeare Press, 1912.

4. Beers, C. W. A mind that found itself. New York: Longmans, Green, 1908.

5. McCall, L. Between us and the dark. Philadelphia: J. B. Lippincott, 1947.

6. Karpman, B. Dream life in a case of hebephrenia. Psychiatric Quarterly, 1953, 27, 262–316.

7. Szasz, T. S. The myth of mental illness. New York: Hoeber, 1961.

8. Scheff, T. J. Labeling madness. Englewood Cliffs, N.J.: Prentice-Hall, 1975.

9. Sullivan, H. S. The

interpersonal theory of psychiatry. New York: W. W. Norton & Co., 1953.

10. Zigler, E., & Phillips, L. Psychiatric diagnosis and symptomatology. *Journal of Abnormal and Social Psychology,* 1961, *63,* 69–75.

11. Sushinsky, L. W., & Wener, R. Distorting judgments of mental health. *Journal of Nervous and Mental Disease,* 1975, *161,* 82–89.

12. Hofling, C. K. *Textbook of psychiatry for medical practice,* 2nd ed. Philadelphia: J. B. Lippincott, 1968.

13. Thorpe, L. P., Katz, B., & Lewis, R. T. *The psychology of abnormal behavior: A dynamic approach.* New York: The Ronald Press, 1961.

14. Mosher, L. R., & Feinsilver, D. *Special report on schizophrenia.* National Institute of Mental Health, April 1970.

15. White, R. W. *The abnormal personality.* New York: The Ronald Press, 1956.

16. Rokeach, M., *The three Christs of Ypsilanti.* New York: Vintage Books, 1964.

17. Lidz, T., Fleck, S., & Cornelison, A. R. *Schizophrenia and the family.* New York: International Universities Press, 1965.

18. Ferriera, A. J., & Winter, W. W. Information exchange and silence in normal and abnormal families. In W. W. Winter & A. J. Ferriera (Eds.), *Research in family interaction.* Palo Alto, Calif.: Science & Behavior Books, 1964.

19. Reiss, D. The family and schizophrenia. *American Journal of Psychiatry,* 1976, *133,* 181–185.

20. Laing, R. D. *The divided self: An existential study in sanity and madness.* Baltimore: Penguin Books, 1965.

21. Meehl, P. E. Schizotaxia, schizotypy, schizophrenia. *American Psychologist.* 1962, *17,* 827–838.

22. Murray, H. G., & Hirsch, J. Heredity, individual differences, and psychopathology. In S. C. Plog & R. B. Edgerton (Eds.), *Changing perspectives in mental*

illness. New York: Holt, Rinehart and Winston, 1969.

23. Matthysse, S. W., & Kidd, K. K. Estimating the genetic contribution to schizophrenia. *American Journal of Psychiatry,* 1976, *133,* 185–191.

24. Lynn, R. Russian theory and research on schizophrenia. *Psychological Bulletin,* 1963, *60,* 486–498.

25. Mattyhysse, S., & Lipinski, J. Biochemical aspects of schizophrenia. *Annual Review of Medicine,* 1975, *26,* 551–565.

Research Methods VII: Correlational Studies

1. Hollingshead, A. B., & Redlich, F. C. *Social class and mental illness: A community study.* New York: Wiley, 1958.

Chapter 22: Conformity

1. Wolfe, K. M., & Fiske, M. The children talk about the comics. In P. F. Lazarsfeld & F. Stanton (Eds.), *Communications research 1948–1949.* New York: Harper, 1949.

2. Riesman, D. *The lonely crowd.* Garden City, N.Y.: Doubleday, 1953.

3. Sumner, W. S. *Folkways: A study of the sociological importance of usages, manners, customs, mores, and morals.* New York: Dover, 1959.

4. Itani, J. The society of Japanese monkeys. *Japan Quarterly,* 1961, *8,* 4.

5. Willis, R. H. Conformity, independence, and anticonformity. *Human Relations,* 1965, *18,* 373–388.

6. Kennedy, J. F. *Profiles in courage.* New York: Harper, 1955.

7. Utech, D. A., & Hoving, K. L. Parents and peers as competing influences in the decisions of children of differing ages. *Journal of Social Psychology,* 1969, *78,* 267–274.

8. Sherif, M. *The psychology of social norms.* New York: Harper, 1936.

9. Jacobs, R. C., & Campbell, D. T. The perpetuation of an

arbitrary tradition through several generations of a laboratory micro culture. *Journal of Abnormal and Social Psychology,* 1961, *62,* 649–658.

10. Asch, S. E. Effects of group pressure upon the modification and distortion of judgment. In H. Guetzkow (Ed.), *Groups, leadership and men.* Pittsburgh, Pa.: Carnegie Press, 1951.

11. Cartwright, D., & Zander, A. *Group dynamics: Research and theory.* New York: Harper & Row, 1968.

12. Gamson, W. *Power and discontent.* Homewood, Ill.: Dorsey Press, 1968.

13. Orne, M. T., & Evans, F. J. Social control in the psychological experiment. *Journal of Personality and Social Psychology,* 1965, *1,* 189–200.

14. Flacks, R. Protest or conform: Some social psychological perspectives on legitimacy. *Journal of Applied Behavioral Science,* 1969, *5,* 127–150.

15. Milgram, S. Some conditions of obedience and disobedience to authority. *Human Relations,* 1965, *18,* 57–75.

16. Milgram, S. Liberating effects of group pressure. *Journal of Personality and Social Psychology,* 1965, *1,* 127–134.

Chapter 23: Prejudice

1. Katz, D., & Braly, K. W. Racial stereotypes in one hundred college students. *Journal of Abnormal and Social Psychology,* 1933, *28,* 280–290.

2. Karlins, M., Coffman, T. L., & Walters, G. On the fading of social stereotypes: Studies in three generations of college students. *Journal of Personality and Social Psychology,* 1969, *13,* 1–16.

3. Brigham, J. C. Ethnic stereotypes. *Psychological Bulletin,* 1971, *76,* 15–38.

4. Sherif, M., Harvey, O. J., White, B. J., Hood, W. R., & Sherif, C. W. *Intergroup conflict and cooperation: The Robbers' Cave experiment.* Norman, Okla.: University Book Exchange, 1961.

5. Daniels, R. *The politics of prejudice.* New York: Atheneum, 1968.

6. Mintz, A. A re-examination of correlations between lynchings and economic indices. *Journal of Abnormal and Social Psychology*, 1946, *41*, 159–160.

7. Rokeach, M., Smith, P. W., & Evans, R. I. Two kinds of prejudice or one? In M. Rokeach (Ed.), *The open and closed mind.* New York: Basic Books, 1960.

8. Byrne, D., & Wong, T. J. Racial prejudice, interpersonal attraction and assumed dissimilarity of attitudes. *Journal of Abnormal and Social Psychology*, 1962, *65*, 246–253.

9. Byrne, D., & Nelson, D. Attraction as a linear function of proportion of positive reinforcements. *Journal of Personality and Social Psychology*, 1965, *1*, 659–663.

10. Stein, D. D., Hardyck, J. A., & Smith, M. B. Race and belief: An open and shut case. *Journal of Personality and Social Psychology*, 1965, *1*, 281–289.

11. Insko, C. A., & Robinson, J. E. Belief similarity versus race as determinants of reactions to Negroes by Southern white adolescents: A further test of Rokeach's theory. *Journal of Personality and Social Psychology*, 1967, *7*, 216–221.

12. Dollard, J., Doob, L. W., Miller, N. E., Mower, O. H., & Sears, R. R. *Frustration and aggression.* New Haven: Yale University Press, 1939.

13. Miller, N. E., & Bugelski, R. Minor studies of aggression: II: The influence of frustrations by the ingroup on attitudes expressed toward outgroups. *Journal of Psychology*, 1948, *25*, 437–442.

14. Mosher, D. L., & Scodel, A. A study of the relationship between ethnocentrism in children and the ethnocentrism and authoritarian rearing practices of their mothers. *Child Development*, 1960, *31*, 369–376.

15. Epstein, R., & Komorita, S. S. Childhood prejudice as a function of parental ethnocentrism, punitiveness, and outgroup characteristics. *Journal of Personality and Social Psychology*, 1966, *3*, 259–264.

16. Stein, A. Strategies for failure. *Harvard Educational Review*, 1971, *41*, 186.

17. Sanchez, D. Testimony before the U.S. Senate Committee on Education. *New York Times*, August 19, 1970.

18. Adorno, T. W., Frankel-Brunswik, E., Levinson, D. J., & Sanford, R. N. *The authoritarian personality.* New York: Harper, 1950.

19. Christie, R., & Cook, P. A guide to published literature relating to the authoritarian personality through 1956. *Journal of Psychology*, 1958, *45*, 171–199.

20. Selznick, G. J., & Steinberg, S. *The tenacity of prejudice.* New York: Harper & Row, 1969.

21. Marx, G. T. *Protest and prejudice: A study of belief in the black community.* New York: Harper & Row, 1969.

22. Delany, L. T. The other bodies in the river. In J. V. McConnell (Ed.), *Readings in social psychology today.* Del Mar, Calif.: CRM Books, 1967.

23. Grier, W. H., & Cobbs, P. M. *Black rage.* New York: Basic Books, 1968.

24. Darrow, C., & Lowinger, P. The Detroit uprising: A psychosocial study. In J. H. Masserman (Ed.), *The dynamics of dissent.* New York: Grune & Stratton, 1968.

25. *Report of the National Advisory Commission on Civil Disorders.* Washington, D.C.: U.S. Government Printing Office, 1968.

26. Grambs, J. D. The self-concept: Basis for reeducation of Negro youth. In W. C. Kvaracens, J. S. Gibson, F. Patterson, B. Seasholes & J. D. Grambs (Eds.), *Negro self-concept: Implications for school and citizenship.* New York: McGraw-Hill, 1964.

27. Dansby, P. G. Black pride in the seventies: Fact or fantasy? In R. L. Jones (Ed.), *Black psychology.* New York: Harper & Row, 1972.

28. Clark, K. B., & Clark, M. P. Racial identification and preference in Negro children. In T. M. Newcomb & E. L. Hartley (Eds.), *Readings in social psychology.* New York: Holt, Rinehart and Winston, 1947.

29. Morland, J. K. Racial acceptance and preference of nursery school children in a southern city. *Merrill Palmer Quarterly*, 1962, *8*, 271–280.

30. Coles, R. *Children of crisis: A study of courage and fear.* Boston: Atlantic-Little, Brown, 1967.

31. Grier, W. H., & Cobbs, P. M. *The Jesus bag.* New York: McGraw-Hill, 1971.

32. Broverman, I. K., Broverman, D. M., Clarkson, F. E., Rosenkrantz, P. S., & Vogel, S. R. Sex-role stereotypes and clinical judgments of mental health. *Journal of Consulting and Clinical Psychology*, 1970, *34*, 1–7.

33. Greer, G. *The female eunuch.* New York: Bantam Books, 1971.

34. Mannes, M. The problems of creative women. In S. M. Farber & R. H. L. Wilson (Eds.), *The potential of woman.* New York: McGraw-Hill, 1963.

35. Salzman-Webb, M. Woman as secretary, sexpot, spender, sow, civic actor, sickie. In M. H. Garskof (Ed.), *Roles women play: Readings toward women's liberation.* Belmont, Calif.: Brooks/Cole, 1971.

36. Koontz, E. D. *Underutilization of women workers.* Washington, D.C.: U.S. Government Printing Office, 1971.

37. Suelzle, M. Women in labor. *Trans-action*, 1970, *8*, 50–58.

38. Levitin, T., Quinn, R. P., & Staines, G. L. Sex discrimination against the American working woman. *American Behavioral Scientist*, 1971 (Nov.-Dec.), 237–254.

39. *1975 Handbook on women workers.* U.S. Department of

Labor, Employment Standards Administration, Bulletin 297, 1975.

40. Bem, D. J. *Beliefs, attitudes, and human affairs.* Belmont, Calif.: Brooks/Cole, 1970.

41. Komisar, L. The image of woman in advertising. In V. Gornick & B. K. Moran (Eds.), *Woman in sexist society.* New York: Signet Books, 1972.

42. Farrell, B. You've come a long way, buddy. *Life,* 1971, *97,* 52–59.

43. *Time,* 1971, *97,* 54.

44. Amir, Y. Contact hypothesis in ethnic relations. *Psychological Bulletin,* 1969, *71,* 319–342.

45. Pearl, D. Psychotherapy and ethnocentrism. *Journal of Abnormal and Social Psychology,* 1955, *50,* 227–230.

46. Rubin, I. M. Increased self-acceptance: A means of reducing prejudice. *Journal of Personality and Social Psychology,* 1967, *5,* 233–238.

Chapter 24: Aggression and War

1. Stark, R., & McEvoy, J. Middle-class violence. *Psychology Today,* 1970, *4,* 52.

2. Buss, A. H. *The psychology of aggression.* New York: Wiley, 1961.

3. Freud, S. *Civilization and its discontents.* New York: Jonathan Cape and Harrison Smith, 1930.

4. Lorenz, K. *On aggression.* New York: Bantam Books, 1966.

5. Eibl-Eibesfeldt, I. The fighting behavior of animals. In R. C. Atkinson (Ed.), *Contemporary psychology.* San Francisco: W. H. Freeman, 1971.

6. Carrighar, S. War is not in our genes. In M. F. A. Montagu (Ed.), *Man and aggression.* New York: Oxford University Press, 1968.

7. Holloway, R. L. Human aggression: The need for a species-specific framework. In M. Fried, M. Harris, & R. Murphy (Eds.), *War: The anthropology of armed conflict and aggression.* Garden City, N.Y.: The Natural History Press, 1968.

8. Morris, D. *The naked ape.* New York: Dell, 1967.

9. Washburn, S. L., & Hamburg, D. A. Aggressive behavior in Old World monkeys and apes. In P. C. Jay (Ed.), *Primates: Studies in adaptation and variability.* New York: Holt, Rinehart and Winston, 1968.

10. King, H. E. Psychological effects of excitation in the limbic system. In D. E. Sheer (Ed.), *Electrical stimulation of the brain.* Austin: University of Texas Press, 1961.

11. Kaada, B. Brain mechanisms related to aggressive behavior. In C. D. Clemente & D. B. Lindsley (Eds.), *Aggression and defense.* Berkeley: University of California Press, 1967.

12. Egger, M. D., & Flynn, J. P. Effect of electrical stimulation of the amygdala on hypothalamically elicited attack behavior in cats. *Journal of Neurophysiology,* 1963, *26,* 705–720.

13. Sano, K. Sedative neurosurgery: With special reference to posteromedial hypothalamotomy. *Neurologia medico chirrwigica,* 1962, *4,* 112–142.

14. Azrin, N. H., Hutchinson, R. R., & Hake, D. F. Pain-induced fighting in the squirrel monkey. *Journal of Experimental Analysis of Behavior,* 1963, *6,* 620.

15. Dollard, J., Doob, L., Miller N., Mowrer, O., & Sears, R. *Frustration and aggression.* New Haven: Yale University Press, 1939.

16. Azrin, N. H., Hutchinson, R. R., & Hake, D. F. Extinction-induced aggression. *Journal of Experimental Analysis of Behavior,* 1966, *9,* 191–204.

17. Kaufman, H. Definitions and methodology in the study of aggression. *Psychological Bulletin,* 1965, *64,* 351–364.

18. Bandura, A., Ross, D., & Ross, S. A. Transmission of aggression through imitation of aggressive models. *Journal of Abnormal and Social Psychology,* 1961, *63,* 575–582.

19. Sears, R. R., Maccoby, E. E., &

Levin, H. *Patterns of child rearing.* Evanston, Ill.: Row, Peterson and Co., 1957.

20. Feshbach, S. Aggression. In P. H. Mussen (Ed.), *Carmichael's manual of child psychology* (rev. ed.). New York: Wiley, 1970.

21. Bandura, A., Ross, D., & Ross, S. A. Imitation of film-mediated aggressive models. *Journal of Abnormal and Social Psychology,* 1963, *66,* 3–11.

22. Berkowitz, L. Impulse, aggression and the gun. *Psychology Today,* 1968, *2,* 18–23.

23. Walters, R. H., Thomas, E. L., & Acker, C. W. Enhancement of punitive behavior by audio-visual displays. *Science,* 1962, *136,* 872–873.

24. Patterson, G., Littman, R., & Bricker, W. Assertive behavior in children: A step toward a theory of aggression. *Monographs of the Society for Research in Child Development,* 1967, *32.*

25. Walters, R., & Brown, M. Studies of reinforcement of aggression: III. *Child Development,* 1963, *34,* 563–571.

26. Kovalsky, N. A. Social aspects of international aggression. *International Social Science Journal* 1971, *23,* 68–78.

27. Levi, W. On the causes of war and the conditions of peace. *Journal of Conflict Resolution,* 1960, *4,* 411–420.

28. Feierabend, I., & Feierabend, R. Conflict, crisis and collision: A study of international stability. In *Readings in psychology today.* Del Mar, Calif.: CRM Books, 1969.

29. Lerner, M. J. The effect of preparatory action on beliefs concerning nuclear war. *Journal of Social Psychology,* 1965, *65,* 225–231.

30. Allport, G. W. The role of expectancy. In H. Cantril (Ed.), *Tensions that cause war.* Urbana, Ill.: University of Illinois Press, 1950.

31. Hammond, K. R. New directions in research on conflict resolution. *Journal of*

Social Issues, 1965, *21*, 44–66.

32. Holsti, O., Brody, R., & North, R. The management of international crisis: Affect and action in American-Soviet relations. *Journal of Peace Research*, 1964, *3–4*, 170–190.

33. Moyer, K. E. The physiology of aggression and the implications for aggressive control. In J. L. Singer (Ed.), *The control of aggression and violence.* New York: Academic Press, 1971.

Research Methods VIII: Controlled Experiments

1. Bandura, A., & McDonald, F. J. Influence of social reinforcement and the behavior of models in shaping children's moral judgments. *Journal of Abnormal and Social Psychology*, 1963, *67*, 274–281.

Chapter 25: Environment

1. Cole, L. C. Man's ecosystem. In J. B. Bresler (Ed.), *Environments of man.* Reading, Mass.: Addison-Wesley, 1968.

2. Von Bertalanffy, L. General system theory—A critical review. *General Systems*, 1962, *7*, 1–20.

3. Egler, F. E. Pesticides—in our ecosystem. *American Scientist*, 1964, *52*, 110–136.

4. Sells, S. B. Ecology and the science of psychology. *Multivariate Behavioral Research*, 1966, *1*, 131–144.

5. Carson, D. H., & Driver, B. L. An ecological approach to environmental stress. *American Behavioral Scientist*, 1966, *10*, 8–11.

6. Selye, H. *The stress of life.* New York: McGraw-Hill, 1956.

7. Mims, C. Stress in relation to the processes of civilization. In S. V. Boyden (Ed.), *The impact of civilization on the biology of man.* Toronto, Can.: University of Toronto Press, 1970.

8. Rahe, R. H., & Holmes, T. H. Life crisis and major health change. *Psychosomatic Medicine*, 1966, *28*, 774.

9. Rahe, R. J., Gunderson, E. K. E., & Arthur, R. J. Demographic and psychosocial factors in acute illness reporting. *Navy Medical Neuropsychiatric Research Unit Report No. 69–35.* San Diego, Calif., 1969.

10. Dubos, R. *Man adapting.* New Haven: Yale University Press, 1965.

11. Huntington, E. *Mainsprings of civilization.* New York: Mentor Books, 1945.

12. Wyndham, C. H. Performance and comfort standards in relation to climate. In *Environmental physiology and psychology in arid conditions: Proceedings of the Lucknow Symposium.* Paris, France: UNESCO, 1964.

13. Eckenrode, R. T., & Abbot, W. C. *The response of man to his environment.* Darien, Conn.: Dunlap and Associates, 1959.

14. Winslow, C. E. A., & Herrington, L. P. *Temperature and human life.* Princeton, N.J.: Princeton University Press, 1949.

15. Edholm. O. G. Tropical fatigue. In W. F. Floyd & A. T. Welford (Eds.), *Symposium on fatigue.* London: H. K. Lewis, 1953.

16. Bursill, A. E. The restriction of peripheral vision during exposure to hot and humid conditions. *Quarterly Journal of Experimental Psychology*, 1958, *10*, 113–129.

17. Cerbos, G. Seasonal variation in some mental health statistics: Suicides, homicides, psychiatric admissions, and institutional placement of the retarded. *Journal of Clinical Psychology*, 1970, *26*, 61–63.

18. Knoblock, H., & Passmanick, B. Seasonal variation in the births of the mentally deficient. In J. B. Bresler (Ed.), *Environments of man.* Reading, Mass.: Addison-Wesley, 1968.

19. Thoreau, H. D. *Walden.* Princeton, N.J.: Princeton University Press, 1971.

20. Muir, J. *The Yosemite.* Garden City, N.Y.: Anchor Books, 1962.

21. Clawson, M., & Knetsch, J. *Economics of outdoor recreation.* Baltimore, Md.: Johns Hopkins University Press, 1966.

22. Shafer, E. L., & Mietz, J. Aesthetic and emotional experiences rate high with Northeast wilderness hikers. In J. F. Wohlwill & D. H. Carson (Eds.), *Environment and the social sciences: Perspectives and applications.* Washington, D.C.: American Psychological Association, 1972.

23. Driver, B. L. Potential contributions of psychology to recreation resource management. In J. F. Wohlwill & D. H. Carson (Eds.), *Environment and the social sciences: Perspectives and applications.* Washington, D.C.: American Psychological Association, 1972.

24. Holland, M. K. Environmental mood inventory. Unpublished manuscript, 1973.

25. Kavanau, J. L. Behavior: Confinement, adaptation, and compulsory regimes in laboratory studies. *Science*, 1964, *143*, 490.

26. Grether, W. F. Psychology and the space frontier. *American Psychologist*, 1962, *17*, 92–101.

27. Walters, H. C. *Military psychology: Its use in modern war and indirect conflict.* Dubuque, Iowa: William C. Brown, 1968.

28. Sharpe, M. R. *Living in space: The astronaut and his environment.* Garden City, N.Y.: Doubleday, 1969.

29. Spivack, M. Sensory distortions in tunnels and corridors. *Hospital Community Psychiatry*, 1967, *18*, 24–30.

30. Wexner, L. B. The degree to which colors are associated with mood-tones. *Journal of Applied Psychology*, 1954, *38*, 432–435.

31. Drechsler, R. J. Affect-stimulating effects of colors. *Journal of Abnormal and Social Psychology*, 1960, *61*, 323–338.

32. Maslow, A. H., & Mintz, N. L. Effects of esthetic surroundings. *Journal of Psychology*, 1956, *41*, 247–254.

33. Wong, H., & Brown, W. Effects of surroundings upon mental work as measured by Yerkes Multiple Choice

Method. *Journal of Comparative Psychology*, 1923, *3*, 319–331.

34. Ittleson, W. H., Proshansky, H. M., & Rivlin, L. G. The environmental psychology of the psychiatric ward. In H. M. Proshansky, W. H. Ittelson, & L. G. Rivlin (Eds.), *Environmental psychology: Man and his physical setting*. New York: Holt, Rinehart and Winston, 1970.

35. Sommer, R. The ecology of privacy. *The Library Quarterly*, 1966, *36*, 234–248.

36. Craik, K. H. Environmental psychology. In T. M. Newcomb (Ed.), *New directions in psychology 4*. New York: Holt, Rinehart and Winston, 1970.

37. Osmond, H. Function as the basis of psychiatric ward design. *Mental Hospitals* (Architectural Supplement), 1957, *8*, 23–30.

38. Milgram, S. The experience of living in cities. *Science*, 1970, *167*, 1461–1468.

39. Lynch, K. The city as environment. In N. Wertheimer (Ed.), *Confrontation*. Glenview, Ill.: Scott, Foresman, 1970.

40. Jacobs, J. *The death and life of great American cities*. New York: Vintage Books, 1961.

41. Doxiadis, C. A. Man and the space around him. *Saturday Review*, December 14, 1968, 21–23.

Chapter 26: Social Space

1. McBride, G. Theories of animal spacing: The role of flight, fight and social distance. In A. H. Esser (Ed.), *Behavior and environment: The use of space by animals and men*. New York: Plenum Press, 1971.

2. Sommer, R. *Personal space: The behavioral basis for design*. Englewood Cliffs, N.J.: Prentice-Hall, 1969.

3. Mowat, F. *Never cry wolf*. New York: Dell Publishing, 1963.

4. Dubos, R. *Man adapting*. New Haven: Yale University Press, 1965.

5. Harlow, H. F., & Harlow, M. K. Social deprivation in monkeys. *Scientific American*, November 1962.

6. Ellenberger, H. F. Behavior under involuntary confinement. In A. H. Esser (Ed.), *Behavior and environment: The use of space by animals and men*. New York: Plenum Press, 1971.

7. Haythorn, W. W., & Altman, I. Together in isolation. *Trans-action*, 1967, *4*, 18–22.

8. Altman, I. Ecological aspects of interpersonal functioning. In A. H. Esser (Ed.), *Behavior and environment: The use of space by animals and men*. New York: Plenum Press, 1971.

9. Ehrlich, P. R. *The population bomb*. New York: Ballantine, 1968.

10. Proshansky, H. M., Ittelson, W. H., & Rivlin, L. G. Freedom of choice and behavior in a physical setting. In J. F. Wohlwill & D. H. Carson (Eds.), *Environment and the social sciences*. Washington, D.C.: American Psychological Association, 1972.

11. Zlutnick, S., & Altman, I. Crowding and human behavior. In J. F. Wohlwill & D. H. Carson (Eds.), *Environment and the social sciences*. Washington, D.C.: American Psychological Association, 1972.

12. Welch, B. L. Psychophysiological response to the mean level of environmental stimulation. In D. M. Rioch (Ed.), *Medical aspects of stress in the military climate*. Washington, D.C.: United States Government Printing Office, 1965.

13. Christian, J. J. Endocrine adaptive mechanisms and the physiological regulation of population growth. In W. Mayer & R. Van Gelder (Eds.), *Physiological mammalogy*. Vol. *1*. New York: Academic Press, 1963.

14. Myers, L., Hale, C. S., Mykytowycz, R., & Hughes, R. L. The effects of varying density and space on sociability and health in mammals. In

A. H. Esser (Ed.), *Behavior and environment: The use of space by animals and men*. New York: Plenum Press, 1971.

15. Thiessen, D. D. Amphetamine toxicity, population density, and behavior: A review. *Psychological Bulletin*, 1964, *62*, 401–410.

16. Christian, J. J. The potential role of the adrenal cortex as affected by social rank and population density on experimental epidemics. *American Journal of Epidemiology*, 1968, *87*, 255–266.

17. Hoagland, H. Cybernetics of population control. *Bulletin of the Atomic Scientists*, February 1964, 1–6.

18. Esser, A. H. A biosocial perspective on crowding. In J. F. Wohlwill & D. H. Carson (Eds.), *Environment and the social sciences*. Washington, D.C.: American Psychological Association, 1972.

19. Calhoun, J. B. A behavioral sink. In E. Bliss (Ed.), *Roots of behavior*. New York: Paul Hoeber, 1962.

20. Calhoun, J. B. Population density and social pathology. *Scientific American*, 1962, *206*, 139–148.

21. Calhoun, J. B. Space and the strategy of life. In A. H. Esser (Ed.), *Behavior and environment: The use of space by animals and men*. New York: Plenum Press, 1971.

22. Marsella, A. J., Escudero, M., & Gordon, S. The effects of dwelling density on mental disorder in Filipino men. *Journal of Health and Social Behavior*, 1970, *11*, 288–294.

23. Hutt, C., & Vaizey, M. J. Differential effects of group density on social behavior. *Nature*, 1966, *209*, 1371–1372.

24. Indik, B. P. Some effects of organization size on member attitudes and behavior. *Human Relations*, 1963, *16*, 369–384.

25. Barker, R. G., & Hall, E. R. Participation in interschool events and extracurricular activities. In R. G. Barker & P. V. Gump, *Big school, small*

school. Stanford, Calif.: Stanford University Press, 1964.

Chapter 27: Sensory Pollution

1. Dubos, R. *Man adapting.* New Haven: Yale University Press, 1965.
2. Swan, J. A. Public response to air pollution. In J. F. Wohlwill & D. H. Carson (Eds.), *Environment and the social sciences: Perspectives and applications.* Washington, D.C.: American Psychological Association, 1972.
3. Dubos, R. We can't buy our way out. *Psychology Today,* 1970, *3,* 20.
4. Schultz, D. P. *Sensory restriction: Effects on behavior.* New York: Academic Press, 1965.
5. Schultz, D. P. Evidence suggesting a sensory variation drive in humans. *Journal of General Psychology,* 1967, *77,* 87–99.
6. Malmo, R. B. Activation: A neuropsychological dimension. *Psychology Review,* 1959, *66,* 367–386.
7. Ruff, G. E. Psychological and psychophysiological indices of stress. In N. M. Burns, R. Chambers, & E. Hendler (Eds.), *Unusual environments and human behavior.* London: The Free Press, 1963.
8. Vitz, P. C. Affect as a function of stimulus variation. *Journal of Experimental Psychology,* 1966, *71,* 74–79.
9. Wohlwill, J. Amount of stimulus exploration and preference of differential functions of stimulus complexity. *Perception and Psychophysics,* 1968, *4,* 307–312.
10. Leiderman, P. H., Mendelson, J. H., Wexler, D., & Solomon, P. Sensory deprivation: Clinical aspects. *Archives of Internal Medicine,* 1958, *101,* 389–396.
11. Rosenzweig, N. Sensory deprivation and schizophrenia: Clinical and theoretical similarities. *American Journal of Psychiatry,* 1959, *116,* 326–329. Copyright 1959, the American Psychiatric Association. Reprinted by permission.
12. White, B. L., Castle, P., & Held, R. Observations on the development of visually directed reaching. *Child Development,* 1964, *35,* 349–364.
13. Dennis, W. Causes of retardation among institutional children. *Journal of Genetic Psychology,* 1960, *96,* 47–59.
14. Butler, R. A. The effect of deprivation of visual incentives on visual exploration motivation in monkeys. *Journal of Comparative and Physiological Psychology,* 1957, *50,* 177–179.
15. Berlyne, D. E., & Slater, J. Perceptual curiosity, exploratory behavior, and maze learning. *Journal of Comparative and Physiological Psychology,* 1957, *50,* 228–232.
16. Krech, D., Rosenzweig, M. R., & Bennett, E. L. Relations between brain chemistry and problem-solving among rats raised in enriched and impoverished environments. *Journal of Comparative and Physiological Psychology,* 1962, *55,* 801–807.
17. Rosenzweig, M. R. Environmental complexity, cerebral change, and behavior. *American Psychologist,* 1966, *21,* 321–342.
18. Scott, T. H., Bexton, W. H., Heron, W., & Doane, B. K. Cognitive effects of perceptual isolation. *Canadian Journal of Psychology,* 1959, *13,* 200–209.
19. Goldberger, L., & Holt, R. R. Experimental interference with reality contact: Individual differences. In P. Solomon, P. E. Kubzansky, P. H. Leiderman, J. H. Mendelson, R. Trumbull, & D. Wexler (Eds.), *Sensory deprivation.* Cambridge, Mass.: Harvard University Press, 1961.
20. Zubek, J. P., Sansom, W., & Prysiazniuk, A. Intellectual changes during prolonged perceptual isolation (darkness and silence). *Canadian Journal of Psychology,* 1960, *14,* 233–243.
21. Zubek, J. P., Pushkar, D., Sansom, W., & Gowing, J. Perceptual changes after prolonged sensory isolation (darkness and silence). *Canadian Journal of Psychology,* 1961, *15,* 83–100.
22. Bexton, W. H., Heron W., & Scott, T. H. Effects of decreased variation in the sensory environment. *Canadian Journal of Psychology,* 1954, *8,* 70–76.
23. Hebb, D. O. The motivating effects of exteroceptive stimulation. *American Psychologist,* 1958, *13,* 109.
24. Zuckerman, M., Albright, R. J., Marks, C. S., & Miller, G. L. Stress and hallucinatory effects of perceptual isolation and confinement. *Psychology Monograph,* 1962, *76,* 30.
25. Cohen, S. I., Silverman, A. J., Bressler, B., & Shmavonian, B. M. Problems in isolation studies. In P. Solomon, P. E. Kubzansky, P. H. Leiderman, J. H. Mendelson, R. Trumbull, & D. Wexler (Eds.), *Sensory deprivation.* Cambridge, Mass.: Harvard University Press, 1961.
26. Smith, S., & Lewty, W. Perceptual isolation using a silent room. *Lancet,* 1959, *2,* 342–345.
27. Heron, W., Doane, B. K., & Scott, T. H. Visual disturbances after prolonged perceptual isolation. *Canadian Journal of Psychology,* 1956, *10,* 13–18.
28. Freedman, S. J., Grunebaum, H. U., & Greenblatt, M. Perceptual and cognitive changes in sensory deprivation. In P. Solomon, P. E. Kubzansky, P. H. Leiderman, J. H. Mendelson, R. Trumbull, & D. Wexler (Eds.), *Sensory deprivation.* Cambridge, Mass.: Harvard University Press, 1961.
29. Lipowski, Z. J. The conflict of Buridan's ass or some dilemmas of affluence: The theory of attractive stimulus overload. *American Journal of Psychiatry,* 1970, *127,* 273–279.
30. Holland, M. K., & Tarlow, G. Blinking and mental load. *Psychological Reports,* 1972, *31,* 119–127.
31. Ettemo, J. H. Blood pressure

change during mental load experiments in man. *Psychotherapy and Psychosomatics, 1969, 17,* 191–195.

32. Zuckerman, M., Persky, H., Miller, L., & Levin, B. Constrasting effects of understimulation (sensory deprivation) and overstimulation (high stimulus variety). *Proceedings, 77th Annual Convention, American Psychological Association, 1969,* 319–320.

33. Usdansky, G., & Chapman, L. J. Schizophrenic-like responses in normal subjects under time pressure. *Journal of Abnormal and Social Psychology, 1960, 60,* 143–146.

34. Wohlwill, J. The concept of sensory overload. In C. Eastman (Ed.), *EDRA: Environmental Design Research Association Proceedings, 1970.*

35. Cameron, P., Robertson, D., & Zaks, J. Sound pollution, noise pollution, and health: Community parameters. *Journal of Applied Psychology, 1972, 56,* 67–74.

36. Kryter, K. D. *The effects of noise on man.* New York: Academic Press, 1970.

37. Anthrop, D. F. Environmental noise pollution: A new threat to sanity. *Bulletin of the Atomic Scientists,* May 1969, 11–16.

38. N.Y. Noise Curbs. *Los Angeles Times,* Sept. 14, 1972, 1.

39. Jet noise suit. *Los Angeles Times,* Feb. 6, 1970, 1.

40. Dubos, R. Man overadapting. *Psychology Today, 1971, 4,* 50–53.

41. Newell, M. The effects of acoustic disruption on short term memory. *Psychonomic Science, 1968, 12,* 61.

42. Sloboda, W. The disturbance effect of white noise on human short term memory. *Psychonomic Science, 1969, 14,* 82–83.

43. Jerison, H. J. Effects of noise on human performance. *Journal of Applied Psychology, 1959, 43,* 96–101.

44. Laird, D. A. The effects of noise. *Journal of the Acoustical Society of America, 1930, 1,* 256–261.

45. Finkle, L. L., & Poppen, J. R. Clinical effects of noise and mechanical vibrations of a turbojet engine. *Journal of Applied Psychology, 1948, 1,* 183–204.

46. Berrien, F. K., & Young, C. W. The effects of acoustical treatment in industrial areas. *Journal of the Acoustical Society of America, 1946, 18,* 453–457.

47. Glass, D., Singer, J. E., & Friedman, L. Psychic cost of adaptation to an environmental stressor. *Journal of Personality and Social Psychology, 1969, 12,* 200–210.

48. Farr, L. Medical consequences of environmental home noises. *Journal of the American Medical Association, 1967, 202,* 171–174.

49. Abey-Wickrama, I., A'brook, M. F., Gattoni, F. E. G., & Herridge, C. F. Mental hospital admissions and aircraft noise. *Lancet, 1969, 2,* 1275–1277.

50. Miller, J. G. Information input overload and psychopathology. *American Journal of Psychiatry, 1960, 116,* 695–704.

51. Meier, R. L. Information input overload: Features of growth in communications-oriented institutions. In F. Massarik & P. Ratoosh (Eds.), *Mathematical explorations in behavioral science.* Homewood, Ill.: R. D. Irwin, 1965.

Research Methods IX: Beyond the Laboratory

1. Sells, S. B. Ecology and the science of psychology. *Multivariate Behavioral Research, 1966, 1,* 131–144.

2. Zimbardo, P. G. The human choice: Individuation, reason, and order versus deindividuation, impulse, and chaos. *Nebraska symposium on motivation, 1969,* 237–286.

3. Barker, R. G. Explorations in ecological psychology. *American Psychologist, 1965, 20,* 1–14.

4. Barker, R. G. *Ecological psychology.* Stanford, Calif.: Stanford University Press, 1968.

5. Barker, R. G., & Gump, P. V. *Big school, small school.* Stanford: Stanford University Press, 1964.

Chapter 28: Mind Control

1. London, P. *Behavior control.* New York: Harper & Row, 1969.

2. Jarvik, M. The psychopharmacology revolution. *Psychology Today, 1967, 1,* 51–59.

3. Freeman, W., & Watts, J. *Psychosurgery.* Springfield, Ill.: Charles C. Thomas, 1942.

4. Milner, P. M. *Physiological psychology.* New York: Holt, Rinehart and Winston, 1970.

5. Delgado, J. M. R. *Physical control of the mind: Toward a psychocivilized society.* New York: Harper & Row, 1969.

6. Heath, R. G. Electrical self-stimulation of the brain in man. *American Journal of Psychiatry, 1963, 120,* 571–577. Copyright 1963, the American Psychiatric Association. Reprinted by permission.

7. Zajonc, R. Brainwash: Familiarity breeds comfort. *Psychology Today, 1970, 3,* 32.

8. Schein, E. H. Reaction patterns to severe, chronic stress in American Army prisoners of war of the Chinese. *Journal of Social Issues, 1957, 13,* 21–30.

9. Brown, J. A. C. *Techniques of persuasion: From propaganda to brainwashing.* Baltimore, Md.: Penguin Books, 1963.

10. Farber, I. E., Harlow, H. F., & West, L. J. Brainwashing, conditioning, and DDD (debility, dependency, and dread). *Sociometry, 1957, 20,* 271–283.

11. Quay, H. The effect of verbal reinforcement on the recall of early memories. *Journal of Abnormal and Social Psychology, 1959, 59,* 254–257.

12. Binet, A., & Féré, C. *Animal magnetism.* New York: Appleton, 1901.

13. Sutcliffe, J. P. "Credulous" and "skeptical" views of hypnotic phenomena: A review of certain evidence and methodology. *International Journal of Clinical Experimental Hypnosis, 1960, 8,* 73–101.

14. Crasilneck, H. B., & Hall, J. A. Physiological changes associated with hypnosis. *International Journal of Clinical Experimental Hypnosis*, 1959, *7*, 9–50.
15. Barber, T. X. *Hypnosis: A scientific approach.* Princeton, N.J.: D. Van Nostrand, 1969.
16. Rogers, C. R., & Skinner, B. F. Some issues concerning the control of human behavior: A symposium. *Science*, 1956, *124*, 1057–1066.
17. Skinner, B. F. *Beyond freedom and dignity.* New York: Alfred A. Knopf, 1971.

Chapter 29: Self Control

1. Wilson, C. Existential psychology: A novelist's approach. In J. F. T. Bugental (Ed.), *Challenges of humanistic psychology.* New York: McGraw-Hill, 1967.
2. Watson, D., & Tharp, R. *Self-directed behavior: Self-modification for personal adjustment.* Belmont, Calif.: Brooks/Cole, 1972.
3. Wooden, H. E. The use of negative practice to eliminate nocturnal headbanging. *Journal of Behavior Therapy and Experimental Psychiatry*, 1974, *5*, 81–82.
4. Shapiro, D. H., & Zifferblatt, S. M. Zen meditation and behavioral self-control: Similarities, differences, and clinical applications. *American Psychologist*, 1976, *31*, 519–532.
5. Boudreau, L. Transcendental meditation and yoga as reciprocal inhibitors. *Journal of Behavior Therapy and Experimental Psychiatry*, 1972, *3*, 97–98.
6. Girodo, M. Yoga meditation and flooding in the treatment of anxiety neurosis. *Journal of Behavior Therapy and Experimental Psychiatry*, 1974, *5*, 157–160.
7. Powell, J. *Why am I afraid to tell you who I am?* Chicago: Argus Communications, 1969.
8. Jordon, T. *P.E.T.: Parent effectiveness training.* New York: Peter Wyden, 1970.

Chapter 30: Revolution

1. Stevens, L. C. *Est.* Santa Barbara, Calif.: Capricorn Press, 1970.
2. Toffler, A. *Future shock.* New York: Random House, 1970.
3. Reich, C. A. *The greening of America.* New York: Random House, 1970.
4. Keniston, K. Counter culture: Cop-out, or wave of the future? *Life*, Dec. 7, 1969, 8–9.
5. Rasberry, S., & Greenway, R. *Rasberry exercises: How to start your own school (and make a book).* Freestone, Calif.: Freestone Publishing, 1970.
6. Graubard, A. The free school movement. *Harvard Educational Review*, 1972, *42*, 351–373.
7. Neill, A. S. *Summerhill: A radical approach to child rearing.* New York: Hart Publishing, 1960.
8. Kozol, J. *Free schools.* Boston: Houghton Mifflin, 1972.
9. *New Schools Exchange Newsletter*, 1971, No. 56, 9.
10. Roszak, T. *The making of a counter culture.* Garden City, N.Y.: Anchor Books, 1969.
11. Communes, U.S.A. *The Modern Utopian*, 5, Nos. 1, 2, 3.
12. Zablocki, B. *The joyful community.* Baltimore, Md.: Penguin Books, 1971.
13. Diamond, S. *What the trees said: Life on a new age farm.* New York: Delta Books, 1971.
14. Landers, R. R. *Man's place in the dybosphere.* Englewood Cliffs, N.J.: Prentice-Hall, 1966.
15. Andrews, L. M., & Karlins, M. *Requiem for democracy?* New York: Holt, Rinehart and Winston, 1971.
16. Huxley, A., quoted in L. M. Andrews & M. Karlins, *Requiem for democracy?* New York: Holt, Rinehart and Winston, 1971.
17. Camus, A. *The rebel.* New York: Vintage Books, 1958.
18. King, M. L., Jr. Letter from Birmingham City Jail. In *Why we can't wait.* New York: Harper & Row, 1963.
19. Seale, B. *Seize the time.* New York: Random House, 1968.
20. Berrigan, D. *The dark night of resistance.* New York: Bantam Books, 1971.
21. Oglesby, C., & Shaull, R. *Containment and change.* New York: Macmillan, 1967.
22. Winborn, B. B., & Jansen, D. G. Personality characteristics of campus social-political action leaders. *Journal of Counseling Psychology*, 1967, *14*, 509–513.
23. Freeman, H. R., & Brubaker, P. Personality characteristics of campus demonstrators compared to nondemonstrators. *Journal of Counseling Psychology*, 1971, *18*, 462–464.
24. Coles, R. A fashionable kind of slander. *Atlantic Monthly*, November 1970.
25. Manoff, M., & Flacks, R. The changing social base of the American student movement. *Annals of the American Academy of Political and Social Science*, 1971, *395*, 55–67.
26. Flacks, R. Protest or conform: Some social psychological perspectives on legitimacy. *Journal of Applied Behavioral Science*, 1969, *5*, 127–150.
27. Mead, M. *Culture and commitment: A study of the generation gap.* New York: Doubleday, 1970.
28. Miller, G. A. Psychology as a means of promoting human welfare. *American Psychologist*, 1969, *24*, 1063–1075.
29. Maslow, A. H. *Toward a psychology of being*, rev. ed. Princeton, N.J.: Van Nostrand, 1968.

Research Methods X: Science and Human Values

1. Weimer, W. B. Overview of a cognitive conspiracy. In W. B. Weimer & D. S. Palermo (Eds.), *Cognition and the symbolic processes.* Hilldale, N.J.: Lawrence Erlbaum Associates, 1975.
2. Kuhn, T. S. *The structure of scientific revolutions.* Chicago: University of Chicago Press, 1970.
3. Rosenthal, R. *Experimenter effects in behavioral research.* New York: Appleton-Century-Crofts, 1966.

Index/Glossary